Also by Edith Fiore, Ph.D.

*You Have Been Here Before*
*The Unquiet Dead*

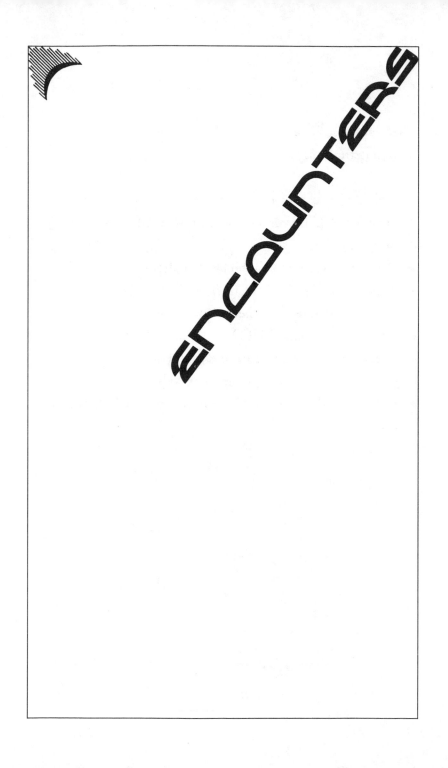

The Ten Most Common Signs of Abductions
by Extraterrestrials

- Inability to account for periods of time
- Persistent nightmares and/or dreams of UFOs and/or aliens
- Sleep disorders
- Waking up with unusual bodily sensations
- Appearance of mysterious marks on the body
- Feeling monitored, watched, and/or communicated with
- Repeated sightings of UFOs
- Vague recollections of a close encounter
- Unexplained healing of ailments or afflictions
- Reacting with fear of and/or anxiety about UFOs and/or ETs

# ENCOUNTERS

A Psychologist Reveals Case Studies of Abductions by Extraterrestrials

Edith Fiore, Ph.D.

Doubleday

New York   London   Toronto   Sydney   Auckland

PUBLISHED BY DOUBLEDAY

a division of
Bantam Doubleday Dell Publishing Group, Inc.
666 Fifth Avenue, New York, NY 10103

DOUBLEDAY and the portrayal of
an anchor with a dolphin are trademarks of
Doubleday, a division of Bantam Doubleday Dell Publishing
Group, Inc.

Library of Congress Cataloging-in-Publication Data
Fiore, Edith.
    Encounters: a psychologist reveals evidence of contact
with extraterrestrials / by Edith Fiore. —1st ed.
        p.   cm.
    Bibliography: p.
    ISBN 0-385-26236-1
    1. Unidentified flying objects—Sightings and encounters
—Psychological aspects.   2. Abduction.   I. Title.
TL789.3.F56   1989
001.9′42—dc19                                    88-35610
                                                      CIP

DESIGNED BY KARIN BATTEN

August 1989

FIRST EDITION

This book is dedicated to Mary Damroth, whose love, friendship, help and patience made writing *Encounters* a joy.

# Contents

# Foreword

It is my pleasure to introduce you to Edith Fiore, Ph.D. Dr. Fiore, a clinical psychologist, has demonstrated her skills not only as a master therapist, but as a master teacher as well. She has contributed her professional experience and knowledge to complex and difficult areas of research.

I am so pleased that Dr. Fiore has turned her writing skills to the timely and controversial topic of UFO encounters. Once again, she shows her ability to identify and formalize basic procedures for personal investigation; she instructs and encourages readers to explore their own UFO memories. Also, she provides information for those who wish further reading and for those who may need additional assistance from professional hypnotists and experienced UFO investigators.

I enjoy Dr. Fiore as a colleague, mentor, and friend because she shares with others her qualities of curiosity, courage and compassion. She is willing to explore paranormal phenomena, which takes curiosity. She is willing to deal with uncertain knowledge, which takes courage. She is willing to listen to the angers, anxieties and fears of others, which takes compassion.

Dr. Fiore is aware of the orthodox scientific paradigm for evaluating UFO reports: Physical evidence is the only basis for "truth"; without physical evidence, there can be no biological evidence, no psychological evidence and no spiritual or psychic evidence! Thus, she knows that she must emphasize her role as a therapist rather than her role as a researcher.

However, in my opinion, the modern scientific paradigm is shifting. Many scientists (e.g., Willis Harman, Ph.D., author of *Global Mind Change)* are considering the hierarchy of physical sciences, life sciences, human sciences and transpersonal sciences, including meditation and spirituality.

My bias, of course, is to regard Dr. Fiore as a true scientist: She follows the trail of the phenomena—regardless of the fears and criticisms of orthodox scientists. She is willing to *explore* (not necessarily *explain)* the ABCs (absurd, bizarre, crazy aspects) of UFO encounters.

The ABCs of UFO reports indicate, over and over, that controversy and ambiguity are the "earmarks" of UFO experiences. Also, UFO experiences indicate repeatedly that there are personal as well as transpersonal aspects in every UFO encounter.

Dr. Fiore knows that paranormal and spiritual aspects of UFO encounters are puzzling but important phenomena. Her case studies reveal the variety of claims about psychic experiences. These same descriptions occur in reports by investigators from all over the planet Earth, from Africa and Australia to the USA and USSR.

Any UFO researcher who has read thousands of reports and listened to hundreds of UFO experiences, as I have, knows that UFO encounters are awesome events. Persons can experience joy and happiness, but they also can experience anxiety, pain, panic, rage and/or terror. The bodily marks and scars of UFO abductees are reminders of their examinations at the hands (or claws) of alien beings. The psychic "gifts" of UFO contactees are a reminder to them of their tasks or missions to assist others around them.

Yes, in my opinion, the evidence for UFO encounters is "real," at several levels. Further, the evidence for a "cover-up" of UFO evidence is impressive. Some writers (e.g., Timothy Good, *Above Top Secret)*, have provided analyses of military and political documents that demonstrate the governmental cover-up of UFO evidence. Others (e.g., Jacques Vallée, *Dimensions* and other UFO books) have emphasized the cover-up by the alien visitors. Other authors, of course, dispute the claims of cover-up either by ETs (extraterrestrials) and/or EDs (extradimensionals), or by governmental agencies.

But there is cover-up at one level of which I am personally aware—the level of individual UFO contactees. I have talked with hundreds and hundreds of UFO experiencers, including many professional persons, who refuse to talk openly about their UFO encounters. Thus, we as individuals are part of the cover-up

—indirectly or directly—if we fail to disclose our own experience(s) or if we fail to listen.

As a counseling psychologist, I understand and respect the wish of any person who requests that I maintain confidentiality of her or his UFO report. However, I claim to be a UFO contactee as well as a UFO observer. (See the 1985 book by Ruth Montgomery, *Aliens Among Us*). As a UFO researcher, I encourage any willing individual to talk to interested persons about his or her UFO encounter. Disclosure is important for three reasons: First, additional information can assist the scientific community to investigate the dimensions of UFO phenomena; second, even if the human community never solves the UFO puzzle, we shall increase our sense of human compassion and social cooperation by sharing our UFO experiences; third, as Dr. Fiore shows in her case histories, most people feel better about themselves if they explore and accept the reality of their UFO encounters.

Dr. Edith Fiore provides competent and compassionate assistance to participants in hypnotherapeutic sessions; also, she provides useful instruction and enlightenment through her perceptive and persistent examination of UFO experiences. Thus, I am pleased to introduce you to a master therapist, a master teacher and an author whose research now provides us all with a clearer vision of the personal and transpersonal significance of UFO encounters.

R. Leo Sprinkle, Ph.D.

# Preface

The sun streamed in my window and onto my face, waking me earlier than I wanted on a Saturday morning in 1950. I stretched sleepily in my four-poster antique walnut bed in the very room where George Washington had slept almost two hundred years before. This was to be a day that would affect my whole life and eventually lead to this book.

"Here's a present for you, Edee," Keith said with a mischievous smile, handing me a hardcover book. Keith Winter had been my family's houseguest at Headquarters Farm for months, preferring it and the fresh, clean air and ambience of Bucks County, Pennsylvania, to his apartment in New York City's Greenwich Village. Keith was a writer and had delighted us on many happy occasions by reading his work, taking the various parts and beautifully changing his voice for each character. My favorite was *The Red Shoes*, the classic film about a ballerina obsessed with dancing.

"What's this, Keith?" I asked, turning the book over and reading the material on the back. "What are flying saucers?"

Keith had introduced me to a subject that would become a lifelong interest. *Flying Saucers Are Real!* was the first book on the topic of UFOs (unidentified flying objects). My reaction to it, having read it that very day, was total acceptance of Major Donald Keyhoe's premise that we were being visited by beings from other planets. I believed that the spacecraft were real and that intelligent "people" were flying here in them. From that time on, I have spent hours scouring the night skies, hoping to see a UFO. I have seen lights doing strange things high among the stars, but nothing so convincing that it couldn't be explained as a natural phenomenon.

In 1979, I joined a UFO study group and became intensely interested in extraterrestrial visitations. I lay in my wine-barrel hot tub many a night at my Light Ranch in Lake County in northern California, delighting in the star-studded sky, occasionally sending messages, even "pleas," to our space brothers to make themselves visible or to give me a message. They never did. However, it was

xv

during that period that I awoke one morning, feeling particularly good, and remembered a fragment of a dream. It was vague and fuzzy, but I did recall being shown around a "room" in a UFO. My hosts treated me as an honored guest and colleague. I sensed that they were humanoid, not the least bit frightening or strange. I also felt that they were males. I didn't remember any other details. The dream did not particularly impress me at the time. I passed it off as just wishful thinking.

After a few years, my focus shifted, and UFOs and extraterrestrials assumed a background position, along with many other interests and hobbies.

I have been a psychotherapist in private practice, first in Miami, Florida, and later in Saratoga, California, since 1969. I stumbled onto hypnosis accidentally in 1973 by agreeing to join my brother, Frank Fiore, at a weekend seminar at Esalen Institute at Big Sur, California. We took a self-hypnosis workshop, and I experienced going into an hypnotic trance for the first time. The following Monday, in my office, I tried it out with a courageous patient and have been using hypnosis ever since.

Hypnotic age regression is an extremely effective therapeutic technique. It gets to the cause of symptoms and problems of all sorts and results in immediate and lasting cures. I have come to believe that a great majority of symptoms are due to repressed trauma. Sigmund Freud stated that making the subconscious, conscious, in other words, bringing repressed material hidden in the dark recesses of the mind to its surface, results in a cure. I had accepted this for many years but now question the process somewhat. For example, many other hypnotherapists and I have found that symptoms could be completely eliminated when, under hypnosis, a patient regressed to the age at which causative events occurred and recalled or relived them. On occasion it was found that when a patient came out of the trance, he or she did not remember the work that had just so painfully been done. This was due to the patient's having been in a very deep, somnambulistic state, in which amnesia upon awakening is frequently experienced. I have also found some patients who had been in light trances were later unable to recall the traumas they had just "remembered." They may have mentally given themselves a suggestion, while still hypnotized, to forget because the events were threatening to their self-concepts.

Even though I don't understand how the cure takes place, I do know that it is important for the repressed event, buried in the subconscious mind, to be recalled, remembered, relived or dealt with in whatever way the person will allow.

During the fifteen years that I have been using hypnotic age regression, I have found many of my patients "remembering" what appeared to have been contacts with and abductions by extraterrestrials in spacecraft. Once the repressed traumas had been brought to light, any symptoms or problems caused by them were immediately eliminated. Generally the patients were surprised, even shocked, to find that they had had close encounters.

In 1987 I was invited to speak at the California Society of Psychical Research by its president, my good friend and colleague, Jeffrey Mishlove, Ph.D., author of *Roots of Consciousness*. When I had finished my talk, I met James Harder, Ph.D., a professor at the University of California at Berkeley. We had a quick chat about his work with abductees and planned to get together as soon as possible to pursue our mutual interest.

Meeting Jim Harder the night of the lecture in Berkeley gave me a person to work with to explore my one and only (remembered) dream of a UFO. My patients' regressions in which dreams played a dominant role and the many accounts of abductions and contacts with repeated references to dreams I had read about made me wonder if my dream could possibly have been the remnant of a remembered experience. I called Jim and set up an appointment for a Saturday. Several weeks later, after a delightful cable car ride up the steep hillside to his house overlooking San Francisco Bay, we met for several very pleasant hours.

Jim offered me some of his home-baked, low cholesterol brownies, and after we settled ourselves in his living room, he asked me, "When did you have the dream?"

"Years ago, and even then it was very vague. I have a sneaking suspicion that it's not a dream."

"Dreams are very commonly the tip of the iceberg of a meeting with ETs," he said, picking up his notepad. "Let's get started and we'll soon find out about yours."

Jim did a gentle, almost whispered hypnotic induction. I could feel my body becoming very relaxed and heavy, sinking down into the cushions of his couch. He had my inner (subconscious) mind select and lift one finger to designate "yes" and another for "no." My conscious mind was not to interfere in any way with the lifting and lowering of the finger. I had used this technique for years with my patients and had already established the responses in myself and had used them during many sessions of self-hypnosis.

Jim questioned my subconscious mind, having it respond through my fingers, which flipped up readily. We quickly discovered that indeed I had been contacted. I had been floated out of the bedroom in my condominium in Los Gatos into a spaceship. Once there, I was treated with respect and kindness and much was explained to me that I was not to remember until later. Then it would filter into my mind, more as memories than as knowledge, and would be very helpful for me. Jim got a description of the aliens and the room. I was in a very light trance and found myself doing exactly what I urge my patients not to do—trying to analyze and critique the material as it came forth. To this day, I am not convinced that I "remembered" an actual happening. I had read a great deal on the subject and had done so many regressions with my patients that I could not separate fact from fiction.

"Edee, most people find it hard to convince themselves that what they bring up in hypnosis is real. We can't really know for sure," Jim explained patiently. "Let's work on it another time. I'll see if I can get you to go deeper." Since then, however, we've both been exceedingly busy, and because it wasn't a top priority for me, we haven't met again.

Several weeks later, a young woman came for a consultation, having been in the audience for my talk that night. I had mentioned a case of abduction that had unsettled her. She had felt extremely nervous when I described the experience of my patient and had battled with herself for over a week before calling for an appointment.

"I've worried about this for several years now," she confided. "I seem to remember being taken on board a UFO against my will. In fact, just talking about it now makes me feel very anxious." Tears spilled down her cheeks as she reached for a tissue. "I'm really scared that I'm losing my mind. Sometimes I think I'm going crazy!"

"You seem fine to me," I told her. "Why do you think that having memories of a possible UFO encounter means that you're not sane?"

"It's my husband. He not only laughs at the whole idea of flying saucers, but thinks that anyone who claims they've been captured by extraterrestrials is a crackpot. He's so sure he's right . . . and if the topic ever comes up, his friends all jump right in and agree. If he ever found out why I'm here, he'd probably kick me out . . . divorce me or have me locked up!"

After more questioning, it did appear that she had seen UFOs on many occasions and had had some close encounters of the fourth kind (CEIVs), those in which there is an abduction by or contact with aliens. We only had time during that session for me to make a recorded tape of hypnotic suggestions to encourage restful sleep at night and to help her to be more relaxed in general and feel better about herself. Unfortunately, her fear got the better of her and she never returned. I have often wondered, particularly since then, how many other suffering people resist the very treatment that could give them the relief they so desperately need, because of their fears of finding out about contacts with the visitors and the consequences of that discovery.

*

Almost one-half of U.S. citizens, according to a 1987 Gallup poll, believe in UFOs, and one out of eleven report having seen them. However, most new ideas and theories throughout history have met with resistance and ridicule. Even now, some Christian groups believe that UFOs are evidence of Satan at work and that those who accept them need prayers for their salvation.

We need to investigate these phenomena and help the people who have been traumatized by their encounters with aliens. I believe it is crucial that we have open minds, being neither gullible nor terminally skeptical, in order to rationally assess the evidence. I feel my work with hypnotized patients who seem to have remembered UFO abductions and contacts adds to the growing fund of data and knowledge of extraterrestrial visits to our planet.

❧

The first chapter of *Encounters* introduces you to the general subject of close encounters of the fourth kind and explains how hypnotic regressions work. It is followed by thirteen chapters, each a case history of an individual who appeared to have had experience with extraterrestrials. Names and identifying data have been changed in order to protect the privacy of my patients and subjects.

Perhaps you have wondered if you have been contacted or abducted. In Chapter Sixteen, I have described a technique for investigation that may help you find out, the pendulum. James Harder, Ph.D., and Leo Sprinkle, Ph.D., both known and respected UFO researchers, as well as others, use this method to help people discover whether they have had contacts with aliens. In the privacy of your own home, you can use a pendulum to tap into your subconscious memories. I have designed questions you can use and also have given you pointers on how to go beyond my questions. If you find that you are an abductee or contactee, you may want to pursue it further. In the Appendix, you will find lists of organizations, researchers and hypnotherapists specializing in UFO sightings and CEIVs. At the end of *Encounters* is a list of books I have compiled, which offers you an opportunity to continue to educate yourself in the area of ufology.

As you read *Encounters*, it would be helpful for you to keep a notepad nearby and record anything at all that you suspect as being evidence of a close encounter. Notice, for example, any signs of anxiety: fear, apprehension, heart acceleration, sweaty palms, dizziness, shortness of breath, etc. Mark the margin or highlight the material and record the page number so you can check back later when you start exploring your own possible contacts. You also may start remembering seeing lights in the sky, or recall a dream you had totally forgotten. This book could bring closer to the surface of your conscious mind experiences that have been deeply buried for years.

*

Having read Whitley Strieber's *Communion* and Budd Hopkins's *The Intruders,* as well as other books on close encounters, I realized that probably thousands of people in our country have been abducted and/or contacted. My patients' and subjects' experiences were similar to, but at the same time quite different from, those reported in the above-mentioned books. Usually their experiences involved being taken against their will and examined thoroughly and, at times, painfully. With some, however, the encounters were meant to educate them, and, in a few cases, even help and heal them.

I wrote this book to expose you to another dimension of the contact/abduction phenomenon. *Encounters* may frighten you. I hope it will educate you. But my greatest reward would be if it helps you.

# Acknowledgments

I wish to express my gratitude to:

The thirteen people who allowed me to present their case studies;

My patients and subjects, whose courage and experiences contributed to my understanding of the close encounter of the fourth kind phenomenon;

Ormond McGill, whose encouragement and friendship helped me keep on schedule with my writing;

Ted Chichak, for emotional support and friendship that go beyond his responsibilities as my literary agent;

Jim Fitzgerald and Mark Garofalo, my editors, for the interest they showed in this work;

Kate Hendon, for her patience, skill, friendship and interest while transcribing the tapes and collating the material.

ENCOUNTERS

# "Empty Your Mind.
# Think of Nothing."

"I was home alone. Scared. As long as I can remember, I've always been frightened of being alone, especially at night. I still am. Then, I was either twelve or thirteen. My parents had taken Bill, my older brother to the junior-senior prom, so I turned on the TV to keep me company. Suddenly my eyes noticed a very bright light out the window right over the TV. It was dark out, about nine. The light was on the hill to the east. A very brilliant single light at the top of the hill. It seemed to be calling to me. I got very scared. I just sat still in the chair. I noticed that my body was immobilized. The TV turned to black-and-white snow. I couldn't take my eyes off of it. I don't know how much time elapsed. Then the TV started blinking and the color came back on. I looked up, but the light was gone . . . vanished. I felt funny. Strange. Heavy. I tried to move my arms and legs. I was so relieved to take my eyes off the TV and to be able to move . . . that I was back."

Sandi "forgot" about her experience for nine years, until a friend, Kathy, told her about a UFO she had witnessed in the desert night sky, as she and her husband were driving in the Southwest. Kathy later remembered having been abducted by extraterrestrials. As she was describing her reactions to it, Sandi began to feel anxious and tingly and commented that she wasn't feeling well. Kathy, having developed some psychic sensitivity since the incident, suggested that Sandi had been abducted.

Five years later, in my office under hypnosis, Sandi reexperienced a very frightening and physically painful two-hour encounter on board a spacecraft, a UFO, in which she had been examined and questioned. You'll be reading her account of this experience in Chapter Two. Officially, Sandi had an encounter of the fourth kind and could be classified as an "abductee."

Sandi is one of thousands of people who have been abducted or contacted by extraterrestrials. As a result of her close encounter, she experienced fears until she remembered the trauma under hypnosis fourteen years later. Many other abductees/contactees have developed phobias, anxiety, depression, amnesia, nightmares and other emotional and mental disturbances. Another, occasional, outcome of these encounters is various types of physical symptoms, which have been reported in the literature. A very common consequence of the abduction/contact phenomenon is that people begin doubting their own sanity. If they remember the experience, instead of being helped with compassion and understanding, they are often ridiculed and treated as though they were crazy, which, of course, further adds to the problem.

Interestingly, in at least one-half of the cases I've been involved in, the people were greatly helped by their encounters. Operations, usually involving lasers, and other treatments relieved symptoms, even correcting some conditions that were potentially fatal.

Despite the often traumatic effects, in almost every case it appears that the extraterrestrials were not motivated to hurt or frighten humans. Sometimes they expressed sorrow when their examinations or treatments elicited pain or fear.

As a hypnotist, it was fascinating for me to hear the verbatim (hypnotic) suggestions the visitors used to invoke relaxation and amnesia. Often they are the very words which any hypnotist uses regularly. In one case, the person was instructed to "empty your mind. Think of nothing." In most cases, just before the experience ended, the people were told, "You will remember nothing. It will be as if nothing has happened. You will forget everything." It seems too that the aliens have devices they employ to induce not only relaxation and cessation of fear, but unconsciousness. You will be reading accounts of individuals being rendered unconscious who still continued to experience what was happening from outside of their bodies, usually from a vantage point above and looking down, observing examinations, operations and treatments. It appears that we have another body, sometimes referred to as "astral," "etheric" or "spiritual," in which we retain awareness. This is consistent with the work of the last decade in the area of the near-death experiences (NDEs), in which people who have (temporarily) died actually left their physical bodies and retained full consciousness, minus the pain and/or fear they had felt prior to leaving them. In *Encounters*, you will see that the majority of my patients/subjects reported similar experiences.

Some of the following case studies may seem like unadulterated science fiction. The case of Dan, whom you'll read about in Chapter Twelve, is especially intriguing. Not only will you see him as a cosmic warrior, but one who totally possessed, by "replacing," a young boy. I found it helpful while working with him to remain particularly objective and nonjudgmental. The interesting thing about his work under hypnosis is that it had a profoundly positive effect on him, helping him to resolve deep inner conflicts (even though he was not a patient) and answering many questions that had troubled him for years. Despite the violence of the material, he felt much better about himself and much more self-confident.

In the next thirteen chapters, you'll be reading the personal accounts of people who have had close encounters of the fourth kind. Some of these individuals were patients who uncovered the hidden experiences in the course of their therapy. Often, the encounters caused the very symptoms that had changed their lives, driving them to seek help. Others were friends, or people whom I heard about through mutual friends, whose "dreams" or sightings of UFOs led me to invite them to my office. Our goals were to investigate their experiences in order to expose possible encounters and/or resolve any resultant symptoms or problems.

I used the technique of hypnotic age regression with each one of these people. Some had never been hypnotized before.

Hypnosis is now being used widely throughout the world as a way of helping people overcome problems and symptoms. There is no agreed-upon definition for hypnosis. However, I believe that every hypnotist would concur, at least, that the patient/subject is in an altered state of awareness, i.e., not in the usual conscious mode of thought. Hypnosis does not invoke sleep, nor unconsciousness. Even in the deepest state, there is awareness, which is focused and heightened. Therapists use hypnosis generally in two major ways: to induce a state of suggestibility in order to impress upon the subconscious mind thoughts and images of wellness and improvement, and as a tool for uncovering repressed experiences, ones that are no longer available to the conscious mind. Hypnosis is an extremely powerful way of helping the subconscious reveal its secrets. When in an altered state, subjects are very susceptible to suggestions. The general suggestions I use in age regression are to go back in time to the event being studied. Since all experiences are recorded in the subconscious mind exactly as they were originally perceived, they are available to be brought to the surface of the mind. However, it must be understood that hypnosis does not improve upon the original perceptions of the encounter, so what is being revealed is only how the person experienced it at the time.

In explaining to my patients how repressed traumas operate, I use the analogy of a thorn in the flesh. While it is embedded in the skin, it is painful, and the wound festers, as the body tries to expel the thorn. When it is finally removed, the healing process starts immediately. The thorn can be held in the palm of the hand and examined. It is not a pretty object, but it no longer causes pain and discomfort. When the frightening memory is brought out of hiding, it is there, usually not forgotten, unless the trance was at the very deepest level, somnambulism. The memory, like the thorn, is not pleasant, but no longer is it doing any damage, and the mind has been healed.

My patients and subjects (the ones coming only to explore a possible UFO encounter) usually went into one of three major levels of hypnotic trance: light, medium or deep. Often, after hypnosis was induced, the person would be in only a light to medium trance, but as the session continued, the level deepened, sometimes to the point of the person's actually reliving the experiences. At these times, the patients/subjects often cried, trembled, flailed about, cringed, etc. On occasion, the experience became too overwhelming, and they brought themselves completely out of the trance, eyes wide open, back to normal consciousness. Usually a few reassuring comments would ease them back into hypnosis so they could continue and benefit from the work we were doing.

Another therapeutic tool I used was finger signals. After the patients/subjects were hypnotized, I asked their subconscious minds to select and lift one finger to designate "yes" and another for "no." Once this mode of communication was established, I was able to ask questions of their inner minds of which their conscious minds were unaware. Although at times unreliable in terms of accuracy, this technique was generally very helpful.

I am a therapist, so my primary goal in doing regressions to close encounters is to help the patient overcome symptoms, problems and difficulties. Recently, I've taken on the additional role of a UFO investigator, in which collecting data (exposing the event) is the primary objective. Often in doing an investigation, I decided to ask questions that may actually have led the person in the suspected direction in order to facilitate our work. If a strict researcher had been peering over my shoulder, he would have frowned and shaken his head, because he would have been after proof of the validity of the contact, whereas my goal may have changed to quickly relieving anxiety that had surfaced.

When you read the cases and verbatim transcripts (which have been edited for clarity and to avoid repetition), you will see how the experiences unfolded for the patients/subjects. Some transcripts show evidence of confusion, contradictions of earlier statements, even flat denials of happenings patients/subjects later revealed. This is because people in trance are still very aware and conscious of what they are saying. If they are in a light to medium trance, they often are simultaneously judging, analyzing and, at times, censoring. Patients have later confessed that they have deliberately withheld material that came to their minds, or, even more confusing for me, have actually lied. Dan, whom you'll meet in Chapter Twelve, nicely summed up his experience under hypnosis the first time as follows:

"I thought there would be more of the sensation of blacking out or going under. And it's so light that it doesn't feel like anything's been done, until you start to let things come out. And you find you're saying things that you're not consciously thinking about. That was a strange experience. At first it was a little disconcerting. But after you relax and accept it, it's not bad. The conscious mind was scurrying around like mad, saying, 'This is not right. You're making this up. You're doing this, you're doing that.' The conscious mind was busy trying to put it down, and the subconscious mind was blabbing its fool head off. It's a very strange feeling, like your mouth is operating on its own, and your mind is saying, 'Shut up, you idiot!' "

In the majority of cases there were very strong resistances to remembering. This came from two main sources: hypnotic suggestions given to the abductees/contactees by the extraterrestrials (often the ones supervising the encounter) that, on waking, they would not remember anything, and from their own inner unwillingness to remember and especially relive an exceedingly traumatic event. Also, many people did not want to feel themselves or be seen by others to be different, to be "weird" and/or "crazy." As Gloria (Chapter Nine) put it before beginning her second regression to an abduction, "It was hard to accept in my mind that this really happened . . . no sense in trying to deny it anymore."

Hypnosis is a less than perfect tool. It is not a "truth serum." But it is helpful. In the hands of a skilled therapist and/or researcher, it can elicit a great deal of valuable repressed material.

When doing any kind of regression, I take a position of remaining very objective within my own mind as to an event's validity;

did it really happen? For example, each week at least three or four of my female patients find, under hypnosis, that they had been sexually abused as small children. They have no conscious memory of these events. We will never know, unless it is corroborated by other family members (which is extremely unusual), whether the material that emerged was an actual memory or a fantasy. What does impress me are the immediate and lasting cures that resulted from their hypnotic work. Besides eliminating debilitating symptoms, age regressions were followed by dramatic changes in many areas of these patients' lives. I often saw the same therapeutic effects after regressions to close encounters. For me, this is clinical validity, and I have no desire to prove that the experiences really happened, any more than I do with my patients who "discover" they've been sexually abused.

The next thirteen chapters are offered to you, therefore, not as proof that the encounters actually took place, nor as accurate portrayals. I am presenting them as case material, accounts of what these thirteen people experienced under hypnosis. You are invited to analyze the material and then to draw your own conclusions.

# "They Put Something
in My Rectum."

 "My friend Sandi thinks she may have seen a UFO when she was a child," Les said, as he put all his strength into the final stretch of my spine. I got off the treatment bench, and, while checking the alignment of my head and shoulders, he added, "She would be glad to talk to you about it. She just told me the other day that she thinks she may have had an encounter." Frowning, he commented, "Your head is just a fraction of an inch off. I think we've almost got it where we want it."

Leslie Szasalay, D.C., is one of the new breed of young doctors who are open to alternative methods of healing. At thirty-four he is developing a private practice in chiropractics in Saratoga and is the kind of person whom I like immediately. During my weekly treatments for low-back pain, we've become good friends and often share tidbits about our lives. After he had told me about an art show at our local junior college he and his friend Sandi had attended, he had asked me what I had done over the weekend.

"I spent both days working on my new book, *Encounters*. I just started it, and it's been very rewarding so far."

8

"What's your book about, Edee?"

"It's about people who have had, or at least appear to have had, close encounters of the fourth kind. Do you know which ones they are?"

"No. I saw the movie, *Close Encounters of the Third Kind.* What's the difference?"

"Let's start at the beginning. Close encounters of the first kind are those in which someone sees a saucer, a UFO, in the daytime and/or nocturnal lights. Close encounters of the second kind involve visual evidence of impressions made by a spacecraft, like burned areas or irradiated soil, grass or trees. Close encounters of the third kind, the ones Steven Spielberg's movie was about, are those in which the witness observes or directly confronts occupants of a UFO. And last, but certainly not least, are close encounters of the fourth kind, CEIV. They're the ones in which people claim to have been abducted or contacted by extraterrestrials. And that's what my book is about. Case studies of individuals who have had this type of experience. Many times they have phobias or other problems that are caused by these encounters, but they have no conscious memory of them, so we use hypnosis to help them recall what's happened. It's been fascinating work."

Not surprisingly, Les seemed very interested and open-minded about intelligent life on other planets and the possibility of our being visited by aliens. However, he is basically a pragmatist and takes a stance of being scientifically objective about such topics.

The following Saturday, Sandi, Les and I met in my office. Despite the relaxed atmosphere, since the building was empty and we were in very casual clothes, Sandi was obviously tense, yet excited about doing a regression.

Sandi is a very attractive twenty-seven-year-old bookkeeper. Trim and petite in her peach sweatsuit, her light-brown hair short and curled away from her pretty face, she smiled a little too often and giggled anxiously as she began her story. You read the beginning of her account in Chapter One, so I'll just summarize it at this point.

As a child, Sandi lived with her parents and older brother, Bill, in Eastern Colorado in a very rural area, where her family had their ranch. On a Saturday evening in the late spring of her twelfth year, she was alone, which was unusual. Her parents had taken Bill to his junior-senior prom. Sandi recalled being nervous, and so, for company and to distract herself, she made a bowl of popcorn, turned on the TV and sat down to watch one of her favorite sitcoms. The large picture window just above the TV looked out over pastures and nearby hills. In the daytime, it created a beautiful indoor-outdoor feeling, but this particular night the darkness was scary, and Sandi made an effort to avoid looking at the window. A few minutes into the TV show, she noticed an intense bright light that attracted her attention away from the set. Looking up and out, she saw what she thought were car headlights on top of the hill, which was about a mile away. No, it can't be a car, she thought, because it is a single light and much too bright. She then reasoned it must be a searchlight that their neighbor, a rancher, used to find lost sheep or cattle. She began to feel fear mounting, for somehow the light seemed to be "calling" her. Gradually she became immobilized. The TV shifted spontaneously to black-and-white snow. She found herself spellbound by it. As she remembered, "I seemed drawn into the TV." The next thing she was aware of was that the TV was blinking, the color had returned and the ten o'clock news was on. When she looked up, she saw that the light had vanished and noticed that she felt "funny" and tingly. A great sense of relief flooded over her when she realized she could move her arms and legs and take her eyes off the TV. A thought flitted in and out of her mind, I'm back!

"Sandi, at that age, did you know about UFOs?" I asked, slipping a tape in my recorder.

"I can't remember even hearing about them as a child. I did tell my parents what happened. Of course, they had no explanation. They thought it was a bad case of nerves. It was only five or six years ago when I first began to wonder about it."

"What happened then?"

"I had lunch with a friend, Kathy, and she told me about an experience she had had in which she had been abducted by aliens and taken aboard a UFO."

"How did she remember it, Sandi? Did she see a hypnotist?"

"No. She just remembered it. Or, at least, some of it. She's a psychic and has had all kinds of weird experiences that we talk about. While she was telling me her story, I began to feel funny again, and it reminded me of that night when I was a kid, with the TV and the bright light. I told her what I was feeling, and she tuned in to me and said she thought maybe I had had an encounter too."

I noticed that Sandi was getting quite uncomfortable; the more she talked about the possibility of her having been abducted, the more uncomfortable she became. "How do you feel about our doing the regression?"

"Scared . . . and excited. I guess it would be best to know for sure. But I've never been hypnotized before and I don't know if I can be," she said, twisting her hands together and looking into her lap.

"Sandi, let's not worry about that. There's nothing mysterious about being hypnotized. Have you ever cried when you saw something sad in the movies?"

"Sure," she said brightening up a little.

"Well, you were in a state of hypnosis. You had forgotten for a while that you were in a movie theater, watching a screen with lights projected onto it. You forgot that the people were only actors and that what was happening was not real. In other words, you had suspended disbelief, one of the things that sometimes happens in hypnosis."

"But I didn't feel hypnotized. I felt like I always do," Sandi said, her brows creasing.

"Almost every single person who has sat in that chair," I said, gesturing toward the reclining chair she was in, "is convinced he or she was not hypnotized. That's because there is such a misconception about hypnosis. It's a very natural state that we slip in and out of probably hundreds of times daily. Let's begin and you'll soon see what it's like."

She nodded in agreement. Les leaned forward in his chair and asked, "Would it be all right for me to stay in the room and watch?"

"With my therapy patients, I never allow it, but this is different. I don't want you slipping into hypnosis, Les, so make sure you stay alert, keep shifting your eyes around and resist any urge to close them."

He smiled broadly, nodded, tilted the chair back and crossed his arms behind his head, looking particularly alert.

After covering Sandi with my lavender-plaid mohair blanket and pushing the chair back to its full reclining position, I began the hypnotic induction. As soon as her eyes closed, her eyelids immediately flickered, a sign of trance. She quickly seemed to slip into a deeper state as her body relaxed, responding to my hypnotic suggestions. When I felt that she was ready to regress back to the possible close encounter, I asked her to go back into her memory banks to the night when she was alone and had seen the light.

I looked over at Les, who was leaning forward resting his elbows on his thighs. He looked a little concerned and gave me a quick smile. He waited, and soon Sandi began speaking in a slow, almost hesitant way.

✦

SANDI: I am sitting in the corner watching TV, and there is something on the hill. I looked up through the window. There is a light. I didn't know if it was on the road or in the pasture. It got brighter, like it was turning toward me. I looked at the light a long time. The longer I looked, the heavier I got. My arms were heavy. My legs were heavy. I felt like a balloon that was heavy. I felt like I was all blown up . . . that I was too heavy to move. I sat there and I looked at the light. I couldn't move . . . I was so heavy. And . . . the TV had gone off. The TV had gone toward snow and it was really loud. It was very loud! I tried to get up to turn it down and I couldn't get up. I was so heavy. Then I started looking at the TV, at the snow, trying to find something in the snow, trying to find a word or a face. [*Sighs*] I couldn't see anything in the snow that I could recognize. But I kept trying, and then . . . then I looked back up at the light. And I looked at it for a long time more. [*Long pause*] I feel like my body . . . is . . . is raising up. It's raising up higher and higher out into the night . . . [*Grimaces and sighs*] My other body is still in the chair, and I feel light. It's like I'm going up, up into the night, higher and higher and . . . higher . . . higher . . . way up into the sky and looking down, going higher . . . higher . . . [*Long pause*] Now I feel like I'm lying down on a slanted board, my feet down toward the ground. Just lying there, feeling so light, feeling so good. [*Pauses*]

DR. FIORE:   And now what's happening?

SANDI:   I'm in a large room with other beds, with other stations . . . and I'm on a slanted board. It's . . . it's big. There's . . . there's about six other stations. And it's oval. Yes, it's oval. [*Long pause*]

DR. FIORE:   Let yourself remember.

SANDI:   [*Sighs painfully*] I don't know . . . I can't . . . I can't see any . . .

DR. FIORE:   Let yourself know everything you experienced. Tell me more about what it feels like to be on the bed.

SANDI:   It feels like I can't get up. I feel like I'm so heavy that I can't get up. I don't think I can see clearly. It's cold. It's really cold, and I can't see. Everything's kind of fuzzy. And there's . . . there's some kind of light up above me, 'cause I'm lying on the slanted board with my head . . . back like it is now.

DR. FIORE:   Tell me more about what's happening. It's crystal clear in your mind.

SANDI:   I just wish it would end. I'm so cold, I just want a blanket. I just don't want to be there. [*Pauses*]

DR. FIORE:   What else are you experiencing?

SANDI: I see a head, and it's got wings on it, the way . . . it looks. [*Sighs*] It's got big wings for eyes, that go . . . they go off the side. They look angry. I see that . . . face. Looking at me . . . I feel like he's . . . he's talking, talking to me. But he's not saying words, he's just talking to my mind. But I don't know what he's saying.

DR. FIORE: You will remember now exactly what he said to you.

SANDI: He wants me . . . to relax, not to be scared . . . [*Shivers*] But it's so cold, and I'm so scared. [*Long pause*] I keep . . . I get messages. It's like he's . . . like he's communicating, but I can't remember what it was. I can't understand what it was. I try to understand it. I try to just let it, let it come in, but . . . I just . . . I can't.

DR. FIORE: Where is he?

SANDI: He's right next to me. He's very close. He's standing over my face, over my body. I think I had a sheet on me, because it was so cold. It would touch me and I would shiver, it was so cold. And I wished that they would just take it off of me, because it was making me colder.

DR. FIORE: Tell me more about the being.

SANDI: I think they might be on both sides of me. I think they are. And there's three of them. Four of them.

DR. FIORE: What are they doing?

SANDI: They just seem to be standing. I think there's three on one side, and there's one on my right side. I think they're just standing there, looking down at me. I'm low to the ground. My head's probably . . . two feet off the ground . . . three feet off the ground. I keep feeling like I'm going to fall off the board, but I don't. I feel like I'm going to slide off, but I don't. I feel like all the blood is rushing to my feet, I wish they'd take me off of that board. [*Pauses and seems to look around*] They're moving around. There seems to be more of them. And they're moving around really fast, just scurrying around. Now they're kind of leaving me alone. I'm just lying there. I can see them, and they're going really fast. They look real cute.

DR. FIORE:   What do they look like?

SANDI:   I'm not sure now. The one with the weird eyes, the wings . . . they don't look like that . . . anymore.

DR. FIORE:   Are you saying that one looks different from the rest?

SANDI:   I thought it did, but I don't see it anymore. A little while ago he was there and he looked . . . he looked very angry and he had great big eyebrow things . . . cute . . . they stuck way out, with . . . deep eyes.

DR. FIORE:   What color were they?

SANDI:   Dark . . . black or brown, I think. They were way deep-set and the eyebrow was way out over it.

DR. FIORE:   You're going to let yourself remember anything they have done to you.

SANDI:   They're turning my head to look at the back of my neck. My neck doesn't go that way. But they're gentle. I feel flat, yeah . . . I'm not on the slanted board anymore. I'm on a level surface. And they're turning my head. [*Pauses*] They might have white robes, I'm not sure. It's like some of them . . . some of them that are looking at me have robes, but maybe the rest of them don't. What else did they do to me? They were gentle. They were cold. When they touched me, they were cold. I didn't like it, but they were gentle. I remember telling them, "No! No, don't you do that to me! Don't you do that to me! [*Cries*] And they were telling me that it would be okay. They were trying to settle me down. And I didn't want them doing that to me. They were going to put something up my rectum, and I . . . [*Crying hard* ] . . . didn't want them to do that to me.

DR. FIORE:    Tell me all about it.

SANDI:    I think it was a needle. And . . . they were pushing me . . . I was on my back, and they were pushing me onto my right side, and I was pushing back as hard as I could. I didn't want them to do that. They were pushing. They were so strong and so cold. At first when they talked to me, I trusted them. They were very gentle, and I trusted them. And then . . . and then they made me do something I didn't want to do.

DR. FIORE:    What was that?

SANDI:    They made me turn over. They made me turn over onto my side . . . and I didn't want to do that, because I was afraid of what they were going to do to me. And they put me on my side so they could spread my cheeks, so they could do something . . . I don't know . . . [*Whispers*] with a . . . probe or something. I don't know if it was sharp like a needle, but it was thin like a needle.

DR. FIORE:    You are remembering everything as though it is happening now.

SANDI:    I think they quit. Maybe they did something really fast . . . and then it was over and they let me go. I was so happy. I laid back down and I was never going to let them do that to me again. I'm so glad it was over.

DR. FIORE:   You are going to let yourself remember everything exactly as it happened. Take it second by second.

SANDI:   I'm lying there, and they're pushing on my hip. They're pushing, and I'm pushing back. And they push harder, and I push harder. And . . . and then they push really hard, and I flip . . . flip over on my side and they push my one knee up. And then . . . then they . . .

DR. FIORE:   Continue speaking out.

SANDI:   I'm so scared. I'm just so scared. [*Crying*] I guess maybe I gave up then. I was so scared. I knew they were so strong. I think I gave up . . . and I just, I laid there and . . . it was a terrible feeling. They put something in my rectum! It was terrible! Whatever they were doing, I didn't want it anymore. And then they pulled it out. And they left. They left me alone, and I was so happy it was over. I pushed back, and I had to lie on my back. I wanted to lie on my back so that they couldn't get to me again. I was still scared, but I wasn't as scared. It was over. I was still cold. I was still really, really cold. It seems like there was a light above me. So I just laid there and looked at the light and tried to think that it's not that bad. Tried to relax . . . tried to relax. [*Sighs*] And then . . . then I relaxed a little more. I looked around the room. It seemed like I was conscious. It's like I was . . . becoming more conscious at that point or something, like I was getting my faculties together. It seems like I had this feeling that I should look around and see what this is. I need to look around and . . . see what it is, see where I am. I have to remember all this. And I just remember a real urgent feeling to . . . to just . . . memorize every detail, but I can't. . . .

DR. FIORE:   What is it you're noticing to remember later?

SANDI:   The shape of the room. . . . The end that I was look-ing at is curved. Again, it was the long end of the oval, I think. It wasn't that huge of a room, but I was looking at the seam. It seemed like it was domed. And the seam, the seam between the top half and the bottom half. I thought, How unusual. I remember thinking, How weird. I don't know what it looked like. How did they do that? What does it do? Things were so weird. But it was . . . it was domed on the top and the bottom. There weren't square corners. You'd fall down if you walked over there, I thought. You would slip and fall because the bottom of the thing was curved. I remember looking at that one wall.

DR. FIORE:   Tell me more about what you're noticing.

SANDI:   I didn't recognize the material . . . I didn't know what it was made out of. It felt like we were in a cave, but it was smooth. You know how the back of the cave is rounded on the top and the bottom—it felt like that, but it wasn't natural like a cave. It was smooth. It felt like maybe . . . maybe it wasn't that tall. I felt that maybe if I stood up, it wouldn't be tall enough for me.

DR. FIORE:   Was it tall enough for the other beings who were there?

SANDI:   Hmmm. Yes, it was fine for them. They must not have been . . . they were so cute. They were littler than me.

DR. FIORE:   And then what happens to you?

SANDI:   I just feel like I'm sinking back down into my chair that I was sitting in. It feels like I'm there and then I'm not, I'm there and then I'm not . . . and then I'm there a little bit more . . . and then I'm not. And then, little by little, I'm there more and more . . . back in my chair . . . back in my living room. And then I just become more whole and more whole. And . . . I was afraid that I wasn't still all there. I was afraid that they had taken something . . . that they hadn't put me back together. [*Cries*] And then they talked to me . . . [*Sobbing*] They talked to me and told me not to be afraid, to be calm, and everything was okay and all that. They were very reassuring again. Just somehow I was sitting in my chair. I was back in my chair in my living room. Then . . . then they just seemed to be gone. I woke up . . . I looked into the TV some more, because it was still snowy. I looked into the TV, still looking for a message, then it blinked . . . blinked and came back on, a program was on. So I was looking down at the TV. The TV was in front of the window that the light came through. I was looking down at the TV, and when I looked back up to check and see if the light was still there, it was gone. And I got up . . . and I went . . . I looked at the window. I went to the front-door window and I looked all over and there was no light . . . it was gone. It was there on the hill, and then it wasn't there anymore. And then I . . . kind of shirked it off, and . . . sat back down and watched TV some more.

DR. FIORE: You're going to let yourself remember if there's anything else they did. Let yourself remember everything that happened. It's crystal clear in your memory, at the count of five. One . . . two . . . three . . . four . . . five.

SANDI: The stuff that felt like cotton was . . . was in a tub . . . was in a big, submarine-looking tub with a big hole in the top. And . . . [Sighs] They put me in there and it felt so soft. It was . . . like . . . jelly, but it was dry. It was so weird. I thought . . . this feels so nice, but what is it? And they put me in there and I kept sinking down. I don't know how deep it was, but it scared me, because I thought, If I sink in this stuff, it's thick enough to suffocate me. I don't want to, so I kept crawling back up. It was thick enough . . . it was thick enough . . . to like . . . grab onto, to get to the top, but it wasn't thick enough to keep me from sinking. It was in a big tank that looked like . . . looked like metal, I guess. It was like a big propane gas tank, like a big torpedo submarine. And it had an opening in the top, not big enough for me to lie out flat. I had to lie kinda with my feet drawn up, a little bit, because the hole wasn't big enough. I don't know how they got me. It seems like they were so gentle. I guess maybe they just lowered me in. They were so nice. The ones with robes were so nice. They seemed like women. They seemed female to me. They were so gentle and so empathetic and so nurselike. They were nice. That was in the corner of the room. The room was basically oval, but it had on one whole side little coves, or quite big coves. It was kinda like the shape of a shell, and in one of those coves was this tank. There was the one cove and there was a big scooped out place on one side. It was like the second cove, and it had a counter, pretty low to the ground. I can't remember them doing anything else.

DR. FIORE:   Did they ask you any questions?

SANDI:   It seemed like they were pressuring me, they were asking me why I was questioning them. "Why are you fighting us? Why are you questioning us?" And I kept thinking, Well . . . 'cause it was weird! [*Laughs*] And I told them, "Just leave me alone." [*Whispers*] And they . . . they kept making me feel really bad. They hurt my feelings. [*Cries*] They made me feel like I was wrong, like I was bad.

DR. FIORE:   How did they do that?

SANDI:   It's just that they kept on me and on me, "Why are you questioning anything we do? How dare you?" And that made me feel bad. There was more.

DR. FIORE:   It's all coming back, it's very easy to remember.

SANDI:   It was that one with the weird face. He wasn't nice. He's the only one that did bad things to me. He's the one that made me feel bad. He's telling me that I was bad, telling me that I was no good, that I didn't matter, that I was expendable, why should I care about my little self so much, and how dare I question him.

DR. FIORE: When he said that to you, how did you feel?

SANDI: I just felt really defenseless. I kind of thought maybe he was right. After a while, he did it to me. I just fought and fought. With whatever communication we were using, I just kept telling him. . . . I tried to fight back, "You know I'm just asking questions because I'm curious." I tried to defend myself, but he was strong. He just kept overpowering me and telling me that I was bad and . . . and finally . . . finally I thought maybe I'd better do what he said.

DR. FIORE: What did he want you to do?

SANDI: He wanted me to . . . he wanted me to empty my mind. I remember him telling me that. He said, "Don't think about anything." And I said, "How can I not think about anything? There's so much here that's going on, I have to think." And then, slowly, he told me to empty my mind of everything. "Don't think about anything."

DR. FIORE: When he said that, how did you feel?

SANDI: I said, "Okay," and he helped me. He talked to me. [*Sighs*] He just kept saying, "Empty your mind. Don't think about a thing. Let it all go away. Just empty it." And I remember . . . [*Sighs*] . . . I remember doing that. And I just . . . I just felt like I was in the blue skies . . . I felt like I was just air. I remember feeling . . . nothing. I guess I emptied my mind, because I thought that I was up in the blue sky . . . just floating . . . just nothing.

DR. FIORE: Now you're going to do something very interesting. You understand now that he hypnotized you, don't you?

SANDI: Yes.

DR. FIORE: You're going to remember what happened when you were under hypnosis. You're going to remember everything that happened. You emptied your mind and then what happened?

SANDI: I see a schoolroom and an American flag. [*Laughs*] Sheep, I don't know.

DR. FIORE: Trust your mind. Where are the sheep, and what are they doing?

SANDI: They're grazing in a pasture with a fence around them. I see a classroom, a little old-fashioned classroom with desks, and a chalkboard and an American flag.

DR. FIORE: Go back to that oval room. Your body was in that oval room, and there was a part of your mind that was observing and witnessing what was happening. You're in the oval room. You've emptied your mind. You're not thinking about what's happened with part of your mind. But the subconscious part of your mind is registering everything exactly as it happened, and now you're going to remember. When this being told you that you were going to empty your mind, did he also tell you that you would not remember anything?

SANDI: Yes.

DR. FIORE: Tell me what he said.

SANDI: It was a threat. He said, "You're not going to remember!" And I kept thinking, Yes, I am! I'm going to remember everything! And he said, "No, you will not!"

DR. FIORE: This is your chance to remember everything. Now you're going to remember everything that he thought you would not remember.

SANDI: He's asking me questions.

DR. FIORE: What questions does he ask you?

SANDI: [*Pauses*] I can't remember. [*Becomes upset*]

DR. FIORE: You can remember. You have every memory in your mind, and the only reason why you think you can't remember is because he tricked you into thinking you couldn't. And he was wrong. You can remember everything. You would like that, wouldn't you? Okay. Now you're going to prove that you are stronger than he is, because you are going to remember everything that happened that he thought you would never remember. What were the questions he asked you?

SANDI: He asked me about water, about the ponds. I didn't know the answers to his questions. It seems like all I had to do was think about things, I didn't have to say things. I remember something about water . . . picture of it, of a dammed pond, ponds that we had all over . . . fish . . . He kept asking me really . . . hard questions I did not know.

DR. FIORE: Like what? What was a really hard question that you did not know?

SANDI: I can't remember.

DR. FIORE: Now you can remember everything. You do want to remember, don't you?

SANDI: Yes.

DR. FIORE: We're going to undo his suggestion. Now he may have told you that you would never, ever remember what happened, but you see you have already remembered, haven't you? So he was wrong. So he doesn't have as much power as he thought he had, because you have already remembered a great deal about the encounter with these beings. Now you're going to remember at this point whether he asked you any personal questions; that would be much easier to remember. Did he ask you anything about your family, or about yourself, or about your life?

SANDI: He asked about my house and my family. He seemed to have been watching me . . . he seemed to know so much about me, and he wanted to know where my . . . I think he asked me where my . . . where my souls were. I think he meant my family.

DR. FIORE: When he used the word soul rather than family, what did you think?

SANDI: I was just trying to interpret what he was asking me. I thought it was kind of strange, but, in a way . . . I was real close to my family and they're like part of me, so maybe he was wondering where the rest of me was.

DR. FIORE: What did you say?

SANDI: I told him they're right here with me, they're inside of me, they're always close to me. And I was afraid he was going to take them away. [Cries] But he said he wasn't going to take them away, he just wanted to know where they were. [Relieved] He wanted to know more about them, he wanted to know a lot more about them. But I thought . . . he just wanted to know more about me. He was very nice. He was very kind. That it would be okay. He told me not to worry, it would be okay. [Pauses] He wanted to know . . . He wanted to know more . . . He wanted to know about the dog. We have a dog, and . . . he asked me if the dog was my soul too. I told him that we loved our dog, but he wasn't my soul. And . . . and then, then he wanted to know about love. He wanted to know about my family. And about love. I had to think about each one. I just thought. He told me, "Just open your mind and think about each one. Think about your mother, think about your father, think about your brother, and now think about yourself." So I did. [*Sighs*] He seemed to be real pleased about that. He was very happy. He said I was doing very well. He had the attitude like . . . now that we've done the part that's uncomfortable, you can do this and it won't hurt at all. He said it wouldn't hurt at all, that it would be fine and I was safe. It was fine. It was okay. It wouldn't hurt me anymore, and he was very nice then.

DR. FIORE: What part had they done that had hurt you?

SANDI: They . . . poked, poked, poked, poked . . . and . . . just poked everywhere . . . every little rib and bone and muscle. I didn't like that very much.

DR. FIORE: This conversation with him was later, is that correct?

SANDI: Yes. I think when I was lying on the flat table with the light up above, when everyone left. I don't think he was really there, he was just talking to me. His power was immense, but I don't remember anyone . . . being there with me. Although he was, you know, he was there, but he wasn't there. I think I was alone.

DR. FIORE: Let yourself know if there's anything else that he said to you.

SANDI: He wanted to know about feathers. [*Pauses*] I see feathers. I see birds. He's making me think about them. He puts his little ideas in my head and then he has me think about everything I know about them. The sheep and the pasture . . .

DR. FIORE: He put that idea in your head?

SANDI:   Yes. He said just relax and let it happen. "Just see whatever you see in a classroom, and the feathers. . . ."

DR. FIORE:   Now I'm going to ask you a few questions at this point. You will remember everything because you want to remember. When you were being poked everywhere, did they do any kind of vaginal examination?

SANDI:   I don't think they did.

DR. FIORE:   Now you're going to let yourself know if they put a needle in any part of your body, other than the rectum.

SANDI:   No. They were carrying needles around, big ones, and I was scared for a while they were going to put one in me, but they didn't. [*Body tenses*]

DR. FIORE:   Now, just let yourself relax. At the count of three you're going to remember whether they did put one of those big needles in you. If they did, know that you're safe, and it's all over, isn't it. And if they didn't, you're going to remember that too, at the count of three. One . . . two . . . three.

SANDI:   They did.

DR. FIORE:   Now let yourself know all about it.

SANDI:   [*Crying in pain*] And they were pushing my head over, and they put it in my neck, in my back. And somewhere. [*Whispers*] I was so scared.

DR. FIORE:   What did they do with the needles?

SANDI:   I can't.

DR. FIORE: You're letting yourself remember. They pushed your head over and they put one in your neck and in your back. Tell me where they put them.

SANDI: [*Winces*] In my neck. In my neck, in my head. In my . . .

DR. FIORE: Did they put more than one needle in your neck or just one?

SANDI: Just one.

DR. FIORE: You said you saw them carrying around big needles. How many needles did you actually see?

SANDI: Ten.

DR. FIORE: And where else did they put the needles?

SANDI: In my arm, in my forearm. They ran it right under the skin.

DR. FIORE: Did it hurt when they put the needles in?

SANDI: Yes. It hurt going in. It didn't hurt once it went in. It just felt like something was in there. It felt like I was deadened. I could feel something hard in there, but it didn't hurt. It just hurt when it went in.

DR. FIORE: Where else did they put them?

SANDI: Between my toes, between my big toe and the next toe. That one was awful! [*Cries in pain*]

DR. FIORE: Did they explain to you why they were doing this, or what they were doing?

SANDI: No.

DR. FIORE: How did you react to the needles?

SANDI: I was scared, but I couldn't react. It was like I was drugged. I wanted to just jump off the table, but I couldn't. I was so heavy. And . . . I'm not sure I cared. I did . . . on the one hand, I did care. I wanted to leave. On the other hand . . . I was so heavy and so sleepy that I didn't care what they did. But when I saw them, especially the one between my toes, I thought, Oh . . . my God!

DR. FIORE: What did they do? Did they put the needle in and leave it sticking in you?

SANDI: They seemed to stick it in and then wiggle it around. They were wiggling it around like they were . . . I don't know. They would wiggle it. And on my arm, they just kept sliding it and kept sliding it in. And . . . I don't know. I don't think they injected anything. It seems like they were just probing in there, to see . . . to see something, to find out something.

DR. FIORE: Were any needles put in your abdomen or your navel?

SANDI: I think so.

DR. FIORE: Tell me about that.

SANDI: [Pauses] It's not so clear.

DR. FIORE: You are going to remember at the count of three. It's so easy. Look how much you've already remembered. One . . . two . . . three.

SANDI: Yes, they did, through my navel.

DR. FIORE:   How did that feel?

SANDI:   It felt like sticking your finger in a balloon. It felt like putting a pin in a balloon. It stretches and it stretches and it stretches and it finally punctures. It was like that.

DR. FIORE:   And when it punctured, how did it feel?

SANDI:   It was fine.

DR. FIORE:   And what did they do once they punctured it?

SANDI:   They wiggled it [the needles] around. I couldn't tell what they were doing. I think some of them were . . . like tubes. And I thought that maybe they were taking something. Yes . . . some of them were like tubes, especially the one in my arm.

DR. FIORE:   What were they taking?

SANDI:   I don't know.

DR. FIORE:   Did you see it?

SANDI:   I didn't look. I was too scared. Then I did look. They [the needles] were metal or stainless steel or something. I couldn't see what was in them. I couldn't see what they were taking. But in my arm, that one . . . that one was like a tube. It couldn't have been blood, because it would have run out.

DR. FIORE:   The male being who was questioning you and put you under hypnosis, did he look like the female type who was very kind and gentle? Did they all seem to be the same species?

SANDI:   Yes.

DR. FIORE:   Did they tell you where they came from?

SANDI: No.

DR. FIORE: Did you ask them?

SANDI: No.

DR. FIORE: When you left your living room, you said you left one body in your chair and floated in another body. I want to know if that's really true. I want you to go back to when you are leaving your living room. See if there's anybody in the living room with you. You're looking at the light. I want you to move to the very moment when you start to leave the chair and tell me everything that you experience.

SANDI: No one's in the room. I don't feel a presence, but someone is talking to me in my brain.

DR. FIORE: What is the person saying?

SANDI: They told me that I would be going up. [*Pauses*] "We're going to . . ." no, "You're going to feel like you're going up. You're going to go up. And don't be scared. Everything's okay." And I started to go up.

DR. FIORE: Tell me what part of you started to go up.

SANDI: Everything . . . it felt like everything was going up.

DR. FIORE: I want you to look back at the chair or the couch you were sitting in. As you were going up, what did you see there?

SANDI: I didn't look back. It felt like I was just leaving maybe a skin on the chair, just like a snake does . . . just a skin.

DR. FIORE: Did it feel like the physical body was going up?

SANDI: Yes.

DR. FIORE: Now what?

SANDI: I just went up and up and up. I didn't think it would ever end. I just felt lighter and lighter. . . .

DR. FIORE: How do you get from going up to being in the oval room.

SANDI: I don't know. It's just like I was there.

DR. FIORE: Okay. Now you're going to let yourself remember if you saw a craft of any sort.

SANDI: I don't know.

DR. FIORE: Now, I want you to remember the very last thing that was said to you by those beings.

SANDI: I think they said, "Goodbye."

DR. FIORE: Did they thank you?

SANDI: In a weird sort of way, I think so. But it wasn't the way we do it. It wasn't so much thank you as it was . . . they knew that I knew. It's like they didn't have to say it. They knew that they . . . had benefited and they knew that I had benefited.

DR. FIORE: Let yourself know how you benefited from that experience.

SANDI: It's like . . . they gave me an experience to make me a more whole person. To experience that, they said, would be good . . . or they implied it would be good for me.

DR. FIORE: Did you ever have any experiences with them or other aliens before that experience?

SANDI: I don't think so.

DR. FIORE: Have you had any experiences with them since then?

SANDI: Maybe . . . I'm not sure. It seems like they've been here again. It seems like they've talked to me and I've talked back. It's a . . . like a warm feeling.

DR. FIORE: A warm feeling?

SANDI: It's like deep inside. Very positive.

DR. FIORE: Are you saying that you may have been telepathically communicated with?

SANDI: I think so, yes.

DR. FIORE: And it's something that you welcomed?

SANDI: Yes.

✿

As I brought Sandi out of hypnosis, I looked over at Les, who had been listening attentively for almost two hours. He looked relieved that it was over and delighted at the same time.

Sandi seemed a bit disoriented at first, which is not at all unusual, especially after being under hypnosis for such a long time. I got her a glass of water, and Les watched her rather apprehensively as she drank it.

"How do you feel now, Sandi?" I wanted to have her start talking and orienting herself to her surroundings. It is very easy for people to slip back into a trance as they mull over what they just experienced.

"Fine. Just a little sleepy." Les moved his chair closer to her, and they smiled at each other.

"You've been under hypnosis for almost two hours, Sandi."

"It seems like just a few minutes. I'm surprised. What time is it?" Les leaned over and showed her his watch. "I can't believe it!"

"That's time distortion, a very common feature of hypnosis. By the way, do you feel you've been hypnotized?"

"No. I didn't go under, but I don't understand how it could have been so long. I didn't feel any different." She looked up and off to the left. "I was pretty scared during some of that. I guess I must have been hypnotized though, because it was so real. And I never knew that all that happened before."

The three of us talked about her regression, and when it seemed that she was back to her normal waking consciousness, I suggested we end our session. Sandi agreed to do some drawings that are included later in the book.

As she and Les were just about to leave, she turned back. "Thanks a lot for clearing up the mystery. I have a lot to think about now."

## "... They're Coming Down Here, Wanting to Mix with Our Race ..."

I agreed to see Mark as a special favor to his grandmother, Betty, a former patient. I work with adults (over the age of twenty-one), and Mark was only eighteen. Since I particularly liked his grandmother and his grandfather, also an ex-patient, I made an exception by taking Mark on for treatment.

Mark was the only person in the waiting room and got up eagerly as I came over to introduce myself. He greeted me pleasantly, and as he walked to my office, I noticed he had a very severe limp, yet there was something graceful about the way he moved his body. Mark was a clean-cut-looking young man, about five feet five inches tall. His body looked somewhat out of proportion, as though the top had grown to manhood, yet the bottom had not caught up.

Once in my consultation room, he got quickly to the point. "I've got arthritis. A couple of years ago it was real bad, now it's in remission." He continued, "I've got it in both hips, my lower back and ankles."

"When did it start, Mark?"

"When I was eleven. I was an athlete . . . in the soccer league. I got kicked in the ankle, but I ran on it. It got worse and I finally had to quit the game. It turned into arthritis, and three months later I was in the Stanford Children's Hospital."

Mark told me more about his life, his goal of going to college in the fall, his frustrations with his disease. As he put it, "It's such a big thing in my life. The doctors just treat the symptoms. I feel it's almost impossible to cure."

After he discussed his grandmother's plans to take him to a special clinic in Mexico, I asked him if he had had any recurrent dreams. He recounted several, but one in particular piqued my curiosity. It sounded like a possible abduction. I asked him to tell me everything he could remember about it.

"It's almost scary, like it wasn't a dream. There's nothing I can do. I'm paralyzed. I see a person for a split second. It's not even a person. He's like the dude on the cover of that book. The one with the picture of the UFO guy."

"*Communion?*"

"Yeah. But not exactly like that one. He has that long face, but in the dream it doesn't have much detail to it. The eyes are round and an emerald green. The body is all one color. After he takes hold of me, it's like I'm shrinking and I'm scared. That's all I can remember."

"How often have you had the dream?"

"Many times over the years."

I suggested to Mark that he might be remembering actual close encounters of the fourth kind and asked him if he was interested in UFOs.

He leaned forward with a lot of excitement showing on his face. "I'm very interested in them. I think about them a lot . . . about their technology . . . the places they hide in the ocean. And how they study us. While I was in Children's Hospital, I was hoping they would come down and take me away. I've taken astronomy classes and I look at the stars a lot. I look for a ship."

"Have you read about abductions? Have you read *Communion?*"

"No. I picked it up in the bookstore and read a few pages."

"Did you have any reactions to the pictures or the cover or what you read?"

After he answered negatively, I decided to continue exploring his dreams. "Have you had any dreams about UFOs?"

"A couple. I'm getting into a ship once and taking off . . . and then the dream is over. They don't make me get on, though. In some other dreams, I'm on the ground and the UFOs fly by me. In some, I'm scared like it's a nightmare and in some I'm not."

We seemed to have gotten off on a tangent. One that interested me greatly, but Mark was seeking my help for his arthritis, and I didn't see any possibility of a connection. I decided to initiate hypnosis at that point in order to do some work on the major issue in his life.

Mark quickly slipped into a moderate trance, and I immediately began to work on his symptoms. After about fifteen minutes, he mentioned seeing a picture of a UFO. Following my intuition, I decided to regress him to the cause of his recurrent dream.

*

MARK: I see my house I used to live in. Here in the Bay Area. And . . . I'm seven. I think this is right after I got diabetes, maybe before. And they're taking me up. They're levitating me up to the ship.

DR. FIORE: Tell me about that in detail.

MARK: I don't have a blanket on me, so I just go up, and part of the roof just . . . I don't know, it's, like it's transparent, and I go through it into . . . and then there's a compartment in the bottom of the spaceship that I go up into. And there's two aliens, one on one side of me and one on the other. I'm a little frightened here. This feels like even the second or third time I've been abducted. And they put me on a little table that has wheels on it. And they roll me down the hall . . . and they're lifting my eyelid back.

DR. FIORE:  What does that feel like?

MARK:  It doesn't hurt. They're not lifting it, they're just pushing it back. I guess they're just looking at me. In the room they put me in, there's another little boy.

DR. FIORE:  What's happening to him?

MARK:  It looks like he's sleeping.

DR. FIORE:  Are they doing anything to him?

MARK:  No. He's just lying there. He's on a table.

DR. FIORE:  What emotions are you feeling at this point?

MARK:  A little frightened.

DR. FIORE:  Where are the aliens in relationship to you?

MARK:  They left.

DR. FIORE:  Are you in the room alone with this boy?

MARK:  Yes. I know the boy is there, but it's like I don't really care if he's there, I'm just worried about myself. I'm lying down, trying to fall asleep.

DR. FIORE:  Why are you trying to fall asleep?

MARK:  Because I think it's a dream and I want it to go away.

DR. FIORE:  And now it's a little later.

MARK:  We're both awake, and we both have our own alien with us. And we're holding hands with it, and we're using it as a crutch and we're walking. I think they're watching the way we walk. And we go back, we go across the room a few times. I'm not really paying attention to the boy. It's like I don't feel like I should.

DR. FIORE:   Why do you suppose they're looking at the way you walk? Did they say anything to you?

MARK:   They don't say nothing. I kinda just know what to do. I kinda read the body language.

DR. FIORE:   Is there anything unusual about the way you walk?

MARK:   Not the way I walk. They're like looking at my knees, ankles and hips. It only happened a couple of times. They put me back up on the table. I'm lying down now.

DR. FIORE:   Now what's happening?

MARK:   I kind of have a feeling that they're coming down here, wanting to mix with our race, you know?

DR. FIORE:   What gives you that idea?

MARK:   Because they're getting like a real small, real thin wire, and at the end of this wire is a tube, and they've been squirting medicine in it, and they stick the wire down my penis and squirt it into me. And I'm out of it though. I'm not awake. I feel like I've got anesthesia.

DR. FIORE:   Where do you feel you are?

MARK:   I feel like I'm on the table. I know what's happening to me, but there's nothing I can do about it.

DR. FIORE:   Do you see what's happening?

MARK:   Yes.

DR. FIORE:   And where are you in relationship to your body?

MARK:   I'm inside my body lying down, and also above it a little bit, above and to the right side.

DR. FIORE:   Do they explain to you why they put the wire in your penis?

MARK:   They keep telling me, this is just going to help us in the long run.

DR. FIORE:   When they say "us," whom do they mean?

MARK:   I guess they mean their race.

DR. FIORE:   What causes you to lose consciousness?

MARK:   They just put their hand on my forehead. Just gently they touched it, and I kinda just went out.

DR. FIORE:   That's when you left your body and went unconscious?

MARK:   Yes.

DR. FIORE:   And then it was after that they inserted the tube?

MARK:   Yes.

DR. FIORE:   Speak out anything that comes into your mind.

MARK:   Kind of like when a doctor presses on your stomach, feels for an ulcer or something like that. I see myself from the top, right now. The aliens are feeling around, like my testicles. I guess they're feeling for the wire or something. It's almost like a fishing wire, fishing line. And they pull it out, real fast.

DR. FIORE: What thoughts are in your mind as you're looking down?

MARK: I don't want no problems with that area when I get older.

DR. FIORE: Are you saying that you don't want them to hurt you permanently?

MARK: I don't want them to hurt me, whatever they're doing. I don't want there to be scars or damage to it later on or something.

DR. FIORE: Now what happens?

MARK: Some of the medicine or fluid or whatever it is leaked out, and they clean it up. It's kind of a pale blue color. Then they're checking my chest area. They're just touching. They take my neck and they move it from side to side. And they cut off a little piece of my hair. [*Pauses*]

DR. FIORE: Just report everything that comes into your mind.

MARK: One of the aliens takes both hands and grabs the sides of my face, gently, and his thumbs or fingers are on my temples, and I wake up.

DR. FIORE: Do you feel that what he did wakes you up?

MARK: Yes.

DR. FIORE: Tell me exactly what he did.

MARK: He uses both hands. He takes his forefingers, puts them behind my head, puts the palms on the cheekbone with the thumb on the temple and kinda just presses, and I wake up.

DR. FIORE: And then what happens?

MARK: He helps me off the table, and he walks me to this little chair. There's a round bowl that comes over my head, like you go inside a beauty shop and it dries your hair. And it covers me. I feel this warm feeling over me. Kind of really relaxing. I fall asleep. It's just so relaxing. And then a guy comes over and picks me up . . . lays me like on the floor, and . . . boom. I'm gone.

DR. FIORE: What do you mean by that?

MARK: He put me back in bed. If I remember correctly, I woke up with a slight headache.

DR. FIORE: Go to any time when they did a healing on you, if they did, of any condition that you have. If they've healed you for a number of things, go to the one that has had the strongest impact on you, at the count of three. One . . . two . . . three.

MARK: They have a big clamp around the left side of my side, my gut. It's sending pulses, shock waves into my pancreas, for my diabetes. I don't know what it's for, but it tickles sometimes, and every time it sends one of these waves through, my body twitches just a little bit.

DR. FIORE: How do you know they're sending it to your pancreas?

MARK: Because that's where it's at, that's where they have this clamp. And I have diabetes, and I have a feeling that's what it's for.

DR. FIORE: How do you feel about them doing this?

MARK: I don't mind.

DR. FIORE:   Do you have any other feelings or thoughts?

MARK:   I just wonder when they're gonna get done with me.

DR. FIORE:   What do you mean?

MARK:   'Cause I felt like I've been there a long time, with them working on me. Nothing they did was painful. I'm just real, real impatient, just to be lying there, having this thing hooked to the side of me.

DR. FIORE:   Are you alone in the room?

MARK:   Yes.

DR. FIORE:   Do they explain what they're doing?

MARK:   No. I kinda feel that they're just putting, this energy in me, this thing that's hooked to me.

DR. FIORE:   How many extraterrestrials are there with you?

MARK:   Just one.

DR. FIORE:   Tell me about this being.

MARK:   His form's kinda flat. It's not round like ours. And he has pretty broad shoulders and a thin neck. His arms are much longer than humans' arms are. His fingers are much longer and more bony-looking, the knuckles are.

DR. FIORE:   How many fingers does he have?

MARK:   Four.

DR. FIORE:   Does he have a thumb in addition?

MARK: Yes.

DR. FIORE: So does he have five altogether?

MARK: No, four. Three fingers and a thumb. It's a big thumb.

DR. FIORE: What does his face look like?

MARK: He has real sharp cheeks, they stick out there. He has a real small mouth. It doesn't open. And his nose is just a little mound. And his eyes look like a cat's almost. They're concave. And his head's almost like egg-shaped.

DR. FIORE: What is his hair like?

MARK: I don't see hair. There's a few little hairs, but not many of them.

DR. FIORE: Does he have eyebrows?

MARK: No.

DR. FIORE: Ears?

MARK: Doesn't really look like an ear, though. They're pretty small. It's like a little piece of skin, sticking up a little bit, with a hole. The hole's bigger than the piece of skin.

DR. FIORE: What color are the eyes?

MARK: Almost black, but also green a little bit, a dark green.

DR. FIORE: And how big are the eyes?

MARK: They're pretty big . . . big eyes.

DR. FIORE:   At this point, what is he doing to you?

MARK:   He's messing with his machinery, his equipment.

DR. FIORE:   You say he's been working on you a long time. What have they been doing all this time? Think back. Remember.

MARK:   He's been hooking me up to his machines.

DR. FIORE:   What part of your body?

MARK:   He was taking blood out.

DR. FIORE:   Where did he take the blood out?

MARK:   He took it out of my arm.

DR. FIORE:   And then what?

MARK:   He put this thing over my chest, like a big thing of rubber, well, it was pretty heavy. Like lead almost, like what they use in X-ray machines. They put it over me, over my chest. And on the machine, it showed my lungs and my heart. And he'd move this thing up and down, and it would show my internal organs, and the bones, you know.

DR. FIORE:   Could you see it too?

MARK:   Yes. I looked over at it. The machine was right by me.

DR. FIORE:   And then?

MARK:   He also has another machine that takes pictures of what this screen had showed on it. It'd keep track of everything that it showed, and as this paper stuff came out, he would mark little x's and o's and he would draw little things on certain areas of the paper, like for my heart or my bones or something. He put this thing on my head, like a bandana, and it made me sweat, and he's scraping the sweat off. He's going to keep it, to study it or something. This thing he put on my head, it's real hot. My forehead broke out in a sweat.

DR. FIORE:   Did he explain why he was doing any of this to you?

MARK:   No. He don't talk to me. I feel that he's going to study it all, examine it, for future reference.

DR. FIORE:   Now he's just scraped off the sweat, now what?

MARK:   That's all.

DR. FIORE:   When does he put the clamp on you?

MARK:   That's not till later.

DR. FIORE:   What does he do in between?

MARK:   He went out for a minute.

DR. FIORE:   During this time, did you think of escaping or protesting?

MARK:   No. It's kinda like being in a doctor's office.

DR. FIORE:   Did you have the feeling that it was familiar, that you had done this before?

MARK:   Yes.

DR. FIORE:   Can you actually remember having done it before, or is it just a feeling of familiarity?

MARK:   Yes. Familiar. 'Cuz that alien that was working on me is real friendly. He seemed like a pleasant person, like he's seen and talked to me before.

DR. FIORE:   Move to the moment when he comes back in the room.

MARK:   He has the clamp with him now. And another person's coming in with him. He put the clamp on me, and then the other alien hooked it up to the machines. Then he left the room.

DR. FIORE:   Did they both leave?

MARK:   No.

DR. FIORE:   Who left the room?

MARK:   The one that hooked the wires and plugs and stuff that the clamp was to.

DR. FIORE:   The one that came in, did he look similar to or very different from the other aliens?

MARK:   He looked a lot alike.

DR. FIORE:   What were they wearing?

MARK:   Nothing.

DR. FIORE:   Could you see their skin all over their body?

MARK:   Yes, something like a chameleon, they can change their colors. It has to do with the lighting. They can change their color. They can't go from like a black to a white, but they can go from a lighter to a darker color from what their skin color is.

DR. FIORE:   They're not wearing any clothing at all?

MARK:  No.

DR. FIORE:  Can you see their genitals, for example?

MARK:  No, I don't look at them. I just see them from the belly up.

DR. FIORE:  Do they have a navel?

MARK:  Yes.

DR. FIORE:  Is it different from ours in any way?

MARK:  It looks basically the same.

DR. FIORE:  Was anything said to you about your diabetic condition? Any questions asked or anything said about it?

MARK:  Nope. But they knew what was wrong with me. They knew I had diabetes.

DR. FIORE:  Did their treatment help your diabetes?

MARK:  Nope.

DR. FIORE:  Did it make it worse?

MARK:  Nope. It didn't do nothing to it.

DR. FIORE:  What do you think they were doing? Why do you think that clamp was there?

MARK:  I think the shock waves were . . . there's something unique inside this shock wave that would hopefully stimulate the dead part of the pancreas to make that start working once again. It didn't work.

DR. FIORE:   Do you feel they have helped your arthritis in any way?

MARK:   I don't think they're helping with it. They're just looking at it and studying it, as I go on. They're not doing nothing for it.

DR. FIORE:   As you have reached maturity, do you feel they have taken any of your sperm?

MARK:   Yes.

DR. FIORE:   You're going to remember that at the count of five. One . . . two . . . three . . . four . . . five.

MARK:   Yes. They have a fishing wire-type of thing. On the end of it is like a miniature thing you stick up a baby's nose to get the mucus out. It's like that, but it's real small. And that was painful. And I guess they used that as a suction. And on the end of it, was like a little camera so they knew where they were going. They must know anatomy pretty well, and they went to the part where the sperm was being made, and sucked some of it out.

DR. FIORE:   And that hurt you?

MARK:   Going in hurt.

DR. FIORE:   But did it hurt so much that you had to leave your body?

MARK:   I was out. They put me out. I'm asleep during this. I see myself from the top now.

DR. FIORE:   How do you know now that it hurts?

MARK:   Just by watching myself, I can tell that it hurt. And I just remember something now. I don't have kidney stones, but when I go to the bathroom, sometimes it hurts bad, and that can be from them doing that.

DR. FIORE:  How many times have they extracted the sperm from you?

MARK:  Twice, I think.

DR. FIORE:  When was the last time?

MARK:  Age fifteen comes to my mind.

DR. FIORE:  Is there anything else you want to remember before we stop?

MARK:  That's it.

*

After Mark was out of hypnosis, he shook his head. "I can't believe all that happened. But it was so clear, and I could feel those scared feelings, just like it was happening right then."

"We'll never know for sure, Mark, but what you experienced is very similar to what other people have remembered about that kind of encounter."

"So do you think my dream was real then? I mean like not a dream, but really happened to me?"

"It's very possible, Mark. There is nothing in your regression that I haven't heard before, or at least heard something very close to it."

*

Mark left my office satisfied that he had done his best and excited about his experience with the aliens. I was very interested in the visitors' efforts to help his diabetes and perhaps his arthritis as well. Yet even their advanced technology could not give him the relief he so desperately wanted and needed. The fact that he had remembered experiences and procedures that were painful and frightening meant that he had healed himself of the negative effects from those buried traumas. Not only had Mark helped himself, he had contributed to our growing knowledge of the most exciting and remarkable happening of our age, the interaction of extraterrestrials and humans.

# "I Wouldn't Let Them
# Make Me Forget."

Barbara eased her huge body into my Danish black leather reclining chair and burst into racking sobs. "I've been real sick. It's all this weight. Three hundred and forty-seven pounds! And now I have panic attacks all the time."

I handed her a box of tissues and waited for the crying to subside. From the biographical data sheet she had returned to me before our appointment, I knew that she was in her early fifties, married, the mother of grown children, and worked full time in a position with considerable responsibility. I saw before me a suffering human being; obese, terrified and probably feeling completely hopeless.

"The moment I arrived in your parking lot, I started to have a panic attack, but I feel better already," Barbara said, blowing her nose noisily. "You're my last hope." Barbara's face reflected the desperation she was feeling. "I've tried counselors and doctors. They just tell me to take off the weight and relax."

She gave me a "laundry list" of her many physical problems, including "heart attacks," hemorrhaging, a hysterectomy, aller-

51

gies, headaches, seven surgeries to repair a bad break in her leg and torn muscles in her knee, and borderline diabetes. As she settled back more into the chair, she described other, psychological problems; a lifelong claustrophobia that had worsened during the past twenty years, and, more recently, the panic attacks. Her stormy marriage of over thirty years was an ongoing source of unhappiness and stress. "I'm sure it's all tied in with my 'iceberg' . . . a lot of anger and hatred that I hold in. I put on a smile and go on with life." She spent some time telling me about her marriage and then appeared to have run out of steam. She looked at me as though the ball were now in my court.

"What's your top priority, Barbara? We have about an hour left today, and we can get started with the treatment now."

"The panic attacks are the worst problem. The others have been around for ages, but these started about three years ago, back in 1983," she said, reaching forward for another tissue. Wiping her face and neck, she gazed up to her left, obviously remembering something. "I was driving home at night, about 10:40. All of a sudden, I saw a flash of light . . . in an instant, twenty minutes had passed. I felt real confused." She leaned forward in her chair and almost whispered as she confided, "I started feeling anxious from that point on. Later, I was in the hospital, when all of a sudden I woke at 3:00 A.M. and something said, 'UFO.' I looked out and saw a strange streak in the sky. I wasn't sure what it was. I started reading articles on UFOs, and they made me really nervous, but I was fascinated at the same time."

"Why were you in the hospital, Barbara?"

"One of those heart attacks I was trying to have," she said, chuckling. "They started about a year ago. My heart would speed up, chest pains were really bad, I'd get faint and just about pass out."

"What does your doctor say about them?"

"He says they're due to stress—pressure. I find if I have a real rough day at the office, they occur."

I wanted to use hypnosis with her before she left, since she lived near Sacramento, about two hours away, and would not be able to come on a regular once-a-week basis. Often panic attacks can be relieved relatively easily, if we are able to "hit the nail on the head" without a whole lot of resistance. But before starting the treatment, I needed a few more clues. I asked her to tell me more about the panic attacks.

"After the first one, I noticed I had sore spots on my body. It was scraped, but I couldn't remember bumping into anything. If I relaxed, my mind would be bombarded with thoughts so fast I couldn't grab onto them."

"Was there any theme?" I asked.

Barbara looked down with a sheepish smile on her face. "Please don't think I'm crazy . . ." She glanced up at me for reassurance.

I smiled at her. "Barbara, you're not crazy and you know it. I'm very used to hearing unusual things. I doubt whether anything can shock me anymore."

"Well, occasionally thoughts of UFOs come storming into my mind and, believe it or not, a day or so later someone will say they have seen one." She let out a big sigh of relief and relaxed back into the chair. "I'm psychic. I've been sensitive that way ever since I was a kid. It's a liability! I get severe headaches before natural disasters, especially earthquakes. I have to call the doctor, and he gives me a shot."

"How frequent are the panic attacks, Barbara, and where and when do they occur?"

"There's one section of the road, just past a bridge, and unfortunately, I have to go that way to get home from school at night. I'm taking some night courses. I have them [panic attacks] there. I haven't had a good night's sleep in three years! I wake up in the middle of the night, terrified." Crying, she twisted a wad of tissues around her fingers and looked up at me beseechingly. "They're crippling me!"

I had planned to make a tape of relaxing suggestions that would help her to sleep and from there proceed into a regression to the cause of the panic. I judged that the remaining fifty minutes would give us enough time.

"Barbara, usually people's body temperatures drop a bit when they're relaxing," I said as I covered her with the mohair blanket and eased her chair into a reclining position.

I settled back in my Danish rosewood chair, slid a thirty-minute tape into the small Sony on the end table, picked up the mike and began speaking to her in a soft, modulated voice, asking her to close her eyes, sink down into the chair and concentrate on her breathing. I studied her face and saw the muscles giving way to my continuing suggestions to relax and drift deeper.

Suddenly, she started squirming in the chair, throwing the blanket off and breathing rapidly. I realized she was panicking and immediately decided to do the regression. Quickly slipping the relaxation tape out of the recorder, I grabbed a ninety-minute blank tape, pushed Record/Play, swung the boom around close to her face and placed the mike in it, to record the session.

✐

DR. FIORE:   Tell me whatever comes to mind, without censoring the material for any reason. What are you aware of now?

BARBARA:   I'm driving along about fifty-five miles per hour. Something in my mind says UFO, and I look around at the sky through my windows, but I don't see anything except a very large bright moon. But the feeling is very strong. There's a flash of light. [*Pauses*] A UFO stops over my car and brings my car to a halt. [*Getting upset*] I am taken out of the car.

DR. FIORE:   How is that done?

BARBARA:   By a light. The light seems to pull me from . . . pulls me out of my car. [*Becoming agitated*] I don't want to go. I'm taken aboard a . . . a . . . ramp. [*Crying*] I'm scared. I can't see anything. I'm scared. [*Pauses*] I'm on a table. I can't move. They keep telling me, "Don't be afraid. We won't hurt you." "I want to leave," I say. They say, "Not yet, not yet. You'll be all right. You won't remember." [*Calmer*] There are people there, but I can't see them. But I know they're there. They have equipment they run back and forth over me. It doesn't hurt. It's just I don't like being in close quarters. I don't like it and . . . [*Much more relaxed*] Then I go down the ramp to my car and I start driving home.

DR. FIORE: Go back to the moment you entered the UFO. You will remember everything that happened accurately at the count of three. One . . . two . . . three.

BARBARA: They are walking with me.

DR. FIORE: Who are "they"?

BARBARA: There's two. I think they're men. I can't tell. They're in gray. I see a gray hood, kinda like . . .

DR. FIORE: Is it like a jumpsuit?

BARBARA: Kinda like that, only it's closer fitting than that.

DR. FIORE: Are they talking to you as you walk?

BARBARA: They're not saying anything, but I hear what they're saying in my mind. "Don't be afraid. We won't hurt you." [*Shivers*] I'm cold. I'm inside now. When they undressed me, I said I didn't like it. "I don't know you guys." They just kind of chuckled and said, "Well, you won't remember anyway, so it doesn't matter." Then I told them I was cold, so they gave me a robe. There was this kind of cabinet under the table, and they got it there. Then they helped me onto the table.

DR. FIORE: Are you lying on the table?

BARBARA: Yes. On my back.

DR. FIORE: Remember exactly how they examined you.

BARBARA: They took a skin scraping.

DR. FIORE:   From where?

BARBARA:   My arm. My leg. They looked at my bad leg.

DR. FIORE:   What did they say about that?

BARBARA:   They said, "You had an accident." And I said, "Yes." They said, "You had your female organs removed," and I said, "Yes." And they wanted to know how I felt about it. [*Becoming upset*] Uh! I don't like the vibration. The rocking disturbs me. I have an inner ear problem, and the motion bothers me. They told me it doesn't take long. [*Jerking her hands away*] My fingernails. They clipped my fingernails and a piece of my hair. [*Pauses*] They took a blood sample.

DR. FIORE:   From what part of your body?

BARBARA:   From my finger. [*Extends right index finger. Long pause*]

DR. FIORE:   Did they examine you vaginally?

BARBARA:   No. They mainly used the machine . . . a big black machine . . . they ran it over my body. It didn't touch me, but it was close. And they were kind. They didn't want me to be upset.

DR. FIORE:   Did they tell you why they chose you?

BARBARA:   Because I was there.

DR. FIORE:   Tell me everything that's happening.

BARBARA:   They say something about my skin. They keep talking . . . something about my skin.

DR. FIORE: Just relax. I'll count to three, then you'll remember. One . . . two . . . three.

BARBARA: How white I am. My skin where it hasn't been exposed to the sun is very white. They keep calling it fragile. They keep telling me it's different.

DR. FIORE: Do they comment on your weight?

BARBARA: No, nothing about the weight. They're more interested in the white skin.

DR. FIORE: Do they say anything else to you?

BARBARA: They put blocks . . . they don't want people to know they're doing this, so they put blocks on the memory.

DR. FIORE: Did they say why they were doing this? Why they didn't want us to know?

BARBARA: They said they were exploring and finding out about other people, and because we're such an emotional people . . . uh . . . I'm fighting the block . . . emotional people, they don't want us to know they're there . . . but they want to find out what we're like. We're similar, but we're different. They tell me they're from Sirius. Uh! Uh! [Squirming] The vibration's getting stronger. [Pauses] The propulsion . . . that's what the vibration is. They take off out of sight of any other cars and then when it's clear, they bring you back to your car.

DR. FIORE: Is there anything else you need to remember?

BARBARA: They told me not to be afraid. That they do not hurt people.

DR. FIORE: Did they say anything about being in further contact with you?

BARBARA: They said I might feel their presence in the area because I have some psychic ability. I might feel their presence when they're there and that I should not be afraid and not let it bother me. They're very kind. They keep telling me, "Don't be afraid. You don't need to be afraid of us."

DR. FIORE: How many people did you see in the ship?

BARBARA: I saw three . . . and I keep seeing a panel of some kind. There's not a lot of light. I can't really tell . . .

DR. FIORE: What shape is the room you're in?

BARBARA: Oval . . . round. Round.

DR. FIORE: Tell me more about it.

BARBARA: There's doors and kinda like . . . I see a big metal wall that comes out into the room. Kinda like covering something. When I come up the ramp, it's kinda like you're in a steel corridor, then you come into the room where the table is. It's kinda like a medical room. It's not the control room of the ship. There's one person who's in charge. He seems to be bigger than the rest of them. He's taller and he keeps projecting kindness. He keeps telling me not to be afraid. He doesn't talk, but I keep hearing him in my mind telling me not to be afraid. They won't hurt me and I feel kindness from him. And he puts his hands on my eyes.

DR. FIORE: He touches your face?

BARBARA: Yes. He touches my forehead. He covers my eyes and my forehead with his hand. He says I won't remember.

DR. FIORE: Did you say anything?

BARBARA: I said I wanted to remember. I didn't want to forget. I'm very interested in things like this.

DR. FIORE: Did you deliberately try to undermine his suggestion to you?

BARBARA: Yes. I kept saying, "I want to remember."

DR. FIORE: You said it to yourself?

BARBARA: Yes. "I want to remember."

DR. FIORE: And now that you've remembered, how do you feel?

BARBARA: I feel better.

DR. FIORE: Do you feel there's anything to be afraid of?

BARBARA: No.

DR. FIORE: Now the panic you've been feeling . . . do you realize it's how you felt when you were going up the ramp?

BARBARA: Yes.

DR. FIORE: You've been having flashbacks. Do you understand that it's because you gave yourself the suggestion to remember? When I hypnotized you today, the memory came right up because you had already told yourself you wanted to remember. All these panic attacks have been your remembering . . . you were remembering the panic you felt as you approached the ship and were forced up the ramp. You didn't feel that way after the tall one in charge calmed you down. Let's go back over that again. You will remember what you experienced. You're going up the ramp again.

BARBARA:   Oh! Jesus! [*Crying and agitated*] Oh God! What are they going to do to me? [*Crying harder*] I'm scared. What are they going to do to me? [*Shouting*] God! No! No! [*Flailing her arms about as though to break free*] I'm trying to run back to the car. . . . [*Becomes calmer*]

DR. FIORE:   What's happening now?

BARBARA:   He's saying, "Don't be scared. We won't hurt you. It's all right. It's okay. Don't be scared. It's okay. It's okay. It's all right."

DR. FIORE:   Do you feel calmer?

BARBARA:   I'm not scared anymore. I know he won't hurt me. I'm looking at the table.

DR. FIORE:   I want you to remember the time you felt the best with him. You've already remembered the worst; now remember the best.

BARBARA:   Just before he put his hands on my head, kindness, just nothing but kindness flowed from him. He said he didn't like to upset people, but it was his job to check people out to see what they were like. And I understood that. I keep feeling kindness . . . kindness . . . kindness.

*

I brought Barbara out of hypnosis with suggestions of well-being and told her she would remember everything.

She opened her eyes and smiled broadly.

"How do you feel?"

"Much better."

"Is there anything to be afraid of now?"

"No," she said softly. "I wouldn't let them make me forget." A big grin lighted up her face.

"That's why you had the panic attacks, Barbara. You were actually reliving the anxiety you had felt during the abduction each time you passed that spot. When you relaxed the guard in your mind, for example when relaxing or sleeping, your subconscious mind tried to heal you of the trauma by bringing it to the surface of your mind. But it was too painful, so you pushed it back down. Have you ever had a boil?"

She leaned forward in her chair, looking puzzled. "Yes, a few times."

"When that happens, what your body is doing is bringing poisons to the surface so they can be released. Your mind has been doing the same thing."

She nodded, understanding.

"When you passed the place of the abduction, or any place very similar to it, the repression holding the memory down was weakened, and it started to come up. You were actually reliving what you had once experienced."

"Why doesn't it fade with time?" Barbara asked, shaking her head incredulously. "It's been just as bad lately as the first time."

"That's an excellent question. The subconscious mind has a memory bank of everything we have ever experienced, exactly as we perceived it. Every thought, emotion, sound of music, word, taste and sight. Everything is faithfully recorded somehow in your mind. Your subconscious mind's memory is perfect, infallible. The charges on traumatic memories are like thorns in our flesh. They fester . . . they cause all kinds of problems and symptoms, until the energy associated with them is dispelled. How this happens is not known, as yet, but that it does is very evident. Now I've given you a psychology lesson," I said, laughing.

"Are the panic attacks gone?" Barbara asked.

"The proof of the pudding is in the eating," I replied. "We won't know what we've accomplished here in the office until we see how you are in your daily life. When can you come back?"

We set up another appointment as soon as possible. As she stood up to leave, we both spontaneously moved toward each other for a hug.

With the door open, she paused, smiled and said, "Thanks. I feel so much better. Best of all, I now have hope."

*

When I saw Barbara ten days later in the waiting room, she smiled and eagerly got up to come into my office. Before she had even settled herself into the chair, she spread out her arms and said, "I'm so much better! I only woke up one night with a panic attack. And I'm not as tired, despite an allergy flare-up and the headache that goes with it."

"How did you feel when you left here?" I asked, picking up my yellow notepad and preparing to take my usual verbatim notes.

"Fine. I didn't feel any dread when I left Sacramento for home. I did a test. I deliberately went past the bridge and the place on the road I told you about. That section still bothers me. I feel some apprehension, but I know why. I have more insight. The first time, I just pulled over and parked . . . and waited it out. No panic, just apprehension."

I commended her for her progress, as well as her willingness to face her fears. Usually when a repressed event is exhumed, it brings in its wake more material that surfaces little by little when the mind is relaxed. Sometimes patients report whole scenes flashing before their eyes on the drive home after a session, or later as they're just about to drop off to sleep, or even when doing the dishes or other routine chores.

"Barbara, has anything more come into your mind about the event we dealt with last time?"

She leaned forward in her chair, bursting to tell me all that had happened. "I remember that two technicians pulled me from the car. They willed me to walk between them. When I got closer to the ship, I started to panic. The same panic I've been feeling. I yelled, "No!" They grabbed my arms, and the third man, the one in charge . . . he was in black, calmed me down. I walked up the ramp into the ship. The two technicians followed behind me. I felt a struggle between fear and curiosity. At the doorway, I stopped. I don't know or remember how I got undressed and on the table." She paused, and her eyes became distant. "The two technicians did undress me, now I remember, and gave me a robe because I complained I was too cold. I became aware of a slight vaginal and anal discomfort. But I don't remember much. There was a rectangular light panel. I hopped out of my body, astrally projected. I've done that since I was a kid, and I stood next to the door looking at my body on the table. The man in black said, "Damn psychics! Get back here!" He was disgruntled and ordered me back. So I went back. The machine is clearest in my mind. The three men looked the same as us. One technician kept talking about my skin and how white and fragile it is. They commented on my blood chemistry, but wouldn't tell me anything more about it." She sat back and took a deep breath.

"I'm impressed with how much you're coming up with. How did your body feel after our session?" I asked.

"My eyes were sore for two days. Not the same day, but the next two. The night of our session, I slept without any panic attack waking me. It was the first time in years!"

"How have you been sleeping since then?"

"Just fine. Oh! Something interesting! They told me it was only twenty minutes, but it must have been more. Since then, I find I'm suddenly distrusting clocks. I'm double-checking them."

"Barbara, how's your energy level been since last time?"

"In the past year, I've been totally exhausted. Since our visit, I'm not exhausted. Of course, I'm sleeping better, but I'm still tired. And I have not been at all depressed since our meeting." She smiled brightly, adding, "And I'm not eating as much."

I felt we needed to review the UFO contact again, since she was not completely free of anxiety. Also I had a hunch there was still more for her to remember. If we had time, I planned to regress her to the source of her claustrophobia, so I induced hypnosis.

*

DR. FIORE: Move back in time to the event responsible for the soreness in your eyes. At the count of ten you will remember. [*Counts to ten*]

BARBARA: The machine . . . the lights on the machine were directly over my face, and that's why I split. I left my body. The one tech said, "Are you about through?" And the other one said, "Yes." And they moved the machine back to my feet, and then the leader covered my eyes with his hand.

DR. FIORE: Let yourself remember what happened that caused you the irritation in your vagina and rectum.

BARBARA: When I was out of my body during the exam, they propped up my legs and did a vaginal and rectal exam.

DR. FIORE: Okay. Go back to one minute before you left your body and see what caused you to leave it.

BARBARA: The light and the machine over my face. I don't like that . . . anything close to my face. They moved the machine over my face, so I jumped out and stood by the door.

DR. FIORE: How did they do the vaginal and rectal exams?

BARBARA: It was something black attached to the machine . . . a round object.

DR. FIORE: Do you know if it hurt or not?

BARBARA: No, I don't. I was just watching.

✦

This session, unlike the first, which was a double session, was only fifty minutes long, and there was no time left to work on Barbara's claustrophobia, which had predated her abduction. We had worked up to the last minute, so I brought her out of hypnosis. After ascertaining that she was fine, I reminded her not to drive for ten or fifteen minutes, and asked her to set up her next appointment with my secretary. We gave each other a hug and exchanged best wishes for the Christmas holidays.

❧

On 15 January 1987, I saw Barbara for the third time.
"No panic attacks! Not one single one!" She announced happily. "And would you believe? I've lost twenty-seven pounds since I first saw you."

I checked my notes and said, "That was only seven weeks ago."

"Yes, and remember, I've been through first Thanksgiving and then Christmas and all the celebrating of the holidays!"

"Did you put yourself on a diet?"

"No diet. My appetite's decreased . . . and I don't feel at all deprived. It really hit me Thanksgiving evening after dinner. I hadn't overeaten. In fact, I left food on my plate without even realizing it. And I only had one helping!"

I was really puzzled, because I have worked with a great many obese patients for years and have always found some plausible subconscious reason for the overweight, which is often a defense against being sexually attractive. I could see no logical explanation for the change she had noticed.

She interrupted my thoughts by saying, "I feel some UFOs are back in the area. I asked, 'Are you there?' I got back a strong feeling that they were."

Barbara and I continued to work on a once-a-month basis for two more sessions. Although our investigation of her UFO experience was over, she still had many things to clear up in her life. Each time I saw her, she reported progress. She was no longer fatigued, the panic attacks were a thing of the past and her relationship with her husband was improving.

In May of 1987, she wrote saying she felt so well that she no longer believed that she needed therapy. In her own words, she was ". . . feeling well. I am happy, and I am losing weight. One of the things that prompted this decision [to discontinue therapy] is my passing a very crucial test recently. In the past when I have been upset or had a problem, I have always headed straight for the refrigerator. This time, I was extremely upset and heartbroken, but instead of heading for the refrigerator, I looked at the problem, accepted it and decided that I was not going to let it bother me. In other words, I have learned for forgive myself for my own stupidity and to forgive others too. As a result, everything is working out great."

I called Barbara just before writing her chapter, to get her permission to use her material, and was delighted to hear that she has continued to make tremendous progress in every area of her life.

# "They Can Come and Take Me Any Time They Want!"

Tom had been my patient for over one year when the topic of CEIVs came up. He is a very warm, intelligent person, a specialist in computer programming, who had sought my help for chronic depression and severe anxiety attacks that had immobilized him from time to time. His basic problem was a real lack of self-esteem and self-confidence. We were making some headway on these crippling issues, but there was still more work to be done before he would be able to actualize his potential and achieve the personal happiness and success that he so richly deserved.

Tom walked over and hung up his navy blazer on the rosewood coat tree in the corner of my office and then settled himself in the chair. He slipped out of his loafers, put his feet up on the black leather ottoman, pushed the chair back into a semireclining position and crossed his arms behind his head.

"What's your new book about, Edee?"

As I described the topic of *Encounters*, he listened attentively. Within seconds, he uncrossed his arms, fidgeted a bit and then folded them across his chest, holding onto himself tightly.

"What are you feeling, Tom, as I'm talking about this?"

"Real strong anxiety. I feel they're out there somewhere and will pick me up . . . again." He frowned as though a little surprised. "Then what will I do? Maybe what I feel is a fear of an impending contact and having to go through that again." He laughed nervously. "It sounds like I've been abducted, doesn't it?"

"It certainly wouldn't surprise me."

"I'm feeling a real strong spooky, spine-tingling, hair-standing-on-end feeling! However, it's totally outside of my belief system that this could happen to me."

"Have you read any books on the subject?"

"Yes. I read Whitley Strieber's book, *Communion*. When he talked about the abject terror he felt, it certainly struck a note with me. It sounded somehow very familiar. Since having read the book, I've had that same spooky feeling more often. I had it before. I can remember times even when I was a kid that I felt like that. I think that it usually happens at night, when I'm alone. One of the recent times was sometime last summer. I was going out to get something to eat. And then, on an impulse, I decided to drive up the road toward Mt. Hamilton Observatory. There are places you can stand and look at the city lights. That particular night I was really feeling good about things. It was a beautiful, balmy night, and I decided I would treat myself to the experience. I did enjoy it. But I was standing to the side of the road, and there were several very gnarled-looking trees. It was real dark, and that feeling came over me: What if they come and pick me up right here? [*Laughs nervously*] That real, absolutely terrified, real spooked, verging-on-terror sensation. I controlled it for a while, but I went back a little sooner than I otherwise would have. I stopped at more than one place. And the feeling kind of ebbed and flowed and came back a couple of times."

"Has it happened often, Tom?"

"Yes. Three or four times a year."

"Tom, it sounds like you may have had a contact and what's happening is that whenever you're in a similar situation or in any way you're reminded of it, you are actually reliving what you once felt. The very best thing we can do now would be a regression."

"Fine, but first there's a possible piece of evidence. There's this funny lump I've got in my nose. And I'm not sure what it is. It's on the inside of my right nostril, on the septum in the center. It feels hemispherical in shape and sort of hard, bony. It appeared overnight. I went to bed one night not having had it and the next morning, got up with it. It was back in late '76 or early '77. I had had surgery on my ear and was still seeing the ENT doctor periodically, so I made a point the next time I saw him to have him take a look. He examined it and then didn't make any comments about it at all. I went away with a question mark in my mind and for some reason decided not to push it."

"Do you remember whether there was any blood on the sheets or anything to indicate a nosebleed or anything of that sort when you woke up that morning?"

"Not to my recollection."

I noticed that our time was slipping away, even though we had a double session. I wanted to do a regression, so I hypnotized Tom and asked his subconscious mind to take him to the event responsible for the "spooky, spine-tingling feeling." I counted to ten and asked him to report whatever came into his mind.

❧

TOM: I'm in a forested area at night, a dark night. And I'm meeting some unearthly looking beings. Rounded heads and generally humanoid, but definitely not human. They have smaller, shorter bodies than an adult human and they're very lightweight. I have the feeling . . . that's an image that I made up, that's not what they really look like. I didn't want to look at them close up, to see what they looked like.

DR. FIORE: Let yourself remember everything that you experienced, just as though it's happening now.

TOM: When it happened, I didn't want to experience it, so the memories I have of it are not complete. I was taken against my will. Had I been given my choice, my choice would have been absolutely not. I'm not ready for this kind of a feeling.

DR. FIORE:   Where were you when you were taken against your will?

TOM:   I may have left the house, intending to just go out into the yard or something, and then I was taken from there. I wish I had never gone out. If I had just stayed inside, maybe I would have been safe . . . but then, maybe I wouldn't have been safe. And the thought went through my mind that I'm never going to feel safe again, wherever I am . . . that being inside isn't safe either. The only way I can feel safe is if I don't allow myself to believe that this ever happened. It's a very frightening feeling to feel like I'm never going to be safe again. I can't quite face that. There's an inner conflict between belief and disbelief. This is something that happens to somebody else, it doesn't happen to me.

DR. FIORE:   Let yourself remember what happened, exactly as you experienced it, at the count of three. One . . . two . . . three.

TOM:   I'm inside some sort of a roomlike area, on a table, undressed, nude, and I don't like this at all. I'm totally out of control. One of the things I really hate about it is the feeling of being out of control, completely in their power, the feeling of being probed. I don't have a recollection of any severe pain, but definitely discomfort and fear. Apprehension. They could do anything they wanted to with me, and I have no choice in the matter. At times being handled kind of roughly, being touched and pressed in different parts of my body with hard, cold objects. Very unpleasant, very disagreeable. My genitals were being handled and examined. That's a real feeling of being violated . . . my person being violated. [*Pauses*] I hate it! [*Squirms*] I hate it! [*Long pause*]

DR. FIORE:   Continue to report whatever comes into your mind.

TOM:   I kicked and screamed and tried to resist, at least initially. They overcame my resistance. Any attempts they made to communicate with me were really limited to trying to calm me down and keep me under control.

DR. FIORE:   You're allowing yourself to remember more of this in order to heal yourself of this trauma.

TOM:   There's definitely resistance within me now to not remember. There's a part of me that does not want to remember that. Part of me that didn't want to believe it in the first place. I think that feeling of being completely out of control is perhaps the most difficult to deal with. The feeling that if I really believe this, then I have to believe that I'm just not in control of my life. They can come and take me any time they want.

DR. FIORE:   Let yourself remember something easier to face.

TOM:   I think the first event was when I was very young.

DR. FIORE:   Let yourself remember that event now. Go back to the very first event, at the count of five. One . . . two . . . three . . . four . . . five. Just report everything that comes into your mind.

TOM:   It was early in the evening. When it began to happen, the sky wasn't completely dark. There was something in the sky. And there's a being in the woods . . . and then it's later. I'm cold and shivery, and that was when they first took my clothes off. That coldness didn't last the whole time, but it was very uncomfortable and unpleasant at the time . . . and connected with that feeling of being out of control.

DR. FIORE:   You're allowing yourself to remember exactly what happened to you.

TOM: A much stronger feeling of this tingling sensation. I'm getting a number of confusing images of different times, kind of mixed together, perhaps out of sequence. Of having been carried through the air, above the trees . . . and I don't know how this is happening. I'm not being supported by them. They're not carrying me physically. I find myself flying through the air all of a sudden. It's exhilirating and frightening all at the same time. It's so strange! And unbelievable. I mean, this must be a dream. And yet I don't think it is. I think it's really happening, but part of my mind doesn't want to accept this as anything happening to me. But . . . it is. I'm looking down, seeing the trees below. And the fear of falling becomes quite strong. And yet, somehow, there's a part of me that knows I'm not going to fall, [but] there's another part of me that's terrified that I am. And if I could just let go and enjoy this, it would be great! If I didn't have all these fears attached to it.

DR. FIORE: Now what's happening?

TOM: I'm still sailing through the air above the trees, in the most inexplicable way. I have no idea what's going on. How in the world are they doing this? [Pauses]

DR. FIORE: Continue to report everything that you're aware of.

TOM: I'm still experiencing that same sensation. I'm trying to let go and enjoy it . . . and I'm beginning to do that.

DR. FIORE: Are you continuing to fly?

TOM: Yes. I'm being carried up to the ship . . . the ship is hovering up above. And it's a dizzying sensation of motion. The trees become a blur below me. I feel like I'm suspended there in midair, being carried along.

DR. FIORE: What do you see?

TOM: I'm looking down at the moment, but the ship is up above. It's a disc with a hemispherical bulge above it. The explanation that comes to me now is that I was in what might be called a tractor beam, a beam that was pulling me up to the ship.

DR. FIORE: Now it's just a little bit later. What's happening?

TOM: I was brought inside the ship. I'm not quite sure how.

DR. FIORE: It's very clear in your mind.

TOM: I'm in a room or a chamber that is somewhat dimly lit, a reddish orange, quite dim. No harsh lighting. I'm in the presence of . . . at least three or four different beings. Because the light is so dim, I experience them as shadowy figures. I don't want to look directly at them. There's a part of me that is very interested, but I think the stronger feeling is uneasiness. Uneasiness and apprehension. [Pauses] Something's draped over my body. Some or all of my clothes have been removed, and some sort of a blanket is being draped over my body. It came down to about my knees, and my feet are bare. They folded it back and exposed my genitals and I'm . . . I didn't like that. And it made me uneasy. It intensified my feeling of uneasiness.

DR. FIORE: What's happening?

TOM: They touched me with their hands. Maybe they had gloves on, a fairly coarse, woven cloth. But they also touched me with instruments. And they were cold, hard, probably metallic. They were prodding and probing and poking. Something was inserted in my penis, and that was distinctly unpleasant, but not painful.

DR. FIORE: You're going to let yourself remember that at the count of three. One . . . two . . . three.

TOM: A real strong feeling, intense feeling, of having my person violated, but surprised that it's not painful. I force myself to try to relax, but I couldn't completely relax. Oh, I think it went really deep. Oh! [*Cries out in pain*] Ah! . . . [*More pain*] It's very unpleasant to even think about. [*Moans*] I want this to be over with! [*Sighs*] It makes me angry too. I don't like being treated that way. They're trying to tell me that it's for a very good reason. I don't really care.

DR. FIORE: Let yourself remember exactly what they conveyed to you.

TOM: They're telling me to hold still. And I don't want to hold still, and yet if I do try to struggle, it's going to result in my being hurt or injured. So I better hold still. [*His body tenses*] And it's the hardest thing in the world to try and hold still and submit to this.

DR. FIORE: Did they give you a reason for what they're doing?

TOM: I don't remember. I think I'm so young that I probably wouldn't have understood. There's a thin, flexible tube. Somehow it's almost like it moves on its own. It went back in through the urethral canal and down into my scrotum . . . it's probing down into my scrotum. [*Squirms*] It's distinctly unpleasant and disgusting to experience that. It was both unpleasant and a relief when it was withdrawn. It kind of stung slightly when they took it out, and yet it was a big relief at the same time. They're telling me that it's not going to have any lasting negative effect. I don't want to think about it anymore. I have the distinct feeling of wanting to block that memory from my mind. So, so unpleasant!

DR. FIORE: Did they suggest that you block it from your mind?

TOM: They were aware of my desire to block it from my mind, and they assisted me in doing that. Without really saying it to me, they were going to help me do that, in order to try to make me more comfortable. [*Sighs*] I was subjected to a rectal probe as well.

DR. FIORE:  Let yourself remember that.

TOM:  I found that also to be unpleasant, but not nearly so unpleasant as the other. Somehow it didn't seem quite so threatening. In fact, that went quite deep too. There were times when I felt a sensation up inside my abdomen that . . . that was not as alarming as the other thing though, but somewhat alarming.

DR. FIORE:  And now?

TOM:  Something's being inserted down my throat, and I'm gagging. And again, feeling a probe inside my chest from that. It's those sensations of something probing inside my body that I definitely find very alarming. I panicked momentarily because of feeling suffocated while it was going on. I wasn't sure I was going to be able to breathe normally.

DR. FIORE:  Let yourself know if you ever saw the beings. If so, remember what they looked like.

TOM:  They're inside that room. Kind of dark, shadowy figures, with some kind of clothing that is like a cloak with a hood. A glitter of light from the eyes, probably reflected light. But they're shorter than . . . Hmmm . . . I think I'm confused with another experience where I was older. They're between three and four feet tall. I didn't look at them very closely, but I do remember a relatively flat face. [*Pauses*]

DR. FIORE:  Continue to report everything that you're aware of.

TOM:  What at first I thought was another type of creature is an instrument or a tool that was connected into the wall of the ship.

A tube with something on the end of it. Two to three inches in diameter. My first reaction to it was that it was some sort of a serpent, but then I realized later it wasn't alive. And now I get the feeling it might have been . . . some kind of a vacuum apparatus. I'm put into a sitting position in some sort of a chair. Maybe the table that I was on folded into a chair, like a recliner chair. [*Pauses*]

DR. FIORE:   And?

TOM:   I'm resting on something that was to some degree form-fitting but it was too big for me. It was like sitting in something that was not completely hard . . . kind of like the feeling of a padded dash in an automobile. And then, for some reason, having my legs strapped down. [*Pauses*]

DR. FIORE:   What is your reaction to this?

TOM:   I'm looking forward to it being over with. A feeling that maybe the worst is over with, that the worst is past. And so, I guess there's some relief from that.

DR. FIORE:   And now what's happened?

TOM:   I'm being dropped back down out of the ship on like a cable or something, in a chair. There's some more of them waiting on the ground below to take me back.

DR. FIORE:   And now?

TOM:   Now I'm feeling really tired, both physically and emotionally. And I want to go back to sleep. And I somehow know that they're going to take me back home.

DR. FIORE:   Now what's happening?

TOM:   I am back in my bed and . . . I'm drifting off to sleep with a feeling that if I remember this, it's going to be like a dream.

*

Before I brought Tom out of hypnosis, I gave his inner mind suggestions to prepare him to remember easily and accurately under hypnosis the next time we met, everything that he needed to remember about close encounters with extraterrestrials. I reinforced the suggestions that this preparation would go on at a very deep level of his subconscious mind and would in no way disturb him. I emphasized that he would feel particularly calm and have a wonderful sense of well-being. Then I counted him out of hypnosis.

*

Two days later, I saw Tom again because he had called my office saying he needed to see me immediately. He got right to the point as soon as he sat down.

"I felt strong anxiety on Monday when I left your building. Since then, my energy level's been down, all day yesterday and today as well."

"It sounds like we stirred up something last time that's not resolved, Tom."

He nodded, looking quite distraught. I immediately initiated hypnosis and regressed him to the event that was responsible for the anxiety.

*

TOM:   It's the UFO issue. I have two conflicting reactions to those experiences. One part absolutely refuses to accept it and resists any further contacts or experiences. The other part of my mind is intrigued and would like to understand and be able to communicate and be at peace with it and look for whatever value might be in those experiences.

DR. FIORE:   Let yourself remember what is causing the anxiety.

TOM: The very initial reaction when it first happens is disbelief combined with a strong feeling of being threatened. A sinister threat to my well-being. Something to avoid at all costs, if possible. But it was not possible. In that initial experience of being carried away from the house, I struggled to the best of my ability, but it was useless.

DR. FIORE: Let yourself remember another experience that has had a strong negative impact on you.

TOM: I'm in the car with my parents. I'm still young. I'm sitting in the dark in the backseat with my brother and sister. I saw the ship again. I didn't have a clear conscious memory of what had happened before, but I was filled with a sense of dread. You see, a part of me did remember and knew I was not able to avoid it. There was a wish that my parents would protect me. The fact that they couldn't increased my sense of helplessness and panic and an extreme feeling of defenselessness.

DR. FIORE: What happened?

TOM: I was taken along with my brother and sister. My parents were temporarily out of commission, unconscious, while this was going on.

DR. FIORE: Then what happened?

TOM: We were taken into the ship and there was a physical exam again. That's the hardest part for me, because it's extremely uncomfortable to think about those intrusions into my body.

DR. FIORE: What happened with your brother and sister?

TOM: I'm not aware of them being in the room, but being taken to the ship with me and our being returned together.

DR. FIORE:   What happened to you during the examination?

TOM:   I'm on that table again, being probed. [*Body tenses*] Into my penis again and a rectal probe . . . a tracheal probe or esophagus or both. [*Gags*] That feeling of something probing inside my body is . . . intensely unpleasant. Especially the genital probe. One or more of those probes, almost like a live thing, a thin, tiny finger moving around and probing. [*Squirms*] Oh! it was just . . . makes me want to squirm and writhe and get away from it. The feeling and having to hold perfectly still is almost too much to bear. At some point on the way back, I compared notes with my brother and sister. She found it much less disagreeable than I did. She was able to exchange information. I was intrigued and envious, and I wondered what was wrong with me. Why couldn't I react like that too?

DR. FIORE:   Then what happened?

TOM:   I thought if I ever had to face that again, I would try to talk to them first to get them to explain to me why it was necessary. And if it was absolutely necessary, why couldn't they render me unconscious? It still makes my skin crawl, thinking I had to submit to that.

*

Tom looked somewhat upset after he came out of hypnosis. We talked for a while, and then I noticed him finally relaxing. After about five minutes, he seemed back to normal and ready to leave.

*

Two weeks later, Tom reported feeling much more relaxed about his CEIVs. Also he had been handling stressful situations very well. We started hypnosis early on in the session, and I asked him to go back in time and space to another CEIV that was still having a negative impact on him.

*

TOM:   There's some sort of a ship, sitting on the ground, and an extraterrestrial standing outside it. And I'm just a very short distance away, just looking on.

DR. FIORE:   Tell me all about it in detail.

TOM:   It's a disc with sort of a bubble shape above it, in the center.

DR. FIORE:   Let yourself know what time of day or night this is.

TOM:   It's dark, so it's nighttime.

DR. FIORE:   What do you feel and think as you're watching it?

TOM:   [*Pauses*] I don't seem to be feeling any real strong emotions, other than interest and curiosity. I was watching this from a hiding place sort of far away. Maybe hiding in some bushes or something.

DR. FIORE:   Let yourself remember it in detail.

TOM:   I'm with someone else, a friend, who told me about it. I went to see it out of curiosity.

DR. FIORE:   How old are you approximately?

TOM:   About twelve or thirteen.

DR. FIORE:   Tell me everything that you're aware of.

TOM:   I'm up closer, maybe even touching it. I don't know . . . [*Pauses*] Maybe I'm confusing two experiences or something. Something's not quite right. This seems to be in the daytime. I'm standing and watching it fly away into the sky . . . in daytime.

DR. FIORE: It's going to be very clear in your mind. You're going to remember it exactly as it happened, at the count of three. One . . . two . . . three. First thoughts.

TOM: I had a flash of being inside the ship. [*Pauses*] That seems to be in the daytime also. Perhaps I came back the next day and . . . went up closer. I was with a friend when I first saw it at night . . . and then I came back the next day alone.

DR. FIORE: It's all coming into your mind. Just report everything that you're aware of.

TOM: I seem to be getting another image, or a slightly different image, again a nighttime image. Of a dark night with a full moon, and hearing a dog sort of howling in the distance.

DR. FIORE: Then what happened?

TOM: I'm walking through a wooded area. But it's a pleasant area to be in, at least in the daytime. And I'm having a mixture of feelings. Some pleasure and enjoyment, because I like that place, and I'm also feeling kind of spooky and anxious at the same time.

DR. FIORE: And?

TOM: I noticed a bright white light that at first I thought was the moon and then realized it wasn't. It's a very, very bright light, like a searchlight or something, except that it's portable. It's like a flashlight, but it's much brighter and bigger than a flashlight. [*Long pause*]

DR. FIORE: What happens? Let yourself remember.

TOM: I'm back and the experience is over with, but somehow it doesn't seem quite real to me. I'm going over it in my mind and I'm trying to figure out what it means. It's almost like I'm trying to decide, Okay, this really happened and this part of it didn't really happen. This was just my imagination.

DR. FIORE: What are you remembering?

TOM: Remembering seeing this strange ship and these strange beings and . . . and remembering watching the ship fly into the sky, into the distance.

DR. FIORE: You're going to go back to the time when you're watching the ship. At the count of five. One . . . two . . . three . . . four . . . five. What comes to mind?

TOM: I seem to have been up close to the ship and possibly even having communicated somehow with the beings.

DR. FIORE: Let yourself remember that clearly. Go down deeper into your mind now and retrieve these memories. Let it happen, at the count of five. One . . . two . . . three . . . four . . . five. What are you aware of at this very moment?

TOM: I'm close to the ship and noticing how big it is. It seems very, very big, and I feel quite small in comparison. [*Pauses*] I seem to have met at least one being that's taller than I am. [*Long pause*]

DR. FIORE: What happened?

TOM: I'm climbing up a sort of a ladder into a hatch underneath and just looking inside and then climbing right back down again. And I'm standing there looking at it disappear into the sky and feeling frustration. The frustration is coming from the fact that my curiosity was left unsatisfied, that I have a lot of questions about where it came from, where it's going, what is it, who are these people? What does all this mean? Combined with a frustrated feeling that I can't talk about it without being subjected to ridicule, that I'll be accused of making up stories or being crazy, or, you know, being off my rocker.

DR. FIORE:   Let yourself know where these thoughts came from.

TOM:   Once before, I tried to tell someone. [*Pauses*] I was really, really laughed at, hooted at, by several friends, and I felt so embarrassed and humiliated that I made up my mind that I was never again going to try to convince anyone who hadn't also seen it. And I was accused of being crazy to a point where I started to wonder myself. At times I questioned my own sanity, in regard to the experience.

DR. FIORE:   Move to the experience you did have, the one you were ridiculed for telling about. Just report whatever you're aware of. Trust your mind.

TOM:   [*Pauses*] I don't seem to be getting any visual images, but I'm noticing a sensation in my hands. A sensation like maybe my fingers were pulled and stretched out over a ball of some sort. My fingers and my thumbs feel like they are pulled into a very painful position.

DR. FIORE:   You're remembering it exactly as it happened to you. What comes to mind?

TOM:   [*His body tenses*] Something is being pressed down on top of my hands. My hands were squeezed between two . . . it seemed like they were both sort of hemispherical surfaces like, part of an instrument. There was enough pressure for it to be distinctly uncomfortable. I was experiencing some fear that it was going to injure my hands. It certainly hurt. [*Pauses*]

DR. FIORE:   Let yourself remember what's being done, just as though you're there right now.

TOM: My ankles are in some sort of a clamplike shackle or vise. My ankles aren't being hurt the way my hands are, except that it's just very disagreeable and unpleasant to be constrained that way. [*Pauses*] Something is being put over my face. And other parts of my body as well, my chest, my genitals. . . . [*Pauses*] There's something around my waist. [*Long pause*]

DR. FIORE: And?

TOM: I have a feeling of wanting it to be over with.

DR. FIORE: What's being done?

TOM: They don't intend to hurt me. But the feeling is they don't really understand that even though it may not permanently injure me, that it is extremely uncomfortable and somewhat painful, and emotionally . . . very disturbing. They don't seem to really understand that. Either they don't understand it, or they don't completely care. Or a combination of both. A feeling of being out of control, of not being able to control what's happening to me, which I find very, very threatening. And fearful. A feeling of being completely at their mercy. They have made some attempts to reassure me, but I don't completely trust them. That's a very frightening thing, because they could do anything they wanted to me. [*Squirms*] A catheter was inserted into my penis and maybe a sample of urine was taken. [*Arches his back*]

DR. FIORE: How did that affect you?

TOM: A feeling of being in someone else's control and having very uncomfortable, disagreeable things done to me and not being able to do anything about it. And having my privacy invaded . . . being violated. I'm able to keep my feelings under control in this particular situation. But I don't like it. It's really disagreeable! I'm not completely panic-stricken, but sort of resigned. I have a very strong wish that I did not have to go through this.

DR. FIORE: Who is doing this to you? Look around and describe who they are and what they look like.

TOM: There's at least three or four. When they were pulling on my hands, there were two on my right and one on my left, and another one moving around or something.

DR. FIORE: What do they look like?

TOM: [*Pauses*] Humanoid appearance. Kind of a cloudy white color. [*Pauses*]

DR. FIORE: Tell me more about them.

TOM: They're about my own height.

DR. FIORE: How tall are you?

TOM: Around four feet.

DR. FIORE: What shape are their heads?

TOM: I'm looking at their heads from the side. They remind me of these dummies that are used in automobile crash experiments. Their ears are not the same as a human ear, maybe more like a crescent-shaped opening. Their features are flatter and less prominent than the human face.

DR. FIORE: What about the eyes?

TOM: I found it disagreeable, somewhat frightening, to look at them directly. They don't have eyelids in the same way we do. The eye seems to be covered by a translucent membrane similar to what I've seen on birds.

DR. FIORE: What's happening to you?

TOM: I'm lying in a semireclined position. I was released from whatever it was that was holding my arms and my ankles and brought up to a sitting position. Something is lowered down against the top of my head. And it feels like it's a very hard surface, probably metallic. The part of it that's against my head is kind of like a ring, a circular shape. It was pushed against my skull with a fair amount of pressure. I found it somewhat uncomfortable, not unbearable. Less uncomfortable than what I've just been going through, so that maybe I'm experiencing a slight sense of relief from being released from what they had just been doing to me.

DR. FIORE: And now what's happening?

TOM: [squirms] My abdomen is being pierced by a needle of some sort, and . . . [He flinches] that caught me by surprise. When it first happened, I felt a very quick, fearful reaction, but that passed very quickly because it wasn't nearly as painful as I would have expected it to be.

DR. FIORE: What are you aware of now?

TOM: Now I'm back outside.

DR. FIORE: Let yourself remember how you got there.

TOM: I was carried back outside by several of these same beings.

DR. FIORE: Let's find out if you were given any kind of suggestion not to remember.

TOM: Several times during the experience something in my mind kept saying, this can't be really happening to me. It's a dream.

DR. FIORE:  Let yourself remember whether the extraterrestrials gave you any suggestions that this was a dream or that you would not remember.

TOM:  They were somehow aware of my thinking that and reinforced it. [*Pauses*] They suggested that it would be easier to think of it that way and to just forget about it. Somehow I was disturbed about that. I felt that's taking the easy way out, and that it would be better if I could really understand it and be able to talk about it with people. [*Pauses*] But if I didn't completely believe it myself, how could I expect anyone else to believe it? And maybe that it would be easier just to forget about it.

DR. FIORE:  Let yourself remember what you did after they took you out of the craft.

TOM:  I walked back home. It was some distance. It was at night.

DR. FIORE:  How do you feel?

TOM:  Still disturbed. My parents are going to wonder where I've been, and I'm not sure what to tell them.

DR. FIORE:  And now you're home and what happens?

TOM:  I'm being confronted by my mother, wanting to know where I've been, what I've been doing. I tried to say that I went for a walk. I am totally unable to give her an explanation that she's satisfied with. She's very suspicious that maybe I've been doing something that I shouldn't have been doing. And I feel like if I tell her what really happened, she'll accuse me of making up a story and that that won't help. I really don't know what to say. She asks me why I went out, and I said I don't know. She's not satisfied with that. I ended up being punished. I felt it was very unfair.

*

I asked Tom's inner mind to bring him back to the present, gave him positive suggestions and then counted him out of hypnosis.

He seemed a little groggy for a few minutes, but calm and oriented to his surroundings.

"No wonder I didn't want to talk to anyone about those meetings. Look what happened."

"It's obvious, Tom, that you've been traumatized by those close encounters. First you were taken against your will and then subjected to painful procedures that were not for your benefit. You were terrified and couldn't confide in the people who were important to you. I feel that a lot of your anxieties, your feelings of vulnerability and helplessness, and even your need to hide in your apartment when you're under stress are all due to these experiences. You should start feeling lots less anxious and more energetic. But we need to explore any more CEIVs that you've had. And as we do, you'll heal old wounds."

"It certainly makes sense. I would like to be over my fear of them. When you think of it, it's really an extraordinary experience to be in the presence of beings from other worlds."

"Exactly! I personally think it's the most exciting discovery of the twentieth century."

# "They Said
I Had Cancer!"

Linda had been my patient for three months when we first discovered she was a contactee. She had sought my help for a number of problems, especially a deep sadness that had swept over her from time to time during the past sixteen years. She is a talented artist and also very sensitive psychically, especially as a healer. During our first session, she told me that her whole family is psychic, that they often worked together as a team doing healings.

Linda, a trim attractive brunette, looks ten years younger than her forty-five years. She is a pleasant person, someone whom one likes instantly because she exudes a goodness and a kindness.

During her months of therapy, Linda developed into an excellent hypnotic subject. During one session, going along with a hunch, I decided to explore the possibility of her having had a close encounter with extraterrestrials.

DR. FIORE: I'm going to ask your inner mind to take you to any UFO experiences you may have had that you have completely

89

blocked from your conscious memory. If you have had more than one, you're going to go to one that is very important, at the count of ten. [*Counts to ten*]

LINDA: It's green inside. There's this light flashing over here somewhere. Somebody's sitting over here. I want to peek around the corner. I'm curious to see what's going on. [*Pauses*] They put me in this room . . . it's really bright and small. [*Pauses*] Ouch! . . . Why are they doing this? Why are they looking at my body? What did I do? [*Crying*] Leave me alone! I can't move! I have to just lie here. [*Getting frantic*] They're opening me up. How can they do that?

DR. FIORE: What part of you are they opening up?

LINDA: They're opening me here, my stomach.

DR. FIORE: How are they opening you up?

LINDA: I don't know, I don't understand what they're doing. There's no blood. They just open me up. It looks real dark inside. They're suctioning something up . . . kind of cleaning me, inside. Getting this dark stuff out of me.

DR. FIORE: Where are you seeing this from?

LINDA: Up above . . . I'm looking down at myself.

DR. FIORE: What do you see when you look down?

LINDA: I see these heads . . . and they're working on my body. And they've opened me up . . . and they're cleaning this black junk out of my stomach region. They said I had cancer! They were trying to help me.

DR. FIORE: How did you feel when they told you that?

LINDA: Confused. I'm all right, there's nothing wrong with me. I don't understand how they could see inside me. [*Pauses*] They put something on me. It's like glass, little round pieces of glass. They aren't like crystals. They're round and smooth and they had little lights on them. And they placed them all over my body. And then somehow they ran something over the top of it, kind of like a sensor of some kind.

DR. FIORE: Did it touch you?

LINDA: No. It stayed about . . . about so far away. [*Six inches from her body*] Until they came to here [*Points to abdomen*] and something was wrong here.

DR. FIORE: How do you know that?

LINDA: I can feel pain there. I just want to be home. My little girl's crying. [*Cries*] They took her too. What did they do to her? They tell me that they are helping us. I don't understand why they're doing this. Why don't they just leave us alone? [*Long pause*]

DR. FIORE: What do they look like?

LINDA: Kind of very, very small . . . very small heads . . . kind of really pointed. And they look . . . not human flesh. It's like greenish, sort of knobby looking. They've got big eyes. I wish they'd hurry and finish up. I want to go home.

DR. FIORE: What are they doing now?

LINDA: Somehow they're pressing my flesh back, and it's going back together. [*Sighs*] I feel I can breathe easier. There's this bright light.

DR. FIORE: Where is the bright light coming from?

LINDA:   Some kind of source over here, to my right. It's like I'm enclosed in a . . . like a capsule kind of thing, and it's moving through a corridor almost like a chute . . . down a chute. [*Pauses*] And then it goes into this . . . some kind of vehicle. And there's other ones too, with people in them. They're putting us in them.

DR. FIORE:   Tell me more about that.

LINDA:   It's almost like a conveyor belt or something, with rollers bringing these capsules with people onto it. And they're closing the door. [*Pauses*] And I just lie there for a while.

DR. FIORE:   Now what's happening?

LINDA:   I'm just lying there. It's dark. I hear some people groaning, mumbling.

DR. FIORE:   How do you feel, and what are you thinking?

LINDA:   I just want to go home.

DR. FIORE:   What are you doing now?

LINDA:   I'm moving. It feels like it's fast. [*Pauses*] We land. They open up the capsules and they help us get out. It's quite a view.

DR. FIORE:   Tell me more about that.

LINDA:   I feel like we're walking. . . . It's more like a desert area, there's not much around. They put us in smaller vehicles. They're full of light. There's lots of lights going. There's about four of us in each one. There's a driver. They take off. We're going over some trees. Aha . . . I'm home. I'm back in my bed.

DR. FIORE:   How do you feel?

LINDA:   Tired.

DR. FIORE:   How does your body feel?

LINDA:   I feel tingling. My hands are tingling. My head hurts still. [*Touches forehead*] I just roll over and cuddle my husband. I'm so glad to be there.

DR. FIORE:   What was that on your forehead that you touched?

LINDA:   They gave me a third eye. It still hurts. It's all tight.

DR. FIORE:   How do you know that's what they gave you?

LINDA:   They pulled it apart. That's what they said they were going to do.

DR. FIORE:   Now go back to another encounter with them, at the count of five. One . . . two . . . three . . . four . . . five.

LINDA:   God, the light's so bright! What's going on? Ahh . . . I can't see. Everything's too bright. [*Pauses*] I don't even know where I am.

DR. FIORE:   Tell me everything you're aware of.

LINDA:   Just this bright, bright light. It hurts my eyes. I wish I could see what's happening. Someone's pushing me back, making me move. [*Pauses*] I'm going in an elevator . . . kind of a glass elevator. [*Sighs*] I feel like I'm way up high and I can see all over. The earth looks real small. . . . I'm way, way up.

DR. FIORE:   Where are you?

LINDA:   I'm in some kind of a bright room. There's other people with me. I don't know who they are. I never met them before.

We're being asked to go in this door . . . down this darker corridor. It's a long corridor.

DR. FIORE:   Tell me about the other people.

LINDA:   We have these white things on. I guess it's kind of like a hospital-type gown. We're just doing what we're told to do, to walk down this corridor into this room at the end.

DR. FIORE:   Is there anybody you recognize?

LINDA:   [*Turning her head as though looking around*] My brother Ralph's there. [*Pauses*] And Mark.

DR. FIORE:   Who's Mark?

LINDA:   My other brother. And my sister Sherry. Looks like a family reunion here.

DR. FIORE:   Are there other people besides your two brothers and your sister?

LINDA:   Ralph and Mark, Sherry, Betty, my brother-in-law, Bill, my niece Barbara, my sister Sally, there's Margie, my other sister. My mom . . . my dad . . . What are they doing with all of us? I don't understand? [*Long pause*]

DR. FIORE:   What are you doing?

LINDA:   We're sitting down on kind of a bench. My family . . . we're all holding hands. It's like the room's spinning.

DR. FIORE:   Besides your family, are there any other people there?

LINDA:   I think my Aunt Eloise is there too, and there's some people I don't know. It's getting more crowded all the time.

DR. FIORE:   How many people would you say there are alto-gether?

LINDA:   Oh, gosh, it's like fifty to sixty people. Now we're going down some steps of some kind. [*Pauses*] Looks like a work center. They're having us do something . . . like working.

DR. FIORE:   Tell me about it.

LINDA:   There's this big machine, it looks like a pump . . . pumping something out.

DR. FIORE:   What are you doing?

LINDA:   I'm turning a wheel. I just keep turning this wheel and turning this wheel.

DR. FIORE:   Who is telling you to do this?

LINDA:   This . . . I don't see him. I don't know who it is.

DR. FIORE:   Move to the first time you do see him.

LINDA:   Sort of a bald head, great big eyes, long nose, pointed chin. Like something out of a comic book or something . . . something someone's made up.

DR. FIORE:   How tall is he?

LINDA:   Very tall. Very, very tall. I feel really tiny compared to him . . . very tall and thin.

DR. FIORE:   What is he wearing?

LINDA:   It looks like a big collar that comes up, and this long . . . long robe. They're wearing similar outfits, but all different colors, very pale colors. They shimmer a little bit. The clothing shimmers. And their hands are long, long . . . thin fingers that come out to about here. [*About five inches longer than her hand*]

DR. FIORE:   What are they doing?

LINDA:   They're instructing us.

DR. FIORE:   Tell me about that.

LINDA:   They're telling us we have to learn these things, it's for our survival. The world will come to an end if we don't learn these things. We've got to help our people. They're going to teach us. [*Pauses*] My whole body's . . . vibrating. Especially my hands. Telling me to point my fingers certain ways. Teaching me to be sensitive. It's all this . . . power coming through my hands. It's like electricity. Strong. [*Pauses*] Oh God! . . . I'm being told I can learn to heal, myself. It's okay to use this power. They've known about it for thousands and thousands of years. I can learn to scan, like they do. But first I've got to be healthy. I've got to take care of myself. [*Long pause*]

DR. FIORE:   What are you experiencing?

LINDA:   I'm being taught . . . how to feel the energy coming through my hands. And to feel what happens when I move the energy around and scan my body. I can feel it inside my body. As I pass my hands over [my body], the energy moves inside. This is fascinating. [*Long pause*]

DR. FIORE:   They said first you have to be healthy, you have to take care of yourself. Did they give you any advice?

LINDA:   I have to watch what I eat. To notice that if something I eat doesn't agree with me, then it's not good for me. And to stop eating it. Chew more carefully. Get more exercise. Meditate every day.

DR. FIORE:   Did they tell you how to do that?

LINDA:   They gave us lessons.

DR. FIORE:   Tell me about that.

LINDA:   We went into some place that looks like a . . . chapel. It's cool there, peaceful and quiet. There's like a crystal, sitting out in the middle of the room. It's really bright and shining. All different colors come out and form a circle around the crystal. We're being told to put our hands up and feel the energy of the crystal. And just go in our minds. Just relax.

DR. FIORE:   Did they give you any other advice?

LINDA:   Be patient. [*Long pause*] My head hurts.

DR. FIORE:   Go back to what is causing your head to hurt.

LINDA:   Something's drilling my head. I don't want these head-aches anymore. [*Cries*] They're telling me I have to let go, not to be afraid. It's the fear that's giving me the headache. Some kind of metal tubing . . . going through my head, right up my ear. [*Pauses*] And there's some kind of fluid being put into the tube.

DR. FIORE:   Who's doing this?

LINDA:   One of those . . . tall people.

DR. FIORE:   Are they saying anything to you as they're doing this?

LINDA:   Trust him, I'll feel better.

DR. FIORE:   How does it feel as they're doing this?

LINDA:   Pressure, like a drill. I just want to pull it out.

DR. FIORE:   Where is it?

LINDA:   It's right here. [*Points to her right ear*] They took it out. [*Sighs in relief* ]

DR. FIORE:   Did they say anything more about it?

LINDA:   Be patient, it'll get better.

DR. FIORE:   Did they tell you what was wrong?

LINDA:   No.

DR. FIORE:   Now let yourself know if anything else was done or said during that encounter.

LINDA:   That I wouldn't remember.

DR. FIORE:   How did you feel when they told you that?

LINDA:   That's not fair. I want to know what's going on. There's too much information, they say, for me to understand at once. I just have to learn it slowly. Just be patient. I'm not ready yet. About five more years.

DR. FIORE:   Did they say anything about having contacted you before or that they would contact you in the future?

LINDA:   Many times.

DR. FIORE:   Tell me verbatim what they said to you.

LINDA:   "We'll be back next month to teach you some more."

DR. FIORE:   How did you feel when you heard that?

LINDA:   Okay. I'm getting used to it now.

DR. FIORE:   What do you mean by that?

LINDA:   They come so often.

DR. FIORE:   How often do they come?

LINDA:   Once a week, for a while. I always feel so tired after they've been . . . and sad.

DR. FIORE:   Why are you sad?

LINDA:   I don't know. I'm confused. [*Long pause*] I'm back home now, back in my room.

✿

Linda seemed a bit disoriented when she came out of hypnosis. After a few seconds, she smiled and leaned forward in her chair, which was now in an upright position. "I've had dreams of UFOs. And when I read *Communion,* I felt it had happened to me. I'm so glad we went into that."

"I was just playing a hunch, Linda. Actually, it seems that psychic people do have contacts with extraterrestrials much more often than people who aren't so sensitive. Also I've found that people tend to develop psychically after close encounters. So I'm not sure which came first, the chicken or the egg."

"As I told you, my whole family's psychic. And there we all were! I can't wait to tell them."

✿

About a month later, Linda came into my office obviously excited about something. "My sister Sherry called to tell me about a dream she had had the night before. And that in itself is unusual, because she rarely remembers her dreams. She dreamed she was taken into a spaceship and they treated her yeast infection with a blue gel. The next morning, the yeast infection was gone. She'd only had it for a few months, and it was pretty bad, but right after the dream it cleared up. She called me in the morning while I was still in bed, so I didn't relate it to myself until that evening, when I realized my yeast infection was completely gone. That's a miracle, because nothing the doctors prescribed did anything except get rid of the itching, never the discharge. It's been gone for a few weeks now. *And* my mother, who had a yeast infection for forty-three years, is cured too, since Sherry's and mine cleared up."

"Well, Linda, it seems like something happened to all three of you. Would you like to check it out?"

Linda agreed that would be important to work on, and so, after she was hypnotized, I regressed her to the encounter in which her yeast infection was treated.

✿

LINDA:   I went to bed early that night. They come . . . there's two of them, they come into my bedroom. There's a tall one. He's got on a long robe. The one with the long fingers, he doesn't have any hair. He has a big cranial section of his head and a large, large forehead. He smiles and says, "Well, are you ready?" I say, "Okay." There's a small one there too. He looks more human. Almost dwarfish. They take me out the front door. There's some kind of a vehicle. It looks about the size of a car and has lots of lights, and it almost looks like a glass with a kind of bubble roof over the top. The three of us get in. They put me in the back part, and we go real fast. And pretty soon we're landing inside a large, large, large spaceship. It's huge! I can't believe the size. It's just huge. I can see the stars.

DR. FIORE:   Where do you see the stars?

LINDA:   Outside of this large spacecraft, I see lots of stars. There's like a cloud of brilliant lights, coming from the top of it, way up here. [*Pauses*] We're still going toward it. I see my brother Mark there. He's greeting me. I get out. He gives me a hug. He tells me that his subconscious will never let him remember this, but he enjoys it when he goes. He tells me that he won't give me a bad time and tease me, but he really does understand . . . because he's going through it too. There's four of us now, the real tall one, the real small one and another one larger than I. We're on a platform or something, and we turn right. Very spacious. Very, very spacious. And I hear a very gentle hum. It's very relaxing. We go into this big theater of some kind, with seats for people to watch a movie screen. They're showing us something, and what they're showing us is a picture of the earth from the way they see it. They see the earth on the screen and clouds surrounding the earth. They're pointing out a particular area on the earth to go to. I can't quite tell where it is. It seems to be some place in Europe. Northern part of Europe. I see where it is. I've dreamed of it before, but I don't know where it is. It's on a hillside, and it's like a big cave with doors that open up. It's a sanctuary, they say, to go there and find peace, comfort and learning. Once we go there, we won't be the same. We will be changed. Our energies will be vibrating at a higher level. I guess we're there with the crystal again. Everybody's holding hands, and we're singing a song. *"Om Shamda, Olom, Vaya, Ovee. Om Shamba Vaya."* I feel tremendous joy. [*Whispers*] It makes me cry, it's so powerful. [*Cries a little*] It's like everybody is being lifted up. It's almost like we're . . . floating. Still holding hands, and we're all . . . being lifted. And the vibrations are getting stronger and stronger and more powerful. I get a little scared. I don't know how much I can take, it's so overwhelming. [*Pauses.*] I'm back in bed.

DR. FIORE:   I'd like you to go to the time when you were being healed of the yeast infection, at the count of five. One . . . two . . . three . . . four . . . five.

LINDA:   I'm on the table, my feet are up. And they use an instrument of some kind. It looks like a big cotton ball on a stick. You know how when they take a throat culture? It's kind of like that, and they're swabbing me inside.

DR. FIORE:   Where?

LINDA: They're going way up into my uterus too. And they're cleaning it out somehow, swabbing it out. They have this jellylike substance that looks like aquamarine blue, and it's clear, it's transparent. How are they doing this? It looks like they're putting it on something that's a squarish, rectangular sort of shape. And they squish it out of the rectangular shape, up inside me. I told them it feels cold. They say that's to help freeze the bacteria. And then they take that out.

DR. FIORE: What do they take out?

LINDA: They take out the applicator which they used to put the jelly in. [*Pauses*] And . . . my legs are still up. It reminds me of the circus, the people that twirl, kind of. And . . . I'm twirling with my feet up. But my feet are together, and they are attached somehow to something. It's not uncomfortable or anything, it's just like the people who, in the circus, twirl up in the air, kind of, and then they bring me back down. And it almost looks like a pad or something they're putting on me, between my legs. And then they put me on another couch. They cover me up for a little while, and I take a rest.

DR. FIORE: Did they explain what they were going to do?

LINDA: They said, "Don't worry, it won't hurt." It's for my own good. But they understand I have been trying to get rid of it by myself. They say now's the time I've got to get completely well, so they're going to help me some more. They say something about an infection of the liver. I don't know how that can have any relation to that.

DR. FIORE: What did they say?

LINDA: Infection of the liver. I damaged it as a child. When I fell from someplace. Damage to my liver, which over the years they have been slowly refurbishing, just as if building, like building it up. The salve penetrates the whole body and generates new cells that will fight infection and in turn will give off new life in my body. They tell me I'll understand more as we go along.

DR. FIORE: Tell me anything else that they say regarding the body.

LINDA: They say there are these portals, where you can gather energy and bring it up through the body, to cleanse and renew each cell. I see. They are showing me a cell and how the energy comes, uses something and is generated out.

DR. FIORE: Where does the energy come from?

LINDA: It comes from the universe. A magnetic system which is generated from the sonar field. I don't understand that. This is the main source of energy for all the universe, for all the one called Eli.

DR. FIORE: Let yourself remember what happens after your treatment for the yeast infection.

LINDA: I go and watch while the other people are being worked on. I just stand and watch them. There's seven, counting me. No, eight, because there's somebody on the table.

DR. FIORE: And then?

LINDA: There's a bright light over here and to my left, about two to three feet across. I'm feeling it shining its warmth on my face. I'm sitting on some kind of a chair and somebody's talking to me on my right. He has my hand and is calming me down. I got scared of something. It's upset me.

DR. FIORE: Move to just a few seconds before you were upset.

LINDA: [*Grimaces*] I feel threatened.

DR. FIORE:  Let yourself remember.

LINDA:  I don't want to. I don't want to!

DR. FIORE:  What is it you don't want to do?

LINDA:  I don't want to go through it again.

DR. FIORE:  Let yourself remember.

LINDA:  It's by the black hole. I fell into it. It feels like a cyclone or something. I'm falling and I'm scared. [*Her voice quavers*] I feel empty. [*Her body jerks*] I'm back in the chair and somebody's comforting me.

DR. FIORE:  Are they explaining something to you?

LINDA:  It was an accident.

DR. FIORE:  What else do they say?

LINDA:  I was in an area of the ship that I wasn't supposed to be in. For my safety, I have to stay with the others. They were able to rescue me, this time, but no guarantee about the future. They do not reprimand me.

DR. FIORE:  Move back to that incident.

LINDA:  I'm climbing up the stairs and I got lost. I thought I would investigate. There's a door at the end. I slipped and fell into the big black hole. I was falling around and around, and some being comes and grabs me. He brings me back up and holds me. He takes me back into another room. And talks to me. And I can see the color of his aura. I was crying.

DR. FIORE:  Move back to the time when you were watching the others.

LINDA:    I see someone on the table, with an instrument over his midriff. Metal goes around him. It's narrow and connected, attached to an L-shaped arm. Attached to something in the wall. That metal thing has parts that touch the person's body. I ask, "What is wrong with him?" And they tell me he has a stomach ulcer, so they are generating energy which is directed at the ulcer. Someone else on the table is tall and thin. Somebody is working on his head, doing something to his head. It's a smaller, circular thing that moves from point to point, and from temple to temple. Just above his eye. They're pulsing it to shrink the tumor, and I can almost see the tumor shrinking as they're working on it. He gets off, and a small child is put on the table. A little girl about five or six. They're scanning her whole body, giving her a physical, checking her out. She has worms, they say. They're going to eliminate them. No, they're going to inject something into her stomach area. It looks like a big syringe in the stomach. [*She points to her abdomen*] They put salve in and carry her off the table, and now they're laying her down and covering her up. They're lifting a big man onto the table. He's about forty. Dark hair, big burly-looking man. They're doing something with his left arm. He has a problem with his shoulder, they said. His shoulder dislocates and gets swollen, like bursitis. He's now inflamed, inside his shoulder. They're raising his left arm, to see the mobility. They're doing something with the left arm, they keep raising it into the air for some reason. The doctor does the same thing. They use an instrument with pulsing light. Then he gets off. My sister Sherry is on the table. I can't see what they're doing to her.

DR. FIORE:    Let yourself remember everything at the count of three. One . . . two . . . three.

LINDA:    They have her legs spread open, and they're doing something to her they did to me, putting salve in. Now they put her legs together, and they're twirling her around and around. Her head is down, and her feet are up there. [*She points into the air*] It kind of scared her. They take her down to the corner and cover her up with a cover. There's a young teenage boy, fifteen to sixteen years old, who lies on the table. He has very large feet. He used to have a hip problem on his right side. His hip is deteriorating, so they are trying to generate energy to promote new cell growth. A large machine with crystallized light. Eight inches around, attached to something on the floor. Like in an L shape. It sends out this green and yellow and blue and pink and white light, into this young man's hip area. They have somebody holding his shoulder because he's squirming. They ask him to squeeze his legs. They use their hands. And somebody's pressing on his side. Somebody else is pressing on the other side. He gets off the table, and he's walking fine. He's still limping, but it seems like an improvement. He's lying down, and they put a blanket over him. They say it's time to go back home. We've had enough for tonight.

DR. FIORE: And then what happens?

LINDA: All of us are walking down a corridor. They have us walk through the door. There are twenty-five other people. We sit and wait for a while for other people. Then they put us into a smaller craft that holds about fifty people. And they close the door, and we whiz off. We land somewhere, way out in the desert. We get out of that [craft] and go into smaller ones that only hold a few people. They strap us in something, and a protective arm comes across. We whiz over the top of trees. The very first thing I see is a lake, over to the right.

DR. FIORE: What time is it?

LINDA: About 2:30 in the night, actually early morning. It's 3:00 before they get me home. Somebody is walking with me. A tall being gives me a hug, and I climb back in bed.

DR. FIORE: Let yourself remember another important encounter, at the count of three. One . . . two . . . three.

LINDA:   The room with a crystal. Standing there. Feeling the energy coming. I know I have to heal myself somehow. They're going to teach me what to do.

DR. FIORE:   Speak out everything that you are aware of.

LINDA:   I'm a little scared. There's a lump in my breast. I'm real worried about it. They tell me they can help me. They said direct the energy from my left hand to where the lump is. Take the right, put it over the top. Take a deep breath. Let energy flow through it. Visualize it getting smaller. I can feel the energy going through. [*Sighs*]

DR. FIORE:   What happened to you then?

LINDA:   It was like the energy suddenly stopped. We're going into some kind of a room.

DR. FIORE:   Just report everything that comes into your mind.

LINDA:   Some kind of a round table, a long table, like in a doctor's office. They're having me get up on it. They have some kind of an instrument over here. It looks like a metal tube with a light on the end, almost like a rounded crystal or something on the end of it. They're putting it over, right where the lump is on my breast. It sends some kind of energy through. They remove it. Get me off the table. There are other people there with me. I don't know who they are, but we're all together, and it's somebody else's turn to get up on the table. Several people taking turns, having different things done. There's just one really tall being with us in the room. He's got on a very dark, almost black robe. I see his long fingers. His hands look very bony. His hands are very long. They come out to about here. Especially the knuckle area is very bony.

DR. FIORE:   What color is his skin?

LINDA: It's whitish, almost iridescent in a way. He's doing something with his hands.

DR. FIORE: What is he doing?

LINDA: His hands are at the top of somebody else and it's like they're cutting right over the top of the forehead a little bit. He's not touching them. I think it looks like Sherry. My sister Sherry. And he's working with her forehead somehow. He's coming around the sides of her ears. He's sending some energy somehow, to the back of her neck. He seems to be reaching over and going along the side of her body, all the way down to her feet. Working with somebody else there too. There's another being at her feet now. And they're both working on her at the same time. She's smiling. She says it tingles. Actually, she's laughing. [*Laughs*] My mother's there too. She says she wishes that we could live closer together rather than have to come together in our dreams. The room seems brighter all of a sudden. There's all this beautiful light coming out of everybody. And we just kind of glow. Now they've taken us back to the crystal again. I want to go and touch it, but they say don't touch it. It's turning purples and blues on the left side and pinks on the right. You just soak it up. It's very powerful. [*Pauses*] I'm back in bed again.

DR. FIORE: Go back into the ship. Let's see if they say anything about your appointment with me today.

LINDA: They say don't tell her.

DR. FIORE: What do you say?

LINDA: Why not? I feel it's important for people to understand. They say that people aren't ready. They'll just laugh. They have to be given time.

DR. FIORE: Let yourself know if anything else was said to you.

LINDA:   You should understand that we mean no harm. We are here to change the world . . . to keep it from disaster. Which is imminent, if people keep living the way they do. We are here to help the people into a new age of living. There will be changes so powerful that only the strong will survive. We are here to give knowledge and understanding to the world of light and the world of children of God. We are here to change the world for a better development in the universe . . . to be closer . . . to surviving planets . . . in the nearby universe. We are here to give to all, new life, new force, a new being, an exciting, wonderful world of knowledge. Peace be with you forever and always.

DR. FIORE:   How do you feel about that?

LINDA:   Curious.

DR. FIORE:   Did you feel that that message was coming through you?

LINDA:   Definitely. I felt that if I had let go a little more, my voice would have changed. And that I would have been completely channeling it. A part of me still doesn't let go enough.

DR. FIORE:   Just let yourself relax. I'm going to ask you to go back in time and space to another important contact. Just report whatever comes into your mind.

LINDA:   Blinking red light over here. They're kind of beings. They're working at an instrument panel over here. It's inside a spaceship.

DR. FIORE:   What do they look like?

LINDA:   Very strange. [Laughs] They're kinda green and glowy and have real tiny eyes. They're real small beings. They have little tiny eyes, no nose at all, just kind of holes where we have noses, and kind of a round little hole where the mouth is, if it's a mouth; I'm not sure. One I see in front of me is working on some kind of an instrument panel. It has these lights, and it has cords coming out of some area, like an electrical type of wire that surrounds them. It looks like a . . . like a telephone type of thing. It has some wires. Like a switchboard. They won't let me go in the room. I can't go in, but it kind of curves around a little bit. And they take me down this hall. I'm walking with some-body very tall. It's like an old friend. I feel comfortable with him. He's got a hand on me, on my back. We're talking.

DR. FIORE:   What are you talking about?

LINDA:   We're talking about what I learned that day. I can't remember what we're saying.

DR. FIORE:   At the count of three, you're going to remember. One . . . two . . . three.

LINDA:   He asks, "Do you know that if you take the energy from your hands and lay it on your third eye, you can send it all the way down . . . through your body to a point of impact, where it will regenerate and come back out again . . . through your ear?" And then I can hear them. Hmm . . . We continue walking. Then we go into the room where Sherry and my mom are, and some other people too, where the table is. There are five other people and two other large, tall beings. And then the table and some of their instruments, all medical instruments, but they're very different from ours. There's a machine over here to the right. It looks like when they take people's blood in a centri-fuge type of machine, and they're taking samples of our urine, and they're putting it in this machine for testing.

DR. FIORE:   Where are you?

LINDA:   I'm over on the other side of the table, and I'm just watching the work right now. It's like they're preparing. This is before they work on any humans. I ask them, why don't they take people who are healthier to do their work? And they say, they're not the right ones. They're trying to prove a point.

DR. FIORE:   What is that?

LINDA:   Trying to change the mental concepts of people. Then I'm back on the table. Someone's at my feet, another tall being's at my head. The one by my head has his hand, not touching me, but kind of directing the fingers toward my head. I feel changes . . . occurring inside my brain and in my head. At one point it hurts.

DR. FIORE:   Did you say anything?

LINDA:   I just told them I felt it go directly in me. It felt like an electrical beam going through my head. They teach me to use the instrument on the lump in my breast.

DR. FIORE:   What instrument is that?

LINDA:   It's a long silver thing with a rounded crystal on the end. And it glows out light. It pulsates, I guess. Somebody is working down at my feet. They're sending energy. It comes up through both feet and just keeps coming in waves. And I feel it at the top of my head, coming all the way through. They say, "You're okay now. You're ready to get off." And so I get off the table. And Sherry says, "I want to go next." So she hops up. And they work on her.

DR. FIORE:   What do you see?

LINDA:   I see them working right around her pubic bone. They're doing something there. It's almost like their fingers are going right through her body and they're cleaning something out of her ovary area over on the right side. It's like a white mass of something that they're pulling out. They bring it out of her and put it in the bag, like a plastic-type bag, and close it up. And somebody dumps it into a pail.

DR. FIORE:   Does she say anything?

LINDA:   She jokingly asks them if they can enlarge breasts too. [*Laughs*]

DR. FIORE:   Where are you?

LINDA:   I'm over on her left side, holding her hand.

DR. FIORE:   Then what happens?

LINDA:   They turn off the lights in the room, and we are directed out of the room, turn right, go down this corridor, and then we get onto—it's like a small spacecraft. And we sit down. It only holds about five people, and one—it's not a tall being, it's somebody small—one of the green ones. Somebody's coming, saying, "Wait. Wait, you forgot something." Giving something to somebody, a bag of something. It's sort of like rocks, but they're not rocks. They're glowing. All different colors, mostly golds and blues and browns. I don't see who they're giving them to. Then we take off. And then I'm back in bed.

DR. FIORE:   Move back to the very first contact with extraterrestrials.

LINDA:   I'm in Seattle. I'm looking out the window. In the sky, there's a light. I stand there watching. And it disappears. And then I don't see it anymore. Beings come into the room. They talk to me like they've known me for a long time. They say that I'm in a different body this time, but we'll continue working together. This will be an exciting time. Wonderful things will be happening. They tell me to not be afraid. I'm sitting on a tall being's lap. I'm four years old. They're telling me something. I don't know what he's telling me.

DR. FIORE:   You will remember at the count of three. One . . .
two . . . three.

LINDA:   His arm is around me like a big father. I feel he cares
about me a lot. He's telling me a story about another place. And
another time. It's a city of lights, and things we do not have here
on this earth. I see a lot of blue, brilliant lights. He is saying this is
where you came from and you can go back when you're
through here. This is your home, but for right now, you have to
be here, on this earth, but they'll come visit me, and I can talk to
them whenever I need them. But I can go home when I'm
through.

DR. FIORE:   What is his name?

LINDA:   Revance. He's leaving now. And tucks me back into
my bed and says goodbye. My little brother's crying. My
mommy comes in and I tell her an angel came to visit me.

❧

When Linda came out of hypnosis, she had tears in her eyes.
"They are so very, very loving. And the energy's so powerful, it
made me cry."

"Linda, I'm concerned about the lump in your breast. Are you
aware of one?"

"Yes. I just found it last night. I'll have it checked out."

"Fine. It's really important to have good medical care. Let me
know what you find. I'll be very interested also in what happens
with your yeast infection."

"It would be too good to be true, if it's cured."

"Do you think Sherry would be willing to come for a regression
to the same encounter? I think it would be particularly interesting
to see what she remembers under hypnosis."

Linda made arrangements with her sister, and Sherry did come
several weeks later. You'll read her account in the next chapter.

Linda had to drop out of therapy temporarily, so I called her
just as I was writing up her case. Her yeast infection has returned,

and she has it recurrently. Sometimes it's a lot better and at times, worse. So it appears that the extraterrestrial "doctors" don't have a permanent cure for it, either. She had the feeling, though, that she is being treated for it by them. Both her sister Sherry and her mother remain free of their yeast infections.

# "I've Let Those People Touch Me!"

 "I don't know whether I can be hypnotized, because I have a very strong will and I don't think I can let someone else take over control." Sherry, Linda's sister, looked decidedly anxious about being hypnotized. Yet I felt she was just as concerned about not being able to do a good job. She had accepted my invitation to come for a regression, therefore she had a lot at stake. First, she wanted to solve the puzzle: How had her yeast infection been cured? And was her dream of extraterrestrials really a close encounter? Second, she wanted to perform well for her sister's sake. And third, she knew my time was valuable and I had given up a Saturday morning for our work. She was under a lot of pressure, especially since she didn't think she could be hypnotized, which is a very common fear.

"That's no problem, Sherry, because you are never under my control and there's no issue regarding will. In fact, the stronger you are, the better, because you can use your will to cooperate. It's really self-hypnosis anyway. I'll give you suggestions, and if you decide to go along with them, and I'm sure you will, you'll hypno-

115

tize yourself. One of the bonuses from our work today will be that you'll have a tool you can use all your life."

Sherry looked much more relaxed and a little curious. Smiling, she asked, "You mean, I'll learn how to hypnotize myself?"

"Yes. By simply giving yourself the very suggestions I'll be using with you, you can put yourself into a trance. In fact, let's have a practice run before we begin the regression and you'll see for yourself what it's like to be hypnotized. I'll teach you how to bring yourself out too."

After she had removed her contact lenses, stretched out almost flat with her feet up on the ottoman and was covered with the blanket, I asked her to close her eyes and concentrate on her breathing. "Just breathe easily and naturally without changing the pattern of your breath. Now imagine a miniature sun, just like the sun in our solar system, deep in your solar plexus. This sun is radiating through you, through every atom and cell of your body, filling you with light. It's shining out beyond you, an arm's length in every direction, creating an aura of brilliant, sparkling, dazzling white light of protection around you." Next I had her imagine herself at the top of a magnificent staircase, and as I counted down from twenty-one to zero, she was to take a descending step with each number, going deeper and deeper within. Once at the bottom of the staircase, I assumed she was in a good state of hypnosis, so I gave her suggestions to remember the three phases we had been through; concentrating on her breathing, surrounding herself with white light and walking down the stairs. I emphasized to her that at this point she could give herself positive suggestions to achieve any goal, and she could strengthen them by imagining the desired result as though it had already been achieved. I pointed out that her subconscious mind couldn't tell the difference between what was imagined and what was actual, that once it accepted the desired goal as a reality, it created a "blueprint" and immediately started to manifest it.

"Now when you are ready to come out of hypnosis, give yourself mental suggestions for well-being, for example, 'I'll be awake and alert and feeling fine in every way.' Mentally count to three and open up your eyes at three. Go ahead and do it now."

Sherry beamed with delight. She had learned self-hypnosis. Quickly, a slight frown of doubt crossed her face. "But are you sure I was hypnotized? I felt like I didn't go under."

"I can be pretty sure you were, and certainly with practice you'd allow yourself to go deeper. It will be very helpful as a way to relieve stress, and it only takes a few minutes. But there's one very important caution: *Do not use self-hypnosis to regress yourself!* It's sort of like opening Pandora's box. In fact, you can make things worse, because undoubtedly you wouldn't permit yourself to reexperience the anxiety involved in the event that's causing the condition you wish to alleviate. You'd only succeed in bringing the repressed memory closer to the surface, and it could cause you more problems. Otherwise, self-hypnosis will serve you well through the years."

Sherry was nodding in agreement. "No. I wouldn't do that, but I could work on a few areas. My weight and procrastination."

"Great! Once at the bottom of the staircase, give yourself positive suggestions and imagine yourself at your ideal weight and see all the tasks you've been putting off as already accomplished." I checked the clock and saw that it was time for us to get started with the investigation of Sherry's "dream."

Having just been in a trance a few minutes before helped her to into an even deeper one very quickly. Within two minutes, she was ready to regress. I gave her inner mind suggestions to go back in time and space to the cause of the dream, emphasizing that she would remember easily and accurately. I counted slowly to ten.

*

SHERRY:   I was lying on a table or some flat surface that seemed like it was stainless steel. I don't remember any faces, but there was a doctor, or someone I perceived as a doctor, and there was some kind of machine that, I was told by mental telepathy, could analyze if there was anything wrong in my body and could also kill bacteria in my body that wasn't good. So I allowed them to do whatever . . . and the next thing I knew, I was being examined vaginally, and it seems like my feet were in some kind of stirrups or in something very similar to what you'd find in a doctor's office. And some kind of cream was being put inside of me. At times I felt feelings of fear, but somebody who seemed to be familiar or whom I trusted would tell me not to worry, that everything was okay. And actually, I think I felt kind of grateful. I was kind of thankful that I was being helped. And then I was put on something that made my head feel like I was spinning. I felt like my whole body was spinning, and that was pretty scary. And I was told not to worry, that it was okay, that I'd be okay, and then I blacked out. When I came to, someone asked me if I remembered anything. I said no. The next thing I knew, I was snapped back into my body.

DR. FIORE:   Where was your body?

SHERRY:   In my sleeping bag. I was camping.

DR. FIORE:   Move to the very first moment when this experience started. Just trust your mind and report whatever comes into your mind. You're in your sleeping bag and what happens?

SHERRY:   It seems like I see a flash of light. I feel this pulsating . . . pulling, kind of sensation. I don't see anything. It's dark except for violet and gold light. [*Long pause*] I keep on getting these feelings that I shouldn't be saying anything. I feel like there's some kind of block that I . . . I don't know if it's my own fear that I'm not going to remember anything or . . .

DR. FIORE:   You're doing just fine. Just speak out whatever comes into your mind.

SHERRY:   I feel real tense, real stiff. It seems like there's some kind of . . . form that seems to be mostly light. I feel kind of frightened. Every time I feel like I'm getting close to something, I start to tense up.

DR. FIORE:   That could be because you're remembering how you once felt, which was tense. So just speak out.

SHERRY:   I feel like I'm lying somewhere and I'm seeing silhouettes above me. It's kind of a silhouette of something that  .  .  . there's no hair or anything, just a form with a head. But it's making me shake like I'm cold. I don't see anything definite, just the feeling of being looked down at, by maybe five or six figures.

DR. FIORE:   Do you remember ETs of different heights? Or were they just one general height?

SHERRY:   It seems like all the forms were about the same height.

DR. FIORE:   How tall is that?

SHERRY:   It's hard to say, because I was lying down. Much taller than I am, maybe  .  .  . eight feet or so. And it didn't seem like there was any clothing. .  .  . There was nothing to clothe, there was nothing to hide. It was just a form. I did see just a brief picture of a  .  .  . a form with very large, dark eyes  .  .  . just very briefly.

DR. FIORE:   You're going to remember that form very well and you're going to tell me the details.

SHERRY:   Hm  .  .  . Now I'm seeing something different. Seems almost like a  .  .  . leathery, almost amphibian-type skin. It's kind of  .  .  . greenish-yellowish and wrinkly  .  .  . large eyes, but they were  .  .  . ooohhh! [*Grimaces*] I really don't want to remember. It's pretty scary.

DR. FIORE:   You're going to allow yourself to remember, because the more you get rid of your fear, the more you will feel good about yourself. It's just because they're different. They did not harm you, so let yourself remember.

SHERRY:   The one thing that I do see is that the eyes are very caring and loving. And  .  .  . I really sense that they are  .  .  .

they really don't want to scare and they really worry about that. The caring is really evident in the eyes. [*Pauses*] The face I saw is gone. It was more amphibianlike than anything else.

DR. FIORE:  Let yourself know if they all look like that.

SHERRY:  I sense that they don't, but I don't really see anything.

DR. FIORE:  Tell me about their bodies.

SHERRY:  They seem to be very trim-looking. It's not like there's any fat. . . . They seem to be the same, I don't see any big differences.

DR. FIORE:  Now let's get back to what's happening. You believed you were lying on something.

SHERRY:  I'm lying flat.

DR. FIORE:  What is your body feeling?

SHERRY:  I feel cold.

DR. FIORE:  What are your emotions?

SHERRY:  I feel afraid, even though I feel like I don't need to be.

DR. FIORE:  Is anything being relayed to you in any way?

SHERRY:  I feel like they're . . . it's like light . . . some kind of light that's making me calm. It's calming.

DR. FIORE:  What color is the light?

SHERRY:  It's purple and gold.

DR. FIORE:  Where does the light seem to be coming from?

SHERRY: It seems to be emanating from whoever is around me. There seems to be kind of a merging of forms or something. It's like seeing an aura around somebody. It's not like actually seeing an actual form, and so the colors merge. But it's mostly like gold.

DR. FIORE: Now you're going to move ahead to the time that something does happen to you.

SHERRY: It's not like I'm actually seeing anything, but I feel like I'm being operated on.

DR. FIORE: Tell me about that in detail.

SHERRY: It seems like they're taking something out of my breast, but I don't know if I'm making this up.

DR. FIORE: Don't be concerned about that. Where do you feel you are in relationship to your body?

SHERRY: I can't feel what's happening. I can't feel . . . there's no feeling of touch.

DR. FIORE: When you say that, do you mean no body sensation or no emotion?

SHERRY: No body sensation.

DR. FIORE: Where do you feel you are in relationship to your body?

SHERRY: It's like being within and also watching.

DR. FIORE: From what vantage point?

SHERRY: From above my head. [*Long pause*] It's like I'm looking at somebody's brain or an X ray of someone's brain.

DR. FIORE:   Tell me more about that.

SHERRY:   It's not an X ray, because I can see . . . It's like there are colors. Light.

DR. FIORE:   Tell me about it in detail.

SHERRY:   I think something was being taken out.

DR. FIORE:   Was that somebody else's brain, or was it yours?

SHERRY:   It was somebody else's.

DR. FIORE:   Was it anybody whom you knew?

SHERRY:   No.

DR. FIORE:   I'd like you to remember how many other people were in the room being examined, treated, and/or operated on.

SHERRY:   There were many.

DR. FIORE:   Tell me about that, you're allowing yourself to remember so very much now.

SHERRY:   There's a child being pushed by me. It looks like I could see light around him. I could see his aura, the golden aura around him. I definitely sense that I'm not alone.

DR. FIORE:   You're going to do more than just sense, you're going to know, you're going to allow yourself to remember now, at the count of three. One . . . two . . . three. You are remembering just as though it's happening now.

SHERRY:   There seems to be one central figure that is like the head. I guess he would be almost like a head surgeon. He's wearing some clothing with a high collar. I . . . just saw him

from the back. He has a large brain . . . a large head. [*Pauses*]
I'm not too concerned about what's going on around me, because it's happened before and it's not like it's new, so . . . I
don't really see anything definite. I suppose I could leave my
body and look around, if I wanted to. [*Pauses*] It's pretty interesting. You can have the opportunity to see what the inside of a
body looks like. It's like I can see somebody with their whole
abdomen opened up. I can see their lungs. I can see the heart
beating. [*Pauses*] There's somebody that had . . . it's almost
like their legs are wrapped. It's not a cast. It's kind of like a
bright, iridescent blue. [*Pauses*] It's pretty busy. There's a lot of
activity. I don't want to get in the way.

DR. FIORE:    How many people would you say are being operated on?

SHERRY:    A hundred come to my mind, but I don't know. It's a
round space and it's pretty full. [*Pauses*] I see something spinning. It's almost like a roulette wheel, but there are different
parts of it going in different directions. It's almost like looking
down from the top. I don't know what it is.

DR. FIORE:    Do you see anyone whom you know?

SHERRY:    Not yet. I feel like I'm moving outside of a certain
space and then back in. I'm not staying in the same place. It's
almost like I can come and go.

DR. FIORE:    What do you mean by that?

SHERRY:    My etheric body can come and go.

DR. FIORE:    Where is your physical body?

SHERRY:    My physical body is on the table.

DR. FIORE:    What's happening to it?

SHERRY: They're still working . . . it seems like they're working on my abdominal area.

DR. FIORE: What are they doing to it?

SHERRY: I'm not sure.

DR. FIORE: Take a look.

SHERRY: [*Pauses*] My mind says they're looking for cancer, but I don't know that.

DR. FIORE: Let yourself know if they conveyed that to you.

SHERRY: They're just looking. There's nothing there. They're just looking to see if there's any obstruction. It seems like they're trying to move things around so my colon is straightened out. [*Pauses*] They fill the space with light. It's not like it's being done with . . . tools, really. [*Pauses*] I can see there's a machine over somebody, and I can see all the bones in their body through the top. It's like an X ray, but it's . . . it's like a fluorescent green, and they're lying on a table. It's a man. They're mostly checking. It seems like they're trying to help people who have problems. There's so many people to help. I get the feeling that as our bodies are healthier, it enables us to better help others. It seems like it's because we won't be worrying about ourselves and we'll be more clear and allow the light to flow . . . flow better, easier. [*Pauses*] It seems like it's all about . . . energy . . . and sharing light and helping others. [*Pauses and looks up*] You can look up and it's like a light show. It's pretty interesting.

DR. FIORE: Let's move to what's been done to you in the way of treatments. You said that you thought they were taking something out of your breast. And then what were you aware of?

SHERRY: I felt like my system was being flushed out, somehow.

DR. FIORE: Is anything being conveyed to you mentally or through speech?

SHERRY: Mostly not to fear, that there's nothing to fear, that they're trying to help.

DR. FIORE: Did they say why they're trying to help you?

SHERRY: I just get feelings of love. But I don't know that there's any connection other than that.

DR. FIORE: Let yourself remember if something was done about your yeast infection.

SHERRY: [*Pauses*] It was like a cream. It was put inside of me . . . real deep inside of me. It was not done with an instrument. It was done, I guess, with a hand and it was a little cold and really messy. It felt . . . gushy. It wasn't really cold, but I could tell that it was like a cream.

DR. FIORE: How did you feel about this being done?

SHERRY: I felt uncomfortable, but I knew what it was being done for. They told me why.

DR. FIORE: What did they say?

SHERRY: They said it would take care of the yeast. [*Long pause*] When I feel like I'm going to remember something, I start to tense up and I . . . feel like I can't. Either I'm not supposed to, or I'm afraid to, I don't know which one.

DR. FIORE: At the count of three, you're going to allow yourself to remember, even if you feel that tension. One . . . two . . . three.

SHERRY: The feeling I get is that I'm out of my body and I'm looking at it as if I were the doctor. And I'm looking at what they're doing.

DR. FIORE: And what do you see?

SHERRY: I'm looking at it like I'm standing in front of my body with my legs spread. And it's almost like I could go inside and see what it looks like . . . inside. [*Pauses*] It seems like I ask them to examine me because I was so worried about this fungus infection. So I don't get the feeling that anything would be done without my consent or asking. I'm being given a different perspective of what is going on with my body. It's almost like I can see the lining inside my vaginal area. Like it's . . . almost like being blown up on a screen . . . magnified. [*Pauses*] But there's nothing really wrong. Hmm . . . It's almost like there's this . . . I can't explain it. It's something that moves along with it. It's kind of like an iridescent green. There's a light on the end of it so you can see. [*Pauses*] It's like I need to know my body and what makes it work so I can understand more. And I get the feeling that the reason for it is so I can help other people. But I don't know if I was told that or it's just a feeling.

DR. FIORE: Let yourself remember if you're told that.

SHERRY: [*Long pause*]

DR. FIORE: Trust your mind and just report whatever comes into it.

SHERRY: It's like I'm being drawn toward a light that's like the light of a candle. And pretty soon, it's . . . not just in front of me, it's like it's within me. [*Pauses*] It's almost like some kind of a ceremony. Something's happening that is very emotional. There's some kind of special group that I'm a part of, and it makes me want to cry. [*Cries*] It's a . . . it's like being . . . all for one for the higher good of all of life. [*Long pause*]

DR. FIORE: Now go to the time when you're spinning.

SHERRY: It was really scary. I didn't understand what they were doing. Now I think there was something connected to me, to my head, and it was making my mind spin. It's just giving me that feeling, like pulsating. I felt like I was going to black out. I knew that was what was going to happen. And when they asked me if I remembered, I said no, even though I did remember.

DR. FIORE: You said no, but you did remember?

SHERRY: I did remember some things, but I said no because I wanted to go back. [*Pauses*] But I don't remember any faces. They didn't want me to. It seems like they only want me to remember them as light. Because that's what we have in common.

DR. FIORE: Why do you think they put that thing on your head?

SHERRY: Because it would erase the memory. It seems like I would not ever allow that to happen again if I knew everything . . . if I remembered everything. I might not allow myself to be open.

DR. FIORE: What do you mean by that?

SHERRY: In a sense, it's like letting yourself be used for a higher purpose. Not like a guinea pig, but because they're helping at the same time it's helping them also to have a deeper understanding.

DR. FIORE: A deeper understanding of . . . ?

SHERRY: Of humans. Of the human body. It's like we're helping each other. Whatever we give comes back in return in other ways. Like the gift of being healed is giving and receiving.

DR. FIORE: Do you feel there have been other experiences before and after? And if so, how many?

SHERRY: [*Long pause*] Hmm . . . Too many to count.

DR. FIORE: Do you feel that they have worked on your body or healed your body either before or since?

SHERRY: I feel that, but I don't have any recollection. Sometimes I'll wake up in the middle of the night and a certain place on my body might hurt and I'll get a distinct feeling that I've just been operated on, and then by the morning it's gone.

DR. FIORE: Have you ever seen any marks on your body that you couldn't explain?

SHERRY: Yes.

DR. FIORE: Tell me about them.

SHERRY: Once I saw a very fine red line, but it was gone in a matter of hours. It was on my abdominal area, on the right side.

DR. FIORE: Do you feel that the ETs have extracted eggs or fetuses?

SHERRY: Eggs.

DR. FIORE: Tell me about that.

SHERRY: It's being used for study. And . . . and I have a concern about pregnancy for some reason.

DR. FIORE: What do you mean by that?

SHERRY: I just felt that there was life inside me before. And . . . I actually consciously feared that some kind of intercourse was taking place. [*Long pause*]

DR. FIORE:  Continue to speak out.

SHERRY:  But I don't know. . . . I just don't know if there's
. . . I don't know. [*Seems very upset*]

DR. FIORE:  Would you like to remember if that has happened?

SHERRY:  No.

DR. FIORE:  But you feel that eggs have been extracted?

SHERRY:  Yes.

DR. FIORE:  How do you feel about that?

SHERRY:  I feel that I don't want it to be used to create a life, but
that for study it would be okay.

DR. FIORE:  Was any explanation given to you?

SHERRY:  It seems like the purpose was for education. But that
. . . concerns me.

DR. FIORE:  What do you mean by that?

SHERRY:  It concerns me because life is . . . is so fragile, and I
don't want to . . . allow myself to be a part of something
that's not . . .

DR. FIORE:  Let's move to the end of that experience, the one
that you had in July. You're going to go to your last moments
with them. Just report whatever comes into your mind, whatever you're aware of.

SHERRY:  It seems like I'm moving. I'm moving toward an all-
consuming kind of light, but it's not real. There seems to be a
sense of excitement. [*Pauses*] I guess they're leaving. I see . . .

heads, through some kind of window area. There's kind of a bright pinkish light, and yellowish. . . . It probably looks like how you would envision a flying saucer.

DR. FIORE:   Take a good look at it.

SHERRY:   It seems to have kind of a dome like. . . . It's funny, this is a smaller . . . only a few people fit in this. Actually, this might be what they bring people back in. It has a lower area that comes around like an upside-down little saucer or something. But there's not very many, it isn't the big one. This is smaller. There's only about five beings in there.

DR. FIORE:   I want you to take a good look at them and tell me more.

SHERRY:   I could draw the outline for you.

DR. FIORE:   Remember what happened. How did you get out of the craft?

SHERRY:   It seems like they're dropping down, kind of like a tube. Hmm . . . It's almost like it's spinning. It's a weird feeling. I can almost feel it, like I'm in it right now, spiraling.

DR. FIORE:   Let yourself know how you got from the craft to where you started.

SHERRY:   [*Pause*] Let's see, it's hard to explain. It's almost like changing matter, like all the atoms were changed. It's almost like there was a physical body there, but the molecules were changed so they could be re-formed in another place and actually be in two places at once.

*◢*

Sherry came out of hypnosis easily. "Their eyes were different from what I remembered from my dream. I immediately backed off when I got a glimpse of them. I would hate to think of someone touching me who looked like that." With dawning realization, she covered her eyes with her hands. "Oh my God! I've let those people touch me!"

# " 'We Need You
as a Contact.' "

"The Pillsbury Doughboy came first. He put his arm around me and I felt better. He didn't talk to me, but did communicate mind to mind. There were three others like him in a row. One was taller than E.T." Ted stood up and showed me how tall they were, putting his hand at about his waist. He walked over to the chair next to my desk and picked up a portfolio of his drawings and began spreading them out on my burgundy-colored carpet. "I brought some of my pictures back. I thought you'd like to see them again."

Ted, mid-forties, tall and attractive, with dark brown hair and startlingly blue eyes, is a former patient. He was here to discover if he had had a close encounter of the fourth kind and had just finished describing a recurrent childhood dream.

I was reasonably sure our visit would be more than productive. When he was in therapy with me, he had shown me many professionally done pen-and-ink sketches, the majority of which were of UFOs. The twenty-odd beautiful drawings of spacecraft now on my floor represented more than ten years' work.

"How long have you been interested in UFOs, Ted?"

"All my life. As a child I used to spend a great deal of time watching sci-fi movies like *War of the Worlds*, and the early Hollywood B-movies of Martians coming to Earth. Then there was one movie that really had an impact on me. I think it came out around 1956, called *Forbidden Planet*. There was a flying saucer in it that was totally fascinating to me. I think that's when I started drawing spaceships, and it carried on in my artwork all these years. When I was ten years old, all of a sudden, I had to know more about stars and astronomy. It got to the point of almost an obsession, where I had to go down and get books constantly. Finally I got a telescope, and then I learned to identify star clusters by sight and by rote memory. The next thing I knew, I formed an astronomy club here in the Valley [Santa Clara Valley] and was active in it for years."

"When do you feel you may have had your first close encounter with extraterrestrials?"

"Probably when I was about two to three and a half years old. I woke up from a nightmare and looked up and there was a person next to my bed. I was terrified! I closed my eyes and went back to sleep. That was a particularly hard time in my life. When I was eighteen months old, I showed the first signs of an angioma, a vascular malformation. Remember we talked about that? I was born with an enlargement of blood vessels in my brain. Later, when I was older, I'd have spells when I'd be out of control, crying, nervous, overly emotional, at times I'd even have some paralysis. My parents took me for my first tests. The doctors said there was nothing that could be done, except medications, barbiturates. They didn't have the treatments forty years ago that they have now, of course. In fact, they told my parents I might be dead in six months, certainly I wouldn't live to adulthood. By then my vision had become very poor, I saw double. I had problems walking, to the point of having to crawl again. I stopped talking and had to be fed. The right side of my body had stopped growing. When I was a little older, about three, I kept telling my folks the doctors had cut the top of my head off. When I was about three and one-half, my parents took me to San Francisco for an exploratory operation. The surgeons were amazed. The growth had shrunk. Nobody could ever figure it out. By then I was walking, talking, feeding myself and could see just fine. I did continue to have some problems with it, though, mainly being supersensitive. My last major spell was in fourth grade, and then they finally stopped."

"Ted, let's start with the nightmare and the night visitors."

"Fine. I hope I can do it."

Ted had developed into an exceptionally fine hypnotic subject during our earlier hypnotherapeutic work, so he was in a trance deep enough for a regression within seconds. I asked him to go back to his very first close encounter. Before I finished counting to ten, he interrupted me.

●

TED:   There's a person here with me. His head is quite large. It's almost like the shape of a peanut. It's larger and rounder at the top. Then it narrows down a little bit and broadens at the bottom. The bottom is a little bit longer than the top. It's very strange looking. I've never seen anything quite like this before. He's got two eyes. They slant upward at about forty-five degrees. The eyes are long and narrow.

DR. FIORE:   What color are the eyes?

TED:   It seems like they're brown. When he opens his eyes, they get quite large. I don't see any ears. The head's very smooth. There doesn't seem to be any hair. The head's very white. It's almost like the texture of . . . like a honeydew melon, but smoother. In fact, it's white, but there's a slight greenish color to it. It's very, very pale green. [*Pauses*] It's very strange, because it seems like there's a number of them, all here at once.

DR. FIORE:   Where are you as this is happening?

TED: I'm in a room in some kind of a craft. And the room is round and there's lights and dials along the wall. On one side there's all kinds of dials and lights in little screens. These dials are built into the wall of the room, but there's a table that comes out like they would use to write information.

DR. FIORE: How old are you?

TED: Three years old.

DR. FIORE: And what are you doing right now?

TED: I'm in this room, and it seems like I'm standing and these people are all around me. Some of them are . . . let's see, they're a little bit taller than I am. They're all different sizes and all different shapes. The ones that are a little bit taller than I am, their heads are very strange . . . kind of like a grasshopper. But the taller ones' heads are a little bit different. They're more like insects.

DR. FIORE: As you're looking at them, how do you feel?

TED: I don't seem to be extremely afraid of them. I find them kind of fascinating. They're not at all aggressive.

DR. FIORE: What are they doing?

TED: Well, they're looking at me. They're fascinated with me. I don't know if we're communicating anything. I can feel some emotions, some tears, almost like I want to just burst out and cry.

DR. FIORE: Tell me more about where you are.

TED: The room is small, but it's not supersmall, but it's not superlarge. I have a feeling it's maybe about twelve feet across. Maybe from the floor to the ceiling it's also about twelve feet.

It's very clean, very smooth, and it's domed. There's almost no furniture in it except for the panels of lights and this table that contours around the room. I believe the door is behind me, and all the people are standing in a semicircle around me.

DR. FIORE: How many are there?

TED: There are two short people, a little bit taller than I am. Then there are two people that are like adults.

DR. FIORE: Now what happens?

TED: There's no verbal communication. I can't tell whether they're saying anything to me. It's like a meeting. Aha . . . what I'm hearing is, "We're here to help you." I ask them, "What do you mean by helping?" And they say, "We are here to help you." Hmm . . . I don't know. "Why are you here?" "To help you." "How?" "With life." "Am I of this planet?" "No." "Why am I here on this planet now?" "Contact." "What do you mean by contact?" "Later, you'll be a contact between them and us." "What do you mean by them?" "Earth people." "Are you going to come back later?" No response. "Where am I?" "In space." "What is this room that I'm in?" "Control room." "What planet are you from?" "No planet. Space station." "Where is your space station?" "Near here." "Are we still close to the earth?" "No." "Do you have a message for me?" "Yes, we will be back later." "What do you mean by later?" "When you are older." "Can you tell me when?" "Older."

DR. FIORE: Now what happens?

TED: It feels like I'm being beamed back down to the earth.

DR. FIORE: Go back through this again to see if there's an examination.

TED:   I see myself lying on a table. I'm out of my body, looking at myself.

DR. FIORE:   Where are you in relationship to your body?

TED:   I'm off to one side, next to them, and I'm watching them. They have a metal probe that's about the diameter of a pencil and about the length of a pencil. It has a blunt end. At the blunt end there is a little . . . almost like a needle that comes out. And they take this probe and they touch different parts of my body. But the needle doesn't go into the body. They just press it up against the skin in different parts. This probe registers information on the dials that are on the wall. As they touch different parts of my body with the probe, the gauges move.

DR. FIORE:   Is the probe independent of the gauges or attached to the gauges?

TED:   It's attached. There's a wire or something attached to one of the instruments on the wall. As they touch me with the probe, the information is being registered on the gauges, and then it's being fed into like a computer for storage.

DR. FIORE:   Then what happens?

TED:   They look into my eyes, look in my mouth, look at my hair. They look at my head. They're doing something to my head. [Pauses] "Is there something wrong with my head?" "Yes, enlarged tissues. If they continue to grow, you will not be able to survive." "Why are you doing this to me?" "To help you. We need you as a contact."

DR. FIORE:   What are they doing to you?

TED:   It seems like they take the probe and they touch different parts of my skull. I don't know whether they're putting energy into the skull or whether they're just registering information. [*Long pause*]

DR. FIORE:   Continue to speak out.

TED:   I'm still lying flat on the table. They bring over an apparatus that's on wheels. There's these little probes and this apparatus that fits around the head. The probes are like little miniature fountain pens attached to the apparatus. These fountain pens can be directed in any direction. There are four of them, two on each side. And at the ends, there's like a glass cover. There are needles that extend out from the glass cover. When they turn the apparatus on, a beam of light comes out. It's very straight and it's very thin. It's needlelike. It's very much like laser light. And it comes out and it strikes my head, but it doesn't hurt.

DR. FIORE:   Are you still in your body when this is happening?

TED:   I'm . . . I'm out of my body. For a few seconds. The beam of light hits the sides of my head, from the back end of the head, all the way up to the front, on both sides. Then they turn off the machine and remove it. Now they awaken me and have me stand up. [*Pauses*] They gather around me.

DR. FIORE:   Your inner mind is going to let you know more about what happened. Let yourself know any details that you omitted.

TED:   What I see now is that I'm in this chair and the top of my head is being removed. And they're looking at my brain.

DR. FIORE:   What do you mean?

TED:   They took an instrument and they cut open the top of the head, all the way around. And they were able to remove that part of the skull and look at the brain.

DR. FIORE: Let yourself remember everything exactly as it happens.

TED: In the beginning, I'm sitting in a chair and there's instruments all around me. They've taken like a laser device and they've cut around the skull. They've removed the top of the head, the skull, and they're looking at the brain. They do that first. Then they put me down on a table. They pick up probes that are hooked up to dials and gauges on the wall and they touch different parts of the brain very gently. The gauges register information. They're finding out something. I don't know what information they want to know. The brain fascinates them, and they're very curious about it. They watch the dials and the gauges, and they record the information. [*Long pause*]

DR. FIORE: What is happening?

TED: They're taking an instrument, it's like a laser, and they're able . . . after they've removed the skull, to heal something. They probe around the brain, they touch all over and they find the enlargement. And with the laser light, they're able to shrink it.

DR. FIORE: Tell me about that in detail.

TED: I watched them, and it's like the light beams out of a little instrument. And it's like fire with a very small beam of light, very thin. It's almost like silk. It's the thickness of a spiderweb, and it beams out and hits that part of the brain. And it just . . . causes it to shrink and change color. Change to bright red, and then it . . . turns to ash. To a grayish ash. And there's another instrument they take, like a suction instrument. And they move it around the surface and remove that ash, and it sucks it up and takes it away. Then they finish. They put the skull back on and fit it, and then with another laser light . . . Oh, the apparatus. They put the apparatus around my head again and they turn it on. And this time instead of cutting, it mends. It mends the skull back together. The atoms go back together, and there's no scar tissue. And when it's finished, there's no indication that the skull has been cut open.

DR. FIORE:   Now what happens?

TED:   I'm taken into a recovery room. There's an attendant there.

DR. FIORE:   Are there any other patients?

TED:   No. I don't see anybody else. I stay there for quite a while.

DR. FIORE:   Where are you in relationship to your body at this time?

TED:   I think I come back in. I feel my spirit coming back into the skull and reclaiming the eye sockets. And I feel my spirit body coming back in and just . . . molding to the skull, to the physical body, almost like pouring milk into a container. I feel myself just gently coming back in and feeling, feeling the skull come up against my spirit body. Feeling myself come back in contact.

DR. FIORE:   Now move to the moment when you were returned to your home.

TED:   I'm on this platform. In the center of a platform is a bell-like jar. I think it's a jar. Anyway, I see these apparatuses coming down from the sides, and they're like laser instruments. They point these at me, and there are four of them, and they beam energy down. And my body changes into a different kind of matter, into light particles. And I travel back to the place where I began, and at that point I materialize.

DR. FIORE:   When you materialize, where are you?

TED: I'm inside of the house. I'm back in bed now. And . . . I wake up. And this person is standing in front of me. And I don't remember what happens, but he frightens me.

DR. FIORE: Which person is this?

TED: He's from the spacecraft. He came down with me to escort me back.

DR. FIORE: When you say you woke up, do you mean you just regained consciousness?

TED: Yes. It was like I was in a very deep sleep, and then I woke up, and I saw this person standing by my bed. He scared me very much. I didn't know what to expect. Then I closed my eyes and the person disappeared.

DR. FIORE: Then?

TED: I went back to sleep.

DR. FIORE: Let yourself remember another encounter.

TED: I see an arm extended out. At the end of the arm there's a television camera, in the center. It's a rectangular lens that fits into the arm and points at me. And there's a sensor in the center of the unit. A robot's moving his arm up and down my body.

DR. FIORE: Where are you?

TED: I'm sitting in a chair in a room in a craft. It's run by a group of mechanical beings. Metal robots. [Pauses] They're checking my body. The room is filled with different kinds of instruments and dials and lights. I'm in a chair that's similar to a dentist's chair, with contoured arms on each side. There's another robot behind me. I'm being studied, but I don't know why.

DR. FIORE:   How old are you?

TED:   Ten years old.

DR. FIORE:   Are they talking to you?

TED:   I'm being examined. I'm in a spacecraft somewhere. The people that are examining me are mechanical. They have artificial intelligence. They don't seem to be very frightening. They're pretty much like the ones in some of the movies I've seen.

DR. FIORE:   How do you know that they're mechanical?

TED:   Their arms are different than mine. They're jointed and they're shaped differently. They're made of metal. It's like a whole series of long, rectangular boxes, hooked together, that move. The body is fairly tall, fairly wide, and it comes to kind of a dome at the top, like their head. But it seems like they're almost all metal.

DR. FIORE:   And you're not frightened by this?

TED:   No. I don't seem to be frightened at all.

DR. FIORE:   Now move back and see if there was a time during this encounter when you were frightened.

TED:   It was in the very beginning, when I was asleep. This was during the night when I was taken.

DR. FIORE:   Let yourself remember all about it.

TED:   I fell asleep. And I was taken aboard. A beam of light came down. I'm not sure, because it feels like I'm a lot older here. It seems more recent.

DR. FIORE:   Let yourself remember.

TED:   Late thirties. It happened in the apartment where I live. It's like a beam of light came down through the apartment, surrounded me and changed me into a different molecular structure, and then it took me back into the small spaceship. And from there I was taken out.

DR. FIORE:   Taken out?

TED:   Taken out into space, away from Earth. And we came to this colony. Where all these different spaceships were.

DR. FIORE:   What happened?

TED:   I was taken on board a larger spaceship or space station. [*Pauses*] I'm in the chair. I'm being examined by the robots.

DR. FIORE:   Tell me more about this.

TED:   There's a robot standing in back of me. The other one in front of me has his arm up, scanning my body. It seems like the end of the arm is like a television screen camera with a sensor. And this sensor is going up and down my body and making readings. But I don't see it being registered anywhere. It's being taken into him and stored somewhere inside of him.

DR. FIORE:   How do you feel?

TED:   It's not frightening. Or is it? I'm not sure, because I feel very numb. I don't have any real emotion.

DR. FIORE:   And now?

TED:   They do the readings and . . . [*Pauses*] I don't know.

DR. FIORE:    Let yourself know at the count of three. One . . .
two . . . three.

TED:    The first thing that comes to mind is really crazy. It's like a
man out of some cartoon. His face is white. It's more like a
human's. His eyes are smaller, more like a human's eyes. His
skin's different. He doesn't have a beard. He doesn't have any
ears. The skin is very smooth. There's no hair. There's two eyes,
they're . . . more elliptical. The eyes are more vertical, up and
down, instead of horizontal like the other beings'. He's in the
room, but he doesn't show himself too clearly, and then he
disappears.

DR. FIORE:    Now what's happening?

TED:    I'm resting. [*Pauses*] I'm still in the chair and I'm in a state
of peace. Everyone around me is not doing anything particular.
It seems like they're getting ready to do something else. They're
extracting some blood. I see this long instrument with some
finger holes on the handle part. It has a long needle. They just
gently stick it in my arm and withdraw the blood.

DR. FIORE:    And now?

TED:    They take the instrument away. I don't know what they
do with it.

DR. FIORE:    Then what happens?

TED:    They take me to another room and they put me on a bed
to rest.

✐

Ted took a while to come out of hypnosis. He stretched his arms,
shook his head as though clearing it and smiled at me. "That was
really weird! I felt like I was reliving it. I could even smell odors
very different from anything I've experienced before."

"I loved the way you asked the extraterrestrials so many questions. What a curious little boy you were. And you obviously felt comfortable enough with them to expect them to treat you with respect, at least enough to answer your questions."

Ted was tired from our long session, so we decided to call it a day. He enthusiastically volunteered to do some drawings for my book. He felt he could draw some of the instruments the visitors used and some interiors of the spacecraft. His parting words were, "It's going to be hard to draw the aliens. They look like a cross between an insect and an amphibian creature." Smiling good-naturedly, he added, "I'll just have to do my best and hope it's not too shocking for the readers."

# "Oh My God!
# They Already Know
# How to Incorporate."

Gloria, a pretty woman in her late thirties, sought my help because of the stress of many family tragedies all happening within a few years.

She began by telling me that she'd been to other therapists but was uncomfortable with them because they were too orthodox. She was tired of their blaming her problems on her mother and her childhood. At any rate, she hadn't improved, and so she wanted to see a hypnotherapist to get at deep layers of her psyche.

Things had not gone smoothly for Gloria for years. At one point, about fifteen years ago, she had so many physical problems that she was hospitalized for a week of testing. She had fever and other symptoms of malaria, but the doctors could find nothing to explain her condition. It was so serious that she thought she would "fade away." She overcame her problems then by becoming a "health nut," and developing a very positive outlook.

Ten minutes into our session, Gloria looked me in the eye, as though sizing me up. "I had a really emotional reaction to a two-day seminar I took with Dr. Richard Haines. It was on UFOs.

Close encounters of the fourth kind." She glanced at me to see if I knew what she was talking about and to see my reaction. When she saw that I was listening attentively, she continued, "He was with NASA for over twenty years. A very credible person."

"Did you undergo any hypnotic regressions during the seminar, Gloria?"

"No, but I became very emotional. I've had particularly bizarre dreams since then, of floating out of my room and strange beings. I had nightmares before, for years actually. Dr. Fiore, are you interested in dreams?"

"Gloria, please call me Edee. Yes. Dreams are very important. I often find that they are not really dreams per se, but actually flashbacks to repressed, forgotten, experiences. Did you have a dream you want to tell me about?"

"Yes. It happened three years ago and it was so incredibly real, I've never forgotten it. I was in bed with my husband, who was asleep. I thought I was fully awake. I couldn't move. The bed was vibrating. There were several figures around me. They were hideous! Gray. Awful! Eyes that were black holes. I told them, "I'm not going to let you control me." I woke up in the morning and the dream was going over and over in my mind. It was *very* real! Less than two weeks before that dream, I witnessed a UFO and was really shaken. I know I've repressed a lot. That's why I want to work with you."

We discussed the possibility of her having been abducted and decided we would spend a future session exploring that area. There were still many things Gloria needed to discuss in laying the foundations for our therapy program. Before she left, I hypnotized her, taping suggestions for relaxation and daily improvement.

After a few sessions in which we worked on pressing issues, Gloria and I decided that we would now do a regression to a possible CEIV.

Using the hypnosis tape to go to sleep with each evening had conditioned Gloria to be very responsive to the sound of my voice. She slipped into a hypnotic trance within minutes, and I asked her inner mind to take her to the event responsible for the dream she had had three years before.

∕

GLORIA: Oh Jeez! This face, it's weird. It's not dead, but it looks dead. Ugh! It looks like a frog or toad. It's not real defined. Not smooth, except around the temple area on the sides. It looks like rolls. Like a scrub board. It's big! A big head. It's like spindly. Ugh! It said something, but I don't want to listen to it.

DR. FIORE: Let yourself remember what it said.

GLORIA: It's like angry because I was acting badly. I said I wasn't acting badly. They don't know me. How could they say I was acting badly. My right leg hurts, up by the thigh. Like somebody kicked me . . . I floated out of there. That's how I got to the sidewalk. Went right through the wall and I was on the sidewalk. [Long pause]

DR. FIORE: Now what's happening?

GLORIA: They're asking questions, and I don't want to answer. Jesus! I can't know everything. [Long pause]

DR. FIORE: Continue to speak out.

GLORIA: There's somebody there, like an attendant, like when you go into surgery. There are people around me at the end, by my left foot. They're standing there waiting. All talking.

DR. FIORE: What do they look like?

GLORIA: The ones that are giving the directions are small. The ones that help are tall. They give that look that they can't talk, even though they can.

DR. FIORE: What are you feeling and thinking?

GLORIA: I don't like it. I just want to leave.

DR. FIORE: What's being done?

GLORIA: I'm okay, but my right leg hurts. It's like being in the hospital when they give you an intravenous. They're taking my blood. They're not trying to stop me from leaving. But they tell me no one will believe me. They will think I'm crazy.

DR. FIORE: What did they say exactly?

GLORIA: "Nobody is going to believe you." I said, "Yes, they will, I'll tell a priest. I'll find a church." [*Long pause*]

DR. FIORE: Now what's happening?

GLORIA: Like I went through a wall. I'm on a sidewalk, and I'm going to go home. I'm back in bed.

DR. FIORE: Let yourself remember more about that same experience. It's all coming back to you, at the count of three. One . . . two . . . three.

GLORIA: The room smells funny. Something's blowing up my nose. It's almost like those tubes they put in you in the hospital. They're doing something. They're opening something. It's like a plastic bag . . . What's in that bag? They're hanging it up. There's that face; that face keeps passing by. [*Pauses*]

DR. FIORE: Describe the face.

GLORIA: It looks like a . . . the skin looks like the skin of a dead person. The eyes are really hollow. Really hollow. Uhhh! It looks awful. It just looks awful! But the others aren't worried about it.

DR. FIORE: The others?

GLORIA: The others that are helping them. They're humans. They don't say anything to them. They just look at each other. And after they look at each other, then the one down by my left foot does something. My leg feels like it's up. It looks like a metal bar. It's got a U on it. It comes from the side of the table . . . I can't feel it, but I know my leg's up there. There's a tube. There's a tube running somewhere. I can't see where that tube is running. I can't move.

DR. FIORE: How do you feel with that tube? Is it connected to your body in any way?

GLORIA: Somewhere. It has to be. I feel like it's my hip. I'm just looking. I . . .

DR. FIORE: What do you see?

GLORIA: There's one coming in the front, in the front of the table. I feel like I'm at a sloped angle, like my feet are up, they're elevated and I'm . . . down a little ways. Because it's hard to lift my head. It's really hard. This one just . . . came in to see how it's going. I think, just to observe. It's like this table is supported on . . . I don't know what supports it. . . . It's easy to move up and down. The tube is in my stomach. Ohh . . . Why is it in my stomach? I don't know how they got it in there. I want it off! [*Pauses*] There's this thing over my head. There's another tube running in it. Maybe that's the one that goes to my nose. [*Agitated*] "Oh, don't touch me!" I want to . . . I just want to leave. I just want that one to get away from my face. I don't like . . . Oh! . . . It's awful. I don't understand! When are they going to let me off of this? Why do they have to be so close? I know . . . they're not going to . . . they're not going to hurt. But it's so repulsive. It's like . . . It's like having dead people walk around you.

DR. FIORE: Do they give you any explanation for the tubes?

GLORIA: I said, "Is that going to help me?" And they said, "Yes." But they said it would help them do more. Then . . . huh . . . this thing that looks like . . . it has light in it . . . and it's coming down. It looks like a whole bunch of crossed wires, little squares with lights in it. It's coming from . . . And it goes to that spot on my stomach . . . and to that spot on my hip, and it's warm.

DR. FIORE: Did you feel anything else?

GLORIA: It was like a tingle. It was . . . just a tingling.

DR. FIORE: Where is the tingling?

GLORIA: All through my middle area . . . and down my leg.

DR. FIORE: How would you describe the beings that are there?

GLORIA: It's those ones that like to come to your face.

DR. FIORE: What do they look like exactly?

GLORIA: Hollow, ugh! . . . They look like . . . how do you describe them? . . . They're . . . they're . . . my height, maybe smaller.

DR. FIORE: What color is their skin?

GLORIA: Grayish, like old people or dead people, grayish, wrinkly. No hair.

DR. FIORE: What about their noses?

GLORIA: It looks like when you look at a skeleton. There's nothing there. There is a nose. They have to breathe. But there's no shape for a nose.

DR. FIORE:   Do you see any nostrils?

GLORIA:   Just little holes.

DR. FIORE:   What about a mouth?

GLORIA:   There's a mouth, but it doesn't move.

DR. FIORE:   When they talk, does it move?

GLORIA:   I don't know what it does.

DR. FIORE:   What about the shape of their heads?

GLORIA:   They're large heads; but it looks okay on them.

DR. FIORE:   Do they all look more or less the same, like the same species?

GLORIA:   Yes, but there are many different other people with them. I get confused.

DR. FIORE:   What do you mean?

GLORIA:   There's human people. There's people like us.

DR. FIORE:   Are they completely like us, are they completely human beings?

GLORIA:   Yes. That's why I couldn't understand why they couldn't tell me nothing.

DR. FIORE:   These people who are like you, do they communicate with you?

GLORIA:   Yes, they're very nice. They relax you. They ask you about yourself. It's almost, it's almost like you go out with a friend for lunch. Very casual, very unalarming. It's like they do this all the time. And then there's the other ones. And you can almost see, you can see their veins, their . . . You can see their veins, very light skin, very thin.

DR. FIORE:  What color is their skin?

GLORIA:  Like our flesh tone, but more transparent.

DR. FIORE:  Are you saying there are ones who have gray, wrinkly skin; then there are ones who are totally human; then there's another group too?

GLORIA:  Yes.

DR. FIORE:  Now these ones who have the totally transparent skin, how tall would you say they are?

GLORIA:  They seem to be about . . . well, they're tall, but not abnormally tall.

DR. FIORE:  Can you tell what sex they are?

GLORIA:  There's male and female. There's a balance.

DR. FIORE:  What are they wearing?

GLORIA:  They're just wearing this cover. It's supposed to protect them.

DR. FIORE:  Now what's happening?

GLORIA:  They were going to take something out of my left arm. I don't know what it is. I'm not dying from it. I was afraid I was going to die.

DR. FIORE:  What are they doing?

GLORIA: It looks like these giant tweezers, and a white cloth. It's like a handkerchief. . . . I don't know why they were mad at me.

DR. FIORE: What do you mean?

GLORIA: Something to do with . . . too smart. I don't know if they meant I was acting smart. It's like it doesn't make any difference if I'm there. They talk . . . they don't care what you think. They don't even ask you.

DR. FIORE: What are they doing?

GLORIA: They're checking my eyes.

DR. FIORE: How are they doing that?

GLORIA: With this little tube. It's not like what our doctors use. I thought that's what they were doing. It's . . . a tube.

DR. FIORE: Does it hurt?

GLORIA: No, it makes this like buzzing noise. And they just move it back and forth. It's like a monitoring device.

DR. FIORE: Are they explaining that to you?

GLORIA: No. They just keep talking to each other, but I can't understand what they're saying. Now they're saying they're finished.

DR. FIORE: How do they say that to you?

GLORIA: They don't say that to me. They say it to the two guys who brought me in.

DR. FIORE: How many are there altogether?

GLORIA:   Two that examined me, and then the two that brought me in.

DR. FIORE:   The two that examined you, what are they wearing?

GLORIA:   They're wearing these hooded things so you can't see them.

DR. FIORE:   What do you mean?

GLORIA:   It conceals them enough so you can't tell what they look like. I see one hand.

DR. FIORE:   What does it look like?

GLORIA:   It looks long and yellowish . . . and that's the one that's got that tube.

DR. FIORE:   Do you see their eyes?

GLORIA:   All I see are black holes. I think it is their eyes.

DR. FIORE:   How tall are they?

GLORIA:   They're like six feet.

DR. FIORE:   The two that brought you in, did you see their faces?

GLORIA:   Yes.

DR. FIORE:   What did they look like?

GLORIA:   They looked like twins, with blond hair. They looked like . . . football players.

DR. FIORE:   Why do you say football players?

GLORIA: Because they were big men. They both looked alike. Not ugly, not attractive, just average, I guess. [*Long pause*] I feel like I'm going to faint. I just want to go to sleep. I feel dizzy, really dizzy. I feel really sick. Maybe if I lie on my right side I won't throw up. I feel sick. [*Squirms and puts her hands on her abdomen*] Uhhh . . . I just . . . I was going to get up to go to the bathroom. No, I'll just stay here until it's over. Then I'll wake up. They told me that it will come easier and I won't be afraid of them. I don't know why they said that. I don't care, I just don't want them to be real close to my face. But I know there's other people that's working with them. I know there is.

DR. FIORE: What do you mean?

GLORIA: People, human people, good people. They don't pick bad people. They can't. There are no bad people. Not with them. You just have to do it that way. They have to work with people that they know will help. And they know those people.

DR. FIORE: And you?

GLORIA: Me? They said I can help. I don't know how. I don't know what I'm supposed to do, but they said it'll come. Can't talk to a lot of people. I don't know what about. But the one in the robe, I want to know who the one in the robe is. He's very, very good.

DR. FIORE: Now what's happening?

GLORIA: They put me in a case after I get up from the table.

DR. FIORE: What is it like to be in that case?

GLORIA: I can't feel anything. And there's a window.

DR. FIORE: Where is the window?

GLORIA: By my eyes, so that I can see.

DR. FIORE: What position are you in?

GLORIA: On my back. It feels like it's curved, because I can feel the sides. Now I'm out again.

DR. FIORE: Did they explain why they were putting you in there?

GLORIA: To go in there and rest for a minute. I don't think it's necessarily rest. I think it's more like . . . it felt like a cleansing. It felt . . . [Pauses] The air was okay, because the difference . . . I could just feel the difference when I came out of the case.

DR. FIORE: Which air did you prefer?

GLORIA: The case. They kept the hoses or the tubes connected to my nostrils. They didn't take those off.

DR. FIORE: They [the tubes] went into the case too?

GLORIA: Yes. The air felt very thick on my arms, very thick.

DR. FIORE: When was that?

GLORIA: When the case opened. When I came out. It wasn't like when I couldn't move on the table. Maybe that's why I didn't feel it.

DR. FIORE: Did they give you any explanation for why they had you on the table and why they did these various procedures?

GLORIA: They said it just would make it easier.

DR. FIORE: To do what?

GLORIA: For me, I . . . don't know. That's what I couldn't figure out. It's almost like . . . I don't know what they were doing.

DR. FIORE: Later you said that you felt that one was very, very good. Was he there during the examination?

GLORIA: Always on my right, talking to me about my feelings, my thoughts. Very beautiful person.

DR. FIORE: What does he look like?

GLORIA: He was human, and he had light brown hair.

DR. FIORE: How was he dressed?

GLORIA: I don't know what it is. It's a tight top, and it covered his arms, and it went down all the way. It's like it was form-fitting.

DR. FIORE: He was completely human-looking?

GLORIA: Yes.

DR. FIORE: What color were his eyes?

GLORIA: Blue. And then there was a little brown on the out-side. Beautiful, they were absolutely beautiful eyes. I'll never forget those eyes. He seemed familiar.

DR. FIORE: I'm going to ask you at this point to go back to your very first contact with ETs.

GLORIA: [Pauses] It's . . . red. Everything's encased in red. I don't know, it's strange. I don't know where I'm at. I'm just feeling things around me. It's all these colors.

DR. FIORE:  What colors are those?

GLORIA:  Reds . . . and golds and . . . then whites coming in . . . then back to red and gold.

DR. FIORE:  Where are these colors coming from?

GLORIA:  They're all around me. I'm waiting.

DR. FIORE:  How old are you?

GLORIA:  I have no age, but yet I'm old.

DR. FIORE:  What position is your body in?

GLORIA:  My legs . . . I'm in a curve, like a little curve, almost a little ball.

DR. FIORE:  Are you a fetus at this point?

GLORIA:  I think I am. I'm floating. And I get to see all these colors.

DR. FIORE:  Remember your contact with the ETs.

GLORIA:  They promised that they would be there. They promised. [*Pauses*] Oh my God! They already know how to incorporate.

DR. FIORE:  Tell me what you mean by that.

GLORIA:  They can penetrate the fetus. They can do that. They can!

DR. FIORE:  Tell me about it.

GLORIA: It's not physical, not in that sense. [*Pauses*] But they can create life. They can change life. They can change life as it's developing. And they can terminate it. But then they can re-create it. [*Pauses*] They don't like termination. They can put it into a temporary status. And then help form its life. Nothing is ever terminated. That's not the whole purpose.

DR. FIORE: When you said, "Oh my God, they know how to incorporate," what did you mean?

GLORIA: Through the mind. They can reach you.

DR. FIORE: What message was there?

GLORIA: That for a while I will not know a lot, but that they would come. They would come again and they would come at the right time. And even then I wouldn't know, but they would help me search, but I would have to come on it myself. I'd have to come on this knowledge myself. They can direct me, but I still have my choice. I felt I was a part of them. [*Pauses*] That's funny, it seems . . . time with them . . . is so much different than time here. Hmm . . . Time here is slowed. It's slowed for a purpose . . . so that we can go through the entire process . . . as our immediate environment, our planet, allows us to. [*Long pause*]

DR. FIORE: Let yourself remember another important encounter.

GLORIA: There's a light. I don't know where it's coming from. [*Pauses*] I'm moving in this light. It's like a magnet. My stomach's upset, just thinking about this.

DR. FIORE: What's happening now?

GLORIA: I'm just moving.

DR. FIORE:  What emotions are you feeling?

GLORIA:  At first, I didn't know if it was something good I was moving toward. But whatever it was, I was drawn to a light, whether it was good or bad, and I guess it was okay. [*Pauses*] I'm in this room, but it's a room with no doors . . . but you can get in and out of it. It's a white room . . . very, very bright room.

DR. FIORE:  What is the shape of the room?

GLORIA:  It's like an egg. That's the only way I can describe it.

DR. FIORE:  Where is the illumination coming from?

GLORIA:  Everywhere, the sides, the top. It's naturally there. It's just there.

DR. FIORE:  What are you doing in the room?

GLORIA:  I'm reading a book.

DR. FIORE:  Tell me about that.

GLORIA:  There's this tool in my left hand. They said it was a tool. It looks like it's made of brass. It's light and it's long, but it's shaped like a triangle . . . but it's not sharp. And you have to point it. You have to hold it at a certain angle as you're reading this book. They say it's a learning tool. It helps you to absorb the knowledge that the book has. Now I know why they use the tool. The book isn't written in our alphabet. It's their alphabet.

DR. FIORE:  Who are they?

GLORIA:  The instructors.

DR. FIORE:  What do they look like?

GLORIA: Actually, they're quite funny-looking. They have very, very white skin. It seems that they may be the same height I am. They've got like . . . a large top head, forehead. Like their ears are pressed against their head. You can see like little blue veins, they're so white.

DR. FIORE: What are their eyes like?

GLORIA: They look like Yodas. They almost don't look like they can be real. But they are. They look like a jellyfish. And their eyes are a yellow and a brown, but dark. Big eyes.

DR. FIORE: What shape are their eyes?

GLORIA: They look almost almond, but there's like a variation to them.

DR. FIORE: What is it you're reading? What is the information?

GLORIA: I don't know if you want to call it Arabic or Hebrew or what. But it's scrolled. And then it looks like it has some variations of Greek. It's bizarre.

DR. FIORE: As you read it with that pointer, you're able to understand the message?

GLORIA: Yes.

DR. FIORE: What is the content?

GLORIA: It has to do with learning the truth and avoiding involvement in false beliefs. There's more. Something about . . . the misconception of time. Something about the unacceptance and misconception of time. I can't make it out. I know what it is, but . . . without that tool . . . it's hard. It's almost like I've seen this page of writing before, or I may have studied it before. There's something familiar about it. [*Pauses*] Wherever they are, they want to be teachers . . . or they are teachers. Our time isn't our time. Not the time we think it is. We're not that old.

DR. FIORE:   I want you to look around the room. Are you the only person in the room who's reading?

GLORIA:   Yes.

DR. FIORE:   And how many instructors are there?

GLORIA:   Three.

DR. FIORE:   And do they all look alike?

GLORIA:   Yes. But they're different.

DR. FIORE:   What do you mean by that?

GLORIA:   They have different personalities, but yet they all help each other. It's like an equal sharing in their knowledge. Almost an enthusiasm, kind of a . . . a happy excitement. [*Long pause*] We just aren't ready to understand or accept, and so it's going to be forced on some.

DR. FIORE:   Is that what happened with you?

GLORIA:   They don't want me to believe . . . the ways that Man has taught . . . in his various beliefs. They said I know better. That's what the tool is for! I feel like I've been to school. I want to be left alone. I want to finish reading. [*Pauses*] I wish I could remember what they were saying.

DR. FIORE:   Now you're going to remember, at the count of three, it will be crystal clear in your mind. One . . . two . . . three.

GLORIA: It's the head instructor. He put his finger on the middle of my forehead. He said that this would protect me. There's just some things that can be understood right now. And he asks if I understood what he was saying. I said, "Yes." Then I said, "I'm so sorry you can't complete your work right now. I'm so sorry that so many people are blinded." But they said that's okay. I feel so bad. They're working so hard. I don't want to leave them. They have to contact you like this. They can't do it any other way . . . not right now.

DR. FIORE: Why is that?

GLORIA: Because of Man.

DR. FIORE: Is this told to you?

GLORIA: No, I know this. Man will fight anything unknown to him. Anything technically advanced, he will take up arms against. They have tried firing a missile at one of the craft.

DR. FIORE: How do you know that?

GLORIA: There was a meeting.

DR. FIORE: What do you mean by that?

GLORIA: Those that are helping them and those that are learning. [Pauses] They won't allow other people to believe that they are real.

DR. FIORE: Who?

GLORIA: Our government, our top officials.

DR. FIORE: Tell me about the meeting.

GLORIA: It was very sad. Very sad. They feel that there are those in higher places, not necessarily good high places, maybe in different planetary structures, who oppose the work of the others. And who assist in the technology of some very destructive machinery. But yet the most destructive is Man himself.

DR. FIORE: When you are talking about this meeting, is this a meeting that you attended?

GLORIA: Yes.

DR. FIORE: Who was in the meeting?

GLORIA: The same instructor and people who have been to his classes. They're learning . . . this is funny . . . they're curious to see how we're advancing. They're curious about how and why we believe. I wanted to bring the tool, because I remembered how good it was, but I couldn't bring it. I thought I had it. Somehow they took it from me. I wanted to bring it, I wanted to show somebody that it was real.

DR. FIORE: Are you in your living room?

GLORIA: I'm sitting on the couch. I can't move. It feels like the air is very thin. Hmmm . . . I can't . . . I wish I could see who was with me.

DR. FIORE: How do you feel?

GLORIA: I was thinking . . . what a really weird dream.

✦

Once back to normal waking consciousness, Gloria leaned forward in the chair, grabbed a tissue and blotted her eyes. "You can't expect them to walk into a room and say, 'Hello, we're here to help you.' Their appearance is far beyond anything that we have physically been accustomed to, much less viewed. They have to do it the way they're doing it now, whether it's through mental telepathy, whether it's through dream states. They just have to do it their way."

# "They Go in There and Dissolve the Damn Clot!"

 "I'm feeling tingly . . . and can't move!" James started hyperventilating, while at the same time he desperately tried to maintain his composure. Within seconds, he arched his back and opened his mouth to bring in as much oxygen as possible.

"You're reliving something important, James. Let's see what it is." I got up and quickly covered him with the blanket as I pushed the chair back to its fullest reclining position in readiness for an hypnotic regression.

James, a darkly handsome physician in his mid-thirties, had sought my help a year before for a drinking problem, which we had actually cleared up in his first session. Since he lived in Southern California, he only flew up as issues arose in his everyday life. During our five visits, we had developed an excellent rapport, and so it was more like two old friends meeting on this occasion rather than a therapist and her patient.

"I guess I'm here to chat more than anything else," he said

166

smiling shyly. "Everything's going very well. And I'm feeling good." He talked about his use of innovative healing methods, especially electric acupressure, and his tremendous success with them.

When I had begun to describe some of the ways the extraterrestrials had healed my patients' physical symptoms, suddenly he had tensed his body and had begun to gasp for air. Some buried memory was being exhumed . . . and fast, leading me to cut short my hypnotic induction and immediately regress him to the cause of his reaction.

*

JAMES:   [*Body tenses*] I feel this intense reaction, but I don't see anything yet.

DR. FIORE:   Just tell me everything you're aware of.

JAMES:   I'm aware of not being able to move, but I don't know why. [*Body becomes rigid*] This is really strange. . . . I feel like I'm in a metal tank, just lying flat on a metal, like a . . . table. I can see . . . [*Breathing accelerates*] some lights on the side. And . . . the things are there. I can intermittently see their forms and . . . but they're not solid forms. Ah . . . I must be a child. [*Breathing becomes labored*]

DR. FIORE:   Tell me everything that's happening.

JAMES:   They're moving around. Doing things. I can feel something on my head. A pressure. For a while it was relieved, now it's coming back. [*Body tenses*] I . . . I'm just lying there like a . . . I can't move, but there's something on my head, like a hemisphere over the top part of my head, and it feels like it's clamped on over my maxilla. There's a little firm pressure there. And . . . because I can't move, it's hard to swallow. And . . . [*Sighs*]

DR. FIORE:   What emotions are you feeling?

JAMES: Fear. But I know nothing bad is going to happen. And I know I don't belong there. Confusion is the only word . . . the single word. And I feel both a terrible fear and a calmness simultaneously. They're doing something to my head. [*Sighs*] And I don't know whether it's energy going in. My nose is really stuffy. There's something in my nose. Now I've read these reports also, but there's something in my nose. Son of a bitch put something in my nose! Right up my nose! I'm afraid to move. [*Long pause*] They're . . . Ahaa . . . It's like an energy transfer. [*Gags*] Doesn't hurt, but I can't move my head and I can't move my body, dammit! It's kind of like . . . [*Sighs*] Okay . . . They're zapping me. There's a needle in my nose and there's energy going through that. It's as if . . . Oh Jeez . . . My frontal lobe is like . . . alive . . . the area where my frontal lobe is. [*Long pause. Body relaxes*] Now I'm feeling very calm.

DR. FIORE: Let yourself know what happened just before you became calm.

JAMES: My nose is really stuffy. [*Pauses*] The energy's stopped. The needle's out. My . . . the front part of my head is just . . . it feels alive. It's really strange. They're moving around. They're not in my vision very easily. I can feel them more than hear them or see them, but they're moving around at a control panel right over my head. They changed some switches. [*Sighs*] I . . . I feel like I'm about five or six years old, but I kind of know I'm a little older, it's really strange. Maybe eight is what I'd say. Maybe this has happened a couple of times. I can see my feet there. They're little boy's feet. I think I'm in my underwear. It's kind of embarrassing. Even though I don't have all my clothes on, it's not cold. It's just a reasonable temperature. And these things are . . . they look green. The color they emit is green, but they don't have a solid form. It's difficult to really see appendages or arms or limbs. They have a head and an oval body . . . but they do have arms. They do manipulate switches. It's very difficult to distinguish facial characteristics.

My memories of this are kind of tainted by pictures I've seen on covers of books, but that's a reasonable depiction, except they're greener, or maybe there's a greener light in the room. Either way . . . very sophisticated panels of lights. My ears are starting to get stuffy. I think there's something in my ears. They've got . . . [Pauses] Well, there's some probes in there too, but they feel like they're . . . that's what's keeping me still, I bet. It's like a . . . a . . . probe in each ear that's generating some frequencies that allow me to be alert. But I can't move. [Pauses] Hmm . . . That's all, except I'm getting nervous about it again. Something's going to happen here. Hmm . . . They're making a decision about something. It feels like . . . I feel mad because they're making a decision about me. But it's scary too. They're . . . [Breathing becomes labored] I have this fear, but I don't know where it's coming from. Something's not right. They're adjusting something. . . . And I think it . . . I think it hurts. It's like a high-frequency sound. I can hear my ears ringing. Maybe it's because my ears and nose are all of a sudden stuffy, but . . . I . . . [Sighs] Yes . . . That ringing is hurting me. They're . . . hurting me in my chest now. . . . Something's going into my chest. This is strange. [Painfully] Oh God! It's like they're putting needles in both sides of my chest! [Seems to be in excruciating pain] Oh . . . guys, I won't move! Ahh! . . . [In agony] I don't know what they're doing. I don't know why, but they've got these things in both sides. It's really strange. It doesn't hurt too bad, but it . . . I can feel this sharp pain. I'm afraid to take a deep breath. And it feels like a clamp on my heart. It feels like the strangest damn thing! I didn't know what it was then, but I know what it is now. They've got these needles on either side. It feels like they go right through my body. And . . . they're . . . doing something with them. [Pauses] Oh . . . is it a big clamp? It's inside me. Okay . . . it's easing. [Body relaxes] I can't tell what they did that for. Dammit! It hurt. Okay, I can breathe again. They're taking them . . . [Sighs] Oh . . . I feel a lot better. [Much more relaxed] It's really strange. I feel better. I'm just lying there semicomatose. [Long pause] I used to get these horrible headaches when I was a kid. Then they went away, and I think . . . either I got the headaches or they went away after one of these treatments. I don't know where that thought came from.

DR. FIORE:  Tell me more about the headaches.

JAMES:  These headaches that I used to have, which were really, really hard, sharp, pounding headaches. I don't understand the sequence, but they relate to what they did to me . . . and I think the headaches went away.

DR. FIORE:  Move back to anything that caused them to go away.

JAMES:  [*Chuckles*] I had a dream once. That I was floating over my backyard. And that dream is as real today as when it happened. And that dream fits in here.

DR. FIORE:  Let yourself remember more.

JAMES:  I'm being . . . I can see down. I guess I look over the side. I'm being transported up on kind of a pallet. I don't understand how it happens, but I'm moving. And I can only remember what the earth looked like before. Maybe I'm in a bubble. I'm going right inside this big thing. Just right up. It looks like your usual depiction of a spaceship, but it's going right up inside this opening. There are these people. They're putting it on. It just kind of moves on its own. They guide it . . . I can't tell, maybe it's got wheels underneath or something, or they're carrying it, but it's moving along. I see other carriers like this, pallets with bubbles over them.

DR. FIORE:  Is there anybody there?

JAMES:  Yep. People. They're just lying there. They have little . . . maybe a strange glow to the atmosphere inside there, but . . . I can move a little bit and look around. Most of them look like they're dead. [*Laughs nervously*] There're . . . just lying there without moving. . . . They're not too many, but it's hard to tell. I can see three or four immediately around me, but . . . they move these [pallets] in and then they take them out after a while and move them into another room. And . . . hmm, they're going to move mine in next. [*Pauses*] Okay. I'm in this room and I'm lying there flat, and I feel like there's something . . . going in both sides of my back. And they . . . all right, that helmet's back on . . . and . . . [*Laughs*] Yep . . . or is it the middle of my back? I can't tell. But there's a needle there. And it does something, because it hurts. I can't understand what it does. That goes on for a few minutes, and then they stop. And . . . I feel sick afterward. That one kind of aches afterward. The other one's . . . I'm not so sure that they didn't do something with my penis too. I'm a little embarrassed to talk about it. [*Pauses*] I'm sure they did, but I'm . . .

DR. FIORE: What do you think they did?

JAMES: I think they put something in it, like a rod, a little probe, or a needle or something. I don't feel that as much as I kinda . . . know that happened. [*Sighs*] It's so strange. I know those things happened. . . . It's easier for me to see myself sitting back on that little pallet afterward than . . . I guess at the time it was very embarrassing. Because that's the way I feel now.

DR. FIORE: Did they give you an explanation of why they're doing this?

JAMES: [*Pauses*] I don't understand . . . any of that. [*Laughs*] I think the answer is yes, but the whole idea was so embarrassing to me at the time that I kinda . . .

DR. FIORE: What did they say to you?

JAMES: [*Laughs*] I guess they were taking some of my sperm or something, but at the time that thought was so embarrassing to me that I couldn't even integrate it into . . . [*Laughs*] All I can say is, it's embarrassing. [*Laughs loudly*] But that's what they were doing! But I'm not old enough. It doesn't make any sense to me, that's what I keep telling them. [*Chuckles. Long pause*] And then I can see myself back in my room.

DR. FIORE:   Let yourself move to the very beginning of the event that was responsible for these terrible headaches that you had as a child.

JAMES:   Oh my God! . . . Oh my! . . . [*Whispers*] This is really strange, Edith. I have to give you some background on this. I don't remember how old I was, but . . . I . . . don't know why this pops into my head, but I . . . I tilted a jungle gym over on its side. I was going to be an astronaut, and I got my brother to push it. And the idea was to tumble over. And I smacked my head and had the biggest goose egg you've ever seen. My dad took me that night to a doctor, and he tried to drain it. It was a big prominent thing. Somehow those headaches are related to this. And somehow that . . . helmet . . . was treating that!

DR. FIORE:   Let yourself remember exactly what happened when the helmet was put on you. It's now being put on you. Let's take it second by second. Let yourself experience whatever was happening to you.

JAMES:   All right. I feel this thing on top of my head. I can kind of see it on either side. And I can feel these little . . . clamps against my cheeks again. [*Pauses*] It's like sound or . . . noise, or . . . I don't understand what's happening. . . .

DR. FIORE:   What are you feeling?

JAMES:   I had this . . . just tension all over and this . . . this heat, inside my head. Not hot, but . . . [*Body arches*] This goes on for a while . . . leaves me very, very tense. I don't know what happened. I don't know what that was.

DR. FIORE: Was anyone standing near you?

JAMES: I see one or sense one, right over on my right side there. [*Points to his right*] Just . . . kinda reassuring me.

DR. FIORE: What is it saying?

JAMES: Comfort and . . . a sense that I don't need to worry, that everything they're doing is okay. That it's not bad.

DR. FIORE: Do they make any references to your headaches?

JAMES: Definitely. I got the definite . . . it's almost a picture as opposed to a . . . I get this picture in my head of a . . . like a thin film that's covering the . . . top and front of my head, of my brain, and what they're doing is going to dissolve that. I mean, I know that now, but I didn't know that then, but that's the picture that's in my head. [*Sighs*] The treatment was uncomfortable, but not in a painful way. It made me, like tense all my muscles, but . . . afterward I feel better.

❧

James opened his eyes, stretched his arms above his head and sat up eagerly. "Those headaches were terrible! Really heavy duty! Then one day they were just gone. I've never known why. As a physician, I couldn't understand it."

"I think it's fascinating. I'm glad you had a positive experience. There's so much that's frightening in most of the books on abductions. It's rewarding to find these healings being done. Were there many others being worked on?"

"I saw a lot of people on those pallets!"

Since our time was up and the little light on the wall was on, indicating the next patient was waiting, we said our goodbyes. I walked James to the door. A little hesitantly, he extended his hand. Instead of taking it, I gave him a hug. "That's what I wanted," he said with a broad smile as he left.

● 

James called me a week later and said that more material was surfacing, mostly in the form of thoughts. "I think we just looked at the tip of the iceberg last time. Are you up to my flying into San Jose and our spending a couple of hours seeing what else is there?"

I blocked out some time, and it was two weeks later that I saw him next. James wasted no time in getting to the point of our session. "For years, I've been interested in UFOs, especially their purpose in being here. For some reason, I think they're interested in our awareness. Maybe they want massive crystal deposits. A friend of mine thinks they're after our fresh water, but I think it's not that simple."

"You said in your call that things are surfacing? What's been coming up since last time?"

"Nothing at all clear. Mostly dreams at night about UFOs that I can't remember. I guess it's a knowing that more has happened to me than we got during our last session."

"Let's check it out."

James slipped into hypnosis easily and quickly. I knew by now that he didn't let himself go into a profound trance, but, even though his conscious mind was right there analyzing, he let the subconscious material come to the surface with no resistance. I asked him to remember the close encounter that had had the greatest impact on him and counted to ten, with instructions to say out loud whatever came into his mind.

● 

JAMES:    I have this image of people or things in the rooms of our house. And it just suddenly struck me that they've been there and I didn't realize it. They look gray and they're maybe five feet tall. And they have oval heads and oval bodies and . . . they're not, you don't see them . . . I kind of wonder if you woke up and looked you wouldn't even see them. It's really strange, they're almost not physical when you're conscious. Or maybe they don't come when you're conscious.

DR. FIORE: What are they doing?

JAMES: Standing there, in two lines with me in the middle.

DR. FIORE: What room are they in?

JAMES: In the bedroom.

DR. FIORE: In the house you live in currently?

JAMES: Yes, we just moved in six months ago. It's a very uncomfortable feeling, but I don't know why.

DR. FIORE: Just keep reporting whatever comes into your mind.

JAMES: I feel trapped, like I can't move. And I keep telling them I don't want to go. [*Pauses*] I don't understand whether it's real or a dream, but it seems like we just move right through the walls. I feel like I'm on a pallet. I'm in kind of a semiconscious state. But the strangest thing is that I'm not sure that my whole form leaves.

DR. FIORE: What do you mean by that?

JAMES: I don't think my physical form goes with them. I think it's lying there in the bed.

DR. FIORE: Take a look and see.

JAMES: No. It's not there. The bed's empty. I mean, my wife is there, but I'm not. I don't think I've been drugged, but narcotized in some way that I feel like I'm floating, but when I look at the bed, I'm not there. [*Pauses*] Okay . . . I'm going out the door . . . and into that big ship that's sitting out over the trees. I don't understand why people can't see that.

DR. FIORE: Now what happens? Tell me step by step.

JAMES: The door opens. I'm being carried in some way. It's as if I've been drugged. . . . It's not drugged, it's done with a . . . some method that leaves you incapacitated. It's a vibrational . . . device that . . . I think it takes two of them pointed at you in a certain . . . it kind of paralyzes you and leaves you feeling . . . helpless, and . . . there's no will to resist. You might as well have been intoxicated with a drug. And I feel like I'm being kind of carried. I guess they open the door. But the entranceway to the ship is kind of conventional. At least it's what you've always seen in the movies. It's kind of a ramp that's lowered, and you just go right up in the center. [*Pauses*] We're sitting . . . [*Laughs*] Strange . . . I feel like I'm sitting at a table having a discussion about our . . . I think they want to understand how we think. Maybe this is where this thought came from. I was sitting one day and had the strongest thought that these people want to contact us, but they're concerned that we're going to self-destruct if they make themselves really . . . manifest. I think that's the point of the discussion.

DR. FIORE: See if you can remember it, word by word, or thought by thought. [*Pauses*] Just report whatever comes into your mind.

JAMES: It feels like I'm sitting there trying to describe the difficulties of introducing ideas of extraordinary change into our culture. It's what I see in our day-to-day lives anyway. It's as if this one alien individual wants to . . . is arguing in favor of becoming manifest to humankind, and the other is saying, "No, they'll retaliate or perceive us as dangerous and would resort to nuclear weapons." He says he can't understand a culture that would live that way. [*Laughs*]

DR. FIORE: What is your role in this discussion?

JAMES: I'm trying to explain the way people think.

DR. FIORE: How do you feel now that you're there? At first you were resistant, taken against your will. How do you feel now?

JAMES: [*Laughs*] Halfway in awe of the situation, I mean of the . . . extraordinary uniqueness of sitting in this environment of a complex machine from another, I assume, planet. And also the awesome responsibility of both trying to explain how we are in terms that will . . . allow . . . I feel like a negotiator. The awesome responsibility of a negotiator.

DR. FIORE: How many beings are in this discussion?

JAMES: I'm kind of focused on two aliens and myself, but there are more people at the table. But they're in kind of a trance. They're just sitting there. They're not actively participating. I get the feeling they get as much information from the mental information as the words. But the other people are just sitting there. It's not an open debate or discussion. They're communicating one at a time.

DR. FIORE: When you say people, are there other human beings?

JAMES: Humans, yes. I think there are four or five. And there are two main people or aliens that I talked to. They're gray skinned and they have the same basic structure that we do, but they're not . . . they're different. There's no neck. It's hard for me to separate their head from their body. [*Becomes tense*] I get the strongest feeling that . . . difficulty in trusting these people. That's . . . without being able to discuss it with my colleagues, it's as if there's a panel, but I feel like I'm being interrogated, not in a bad way, but, I feel tremendous . . . [*Squirms*] There's both good and bad that's at stake here in terms of the discussion. They're probing for weaknesses, at the same time they're probing for the strength to communicate.

DR. FIORE: What do you feel in your body? I notice you're squirming.

JAMES: I can't explain it. I don't know. Fear. I feel like . . . [*Labored breathing*] I guess I was getting kind of irritated and began to show anger, and they . . . they won't deal with that. The way they handle that is to put you back into that . . . state of . . . whatever. You can't move. It's as if you're being strapped down, but you're not, literally. You feel enclosed in something. I think that's how they take you back to the . . . I feel like it's a tube. And then. . . . I wake up in bed. It's really strange.

DR. FIORE: How do you feel when you wake up?

JAMES: Relaxed and . . . they must do something when you're in that tube.

DR. FIORE: Let's go back into that tube. Let yourself remember, at the count of three. One . . . two . . . three.

JAMES: Okay. The whole tube is sitting on a table. There's like a cover, just goes from top to bottom. And afterward you feel . . . kind of recharged. I mean, it's not a bad feeling at all. That's the feeling you're left with, and . . . while I'm in bed, it's really difficult to remember.

DR. FIORE: Let's see if you were given any suggestions or commands not to remember.

JAMES: There's somebody standing again, at the top, just off to the side of whatever that thing is that goes over you. I get the feeling he's being very reassuring and almost talking as if he's talking to a child and telling him how important it is that nobody knows about the discussions.

DR. FIORE:   Did he explain why it's important?

JAMES:   He just says they wouldn't understand. [*Pauses*] This guy's someone I've spoken with several times. His name begins with an *M*. He's got a funny name.

DR. FIORE:   You're going to let yourself remember his name at the count of three. One . . . two . . . three.

JAMES:   Mogwan. That's the name M-O-G-W-A-N. I get the strangest feeling about the shape. I don't understand why I have so many images of their shape, unless they're . . . different. Maybe they're different. . . . This one has more of a physical form than some of them I've talked to, like at the conference table. I don't know if they're different. . . .

DR. FIORE:   Could they have been wearing anything that obscured their physical form?

JAMES:   That would certainly make sense.

DR. FIORE:   I want you to remember. Something that obscures their body. Look at the one that doesn't have a neck, for instance.

JAMES:   It's interesting, because even this fellow, this Mog fellow. I can see his lower body and his legs, but his . . . he's got kind of like a halo. It's almost as if it's a hat that extends down like a shield. Goes up above his head a bit and then down. It's like an arch he's wearing on his head. Because I can see his feet. I mean he's got kind of spindly feet and toes, and his fingers are a little longer . . . his hands are a little longer than ours. And I'm not so sure if they have only three, or four, fingers.

DR. FIORE:   Take a look.

JAMES:   They have three fingers.

DR. FIORE:   Let yourself remember if they have given you help as to techniques to use in healing people.

JAMES:   It's in the ship. [*Pauses*] They use kind of a plate, or maybe a . . . [*Pauses*] It's like a big U. And you can select the frequencies. They have both a plate and a big U. The U they use for the extremities and the plate . . . I feel like I'm sitting there in a chair discussing this stuff.

DR. FIORE:   Did they demonstrate it? Or did they just tell you?

JAMES:   They're demonstrating it on somebody. First an alien and now a human. What you can do is you pick up the . . . [*Pauses*] Oh, no wonder! You . . . [*Laughs*] On the screen, like a beautiful . . . television screen, you can see the different energy channels, just like they're interspersed with arteries and veins. It's like our MRI, except it shows not only tissues, it shows the energy channels, and they're . . . graphically depicted. Where they're weak, you can see the multicolors, and . . . and the ones that are . . . not flowing well, you can actually stimulate with selected frequencies. Very interesting. [*Pauses*] The incredible thing is how you can do this same thing with . . . I mean that's the key to . . . [*Pause*] We've been doing that for a long time with . . . [*Long pause*]

DR. FIORE:   What are you talking about?

JAMES:   Repairing those energy channels, or . . . there're techniques present now that have been handed down for such a long time. Acupuncture techniques, for example. But they've got techniques that allow you to . . . put that graphically right up on the screen.

DR. FIORE:   Did they explain why they are showing you this?

JAMES:   There's something that makes me very nervous about this. I think they're asking for something in exchange and I can't figure out what it is.

DR. FIORE:   You're going to let yourself remember it. It's crystal clear in your mind. At the count of three. One . . . two . . . three.

JAMES:   They want me to use it to . . .

DR. FIORE:   They want you to what?

JAMES:   They want to show me the control techniques. And I refuse.

DR. FIORE:   Why do you do that?

JAMES:   Because they want to use it to . . . subvert our population.

DR. FIORE:   Let's go back to what they're teaching you that you are able to understand and perhaps use. Are you learning anything new from them?

JAMES:   No question. It's a synthesis of ideas. But maybe it's a demonstration of how those ideas can work. In the situation I described, I think they have it, where we . . . can use it both for healing and also for control. And it's really . . . not the same techniques, but they're different applications. And it's not automatic. [*Pauses*] I don't understand the anxiety that this provokes, but it . . . [*Pauses*] I'm refusing to do something.

DR. FIORE:   What is that?

JAMES: [*Pauses*] They want me to help them in some way, but I can't figure out exactly what they want. It's kinda like they're saying, "We've shown you what good this will bring your people," but there's something else I can't put my finger on that they want me to agree to.

DR. FIORE: You're going to let yourself remember at the count of three. It's very easy to remember. One . . . two . . . three. First thoughts.

JAMES: They want me to do some work with a really innocuous looking device that enhances their ability to . . . communicate.

DR. FIORE: Do you feel any anxiety when they propose this?

JAMES: Yes, because I'm not sure what their real intent is, whether it's to . . . [*Pauses*] It's a real conflict in that there's a lot of good to be shared, but also you have to be careful to not just accept the whole thing immediately, because it's not clear what their whole intent is. I just have concern that they're no different than we are in terms of different factions. And while the stated purpose may appear peaceful, there might be other motives involved. Just a simple-looking device that they claim would enhance our ability to see and communicate with them more easily. Maybe that's what they're wearing. This thing is kind of like a cone. And it emits that same kind of whitish glow.

DR. FIORE: And how do you deal with this, as they're proposing this to you? Do they want to give you one of these devices? Do they want to teach you how to make it?

JAMES: The latter. I don't know if they want to teach me or if they're asking my thoughts on how to get it accepted. If it were available. This is really strange. Marketing their device. [*Laughs*] It's not a direct question to me, but I'm aware that that's what they want. I guess I'm not in the main part of the discussion about that. I'm not brought into that. But I can see one of these things sitting there, and I know what it does. Not that it happens immediately. It's kind of like some kind of . . . stimulator, and it does that by frequency emissions.

DR. FIORE:   Did they discuss any illnesses with you? For instance, did they discuss AIDS?

JAMES:   Not specifically. It's more in terms of demonstrating what it takes to support these deficient [energy] systems. And I'm not really sure [whether] the thoughts that question brings to mind are directly discussed or secondary to the work I've been able to do with . . . you know, greater understanding of what's happening with people. But the work that they do . . . clearly shows an effort to support deficient systems at the same time that they try to remove the cause of the deficiency, the irritant factor, replacing the deficiency. I get the feeling that's a secondary observation, using the increased awareness.

DR. FIORE:   Let yourself go back in time and space to any meeting that you had with them in which they instructed you or gave you some understanding of the body, health, disease. At the count of five. One . . . two . . . three . . . four . . . five. Just report whatever comes into your mind, whatever you're aware of.

JAMES:   It's the same kind of meeting room.

DR. FIORE:   Tell me all about it, how many people are there, who's there, what beings are there?

JAMES:   Basically, two alien beings. [*Pauses*] One is an expert on diseases and health. And on the screen they're showing the diagrams of the studies that they've obtained on people. Different, what we call, disease states. As these people talk, what they say begins to explain centuries of concepts, more in an Eastern sense of medicine, in terms of energy flows. But the really intriguing thing is that the diagrams can demonstrate right on the screen how the energy flow changes through different organ systems with just various exposures of materials. [*Seems anxious*]

DR. FIORE: Are you feeling any anxiety right now?

JAMES: Yes, but I'm not sure why.

DR. FIORE: You're remembering everything that's happening. You're sitting there and you're seeing them change the energy flow, using different substances.

JAMES: The diagram shows how, in a very graphic way, with someone just lying there, exposures to different materials can cause changes in energy flow in our system and how that begins to happen long before the material begins to enter our physical frame. How you begin to react to things across the room.

DR. FIORE: Can you give me an example from what they showed you?

JAMES: They're bringing a plant that emits a strange perfume. [*Body tenses*]

DR. FIORE: What are you feeling in your body right now?

JAMES: I feel a lot of anxiousness.

DR. FIORE: Is anything being done to you?

JAMES: I think it brings up the memory of when this was done to me, when I'm watching.

DR. FIORE: Let yourself remember what was done to you.

JAMES: When I was young . . . [*Cries*] . . . I can remember being so scared. [*Shaking*] In the tube . . . I thought it was a coffin. I thought I was dead. I couldn't get out. I wakened and lay there for a while, afraid to scream. [*Panicking*] Ah! . . . Ah! . . . One of them's touching me on the head! Oh! . . . Their skin looks like it would feel so slimy. Ah! . . . Ah! . . . Okay . . . He's trying to soothe me. It's a he. I don't know why I know that. The words are strange, but what they say is, they're not there to hurt me. [*Pauses*] Ah! . . . [*Choking*] They needed . . . to help make it better. Talking about that accident I described before. And they were afraid to . . . totally sedate me because . . . they weren't sure how bad the damage was. And that's why I woke up. And they're sorry, that it frightened me. [*Pauses*] We've been so conditioned by the movies to be afraid and to fear them, and they're not very appealing in the usual sense of what appeals to us without their . . . mask on, they're frightful! [*Voice shakes*] Okay . . . I figure, if they were going to hurt me, they would have, so I just . . . slowly begin to relax. I think the machines they have now are much better. They look more modern than the ones they had thirty years ago.

DR. FIORE:    Continue to speak out.

JAMES:    I've been moved to the table again. . . . When I look at this person on the table, I can remember being there myself, and I try and tell myself that they're not going to hurt them. It's just so scary, so strange, so frightening. It doesn't really hurt. It's cold . . . my arms and legs are gently strapped in so I won't move and writhe around. That thing's back on my head, I remember that. I think that damn thing's a coaxial laser. And they go in there and dissolve the damn clot. I can't believe it! [*Sighs*] It takes a long time . . . you gotta lie there in this thing. It's pinned to my head. First they scan to see the size and location. Then there's two beams, and when they cross, it creates heat at that exact location. And it takes a long time, because as it dissolves the clot, gasses form, and they don't want to obstruct the blood flow. So, in essence, what they're doing is speeding up the process that would occur naturally, by removing the pressure much more quickly than it would have happened. And they don't have to cut, he says, because there was no immediate danger. Just to keep the pressure off. [*Pauses*]

DR. FIORE:   How is this being done? Is he explaining it to you?

JAMES:   Yes.

DR. FIORE:   Does he explain the coaxial laser, for example? Does he use these terms?

JAMES:   No. Just says that there's some beams of light that'll help take care of things. I didn't understand it before, but it makes sense now. They rotate around this big circular frame. And they stop and scan. And he's saying something about the front part of humans' brains. He says you barely have enough room to expand in there as it is, without having this extra stuff. I don't understand. They're kind of laughing. Two or three of them are laughing about that. [*Long pause*] I saw a picture of a mouse in the newspaper that they had transplanted some of the human immune system into for research, and that's what's happened to us. They're doing it to us to reproduce some problems that they've got, so that they can study ways to treat it. [*Flinches*]

DR. FIORE:   What are you feeling in your body right now?

JAMES:   I don't want them to take my arm. I'm holding on to my belt, so they can't take my arm. I don't want . . . I think they're going to inject something into me.

DR. FIORE:   Is this happening to you as a child or as an adult?

JAMES:   I think it's as a child. [*Shaking*] I'm not sure. I think it happened before, but it's . . . won't do it again. . . . [*Struggling*]

DR. FIORE:   When is this happening?

JAMES:   It's happening recently.

DR. FIORE:   Tell me everything that you're aware of.

JAMES:   I don't know what it was. They took some blood and also gave me something.

DR. FIORE:   Did they give you an explanation?

JAMES:   Yes.

DR. FIORE:   What did they say?

JAMES:   They want to know how I survived. [*Pauses*] An inoculation from twenty years ago.

DR. FIORE:   Remember everything that they're telling you. Are they implying that you should not have survived that inoculation?

JAMES:   Yes.

DR. FIORE:   Did they explain why?

JAMES:   Because it kills their people. And they had to see if the theories were right on the combined forms. [*Relaxes*]

DR. FIORE:   What happened just then?

JAMES:   I relaxed, and the whole thing started to make sense.

DR. FIORE:   Tell me about it.

JAMES:   The sedative they gave you has kind of a hallucinatory effect. It's like a mind-expander. But I think that some of us are humans . . . and aliens combined. And the ones that develop close enough to be accepted in the society get implanted.

DR. FIORE:   So they need to make sure that the virus would not kill this hybrid, is that it?

JAMES:   Yes. And the hybrid's really the . . . combination of the parents. But it has . . . some significant pieces added so that it'll represent the vulnerable portions of the aliens . . . what they think is the vulnerable portion in their immune systems. And they're trying to figure out how our system can adapt to it. [*Pauses*] Because their race isn't able to. [*Long pause*]

DR. FIORE:   Speak out whatever comes into your mind.

JAMES:   And they run correlations on so many factors that affect energy flow. And they've looked at the heavy metals. It looks like a debate . . . the research being worthless because of cofactors on the planet, the heavy-metal cofactors being one that they can't control for in their experiment. [*Laughs*] I get this image of this one . . . younger researcher trying to explain to the professor, if you will, the director of the project, that that is invalid because the subject is so contaminated.

DR. FIORE:   Are these aliens having the debate?

JAMES:   Yes. They're standing in the conference room, and they had been asking me about what our awareness of heavy-metal exposures is. And I told them that wasn't an area that I was really expert on. He didn't explain it to me, but it seems like it screwed up his data, that's all. [*Laughs*] I don't know why I find it comical, but maybe it's a scene you could see anywhere, in any society.

DR. FIORE:   Before, you were telling me about how we could be affected by things that did not enter into our physical frame, and I asked you for an example and you told me about a plant emitting an odor from across the room. Will you go back to when this was being explained to you?

JAMES:   Somebody's lying on the table and . . .

DR. FIORE:   Human?

JAMES:   A human. And they're being scanned. And that scan's graphically depicted in terms of the energy channels, the support structures are barely visible. The bones and tissues are like a faint outline or a background on a piece of paper, but the energy systems are graphically depicted. I guess they can do this on a limb, but not as well through the whole body, because I don't see the whole-body scans. Maybe it's too hard to put together, but when the material is brought closer to the patient, as it gets closer, one of the systems fades, as if the energy flow is not continuing as strong as it was before. It was already not as intense in terms of the intact systems represented by a nice bright color.

DR. FIORE:   What colors do you see?

JAMES:   Red, blue, yellow. It's the yellow one going out of this one. There's green.

DR. FIORE:   You said yellow is fading?

JAMES:   Yes, in this system, I don't know why.

DR. FIORE:   Do you see all those same colors in the same area?

JAMES:   No, they're separate. They're like cables. You can think of them as cables of different colors.

DR. FIORE:   What is being explained to you? Are they demonstrating on this person?

JAMES: Yes, they're showing how different materials natural to our environment can both help and . . . it's almost as if they're demonstrating the impact of a concentrated material versus the dilution of a material. That in the natural form it may be harmful, and someone very sensitive to it in a naturally occurring concentration reacts very strongly, but if you deliver [it] in an extremely diluted dose, it has a strengthening effect as opposed to a weakening one.

DR. FIORE: Does that make sense to you?

JAMES: It does based on what I've seen subsequently.

DR. FIORE: Do they explain what is wrong with that person lying there?

JAMES: Liver.

DR. FIORE: What do they say has happened to him?

JAMES: He's dying of inflammation of the liver. And that system has become so weakened that even exposures to materials that you normally wouldn't consider toxic, he's reacting to.

DR. FIORE: Such as?

JAMES: Looks like a cactus plant.

DR. FIORE: Did they demonstrate anything else?

JAMES: They're going to use synthetically generated energy forms to treat it. I guess the question is, can they resolve this episode? But they're not sure they can. What they're asking me is why don't they stay stable?

DR. FIORE: What do you say?

JAMES: I told them it looks like the cofactors they were talking about. I'm not so sure that the virus is the problem. They don't like hearing that either.

DR. FIORE: What do they say then?

JAMES: They tell me, what would I know, I'm just a human.

DR. FIORE: How do you feel when they say that?

JAMES: I try to keep from laughing, because it's the same thing I hear from my fellow humans. [*Laughs*] I keep trying to tell them I'm not so sure there's so many differences, but they don't want to hear that.

DR. FIORE: How do you know that they don't want to hear that?

JAMES: Maybe they choose to ignore it. [*Laughs*] I just draw some glances of reproach. I'm expected to sit there quietly, I should be seen and not heard, that's it. [*Laughs*] So I'm sitting there in this chair at this table. There's a group of aliens, and there are several humans interspersed. Experts from various fields, people who have become experts in various fields that are part . . . alien, also. And by that, I don't mean they look like that, but they've got some common . . . as if they were once part of a big experiment, but the magnitude of the problem is such that they now need input, even from the experimental subjects. And they're really uptight about it.

DR. FIORE: Who's uptight?

JAMES: The aliens. I mean this is a high-priority project. And humor has no place in it, I'm told, especially from a human. And I can tell that's coming from the head of the table. It's a very authoritative comment from one of the aliens in charge. I don't know if he's in charge of the project as much as he's some kind of representative overseeing, inspecting the project. But I can tell from the glances of the other aliens that they're not in total support of his assertion that the problem isn't the cofactors, as we refer to it. On their own planet. [*Pauses*] But I guess I feel comfortable enough to . . . slip that in. It doesn't bring as much fear as it might have at one time.

DR. FIORE: What's happening to the sick person?

JAMES: It looks like he's going to die after all. They're not having as much success reversing it as they anticipated. He looks very sick, both physically and on the screen with the colors.

DR. FIORE: Do you think he might die right there on the ship?

JAMES: Yes. I've never seen that before, so it was hard for me to imagine that, but it's creating a big consternation. Some problem with getting him back. And explaining the whole issue, that creates a big problem. They don't understand why the usual reversal techniques aren't working. They ask me if I had any ideas. That's one reason I'm there. [*Pauses*] I feel a tension at the moment . . . just like I would if I were standing in front of my own colleagues trying to solve the problem. [*Laughs*] I keep telling them to get the congestion out of his liver, but I don't think we can do it. It's as if you're watching the whole system start to fail. This one's dying.

DR. FIORE: What happened to the colors you were talking about?

JAMES: They went out.

DR. FIORE: Are there any colors left, anything at all?

JAMES: Not on the screen, maybe the faintest . . .

DR. FIORE:   Can you still see his bones faintly?

JAMES:   Yes, the tissues are all there, the thing I'm referring to are those conduits. They look like conduits. You know, it's a graphic representation. So they look like pipes.

DR. FIORE:   And what happened to them? Are the colors gone?

JAMES:   Yes. There's some faintly glowing red, and maybe this light is blue, the yellow's just flicker, flicker, and then it went out. It was kinda just like watching a light bulb burn out. It wasn't ever that bright, but it's just the same thing. They don't go out totally. Maybe they're smoldering, but this guy was in bad shape to begin with.

DR. FIORE:   What is the reaction of the aliens? Are they looking at the screen?

JAMES:   Yes. There's a lot of disappointment and also a lot of maneuvering to figure out who's going to take care of the disposal [*Laughs*] . . . of what they consider to be a contaminated form. I mean, they think that thing is contagious. Somehow they've got a waste-disposal problem. [*Laughs*] And ideally they put it back in the place where they got it, but they're not so sure they can. . . . some transport problems because the . . . [*Laughs*] Nobody wants to be involved with a contaminated human form. In terms of taking it back. So there's a little bit of a . . . it turns into a . . . chain-of-command issue. He's back in the tube and back on the pallet. I'm not standing right there as they do this, but I know it's happening. And you've got a . . . a detail. To take it back.

DR. FIORE:   They're concerned about their image?

JAMES:   Two things. One, they're concerned about the apparent failure of the project and the techniques to reverse the different systems, and . . . the first thing that came into my mind was that they're concerned that they were involved, being involved with somebody who died . . . It's almost like a political event. I mean, they didn't do this, but they are very worried that they would be perceived as doing this. I get the feeling that there's two groups kind of negotiating. With . . . humans as a people. [*Pauses*] They're both demonstrating their technical prowess and also their goodwill. I think one group has generally got goodwill. I'm not so sure about the other. I mean, in terms of its impact on us.

DR. FIORE:  What happens to the meeting? What happens with you?

JAMES:  I'm taken back also.

DR. FIORE:  When did this happen?

JAMES:  I think this happened two or three months ago.

DR. FIORE:  Were you given any instructions or commands that you would not remember?

JAMES:  The usual.

DR. FIORE:  What are the usual?

JAMES:  I feel like I'm sitting in a little cubicle. And it's kind of an automated process now. I think they used to do this individually, but it's a combination of lights and sounds and like a posthypnotic suggestion to . . . or some kind of suggestion to wipe the memories out of the easy-access part of my memory. As well as the fact that if I do bring them up, if I do share them, there could be recriminations. I think that's part of the anxiety I feel as I go through talking about some of this.

DR. FIORE:  Do you feel that the recriminations would be against you or them?

JAMES: I never thought about that. What they leave me with is the feeling it would hit on me. It seems like the relationship is much more relaxed, and this is almost a formality now, the suggestion part, but it leaves me feeling very anxious in discussing it.

DR. FIORE: Tell me how you were going back.

JAMES: I feel like I'm sitting in a chair. Some kind of a bubble. [*Pauses*]

DR. FIORE: And what happens?

JAMES: I get out and I'm led by one individual who accompanied me, maybe he was driving or steering or whatever you do to this thing. It kind of glides or floats. It's really strange. But I'm in kind of a buzzed-out state, so it's really hard for me to remember those details well. I might even be undergoing that suggestion period while we're moving, so it's really difficult for me to even be aware of what's happening. God, that craft is huge.

DR. FIORE: How big is it?

JAMES: Two blocks.

DR. FIORE: What shape is it?

JAMES: It looks oblong. I mean it is big! I can't understand why we can't see it.

DR. FIORE: Does it have any lights on it?

JAMES: Not now, because it's really close to the city, to the populated area. I get the feeling that I've seen multicolored lights.

DR. FIORE:  Where were they?

JAMES:  Around the perimeter on the bottom. It's kind of like a big elongated oval shape. And it's as if there are windows on the bottom as well as on the sides. And the lights are not directly on the very bottom, but kind of halfway between the two. I don't understand. Maybe what you see is the lights from inside coming through those windows, I don't know.

DR. FIORE:  What brings you home?

JAMES:  A small, round-shaped craft of some kind. It's got kind of a clear canopy in front. It's not very big.

DR. FIORE:  How many people does it hold?

JAMES:  I think there's just one driver, one flier. It's hard for me to tell because we're kind of in the front. I don't think it's very big.

DR. FIORE:  And now what happens?

JAMES:  It lands in the backyard. And I am kind of led because I'm in a semiawake state. I'm led back to my door. The doors open and they wait there while I get in bed.

DR. FIORE:  Do they go into the house with you or just wait there?

JAMES:  Just wait at the door. Just one.

DR. FIORE:  Can they see you go into the bedroom from the door?

JAMES:  Oh yes. There's a door from our bedroom. My wife stirs. And it's like he . . . he does something that kinda . . . I don't know if he's got a device in his hand or something. . . .

My wife's always complaining I don't sleep anymore. She's always saying I'm up all the time at night, that I never sleep all the way through the night. [*Laughs*] She's right more than she knows.

*

James came out of hypnosis and was fully alert, even though he'd been hypnotized for almost two hours. He immediately started to chuckle. "My wife has really been complaining about me waking her up, and she's a light sleeper. I wonder if she'll believe me?"

"Does she believe in UFOs? Almost half of Americans do, according to a recent Gallup poll."

"She believes in them, but this is pretty far out. I think she's ready for it, though." James glanced at his watch. "My flight leaves in about an hour, I'll have to go. I'd love to be able to run some of this by you, but I don't think USAir will hold the plane for me," he said, laughingly. A quick hug and he was gone.

I opened the sliding glass door to my redwood deck and breathed in some fresh air and watched a few leaves floating down the trickle of a creek. A bad drought had almost dried it up. I was savoring our session and wanted to skim through it again before my next patient arrived. I enjoyed James's sense of humor in the midst of such seriousness. I could just visualize him slouched down in his seat at the conference table, stifling a chuckle and making mental comparisons with the power ploys that go on at board meetings on Earth. I could imagine the silencing frown of the alien at his unwelcome observations. It had been a particularly intriguing session for me and one that I knew would benefit James in many, many ways.

# "They Take My Eggs!"

"My top priority is to lose weight. I've lost as much as ninety-five pounds at one time. Of course, I gained it all back. Last year I took off sixty pounds and regained thirty-five . . . twenty in the last two months."

Victoria, an artist in her mid-fifties, sought my help for her lifelong weight problem. Her five-feet-four-inch body was about 150 pounds too heavy.

During our first session, we covered the important areas of her life; her marriage with its frustrations, the lack of sex for many years and her struggle as an artist. Before she left, I made her a tape to use as she drifted off to sleep, suggesting that the healing force within her be mobilized to resolve her many difficulties.

I used hypnosis with Victoria in each of our next few visits and found that she was an excellent hypnotic subject. She went into a deep level of hypnosis readily and very easily established rapid and clear finger signals.

Victoria sailed into my office for our fourth session with a big smile on her face and radiating an aura of self-confidence. "I've lost eight pounds in the last two weeks. There's a real change in my way of eating. I've cut out the snack in the evening . . . and I'm not picking in between meals. I'm delighted! It's never been so easy!"

After she had been hypnotized for ten minutes and we had come to the end of our work on her weight problem, I followed a hunch and asked her subconscious mind if she had had any close encounters with extraterrestrials. Her "yes" finger popped up immediately. By a twenty-questions approach, I found that she had had a total of three close encounters of the fourth kind, the first when she was only five years old. We had time for one regression before the end of the session so I asked her inner mind to take her back to the very first encounter.

*

VICTORIA:   I'm floating, but I'm floating fast. [*Pauses*] I didn't know anything could go this fast. I'm zooming out.

DR. FIORE:   Tell me more.

VICTORIA:   It's real light. Real bright. All I can see is a bright light . . . and I'm just spinning. I feel like I'm spinning around and around and around. And I feel like there's something there. Something's looking at me. They're watching me, but I can't see them. This bright light's there. It's there, it's so white and I'm just spinning, and they say, "It's okay, it's okay. We're not going to hurt you. It's okay." But I can't see anything, I'm just spinning. Now we're going zooming back. I feel like I'm going backward. [*Long pause*] I'm slowing down. [*Pauses*] This hand, I think it's a hand, it touches my shoulder . . . and . . . Ah! I've slowed down and I've stopped. [*Pauses*] I'm sleeping now at home, in my bed.

DR. FIORE:   You're going to remember the very beginning of this experience. Let's see where you were just before it began.

VICTORIA: I'm looking out the window at the stars. And this one star comes down. It just comes down. It just gets bigger . . . and it comes down. And I'm saying, "Twinkle, twinkle little star." [*Long pause*] But it gets bigger. It's a big star! And I just keep watching it. And now the light's real bright. Real bright.

DR. FIORE: Where is the light?

VICTORIA: At my window. And I go to the light.

DR. FIORE: How do you do that?

VICTORIA: I just kind of went. It just kind of drew me there, because it was so bright. I can't go through that window. It's closed. [*Pauses*] They opened the window.

DR. FIORE: Tell me about that.

VICTORIA: The window opened and I climbed out. I didn't fall. I just climbed out. And then we went zooming. That's when I started zooming.

DR. FIORE: Who are they? Tell me about them.

VICTORIA: I don't know who they are.

DR. FIORE: But you said that they went with you. Who are they?

VICTORIA: The people in the bright light.

DR. FIORE: What do they look like?

VICTORIA: Shadowy. Tall . . . and shadowy.

DR. FIORE: How many would you say there are?

VICTORIA: A lot.

DR. FIORE: What do you mean by that?

VICTORIA: They stand around me in a circle. That's why I keep going in a circle. They keep spinning me around and looking at me. They've got real round heads. And they don't have any hair. But they don't hurt you, they just look at you. They don't hurt you. You don't have to be afraid. [*Pauses*] "You'll think it was a dream." That's what she said. "You'll just think it was a dream." And she puts her hand on my shoulder . . . and I'm in bed. [*Long pause*]

✿

I counted Victoria back to the present and, after giving her suggestions for well-being, brought her out of her trance. I asked her how she felt, because I didn't want her to leave my office still partially in a trance.

"Real kind of light. Real calm. Really peaceful."

"Have you read any books on UFOs?"

"Never. I've never read any on the subject . . . I'm so surprised!"

I reminded her that her finger signals had indicated she'd had a total of three experiences and told her that we would have to explore each one. "It's important that we deal with all buried traumas. So many times these events cause problems and anxieties in people's lives. Think of them as thorns in your flesh. We need to pull them out."

She nodded with the smile of an adventurer and, at the same time, an expression of reluctance that silently said, "I wish I didn't have to."

✿

One week later, Victoria filled me in on some background material that seemed to support the probability that she had been abducted as a child. She told of waking up more than once watching a star change colors. Then it would seem that it didn't change any longer, and she'd go back to bed.

Suddenly she burst out, "They own me! My body belongs to them, not me." Tears rolled down her face. "That's why I hate my body!" She leaned forward and angrily yanked a tissue out of the box. Drying her eyes and wiping her nose and cheeks, she added, "I've been fighting an inner battle all week long. It seems that forces are pulling in each direction. I've been concentrating on surrounding myself with the white light and telling them . . . and me that I'm in power."

I suggested that we use hypnosis at that point, to see what had been affecting her during the week, what had been causing the inner battle. She quickly slipped into a trance and soon was going back in time again.

✦

VICTORIA:   I'm not at home. I feel like I'm outside. I'm floating to meet this . . . And the light's getting brighter. And my head's . . . my head's heavier. He's calling. And the light's bright. [*Pauses*] And I feel a sinking feeling in the back of my head. They want to connect, and I don't want to. I never want to, but they always win. They tell me, "You know we always win." And they're pulling, and I'm going. [*Cries*] And they're saying, "It's okay." And I'm saying, "It's not." And they just keep pulling. [*Cries harder*] They've got me . . . again. [*Long pause*] But we're staying here this time. We're not zooming out. We're just hovering. We're hovering around. There's the table again. It's the table you always lie on. It's a . . . golden-glow color. And they circle around you. And you spin on this table. And as you spin, they're taking . . . what are they taking? [*Cries very hard*] They're always taking! [*Becomes calmer*] I don't know what they're taking, but they're taking my thoughts. They take my thoughts. And the light gets brighter. And the brighter the light gets, the faster everything happens. There's one that has more power than the rest. He's the one that pulls everything. Everything! "We want everything." "Everything . . . come on, everything. You're going to give us *every* . . .

*thing."* But I don't. That's why they get so angry at me. I keep part of me, and they get real angry at me. He tries to penetrate all of it. With . . . his eyes. His eyes beam in . . . They all beam in, but his are the most penetrating. And that's how they absorb what I know. I'm not sure why they have to know all this. "You don't have to know. Only we know, you wouldn't understand." [*Pauses*] "When does this stop?" "You don't ask questions. You aren't here to ask questions. You're here to do what we say." The back of my neck hurts again. "What are you doing to the back of my neck?" [*Cries*] "Don't do it! Please don't do it! I don't want you to do it! You make me hate you! I hate you! Don't! Don't!" They always do it. It's so hard to fight them. You can't win. They don't let you, because they won't let you go home. I can go home if I do what they say. . . . It isn't fair. [*Stops crying*] That's what they can't get from me. And that's what they keep trying to get. I never give them . . . the inner me. And they want it. But I have a stronger power . . . that doesn't give it to them. And that's why they get so angry at me. They say others let them have it. "Others can do it, you can." But I won't. I won't! My neck hurts again. They're trying again. [*Angry now*] They just keep trying, and I won't. I won't! No matter what, I won't. I've got God on my side, and I can do what I want, and they can't have that part. "Someday," they say. "Someday." He said. "Someday you'll be totally mine." And I always say, "Never!" That's why we constantly fight. That's why part of me hates the other part of me. The part he has control of. The others watch. They watch and observe. He's their teacher. I'm their subject. One . . . one always has compassion for me. And she's not supposed to. She's the one that told me it was okay when I was little. She's always there. [*Long pause*] Maybe it's always part of the plot. Maybe her telling me it's okay is part of . . . that's it . . . is part of him trying to get to me by telling me it's okay and they won't hurt me. Because they do hurt me. They hurt my body. They hurt every part of me.

DR. FIORE:  How do they hurt your body?

VICTORIA:   They put things in it. And they take things out of it.

DR. FIORE:   Tell me more about that.

VICTORIA:   They put . . . they put something in . . . that's how they control me. That's how they make me come. That's how they make me watch. That's how they call me. . . . And they do other things. They check my body, with different things to see how it functions, what it's doing. They're keeping a recording of me. It's a record of my progress as a human being. They're studying human beings. I'm one of their experiments. They want to know how we function. They find the physical. That's it! That's what I don't give them, the spiritual. I just give them the physical. And they want all of it. But you can't give that without completely losing yourself. And you have to be a strong, spiritual person to keep it. The weaker ones, they get. And that's what they want, because then they can be total, total . . . total what? I don't know what total is, because . . . I don't give in. My and's real cold, like ice. [*Pauses*] "So . . . we'll control your body . . . we'll control your body." That's what they do. They spin you around. . . . And as you're spinning, they're drawing everything they want out of you. Sometimes they use instruments, and they hurt. They're . . . they're weird. I don't know what they are. [The instruments are] always cold. The coldest is in my hand. It's something they put in. [*Cries*] They put it in so they can draw out everything. Oh yuck! They come in and out. They come in and out. [*Cries harder*] That's what they do! They come in and they use . . . they use your body. They use your body to stay alive. They come in and out, so they can watch. [*Sobs*] That's why it hurts. That's why you go back. You go back so they can change. Because if they can't get all of you, they have to change. They have to keep changing. That's why. That's why it hurts. That's why they make you hate yourself. That's why you don't feel good. You don't feel good about yourself. You're never worthy of anything. They don't want you to be . . . because then they can't be in control. So they fight you, to be in control. Oh . . . they're hating me for this. But I've got a stronger power than they have, and they're hating me for that. And I'm going to win. Because I can see this white light, and this white light always lets me know . . . I'm . . . okay. They really try to hide that, and I constantly battle them on this. Constantly. They don't want to give . . . me . . . up. And I don't want them to have me. [*Pauses*] We're battling to see who's in control. They want to be in control. In *con-trol.* "No . . . No . . . No . . . I said never, and I mean never. Never!" [*Long Pause*] The back of my head isn't hurting anymore. They're leaving. They're zooming out, and I'm staying here.

DR. FIORE:    You said they come in and they go out. What do you mean by that?

VICTORIA:    [*Pauses*] They come . . . when I'm off guard. They come in and out of my body while I'm there. They come in and they draw things out of my body. Then they come in and they draw more . . . things . . . out. They come in, and they come down, and they stay, and if they can't get what they're supposed to get, then I go back, and they trade. They trade energies. They trade energies. . . . in me. They all come in and out, as part of rejuvenizing energies. They draw . . . that's it, they draw the energies out of me. And at times they need it more. And as they draw out energies, I have less defense and have to fight harder.

DR. FIORE:    Are you saying that they come back with you, that the others will go off and somebody remains with you in your body?

VICTORIA:    One remains with me, as a controller. [*Pauses*] Oh! . . . It's what they've put in my hand. It's that feeling in my hand when my hand gets cold. One is part of me. Whatever it is that they use to control me with is what comes and goes.

DR. FIORE:   Is there anything or anyone controlling you at this moment?

VICTORIA:   [*Pauses*] It's like it's neutral. They were battling me all week. I kept fighting them. They don't want to lose. I can feel the pulling in the back of my neck. It's getting stronger. [*Long pause*]

✦

Despite my suggestions to feel good in every way as I brought her out of hypnosis, Victoria felt tired from the struggle and her hands were still cold. I made a mental note that there may be some repressed material associated with the regression that we would probably have to return to at a later date.

✦

When I saw Victoria in the waiting room the following week, one glance told me that things had not gone well with her. Once in my office, she sank into the chair and shook her head. "I've been really depressed all week. It was hard for me to pull out of it on the way home last time. There's something nagging at me. Something I don't want to face. I didn't want to come today. But I knew I had to."

I put her into hypnosis immediately and regressed her to the event that was causing the depression.

✦

VICTORIA:   They're coming in. And I'm getting on.

DR. FIORE:   On what?

VICTORIA:   Whatever it is I get on. What they're on. It's just all . . . shiny and light. [*Big sigh*] I'm back on the table. Now we're going. Not as fast this time, but we're moving. It's faster. Now we're starting. They're all circling again. . . . I'm really afraid this time. It feels . . . different. Like there's been a change. It's not them, it's me. I'm older.

DR. FIORE: How old are you?

VICTORIA: Twenty- . . . five. Someone says, "Go with it. It won't hurt you. Just go with it." My legs feel . . . heavy, but the rest of my body is light. [*Pauses*] I can feel their eyes piercing. [*Pauses*] I get numb for just a little while. Only while I'm spinning and spinning and spinning.

DR. FIORE: Tell me about the spinning.

VICTORIA: I feel like I'm spinning in a circle real fast.

DR. FIORE: What position is your body in?

VICTORIA: I'm on my back and I just spin around in a circle. I feel like there's something under me, but there's nothing under me.

DR. FIORE: And how do you feel as you're spinning?

VICTORIA: Light. I feel like everything is coming out. All my thoughts . . . are just spinning away. . . . That's why it's different. The controller wasn't there right away. Now he's here. It's his time to take power. He's letting the rest see what they could do, how much they could get. He's testing to see who's the strongest. That's what he says, "Who's the strongest?" He's still the strongest. If he can totally take me over, he can stay. They want to use my body so they can stay on Earth. [*Cries*] If I don't fight, I lose. And you can't lose. This is the final test of who's going to win. [*Pauses*] I can hear my voice saying, "I'm stronger. I'm stronger. I'm stronger!" And with each time I say, "I'm stronger," the light gets brighter. It gets brighter . . . and brighter. He wants someone to be able to control me all the time, and they're arguing. [*Big sigh*] I feel far, far away. Everything's far away. I'm floating. I'm floating, and they're pulling. They're removing something. [*Grimaces in pain*] And it hurts. Oh!

DR. FIORE:   Where does it hurt?

VICTORIA:   I feel it in my neck, and in my arm and my legs. It's like it's pulling. Pulling. Oh! [*Cries*] Now my stomach hurts. I feel like something is holding my shoulders. And pulling my head back. They're holding me down at my waist. They won't let me go! [*Cries hard*] They're just holding me down! It's so hard. [*Breathes heavily*] It's so hard when they hold you down. It hurts! [*Cries*] It's cold, and it hurts! [*Shouts*] They pierce and they pull!

DR. FIORE:   Where do they pierce?

VICTORIA:   My stomach. [*Points to abdomen*] They need to know . . . Oh no. . . . [*Cries*]

DR. FIORE:   What is it they need to know?

VICTORIA:   How I function. They want . . . to know . . . what . . . causes . . . the reproduction. How we reproduce. They're trying to study . . . Oh! That's what they want to know . . . how we reproduce! [*Breathes hard*] It isn't the sex they want. They want the reproduction.

DR. FIORE:   How do you know this?

VICTORIA:   By the tests.

DR. FIORE:   Do they explain this to you?

VICTORIA:   She does. She says, "We have to know. It's okay." It's someone that always tells me it's okay. "We have to know." They want to find out how to reproduce us. . . . [*Pauses*] They . . . Oh! . . . That's . . . [*Cries*] . . . what they did. The probing was taking the egg. They're going to try and reproduce us. I wasn't really supposed to know. If they can reproduce us, they can come back . . . with the people they reproduce. The controller says he will win . . . the battle. Because I can't have any control over what he takes. [*Cries*]

DR. FIORE:   What are you thinking?

VICTORIA:   I don't want them to have any part of me. [*Cries hard*] And I really feel robbed because they took it!

DR. FIORE:   What did they take?

VICTORIA:   Part of me.

DR. FIORE:   What part is that?

VICTORIA:   They take my eggs! They knew how to probe and get them. And that's mine. Not theirs. [*Cries*] That's why they have control. And I don't want to go back. I don't want to go back!

DR. FIORE:   You don't want to go back where?

VICTORIA:   They took me back. When I ovulated, they took me back . . . and took the egg.

DR. FIORE:   How many times did they take you back?

VICTORIA:   Six . . . ten. Ten times.

DR. FIORE:   Did they take an egg each time?

VICTORIA:   Yes.

DR. FIORE:   Did they tell you what they were going to do with the eggs?

VICTORIA:   No. Try . . . try experiments. [*Pauses*]

DR. FIORE:  When you say try experiments, are you reporting what you heard or what you think?

VICTORIA:  What I heard.

DR. FIORE:  Were they talking to you?

VICTORIA:  No.

DR. FIORE:  What are they going to do with these eggs?

VICTORIA:  That's how they're trying to reproduce [us].

DR. FIORE:  This is the female component. How do they get the male component?

VICTORIA:  From the males.

DR. FIORE:  What males?

VICTORIA:  Ours. That they take. That's who else is there.

DR. FIORE:  Who is there?

VICTORIA:  A male.

DR. FIORE:  Is it someone whom you recognize?

VICTORIA:  No.

DR. FIORE:  What's being done?

VICTORIA:  They take his sperm.

DR. FIORE:  Do you see this being done?

VICTORIA:  Yes.

DR. FIORE: And how do they do this?

VICTORIA: I don't know what it is that they have. But they . . . it's like a suction. They have on him.

DR. FIORE: Where?

VICTORIA: On his . . . penis.

DR. FIORE: Is this being done at the same time they're removing your egg?

VICTORIA: Yes. Only he's, he's . . . not by me. There's another circle of people around him.

DR. FIORE: What's happening to you at this point?

VICTORIA: They're through with me and they're waiting for him.

DR. FIORE: And what's happening to you?

VICTORIA: I'm just lying there and I'm cold. I'm cold all over. Whatever they gave me made me real . . . cold.

DR. FIORE: What did they give you?

VICTORIA: They put something in that was so cold.

DR. FIORE: Where did they put it?

VICTORIA: In my tubes, and it was so . . . cold. Like they're freezing. It just makes you cold all . . . over. I don't know exactly what all they did to him. I only saw the end. Just the suction and the end.

DR. FIORE: How did he seem to react to it?

VICTORIA:  He fought too. That was the other yelling I heard.

DR. FIORE:  And now?

VICTORIA:  And now . . . I'm home.

DR. FIORE:  Remember how you got home.

VICTORIA:  Just going fast. Real fast. [*Pauses*] And then . . .
the machine opens and I'm out.

DR. FIORE:  Where were you?

VICTORIA:  In my backyard. In San Bernardino.

DR. FIORE:  Was anybody else in the machine with you?

VICTORIA:  [*Pauses*] They had my daughter. They had Susie.
She came out with me. We're sitting in the patio, and I'm just
holding her, and she's telling me about the little blue man.
That's where she got that little blue man! She's always telling me
that she was talking to a little blue man, and I just thought it was
her imagination.

DR. FIORE:  How do you feel now?

VICTORIA:  I feel . . . like they're through. I feel calm. And like
it's finally over.

✐

Victoria opened her eyes as I counted her out of hypnosis, and
smiled in relief. "Do you think they really do those things?"

"Budd Hopkins, an artist who wrote the book *Intruders*, reported many cases of people being used for genetic experiments
or possibly for breeding purposes. Have you heard about this before?"

"No. It seems incredible. Why would they do that?" Victoria frowned and leaned forward expectantly.

"I'd rather not go into it now. I don't want to influence any further work we may do on this. Later, when we're through, you should read his book and Whitley Strieber's *Communion.* You'll find them fascinating, I'm sure."

As I walked Victoria to the door of my office, she turned and gave me a big hug. I felt relieved that we had gotten to the cause of her depression, especially since I was going on vacation and wouldn't be seeing her for three weeks.

*

Victoria couldn't wait to tell me how good she felt as we walked from the waiting room to my office. "Edee, I feel really great!" She quickly sat down and reached into her purse. "I've kept some notes for you. I was afraid I might forget since it would be a while till I saw you again." She put on her glasses and looked up. "Is it okay to read them to you?"

"Sure. I find it very helpful when people keep records. I always need to know how they do, especially on the way home following our sessions. It gives me valuable clues about what we've accomplished and what needs to be resolved. What do you have there?"

Victoria read from two three-by-five-inch cards. "I have not been depressed. I feel great. I feel that my life is going in the right direction, with new opportunities and new doors opening up more every day. I really feel in contact with my core and true feelings. I'm taking each day as it comes, with great joy and thankfulness for all the new energies around me." She stopped and her whole face lit up with happiness.

"I'm absolutely delighted for you, Victoria. You must have released some pretty powerful blocks last time. It sounds like you've got your power back as well."

"Yes. And more good news! I just saw the doctor yesterday, and I've lost fifteen pounds since I started my therapy. Without trying. That's the best part."

I got up and walked over to my desk and checked her file.

"That was about six weeks ago. Wonderful! That's a safe rate of weight loss too."

As I sat back down in my Danish rosewood chair, I noticed Victoria frowning.

"There was only one negative thing in these three weeks." She read from the other card. "On August second I was sitting outside on the patio with my ten-year-old grandson, waiting for his parents, my son and his wife, to return. It was a lovely summer evening. We were relaxing, looking at the moon and clouds. Then I saw the stars and was afraid to look at them. So I stopped looking at the sky. I have always loved looking at the beauty of the moon, clouds and stars, as an artist. Maybe there's still something, I haven't remembered." She looked up anxiously. "Aside from that one night, everything's been great."

"Tell me exactly what happened. You said you were afraid to look at the stars?"

"My eyes wanted to focus on one star . . . and yet I didn't want to. I began to feel real anxiety with this business of looking at the star. My heart was pounding. I could feel the fear mounting up with the urge to look at the one spot. I was fighting myself. A part was telling me, You have to look. There was a real battle within. I chose to turn around and think of something else and not look at the sky. In fact, it bothered me for a couple of days. And, ever since then, I haven't really wanted to look at the sky at night. Actually, I forced myself finally to look a week ago. Again, I was outside with my grandson on the patio. There was a full moon. I could look up at the stars for a while, but if any star started to twinkle, I didn't want to look at it. I felt fear, but not as strong as that first time."

"There's something still hidden, repressed. We need to deal with it," I said.

Victoria looked scared. Her body tensed and her face stiffened as she looked down into her lap. "I was afraid so. I was real depressed as I got ready to come to this appointment. I started thinking about UFOs and felt worse. I had to put them out of my mind."

After she had been in hypnosis for a few minutes, I regressed her to the event responsible for the fear she had felt on the evening of August second.

✦

VICTORIA:   I just see this real bright light. It's coming toward me. It's getting brighter and brighter, and as it gets brighter, the lights keep changing in it. They twinkle red and green and blue. But there's a white light that's more penetrating . . . and they're here.

DR. FIORE:   What do you mean by that?

VICTORIA:   They're here and they're opening the door, and I'm going in. I don't want to go in, but they're just making me come in. They've got me by each arm and they're taking me in. And they glow in the light also. It's like it's all an illumination. I'm just not sure where I was when they got me.

DR. FIORE:   Let yourself remember.

VICTORIA:   It's my backyard.

DR. FIORE:   Tell me about them.

VICTORIA:   They don't feel like they are the same; they're not the ones I was with before. They're different.

DR. FIORE:   In what way?

VICTORIA:   They're taller, they're shaped different. [*Pauses*]

DR. FIORE:   Tell me whatever comes into your mind.

VICTORIA:   I feel trapped.

DR. FIORE:   What else are you feeling?

VICTORIA: Fear . . . because they're different. Fear that it's starting all over again, only a different way. It's like I'm just, I'm just kinda . . . hovering . . . The inside's different too.

DR. FIORE: What's happening?

VICTORIA: I'm standing there, and they're just holding me. They've got a hold of me, but I don't feel the pressure. Everything's light. And I feel we're moving, but we're not moving real fast. They aren't leaving our gravity area. They're just kinda staying in this [area]. I'm not the only one they're picking up, that's why.

DR. FIORE: Did they explain that to you?

VICTORIA: No. We stop and other people get on. I don't know the others. [Pauses] There's something they want from us. They seem to be kinder than the others. But I'm still afraid, 'cuz I'm not sure if that kindness is a deception. They're superintelligent, a lot more advanced than we are here.

DR. FIORE: How do you know that?

VICTORIA: I can just sense it. Now my ears are ringing. And I feel tingly. But I'm not afraid. I'm not sure what's happening.

DR. FIORE: What position is your body in?

VICTORIA: I'm standing up, but it doesn't feel like I'm standing up. It feels like I'm starting to tilt . . . backward. I don't feel like there's anything holding me there. I'm just kind of being there. I feel like I'm just sort of elevated there. The other people are in the same position. We're all just kind of at this angle.

DR. FIORE: How many other people are there?

VICTORIA:   I don't know. There's a row of us. I can't see the end. We're from all over, I know that.

DR. FIORE:   What do you mean by that?

VICTORIA:   I know we're just not all from our country . . . we're from all over the world. That's what we were doing. We were hovering and picking up people from all over the world. And now we're all lined up in this weird angle. I feel like they're taking something, but I don't know what. They're not letting us know. We're afraid and at the same time, we're calm. They've made the calmness. It's like they've got us in a spell. [*Pauses*] I feel like . . . I'm just not me. I feel like my body's there, but I'm not. But I don't know where I am. I feel like I'm looking at my body, lying there.

DR. FIORE:   Where are you in relation to your body?

VICTORIA:   I'm above it, looking down at it.

DR. FIORE:   When you look down at it, what do you see?

VICTORIA:   I'm just lying there. I don't feel like there's any life in my body. I'm just lying there like . . . a dummy. Like it's not part of me. I feel like I'm just floating up there, looking down at this row, and everybody else is doing the same thing. We're all up there, looking down at our bodies.

DR. FIORE:   Look at your body and see what's happening.

VICTORIA:   [*Cries out in pain.*] They're putting different rays on us. I don't know what they are, but they're zooming to different parts of our body.

DR. FIORE:   Tell me more about that.

VICTORIA:   It hurts when they do this.

DR. FIORE: How do you know that?

VICTORIA: Because at first . . . at first, I was there . . . when it started hurting . . . before I started floating and looking down. It's just hard to breathe. I feel like everything's being pulled out. My energy is low. My neck aches . . . my shoulders are heavy. I feel like there's nothing in my stomach . . . that everything's been taken out.

DR. FIORE: When you say your stomach, what do you mean?

VICTORIA: My stomach. The intestines . . . and my whole abdomen. It's like they've drained everything out. I feel like they've put something in that's making us glow. They can see everything and all of our functions inside. We can't see it, but they can. It's like a glowing substance. And I just feel hollower . . . and hollower.

DR. FIORE: At this point are you still in your body?

VICTORIA: Yes . . . [Long pause] Our bodies just look like they're dead mummies in a row. [Pauses] Now I feel like I'm not up there anymore. I'm starting to feel warm. I'm not cold anymore. I feel like I'm starting to fill up and that everything's working again. [Pauses] We're just lying there, and everything's coming back . . . to normal.

DR. FIORE: Describe these beings.

VICTORIA: They're taller than me. About half as much taller than me. Their bodies are shaped similar, but real thin . . . superthin, like half what we would consider normal. Almost like a skeleton frame. They're smooth-looking. I don't think they have any hair. They don't have it on their heads. Everything is real smooth. They're sort of a creamy white.

DR. FIORE: Tell me about their facial features.

VICTORIA:   Real high cheekbones. Their eyes are more sunken in than ours. More round.

DR. FIORE:   Tell me about their noses and mouths.

VICTORIA:   The ears are kind of flat to their heads, they don't protrude out at all. You hardly see them. They don't have noses like we do. They're very . . . kind of flat, with just little openings.

DR. FIORE:   And their mouths?

VICTORIA:   Their mouths are larger than ours. They're wider. They're like almost clear across the jaw line, but very thin. And the same color as their skin. They're all the same color. There's no variation. Everything's the same color.

DR. FIORE:   What color are their eyes?

VICTORIA:   A blue . . . green.

DR. FIORE:   And what are they wearing?

VICTORIA:   Silver. Glowing silver. Not the kind of silver we know. It's almost iridescent . . . it's a shimmering iridescence.

DR. FIORE:   Can you tell if they're males, or females, or both?

VICTORIA:   I feel they're mostly male. There's a few females. But they don't do very much. It's the males that do everything. The females assist.

DR. FIORE:   What do the males do?

VICTORIA:   They're the ones that work on our bodies.

DR. FIORE:   Do they communicate with you in any way?

VICTORIA: They just gave you an overwhelming . . . power-ful feeling that you're gonna stay calm, that you weren't to be afraid. Now when all of this was happening, you felt . . . even when you were hurting and everything . . . you felt a gentle-ness.

DR. FIORE: From them?

VICTORIA: From them.

DR. FIORE: Did they communicate with each other?

VICTORIA: Yes, but with their eyes.

DR. FIORE: Did you hear any sounds?

VICTORIA: No. I felt they could look at each other and just communicate.

DR. FIORE: Did they use any gestures?

VICTORIA: They touched. And when they held us, the touch wasn't strong. It felt forceful, but it wasn't forceful. It was . . . like you knew that they had you . . . but you didn't feel . . . you felt harmed, but you didn't feel harmed.

DR. FIORE: After you return to your body and it's all over, what happens?

VICTORIA: Now they're dropping us off. I'm still there, 'cuz I'm waiting for them to take me next, but they're leaving others off along the way. They're just dropping us . . . all . . . back. [*Long pause*] I feel like I'm drifting now. And I can see the light again and I can see them zooming off.

DR. FIORE: And now what do you do?

VICTORIA: I don't realize I was there with them. I go into my house.

*

One month later, Victoria came into the office obviously upset. Her whole being reflected depression.

"What's wrong, Victoria?"

"It's those UFO drawings! I got upset and disoriented doing them. I had a superhard time. I got so depressed, I couldn't finish them." She looked up at me with tears in her eyes. "Do you ever get rid of them? They'll just have me the rest of my life. Is it over? I want to believe it's over." Her eyes were pleading with me to reassure her.

"I wish I could tell you it is over, but I have no way of knowing. Probably there's still some repressed memory festering inside. If it's not over, I can help you become stronger."

She managed a weak smile. "The first pictures were a release. The UFO and the operations. It even had a calming effect. I actually felt a lot of love. But then I got into this set." She spread out some sketches on the carpet. "This one's the hardest. I couldn't draw the ship. I could see it in my mind's eye. It had a radiant haze, a glow. I just couldn't finish it. That's when I got so depressed."

"I think you've solved the riddle. Something happened on that ship that was very depressing. So it probably is over. You are just responding to past history. Let's bring it up to the surface of your mind so it won't bother you any longer."

Victoria was ready for the regression in three minutes. I asked her inner mind to take her to the cause of the depression.

*

VICTORIA: It's their bodies in mine. They have a way of entering your body and staying with you for as long as they want.

DR. FIORE: Let yourself go to when that happened.

VICTORIA:   I didn't want them to enter, and they held me down and said, "We do this to everyone, and you're the same." And they just enter you and stay there. They enter you to find out how you function, and so that they can become a part of this earth.

DR. FIORE:   Get in touch with how you felt when they held you down.

VICTORIA:   I felt . . . deprived. I felt like I was not me. Like I wanted to hide. That I wasn't in control. I had no say over my life.

DR. FIORE:   Tell me more about this particular contact. Tell me where it's taking place and everything that's happening.

VICTORIA:   It starts in their ship. With . . . blue lights all around. It's a weird blue, I can't describe the color. It's sort of a mixture of blues. And it's like their bodies enter you, and at the same time they enter you, you also feel like you're being molested sexually. But it's from within. When they enter you and they're a part of you, you just feel like you've been raped, not just physically but mentally also. And you feel like there's a constant battle of who's in control. You feel pinned down. And I don't know if the pinned down is the fear you feel or if you're being held down, or a combination of both. But you also know that when you leave the ship, that they're going to be with you.

DR. FIORE:   Let yourself to back to the very part of the event that caused you to have difficulty drawing the ship. What did that drawing bring up in you?

VICTORIA:   That's the ship where they took control. And I lost. I lost the battle. [*Cries*] And they took control. And they didn't let me go. [*Cries more*] And the glow, the glow around the ship is red. And no matter where that red glow is, it brings back fear, and I know they're there. Not maybe physically, but subconsciously I know they're there. They're there again. The red glow at Ann's that I saw in her kitchen is why I was so afraid. It's the first time I think I've been really awake and aware of that red glow, and I don't know if I was afraid because I just came back or because I was going to go. I could lie there and see it, and I knew I was terrified of it. And I felt if I didn't breathe and I stayed where I was at, they couldn't get me. But they didn't have to get me, because they had already had me, and they had just brought me back. I just want it to stop happening. Every time I think of the red glow, I can feel the pressure in the back of my neck.

DR. FIORE: What happens to the back of your neck?

VICTORIA: It just feels like there's a pressure right at the bottom of my skull.

DR. FIORE: What is that part of your body remembering? Let yourself know.

VICTORIA: It's remembering that there was something placed there. It's placed there and it's taken out more than once. It feels like a . . . It's a pressure that feels like it makes something stop or turn on or something. I don't know what it's supposed to do. Maybe it records whatever they want.

DR. FIORE: Are you saying that it's embedded in your flesh somehow?

VICTORIA: Somehow it's there. It's either something embedded or it's something they have that can control. But it's more powerful when they're present. It's a . . . it's like a fluid.

DR. FIORE: Let yourself remember when it was placed there the first time.

VICTORIA: The very first time I had an encounter with them. When I was little in Schafferstown, the very first time they came.

DR. FIORE: How did they implant it?

VICTORIA: That was when they kept telling me, "It's okay, it's okay, it's okay. We're not hurting you, it's okay." They try to make you believe they love you and that everything's okay. But it's not. They just want control. They apply something to find out what they need to find out. But it really hurts the back of your neck. [*Pauses*] I have never known fully what they want. Because they won't let you know. [*Pauses*] I feel a distance. Like I'm way out somewhere. Far out. And they're holding me there and just having me look down. Saying, "You want to go back, you do as we say." And you want to come back, so you have to do as they say. [*Cries a little*] Every time that door opens, when they come, you have no control. It just pulls you in.

DR. FIORE: When you say the door opens, what door is that?

VICTORIA: The door on the ship. It comes down and they draw you in. They don't come out, they just have a power that pulls you in.

DR. FIORE: Where are you when this happens?

VICTORIA: I've been in different places. At home.

DR. FIORE: How do you get from your home to the ship?

VICTORIA: This glow is all around, and the glow just pulls you into the ship.

DR. FIORE: What color is the glow?

VICTORIA: Red.

DR. FIORE:   Tell me how you would get from your bedroom into the ship. Tell me exactly how that would happen.

VICTORIA:   Usually I see the glow and get up and I remember I'm afraid. Then I look to see what the glow is. And then I don't remember anymore. I don't remember. I just remember the glow pulling me to the glow, and when I look at it, I don't remember anything until I'm on the ship. I can remember trying to hide from it and saying, "I'm not going to look. It's not there, it's my imagination." But something always makes me look.

DR. FIORE:   Let yourself go to anything else that is causing you anxiety or depression in regard to the drawing you were doing. Anything else that was being stirred up in you. At the count of three. One . . . two . . . three.

VICTORIA:   The tubes they have attached to my hand.

DR. FIORE:   Tell me more about this attachment.

VICTORIA:   In the tubes are different chemicals or something that they use. Each one has a different substance. And they control the substances and what they want to use from a big panel.

DR. FIORE:   Where does this tube enter your body?

VICTORIA:   They enter your hand on the top. They go into the vein.

DR. FIORE:   Do you feel anything when this is put in there?

VICTORIA:   You feel different. With each one you feel different.

DR. FIORE:   Tell me about that.

VICTORIA: With some, you shake. With others, you're cold. With others, you're numb. Then you can get hot. And then with some you can't feel at all. And then they have a wire or some type of tube that's fastened by your heart, on your breast. On your navel. And usually three tubes that go into your pelvis. They control what they're doing with these with what they put in your hand.

DR. FIORE: How old are you when this is being done?

VICTORIA: I'm in my twenties.

DR. FIORE: How many times has this been done to you?

VICTORIA: Ten.

DR. FIORE: Do they give you an explanation?

VICTORIA: They need what I have.

DR. FIORE: Are they communicating with you?

VICTORIA: They're just taking what I have. They want to try to reproduce us . . . there. And become them, so they can mingle here and not be noticed.

DR. FIORE: How do you know this?

VICTORIA: They told me. That's why they're going to use . . . they can reproduce us by getting the reproduction from . . . eggs from us and the sperm from the men, and reproduce us on their ships, and that's what's scary, because you never know, and you hope that . . . you don't want to be one of them.

DR. FIORE: What do you mean by that?

VICTORIA: You don't want to be one of them. You don't want to be the ones they've reproduced. And when they're taking all of this, you wonder if you are or not. [*Cries*] But they won't tell you if you are or not. And you've got that fear that you are, and you don't want to be. [*Cries harder*] You don't know. You don't know! [*Sobs*] And you don't know if you are or if it's good or bad.

DR. FIORE:  But you remember being brought up by your family, don't you?

VICTORIA:  Yes.

DR. FIORE:  And there are pictures of you when you were an infant?

VICTORIA:  Yes.

DR. FIORE:  So obviously they did not raise you through those years.

VICTORIA:  That's right. But they still took me on their ship.

DR. FIORE:  They took you on their ship, as they have taken hundreds, maybe thousands of people on their ships, because they're studying us. And when you became older, they wanted something from you, they wanted your eggs. But that does not make you one of them, does it?

VICTORIA:  No.

DR. FIORE:  Do you have the genetic qualities of both of your parents?

VICTORIA:  Yes. And I've been afraid that they can make me have those, so I'd think I belong here.

DR. FIORE:   Does your mother remember being pregnant with you?

VICTORIA:   Yes. I am from here. [*Cries in relief*]

DR. FIORE:   I'd like you to look at the very cause of your greatest fears. At the count of three. One . . . two . . . three.

VICTORIA:   The fear of who they were going to reproduce with my eggs. The fear of what they were going to do with them. [*Cries*] And that they were part me, but they didn't belong to me anymore. They weren't mine. [*Cries harder*]

DR. FIORE:   So what you didn't like was the lack of control over the outcome for your eggs, is that right?

VICTORIA:   Right. I just wanted them to leave me alone.

DR. FIORE:   And you believe that the white light can protect you from them?

VICTORIA:   I believe it can, but I feel . . . this week, when I tried to protect myself from them, I had a hard time concentrating on the white light, and I was afraid it wasn't strong enough. In my mind, I kept trying to make it stronger and stronger and stronger all week.

✦

Victoria wiped her eyes with her hands and then took the tissue I offered her. "I do feel better. I'm much calmer now. I feel I can finish the drawings. I'll have them for you next time."

"Please notice if you have any problem with them. There may still be something you haven't dealt with. The proof of the pudding is in the eating."

✦

I called Victoria to see how she was doing as I finished writing up her material. I had taken off two weeks to finish the manuscript, and so it had been three weeks since we last met.

She reported that she hadn't been depressed at all. In fact, things had gone well for her, despite some stress from family problems. The weight she had regained on a vacation, she had lost as soon as she was home . . . without dieting. She feels her eating is now under control.

She had been able to easily finish the pictures for *Encounters* and while she was drawing the spacecraft, she remembered something new. As she was brought to the opened underside of the UFO, there was a very strong light that came out of it that "pulled" her into the ship.

She said in closing, "I feel resolved about the abductions. There's no fear anymore. No depression. I just have a feeling that there's a reason why I chose to have those experiences."

# "To Be Back . . . Would Be Fabulous!"

 "I've always had a deep and abiding interest in UFOs. Ever since I was a kid, I was interested in exploring beyond this earth." Dan, an attractive blond man in his mid-forties, seemed very comfortable talking about the topic that was the reason for our meeting. I had invited him to explore the possibility of a close encounter of the fourth kind.

Dan was a friend of Gloria, whom you met in Chapter Nine. In fact, he was the only person she allowed herself to confide in. She had mentioned him and his openness to the whole subject of UFOs and extraterrestrials many times during our work together. I had a hunch that he himself might have had encounters, so I asked her to have him call me if he wanted to look into his interest in depth.

"Dan, is there anything that you feel you've experienced that could be evidence of a close encounter of the fourth kind? CEIVs are when someone's been abducted or contacted. It's always fasci-

230

nating to find out what a person remembers or understands before
we use hypnosis, compared to what comes out later. For example,
have you had any dreams of UFOs?"

"No, and I've never even seen one. That's a big frustration. I
fly and I'm always scanning the night and day sky. But nothing, so
far." He chuckled and added, "But I keep hoping."

"I do the same thing. I travel long distances a lot, on planes,
and I usually take the red-eye. I'm always looking out the window,
but I've never seen one either. Is there anything that gives you a
clue about a possible CEIV?"

"I don't accept anything on blind faith. I try to remain open
and objective. But it's odd. I've always had the feeling that I'm
not native to here. Every time I look at the night sky, I have a
nostalgic feeling, really at a gut-level, that I want to go home."
Dan's voice had become softer, filled with emotion. I wouldn't
have been surprised to see tears brimming in his eyes.

Dan continued to discuss his interest in flying. As a child, he
spent hours building model airplanes, and, since he lived near
Boeing Aircraft, he "hung around" planes as much as possible.
They were the love of his young life. He started flying in high
school, with a friend who was a pilot, and soon got his license.

"Do you have any interest in sci-fi, Dan?" We had just a little
time left before we had to begin using hypnosis, and I felt this
might give us a clue.

"I've read a lot of sci-fi, but I don't feel a kinship with it.
Except one thing. It boggled my mind. I have always noticed
Chesley Bonestell's work—do you know it?"

I shook my head. Science fiction doesn't hold an interest for
me.

"He's a sci-fi illustrator and did covers with planets on them.
This was even before Sputnik. When the close-ups came in from
Pioneer and others, his paintings, done long before, were perfectly
accurate. For example, he was dead-on with the colors and patterns on Jupiter. That stunned me!"

I would have enjoyed talking with Dan for hours, but we had
work to do. I explained hypnosis to him, since he'd never experienced it. After a few minutes of suggestions to relax, I could see

his body letting go of tensions as he concentrated on his breathing and listened to my voice. When the hypnotic induction was completed, I set up finger signals and asked him about CEIVs. His inner mind, through his "yes" and "no" fingers, told me that he had had 627 CEIVs! My policy is to keep an open mind, so I recorded the number on my notepad and then asked him to go to a particularly important encounter.

⬦

DAN:   I'm inside, waiting to get out. Nobody's around, just me. I'm waiting for some sort of a signal. Or an okay, a release. It's like I'm leaving an office. I go out into the corridor through the door, down to the docking base . . . Aboard a ship . . . [*Pauses*] We make dirt in twenty minutes.

DR. FIORE:   What do you mean by that?

DAN:   We land, from orbit, drop. And clean everything out. Nothing's standing. Nothing's left. Totally. Everything's gone.

DR. FIORE:   What do you mean by that?

DAN:   It was a small settlement. It's gone.

DR. FIORE:   What happened?

DAN:   We wiped it out.

DR. FIORE:   Where was that settlement?

DAN:   It was on the seacoast, small bay, flat ground.

DR. FIORE:   What was your role in it?

DAN:   Captain, one of the landing ships.

DR. FIORE:   Do you know the reason why you did this?

DAN:   Orders. I never saw the people, if there were any.

DR. FIORE:   How did you wipe them out?

DAN:   Weapons.

DR. FIORE:   What kind of weapons did you use?

DAN:   Force beam.

DR. FIORE:   Do you have any remorse about doing this?

DAN:   None. Duty.

DR. FIORE:   This was on a seacoast. Whereabouts?

DAN:   Deneb. System Deneb. Third planet. Easy job. No resistance.

DR. FIORE:   Have you done this sort of thing before?

DAN:   Many times.

DR. FIORE:   Do you know the real purpose for doing this?

DAN:   Control. Planetary control. Teach them a lesson. They're terrified of us. It doesn't take too many.

DR. FIORE:   What do you mean by that?

DAN:   Drop out of the sky and kill a few and leave. The rest of them come around, real quick. Kind of fun, if you don't think about it. Now I remember where I've seen that red sky before.

DR. FIORE:   Where?

DAN: Curious atmospheric phenomenon, not on Deneb, not in that system. Another drop, another time. [*Pauses*] No problems, no losses. One guy hurt.

DR. FIORE: Do you sometimes have losses?

DAN: Rarely. Occasionally a mistake. Somebody screws up. Somebody dies. Nobody has the weapons we have. Occasionally they get lucky. It costs them. [*Pauses*] Hop in the bay and everybody's laughing, kidding around, cleaning their boots. Decontamination. Some of them are nasty. The guys joking about finding a planet with nothing but women. The women joking about finding a planet with nothing but guys. Everybody hungry. Go to mess. Settle down into the ship routine. Two weeks till the next one. Not much to do between them. Nobody's told us where we're going yet. It doesn't make any difference. We don't know where they send us. Not a bad life, really. Better than being on one of those planets we hit. A lot of fun on the ship.

DR. FIORE: Tell me about that.

DAN: Mixed crew. Women get wired from the combat. Keeps you busy for the first three or four days after. Then the captain usually squashes things a little bit, calms us down, gets us ready for the next one, back to training. Briefing films, tapes, precautions. Weapons status of the planet. Their level. How far along. What's dominant. What to shoot and what to leave alone. Some of them aren't humanoid. Weird. Everything thinks the same. Everything wants to live. It doesn't make any difference where you go, same story. Kind of fun.

DR. FIORE: Did you ever have any feelings for the planet Earth?

DAN: I don't know it. I've never been there. They'd know it if we got there. [*Pauses*]

DR. FIORE: What are you doing now?

DAN: Relaxing in my room, looking at tapes, reviewing them. The landing formation, seeing why that guy got hurt. See if we can keep it from happening next time. He could have been killed. The stupid shit fell out of the ship, missed the gangway. Full gear, into the ground, face first. Doesn't happen very often. New recruit. He'll fall into it. He won't forget that one. Hell of a thing to happen on your first drop. Kind of funny, watching the tape of him taking a fall. He don't look quite as good as he did when he left. Some gal someplace will like it. [*Pauses*]

DR. FIORE: Just let yourself relax deeper and deeper. We're going to move now to the first time that you were aware of the planet Earth. At the count of five. One . . . two . . . three . . . four . . . five.

DAN: Standing in the middle of a logging trail. Washington State Cascades. Looking at the Douglas fir. Watching the clouds move through the tops of the trees, smelling them, listening to the animals in the bushes. First time out. It's beautiful.

DR. FIORE: What kind of preparation have you had for this?

DAN: None. Woods behind the house. Just kind of took off, took a walk. [*Pauses*] Just walking up the trail, the road, really. They don't log there anymore. Nobody out there. Nothing around, really nice. Peaceful, quiet. All alone.

DR. FIORE: Why are you there?

DAN: Just to see what's there.

DR. FIORE: And where's your ship?

DAN: I'm a little kid, no ship, no responsibility. Just a nice summer day. Nothing to do. All day to do it. Just exploring.

DR. FIORE:   Now we see you as this child. I'm going to ask you to make the connection of how you became this child.

DAN:   Two different people. The child has all the memories. It's like retirement. You get a chance to do nothing if you live longer. Be at a nice pretty place.

DR. FIORE:   How did you get to be this child.

DAN:   I don't remember.

DR. FIORE:   I'm going to ask you to remember everything, at the count of five, we'll go to the very moment when you either joined this child or you somehow are this child. At the count of five. One . . . two . . . three . . . four . . . five.

DAN:   I joined him on that road. Replaced, really.

DR. FIORE:   Let's go back to before you joined him, and let's see how you got to be on that road.

DAN:   Drunk. Horribly, horribly drunk. Good party. Next morning . . . tour the bridge. Say goodbyes.

DR. FIORE:   Then what happens?

DAN:   Just me today. One at a time, pick your planet. Pick an easy one. Everybody's laughing.

DR. FIORE:   You say that you were drunk?

DAN:   The night before, terrible hangover.

DR. FIORE:   Where did you get drunk.

DAN:   On the ship, officers' mess . . . Confusion, drinking.

DR. FIORE:   What kind of ship is this?

DAN:   Class M. Large. Battlecruiser; fourteen drop ships; 3500 people. Armed to the teeth.

DR. FIORE:   Where are you from?

DAN:   [*Pauses*] Try and remember home; it's been a long time.

DR. FIORE:   The first ship, where does it travel?

DAN:   Space.

DR. FIORE:   And then you landed in the state of Washington, on the planet Earth, is that what you're saying?

DAN:   Never touched down.

DR. FIORE:   I see.

DAN:   No need. The ship's too recognizable.

DR. FIORE:   How did you get from that ship to the loggers' trail?

DAN:   No need for physical transport. The body never leaves the ship. The mind.

DR. FIORE:   Part of you, the mind, goes?

DAN:   Right.

DR. FIORE:   Do you know the purpose of going to that particular area?

DAN:   Retirement.

DR. FIORE:   Did you know that you would be joining the boy there?

DAN:   Sure.

DR. FIORE:   Was this all planned beforehand?

DAN:   Yes.

DR. FIORE:   Go to the very moment when you see that boy for the first time.

DAN:   From behind. He doesn't know. He couldn't see me anyway.

DR. FIORE:   Do you know the boy's first name?

DAN:   No.

DR. FIORE:   But he has been selected, this has all been planned?

DAN:   He's my choice.

DR. FIORE:   You chose him?

DAN:   No. At random. Looked around.

DR. FIORE:   Now you've seen him from the back, tell me step by step what happens.

DAN:   I replace him.

DR. FIORE:   What happens to him?

DAN:   Gone.

DR. FIORE:   How is this done?

DAN: I don't understand it.

DR. FIORE: Have you ever done this before to anyone?

DAN: I've seen others.

DR. FIORE: What do you mean?

DAN: Other retirees.

DR. FIORE: Other retirees do this?

DAN: Yes.

DR. FIORE: So you take over this boy's body, is that it?

DAN: Yes.

DR. FIORE: Do you have all of your memories from before?

DAN: You lose them, they fade with time.

DR. FIORE: Do you have his memories?

DAN: Yes.

DR. FIORE: What kind of reaction does he have when you enter him, when you take over?

DAN: Fear, then he's gone.

DR. FIORE: What does it feel like for you to be in this particular body?

DAN: Strange, very strange.

DR. FIORE: Tell me about it, in what way is it strange?

DAN:   It's small. It's not strong.

DR. FIORE:   Was your body much bigger?

DAN:   Yes, adult. Seems funny, it's so soft. [*Pauses*] Things look so pretty, though. I made a good choice. Good thing too. Can't be reversed.

DR. FIORE:   Now what happens?

DAN:   Thinking. It was a lot of fun. Wondering what's ahead. Wondering what it's going to be like here. No choice now. Just go ahead, do it. Wondering if it's a great idea or not, this method. Can't change your mind. It's kind of funny, sure changed that kid's mind, permanently. Now I'm him. I'm stuck, and no way out.

DR. FIORE:   Do you have some instructions or some game plan?

DAN:   No plan, just play it as it comes. No instructions.

DR. FIORE:   Was there some purpose in your being in this particular place, on this planet?

DAN:   No, it's just easier to get rid of retirees, than pensioning them off on the state. No welfare. It's funny, here they take care of everybody; can't get used to that.

DR. FIORE:   Are you planning to go back sometime?

DAN:   No. That won't be. They told me, only if needed. Unlikely. I wasn't that valuable. Probably be here forever.

DR. FIORE:   What are you doing now?

DAN:   Go home, go back where he lives.

DR. FIORE:   How do you know where he lives?

DAN:   I have all his memories.

DR. FIORE:   Tell me about your first minutes at his home.

DAN:   Open the door, walk in. My mother's standing there in the kitchen. Seems kind of funny. She seems nice. We get along all right. It's going to take some time for the memories to fade, become a kid again. Smells funny in the house. It's different. There's a dog. [Pauses] Kind of a lost feeling. [Pauses] I find my room. It's okay. I plop down on the bed and just relax, go to sleep.

DR. FIORE:   Move to when you wake up.

DAN:   Strange surroundings. Real strange. Hungry. I go out, she fixes me something to eat. I go out and play. [Pauses] The ship's gone, everything's gone. Put that behind me. Just forget it.

DR. FIORE:   Now what do you do?

DAN:   Go out and play. Find a friend or something. We go down by the creek. Mess around. Have fun.

DR. FIORE:   Does anyone notice anything different? Do they seem to react to you in any different way, to indicate that they know something has changed?

DAN:   No. They couldn't know.

DR. FIORE:   Why is that?

DAN:   I have all his memories, all his patterns, and mine will fade.

DR. FIORE:   How do you feel about the fact that yours will fade?

DAN: I'm sorry. I think maybe it wasn't such a great idea. I had a lot of fun. Did a lot. Saw a lot of places. Miss some of my friends. That's supposed to go away.

DR. FIORE: Is his body any different from yours, basically?

DAN: No. The same.

DR. FIORE: Are you saying that you had a human body before?

DAN: Yes.

DR. FIORE: On that ship?

DAN: Yes.

DR. FIORE: Move ahead, to a time when, as this new person, Dan, you had your first close encounter, at the count of five. One . . . two . . . three . . . four . . . five. Just report everything that comes into your mind.

DAN: There's nothing, I can't see anything.

DR. FIORE: How do you feel?

DAN: Sweaty, tingly. Tight chested.

DR. FIORE: It's all coming back to you, crystal clear.

DAN: I hope not.

DR. FIORE: Every detail of that first encounter.

DAN: I can't quite make it out . . . meeting with someone.

DR. FIORE: It's coming clearer and clearer into your mind.

DAN: He's not human, he's familiar. I'm not afraid, except for what he's going to do.

DR. FIORE: What is he going to do?

DAN: I'm not sure. He's not nice.

DR. FIORE: What do you mean by that?

DAN: He's not one of those we like. Treacherous. Hard to deal with. Wants information.

DR. FIORE: How old are you at this point?

DAN: Eighteen. I want information from him. He just laughs, won't give it to me.

DR. FIORE: Just speak out whatever you are aware of.

DAN: I don't have the information he wants. Very risky. Accidents can happen. Seems stupid, all he's asking.

DR. FIORE: What is he asking?

DAN: I only remember that it seems so dumb. Probably a test. There's nothing here he wants. [*Pauses*] These people are backward. He must be just testing. He leaves me alone. It's a good thing nobody here can see him, they'd have nightmares for a month. He's not an air-breather. I wonder why they sent him. Strange. Frightening. I hope they don't send him back. They told me they'd leave me alone. Something must have gone wrong. I can't remember enough about it to do anything. I can't even remember how to build a goddamn weapon. It's awful. Can't defend myself. I don't want to have that experience again. I'm glad it's over.

DR. FIORE: What happened?

DAN: Just interrogated.

DR. FIORE: And where are you now?

DAN: Standing someplace, at a school crossing.

DR. FIORE: It's all crystal clear in your mind. You're remembering everything.

DAN: On the sidewalk in front of the school. Waiting for the bus. Nobody around me notices anything. Everything's fine, back to normal.

DR. FIORE: Where were you when you were interrogated?

DAN: Not sure.

DR. FIORE: Let yourself remember the very beginning of this interrogation, of this encounter.

DAN: Mental interrogation.

DR. FIORE: What's the very first thing you notice?

DAN: This face in my mind.

DR. FIORE: How do you feel when you see that face?

DAN: Oh shit! It's not supposed to happen.

DR. FIORE: So you're remembering.

DAN: They said they'd leave me alone. I want to go back. Not with this guy. [Pauses] Maybe if I give him the right kind of lie I can get out of it. I don't have the information he wants anyway.

DR. FIORE: What kind of information does he want?

DAN:  It seems stupid.

DR. FIORE:  What is he asking you?

DAN:  I can't remember.

DR. FIORE:  You're going to allow yourself to remember, at the count of three. One . . . two . . . three.

DAN:  He did a good job. He was good at what he did. I can't remember. I don't know what he wanted.

DR. FIORE:  Why do you say he was good at what he did?

DAN:  He took the memory with him.

DR. FIORE:  Do you feel that maybe he created amnesia in you?

DAN:  No, he just took the memory, that part.

DR. FIORE:  Now you're going to go to the very next encounter, at the count of three, whatever form that encounter takes. One . . . two . . . three. First thoughts.

DAN:  My old captain, friend, familiar. Good person. He apologizes. For being there. Just a chat. Against the rules. The other side's worried. That's why the questions seemed dumb. They're paranoid.

DR. FIORE:  Is he explaining this to you?

DAN:  He's asking me what he asked. And I'm telling him. But I don't remember what I told him. That part's gone.

DR. FIORE:  Do you want it to be gone?

DAN:  No. I want to remember it.

DR. FIORE:   Then you'll be able to remember it. You see, they can't take the memory away.

DAN:   They can take the memory. Just as I replaced the child. The memory can be erased.

DR. FIORE:   Did you tell your captain what he asked?

DAN:   No, I didn't. I couldn't tell him.

DR. FIORE:   Does your captain give you any instructions?

DAN:   Not to talk to them again. I laugh and tell him that I have no choice. He laughs and tells me to get drunk, I'll feel better. And goes away.

DR. FIORE:   How did you make this contact with him?

DAN:   Mental. I'm in bed.

DR. FIORE:   How soon after the first contact is this?

DAN:   A couple of weeks.

DR. FIORE:   Now move to your very next contact.

DAN:   I don't think I want to remember that one.

DR. FIORE:   Why do you say that?

DAN:   Just not a good memory.

DR. FIORE:   Is it frightening?

DAN:   I don't know if it's frightening or it's bad or wrong, or . . . what. Just doesn't want to come, and I don't want it to.

DR. FIORE: Okay, that's fine. You're in charge of what you remember and what you don't want to remember. Let's move you to a memory of an encounter that's perhaps more recent, that you do want to remember, one that you will allow yourself to remember, at the count of three. One . . . two . . . three.

DAN: I open the front door, and there's one of them standing there. I never met this one. He's humanoid. I know the type. I'm not afraid. They're not violent. Intellectuals.

DR. FIORE: What does he look like?

DAN: Silver. The suit. It's not really that way. They need protection. He comes in. We sit and talk. Old times.

DR. FIORE: Does he realize that you've replaced the boy?

DAN: Yes. He knows me. I don't know him. He's been reading records.

DR. FIORE: What do you talk about?

DAN: He's asking me what's going on. What I'm doing. How I like it. I'm begging him for the secrets that I used to know. He won't tell me. I can understand he wouldn't give me the weapon. I'm trying to get him to tell me. It's so simple. I can't remember. So damn simple a child could build one, and I can't remember. I can't remember the damn way to put the thing together, and he's not helping me.

DR. FIORE: What is the purpose of that weapon?

DAN: It's not a weapon.

DR. FIORE: What is it?

DAN:   It's the drive for the ship. It's simple, so simple. And I tell him I think I can come up with everything I need here. And he won't tell me. He just laughs and says, you made your deal, you're stuck. And I tell him I'm not stuck or they wouldn't keep coming back. It's pointless to argue with those people.

DR. FIORE:   Why is that?

DAN:   They're too intelligent and they're way ahead of you.

DR. FIORE:   What does he look like?

DAN:   If you peel off the suit, it'd be brown. Rather large eyes, small mouth. Pretty nose. Slight build.

DR. FIORE:   What color is his skin?

DAN:   Brown. Doesn't tolerate temperature extremes well.

DR. FIORE:   Is any part of his skin exposed, or is it covered?

DAN:   It's covered. Just holes for the eyes. They're not really holes. They've got . . . covering across them, just to protect them.

DR. FIORE:   What color does his skin look like with the suit on?

DAN:   Silver.

DR. FIORE:   But underneath it's brown?

DAN:   Underneath it's brown, medium brown.

DR. FIORE:   What else do you talk about?

DAN:   Women. Differences.

DR. FIORE:   Do you feel there's more to it than just a social get-together?

DAN:   There always is with those. They only socialize with each other.

DR. FIORE:   What does he want from you?

DAN:   He seems to be interested in my attitude toward . . . my feelings about being here. He's probably some sociologist on a field trip. I tell him that. He laughs. They never give you a hint whether you got it right or not. You could guess dead-on. They never tell. Makes me nervous after a while. He's staying too long. I'm afraid somebody's going to walk in. Then he gets scared. Sees I'm nervous. And scared. Accuses me of setting a trap for him. I invite him to leave. Then he goes. A little paranoia. He's worried that the rest of the family's going to come in and find him. I tell him just sit there and I'll go get them. They'd love to meet him. Against all the rules. Can't do that. Don't think the wife could handle it anyway. The kids would love it. I don't feel him take any memories when he goes. They're pretty good, though. Huh . . . They don't usually come and go through the front door. Strange . . . Seems funny . . . Treat him like anybody else. Back in the old days, he wouldn't have even talked to me. Brings back the old feelings. I'd like to go back.

DR. FIORE:   Let's move on to another encounter, a recent one.

DAN:   Same one, only this time less chat. Same guy.

DR. FIORE:   What's happening?

DAN:   Been messing with the computer, and he's taking some printout of some program. He doesn't need it. It's a toy for him. Won't do anything for him.

DR. FIORE:   What computer is this?

DAN:   Personal computer at home.

DR. FIORE:   What's he taking?

DAN:   He's taking printouts of my programming. It's silly. I use it in my work. Probably just doing it for a laugh. He says it'll help him. Not unless he's going to retire here or what. Then he's gone.

DR. FIORE:   How did he get there?

DAN:   He didn't use the doors this time.

DR. FIORE:   What was the date when this happened?

DAN:   Twenty-fourth . . . August . . . '88.

DR. FIORE:   Move to another encounter.

DAN:   I don't know how I got here, back aboard the ship. Party time. People I haven't seen for a long time.

DR. FIORE:   What's it like for you?

DAN:   Like being alive again. Everybody's laughing at the way I'm dressed.

DR. FIORE:   What are you wearing?

DAN:   Blue jeans, cowboy boots. They made me take them off to prove my feet weren't that shape. Lots of people. Good friends. Lots of war stories. Good party. Lots of pictures. Some of the old drops. They save the one where the guy falls off the ship. He's a captain now. [*Pauses*] We get a tour of the ship, just for old times.

DR. FIORE:   Same ship?

DAN:   Same ship. Same one I served in.

DR. FIORE:   Tell me about the tour.

DAN:   Start with the bridge. All different people. Crew's changed. Look out through the windows. I remember what it was like. Just traveling. Sit up on the bridge and talk. Just watch the stars. Drop down through the ship. Past the old quarters. Down into the bay. Then home. I wanted to stay. I just wish they'd let me stay. I'm getting tired of being jerked around.

DR. FIORE:   Is there any chance of your joining them again?

DAN:   Possible. Possible. Mention drops coming up. Needed the experience. Don't have it anymore. Memories are gone. I don't know if I could get them back. [*Pauses*] I spend time with the captain. We talked in his quarters for hours.

DR. FIORE:   What do you talk about?

DAN:   I want to come back. He wants me to. Against the rules. Can't do it. He'll look into it and let me know. [*Pauses*] Talked about the big drop out on the far side. Sounded like old times.

DR. FIORE:   What do you mean by drop?

DAN:   Swing into orbit. Set up. Load up. Open the bays, let enough landing ships out to do the job. Drop down through the atmosphere.

DR. FIORE:   Are these drops always hostile?

DAN:   Always. That's what makes it so much fun.

DR. FIORE:   How many ships are involved in the big drop?

DAN:   Four or five ships.

DR. FIORE:  How many men are in each ship?

DAN:  Thirty-five hundred. All class M. Go for it. All fourteen, each ship.

DR. FIORE:  Fourteen smaller craft in each ship?

DAN:  Yes.

DR. FIORE:  And how many personnel in each smaller craft?

DAN:  A hundred. One hundred people on that ship, take care of anything.

DR. FIORE:  The big ships hold 3500 people?

DAN:  Yes.

DR. FIORE:  How big are they?

DAN:  A mile and a half long, approximately.

DR. FIORE:  What shape are they?

DAN:  Basically, hard to describe.

DR. FIORE:  Are the big ships circular or disc shaped?

DAN:  No. That shape won't work in the atmosphere.

DR. FIORE:  Are you interested in the big drop the captain talked about?

DAN:  Yes. Sounds like a good time.

DR. FIORE:  What will happen?

DAN: Showed me reconnaissance photos. Have to take on about three cities at a time. I don't know what these people did. Must have been bad, because they want that place clean.

DR. FIORE: Do you know what planet that was on?

DAN: No.

DR. FIORE: Do you know what galaxy it's in?

DAN: Same galaxy as Earth, other side. Out on one of the arms. I don't think Earth has a name for it.

DR. FIORE: When will it occur?

DAN: It's coming up. There won't be any resistance. Big operation.

DR. FIORE: Would they make a drop on Earth?

DAN: No, they won't. There's no need to.

DR. FIORE: Why is that?

DAN: Earth is of no significance.

DR. FIORE: Tell me more about that last experience, that encounter.

DAN: I had a couple of drinks with the captain. Says they want somebody to coordinate it. I ask him why he didn't. He says he was told to ask me. I ask him how he's going to do it, since it's against the rules. He says he doesn't know. We're getting a little drunk and a little confused at this point. I think we're getting a little fuzzy. All I can think of is that it sounded like fun. I need the excitement, to feel alive again. Then the discussion's over.

Nothing's resolved. Go down the corridor. Down a deck. And I'm home.

DR. FIORE:    How do you get home? Let yourself remember that.

DAN:    Through the door. Close the door behind you, and you're there.

DR. FIORE:    How do you get from that ship to your own home?

DAN:    I don't know how it works.

DR. FIORE:    You're going to let yourself remember.

DAN:    I don't think I ever knew. It's too technical.

DR. FIORE:    Were you taken on another ship?

DAN:    No, there's no transport. You simply walk in the door and close the door behind you. When you close the door, you're there.

DR. FIORE:    When you're there, do you remember what you've just experienced?

DAN:    Briefly. I remember it's unnerving. Sudden change of scene. I didn't realize I hated to travel that way.

DR. FIORE:    Let yourself remember another encounter on the ship.

DAN:    Just once in a while, the parties. They played some tapes of some of the things I was involved in. Showed the pictures. Got a chance to relive the old days. That was fun.

DR. FIORE:    Let yourself remember if you've ever had any close encounters on a different ship.

DAN:   Shore leave. [*Pauses*] Lots of different places. Different races. [*Pauses*] Not too much visiting between the ships. Most of the time too far out. Only when you come back. Too many people to know them all. [*Pauses*] Don't talk too much to the other people on the other ships, no chance, no opportunity.

DR. FIORE:   When did this happen? Did this happen after you assumed the body of Dan?

DAN:   No.

DR. FIORE:   Before.

DAN:   Yes.

DR. FIORE:   After you took on the body of Dan, the identity, have you had any other close encounters with other types of extraterrestrials?

DAN:   Just the intellectual and the treacherous ones. Those are the only two that I've seen.

DR. FIORE:   Are you ready now to remember that encounter that you avoided before?

DAN:   I don't like that one. I don't like that one at all.

DR. FIORE:   Let yourself remember a little something about it.

DAN:   If I had the right weapon, I'd kill him.

DR. FIORE:   What was he like?

DAN:   All I remember is the protruding face, oversized teeth. A coarse fur. Grease. Stink.

DR. FIORE:   Where did this encounter take place?

DAN: I don't know where it took place.

DR. FIORE: Did it take place in your home, or on the ship, or outside?

DAN: I think this one was mental. That one couldn't ever come down here.

DR. FIORE: Why is that?

DAN: He'd never be able to fit in, never blend. He just couldn't do it. He's too strange. He wouldn't want to anyway.

DR. FIORE: You've run into that type before?

DAN: Yes.

DR. FIORE: Was that before you came into Dan's body?

DAN: Yes.

DR. FIORE: Will there be any drops on planet Earth? Or have there been in the past?

DAN: No, not to my knowledge. Earth is backwater, it's the outback. It's a retirement planet.

DR. FIORE: Do you feel like there's many people here who are retirees?

DAN: Probably quite a few.

DR. FIORE: In your last encounter with the intellectual type who wanted the printout, did he want actual paper from your printer?

DAN: Yes.

DR. FIORE:   And why did he want it?

DAN:   I have no idea why he'd want it. It doesn't seem to make any sense. Of course, with them, you never know.

DR. FIORE:   Was there something unusual you had printed out?

DAN:   No. It was just basic language programming. He doesn't even need programming. I don't understand why he would even want it. Maybe a curio.

DR. FIORE:   He was there in your room?

DAN:   Yes.

DR. FIORE:   Did he sit down at the computer?

DAN:   No, he just stood beside me. Watched me work. Asked me to print it out, so I did.

DR. FIORE:   Did you give it to him?

DAN:   Yes, there's no harm in it. He can't do anything with what he got. At least not that I know of.

DR. FIORE:   You've seen the cover of the book *Communion*?

DAN:   Yes.

DR. FIORE:   Does that face look familiar? Does it look like anything that you'd recognize?

DAN:   Similar, but it's very elongated. Eyes are much too big.

DR. FIORE:   Is there anything else you want to remember?

DAN:   I could spend all night going over the ship, I love it.

DR. FIORE:  Why don't you describe the ship some more. Where did you sleep?

DAN:  A bed about the size of a single bed, adjustable, at an angle, so you could read. Screen on the wall. So you could watch entertainment or reviews, whatever.

DR. FIORE:  Was there other furniture?

DAN:  Yes, same kind of things. And . . . storage cabinet. If you walk in the door, it's to your right. Bed straight ahead. View screen on the right-hand wall. Storage cabinet in the right-hand corner. Locking drawers. Very plain, maybe ten by twelve.

DR. FIORE:  What are the walls like?

DAN:  Painted, feels like steel.

DR. FIORE:  You said painted?

DAN:  It's painted over.

DR. FIORE:  What's on the floor?

DAN:  Carpet.

DR. FIORE:  What color is it?

DAN:  Dark brown, cream-colored walls. Whole ceiling illuminated. Adjustable switch by the door, and one by the bed.

DR. FIORE:  When you're on this ship, how long is your tour of duty?

DAN:  A year.

DR. FIORE:  And then what happens?

DAN: Rotate back to base, shore leave, then another year.

DR. FIORE: Is that on your home planet?

DAN: No. It's a station.

DR. FIORE: In space.

DAN: Yes. Trying to remember how long. It's been a long time.

DR. FIORE: When you're on this ship, are there women, as well as men?

DAN: Oh yes.

DR. FIORE: What's the function of the women?

DAN: Same as the men. Fight. Any duty the man does.

DR. FIORE: You were talking about having a party, with alcohol.

DAN: Yes.

DR. FIORE: What kind of food do you eat?

DAN: I'm trying to remember.

DR. FIORE: Just try to remember a meal, sitting down to a meal. Maybe it's a special meal.

DAN: I'm trying to remember eating in my quarters.

DR. FIORE: Is that where you ate?

DAN: Yes. Not always. I'm just trying to remember sitting on the bunk, eating, a metal tray with about eight compartments cut into it, like a stamp, like an aluminum-foil tray.

DR. FIORE: And what utensils do you use?

DAN: It's like a fork, sharp on one edge, for cutting. And . . . food's pretty similar, looks a little bit different.

DR. FIORE: Do you eat meat?

DAN: Yes.

DR. FIORE: Vegetables or fruits?

DAN: Yes, vegetables, some fruits. Some special treats. Takes a lot to feed them.

DR. FIORE: What do you mean?

DAN: It takes a lot to feed a ship that size.

DR. FIORE: Do you have sexual contacts between the men and the women?

DAN: Every chance we get.

DR. FIORE: Is there any homosexuality?

DAN: Some.

DR. FIORE: And how is that seen?

DAN: Tolerated. Not favorably, but tolerated.

DR. FIORE: Is there any problem with contraception?

DAN: No.

DR. FIORE: Why is that?

DAN:   Medicines, injections.

DR. FIORE:   How often is it given?

DAN:   Every tour.

DR. FIORE:   Just once?

DAN:   Just once.

DR. FIORE:   When you're back at the home base, do you have sexual contact with the crew?

DAN:   Yes. It's part of the normal routine.

DR. FIORE:   Do you have one partner, or do you have many partners?

DAN:   Individual preference. Some pair up. It's not a good idea. You get too attached. They get killed, and you go nuts. You'll become ineffective. Doesn't work.

DR. FIORE:   So it's discouraged?

DAN:   It's not discouraged. Most people just assume it's not going to work, they can't get that close to somebody.

DR. FIORE:   How are they killed?

DAN:   Somebody screws up on a drop.

DR. FIORE:   What percent per drop have some kind of injury?

DAN:   Drop a hundred in, somebody might stub their toe. Occasionally you lose one.

DR. FIORE:   How many drops do you have, say, per year?

DAN:   One every two to five weeks.

DR. FIORE:   What is the biggest drop that you were ever involved in?

DAN:   Two ships.

✎

When Dan came out of hypnosis, it was nine o'clock and black outside my window. The lighting was dim in the room, and we both had skipped dinner, so there was a feeling of it being later than it was. My day at the office is usually over at five, six o'clock at the latest, so it was an unusual feeling to be there at that hour.

Dan stretched and rubbed his eyes as though waking up from a nap. I asked him how he felt.

"Like a thoroughly dangerous person until I realized exactly where I am. The regression put me back into a different mind-set. It's not one you carry around with you, except in a situation where you are allowed to kill, and where you are rewarded for it. It's your job, being a soldier."

"Dan, were you ever in that situation in this lifetime? Were you in the service?" So many of his terms sounded like Navy jargon to me, that I was sure he would reply in the affirmative. In fact, because of terms like "bridge," "bay," etc., I had wondered at one point if he weren't retired from a professional career in the Navy.

"No, thank God! I'm glad that I never got into the service here, because I knew intuitively, even long before this session, that I would have enjoyed it too much. I don't know if I would have been able to make the transition from one minute you're killing somebody in some field in Asia, and three days later you're back on the streets in America. I don't know if I could have done that."

He commented on how his conscious mind had constantly critiqued the material that was coming forth. (I quoted him at some length in Chapter One.) My favorite line was, "It's a very strange

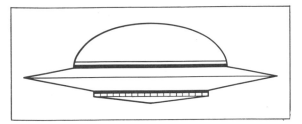

The alien space shuttle used to transport Ted to and from the space colony (Chapter Eight).

The spacecrafts that Victoria was taken to for the extraction of her eggs (Chapter Eleven).

Linda was taken to this space colony via a smaller craft (Chapter Six).

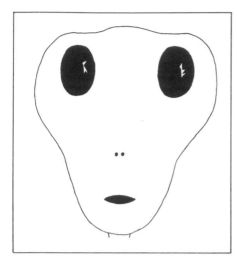

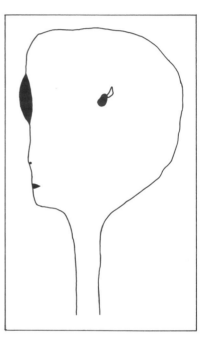

Face-forward and profile views of the extraterrestrial who communicated with Mark on the spacecraft (Chapter Three).

Gloria's sketch of the teacher who was in charge (Chapter Nine).

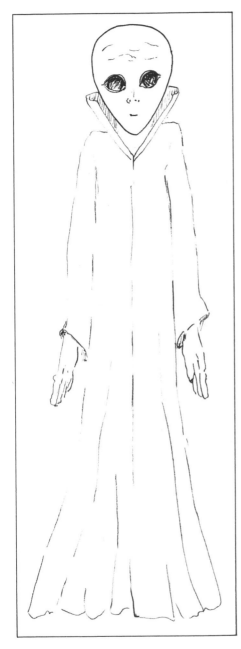

A part-amphibian, part-humanoid female alien Ted encountered on the shuttle (Chapter Eight).

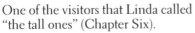

One of the visitors that Linda called "the tall ones" (Chapter Six).

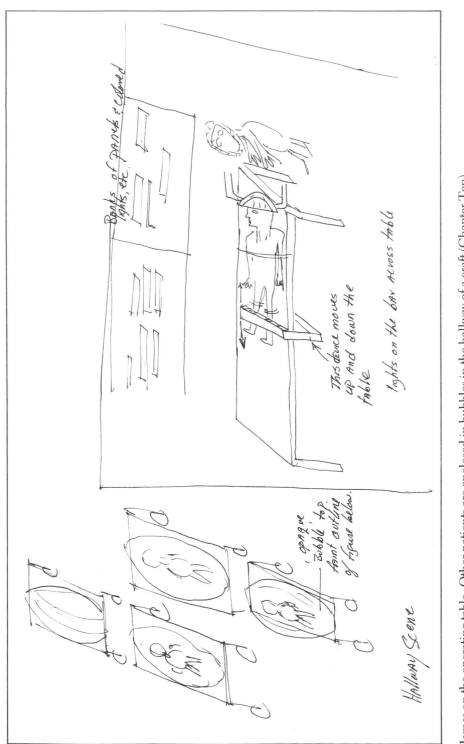

Banks of panels e others
lights, etc.

This device moves
up and down the
table

lights on the bar across table

opaque
"Bubble" top
front outline
of figure below.

Hallway Scene

James on the operating table. Other patients are enclosed in bubbles in the hallway of a craft (Chapter Ten).

Victoria observing her body as her eggs are being removed (Chapter Eleven).

Sandi's view during her examination of the interior of the room and the night sky outside (Chapter Two).

The medical instrument with a crystal on one end that was used on Linda (Chapter Six).

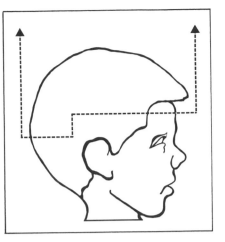

Ted's skull was cut by lasers along the dotted lines and removed before the operation (Chapter Eight).

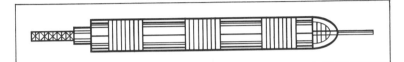

The laser instrument that cut and later welded back together Ted's skull. During the surgery it disintegrated Ted's tumor (Chapter Eight).

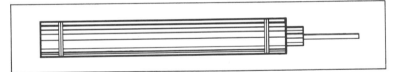

This medical instrument, an energy indicator, was used to probe Ted's skull (Chapter Eight).

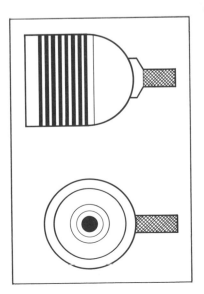

Two views of the suction device used during Ted's surgery (Chapter Eight).

Linda with other contactees and visitors in front of the healing crystal
(Chapter Six).

feeling, like your mouth is operating on its own, and your mind is saying, 'Shut up, you idiot!' "

I reassured him that he had done an excellent job of just letting it flow. I felt that his conscious-mind analysis hadn't interfered at all.

"It was an interesting experience. I didn't know that I would still be aware of my body, as much as I was. I was amazed at the physical reactions to the memories."

This intrigued me and added to my impression that it was not just one big fantasy.

"There was great tensing of the muscles. Like the fight-or-flight reflex. This feeling that you're sweating, but you're not."

"Did you feel any anxiety?"

"Yes. But much to my discredit here on Earth, I felt a lot of fun too. A lot of joy at making the drop, going in, hitting the dirt, going out, and feeling alive and like this was great fun. And that's not exactly your Saturday night entertainment in San Jose, California." He laughed heartily.

It was time to stop for the evening, but we decided to get together one more time to see what else we could find.

❧

Two weeks later we met again at the end of the day. I wanted to have plenty of time available in case we needed it. The last time he'd been under hypnosis for almost two hours, which is long for one sitting.

"Dan, how did you feel when you left here?"

"On a real high. I was very comfortable with it. It put everything into place, nice and neat. Everything's explained now. I don't worry about where I came from or what I'm doing here." Dan seemed relaxed and excited at the same time. Our session had obviously been a very positive experience for him.

"Have you noticed any changes in yourself? I know it's only been two weeks, but sometimes these regressions lead to rather dramatic results immediately."

"One of the smaller changes has been not worrying about things nearly as much. They don't seem as important as they used to. I'm more able to deal with crises that are going on around me. I seem to be a more objective observer, rather than a panic-stricken participant. I think that, coupled with having some of the answers, has given me more self-confidence. I'm a little more assertive than I was, simply because there's not this great sense of having something to lose. To sum up, I think that one of the major changes is an increase in self-confidence."

I was curious about how his self-confidence could have been so enhanced. I suspected his identifying with who he had been before he took over Dan's body was the obvious answer, but I was interested in his insight into the change. "What do you feel caused you to feel more self-confident?"

"It's due to his character. There was *no* lack of self-confidence. I don't feel an arrogance, but rather a surety in his own mind of a near invincibility. And he never had to deal with anything that he couldn't overcome through superior force or any other means. I think realizing that side has filled in the self-confidence a lot. I know I came out of here just really hyped. I really enjoyed it. I felt good. When I talk about it now, I still get tingles up and down the spine, and it still fills me with a sense of power and strength." He looked up at me gratefully. "It was great. I don't think, when we separated last time, you realized how much it had done for me."

I felt extremely happy that he had gotten so much out of the session. I knew his material was really exceptional and different from the other cases I'd be presenting in *Encounters,* and I was more than glad that it was so rewarding for him.

As I was covering Dan with the blanket, I explained that his body temperature would probably drop when in hypnosis. He suddenly remembered something. He was already in a reclining position, so I asked him to sit back up and not let it wait for later.

"I'm not sure, Edee, what this means, but I think it has to do with what we've been working on. When I'm asleep, my body temperature and my heart rate and my respiration will drop way below normal levels. If you were to touch me, I would be quite cold to the touch. It's scared the living chickens out of the wife a number of times when she touched me in the middle of the night. She couldn't wake me. And she was afraid I was gone. She told me she put her hand on my chest to make sure I was breathing. I was, but very slowly. In that stage, if I'm awakened, brought out of it suddenly by a calamity or a sudden loud noise, I can't see for two or three minutes. I'll run into walls. I can barely coordinate to walk. It's almost like I'm so deep asleep that it just won't come back. But it never bothers me. It's never given me any difficulty or problems. It is so restful." Finishing, Dan looked almost blissful. Then he glanced over to me for an explanation.

"It sounds like you're out of your body at those times. The physical body goes almost into a state of suspended animation while your energy is being used in your other body. The other body's called by various names, mainly an "astral" body, because even in ancient times, it was understood that this body was capable of traveling through the stars, while the physical body remained where it was. This traveling is called, "out-of-the-body" travel or astral projection. You're right that it's related to what we found out last time, because you did remember visiting the spaceship and the space station. So you probably did it in your astral body."

Again, I pushed Dan's chair back to its fullest reclining position. I made a special effort to tuck him in with the blanket, since his body temperature would undoubtedly drop more than most people's do when they're under hypnosis. I wasn't expecting him to leave his body, but I wasn't taking any chances of his being chilled, if he did, as has happened before with some of my patients, while in a particularly deep trance.

Once he was hypnotized, I asked his inner mind to take him to an especially significant event. I wanted to leave the suggestions fairly undefined in order not to miss something important to him. I counted him back in time and space and asked him to speak out whatever came into his mind.

❦

DAN: I'm kneeling next to an open hatch, with another man, looking into the side at the machinery. Neither one of us knows what's wrong. We're trying to figure it out. I can't come up with the answer. Something's wrong with the ship. It's not working right. We're worried about being stranded. Neither one of us is an engineer. Can't repair the silly thing. We're under pressure of some sort. Need to get out of there. We're struggling to fix it, do something with it. Neither one of us understands what. I can't seem to quite get it done.

DR. FIORE: Is there anyone else there with you, on the ship?

DAN: It's just us at the hatch. On the outside. The ship's on the ground.

DR. FIORE: Where is it?

DAN: It's in a forest.

DR. FIORE: Do you know the name of the planet you're on?

DAN: Something like Markel. It's getting dark. We give up and close the hatch and go inside. Some success; it lifts. We make it back. Laughing at our success. But we didn't even know what we were doing. Complicated things.

DR. FIORE: What did you actually do?

DAN: Reached in and . . . just tugged and pulled, twisted and wiggled things around, looking for loose tubing, connections. Must of wiggled the right thing.

DR. FIORE: How did you feel when you felt the ship lifting off?

DAN: Apprehensive, scared. It might not lift all the way, or it might not continue. It's the only way out, though. Take a chance. Go for it. Have a couple of drinks aboard the ship, when we get back; try to relax, calm down. Close call.

DR. FIORE: How long did it take you to get back, in Earth time?

DAN: Ten minutes.

DR. FIORE: Let yourself remember another encounter, one that's still having a negative impact on you, at the count of five. One . . . two . . . three . . . four . . . five.

DAN: Interrogation with one of the violent ones. Stupid questions. No way to know the answers, from my position. Keeps pressing.

DR. FIORE: What kind of questions are you being asked?

DAN: Where are you living? What are you doing here? Questions I shouldn't answer. Not to him. Too dangerous. Can't trust him. I'm afraid he'll see through it. He shouldn't be here.

DR. FIORE: Where is this taking place?

DAN: Seems to be in front of where I went to high school.

DR. FIORE: How old are you when this is taking place?

DAN: Fourteen.

DR. FIORE: Tell me more about the interrogation.

DAN: It's like a test. He's not one you mess with. No answers. Don't want to give him any answers. He's mad. Can't really do anything now. Breaks it off. Leaves me standing there. Shouldn't talk to them.

DR. FIORE: Tell me about that.

DAN: Vicious. Untrustworthy. The worst. A race of killers. Born that way. Useful and troublesome.

DR. FIORE: What do you mean by useful?

DAN: They have their uses. Troublemakers. Difficult to control. I'm defenseless here. He really shouldn't even be here. I don't know how he got here. I'm glad he's gone.

DR. FIORE: Let yourself remember another contact that's having an effect on you.

DAN: Conference on the ship, talking with the captain. Old friend. Sitting in his cabin. Comfortable. Feels good to be there. No, I can't stay. Sorry about that. Laughing. Just kidding with each other, remembering old times. He's human. Just like me. We're discussing the troublemakers. He doesn't know about the contact. Finds it upsetting, it's been too long ago to do anything about it. No more trouble. It's all over. They won't be back for a long time. It finally became too much trouble. To put up with it. Talk late into the night. Lots of stories. Good times. He says good night. Walks me down the corridor. Into the room and closes the door behind me. And I'm back.

DR. FIORE: How do you get back?

DAN: Just close the door.

DR. FIORE: What happens between the time you close the door and the time you get back?

DAN: I just change positions.

DR. FIORE: Once you're back, what do you remember?

DAN: Just a warm feeling.

DR. FIORE: Where are you when you get back?

DAN: Back in my house.

DR. FIORE: What are you doing there?

DAN: Walking down the hallway.

DR. FIORE: How long would you estimate you've been gone?

DAN: All night, ship's time.

DR. FIORE: Go back to the beginning of that encounter and get in touch with the very first thing you experience.

DAN: Dizziness as I go through the bedroom door, brief dizziness. As I walk out into the hallway, brief dizziness.

DR. FIORE: And then?

DAN: Then aboard the ship. And then back down, halfway down the hallway, I'm aware again.

DR. FIORE: How much time elapsed altogether, in Earth time?

DAN: Maybe fifteen seconds, walking down the hall.

DR. FIORE: And how much time in terms of the ship's time?

DAN: Eight hours.

DR. FIORE: Just continue to report everything that comes into your mind, as you remember more and more of your encounters.

DAN: There's a friend at the door, the front door. One of the intellectuals. Comes in. Social call. Just to say hello.

DR. FIORE: What is your reaction?

DAN: Glad to see him. Good to hear . . . any news of the ship. He's in a hurry to leave. I want him to stay and talk some more. He says next time. Goes. Disappointed.

DR. FIORE:   Why was he in a hurry this time?

DAN:   Busy. Duties.

DR. FIORE:   Where were you when he visited you?

DAN:   Front room.

DR. FIORE:   Was there anybody else there in the room with you?

DAN:   No.

DR. FIORE:   Let your mind help you to remember another encounter, an important one that is still affecting you in some way.

DAN:   Talking with the captain. On a possible recall. Makes me hope. Nice to think it might happen, so I might get back. I'd be doing something I really like. No schedule. No timetable. It's coming up. They want experience. They want people. Makes me feel good.

DR. FIORE:   What is he saying about a recall?

DAN:   Talking about the big operation. Possible. Needs a lot of people. I'm falling all over myself trying to volunteer. It's important enough to break some rules to do it. No promises. Just a maybe. I'm anxious. Want to be involved. Telling him that. Who knows? They'll let me know.

DR. FIORE:   Did he say how many ships would be involved in the drop?

DAN:   Four or five.

DR. FIORE:   How many planets would be involved?

DAN:   Just one. This time the whole planet. Major action.

DR. FIORE:   Did he tell you the name of this planet?

DAN:   No. Have to go to base to regroup. Standing on the bridge looking at the base. Beautiful, just hanging there in the blackness. Other ships all nosed in all around it. Huge. Beautiful sight!

DR. FIORE:   How long is it?

DAN:   It's a couple of miles across. The whole ship's up against the outer ring, nose first. Quite a sight.

DR. FIORE:   What shape is it?

DAN:   Large . . . almost disc shaped . . . thicker in the middle than at the edges. Circular. Ship's nosed up against the outer rim. It's pretty.

DR. FIORE:   Where are you when you're watching this?

DAN:   Standing out on the bridge of the ship, looking in toward the center of the station.

DR. FIORE:   Has it been decided that you will be recalled?

DAN:   No. They'll let me know. No word.

DR. FIORE:   What are you aware of now?

DAN:   Bridge. It's all quiet. Everybody's busy below. Just one or two people on the bridge. Just relaxing, nothing to do. Just enjoying the view. Back home again.

DR. FIORE:   Let yourself know the date when this happened.

DAN:   August fifteenth.

DR. FIORE:   What year?

DAN:   It's '87.

DR. FIORE:   Let yourself know if they have informed you as to whether you're going to be recalled or not.

DAN:   No. No, still waiting. No further word. I just hope they didn't go without me.

DR. FIORE:   What would happen to your life here if you went?

DAN:   Just take this body, everything, as it is.

DR. FIORE:   Would you just disappear, be a missing person?

DAN:   Right.

DR. FIORE:   How would you handle this with your family?

DAN:   It wouldn't be important. A few minutes of worry. I wouldn't be important anymore.

DR. FIORE:   Would you return to Earth again?

DAN:   No. This would be it. Memories come back.

DR. FIORE:   Who is making this decision?

DAN:   Command leaders.

DR. FIORE:   What outcome do you want, in terms of the decision?

DAN:   Only one! I want to go!

✒

Once he was back to normal waking consciousness, I asked Dan how the regression had been for him.

"It was difficult dealing with the memory of the violent ones. But I realized we got even, and I won't have that problem again. I got that understanding from the captain. So I know that it's been taken care of. They're not going to be a problem for anybody for a long, long time. They're not going to be able to get into space for generations. So I don't have to worry about that, nor does anybody else, which makes me feel better. Last time, that kind of bothered me. It had drifted in and out of my mind since then."

Going along with the material that had emerged, I was concerned about the possibility of Dan returning to space. I knew he had a wife and children. He also had a specialized job in construction management and an expertise that few others could match. "Dan, what would you do if presented with the chance to go back?"

"I want to go back. It's not that I don't love the wife and children and all that sort of thing. It's just that it's so far superior to be there than to be here. And I know that if I were there, I'd be involved in something so grand, that what happens here means nothing. Means nothing! To be back, to be able to do that again, would be fabulous!"

"How would you arrange it with your family, Dan?"

"A couple of months ago, the wife and I were standing out back, looking up the stars. It was a nice clear night. And I told her, 'Someday I'm going back.' And she said she'd really like to also. And I said, 'No, you don't understand. Someday I'm going home.' And she said, 'I'd like to go up there.' But she doesn't consider it her home, and I do."

"Did you know any of what we uncovered tonight, then? Or did you just have a very strong feeling?"

"I couldn't have possibly had any idea. I just always had this very strong feeling that that was where I belonged, that that was home. And I can't think of any other possible reason to say it to my wife, other than to prepare her."

"And to prepare yourself too."

"Yes! I'm ready!"

# "They Call Themselves the Planters."

Diane Tai is an exceptional person. She's been a gifted psychic since childhood. When I mentioned to a mutual friend that I was writing *Encounters,* she told me I should have Diane in the book because she's probably been a contactee for years. I called Diane, and she graciously agreed to come over to my office for a regression as soon as possible.

Diane arrived early for our appointment. She is a beautiful woman, just over forty, petite, with curly dark-brown hair and sparkling brown eyes. Her flowing white cotton dress and brilliant blue beads added to the general impression of her being special. She has had to cope with a serious physical condition since she was a child. She was diagnosed as having spinal muscular atrophy, a genetic disease. The doctors she's consulted through the years are amazed, first, that she is alive and, second, that she can walk and is actually quite active and mobile. Her sister died of the same disease at the age of nine, never having walked. So Diane has overcome many obstacles.

After a few minutes of social chitchat, we got down to business.

274

Diane had mentioned during our phone conversation that she had had a particularly exciting thing happen after a dream nine years ago, while she was still married to her former husband, so I decided this would be a good place for us to begin our investigation into a possible close encounter of the fourth kind.

"Edee, this kind of thing is always happening in my life. You won't believe it. Oh yes, you will, but nobody else would!" Diane laughed and continued, "I just talked to my ex-husband today, whom I hadn't spoken with for two years. He said, 'I was just thinking about you yesterday and today you call.' And then I said, 'I'm going to see Edee about this UFO thing. Remember that incident that happened and you laughed at me?' And he said, 'Oh, my goodness. I was just thinking about that yesterday, and here you're telling me about it today.' So I thought, We're either telepathic or something's going on here."

Knowing Diane, I wasn't in the least surprised. I've also experienced that sort of thing many times myself. I wanted to know about the UFO incident. "What happened, Diane. Tell me about the dream, and you said on the phone that something special happened after it?"

"On a Wednesday night, I think it was about nine years ago, I had a dream that a UFO was over my house. I had awakened from the dream, sat up in bed and told my husband, 'The UFO is here and they're over the house and I have to pack and get ready to go.' I was getting out of bed, and Dick said, 'It's a dream. You're okay. Go back to sleep.' He laughed at me, and I was half-remembering that I was in this spaceship. So I realized it was a dream and went back to sleep. The next day I was talking to my son, Ronnie, about it, and he and Dick were laughing and teasing me all day, saying, 'Here comes the UFO.' That night, Thursday, we were all watching '20/20,' when the first words out of Hugh Downs's mouth were, 'This is "20/20." A UFO was sighted over Cupertino, California, last night.' I thought, this is not true! I must be dreaming. I remember sitting there, and Ronnie and Dick turned and looked at me like I was an alien." Diane was really laughing at this point. She composed herself and continued,

"He went on to explain that it was an official sighting and had been picked up on radar at the San Jose Airport."

"Diane, we'll regress you to your so-called dream in a few minutes, but for the record I'd like to know more about your psychic abilities. When did they start?" Often psychic sensitivity is a consequence of CEIVs, and I was trying to get an idea of how long she might have been a contactee.

"I had an eye operation when I was seven, so I had bandages around my eyes while I was healing. They had taken the eye out and done the operation on my muscles because I was cross-eyed. It didn't take long before I realized I could see other things without my vision."

"You mean you could see things that weren't there?"

"No. My parents would try to test me, 'Okay, what's the neighbor got on today? Who's here, Diane? What do they look like?' I could see a lot of things. I was using a different sight. My parents didn't understand these things. They were simple people and they just thought it was fun. And it was."

"Thank heavens they didn't squelch your development. That's what usually happens. Parents are threatened by children who are different, so they wash their mouth out with soap or tell them they're lying. I've heard some pretty pathetic tales. That usually drives those abilities underground. If they ever surface again, it's usually in adult life. When did you next notice something special?"

Diane thought for a few seconds, and then her face lit up with a mischievous grin. "In junior high I began to have these strange feelings that I was communicating with an alien. I was about thirteen, maybe fourteen. And the psychic ability was really getting strong at that time. I didn't even know what the word 'psychic' meant. Sometimes I would look at the kids and say, 'This is going to happen to you.' And it would. So I went to school and I started to tell them I was talking to this woman from another planet who was giving me all this information about the planet, and she also knew things about other people. And they'd say, 'Well, what does she know about me?' And I'd say all these things. And finally it got so big that everybody was talking about it. You know how things can go fast in school. One day my gym teacher had me stand up in class and she said, 'Today we're going to ask Diane about this planet, and she's going to talk to her alien.' And they were asking me all these questions. And I don't know where the answers were coming from. I just stood there for an hour answering questions and looking at the kids and saying, 'This may happen to you,' and 'This is coming in your family.' The things started coming true, so they had some PTA meetings about me, because a lot of the children were upset. Some people said I was a witch. They called my dad down to the school and told him I would have to leave, if I didn't stop. I carried it to extremes just before that. I drew my eyebrows way up and made my face up like the woman I saw. I would just sit quietly and talk to the woman in my mind. I could see her and what she looked like. She said she was hundreds of years old. They all lived hundreds of years on her planet. So that was quite interesting. But my father got really upset with me and said how embarrassed he was. He told me I had to knock off that stuff and stop making up all these stories. So that was the end of that."

"That's too bad, but understandable, Diane. Let's get back to what we'll be starting with today, your dream of the UFO nine years ago. Did anything happen after that '20/20' show?"

"After that UFO incident, I began to realize that possibly what I'd thought or felt as a child might also be true. Maybe I had been contacted. Then I started to hear a lot on television, and I felt that possibly those contacts could have been real. Whenever those things happened to me, it was always something good. It was never fearful or negative. I would get a lot of comfort."

"Do you feel you have been contacted since you were a child?"

"One interesting thing comes to mind. One time in Washington, D.C., I was about twenty, and I was standing with a man, talking in the parking lot of my apartment. We were looking at the stars. It was a beautiful night. We were looking up and talking about something else, and we saw a UFO. I mean we saw it! This was not imagination or anything. It was red, glowing, and it was moving in straight angles across the sky. It would stop and move, and stop and move. We watched it for about five minutes, and then it zoomed away. So I went in and turned on the television set. I was shaking, because I thought, Oh God, the UFOs have landed! There was a news bulletin that came on and interrupted the channel and said, 'A UFO has just been sighted over Washington, D.C.' And I thought, Oh my God, we really saw this thing. He said, 'Details on the eleven o'clock news.' And you know, they never mentioned a word about it, not a word. So the government, I guess, covered it up."

I got us each a glass of water. It was good to stand up and stretch a bit. I told Diane about Timothy Good's book that had just come out, *Above Top Secret.* He had spent years collecting data on the worldwide cover-ups of governments of their own investigations of UFO sightings.

As soon as Diane had finished her water, she leaned forward excitedly. In a conspiratorially lowered voice, she said, "Now another thing I'm going to tell you, Edee. Darn, I wish I had those letters! One day, about four, five years ago, Paul [Diane's husband] came home and he was shaken. He said, 'I want to show you something that came in to the company by mistake.' It was addressed to a different company, Technical something; his is Technical Analysis. We opened it up, and it was letters from an Air Force colonel to Barry Goldwater and some other people. And there were these letters back and forth about how this colonel had seen UFOs. He knew of other Air Force people who had seen UFOs, and why wasn't some of this information out, and what was going on at some Air Force base in California where they had a UFO and some alien bodies. This was all in these letters. There were all these different letters back and forth, and copies of letters. Paul said, 'I'm really scared about this. I don't know what I should do.' And I said, 'Oh, this is wonderful! I can't wait to show it to this one and that one.' He took the letters, and I never saw them again. He said he got rid of them."

I was totally fascinated by what Diane was telling me. I had known her for years and knew she was telling me the truth. It would be completely out of character for her to be making up a story about this. Also, since it was so recent, I felt that her memory of it was probably accurate. Further questioning brought out that there were about seven letters and that Barry Goldwater knew all about the issue. Paul had figured out to whom the letters should have been sent originally and had mailed them on without making copies.

I would have loved to have seen those letters and for them to have been made public. We had gotten off onto an intriguing tangent. But it was now time for us to see about Diane's "dream."

Diane meditates daily, does regressions herself and, under hypnosis, gave birth naturally about two years ago to a beautiful baby girl. I helped her with the birth by giving her hypnotic suggestions. It was a peak experience in my life. I knew Diane was an exceptionally fine hypnotic subject. Within a few minutes, Diane was ready to be regressed. I asked her to go back to the night about nine years ago when she had had the dream of a UFO. I counted to ten and asked her to report whatever came into her mind.

＄

DIANE: I'm in bed, I can feel the bed and the room. Dick's there, he's sleeping. This is the first time I remember this, but I get up and I go out to the backyard. I thought I heard something. So I go out to the backyard. It's very, very quiet. And what I heard, now I can hear it . . . it's humming. It's a hum. So I thought it was the pool, maybe the pool was on. [*Pauses*] The next thing that happens is I start to feel very, very heavy. There's this heaviness coming over me. My whole body feels kind of funny and heavy and numb. And I look up and I see this light, just a light. So I think, well maybe it's a helicopter, a light from a helicopter. It's shining down on my face. And then I feel this numbness, so I'm afraid. [*Pauses and frowns*]

DR. FIORE: Tell me everything that you're aware of.

DIANE: I feel afraid. I don't know what's happening to me. I'm in this light, and I can't see out of the light. I don't see around me. [*Long pause*] Now I see okay. There's been a gap somewhere, because now I'm walking in this large ship and there's these . . . about twenty black people, sitting down in the ship, on this, almost like a bench.

DR. FIORE: How are they dressed?

DIANE: These black people are dressed in a Western American style. They look very confused and disoriented. And there's this man . . . now I see him beside me, but he's tall, and I said to him, "Why are all these black people here?" And he said, "Well, these people were sent down into the most difficult of circumstances, like poor ghetto places, for a very high service there. These are different souls." And I'm really confused, I don't understand what he's saying. And now we're going into this room. Oh, I understand. . . . Okay, there's a time difference. I'm really there for a long time, but when I'm put back, the time hasn't changed much. I don't understand this difference, but it's like we've left the atmosphere and we've come back.

DR. FIORE: You're going to go back to before you're in the ship, and you're going to take it moment by moment, without any gaps. You're going to allow yourself to remember everything that you experienced.

DIANE: The numbness first and the heaviness. It's like I'm lifted. I can't stop it. It's like a magnet, and I can't stop it. It's pulling me away. And I think maybe I must be dying. Because I'm going . . . away from the ground. [Pauses]

DR. FIORE: What emotions are you feeling as this is happening?

DIANE: Confusion. Like am I going to be okay? Am I going to see God? Or am I dreaming? Maybe I'm dreaming. But it happens very quickly, and I'm in this room. It's a strange room and it's got a very strange metal all around it. Now I can see this room. It's almost circular and it's small and I'm seeing it better now. I see these blue lights, about eight or ten blue lights on the ceiling and they're turned on . . . they cover the whole ceiling. They go through the whole room. And something's happening from these lights. It's like my body feels . . . the air smells funny. The air I'm breathing has a sweet smell to it. [Sniffs] Almost like honeysuckle. And I'm alone. It seems like I'm here a long time, but I guess not.

DR. FIORE:   What are you doing?

DIANE:   I woke up on this table. And . . .

DR. FIORE:   What position are you in?

DIANE:   I was lying down on this table. On my back. And it's cold. I look around. Now I don't have . . . I don't have on the same clothes.

DR. FIORE:   What do you have on?

DIANE:   I have on these . . . it's like a white, almost like a white pair of shorts, and it ties right here. [*Points to her waist*] And a little top . . . that ties here and here. [*Points to the center of her chest*] I don't understand this, I really don't. The door is opening. It goes inside the wall. And there's this very tall man with dark hair. And I think he's a doctor. For some reason, I think he's a doctor . . . I don't know why. Now I've been here for a while, I don't know what happened. So I said to him, "Can you make my muscles grow? Can you help me to get over this disease?" [*Long pause*] Now we are walking down this hallway. . . .

DR. FIORE:   How did he answer you?

DIANE:   He says, "The body is not as important as the spirit. Your spirit is already well, and your body will follow. And you're here. We're watching our children." That's all he says, "We're watching our children."

DR. FIORE: How do you feel when you hear that?

DIANE: He's so special. He's so wise. When he talks, it's very low and very soft. And comforting. And he touches so nice. I don't have to be afraid of him. But the black people are a little afraid. They're the first people I see. "And they're up there," he said, "to refresh their minds." I don't understand what he means. But they've been planted . . . their souls have been planted in specific places of high need.

DR. FIORE: Are they in the same room with you?

DIANE: No, I was alone. I asked him, "What are the beautiful blue lights?" It's almost like a violet-blue. And he said, "We put everyone here first so that their bacteria won't hurt us." I don't understand that, but it's like a cleansing room. When you first come up, you come in here . . . and it's like you're sleeping and you're breathing and these lights are killing something. And he said, "We checked you." I don't know what happened. That's why my clothes were different. They took my clothes away, my pajamas. And it's warm out. It's cold in that room, but it's warm out in the corridor, where we're walking. We're going to some other place.

DR. FIORE: Where are the black people?

DIANE: They're sitting, waiting to go in this room. Not the blue-light room, but there's another room. There's so many of us, there's a lot of us up here. This must be a huge ship.

DR. FIORE: How many would you say there are?

DIANE: The corridor that I walk through is filled with people. There's like twenty here, and over here there's thirty or forty. And we're being . . . it's like this contact is made every so often, to give us strength and to see how our bodies are doing physically. I don't understand. We're part of this group that comes into the physical body that sometimes has trouble adjusting to the vibration of the physical form. And it's like, it's . . . we have to learn to stay focused.

DR. FIORE:   How do you know this?

DIANE:   That's what they're telling us.

DR. FIORE:   Who are they?

DIANE:   They call themselves the Planters. They go to different parts of this world and different parts of other worlds to check up on their . . . it's like we're distant cousins. It's like we were planted here thousands of years ago to start the colony. And there were different planets that planted different things here. It's not like an experiment, although I'm starting to feel like one. He says, "No, no, no." I feel not as evolved as they are. And I feel a little uncomfortable that I'm not on their level, like my dog might feel around me or something. I'm feeling that I hope they'll be kind, because they're so far advanced. I want to be like they are, but I'm not on that level. I'm just still growing. They can do so many things. They can . . . they can materialize themselves. They can levitate things. They can travel in this ship by making this ship change form and then beaming it on this laser beam of light to another destination. And that's how they go from planet to planet. And when they take us out of orbit, we go . . . we go away. I see the earth through this little window . . . it's green. But the time is stopped. And when we come back, it's just a few minutes difference. They can do anything. They're so incredible!

DR. FIORE:   Tell me what happened to you. You're walking down the corridor, and you see the black people and the other people, and then what happens?

DIANE:   They said they want . . . they must keep making contact, because certain people . . . policemen and doctors and healing professions and psychics, social workers, and people who care, those people are drawn to try to change the negative force that is on a self-destruct cycle . . . the people who don't care about pollution and don't care about the natural way of the planet. And the others are waking up, and they want to try to counter that, to save the planet so we don't destroy it through some ignorance of the others. So he's saying to me that I need to pray for communication. There is a part of my brain, somewhere in the middle of my brain, that enables me to tune in to a different frequency. Be careful how I use it. Never think a negative thought toward another, for that thought is energy, and the higher the vibration of the one using it, the faster the energy can be created in the physical form. We're all in this big room, and we're listening to this man talk. "Go out and be of service. And talk to us. We are always here. You will hear us, and you must come from time to time." For this . . . it's like a renewal somehow in this room. . . . I don't understand what we go through, but it's a renewing process to help us deal with this dimension. Sometimes the chemical imbalances can throw us off, if we're not getting the right light foods. The energy waves from the televisions and the radio frequencies can disrupt us. It's too much going on. It's like we can't make our brains quiet, so we become agitated and irritated. The only way we can protect and balance is turning on that little thing in our head and changing our frequency. This enables us to help transcend time and space, to see the future, to see the past, and to help bring about healing within an individual's mind and body. When they came here, and it was like 40,000 years ago when they first came . . . they took up many people.

DR. FIORE:   Is this being explained to you? And if so, is it being explained to you individually or to all as a group?

DIANE:   As a group.

DR. FIORE:   And is one person explaining this or are there several?

DIANE: No, there's just that one "doctor," I call him, but I don't know why I call him a doctor. When they bring you up, they do something in your brain.

DR. FIORE: Let yourself remember what was done to your brain, at the count of five. One . . . two . . . three . . . four . . . five. Just report everything that comes into your mind.

DIANE: [Pauses] It's hard.

DR. FIORE: Don't try. Just let yourself remember. Remember where you are when this is being done and what's happening.

DIANE: I'm back on the table. [Pauses] And I'm awake, but I can't move. There's this, almost like an X-ray machine that goes from the top to the bottom. I said, "Are you going to take blood?" And they said, "No, we don't have to do that." [Pauses] "What are you looking for?" "We're looking for the way that you have evolved in physical form over the thousands of years." "Did my soul evolve with the body?" And I'm not understanding how the connection is made between the soul and the body. If the soul comes in a body, that body begins to form, like a response from the thought of the soul. And the vibration of its environment and that's what makes you look the way you do. And they're interested in my reproductive system. Especially. They want to make sure that there's not a weakness for a new generation. They're speeding up production of something in my brain. It's like a radio turned on that hears frequencies, intercepting thoughts, intercepting your music, the way a radio does when you turn it on, and that's the way you explain it. It's almost like a needle, but it's not. It goes in through the top of my head, into my brain somewhere. It's not really painful, but there's something going in there. And then I feel . . . I feel calmer. And they told me I would have another baby. And I said, "But I've had my tubes tied." And they said, "No, that doesn't matter. You will have a healthy baby." And I keep asking them to heal my body. I keep asking them, "Please, can you make my muscles grow?" They said, "You will not get worse. Eat foods with the highest vibration on your planet; they will nourish you. And you must talk to us. Talk to those of the light. That's who we are. And when you feel the light, you will get your nourishment. Bathe in the light. That is the force of love." And I feel this heat in my body, in my reproductive system. And it's like starting from there and going out. It's in my ovaries. I don't want to go home. I want to stay here. Because I feel lighter and I walk so easy here. I feel like I weigh fifty pounds less, and I said, "On the planet, I feel heavy. I can walk here, I can bend down and get up." But I cannot go. I can't go with them.

DR. FIORE:   How do you know that?

DIANE:   My vibration is not up to theirs. I can't yet disappear and reappear, the way they can. He says we will all do that, eventually, and the more we pray in the light . . . this accelerates our vibration. That is the key to our evolution . . . is that contact with God, who created the universe. And those who have gone before us who walk in this light of love and service. So communication is the key to our evolution, through quietness, just being quiet and feeling that part of the brain inside the middle, asking it to turn on, like a radio, and then waiting to receive our information. All things are known through that receiver. Those who don't do it become pulled down to the force of a lower vibration, and they'll become angry and hurtful. You must awaken that part of the brain. They say, "Turn that on and join the light, and then help others to awaken their light as well." We all then hold hands and affirm our missions, and we would be strong together.

DR. FIORE:   Who holds hands?

DIANE:   All the people in the room from all over our area, the Bay Area. They work this area today. And they only come back every so many years, it feels like. But this trip is the biggest one. They seem to be concerned about the bombs and the lack of love between countries. And so people have to be stronger in order to little by little, raise the vibration of the planet.

DR. FIORE:   How do you know this?

DIANE:   That's what we've learned, and we feel it in our hearts. They say that the animals are also part of this. We are to the animals, as they are to us. They're in our care. And if we can love those things that are evolving toward the light, that will enable love to come to us more, as well. How can we kill our animals and destroy our nature? If we can learn these lessons, we can go on into a different vibration where we will be able to drop the heaviness of physical form and travel among the stars, free of disease, free of aging. [*Long pause*] We all want to stay, but we wake up. I wake up in bed, and I remember only part of the dream.

DR. FIORE:   Let's see how you got from the ship to your bed. Let yourself remember at the count of five. One . . . two . . . three . . . four . . . five.

DIANE:   I'm standing on this disc. It's a circle about four feet by four feet, and the ship seems to be very high up in the sky. I mean, I can see the outline of California, I'm so far up.

DR. FIORE:   Are you in the ship at this point?

DIANE:   I'm in the ship, and we're standing on these discs, and then I feel that numbness again and I see that bright light again, and then I'm in my bed. And this metal thing I'm standing on in the ship is very, very dense. It's a different feeling, of a metal I've never stood on before. And I don't have any shoes on and I'm in my pajamas.

DR. FIORE: Let yourself know how you got from wearing the shorts to wearing your pajamas.

DIANE: [*Pauses*] The pajamas were waiting for me in this large open area, where we all come into to go back home. That's where our clothes are, and we just put them on there. It was so warm in the ship. It felt like it was eighty-some degrees, and we didn't need to have a lot of clothes on. Only in that blue-light room, it was cold. It was very cold there, but the rest was very warm, almost like the sun was shining on you.

DR. FIORE: Let yourself remember if you were given any suggestions that you would not remember.

DIANE: I don't remember that.

DR. FIORE: Okay. Approximately how many people were in the room where you were all together?

DIANE: In the room where we were holding hands, there seemed to be about fifty or sixty people.

DR. FIORE: Did you recognize anyone?

DIANE: No. And there was . . . in that corridor, a lot of black people, all together.

DR. FIORE: Were these same black people together in the room where you were all holding hands?

DIANE: Yes, they were there, and when I looked at them, they were the most beautiful people. Their eyes were so beautiful, and they seemed so wise. They were evidently in more distressed areas of our area, and they were working with people who had really gotten out of balance. They were very religious and very filled with such joy in the face of what seemed to be a lot of obstacles to overcome. So I felt very good where they were. They were beautiful spirits. And they needed a lot of extra encouragement.

DR. FIORE:   Were you given any information about your specific role?

DIANE:   We all seemed to be taught that we were here to show others how to awaken that part of them inside their brains that helps to communicate with the light. I remember asking if the light had to do with the earth and it was the universal light. In other words, there seemed to be one light for everybody, and even them [the extraterrestrials]. Even though the planet was still young, they had come and had children with some of the people, so some physically were a little more evolved. But the light was for everybody, and it would renew and strengthen on all levels, no matter what the evolvement was. So it seemed like there was a central point for this light that radiated out to the planets. And that light is high consciousness . . . of thought that is pure in every sense of the word. We call it God on this planet. They never mention too much about specific religions or anything like that, just universal light. It was in each of us. And all we had to do was ask for it to waken and to grow. That's all we had to do, nothing else. [*Long pause*]

DR. FIORE:   Go back in time to when you were a little girl, to the very first time when you met with the woman, with the extraterrestrial who guided you, at the count of five. One . . . two . . . three . . . four . . . five.

DIANE:   Right now I'm fifteen, and my sister, Denise, is lying on the bed. And she's ill. She's almost nine. She says to me, "Diane, who is that lady standing there?" But I don't see her. And she said, "She's so beautiful, I've never seen anyone that beautiful." I could sense something, but I didn't see anything. And I just held her hand and said, "It's okay, Denise." And then that night she died. And I kept thinking about that woman she saw. Who was she? Now that, that's fading away, and I'm going back

. . . I must be . . . six or seven. I'm in my room. Upstairs, alone. [*Pauses*] And there's . . . there's somebody in my room and I start to feel afraid. And I wonder if it's the bogeyman that my baby-sitter said would get me. But there's this light, and I don't understand why I see this light in the corner. It gets brighter. There's almost like an outline in the light. I can't see the face. I just see this outline of this woman with dark hair. She has her hands out. And so I put my hands out. And when I put my hands out, with my palms up, my hands start to tingle. And I think she's very nice. And she's smiling. And I feel the tingling in my hands. [*Smiles*] And then I also feel the warmth in my head. And then she's gone. And she never said anything to me then.

DR. FIORE:    Let's move to the time when somehow you are informed that she is from another planet, that she is an extraterrestrial. At the count of five. One . . . two . . . three . . . four . . . five.

DIANE:    I'm in Mount Ranier. I have to walk to school a long way. It takes me almost an hour, every day, back and forth. Something happens, I don't remember where. This woman . . . it's as if she begins to merge with me. For a short time. To feel the earth energy. And when I look in the mirror, it's almost like I see her too. So she's there, sometimes out of me, and sometimes she comes in me.

DR. FIORE:    What is your reaction to this?

DIANE:    When she comes in me, I start getting A's in school, because it's easier when she's there. And I also can see into people easier. It's as if I feel their thoughts. I begin to ask her questions about our planet. And I'm talking to her when I close my eyes when I sit in the park. And she tells me all these things. But I didn't listen to some things she told me.

DR. FIORE:    Why is that?

DIANE: I was telling everybody about her, and some people were laughing. And I feel very bad about that. And they didn't want me to talk about it to everybody.

DR. FIORE: Whom do you mean?

DIANE: Those people on the . . . where she came from. I wasn't supposed to say all those things, because people laugh, they don't understand. And I did get in trouble, like she said, but she said not to worry about it, that they would know someday. And she was only there a short time, and then I didn't see her anymore.

DR. FIORE: How long was she with you?

DIANE: It seemed like maybe a month.

DR. FIORE: Let's see if you ever were taken anywhere, into a ship or anything of that sort, during your contacts with her. Let yourself remember.

DIANE: I remember now. I had forgotten this, but now I remember. I'm in this big funny kind of see-through tube, and I'm standing up. And when she decides to join with me, we get into this tube together. And when she left, we got into the tube again, and then she was gone.

DR. FIORE: How many times did that happen?

DIANE: It feels like I went up twice, once when we went in the tube, and once when we went back into the tube, and she left.

DR. FIORE: Let yourself know what happened just before you got into the tube, and where the tube was.

DIANE: [Pauses] Well, it's in a ship . . . the tube is in a ship.

And . . . I can't remember how I got there, but I think it was when I was walking.

DR. FIORE:   You're going to let yourself remember, it's very clear in your mind. You're going to take it step by step and remember everything. At the count of five. One . . . two . . . three . . . four . . . five.

DIANE:   Okay . . . I'm waking up now, and it's late at night and everybody's asleep and I hear a humming. So I'm going out to the backyard, and it's very clear; there's no clouds. And I'm wondering where is the humming. It's louder and louder. And then there's that light again. It's the same feeling like before, the numbness and the light getting brighter and then everything around me getting darker . . . and then I'm in the ship.

DR. FIORE:   Is this the first time you've ever been in the ship, or does it feel familiar?

DIANE:   No, it's the first time. I feel like I'm dreaming. It feels like I must be . . .

DR. FIORE:   What's happening to you?

DIANE:   [*Pauses*] I said, "Am I in a dream?" I'm only thirteen, fourteen. "Oh no, child, this is true." There's another man, but it's not the other one, the doctor. He's different. He takes my hand and we go down like little corridors that are short and circular. I feel lost very quickly. I don't know where I'm going. Now I see this woman . . . dark hair, dark eyes. Very straight hair. No curls. Very white face. Her skin is so white and pure. And then we hold hands. And she said, "Do you remember me?" And I remember her from when I was little. And she talks different than everybody else. I can hear her talking even though she doesn't move her mouth. The others, they talk to me, but she thinks to me, and I can hear her. So she must be special. [*Long pause*] That's when . . . I begin to change.

DR. FIORE: Where are you at this point?

DIANE: I'm just holding her hand, but I can't remember . . . everything's going black after that. I can't remember what happened.

DR. FIORE: You're going to let yourself remember. It's crystal clear in your mind at the count of three. One . . . two . . . three. Just speak out whatever comes into your mind.

DIANE: [*Long pause*] I'm in the theater. It's almost like that other auditorium we all went to, but it's a little different. It's longer, and there's this big screen. It's like a movie. I don't know why I'm looking at this screen. All these things are flashing so fast on the screen, one after another, words and pictures, and words and pictures. And I'm just supposed to look at it. And it's almost like, as fast as it's flashed on the screen, I know it. I'm just watching it. I don't know how long I'm there. There're several people there, looking at this screen. Now the lights are on, and . . . and I'm back on this different table, and they move this funny thing up and down my body again. They're looking for something, but they don't really tell me anything. They just go up and down my body with this machine. And again, they're interested in my ovaries. Because I can feel that heat, when the machine stops there.

DR. FIORE: When did they do this examination?

DIANE: The first time I went up. I didn't say too much, like I did when I went up the other time. Then I said many things. But when I was little, I just sat there mostly and watched. And the beautiful lady didn't talk that much to me, she just looked at me and smiled, and I could feel things.

*

Diane came out of hypnosis feeling a little groggy. She had been under for just short of two hours. She was tired, but very interested in what had emerged. There were many unusual aspects to her work; the female alien "possessing" her for a month, the information she had been given, her many contacts over the years. I suspected that there also were many more we had not delved into. It had been a delightful experience working with her and one that she felt had enriched her life. Additionally, it had answered some questions she had had for years. She left feeling good, and feeling good about what she had learned. In fact, we both felt uplifted.

# 14

# "I Went Through
# Those Venetian Blinds!"

 "I was extra sensitive. Every time I read a newspaper, saw a TV news show, or heard people talking, I would pick up on parts of the conversation that would start what I call the nagging. I would have this overwhelming desire to say, 'But you're wrong,' or, 'I need to correct you.' 'If you do this, a hundred years from now, this is what we're going to have.' So I started drinking."

"To try to cope with it?"

"Yes. I found that when I drank, I could be normal. I could have a social relationship with people. I could listen to their babblings and conversations and be a part of it, and this other thing didn't bother me."

Fred had come to my office just after I had finished writing *Encounters*. A colleague, Josie Hadley, had told me about him over dinner one evening about a month earlier. He had seen her several years before and had benefited greatly from hypnotherapy. During their work together, he had related to her a remembered close encounter of the fourth kind. That in itself was unusual. She and I and other hypnotherapists with whom I had discussed the topic found that abductions usually became known only with hypnosis. Josie gave me his name and suggested I contact him.

Fred and I couldn't meet sooner because he was in Europe, and when it was possible for us to get together, the finished *Encounters* manuscript had already been sent to my agent and editor. But I felt that it would be very interesting to include him in the book, because he had recalled the abduction experience without the aid of hypnosis. I planned to interview him and then check his remembered account against the material that emerged with hypnotic regression. If it proved to be as unique as I suspected, it would be well worth adding his chapter at the last minute.

✒

The nagging that Fred had referred to was a consequence of his remembered CEIV. At this point, fifteen years later, it no longer troubled him. In fact, it appeared that very little troubled this dynamic businessman and author. At fifty-three, he seemed the picture of health and was full of surplus energy. He talked so rapidly, I was glad I had a reliable tape recorder to back up my verbatim notes.

"Fred, before we get into the details of the abduction you told Josie about, I'd like to know if you have any evidence of having been contacted before, maybe when you were a child."

"Something happened to me in the Boy Scouts when I was eleven or twelve years old. We were out hiking at a Boy Scout camp in Riverside County in Southern California. We were walking along, and I heard a voice saying to me, 'Gregory. Have you noticed that Gregory's not with you?' And I looked around and he wasn't there. And I hollered out to the guys, 'Where's Greg?' 'Oh, he'll be along.' And I said, 'No, there's something wrong.' And then we all laughed and joked about it a little bit. But it concerned me, and I went back the way we had come. There was a ledge, and I heard this noise, crying. And I went over to the ledge. I saw Greg. It was a good eighty-foot drop. And he was hanging on to a dead mesquite bush. He couldn't move. And he said, 'Help me, help me, Fred.' I helped him get up. He got up and he said, 'I was scared to death. I was afraid if I yelled out I would fall. And I was afraid if I did anything I would fall. All I could think about was that I was going to be here forever.' And that night when we were sleeping, or one night during that week of camp, was the first time those people were around."

"Do you remember seeing them?

"Sort of. But I'm concerned that this is being fabricated in my mind because of the Mountain View incident, which happened later."

"Something gave you a warning about Gregory being missing. That in itself is remarkable, whether it has anything to do with aliens or not, Fred."

"In my growing-up years of junior high and high school, if I was with a group of people socially, adults or children, it made no difference, if I spent some time with them, I would sit there in my little mind and say, I know what's going to happen to them. And my father, the typical Italian father, would say, 'Don't think. What are you doing there sitting and thinking?' But that was a very minor type of thing. This perceptiveness helped me in the beginning of my career in sales. I could sit with someone, a customer, and he would discuss with me something that was going on in the business, and I'd say, 'Well, if you do that, this might happen. Of, if you expand the business, have you taken into consideration what that's going to do to your existing customers?' But it wasn't as powerful then as it was after the Mountain View encounter. That's when it really started coming in strong!"

"What happened to you? Josie told me you apparently had a close encounter that you remembered without hypnosis. Is that right?"

"Right. Well, I'll tell you about it. One night after a meeting, I had gotten home, was quite tired and went to sleep. During the night, I was awakened. I looked around and there was nobody in the room. The bedroom faced the street. It had a large window, an eight-by-six-foot window, with those old-style venetian blinds. Remember the wide ones, two inches wide, that were so hard to clean? The blinds were open. I was lying there and I started to move. This is the one thing about the whole experience that I have never been able to fully accept or understand. And I probably never will. I went through those venetian blinds! I was absolutely terrified. I went through them. They didn't open. The window didn't open. I literally went through those blinds. To this day, it astounds me! The next thing I saw was a sign saying Church Street. There is a Church Street in Mountain View. Then I saw the building. GTE Sylvania had a light, inflatable building that was kept up by two large fans on each side, and I was over the top of that building. I could see that building, and that's what gave me my bearings. That's how I knew I was still in Mountain View. And I'm looking down at those buildings and down at the Sylvania complex and the Central Expressway. I was thinking, oh my God, what if people see me? I'm nude. Then the next intelligent memory I have is being inside the building. At that time, I thought it was a building. It was a large round room with these people walking around, the aliens."

"Did you know they were aliens?"

"Oh, absolutely!" He laughed and continued, "In the beginning I thought I was inside that inflatable building, and these people had clean-suits on. But I thought, either there's a whole bunch of five-feet-one-inch people working in this building or . . . These things were going through my mind. But this UFO group wanted me to give them technical data. But I had no technical . . . I'm not a technical person. But I'll describe the room to you. It was round, and you couldn't see any light, like a light bulb or a lamp or a chandelier or anything. It had sort of like this backdrop all the way around, with fluorescent-type tubes or something on the other side. That's where the light in the room emanated from. And it was in gray tones. You're seeing color, but everything looked like tones of gray and black, like a very soft black-and-white photograph. And they put me on a table, and that's when I started getting nervous, and I said, 'What are you doing?' We were communicating in a strange way."

"Were you speaking out loud to them, Fred?"

"I was, but they weren't. But I understood everything they were saying to me."

"Were they communicating telepathically?"

"I guess so, because I heard them, but I didn't hear them. My ears didn't hear what they were saying, I did. And, of course, they had those outfits on. They have to wear those, the prophylactic outfits. That's what makes them look weird."

"So you talked to them?"

"Yes, we talked. Of course, I'm an inquisitive person. When they put me on the table, I told them I didn't want to. I asked them what they were going to do, and they said, 'We're not going to hurt you.' And I said, 'I don't want to be on this table. Can't we go sit somewhere?' There's no chairs. 'Let's go sit somewhere.' 'Well, no, we have to do this. We have to take care of this first.' I'm paraphrasing this, but that's what they said to me. And I said, 'No.' That's when I realized that what I said didn't make any difference. That's really hard to deal with, when you're a person who likes to sense that you have control of your life, and you've spent thirty-eight years of your life making decisions in relative freedom, practicing some self-government. But you're practicing it on yourself, self-discipline. To have someone else say to you, 'You haven't got the choice. We have to do this.' There is no choice. That's the hardest thing, Edee, to experience. You have no choice. Well, then they brought a clear Plexiglas dome down. I was lying on my back. I could see through it. I could see everything that was going on. They had some things they used to reach inside. And they were messing with me, but nothing hurt. They were messing with my genitals and my nipples and my teeth." Fred chuckled, "My nipples! It was weird!"

"Were you still nude?

"I don't wear anything to bed. It's one thing to be that way in your bed, it's another to be that way in public. By the way, that's another interesting point. When I was looking down at the building, I was looking down for people. I wanted to shout, 'Hey look at me.' Until I got in front of Sylvania. Then the first thought was that they might see me naked." He looked a little sheepish and smiled. Then, growing serious, he continued, "So they're working on me."

"You're on your back and there's a Plexiglas cover over you, Fred?"

"Yes. A Plexiglas-type of thing. They had a way of manipulating tools inside of that chamber. They could put their hands in, down at the bottom, because I felt that. Not their bare hands, but they could put them in, and they were messing with my feet. I don't know exactly what they were doing. They were looking at me. And then, just like that, the air left that chamber. It was a total vacuum. Caught me completely by surprise. I couldn't breathe. My chest wouldn't move. I was absolutely panicked!"

Fred's hands gripped the arms of the chair. His breathing stopped momentarily. Then he took a deep breath and continued, "She said to me, 'Don't worry. It's going to be okay. This isn't going to last long.' I couldn't talk, but I was thinking, You've got to stop this or I'm going to die. I'm a human. I'm a human. And she was saying, 'So are we.' Then, when that stopped, whatever that vacuum was, there was the greatest feeling, to be breathing again. That it was over! It was like a great physical release for me." His body relaxed and he smiled in relief. "We talked after that. I could tell the males from the females. The females had breasts. The woman, the one who seemed to spend the most time communicating with me, said, 'Of course I have a vagina.' And I said, 'Why did you say that?' And she said, 'Well, you're wondering if we have . . . if we are like you are. I'm just like you and just like everybody else. We're the same. We have children, but we don't have families. We think sometimes that you are children, because of the way you portray us.' And she explained to me why they wear the uniform. It keeps them immune from everything. They may have something. I'm not a doctor, but they may have some bacteria or virus in their system that's perfectly okay for them that could kill us if one of us got it or it spread amongst us, and vice versa. So they wear these outfits. They're white, and they have like sunglasses that are right on the uniform. They're dark, but you can see the eyes in there. You can see the mouth. These uniforms were really tight on their skin. I was trying to figure out how they were breathing, why they weren't suffocating."

"Fred, you must have seen the picture of the alien on the cover of *Communion*. Do you feel that he's of a different species, or do you feel he looks that way because there's a uniform that's covering him?"

He shook his head and rubbed his hand over his mouth. "This is my opinion. That's the way the uniform is. I saw that, the artist's rendition on the cover of *Communion*, and I've seen other renditions. That's the way you and I would look if we had one of those suits on."

"Do you think the reason they don't appear to have hair is because their heads are covered?"

"I don't know whether they have hair or not. But, for instance, most of your hair is on the top of your head, and if you had that outfit on, your hair would be bulging inside of it, and there was no bulging. It was tight, all the way down. I could tell the age of those fellows. I could sense they were in their late twenties, early thirties. And I could tell she was pretty and very feminine. Yet when they were away from me in the room, talking in some other areas, from the rear they all looked the same, except for a little difference in the woman's figure. We discussed the similarities between us and them. There is no difference except for height. They're just like us. They have eyes and teeth, and they eat food, and breathe air and things like that."

"And you know that from the conversation?"

"Yes. I really learned a lot. They treated me like I was a child."

"The sequence is that they brought you in, then they put you on the table, then they talked to you afterward?"

"When I first came in there, the conversation was very curt, polite but curt, sort of reassuring. Then they went through this messing with my body. After that, it seemed to be more like we're talking now, except I was lying there talking. I'm talking, they're not talking, okay? And another thing, Edee, when I was inside the case, whatever it was, we could still communicate. In other words, they either had a microphone in there or they were using whatever it is they use. Which reminds me, she seemed to be the one who was doing most of the talking. Everybody else was kind of busy. Have you ever had an operation?"

"Yes."

"You know how it is when they first give you the gas or whatever it is they give you. You see people walking around doing things, and you wonder what they're doing. It's very similar to that. A lot of activity. Nobody's just sitting there."

"How many people were there?"

"In that chamber, in the beginning there were about a dozen and at the end there were probably five, including her."

"Were all of them interacting with you? Were they all doing things related to your presence?"

"I think so. There were some of them over there working on a table, and there was some equipment. That is when I saw their backs. But my sense is that everything that was going on had to do with me. She was the one who began the conversation about oneness and how we've got them wrong."

"I'd love to know more about that in detail."

Fred chuckled and leaned back in the chair, crossing his arms behind his head. "I guess I started my usual wisecracking, typical salesman. I was making comments to myself, but she heard them, can you understand that? I had thoughts about her. Of course, she picked up on them. Then she would respond to me, you know, very professionally. But I could tell when she was feeling humorous. When they were talking back and forth, I could sense the humor. By the way, I couldn't understand what their conversations were at all. I don't even remember if it was verbal or mental, except I knew they were talking. She would talk to them and then talk to me, or he would talk to me and then talk to somebody else. And I'm getting it when they're talking to me, but not getting it when they're talking to someone else. Yet I knew they were talking, they were communicating."

"But it seems you could pick up that they were being humorous with each other."

"Yes, and with me. And our kind of humor. The real emotion of humor. Then she said, 'You've got it all wrong.' I don't, but she meant people. She explained, 'We're not invading anybody. And we're not here to stop people from causing a nuclear holocaust. All the different things that you think about us are false. We're the ones with the problem.' And that's when I came unglued. 'We're the ones with the problem. We want to know more about where we came from so that we can resolve this problem, the oneness problem.' As best I understood it, they're technologically and intellectually ahead of us, but the things that make up the elements of a human are the same universally. The emotions, the feelings, the bad as well as the good, the quest for power, for domination. We're all linked that way. She said they had reached a point where they had eliminated almost any form of discrimination, prejudice or conflicts, because of years and years and years of working the way we're working toward this goal, one race, one nation, one world type of thing. Those are my words, not hers. They don't have religious conflicts. They don't have wars. They haven't got affirmative-action programs. They don't need them. We didn't need them either then. But using that to illustrate, they don't have race wars and KKKs and all that kind of stuff. But what they've done to themselves is that they've lost their identity. They've lost their individuality. There's an emotion in her when she's discussing this with me. And what they're leaving with me is, first of all, I wasn't picked because I have anything special about me. Those people in that laboratory didn't know how the selection process worked."

"What do you mean by the selection process? How were you selected?"

"Yes. I mean, it's not that I might be smarter than someone else or more available, or dumber than someone else. That wasn't their decision to make. They had these random selections that were going on. According to her, they had been doing it for a couple of years at that point. So we talked, communicated about this oneness thing. And they see our conflicts from an admirable point of view. They don't see anything wrong with people having differences in beliefs or philosophies of life, but as the essence of individuality. So what has happened with them is they lost their identity, their individuality and their uniqueness. Maybe they have lost the sense of destiny and of individual achievement, all

these individual things that we take for granted." Fred took a
deep breath and leaned forward. "You can imagine what it was
like for me, after having that experience. I had some prejudices
before, and they were gone. All of a sudden, I looked at some
people whom I had held in a prejudice, and now I said, this is a
unique person. I can't be who I am, if he's not who he is. Because
if he and I were the same, I would lose my identity, my individuality."

"That's pretty powerful thinking, Fred." I was mentally planning the regression we would be starting soon. I asked Fred for
more details about the sequence of events.

"It seemed like we conversed for a long time. I was very comfortable. I was not self-conscious of the fact that I had no clothes
on. I wished it could have gone on longer. But I thought that
must be what it's like to be raped, because someone else controls
your body, and there's nothing you can do. Nothing! But I didn't
feel that way afterward, when we were talking. Then it was like
just talking, like we're talking, sharing ideas and things like that. I
have this thirst to know more, to know as much as I could. And
some I forgot, by the way. It comes back to me every once in a
while. Then, Edee, I don't know when I left. I do remember
being back in bed and saying to myself, Oh God, you just had a
nightmare. And I fell asleep. When I woke up, I remembered it.
But I went around during the first week almost in a state of
euphoria." He frowned and continued, "With the exception of
when I was listening to people saying things that I knew were
taking them in a direction that was dangerous, dangerous in relation to the understanding I had from the aliens, of what they
considered danger to be. So I started to be one of the boys." He
shook his head resignedly.

"What do you mean by that?"

"Started drinking and denying the thing. I got ahead of myself,
Edee. I was going to say that first week was euphoric, but after
that I really felt violated. I felt that I had been personally violated.
And it took a long time to get over that. That's a weird emotion.
On the one hand, there's the excitement of the experience and

what it has done, and at the same time, feeling that you really have been abused."

"Do you feel that there are any other negative consequences of that incident still affecting you? Any symptoms or vulnerabilities that you would consider negative changes?"

"Yes." He paused and scratched his head. "It's this uncanny ability I have to make projections. It's a plus and a liability."

"Fred, are you still drinking excessively?"

"The alcoholism's not an issue anymore. That was dealt with successfully through hypnosis. By the way, one more thing of interest. It's New Year's Eve, and my wife and I and another couple are on Front Street in Lahaina, in an open restaurant, looking out to the ocean. New Year's Eve is a big celebration in Hawaii. There was a bit of a storm, and the power went out, and we're sitting in the restaurant with a minimum of fifty people, plus people walking up and down the street, celebrating. I looked up and saw a UFO. Actually I saw three of them, in formation, and I nudged my wife. I said, 'Look!' And she said, 'I'll be darned!' And she turned to our friends and said, 'Hey, you guys, there's three of them up there!' And they looked up and saw them, and then we talked about it for a little while. And we said, 'We saw some of those when we were in Scotland.' And this was just a casual, midnight-snack conversation amongst four people. I would estimate there were a minimum of sixty thousand people who were awake at that moment on the island of Maui. Some of them must have been looking in the sky. We were the only ones that saw them, as far as we know. Because I didn't see anything in the paper the next day. There was nothing on the radio about it."

"What did the UFOs look like?"

"These were what I call the triangle-style, because you can see the three engines on the bottom of the ships emitting exhaust and fire. So it looks like three triangles flying in the sky. But since it's dark, you can't see the shape of the ships, all you're seeing are the engines, but they were flying in formation. What you're looking at when you look up there are three little round balls of fire in the shape of a triangle, flying in a group of three. In our type of formation, the V-formation. Isn't that cute?"

"Fred, our time is slipping away. Let's do the regression now."
Fred was a naturally good hypnotic subject. His work with Josie
had enhanced his ability to slip easily and quickly into an excellent trance. I asked his inner mind to take him to his first close
encounter with the visitors. After a brief pause, he began speaking
slowly, in a higher, childish voice.

✱

FRED:   I'm in the Boy Scouts. I'm eleven years old. We're on a
survival trek, having a ball, singing songs, talking about the girls
over at the camp on the other side of the mountain. And
Gregory's not there.

DR. FIORE:   What makes you think of him?

FRED:   I don't know, we're just all together on the trail, having a
ball. I don't even know him.

DR. FIORE:   Go to the very moment when you think of him.

FRED:   I had to go find some sticks. That's how we cook. No
forks or anything. We gotta learn how to survive. We have to get
these sticks, birch, hardwood. There's not much birch around.
And I was out scrubbing around, and there was a guy sitting
there on a rock.

DR. FIORE:   What do you think when you see him?

FRED:   "Hi! I'm looking for birch." He has black hair, white
skin, black eyes. Kinda skinny. [*Whispers*] Not much bigger
than me.

DR. FIORE:   How is he dressed?

FRED:   He has on a shirt and pants and shoes.

DR. FIORE:   He's just dressed normally?

FRED:   Except he's really white. He needs sun bad.

DR. FIORE:   Are you startled when you see him?

FRED:   No. The guys are around. I could holler out. I don't think that's real hair. It looks like somebody painted it on there. No beard, no hair on his face. No smile either. "What do you want?" "You're special." "Why me?" [*Whispers*]

DR. FIORE:   Go back to the very moment you saw him, and take it second by second.

FRED:   There's all this mesquite and tumbleweeds and stuff, and I'm trying to find some hardwood to make my utensil out of. And I come walking around, and there he is, sitting there. [*Pauses*] "What do you want? What do you want me for? Oh God . . ." [*Cries*] "I'm not going to hurt you. Everything's going to be fine." And before the day's over, I'll know that we've talked to each other. He's going to prove it to me. "You're going to make me some kind of Captain Midnight?" "No. . . . We need you to help us. You're going to help us. And you're not going to say anything to anybody." "How do you know that? I'm going to go tell Mr. Foster." "No you won't." [*Whispers*] He's not any bigger than I am. [*Long pause*] Now he's gone. What a weirdo! [*Cries*]

DR. FIORE:   What are you feeling?

FRED:   I waited until he was gone before I cried. [*Cries*] 'Cause he scared the shit out of me.

DR. FIORE:   Do you know why he was scary?

FRED:   No. [*Trembles*] I don't know what's going to happen, and he said I would. And I'm scared. It's all stupid stuff!

DR. FIORE: Let's find out what happened. Move ahead in that same day to the next significant event.

FRED: We're on our survival hike. And I notice that this kid, Gregory, isn't there.

DR. FIORE: Move to the very moment when you notice that.

FRED: Holy shit! Aha . . . The guy is over there on the other side of a tree. Spooky. And I see him and he sees me with those little beady black eyes. And I look and there's no Gregory. And I have this feeling that Gregory's in trouble. I told the guys.

DR. FIORE: Move to the moment when you had the feeling that Gregory is in trouble.

FRED: I'm looking right into those little black eyes, right in those eyes, yeah, yeah. . . .

DR. FIORE: What thoughts come into your mind?

FRED: Gregory's gone, Gregory's going to die. I've got to check. Then the little guy's gone. And I say, "Aren't some of you guys going to go with me." They say, "No." And I went back. And I heard him, like whimpering. And Greg's big. And my first thought was, I'll bet he's down there. And what am I going to do if he's down there? I can't help him. He's going to pull me over if I stick my hand down there. I looked over the edge, and there his face was, right there. I could almost reach him, and he's crying. He says, "Help me, Freddie." And I look around and the guys are gone, and I can't find the little beady-eyed guy either. And I finally figured out how I could help him. I wrapped my legs around this massive tumbleweed. It was sticking in my legs. And I got ahold of his arm and his neck, fricking near choked him. [*Long pause*] I got a badge from Mr. Foster. But I don't want badges and stuff. I can see Mr. Foster standing up there with his little badge, chewing everybody's ass out. "You always take a count before you leave," he said.

DR. FIORE:   Now move to the encounter that you call the Mountain View incident. Let yourself remember it exactly as it happened.

FRED:   [*Pauses*] I'm looking down at everything. I'm looking at me. I'm looking at me lying in bed.

DR. FIORE:   How do you feel as you're doing that?

FRED:   Silly. Yes . . . Not bad-looking. I'm trying to hide from . . . going through those venetian blinds, because I know that's going to happen. [*Whispers*] Oh no! [*Pauses*] Okay, take me where you want me. Take me. [*Long pause*]

DR. FIORE:   Continue speaking out.

FRED:   I'm scared to death. I'm floating. I had pizza after the meeting. Maybe it's the pizza. I'm floating, and I'm naked. And there's the House of Pancakes . . . Payless. I'm over the top of the Leisure Arms. Wow . . . El Camino, the Chevy Dealer. There's the building. It's kept up by air, you know. Like a balloon. Church Street. [*Long pause*]

DR. FIORE:   You're going to let yourself remember this exactly as it happened.

FRED:   I'm scared. I'm inside. I know I'm inside, but I can't see anything, and there's people here. Oh boy! The lights! I'm on the table.

DR. FIORE:   How did you get on the table?

FRED:   I don't know.

DR. FIORE:  Let yourself remember.

FRED:  It was black, like going inside of an armadillo shell. And now, here I am. But I'm smarter this time. It's not like I thought it would be. I'm not living it. I'm seeing it like a movie.

DR. FIORE:  From what vantage point are you seeing it?

FRED:  I'm on the table, but I'm standing here. Very nice, clean place, circular. No direct lighting anywhere. Gray. It's like being in a black-and-white movie, but it's not. Equipment all around the room, a lot of space. Small people.

DR. FIORE:  How tall are they?

FRED:  Four feet eight to five-two. And everything's clean, spotless clean. No pictures anywhere, no calendars, nothing. Trying to see the gauges. I got the message I can't go over there. I'm to stay right here. But I'm outfoxing them. Because I'm standing up, looking down at me. Now I can see what they're going to do. She knows everything that I think of and everything that I'm saying. I am not going to spend my life as a living test tube. No matter how good it might be for me. And I'm getting hot. It's hot in here. [*Whistles*] "Could you cool it down a little bit?" "No." "I'd like to get up." They're not going to let me. I feel kind of foolish. And now, all I want to do is get it over with.

DR. FIORE:  What's happening?

FRED:  They put this cover over me that's made out of some kind of clear like glass. God, I feel naked! No clothes. And now they're messing with me.

DR. FIORE:  What do you mean by that?

FRED: They have some way of getting inside here with probes. Poking at me. Poking at me! I'm not circumcised. [*Laughs*] It's embarrassing.

DR. FIORE: At this point, do you feel you're in your body?

FRED: Yes! Boy, oh boy! Is it hot in here! Phew! . . . "Oh, thank you, thank you, thank you." [*Whispers*] I gotta help you. They're taking it off now. Just—white! Tight to the skin. Outfit. And those girls have got nice bodies. Small, but nice. I feel like a fool, because whatever I think, I know they're hearing. [*Pauses*] And we should not be that way about them. They are just like we are, just smaller. And that could have happened in any galaxy in the universe. It all depends on how people breed, whom they select for their mates. And the head is normal, maybe a little bit bigger. So don't expect any new great mystery. [*Laughs*] And they do it! And they have babies. And . . . yes, the fingers are small.

DR. FIORE: How many fingers do they have?

FRED: Four and a thumb. And it's warm. I can feel it through the uniform. It's just small.

DR. FIORE: What's small?

FRED: They're just small. [*Long pause*] Yes . . . I feel very good. I wish I could just stay here for a long time. Taste, smell, taste, smell, taste, smell. [*Whispers*] It's like the inside of a scuba mask. That's what it tastes and smells like, the inside of a scuba mask.

DR. FIORE: Go to the feeling of the vacuum that you described before.

FRED: I beat it this time. I outsmarted them. When I knew they were going to do it, I beat it, somehow.

DR. FIORE:   How did you know what they were going to do?

FRED:   Because I've been here before. I know how they operate.

DR. FIORE:   How did you beat it?

FRED:   I closed off. This is gonna kinda screw things up, I'm afraid. Can't have one without the other. Can't have the sharing without the vacuum.

DR. FIORE:   Where do you get that idea?

FRED:   From her. I feel like a little kid, trying to beat my mommy at something and I got caught. So it's going to come back down. It's going to come back down. [*Whispers*] Shall I just give in to it? [*Pauses*] Oh yes. They don't use anesthesia. They don't use that kind of stuff. They can put you in this, and they can just hack away and do anything they want. And when it's over, you feel good instead of sick. [*Pauses*] I can't get away from the table. They won't let me. [*Long pause*] I wish I knew why it was me. I wish I could be of more help. And I wish I could bring this little lady back to my apartment tonight. [*Smiles*]

DR. FIORE:   How did she respond when you had that thought?

FRED:   She laughed. Have you ever heard a person laugh and not seen the mouth move? Quite an experience. Isn't it funny how we develop concepts about things and people and all that, and then when you get right down to it, everything is so logical. Like humor. He's . . . oh, the guy down at the end where my feet are, I'll bet if I got that mask off, he'd be that little beady-eyed guy. [*Pauses*] They really don't want to hurt anybody. They really don't want to mess up things or alter the course of our lives. That's why they stay up here the way they do, instead of landing somewhere. They don't trust . . . the nature of man, because they are like us. They know that the people would get ahold of those things and they might use them for the wrong reasons.

DR. FIORE:   Is that what they're telling you?

FRED:   Yes. And I'm a simpleminded man, and that's why I'm here. I thought that was pretty unique to us Americans, and that's why I'm here. I want to know how I was selected. They say they have no choice, that that's taken care of before they get here. [*Pauses*] I wish we could do some things together. I'd like to take them to a football game. [*Shakes his head*] They've already been to a football game.

DR. FIORE:   How do you know that?

FRED:   They've seen everything.

DR. FIORE:   How do you know that?

FRED:   She told me. "We can travel at the speed of thought. And if you would just think about it logically, you would understand." And they eat food.

DR. FIORE:   Did you see that happen, or did she tell you that?

FRED:   She told me that. I can't see anybody eating. I can't see how they could eat anyway.

DR. FIORE:   What's happening now?

FRED:   There's a round like door over on the wall. There's like a uniform stretched around the door. They climb into the uniform from outside, so that when they're into the room, the uniform is around them. And there's this guy helping them. Then they shut the door, and then the next time somebody comes in, the same thing is repeated. They put this white uniform around the door, the way you'd put a balloon on a whistle. And the other side is similar. The door is gray. And when they open that door, when they go out, they leave the uniform inside.

DR. FIORE: Now what's happening?

FRED: Cholesterol. I don't even understand what that word means. My first exposure to the word cholesterol.

DR. FIORE: Who mentions that word?

FRED: The guy at my feet.

DR. FIORE: What does he say to you?

FRED: He says, "Cholesterol!" It's negative. It's . . . ewww . . . cholesterol!

DR. FIORE: What is he implying?

FRED: Like he's saying, "Ewww . . . gonorrhea. Yuk!" He's not saying gonorrhea, but he's saying cholesterol in the same . . . way. It's disgusting to him. [*Long pause*] I'm feeling like I'm waking up. I just had the wildest dream of my life! That's what it was. It's nothing more than a dream, an illusion. Because there's absolutely no way in the world that I can go through those venetian blinds.

DR. FIORE: Go back to just before you wake up.

FRED: Cholesterol.

DR. FIORE: What happens next?

FRED: Cholesterol. Then she puts her hand on me, and it's warm.

DR. FIORE: What part of your body does she touch?

FRED: She's touching my stomach. And . . . I don't know what he's doing down there. My feet are kinda gross. Doesn't seem to bother him. I want to know if we're ever going to see each other again.

DR. FIORE: Whom do you mean when you say that?

FRED: The girl and . . . I'm not really supposed to say "girl," you know.

DR. FIORE: Did she say not to use the word "girl"?

FRED: Yes, and "man" too. But I don't know how else to communicate. Think. And I really want to know what this is going to do to my life.

DR. FIORE: What do they say to you?

FRED: There will be no harm, and that it will be good. That woman was right. They had been with me before. And there'll be no harm, and I'll be wiser. I was chosen. They don't know how. I mean, they do what somebody else tells them to do. The people who are chosen are people who will not exploit the experience. Can you imagine that word? Exploit the experience. How in hell are you going to exploit it? And I'll be taken when my work is done.

DR. FIORE: What does that mean to you?

FRED: I don't know. I say, "What do you guys think about God, G-o-d?" [Pauses] They have God, same one. But there hasn't been a Jesus there.

DR. FIORE: Is that what they told you?

FRED: Yes. And all the elements are the same. Minerals, and the chemistry of the body, the uniqueness of the human.

DR. FIORE:   Did they tell you where they're from?

FRED:   No.

DR. FIORE:   Did they tell you what galaxy they're from?

FRED:   This one. "Do you know if there's any more [earth's]?" Yes. There's more earths, not E-a-r-t-h, in this galaxy.

DR. FIORE:   What does that mean to you?

FRED:   There's consistency of creation in the universe. And that maybe I should have spent more time in my science classes.

DR. FIORE:   Is that what they told you?

FRED:   No. That's what I said, and it brought a laugh. There's a black guy and a white woman who're married, and they went for two days.

DR. FIORE:   How do you know that?

FRED:   She just told me.

DR. FIORE:   Who told you?

FRED:   My friend here. She was trying to make me feel better about not doing well in science. I guess I better start reading books about this stuff, huh? I don't know anything about those people. I'll find out later.

DR. FIORE:   Continue to speak out.

FRED:   I'm just getting to feel better all the time. I'd like to spend a little time with the guys, but she seems to be hanging on here. I feel like they're not going to let me off this table. And I'm lying here thinking that I'm in control of the situation, and yet I have no control. My friend here, at my feet, tells me that they don't rule my emotions. They don't rule each other's either. And that . . . that would be the ultimate disaster for anybody. They're just like we are when it comes to that business. Water. Must have water and oxygen and food. "And I need to know how you can communicate the way you do, because I think that would be a wonderful thing." And I am told that outside of the experiment, they communicate just like we do. I mean noise comes out of the mouth. They don't speak English, but we could learn their language. "Why do you keep it so warm in here?" "Your bodies have to be warmed up." "Tell me what it looks like over there." And that's the simplicity of it all, no methane gas floating around in the sky. They have oceans, salt, and water and clouds, everything.

DR. FIORE:   Now what's happening?

FRED:   [*Smiles*] I want to hold them. That's an earthling emotion. "But I really would like to give you guys a hug. Because I believe that you really are who you are, and you really are here for the reasons that you've told me, and I'd like to give you a good old-fashioned hug." And I'm sitting up, and he's saying, "Don't leave the table." And I'm hugging him. You can almost feel right through these things. Nice hug. And she's telling me to remember to look for the logical, simple things to find the answers and stuff. And I said, "How can I go home without getting off the table?" I see little flashes. Vividly! Like shooting stars or something, and . . . I'm lying in my bed.

DR. FIORE:   Are you back in your home now?

FRED:   Yes.

DR. FIORE:   How do you feel?

FRED:   Great.

✎

Fred took a while to come completely out of hypnosis. There was something obviously still bothering him. "I realized with the Gregory incident that nobody else was going to either believe me or help me. I started back down the path. I don't know how, but I knew he was in trouble. It was like a dream. I heard him sobbing, but I couldn't see him. I knew he was down on the side of that ledge, somewhere. My first reaction was to pretend that I didn't hear him. To pretend he really wasn't there and to run away, so that I wouldn't have to help him. The reason I didn't want to help him was he might pull me over." Fred smiled guiltily. "Maybe the real reason was that I didn't want to accept that the beady-eyed man was real. I didn't want to accept that he could arrange Greg's accident." He turned in his chair and looked out the window at the creek. With his back to me, he said. "But most of all, I didn't want him to single me out."

After a few seconds of silence, he rotated the chair back and looked deeply into my eyes. There were tears welling up in his. He stared down at his lap as though weighing something in his mind. Then, seeming to have resolved a conflict, he looked up at me again and smiled broadly. "I guess they have. And I'm glad they have. I wonder what's next?"

**15**

# "... The Signs and Symptoms That Are Indicators."

As you were reading in the preceding chapters how thirteen people experienced their close encounters of the fourth kind, you may have noticed certain features that many accounts of abductions had in common, as well as some features that were unique to a particular case.

In order to help you assess whether you have had a close encounter with extraterrestrials, I'll describe the signs and symptoms that are indicators. It is not necessary to have experienced all of them, sometimes just one important indicator can give you a very strong clue about the repressed event. Often, that one may be only the tip of the iceberg.

1. One of the most telling signs of a CEIV is the phenomenon of missing time. As you can imagine, the experience of being removed from one's home or car, for example, and then transported into a craft, the subsequent meeting with ETs and being returned, takes time. It is a very common finding that there is a gap, usually of about an hour or more, though sometimes less.

One of the very first cases I studied involved a loss of about one

319

and one-half hours. Two women were in their car when the CEIV occurred and were surprised to find that time had elapsed, though they had no memory of what had happened in the interim, and also to find that their vehicle was on a road going in the opposite direction from their destination. They had been abducted, car and all, and deposited in a remote area.

Missing time is usually noticed after day or evening abductions, which took place while the person was awake, as contrasted with the frequent CEIVs that begin while the person is sleeping and therefore has no concept of time.

2. As you may have seen in many of the cases you've read about in *Encounters,* nightmares or dreams of UFOs or aliens (or monsters with large eyes) were later revealed to be memories of actual happenings. ETs often give hypnotic commands to contactees that they will only remember the experience as a dream. Sometimes they give suggestions that the event will not be remembered at all, but the mind tries to heal itself through the dreaming process, so the flashback is remembered as a dream upon awakening. Take seriously even one dream, especially a nightmare. *Write it down as soon as you awaken. Do not wait!* Dreams, no matter how vivid, have a way of evaporating.

3. Sleep disorders are often strong indicators for many reasons. If you consistently wake up at a certain time, for example 1:43 A.M., you can be reasonably sure that something traumatic happened at exactly that time. If you are unable to go to sleep easily and naturally, it may be that your subconscious mind is seeing to it that you do not put yourself in a position for the traumatic event to be repeated. That's the subconscious's job. Likewise, sleeping very lightly may be a way of avoiding vulnerability. However, as you have seen, it certainly doesn't matter whether a person is asleep or not for an abduction/contact to take place. But the subconscious mind does not operate with the same logic as the conscious mind.

Of course, sleep disorders may be due to many causes that have nothing to do with CEIVs, and if disturbing, should be treated by competent medical and/or psychological specialists.

4. If you wake up during the night or in the morning with

unusual bodily sensations, even once, you may be experiencing the aftermath of a CEIV. Actually, this telling sign may occur other than on awakening. Remember Sandi from Chapter Two? She "came to" from her CEIV on her living-room couch in the evening. The most common bodily sensations are tingling, numbness, dizziness, heaviness and paralysis. These are often accompanied by disorientation. All of these sensations are temporary. Take note of them, especially if you experience this sign in addition to others. But be warned: Like sleep disorders, these sensations may be due to physical conditions requiring medical attention, perhaps urgently.

5. In a few of the cases in this book, and in others that I did not include, individuals found unexplained marks on their bodies. These were due to procedures done during an examination and/or operation or treatment. Scrapes, fine red lines, little scooped out marks, bruises which suggest that blood was drawn are all frequent indicators of a CEIV. Nosebleeds, bleeding from the ear, finding blood on the sheets that cannot be explained are signs that should be noted. These may be due to insertion of tracking implants. One of my patients reported she had a little extra "cartilage" at the base of her nose, almost between her eyebrows. Medical tests could not determine what it was. She suspected it was some sort of tracking device that had been inserted by the visitors. And remember the case of Tom of Chapter Five. He also found something had appeared in his nose overnight.

6. ETs are monitoring and watching people throughout the world. If you suspect that they are monitoring you, you could be correct. On the other hand, many emotionally and mentally troubled individuals believe they are being monitored by the CIA, FBI, the television or aliens.

It appears that the visitors communicate with us by telepathy (mental talking). We are told to go outside, to drive to a deserted area, to look into the sky, etc. Unfortunately, the issue again becomes cloudy, because many emotionally and mentally disturbed people feel they are being communicated with and controlled by others, including extraterrestrials. These paranoid ideas come from within themselves and have no basis in reality. Also, to add to the confusion, CEIVs and subsequent communication and monitoring can lead to emotional/mental imbalances. This is why I have emphasized the need for finding a competent therapist or investigator.

7. Many abductees/contactees report seeing UFOs repeatedly. Even one sighting can be the remembered part of an abduction, the major part being repressed. However, if you often see UFOs, it is quite probable that you have had one or more CEIVs.

8. Some people remember their CEIVs clearly, exactly as they would any other significant experience. Most only remember the event vaguely, even doubting that it actually happened. If you remember anything at all resembling the encounters you read about in this book or in others, you are probably recalling an experience that actually happened.

9. As you saw, for example in the cases of James (Chapter Ten) and Ted (Chapter Eight), healings took place. In about one-half of the cases I've been involved with, there have been healings due to operations and/or treatments. Sometimes the cures are permanent. At other times, the conditions recur. There can be many other reasons for spontaneous cures or improvements of physical conditions. But if you have noticed a healing or inexplicable improvement, and you see other signs of a probable CEIV, you may have had help from the visitors.

10. Reactions of fear, anxiety, unusual bodily sensations (tingling, numbness, heaviness, etc.) to pictures of, movies or documentaries about, of discussions of UFOs and CEIVs are very clear indicators of abductions by aliens. A friend of mine noticed she felt faint and her heart started beating wildly when she picked up a book, *Communion*, at a local bookstore. As an experiment, I showed her the cover of the Time-Life book *The UFO Phenomenon*, and she was again overcome by anxiety. A later regression under hypnosis revealed a CEIV.

I'll now give you a checklist of the ten most common indicators of CEIVs.

1. Missing time
2. Nightmares and/or dreams of UFOs and/or aliens

3. Sleep disorders
4. Waking up with unusual bodily sensations
5. Unexplained marks on the body
6. Feeling monitored, watched and/or communicated with
7. Repeated UFO sightings
8. Vague recollection of close encounter(s)
9. Unexplained healing
10. Fear of and/or anxiety about UFOs and/or ETs

While the foregoing are the most common signs of a CEIV, there are many other less frequent indicators that I'll briefly touch on now.

When people are abducted or contacted, they are often told of a mission or task that they are to carry out immediately or in the future. Since the experience is repressed, the feeling of needing to do something important nudges at them, yet they do not know what they are supposed to be doing.

A number of fears, all related to the buried traumas, present problems of varying degrees of seriousness. Fears of needles, being kidnapped, UFOs, monsters, aliens, creatures with large eyes—like owls—the dark, certain places in the home or outside, and many other fears and aversions, have been traced to CEIVs.

People often develop psychic abilities (telepathy, precognition, clairvoyance, etc.) after CEIVs. Since these experiences may have occurred very early in childhood, it is not unusual for these individuals to feel they were born that way.

Seeing a beam of light or balls of light in the house is often the remembered part of a CEIV. Sometimes people just remember waking up with the room full of light.

If you have found yourself outside at night without remembering how you got there, it could very well be that you had just been returned from a CEIV. Or, if you've felt an irrepressible urge to go outside at night, you could have been given a telepathic command to do so by aliens.

It is commonly found that UFO buffs or others with an intense interest in ufology and CEIVs are contactees. Leo Sprinkle, Ph.D., known throughout the world for his research into the contactee phenomenon, discovered only recently through hypnotic regression that he himself was a contactee. I believe that most researchers and therapists specializing in this area have been contacted or abducted.

As I mentioned previously, any anxiety reactions experienced while reading this or any other book on UFOs and CEIVs is a strong indicator. What is happening in this case, as with any reactions of anxiety in relation to this topic, is that you are actually partially reliving the original traumatic experience during which you felt anxiety, maybe even terror.

◢

Now that you know the signs and indicators of repressed close encounters with extraterrestrials and have determined that you've experienced one or more signs yourself, you are ready to discover if you have had a CEIV and, if so, what happened during it. The next chapter gives you a simple technique you can use in the privacy of your own home to explore this amazing possibility.

**16**

# "You Can Discover
# Your Own Close Encounters."

By now you realize that your subconscious mind has a perfect memory. *Everything* you have ever experienced is recorded in your subconscious memory banks exactly as you perceived it. The inner mind can be seen as your own personal computer. With a computer, you can access files. With your subconscious mind, you can retrieve memories. Therefore you can discover your own close encounters of the fourth kind. Later in the chapter, I'll show you a simple, time-honored method for exploring forgotten memories.

You have seen in previous chapters how people under hypnosis recalled and, at times, vividly relived experiences that they were totally unaware had happened. Repressed memories, those that the conscious mind cannot access, sometimes spontaneously surface in dreams or meditation. On occasion, something will trigger them and they will break through to conscious awareness on their own. The trigger is usually something strongly reminiscent of an aspect of the buried event: a picture, an account, smell, place, anything so similar to what has been repressed that the forces keeping it forgotten are overcome.

325

The *only* method that I consider safe for you to use on your own is a form of dowsing, using the pendulum. The pendulum, as a dowsing tool, has been used over the centuries for many different purposes: to find missing people (by holding the pendulum over a map); to ascertain the health of the body; to find gold, silver and other minerals; to discover underground water, etc. There are many theories about why and how it works. I personally feel that it taps in to a part of our subconscious mind that is omniscient. In exploring your own possible close encounters, you will be using it as a means of accessing your memory banks.

However valuable and remarkable the pendulum can be, it is *not* infallible. At times, the answers obtained are wrong, misleading or contradictory. However, I and other UFO researchers have found it to be very helpful for exposing repressed sightings and encounters. When you use it, consider the responses as probabilities, not as gospel. It helps, in terms of validity, to double-check, by going over the same questions again on another day and seeing how closely the answers match. Remember, you are using your subconscious mind, and your conscious mind may be interfering. For that reason, *it is imperative to remain as neutral as possible, to leave emotions out,* as you are questioning your inner mind. Also, do not allow a conscious answer to remain in your mind. Take the position of really asking a question, not trying to confirm a preconceived idea. You may be very surprised by the answers you receive.

By using a pendulum, you can discover whether you have ever seen a UFO and especially if you have had one or more encounters of the fourth kind.

Most bookstores and/or shops that specialize in metaphysical subjects and/or crystals or minerals have pendulums of many kinds and different sizes. Some are made of quartz or other attractive minerals set in gold or silver so that they can be used as necklaces. Others are made from various woods or metals. I have an assortment of pendulums that I've collected over the years. One of my favorites is a small clear quartz crystal suspended from Indian beadwork that covers one end.

It is, however, very easy to make your own pendulum in a

matter of minutes. All you need is a string or heavy thread between six and ten inches long. Tie a button, bead, ring, pendant, or even a small cross to one end of the string. Any slightly heavy object may be used, but it is better to use one that is symmetrical.

Once you have an adequate pendulum, sit at a table or desk, hold the end of the string between your right thumb and index finger if you are right-handed (left thumb and index finger if left-handed). Rest your elbow on the table or desk. *Without consciously* moving the pendulum, think the word "yes" and will the pendulum to move back and forth in front of you. When you nod your head indicating "yes," you are moving it in the same plane or direction as the desired swing of the pendulum. To establish the "no" response, use the same technique. *Without deliberately* moving the pendulum, think the word "no" and will the pendulum to swing from right to left, or left to right, in a side-to-side movement, just as when you shake your head "no."

At first, the pendulum may not budge. Keep thinking "yes," and imagine it moving back and forth. Soon it will easily and freely swing back and forth in front of you as you think "yes," and from side to side as you think "no." When this happens, you are ready to ask your subconscious mind questions.

While you are establishing the pendulum responses, remain calm and patient. *Know that you can do it!* If you do not succeed the first time, keep trying. Everyone can eventually develop this technique. Once you have the signals working for you, you will have a wonderful tool for exploring your own subconscious mind!

If you use the pendulum on more than one occasion, start each session by reinforcing the yes and no responses. I have used it innumerable times, and each time I get it swinging strongly in the yes and no responses before I begin.

If you become upset while working on your list of questions, stop for a while. Calm yourself. Do something else, and later, or on another occasion, try again. If you are entirely too upset to continue, you have already answered a major question by your reactions. You probably have had one or more encounters and should seek help. The Appendix lists organizations and people who can work with you.

I have designed a list of fifty questions, which follows. You may use these questions or write out your own. If you use the ones here, place a sheet of paper next to you and write the numbers corresponding to the questions, 1 through 50, down the left-hand side. You will record your responses, yes or no (Y-N), next to each number. At the top, you may want to record the date. Then, if you later double-check the answers, write the new date next to the new answers. That way you can compare the responses on each occasion. If you do seek additional help with your exploration, the dates may be important.

I suggest that you have another sheet of paper handy for questions or thoughts that occur to you as you are reading and answering the questions on the list. Another way to go beyond my list is to remember any questions that came up in your mind while you were reading *Encounters*. You may want to reread it, all the while very carefully monitoring your reactions, physical, mental and/or emotional. From these responses, you can compose your own questions.

1. Have I ever seen a UFO?
2. Do I have a subconscious memory of seeing a UFO?
3. Have I had a UFO experience that I do not remember with my conscious mind? (More than one—two, three, etc.?)
4. Have any dreams actually been memories of a CEIV? UFO sighting?
5. Was I alone when I had the UFO experience(s)?
6. Was the experience(s) traumatic? (Emotionally? Mentally? Physically?)
7. Did the experience(s) involve ETs?
8. Where was I first contacted by ETs? Outside? Inside? (Backyard, bedroom, living room, etc.?)
9. Was I taken aboard a UFO?
10. Was I examined physically? (Genitally?)
11. Were instruments used in the examination?
12. Was a needle(s) inserted into any part of my body? (Navel, head, nose, ear, etc.?)
13. Was a "medical" treatment done?

14. Was an operation performed?
15. Were lasers involved?
16. Did any treatment or operation help me?
17. Was I cured of a physical problem?
18. Was I questioned?
19. Did the ETs speak?
20. Did the ETs use telepathy? (Communicate without speech.)
21. Was I given an explanation for the abduction/contact?
22. Was I given information?
23. Did the ETs look like humans?
24. Were they over five feet tall? (Under five, four, three feet?)
25. Were there ETs of different sizes involved?
26. Were there different kinds (species) of ETs involved?
27. Was there more than one ET involved? (Two, three, etc.?)
28. Did the UFO encounter (or first encounter) occur before I was twelve years old? (Five, four, etc.?)
29. Did the last encounter occur less than one year ago? (One month, week, etc.?)
30. Was I told of a mission I was to carry out for (or with) the ETs? (Now? In the future?)
31. Did the encounter last more than one hour? (Two hours, three, etc.?)
32. Was hypnosis used?
33. Was I told not to remember the experience?
34. Was I told not to remember the examination?
35. Did the ETs put a tracking device or object through which they can communicate with me in my body?
36. Have I received telepathic messages from ETs?
37. Are any of my problems (fears, phobias, anxieties, etc.?) due to experiences with ETs? With UFOs? Both?
38. Does my subconscious mind know if someone else I know (brother, sister, mother, father, spouse, friend, etc.) has been involved in encounters with ETs? UFOs?
39. Have I developed any psychic abilities as a result of the encounter/contact?
40. (For women) Have any of my eggs been removed by ETs? (If so, before, after fertilization? More than once—twice, three

times, etc.?) (For men) Was an instrument inserted into my
penis? Was sperm removed?

41. (For women) Have I had a sexual experience with an ET?
    Intercourse? If so, did a pregnancy result? Was the fertilized
    ovum removed? Naturally aborted? Was the fetus brought to
    term, born? (For men) Was I forced to have intercourse with
    a female ET? (Once, twice, three times, etc.?)
42. Have I received information about or visions of future events?
43. Have I received information about or visions of planet Earth
    changes?
44. Have I received information about or visions of future politi-
    cal and/or social changes? Personal changes? Scientific
    changes?
45. Am I a human-alien hybrid? An ET?
46. Have I been incorporated by an ET? In the past? Now?
47. Have my experiences with ETs shown them to be hostile?
    Uncaring? Scientifically objective?
48. Have my experiences with ETs shown them to be loving?
    Compassionate? Concerned about the welfare of planet
    Earth?
49. Have I been seriously damaged or hurt in any way by my
    experience with ETs?
50. Have I benefited in any way by my experience with ETs?

If any thoughts, images, bodily sensations, etc., came up as you
asked and answered the questions, be sure you recorded them.
These may be excellent clues to, and even bridges into the repressed material that you can use later while working with a quali-
fied UFO researcher or therapist.

If you have uncovered one or more close encounters of the
fourth kind, you have confronted something that undoubtedly has
been affecting you in many ways. Just by tapping in to it to this
extent, you may very well have released the "charges" associated
with it and freed yourself from its negative impact. In which case,
you should notice across-the-board positive changes in yourself. If
not, then you do need to get in touch with a hypnotherapist

competent in this field and/or a UFO abductee/contactee researcher. (See Appendix.)

There are also a growing number of support groups for abductees and contactees. The Rocky Mountain Conference on UFO Investigation (annual contactee conference) is a way for people who have had encounters to get together, have counseling, hear speakers and generally share their experiences. You can find out more about it by contacting Leo Sprinkle, Ph.D., Institute for UFO Contactee Studies, 1425 Steele St., Laramie, WY 82070.

# 17

# ". . . The Evidence Can
No Longer Be Squelched."

Are close encounters of the fourth kind real or are they fantasies? This is a question that has bewildered people for centuries. It is intriguing to read the accounts from ancient times of the wee people, gnomes, fairies, angels and mysterious folk who kidnapped or helped humans.

In the 1950s, when Major Donald Keyhoe's book *Flying Saucers Are Real!* came out, there was great controversy about UFOs that lasted for decades. Only in the last ten years or so has it become blatantly obvious that governments around the world have been doing their best to cover up the UFO phenomenon, including their own investigations into it. In order to accomplish their goals, they have discredited witnesses and silenced experienced air-traffic controllers and pilots, even our astronauts. The cover-up surrounding this exceedingly important topic makes Watergate look like child's play. The net effect is that citizens are still confused. However, the cover-up is not working! As I mentioned earlier, approximately one-half of the people in the United

States believe in UFOs and one out of eleven thinks they have seen them.

Not only do people believe in the existence of UFOs, many accept that thousands among us have been abducted by extraterrestrials. And as more books and reports are published, the evidence can no longer be squelched.

As a therapist, I have been impressed with the very positive results of regressions under hypnosis to CEIVs. People who have undergone one or more regressions have experienced profound changes in their lives. Often symptoms of many years' durations, such as phobias and depressions, were immediately resolved when the patients remembered being abducted and traumatized. In my opinion, the only way these severe problems could have been eliminated by regression is by an *actual* event having been dealt with and the negative energy associated with it discharged. Besides these exceedingly obvious changes, there were frequently minor positive improvements, leading to a general enhancement of people's lives.

Even in those people whom I worked with more as an investigator than as a therapist, and even when the encounters had not been traumatic, I found positive changes following regressions. The case of Dan (Chapter Twelve) is an excellent example of this point. He felt very little anxiety during his regression. In fact, it was a thrilling experience for him. He noticed immediately after our first session a definite improvement in his self-confidence and a wonderful inner peace of mind that he had not felt before.

I believe the experiences that I have reported in *Encounters* are real, that they actually happened very much as they were remembered. By that I mean that the experiences were remembered as they were originally perceived. There were CEIVs, and any distortions or misperceptions were part of the confusion of being in a totally unfamiliar situation that was traumatic. Additionally, the visitors very well could have deliberately done things, used devices and/or given hypnotic suggestions to erase memories or to have what was experienced distorted in certain ways.

Because my main concern is to help people, it is not important to me if the patients/subjects report correctly the color of the aliens' skin, for example. What is important is that the negative effects of encounters be released through regressions.

It has been fascinating for me in working with abductees/contactees to learn that the extraterrestrials can incorporate, either temporarily or permanently. Incorporation, the actual taking over or possession of a human's body by an alien, was temporary in Diane Tai's case and permanent in Dan's. From the accounts of my patients/subjects, it also appears that there are human-alien hybrids living among us. I'm sure that more about this will be revealed in the future and will prove to be very exciting.

One of the most interesting findings that emerged from this work was the many healings and attempts to heal on the part of the visitors. Even when lasers were not yet being used by Earth people, the extraterrestrials were using them on humans in their spacecraft. I wonder if some of the modern developments in medicine, technology and space exploration can be credited directly or indirectly to the intervention of our space friends. Remember telepathy! Wouldn't it be interesting if our top scientists were being helped with their research and development?

I feel that the discovery of visits to our planet Earth by beings from other worlds and their interactions with humans is the most exciting and significant happening of the twentieth century.

Appendix

Organizations

J. Allen Hynek Center for UFO Studies. (CUFOS)
1955 John's Dr.
Glenview, IL 60025

Dr. Hynek was respected as one of the United States' leading UFO researchers. Since his death, the center continues
to investigate reports of UFO sightings. It also publishes the
*IUR (International UFO Reporter)*, a bimonthly journal for
UFO research, edited by Jerome Clark.

Mutual UFO Network (MUFON)
103 Oldtowne Rd.
Seguin, TX 78155

Walter Andrus, Jr., Director. This organization has the largest membership of any UFO organization. It publishes a
journal and conducts an annual conference for international
exchange of UFO information and research.

National Investigations Committee on UFOs
P.O. Box 5
Van Nuys, CA 91401

This information center publishes books and a newletter
based on alleged contacts with a Venusian.

Guardian Action Publications
P.O. Box 27725
Salt Lake City, UT 84101

This organization offers a free catalog of UFO material.
They claim to be channels for the Space Command, extraterrestrials supposedly orbiting around our planet.

335

Fortean Research Center
P.O. Box 94627
Lincoln, NE 68509

This group investigates UFO reports and other metaphysical miracles.

Institute for UFO Contactee Studies
1425 Steele St.
Laramie, WY 82070

This organization counsels people who feel they've had a close encounter. It sponsors an annual contactee conference each summer.

The New York Center for UFO Research (NYCUFOR)
134 W. Houston St., Suite 1
New York, NY 10012
(212) 995-0384

Michael Luckman, the director, sees this organization as a vehicle for disseminating information about UFOs and extraterrestrials. Conferences, lectures, media presentations are the main emphasis. However, there is a referral service for those seeking help with problems arising from their abductions/contacts.

Church of the Seven Arrows
4385 Hoyt St., 3201
Wheat Ridge, CO 80033

Rev. George Dew is a shaman and pastor of this church. He and his coworkers use shamanic and modern psychological techniques to help abductees.

Publications

The MUFON Journal
103 Oldtowne Rd.
Seguin, TX 78155

Walter Andrud, Jr., is the director of MUFON. The journal contains articles about international information and research.

Flying Saucer Review (FSR)
P.O. Box 12
Snodland
Kent ME6 5JZ
England

Edited by Gordon Creighton, FSR is published quarterly (U.S. $30 subscription, plus $10 for airmail). The journal features photographs and articles by an international network of UFO researchers.

UFO Magazine
1800 S. Robertson Blvd.
Los Angeles, CA 90035
$15.00/Bimonthly, six issues

This newletter gives information about UFO news and related items of interest.

Quest: The Journal of UFO Investigation
106 Lady Ann Rd.
Soothill, Batley
England
$25.00/Bimonthly, six issues airmail

This magazine contains articles on the latest worldwide UFO research regarding sightings and government reports.

Fate Magazine
3510 Western Ave.
Highland Park, IL 60035
(312) 433-8100
$1.50 per issue/Monthly

This magazine often has articles about UFOs, personal accounts of both sightings and abductions, as well as summaries of the latest theories and information.

The Star Beacon
P.O. Box 174
Delta, CO 81416

Edited by Ann Ulrich, this newsletter presents information about UFO abductees and contactees and related topics.

Contactee: Research of UFOs by Direct Observation
P.O. Box 12
New Milford, NJ 07646

Published quarterly by Ellen Crystall, this newsletter provides information about UFO abductions, contacts and related topics.

The Star Network Heartline
P.O. Box
Poway, CA 92064

Edited by the Rev. Diane Tessman, this newsletter provides channeled information (Tibus) about "star people" and New Age prophecies.

White Star
P.O. Box 307
Joshua, CA 92252-0307

This newsletter provides channeled information about Earth changes and prophecies about UFO/ET encounters.

Hypnotherapists Working With Abductees/Contactees

Aphrodite Clamar, Ph.D.
30 E. 60th St., Suite 1107
New York, NY 10022
(212) 988-8042

Beverly J. Carter
4491 South Yates
Denver, CO 80236
(303) 794-7626

Ann Druffel
257 Sycamore Glen
Pasadena, CA 91105
(213) 256-8655

Stephen Field, Ed.D.
800 Oak Grove, Suite 207
Menlo Park, CA 94025
(415) 325-46788

Edith Fiore, Ph.D.
20688 Fourth St.
Saratoga, CA 95070
(408) 867-1100

✓ Josie Hadley
2443 Ash St., Suite D
Palo Alto, CA 94306
(415) 321-6419

✓ Richard Haines, Ph.D.
P.O. Box 880
Los Altos, CA 94023-0880

✓ Tisha Hallet
450 San Antonio Rd.,
Suite 27
Palo Alto, CA 94306
(415) 857-0638

✓ James Harder, Ph.D.
2800 Hilgard St.
Berkeley, CA 94709
(415) 848-6043

✓ Barbara Levy, Ph.D.
317 Eureka St.
San Francisco, CA 94114
(415) 826-2250
(415) 751-3971

Linda Marie Martin
152 Olive Springs Rd.
Soquel, CA 95073
(408) 479-3493

Jeffrey Mishlove, Ph.D.
48 St. Francis La.
San Rafael, CA 94901
(415) 456-2532

Raymond Moody, M.D.
205 Tanner St.
Carrollton, GA 30117
(404) 834-6393

Sharon Moss, Ph.D.
2947 Eastmoreland
Oregon, OH 43616
(419) 691-4926

Jean Mundy, Ph.D.
33 Windward
East Hampton, NY 11937
(516) 267-8896
and 105 West 13th St.
New York, NY 10011
(212) 741-1278

June Parnell, Ph.D.
2219 Rainbow Ave.
Laramie, WY 82070
(307) 742-3394

Alice Rose, Ph.D.
4651 Roswell Rd., Suite
I-8013
Atlanta, GA 30342
(404) 255-7051

Patricia Shaw, Ph.D.
225 S. Meramec Ave.,
Suite 506
St. Louis, MO 63105
(314) 863-3588

Richard Sigismund
1557 9th St.
Boulder, CO 80302
(303) 447-9170

✓ June Steiner
987 University Ave., Suite 6
Los Gatos, CA 95030
(408) 395-9209

Jo Stone, MFCC
P.O. Box 2828
Los Angeles, CA 90078

Sue Street, Ph.D.
University of South Florida
St. Petersburg Campus
140 7th Ave. South
St. Petersburg, FL 33701
(813) 893-9129

✓ Keith Thompson
P.O. Box 5055
Mill Valley, CA 94942
(415) 388-9008

Mary Ellen Trahan, Ph.D.
205 Tanner St.
Carrollton, GA 30117
(404) 834-6393

Norma Triggs
10 Willow Creek
Richardson, TX 75080

Thomas J. Zinser, Ed.D.
2041 Raybrook SE
Grand Rapids, MI 49506
(616) 957-3168

# Suggested Reading

Andrews, George. *Extra-Terrestrials Among Us.* St. Paul: Llewellyn, 1986.

Berlitz, Charles and W. L. Moore. *The Roswell Incident.* New York: Grosset & Dunlap, 1980.

Druffel, Ann, and D. Scott Rogo. *The Tujunga Canyon Contacts.* Englewood Cliffs, N.J.: Prentice-Hall, 1980.

Editors. *The UFO Phenomenon.* Alexandria, Va.: Time-Life Books, 1987.

Emenegger, Robert. *UFO's: Past, Present & Future.* New York: Ballantine, 1986.

Flammonde, Paris. *UFO Exist!* New York: Putnam, 1976.

Fowler, Raymond E. *The Andreasson Affair.* Englewood Cliffs, N.J.: Prentice-Hall, 1979.

————. *Casebook of a UFO Investigator.* Englewood Cliffs, N.J.: Prentice-Hall, 1982.

Fry, Daniel. *The White Sands Incident.* Louisville, Ky.: Best Books, 1966.

Fuller, John. *Aliens in the Sky.* New York: Medallion/Berkley, 1969.

————. *The Interrupted Journey.* New York: Berkley, 1966.

Good, Timothy. *Above Top Secret.* New York: Morrow, 1988.

Hopkins, Budd. *Intruders.* New York: Random House, 1987.

————. *Missing Time.* New York: Richard Marek, 1981.

Jung, Carl G. *Flying Saucers: A Modern Myth of Things Seen in the Sky.* New York: Signet Books, 1969.

Keyhoe, Donald E. *The Flying Saucers Are Real!* New York: Fawcett Publications, 1950.

Kinder, Gary. *Light Years.* New York: The Atlantic Monthly Press, 1987.

Larsen, S. J. *Close Encounters: A Factual Report on UFOs.* Milwaukee: Raintree, 1978.

Lorenzen, J., and C. E. Lorenzen. *Abducted!* New York: Berkley, 1977.

Montgomery, Ruth. *Aliens Among Us.* New York: Putnam, 1985.

341

Puharich, Andrija. *URI: A Journal of the Mystery of Uri Geller.* Garden City, N.Y.: Anchor/Doubleday, 1974.

Rimmer, John. *The Evidence for Alien Abductions.* Northamptonshire: Aquarian Press, 1984.

Rogo, D. Scott, ed. *Alien Abductions.* New York: New American Library, 1980

Rutledge, H. D. *Project Identification: The First Scientific Field Study on UFO Phenomena.* Englewood Cliffs, N.J.: Prentice-Hall, 1981.

Sachs, Margaret. *The UFO Encyclopedia.* New York: Perigee/Putnam, 1980.

Sagan, Carl. *Cosmos.* New York: Ballantine, 1985.

Sprinkle, R. Leo. "Hypnotic and Psychic Implications in the Investigation of UFO Reports." In *Encounters with UFO Occupants,* edited by C. E. Lorenzen and J. Lorenzen, 256–329. New York: Berkley, 1976.

Steiger, Brad. *The UFO Abductors.* New York: Berkley, 1988.

Steiger, Brad, and Frances Steiger. *The Fellowship.* New York: Dolphin/Doubleday, 1988.

———. *The Star People.* New York: Berkley, 1981.

Strieber, Whitley. *Communion.* New York: Morrow, 1987.

———. *Transformation: The Breakthrough.* New York: Morrow, 1988.

Vallée, Jacques. *Dimensions: A Casebook of Alien Contact.* Chicago: Contemporary Books, 1988.

———. *The Messengers of Deception.* Berkeley, Calif.: And/Or Press, 1979.

———. *UFO Enigma: Challenge to Science.* New York: Ballantine, 1966.

Von Däniken, Erich. *Chariots of the Gods?* New York: Berkley, 1984.

———. *Gods From Outer Space.* New York: Bantam, 1972.

Walton, T. *The Walton Affair.* New York: Berkley, 1978.

Wilson, Clifford. *The Alien Agenda.* New York: Signet/New American Library, 1988.

How is the pattern of **life** ordered and followed?
How are **family** and marriage defined? How much sa
How are manners, **etiquette**, and rules set? How flex
To what degree is **education** emphasized? For both s
How are **groups** created and identified? Which are m
What **professions** dominate, and how is work viewed
How is **information** gathered and spread?

D0382651

**Beauty**

What is the **look most aspired to** in this group?
Who are the contemporary **ideals** of male and female perfection?
What are the most **coveted** skin types, hair color and styles, and physical proportions?
What part does physical **fitness** play in physical attractiveness? What is the relationship between beauty, health, and **comfort**?
Which **colors, shapes, textures**, and **silhouettes** are favored in clothing, furnishings, props, hairdos, and jewelry?
How important is **fashion**? How fast does it **change**?
To what degree is **nature** altered to create a thing of beauty?
How is **taste** defined?
What are favored modes of **artistic expression**?

**Sex**

How significant a part of the collective **consciousness** is sex?
What do most people consider **turn-ons** and **turn-offs**?
How is **seduction** defined?
How is **sexuality** acceptably **communicated**? What are the sexual **stereotypes**?
Which parts of the **anatomy** are revealed, concealed, and emphasized?
Is the **emphasis** on the act or the chase? On pleasure or procreation?
What is the standard **courtship ritual** and its significance?
How much is **deviation** tolerated?
What are the accepted attitudes toward **infidelity** and **promiscuity**?
To what **degree** is sexuality **suppressed or expressed**?

**Recreation**

What is most people's idea of **fun**?
What would be an **ideal social occasion** in this world?
What is the **participation** level? Are they doers or watchers?
What is **intellectual** life? Are they thinkers or mindless hedonists?
What are the common **shared** hobbies, **pastimes**, and concepts of having fun?
What is most people's **vision** of an enjoyable evening, vacation, or day?
What are the differences between the **sexes**?
**Consumption**? What are the favored and coveted food, drink, drugs, and snacks?
What is the relative **importance** of recreation in life? The standard view of **indulgence**?

**Sight**

How do all the above manifest themselves in the way the world of the play looks, in **shapes and angles**, **light** and **shadow**, **in dominant patterns**? In **standing, sitting, facial expressions, ways of walking, touching**, and **being touched**?
What is the pattern of **movement** and **contact** and its significance?

**Sound**

How does it all come out in common **speech** and **nonverbal** communication?
To what degree are **listening** and **speaking** prized?
What is most desired in terms of **voice quality, timing, articulation, pronunciation, use of pitch and volume, choice of words**, and **vocal patterns**?
What is the role of **music** and **dance** in life?

# FOR ACTORS

ROBERT BARTON

UNIVERSITY OF OREGON

MAYFIELD PUBLISHING COMPANY

Mountain View, California
London • Toronto

*In loving memory of F. Carrow De Vries*
*for what he showed me about writing and truth*

Library of Congress Cataloging-in-Publication Data

Barton, Robert
　　　Style for actors / Robert Barton.
　　　　　　p.　　cm.
　　　Includes index.
　　　ISBN 0-87484-958-6
　　　1. Acting.　2. Drama.　I. Title.
　　　PN2061.B295　1992
　　　792′.028—dc20

92-16227
CIP

Manufactured in the United States of America
10 9 8 7 6 5 4 3 2

Mayfield Publishing Company
1240 Villa Street
Mountain View, California 94041

*Sponsoring editor,* Jan Beatty; *production editor,* Sharon Montooth; *manuscript editor,* Sally Peyrefitte; *text and cover designer,* Anna George; *illustrator,* Robin Mouat. *Cover photo:* Kenneth Branagh as he appeared in the title role in *Henry V.* © 1992 Motion Picture & Television Photo Archive. This text was set in 10/12 Galliard by Graphic Composition and printed on 50# Finch Opaque by Maple Vail Book Manufacturing Group.

**Photo Credits**
　　Chapter opener One, © Henry Kranzler; Chapter opener Two, © Robert C. Rags-dale, courtesy of the Stratford Festival; Chapter opener Three, © Henry Kranzler; Chapter opener Four, © Henry Kranzler; Chapter opener Five, © Henry Kranzler; Chapter opener Six, © Zoe Dominic, courtesy of the Stratford Festival; Chapter opener Seven, © Douglas Spillane, courtesy of the Stratford Festival; page 224, © Henry Kranzler; Chapter opener Eight, © Christopher Briscoe; Chapter opener Nine, © Robert C. Ragsdale, courtesy of the Stratford Festival; Chapter opener Ten, © Christopher Briscoe. Back cover photo by Cliff Coles.

This book is a guide for the intermediate actor who is ready to move beyond contemporary American realism into the less familiar acting territory of historical periods and genres. At the introductory level, actors learn to perform in a familiar world. This book is about performing in new worlds.

Greater emphasis is placed on *tools* than on *rules*. The guiding assumption is that it is more important for an actor to know how to ask questions, vigorously investigate and bravely experiment than to have ready answers, since answers change from production to production. This book attempts to prepare actors for a variety of directorial approaches, without restricting their choices. Although style is an extraordinary challenge, there are many right ways to meet it.

The text is distinct in many ways:

1. Style is presented as situational, flexible, and ongoing rather than as a set of laws. Actors are encouraged to approach each new production freshly, without preconceived notions of stylistic conventions.

2. The styles included are those most performed. Far more space is devoted to the works of Shakespeare and Molière than those less likely to enter the actor's life (e.g., miracle plays, Roman tragedy).

3. Familiar styles are used as bridges to less familiar ones, with current music, clothing, language, and "stylized" encounters, such as courtroom trials and marriage ceremonies, serving as lead-ins to performing the classics.

4. Interviews with imaginary persons from each historical period— a Greek seer, an Elizabethan noble, a Restoration courtier, a Mo-

lière actor, and a Georgian merchant—convey the ways in which beliefs support and change acting.

5. A ten-step investigation into the period's time, space, place, values, structure, beauty, sex, recreation, sight, and sound allows the actor to look at a play the way an anthropologist might look at an undiscovered country and to investigage it with the same urgency.

6. What the actor is most likely to be asked to do in production is always favored over what was believed to have been done in the original productions. The world each playwright creates is favored over the one in which he may have been living.

7. Period or classical styles, which strike young actors as remote, receive far greater emphasis than do contemporary styles, which always have the advantage of starting in familiar territory.

8. Improvisation is offered as a primary means of entering each period. Actors have a chance to explore a style within a strongly defined context while momentarily free of text by participating in the nearly 150 exercises.

9. Issues often omitted when style is addressed, such as translations, Eastern theatre, musical theatre, scansion, and displaced plays (those written in one period but set in another, such as *Amadeus* and *Les Liaisons Dangéreuses*), are included if they are likely to involve the actor.

10. A list of scene suggestions for workshop and showcasing accompanies the discussion of each historical style. A full annotation of all the scenes in the plays of William Shakespeare is included.

The text begins with two chapters about style in daily life: recognizing it, analyzing it, and using it to understand one's own experiences. Chapter 2 also presents ten categories for examining and entering a world—in the theatre or outside it. These ten categories are carried forward through the remainder of the book and are presented in a checklist format on the inside front and back covers. Chapter 3 analyzes the differences between a limited contemporary realistic actor and one who comfortably performs the classics to determine what characteristics all good style actors share. The next four chapters address periods most produced on stage: Greek, Elizabethan, Restoration, Molière (neoclassic), and Georgian (eighteenth century). Chapter 8 deals with scripts written in one time but performed or set in another, it addresses the varieties of translations, adaptations, and editions and offers a system of connecting any script to the audience for which it is being presented. Chapter 9 surveys the genres (the isms from romanticism through postmodernism) that define today's theatre. The final chapter examines personal style, both in performance and in life, so that the text ends as it begins, with the actor's examination of self.

The book strives for a tone that is personal and empathetic, addressing the readers as human beings, with respect for their own inherent wisdom.

It attempts to connect frankly with the person who has to go out there (sometimes struggling with panniers, feathers, fan, cape, sword, doublet, and couplet) and *do* it—the actor.

## USING THIS TEXT

The reader will have no trouble exploring this material independently even though it is designed for a class or cast. For the interactive material, a partner will be helpful.

We instructors all teach style under different circumstances. Within the ten-chapter organization, much flexibility is possible. Advanced or sophisticated groups can skim Chapters 1 and 2 for possible new questions, but the activities are not necessary, unless they wish to renew a sense of exploration or awareness of style in everyday life. Because so many actors are terrified of the subject, these chapters offer reassurance that style exists all around us, that none of us is totally ignorant, and that all of us do have style knowledge on which we can draw. The book is deliberately filled with more questions to ask and exercises to try than any group would wish to undertake so that classes can pick and choose favorites without impeding their progress in any way.

The chapters that deal with significant style issues that influence *all* periods and genres are Chapter 3 (Mastering Style) and Chapter 8 (Displaced Style), which contain exercises for vocal, physical, and psychological preparation as well as methods for rehearsing text. Those who are limited by time or desire an overview can isolate these two chapters for intensive work. Groups who wish to focus on one major historical period can combine these chapters with Chapter 4 (Greek), Chapter 5 (Elizabethan), Chapter 6 (Restoration), the first part of Chapter 7 (Molière), or the second part of Chapter 7 (Georgian). In this scheme, the class reviews general principles, then applies them in one clear context. Those who are interested in the concept but not the history can combine Chapters 3 and 8 with Chapter 9 (Isms) to explore modern styles alone. Other combinations are certainly possible. One class might elect to do just Greek and Elizabethan for heroic perspective. Another might do just Restoration and Molière for exploration in wit.

Chapter 10 brings all the material into the actor's offstage life. It is an optional excursion. Those who have read my text *Acting: Onstage and Off* will recognize my bias for the application of theatrical principles in daily life, but you certainly are under no constraint to share it. In our own program, this chapter is like frosting. Students find it stimulating, funny, and moving, but time and focus constraints could limit it to a reading/discussion assignment. The primary pragmatic issue this chapter deals with is the way style or lack of self-knowledge may be blocking his or her entry into the world of the play.

Ideal circumstances would allow you a year to explore all the material here. Unfortunately, few of us teach under ideal circumstances. At the University of Oregon, we have only one ten-week quarter for this subject, but we do review all the material, with each actor performing a scene from two separate periods. A vocal technique course that addresses verse and classical speech precedes this course. It is part of a curriculum in which Shakespeare and improvisation are used in every course beyond Acting One, so students are familiar with both. I offer this information to suggest that it is possible to overview the whole text in a short period of time, varying the amount of attention given to any particular section according to each program's circumstances. Any serious actor will return to this material again and again over the years, so a brief overview can alert him or her to what is ahead and frame future exploration. Style is a lifelong subject of study for which this text can provide a basis.

## ACKNOWLEDGMENTS

Over two hundred students (particularly Karin Clarke, Russel Dyball, Barbara Embree, Kendra Fanconi, Heather Herion, Terry Hunt, Erin Malecha, Gwennis Mc Neir, Shawnna Pledger, Clara Radcliffe, Heidi Reeder, Jeremy Southard, Lenanne Sylvester, Amy Thompson, Paul Verano, Tim Baxter-Ferguson, Jeff Charlton, Melissa Durel, Jon Egging, Michele Fox, Rebecca Kimball, Jean Kramer, Angela Larson, Adrienne Peden, Matt Pidgeon, Tricia Rodley, Rebekah Shelley, Heidi Schreck, Jill Snyder, Tanya Van Sant) and fifty teaching assistants (particularly Janet Gupton, Bettyrae Hanner, Andrew Longoria, Todd Luedtke, Dei Olson, James Queen, Suzanne Seiber, David Mason, Hilary Mosher, Justina Mattos, Marion Rossi, Amy Sarno, Jay Pyette, and Rob Urbanati) helped shape these ideas in my classes over the past decade, served as patient guinea pigs and perceptive advisors in the final stages of writing and, in some cases, contributed both research and ideas for exercises.

Stratford Shakespeare Festival and the Oregon Shakespeare Festival artists gave time for invaluable interviews and observations. Thanks to Libby Appel, Marco Barricello, Kirk Boyd, Deena Burke, James Edmunson, Eric Johnson, Joan Langley, John Leistner, Michelle Morain, Mark Murphy, James Newcomb, Paul Vincent O'Connor, Victoria Otto, Pat Patton, Demetra Pittman, Rex Rabold, Remi Sandri, Jerry Turner, Holly Weber, Derrick Lee Weeden, and Henry Woromcz at Ashland, and to Marion Adler, John Broome, Tandy Cronyn, Colm Feore, Michael Hanrahnan, Richard Monette, John Neville, Robin Phillips, Lucy Peacock, Nicholas Pennell, Stephen Russell, Albert Schultz, and Dorothy Ward at Stratford. Thanks also to the festivals for the use of their production photos herein, and to archivists Kathleen Leary and Lisa Brant for assistance in securing photos.

I would particularly like to acknowledge the assistance of the late Rex Rabold who provided not only information, but served as a model and an inspiration to countless young actors.

Help in finding or synthesizing resource material was given generously by Carrol Barton, Mary Donohoe, Terra Pressler, John Schmor, Jack Watson, Barbara Sellers Young, and Annie MacGregor. Responses to the manuscript in various stages were provided by Libby Appel, Artistic Director, Indiana Repertory Theatre; Patricia Boyette, California State University, Long Beach; Ramon Delgado, Montclair State College; Alan C. English, Ball State University; Jeffery Huberman, Bradley University; Richard L. Jennings, University of South Carolina; Rex McGraw, Ohio State University; Malcolm Morrison, University of Wisconsin, Milwaukee; Leslie Rivers, California Polytechnic Institute, Pomona; Jon Sidoli, Orange County College; Suzanne Trauth, Montclair State College; and Ron Van Lieu, New York University. Thanks to all these collaborators.

# CONTENTS

## 5. ELIZABETHAN PERIOD STYLE: THEATRE OF EARTH AND STARS   *115*

# RECOGNIZING STYLE
## The Eyes of the Beholder

Style is something we all both want and fear. We want to have "real style," but we want to be more than just "stylish." We want to master style, never be slave to it. We want to create, transcend, or play with style, not succumb to it. We want style, but we don't want to mistake style for substance. Because our feelings about style in our own lives are ambivalent, most of us are tentative in our early efforts at style in the theatre. To understand style in acting, we must recognize it in living, where the word is used synonymously with *form, manner, method, way, fashion, vogue, mode, chic, craze, fad, rage, practice, habit, air, distinction, presentation, behavior, elegance, wording, means of expressing,* and *execution.*

Style is the way something is done rather than the core act itself. In writing classes, for example, teachers often give separate grades for style and content. A beautifully written essay may say nothing; conversely, an awkwardly expressed paper may have profound insights. In theatre and life, style is more complex than in basic writing, because design, interpretation, timing, and communication all influence the meaning of the words. We perceive style in terms of our expectations. Contemporary American realistic theatre, where each actor in the company is cast close to age and type, is standard. It is our dominant, expected style. Any show that moves away from this standard is called "stylized" or is described as done in "the _ style." We stylize an event by boldly removing it from everyday expected behavior. The more stylized a production, the more rules of make-believe the audience must accept to be able to appreciate it.

For an actor, "style work" may refer to any journey from mastered, known territory into new ground. This often involves changing (or en-

Derek Lee Weeden (Oberon) and Henry Woronicz (Puck) in *A Midsummer Night's Dream,* Oregon Shakespeare Festival

hancing) yourself enough to enter another world unfamiliar to you or to most audiences. The same happens in everyday life, too; people who are thought of as having "real style" are those who move between worlds with relative ease.

## DEFINING STYLE

### Understanding the World

*Style is a way of understanding the world and then entering it based on what you see.* If you see the world as a vicious concrete jungle, you might wear leather and studs and often use the "f" word. If you see the world as an enchanted romantic garden, you might wear flowing chiffon and improvise poetry. If you suddenly change your mind (imagine yourself stuck in chiffon while spouting obscenities), you have trouble reconciling feelings with presentation. Style is the external manifestation of some inner drive. It is a set of choices in action, a relationship between what you feel and what you present to the world. The world may be a club, a country, a period, or a play. It may be all of the above.

A belief shared by enough people is perceived as the dominant style. Consider this example. A recent article tells us that mounting serious plays about infidelity in France is difficult, simply because the French tend to view the subject humorously or ironically. If you see a character in a French film being told about a neighbor's affair, what do you expect that character to do? Shrug? Smile? Wink? Briefly philosophize? Probably. Express outrage? Weep? Register shock? Get a gun? Probably not.

Too often in the theatre, outward manifestation of inward belief is picked up without the belief itself. When you attend a bad production of a period style play, you may see a series of poses without gaining a sense of anything going on behind them, as if the director had said to the actors, "You should all shrug a lot and then smile, because that's what French people do," neglecting to explore the various *motives* in the culture that might prompt the act. Without belief, the whole venture looks hollow. The actors are likely to shrug in all the wrong places.

### Sharing with Others

*Style is what characters in a play (or people in a group) share, whereas characterization is what distinguishes them from each other.* All characters in a play share qualities. There is a collective characterization, a union, a brotherhood or sisterhood that ties them together. In some musicals, *all* characters wear sequins and tap shoes (even to the office), and when someone says, "I've got an idea!" they *all* lean toward that person and shout, "What?"

simultaneously. Yet the sweet hoofer from Kansas is clearly different from the temperamental, vamping star, even in this stylized world. They share style as distinct entities.

The balance between interesting, idiosyncratic, or even quirky character work and consistent, detailed style work is what makes an exciting production. We want all of the characters in the play so clearly defined that we won't confuse them, but we also want them to share enough to tie the play together. Offstage, most of us wish to "fit" into our communities comfortably while still distinguishing ourselves as unique, special people. We like to be part of the neighborhood without being mistaken for our neighbors.

Many plays and films are about group style wars. On the back shelves of your local video store you'll probably find the movie *Valley Girl,* which is about a girl and boy who are in love but whose peer groups are at war. The fact that the two styles involved, "valley" and "punk," are now both dated, helps us realize how often each of us may have mistaken, in our own lives, someone's style choices for the person's real self. *Valley Girl* is the umpteenth version of *Romeo and Juliet,* a story of two families, who seem very similar to most of *us,* warring over their differences, which seem so obvious to *them* that nobody in the play ever bothers to say what they are. In most productions, it looks as if the whole problem is merely that the Montagues don't like the Capulets because they wear red and that the Capulets don't like the Montagues because they wear blue; this is what ultimately leads to the death of hero and heroine, who are color-blind.

## Working in a Group

*Style is what works in a group.* There is one group around the breakfast table at your house, another on the bus, and others in each class, the cafeteria, the gym, the library, your job, and the rehearsal hall on an ordinary day. You spend the first few weeks of school adjusting to each of these groups, sending out and picking up signals, antennae alert to see what will get you by. This process of discovery is what makes these weeks so exhausting. On a wider scale over a longer period of time, you try to grasp the style of your new school, city, department, and chosen art form or profession. In trying to figure out who you are, you use groups as a gauge, joining some, avoiding others.

Consider an example. Imagine that during Rush Week at a large university you overhear someone say to her companion, "That look is *great* for the Kappas but much too sleazy for the Deltas." Imagine this poor freshman, taking the advice, running into the rest room, unteasing her hair, wiping off most of her make-up, and tugging desperately at her spandex micro skirt, hoping to make it look somehow demure, before moving on to the next open house. Trying to fit into a group's image is deceptive. Are the Kappas really sleazy and the Deltas demure? Who knows? It's doubtful that either group would choose to describe itself that way. And the poor potential pledge is probably just trying to find a group that may help her figure out *what* she is.

We choose some groups (religious, political, social, academic) but are thrust by fate into others (race, class, family). People who are nothing but their groups are bores. Is there anyone more tedious than the person who seems to be *only* gay, Jewish, black, Republican, Capricorn, a Shriner, a square dancer, or a stamp collector? Those who talk of nothing else and press their group identities into every occasion and conversation are a pain. Most of us want groups to define us, not submerge us.

Yet membership in groups is a social necessity, a tool for survival. Style is an ongoing struggle to fit in, rather than an accomplishment. Suppose you are pulled over to the side of the road far south of the Mason-Dixon Line and two police officers saunter over to you. You turn into as close to a "Good Ole Boy" as you can get away with in order to minimize your fine and avoid the county jail. You may start using the word "sir" for the first time in years. Because the stakes are high, you may amaze yourself at how *deeply* Southern you can be. In tense situations, stylistic maneuvers can be critically important.

## Making Effective Choices

*Style involves effective strategic choices. It is a latitude, with some limits but much creative space.* All of us return to and repeat what succeeds. You use a great opening line until it falls flat; you frequently wear an outfit that gets compliments and stick to a tone of voice or way of moving that gets the results you want. You settle into choices that serve you well; they become habit. The more ingrained the habit, the harder it is to change once it stops working. People can get *stuck* in style choices that served them in another era but no longer wear so well. They fail to stay alert for what works here and now.

Style involves understanding both rewarded and punished behavior in any set of given circumstances. Your household probably has a style based on desired and undesired actions. Your parents just *love* it when you do or say certain things. Other acts are not tolerated. There were (and probably still are) degrees of reward and punishment. Some offenses get a time-out, others a spanking, others deprivation of privileges. Some maneuvers perhaps make your mom smile warmly; others get her cooking your favorite foods; others result in major toys. You learned to function within these two extremes—grounded and glory—most of the time.

This pattern continues with every other group outside the home. If you do A, you will be punished in this group's worst possible way, but if you do B, you will be honored. These are relative terms. For the Deltas, A may be being blackballed from Sorority Sing for three months (horrors!), whereas B may be getting chosen to play Cupid at the Sweetheart's Ball (heaven!).

As long as you comply with certain issues and don't push certain others, you're OK. But within these limits is a big space, a comfort zone in which you are free to do pretty much what you want. Actors often want to know *exactly* what to do to act Sophocles or Shakespeare. They live in terror of making critical mistakes. They visualize the audience laughing at how stupid they look and throwing things. They fail to realize that there is a giant playground and many ways to win.

### Natural versus Unnatural

*Style is behavior perceived by the individual as natural, while others (of unlike style) are perceived as artificial and contrived.* Mastering any new style is a challenge, but we all have an amazing capacity, once we've got the new style, to forget the old one. Suddenly this is the *only* way to act. Those who act otherwise are perverse, retarded, or both.

Just as each person views his or her own behavior as normal, so does each era. When you look at old photographs of yourself, for instance, you're often appalled at what you once thought attractive. Plays match how the people *feel* about themselves. It is only when the group's view of itself alters that the old behavior suddenly seems stylized. Elizabethan actors had no trouble shouting above the groundlings, because they thought of themselves as larger than life and ready to conquer the rest of the globe. But in the present day, we tend to think of ourselves as small grains of sand on the beach of life, in need of therapy or at least a back rub; consequently, what we consider "normal" behavior is cautious, defensive, and even neurotic compared to that of the Elizabethans. When reality is the issue, you need to ask, Which one? When normality is concerned, you need to ask, On whose terms?

### Journeying into the Play

*Style is the journey from tourist to native. It is living in the world of the play, not just visiting it.* Style is the path by which we (or our thoughts and feelings) travel, the means we use to put ourselves (or our points) across. The path is not the starting point or destination; it is what connects them. Actors enter the play like tourists, get their rehearsal passports, immigrate, buy property, settle, acquire citizenship, and prosper. If all goes well, they appear comfortably native by opening night.

Rehearsals for plays are psychic relocations. No one walks into the first read-through with mastery. The process is like moving into a new neighborhood or country. Even directors and designers, who have mapped out some of the territory, are still finding out what this play is about and how its world comes to life. But the whole process goes more smoothly if you pack well, learn some language and customs, and get all your shots. The rehearsal is a journey, the performance the destination.

But before you set off on any journey, you should learn something about where you're going. The following categories are the sort you would find in a traveler's guide for visiting a foreign country. They will be useful to you when preparing for a journey to a different world of drama, such as Shakespeare's Navarre, Illyria, or the Forest of Arden (the settings for *Love's Labor's Lost, Twelfth Night,* and *As You Like It*). The traveler's guide can serve as a guide through any play. If you prepare with the same enthusiasm you would give a trip, research comes easily.

### Travel Guide to Shakespearia

A BRIEF HISTORY—WHAT TO SEE—EXCURSIONS—SHOP-PING—WINING AND DINING—RELAXING—HOW TO GET THERE AND WHEN TO GO—PLANNING YOUR BUDGET—BLUEPRINT FOR A PERFECT TRIP
SPEAKING THE LANGUAGE
Articles, Nouns, Adjectives, Adverbs, Possessive pronouns, Demonstrative pronouns, Personal pronouns, Verbs, Negatives, Questions, Expressing agreement and disagreement
GUIDE TO PRONUNCIATION
Spelling and sounds, Elevated classical speech, Scansion, Historical rhymes, Basic expressions, Greetings, Good-byes, Questions, Forms of address, Dismissals, Commands, Oaths, Parentheses, Useful words
ARRIVAL
Customs, Baggage, Directions, Reservations, Transportation
ACCOMMODATIONS
Decisions, Bills, Tipping, Registration, Service
EATING OUT
Types of establishments, Mealtimes, Eating habits, Asking and ordering, Menus, Beverages, Snacks
TRAVELING
Horse, Carriage, Foot, Barge, Boat, Magic, Other means of transport
SIGHTSEEING
Attractions, Religious services
RELAXING
Entertainment, Music, Dancing, Fights, Bearbaiting, Hangings, Madrigals, Masques, Versification, Sports
MAKING FRIENDS
Introductions, Follow-up, Weather, Invitations, Dating
SHOPPING GUIDE
Shops and services, Bartering, Bookshops, Crockery and cutlery, Chemists, Toiletry, Hair, Clothing, Size, Fit, Accessories, Jewelers and watchmakers

SOUVENIRS
Weights and measures, Currency, Credit, Monetary units, Deposits and withdrawals
POSTING
Notices, Mails, Edicts, Seals, Proclamations, Information sources
DOCTOR
Symptoms, Illnesses, Wounds, Prescriptions, Dosages, Potions, Alchemists, Witches
REFERENCE
Regions, Times, Months, Seasons, Holidays, Temperatures, Conversions, Signs

Is all of this information at the library? No. You start there, but the more you find out about historical Illyria, Navarre, or Arden, the less it seems to match Shakespeare's. So you move from investigation (research) to inference (making connections) to invention (making it up). The information *is* available in your imagination. The big difference between traveling to Shakespearia, Sophoclia, or Molièria and traveling to England, Greece, or France is that the former are kingdoms of the mind. They are *based* in history, literature, and theory, but they *actualize* only in production. Much creation must take place. And you will be one of the creators.

Ironically, what was easiest during childhood, "let's pretend," is often hardest now. Transforming the acting space by sheer power of belief and deciding to live there test both imagination and concentration. The audience always knows which actors feel like aliens, which are not entirely foreign but still haven't "gotten their papers," and which have decided they *belong*. These last actors own the stage.

The power to do this is based on the willingness to believe. Small children *believe* they are the fairy-tale, legend, or cartoon figures they play, so they are believable and fascinating. You *are* a prince, a sage, a monster, or even a god if you have the imagination and courage to let yourself be. The great period style plays allow a glorious return to Once Upon a Time.

## Being Good Enough to Be Bad

*Style is being good enough at being good to get away with being bad.* By the time actors have mastered style, they feel confident, versatile, commanding, and maybe even cocky. Once you understand what works in a culture you can begin to *play* with it. If you know how to charm, impress, inspire, intimidate, move, amuse, and seduce, you can get away with almost anything.

Think about Peter O'Toole's entrance to the throne room as King Henry II in the film *Becket*. He dashes across the room, whips off his crown, tosses it over one corner of the back of his throne, and then throws himself on the throne, one leg hanging over the arm of the chair, ready to hold court. Of *course* a young, cocky monarch would act this way! He clearly knows protocol well enough to tweak its nose. Only a man who understands pomp and majesty would recognize when to mock ceremony and create his own court. The long hours you spend learning the customs and manners of the period give you the confidence to create and expand, realizing that there are many ways to make the performance work, some yet to be invented—by you.

### Entering the Play

*Style is knowing what play you're in.* Have you ever found an actor's work striking and skillful, but not right? As if the actor were imposing a world of his own on the play? As if he were not in the same show as the script and the other actors? In the theatre, you need to know what play you're in; otherwise, survival is unlikely and success impossible. What works in the back alleys of a Detroit slum doesn't work at all in the salons of St. Tropez. And what works in a Sam Shepard play is unlikely to cut it in a Noel Coward. In one play, an actor might rip off his clothes and flaunt his naked body to impress someone he desires. In another, this tactic would be disastrous, and anything less than a subtle, witty remark delivered with panache would send his intended exiting with laughter and disdain.

Figuring out the predominant style is what most characters in recent films do. Critics have called this movement "fish out of water" films. Consider these examples:

Time travel: *Field of Dreams, Back to the Future* (and its sequels), *Peggy Sue Got Married, Star Trek IV: The Voyage Home, Time After Time, Bill and Ted's Excellent Adventure, Bill and Ted's Bogus Journey, Freaky Friday, Radio Flyer, After Hours, Encino Man*

Body travel: *Switch; Honey, I Shrunk the Kids; Truly, Madly, Deeply; Defending Your Life; Like Father, Like Son; Vice Versa; Eighteen Again; Dream a Little Dream; Back to School; The Incredible Shrinking Woman; All of Me; Big; Ghost Dad; Ghost*

Species and/or planet travel: *Total Recall, Teenage Mutant Ninja Turtles, Mannequin, The Little Mermaid, Edward Scissorhands, Starman, Who Killed Roger Rabbit?, E.T.: The Extraterrestrial, Splash, Brother from Another Planet, My Stepmother Is an Alien, The Terminator, Altered States, Robocop*

Culture travel: *Dances with Wolves, King Ralph, City Slickers, Dutch, Doc Hollywood, The Hard Way, Pretty Woman, Green Card, Trading Places, Desperately Seeking Susan, After Hours, Red Heat, Twins, Rain Man, Baby Boom, Being There, Die Hard, Things Change, Private Benjamin, Chariots of Fire, Down and Out in Beverly Hills, Risky Business, Troop Beverly Hills, Beverly Hills Cop, Coming to America, Big Business, Working Girl, Dead Poets Society, Crazy People, My Left*

*Foot, The Fabulous Baker Boys, Crocodile Dundee, The Russia House, The Rescuers Down Under, Baghdad Café, Vibes, Pow Wow Highway, Withnail and I, Sister Act, Class Act*

In all these movies, the central character is thrust into a new world and has to figure out the right style to survive there. Some actors (for example, Arnold Schwartzenegger, Goldie Hawn, or Eddie Murphy) have based their careers on playing characters who struggle with style as aliens in a strange world, usually triumphing in the end. Albert Brooks and Woody Allen create gentler comedies, often called "neurotic" because the insecure central character often second-guesses style choices.

Style is *always* a struggle. Nobody ever has it down perfectly. No one ever quite masters it, and everyone keeps trying to refine, polish, renew, or reinvigorate style choices. Even people who seem to have style are struggling to get better at it and to survive the next challenge. So it is an ongoing, dynamic process. Characters in brocade clothes uttering rhymed couplets do not have their lives all figured out, and neither need you and I. What we do need is to understand how each of these people feels and to experience their worlds from their perspectives. By asking the following questions, you will get information on how to survive and succeed in the world of the play.

*It's an interesting world we live in when Arnold Schwarzenegger can kill 115 people in a movie and he's fine. I drive around a woman's house twice, and I'm neurotic. Go figure.*

—ALBERT BROOKS

- How do these people understand or perceive the world around them?
- What do they all share? How much the same do they seem to be?
- What works in this group? What do they reward and punish?
- What is the most effective strategy for me here? Where's my free space?
- What have they learned to think is natural? What to them seems contrived?
- What is the most expedient way for me to move from tourist to native? How could I live here?
- Who gets away with things? How do they manage to? What did they have to learn?
- Do I really know what play (world) this is? Am I fully here?

## SIGHT AND SOUND—FIRST STYLE IMPRESSIONS

The way you look and dress creates a first impression, followed by the way you speak. Physical signals are backed up or contradicted by vocal ones, and we make instant judgments. Researchers report that in the first sixty seconds after spotting someone, we predict their level of education, social standing, political views, organizational skills, trustworthiness, income, maturity, background, and health. In our relationships with acquaintances or associates, we may never look beyond this first evaluation.

Industries are devoted to how to look. Magazines, from *Vogue* and *Gentlemen's Quarterly* through those aimed at readers of lower income, status, or expectations, offer advice, not on what to believe or feel, but on what to wear and how to present oneself. Ours is a visual culture. Before a big occasion, we narrow what we're going to wear down to several choices. Often, our final decision is based on the kind of person we want to *seem* to be, whether that is what we are or not.

We make some style choices to mislead (to show, for example, that I'm more sophisticated than you are), some to lead people to the real us, and some to send out mixed messages. Sight now virtually overwhelms sound. Former President Reagan's skilled support staff now openly acknowledge that if they provided a visual clip contradicting unflattering news, most of those watching would never hear it.

After sight comes sound. The language of style changes as rapidly as each season's look. The most vivid words are *about* looks.

*The eye wins every time. Image has replaced word as the grammar of our culture. Good visuals are often more valued than good journalism.*

—BILL MOYERS

---

**E X E R C I S E**

**Levi Lingo**

This exercise is based, in part, on an annual survey of what is in and out among college students. Divide the class into two teams, "good" and "bad." Review this list:

| *Good Dresser* | *Bad Dresser* |
|---|---|
| bad | wonk |
| babe | brutal |
| crisp | clueless |
| stylin' | dirtbag |
| ham | doorknob |
| happening | dressed in the dark |
| hip | fashion nightmare |
| whip | hairball |
| tree | serious student |
| stud mom or stud dad | stanko |
| silk | fashion faux pas |
| well-ironed | heinous |

1. Decide which terms have become passé since the survey came out and what they should be replaced with.
2. Have each member of the team use one of the terms in a sentence with a context and try to adopt appropriate body language and attitude.
3. Go back and identify which terms have been around for a long time and which are new. Double-check your decisions with others over the next few days.
4. Make up at least three terms of the future, and have three classmates present them to the class in a definite context.

Now consider these terms, which were popular among middle school students:

| *Good* | *Bad* |
|---|---|
| totally cool | bummer |
| neato | gross |
| radical | barf-a-around |
| far out | sickening |
| all right | evil |
| out of sight | slashed |
| outstanding | gross |
| fresh | uncool |
| gnarly | bogus |
| dudical | magu |
| sweet | the worst |
| boss | no way |
| magical | pathetic |
| jammin' | oldtimer |
| poppin' | fashion |
| clean | hideous |
| coolsome | boohoo |

1. Repeat each of the steps in the exercise above with the new vocabulary.
2. Pretend you and your classmates are all seventh-graders sitting in the school cafeteria. Limiting conversation topics to the food and each other, use as many terms on the list as possible.
3. Identify which terms are "revivals" of old ones.

There may be no culture in which words change faster or which employs more euphemisms than the film industry, particularly the people (writers, agents, publicists, and producers) who put together deals. By the time you read this list, many will have changed again. Which ones do you recognize as now dated? Which ones passed you by the first time around?

| *Out* | *In* | *More in* |
|---|---|---|
| take a meeting | I have a 12:30 at Fox (*never say the "m" word*) | |
| call you on the car phone | call you in the car | call you from the field |
| close up shop | do a Dino | out of there |
| in the dark | out of the loop | |
| hot | has heat *or* is on the cusp | happening |
| selling a project | shopping a project | |
| client relationship | attachment | |
| non-box-office client | encumbrance | |
| getting in bed (making a deal) | making a marriage | |

| | | |
|---|---|---|
| highly commercial | no brainer | |
| credentials | auspices | the 411 *or* What's her story |
| high concept | marquee value | |
| rewrites | fleshing out the character signature, firming up the arc | |
| producer turns you down | producer takes a Pasadena | producer bails ("He bailed on me") |
| I'm not going to produce it | It's a real character piece; It's for specialized audiences; *or* It's a very cast driven movie | |
| definite refusal | hard pass | |
| tentative refusal (worth rewrite) | soft pass | |
| uncooperative actor | on his own agenda *or* not on the program | |
| strong initial box office prospects | will open | should open big |
| advance publicity | front loading | |
| selling out at box office | going clean | |
| legs | playability | second weekend |
| doubtful film | a brave movie, a human story, *or* a relationship movie | |
| bomb | craters | Hudson Hawk |
| unemployed | between jobs, on hiatus, in development | at liberty |
| You'll never work again | You're off the sports list | You're out of here |
| You're on the beach | You're off the sports list | |
| You're history | You're toast | You're history (*again*) |

Improvise a scene in which two professionals struggle to one-up each other. Be sure to invent terms your opponent has never heard.

E X E R C I S E
**━━━━━━━━━**

**The Euphemizing of America**

The following is a list of old terms with their newer replacements. The new choice softens the impact.

| *Old Term* | *New Term* |
|---|---|
| help wanted | employment opportunities |

| *Old Term* | *New Term* |
|---|---|
| poor | functioning on a limited income |
| divorce | dissolving a marriage |
| used | previously owned |
| secretary | administrative assistant, office specialist, support services agent |
| junkie *or* drunk | substance abuser |
| cheap *or* a bargain | affordable |
| possible weirdo | alternative life-style |
| having sex | in a relationship |
| bus | motorcoach |
| uninhabitable | fixer-upper |
| easy to run | user-friendly |
| hard to put together | some assembly required |
| garbage collectors | sanitation engineers |
| massage parlor | adult social service center |
| laundry | fabric care center |
| old | chronologically gifted |
| dating others, playing the field, *or* sleeping around | nonmonogamous relationship |
| crippled | physically challenged |
| _____(*insert atrocity*) victim | _____(*insert atrocity*) survivor |
| poor *and/or* retarded | disadvantaged |
| disadvantaged | special |
| fat | has a weight problem |
| broke | overleveraged |
| clumsy | vertically challenged |

1. What euphemisms can you add to the list?
2. Probably the most euphemized subject in the world is the bathroom. How many terms can you think of for the place and what usually goes on in it?
3. Second place would go to the sexual act. How many terms can you come up with for it?
4. In what instances is it now in style to reverse the above trend and use a more blunt term (as in *alcoholic* instead of *heavy drinker*) in conversation? What are the blunt terms for (2) and (3) above? When are they most likely to be chosen?

The terms "boyfriend" and "girlfriend" are largely unused, so there is some confusion about what terms should be used. Some cultures use the term "mistress" (no known male counterpart) or "lover." We struggle most for the appropriate style

**E X E R C I S E**

**Couples Coupling**

choice when the people involved share the same quarters. A cohabiting lover may be called any of the following:

partner
main squeeze
the man/woman I'm living with
significant other
spousal equivalent (*state systems*)
domestic associate *or* affiliate (*used by some yuppies*)
POSSLQ (Person of Opposite Sex, Same Living Quarters) (*used by U.S. Post Office*)

1. What other terms have moved in and out of style during your lifetime?
2. Do your parents use any terms that you and your friends never use (that you would in fact never be caught dead using)?
3. How do you introduce someone whom you are dating but not sleeping with? Someone with whom you are sharing the same house but not bed? To what extent does this issue matter to you or to your friends?

**E X E R C I S E**

**Misread Signals**

You choose your clothes and your words to project a certain image. But people form impressions based on other signals you project, too—signals that you don't necessarily choose consciously. These include such visual signals as your stance, facial expressions, walk, gestures, and use of space; and such sound signals as your vocal quality, timing, articulation, pronunciation, pitch, and volume.

1. Sit with your classmates in a circle on the floor.
2. Take a minute to look at each person and recall your first impression of that person.
3. Compare your impression with those of your classmates, and identify collectively how your first impression was off and how it has changed.
4. What style signal does this person send off (what signals does he or she project that made you form an impression different from the lasting, deeper evaluation you formed later)?
5. Keep free of judgment. Take time to make sure there is a consensus before moving on to the next person. Remember that this information is meant to help the person. It is not given as a suggestion for change; it is just given.

## RITUALS AND LIFE-STYLES—FINDING PATTERNS

Since we think only of *others* as stylized, we often don't notice stylized events in our own lives—ceremonies, formalities, prescribed patterns, rites, and sacraments. When a visiting relative leaves your home, for example, does each member of the family walk to the car and hug or shake hands before the visitor gets in the car and takes off? Do you all stand and wave until the car is out of sight? Is anyone who *fails* to take part in this ritual chastised and given the cold shoulder later? Even though the *real* good-byes may have taken place earlier, this ritual seems essential, especially if the visitor has come a long distance and has not been seen for some time. Many feel cheated if an important experience is not stylized into a ritual, possibly even a full ceremony.

Only the truly insensitive would deliberately fail to observe family and social protocol. If some stylized event has become important enough to become protocol, the ceremony is just the surface expression of something deep in the bones and hearts of the people performing it.

---

Select someone in class to play a child from birth to death. Call the child "Adam" or "Eve." Devise as many formal rituals as possible for the child. Cast a mother and father, and devise other rituals in groups of two. Pass through a whole life in no more than ten minutes, so that only the ceremonies are included. Be sure to include these events:

1. Cutting the cord
2. A christening
3. An important birthday
4. An initiation rite
5. Facts-of-life talk
6. A graduation
7. A job interview
8. An engagement
9. A wedding
10. An arrest
11. A court trial
12. Receiving an award
13. A retirement ceremony
14. A funeral.

**EXERCISE**

**Life Cycle Ceremonies**

Your life-style involves all your observable choices, from music to appliances. It is how you use time, at work and at play.

The following changes were widely and accurately predicted for the 1990s: (*a*) Women will wear more white and cut their hair shorter; (*b*) men will wear wider ties and grow their hair longer; (*c*) portraits and statues of affluent people will become popular again; (*d*) there will be more New Age radio channels and less overamplified music; and (*e*) "wet" beer (designed to be drunk on the rocks) will appear.

**EXERCISE**

**Backing into the Future**

1. Discuss the basis on which researchers may have made these predictions.
2. Identify which trends you believe are most and least likely, which seem absolutely new, and which are retro.
3. Come up with a list of at least five additional trends you as a class would be willing to predict.

4. Identify any trends you see in the theatre itself.
5. Some groups get national attention. In the 1970s, it was the preppies; in the 1980s, the yuppies. Which do you see on the horizon? Predict the most likely group to replace these two in public fascination.

---

The more public a job, the more style demands are placed on the person holding it. We have strong ideas about how heads of state, network anchors, and superstars should look, sound, and act. We adjust when a new phenomenon comes along, but we keep our expectations and react when someone violates them. Consider the British royal family. One of the reasons for the massive popularity of the Princess of Wales is that someone *finally* joined that group who looks and acts like a princess! We were all so relieved after years of pretending to find the other members of the family royal (and attractive) that when Diana came along, looking as though she had come straight from central casting, things suddenly seemed right. Can you imagine a job listing for someone in a position like hers?

> WANTED: Attractive young blue-blooded female capable of (1) bearing two male heirs as rapidly as possible; (2) dressing with some flair; and (3) handling idle chitchat in receiving lines. Remuneration will include jewels, personal wealth, and the adoration of most of planet Earth.

Spouses of heads of state hold crucial style setting positions, largely because their job consists *entirely* of style. They do not officially set policy but influence taste. The shift from the Nancy Reagan to the Barbara Bush White House received massive media attention. It sent out a message about hair color, dress size, candor, and the values behind these style choices.

---

**E X E R C I S E**

**Changing Worlds**

Each improvisation has three characters, two who are familiar with the world and one newcomer.

- A college student interviews for an executive business position requiring experience and maturity.
- An ardent feminist tries to make it to the Miss America finals without compromising her principles or offending the two key judges in the crucial interview.
- A journalist tries to pass as a member of a satanic cult in order to get the story.
- A Democratic political supporter of John F. Kennedy falls asleep in 1960 and wakes up at 1992 campaign headquarters (based on *Rip Van Winkle*).
- Somehow, while reading, a student falls into a time warp and appears in Camelot, behind a canopy in Guinevere's chambers, during a clandestine visit by Lancelot (based on *A Connecticut Yankee in King Arthur's Court*).

1. Working in threes, devise similar predicaments based on the sudden shifts that take place in *The Prince and the Pauper* and *Alice in Wonderland*.
2. Find other classic examples in literature or current examples in the news of someone's sudden need to adjust style habits to survive in a changing world.
3. After trying these, let members of the class suggest other struggles for survival they have experienced or observed.
4. Discuss what specific adjustments the outsiders make in order to fit in. Which elements of learning a new style seem to come quickly? Which are the toughest to crack?

---

People go about the same fundamental acts in different ways. Acts and people are not really different. The style is. This knowledge makes it easier to stop judging others on surface issues and to take the time to find out who they are. It also makes it easier to find the connections between you and characters you play and then confidently "refine" yourself around the differences without being intimidated by them. One of the best ways to achieve this is to imagine a wide range of choices surrounding a single, simple act.

---

**EXERCISE**

**Song Style**

Agree on a classic everyone can sing a cappella (possibilities: "Row, Row, Row Your Boat," "You Are My Sunshine," "I've Been Workin' on the Railroad," "Take Me Out to the Ballgame," "A Bicycle Built for Two," "My Bonnie Lies over the Ocean," "Comin' 'round the Mountain," "Yankee Doodle," or "Happy Birthday").

1. Sing the song together, without making any conscious style choice.
2. In groups of three, do a verse in the style of these genres: reggae, blues, country and western, rap, opera, lounge singer pop, acid rock, others.
3. Select someone or volunteer to do a verse in the style of these performers: Hank Williams, Jr., Ethel Merman, Carol Channing, Elvis, Jimmy Durante, Bob Dylan, James Brown, David Bowie, Julio Iglesias, Rex Harrison, Louis Armstrong, Willie Nelson, Madonna, others.

**EXERCISE**

**Same Game**

1. Work with partners. Half the class watches, and half plays.
2. Agree on an imaginary physical game—shooting baskets, throwing and batting a ball, tennis, ping pong—anything two can do and that is easy to mime.
3. Begin as if your partner is really your partner. Then, as a side coach calls out, imagine that your partner is
   • The person you idolize and revere most in the world
   • Someone you believe to be evil
   • A parent whom you are planning to ask for a special favor
   • Someone you want to love you

- Your servant, who has not been working hard enough
- Your boss, whom you want to give you a raise
- A retarded or learning-disadvantaged person
- Other suggestions called out by the observers

4. Switch, and have observers become players.
5. Discuss how the act in each case changed in style simply by your attitude toward the other person involved.
6. Now play the game with the class shouting out types of films. Within the rules, fit the film style. How does the game change?

**E X E R C I S E**

**Same Story**

1. Sit in a circle, and begin to tell a familiar story or a well-known fairy tale or legend.
2. When the teacher or a designated classmate calls out one genre (musical comedy, silent slapstick, sitcom, gothic romance, murder mystery, Sunday cartoon, network news broadcast, buddy movie, soap opera, slasher movie, *Masterpiece Theatre*, Western, horror flick, documentary, game show), change the way you tell the story but not the actual plot details. For example, you might refer to Cinderella as "the little filly," "the perpetrator," or "contestant number three," but she still goes to the ball and gets the prince.
3. Variation: The "Die, Die, Die" game. A student who does not pick up the new style is "caught" by the rest of the class, who shout the line "Die, die, die!" This student must then drop out of the circle by dying the appropriate death of someone living in that style.
4. Discuss not only the variations but also the circumstances under which you felt most and least secure with the challenge of changing style while keeping plot identical.

## GROUPS AND INDIVIDUALS—YOUR OWN STYLE

Style is associated with groups but is embraced by individuals. You need to know what impressions your own style choices leave in the world to recognize when your style may be infringing on rather than serving the character you are playing. To help you do this, think about the following questions:

- Of which groups do others "think" you are a member, whether it is so or not?

- When in your life so far have you altered your own style most radically to get out of a sticky situation?

- In what contexts can you get away with being bad? How did you get this control?

- How would you describe your own standard way of dressing? How would others describe it?

- What single article of clothing would others most likely associate with you? What kinds of people wear this kind of clothing?

- What do you work hardest at altering about yourself before you present yourself to the world each day?

- Do you embrace any particular lingo? Which category of speech in the preceding exercises comes closest to your own style?

- When you want to avoid being blunt or crude, what euphemisms do you favor?

- How much do you influence the way others speak, dress, or relate? How easily influenced are you, and by whom?

- When you have traveled, where have you felt most at home and where most like an alien?

As you explore new group styles in subsequent chapters, ask yourself how your style fits into each one. Use the questions in this section as a reminder. Remember that if a style gives you problems, you may be imposing your own on it. You may have not yet decided to enter the new world completely. Or you may have not yet unearthed those parts of your own style which fit.

Recognizing style is rewarding, touching, and often amusing. For two years in a row, my wife and I have, by accident, eaten out at an elegant restaurant on Prom Night. We watch high school students struggle with style, like brave explorers venturing into unfamiliar territory: tuxes, evening gowns, corsages, borrowed or rented cars, an ambiguous and expensive menu, a formal atmosphere, starched collars, wobbly high heels, intimidating waiters, polite and studied conversation—a barrage of new experiences as high school ends and life begins. Each year we've asked ourselves, "Were we ever really that young? Did either of us ever drop our napkin that many times?" The answer "Yes!" comes resounding back. And we wish we could let them know that they *can* survive this, master it, and even learn to enjoy it.

Some look as though they've decided to be intimidated and have a terrible time on this supposed night of celebration. Others ignore the style changes and act as though they're in the school cafeteria. Others are full of discovery, *appreciating* their own newness and awkwardness in unfamiliar territory and even being able to laugh at it, but also experiencing little victories of elegance and adulthood.

For some of these people, tonight is a nightmare, and they will never venture this far from jeans and fast food again. For others, it is an introduction to one more way to have fun. Style is an ongoing discovery. You are always getting better at being who you are in public. You are always at least striving. If you recognize that possibility for growth you make the experience a great adventure.

**E X E R C I S E**

**Style in a Nutshell**

1. Draw names for classmates.
2. Between one class and the next, find a short phrase (no more than five words total) that seems to capture the style of the person you drew.
3. To gauge the accuracy of your own impression, check with as many other people who know the person as you can.
4. Try to predict what someone else will say about your style.
5. Gather in a circle, and share the results.
6. Note which of your classmates' impressions most and least surprise you.
7. How do you feel about your style? What does this tell you about what you send out?

**E X E R C I S E**

**Style Signals**

Write a one- or two-word response to each of the following as they relate to impressions you leave: (1) sight, (2) sound, (3) ritual, (4) life-style, and (5) group membership. Keep your answers to yourself, but try to watch more carefully to see whether you send out the same signals you think you do. Consider the ways in which your reputation may or may not reflect who you actually are.

**E X E R C I S E**

**Style Abstract**

To find out how you present yourself, ask others. But to make sure they are candid, ask them to think of you in abstractions. In this way you remove yourself from literal, linear, blunt, and potentially embarrassing interaction so that they can answer truthfully. Abstraction allows them to call it as they see it. Pick an answer in each of the following categories that reflects how you are perceived in the world. Answers are not what you would *choose* to be but what you *appear* to be. You may *like* warm, sunny summer days but *project* chilly, rainy autumn nights. Abstracting captures essence, which may be different from taste. (The form that follows can be used for four subjects at a time if the group chooses to analyze the entire class or cast.)

1. Analyze yourself first, attempting to predict the responses of your classmates.
2. Make one copy of the form for every four subjects, plus one copy to use as a worksheet for yourself.
3. Each week, fill out forms on four classmates. Make them all due on the same day, but do not return them to the subjects until the last week of the term.
4. Assign a classmate to analyze the answers, looking for trends, rejecting categories that seem indecisive, and focusing on those where there is either uniformity or remarkable diversity.

## Abstract Form

*due* _____

|  | Subject #1 | Subject #2 | Subject #3 | Subject #4 |
|---|---|---|---|---|
| | \_\_\_\_ | \_\_\_\_ | \_\_\_\_ | \_\_\_\_ |

1. fabric _____
2. animal _____
3. bird _____
4. beverage _____
5. mode of transportation _____
6. city _____
7. tree/vegetation _____
8. color _____
9. play/film/TV show _____
10. scent _____
11. type of day _____
12. decade or era _____
13. song _____
14. mythological/fantasy figure _____
15. landmark or building _____
16. snack _____
17. spice/flavor _____
18. musical instrument _____
19. painting/photo _____
20. toy _____

# ANALYZING STYLE
## Survival Questions

**THE WORLD ENTERED**

An astronaut steps onto the moon, Dorothy into a Technicolor Oz, and a freshman into something called a dorm. None of them knows exactly what to expect in this new world. An actor is cast in a Greek chorus, a Shakespearean romance, or a rock musical fantasy. All offer adventure beyond real life. So why do some adventurers survive, prosper, and conquer while others are squelched, humiliated, and eliminated? Why are some travelers Indiana Jones, some Walter Mitty, others Accidental Tourists? Some are better at figuring out what is going on in a world and then acting.

Here are some categories in which great travelers and actors make style decisions to ensure their survival and long-range success in the worlds they enter:

1. Time: tempo and history
2. Space: public and private
3. Place: surface and safety
4. Values: truths and beliefs
5. Structure: control and change
6. Beauty: models and expression
7. Sex: recreation and procreation
8. Recreation: doing and watching
9. Sight: looks and image, movement and contact
10. Sound: speech and song, music and dance

Brian Bedford (Alceste) and Sherry Flett (Celemene) in *The Misanthrope*, The Stratford Festival

Over years of trying to tie together the various style concepts of the theatre and the behavioral sciences, it gradually dawned on me that all style issues fall into these fairly simple categories. Actors and anthropologists are kindred souls in style. No single category is more important than another. The first eight cause the last two. The last two, however, are the first by which style is judged.

You can achieve membership in almost any universe you choose, if you know how it works. As you read more about these style categories and apply them to the world you want to enter, keep in mind two crucial points. First, when you travel to a new place, you need to look for the style choices the majority makes. So whenever a new issue comes up, try to determine how important (or insignificant) it is to the people in this play (world). The number of questions you will encounter on the following pages will seem overwhelming until you realize that in any given world, there is a hierarchy of concern. These questions merely provide a framework for you to scan and determine which subjects the people of that particular world really care about.

Second, you need to determine how polarized or uniform the characters (people) are in their views. In the sixties, for example, American culture was polarized in the extreme. The contrast between the Nixon White House and Haight Ashbury, between White House princess Tricia Nixon and young women who renamed themselves Tree or Seagull, was as strong as any such contrast in memory. Yet the sixties followed a decade of almost complete conformity. Ask how close or far apart people are in the way they see life.

### Time: Tempo and History

*In what point in history is the play set, written, and performed? How do these factors interact? How far does the audience or play move out of its own time?* Plays that are set in other eras present several problems. Do we update the script to make it "relevant"? Do we play into its period charm? Do we pull the audience back into history or push the play forward? Note what one writer says about this issue:

> Playwrights—even great ones—do not write for the ages. They write for their specific audiences at their specific times. . . . special problems arise when a play is done for an audience other than the one it was written for.
>
> For example, twentieth-century Americans often read *Hamlet* as a play about Elizabethan English with characters (dressed in Elizabethan clothing) behaving as if they are English. But Shakespeare set the play in Denmark, knowing his London audience of 1601 had specific thoughts and feelings about Danes. Modern Americans don't share those thoughts and feelings; they aren't even aware of them.
>
> In 1601, Shakespeare's Londoners had reason to think Denmark a terrifying place, peopled by warlike, bloodthirsty savages. Londoners knew that a few centuries earlier Danes had sailed up the Thames and set fire to Lon-

don Bridge (hence the nursery rhyme "London Bridge is Falling Down"). And even in the sixteenth century Danes frequently landed on England's shores to attack isolated villages—killing, raping, and plundering before disappearing back to sea. To Elizabethans Denmark meant destruction, primitive brutality and terror.

Into the midst of such a world Shakespeare puts Hamlet . . . a *man* of introspection and considered thought versus a *society* of impulsive, arbitrary brutality. This conflict partly explains Hamlet's "inability" to act, without resorting to modern psychological theories about melancholia disabling the prince. It may be coincidence that no one thought Hamlet incapable of action until a hundred years after the play was first staged—right about the same time that the English perception of Denmark as bloody and brutal started disappearing.

For every play from a time and place other than your own, *consider what the original audience thought and felt about the world portrayed in the play.* Sometimes this takes a lot of research, but the result will be worth the effort (*David Ball in* Backwards and Forwards.)

In successful productions, there is movement in every direction. The play moves up in time, the audience moves back in time, and they meet at an exquisite point in the imagination.

*How rapidly does time move for most people? How conscious are they of time passing? How do they record or note time? What is the dominant tempo/rhythm?* When I moved from a big East Coast city to a small West Coast one, I thought at first that most people I talked to had slight brain damage. They took *so* long to answer. Clerks would finish conversations they were having before waiting on me! And everyone would easily be distracted by a cute child or something in the sky or coming up out of the ground. Many didn't even wear watches. Perception of time and its proper use varies radically from place to place, and from play to play. Time can be thought of in generations, seasons, and full moons or in split seconds, deadlines, and cost. Tempo may move from speed-of-light to barely perceptible. Rhythm may insistently throb or softly undulate.

*Do people focus mainly on the moment or on whole lifetimes? On the future or the past?* The Greeks dwell on the past, the Restoration on the moment, and Elizabethans almost breathlessly on the future. Where you focus in time can change the way you see and live—it determines whether you are always making plans, savoring what is, rehashing what is over, or some combination. The past may mean bygone eras or the last half hour; you may look at it with longing or regret.

*What length of attention span do these people have? Is age revered or feared? What is the relationship between youth and maturity?* Time passes according to how engaged you are. If you love to listen to a well-developed argument and complex processes of thought, someone can talk forever and keep you enthralled. If you are illiterate, you *must* listen carefully, because you cannot write down what you hear or look it up. If you're used to ten-second commercials and sound bites, you have little patience for exposition.

In some worlds, youth is associated with stupidity, in others with freshness and purity of insight. Which ages are honored, ignored, and merely tolerated? What is considered the peak of life?

---

**E X E R C I S E**

**Change Time**

1. Imagine the same activity performed in different times, based on different views of the world. Agree on a simple everyday activity, such as setting the table for your family dinner.
2. In pairs, perform the event as if you are living in the following eras: the fifties, the sixties, the seventies, the eighties, the nineties, prehistory, science fiction future.

**E X E R C I S E**

**Same Plot, Different Time**

1. In teams of three (with at least one member of the opposite sex in each group), draw one of the times above.
2. With no more than ten minutes' preparation time, present a simple proposal of marriage and an acceptance. The third person may be a human who is involved, an inanimate object, a narrator, a pet, or any key third element that might be at the scene.
3. With the same amount of preparation time, immediately go back and present the proposal and a refusal.
4. Discuss the comparative values in the scenes and in the two versions of the same scene.
5. Draw two other style groups, and repeat the exercise.
6. Try these two variations based on a woman telling a man she is going to have a baby. In the first version, the news is received joyfully. In the second, it is received as bad news. Note that the events (marriage and birth) in the exercise above are universal but that the style in which the event is enacted can vary tremendously. The act is identical, but the styles are myriad.

**E X E R C I S E**

**Time Games**

In this exercise, the class will be creating an imaginary culture. Be yourself, except where the time issues are concerned. Two people step out of the room so that they do not know what is being created. As a group, the rest of the class chooses one from each category below. The group should perform each of the following activities without digression but may agree to change itself at any time (becoming fast after having been slow, for example).

Point: distant past, recent past, present, immediate future, distant future
Rate: fast, slow, medium, variable
Focus: past, present, future
Attention: short, long, moderate, visual, aural
Age: revered, feared, polarized

1. Without preparing, three people get up and do the marriage proposal, with both responses.
2. Three others do the pregnancy announcement, with both responses.

3. Everyone else now gets up and functions as an entire group within the time style:
   a. Together decorate a vehicle for the honeymoon of the couple in (1).
   b. Together choose a collective shower gift for the baby in (2).
4. Everyone in class now forms the total culture, keeping any identities adopted so far:
   a. Choose a community leader to serve for the next year.
   b. Pick someone to deliver a dangerous message to another foreign community, one about which you know little, except that they threaten you.
5. The two people outside become immigrants from the foreign culture while those inside proceed to inaugurate their leader from (4a).
6. The foreigners enter in great need of help, with a secret agreed on by the two of them that may not be discussed. They try to get results without revealing the secret.
7. Discuss what happened.

---

## Space: Public and Private

*How is space defined and viewed? Is space simply literal, or do people think in terms of spiritual, philosophical, or abstract space? How large a bubble do most people carry around? In what ways do personal spaces alter? How flexible are they? To what degree are privacy and personal space respected? What are attitudes toward invasion and physical force? How is space violated?* In the seventies, a person asking for "space" did not (usually) mean a larger bedroom or den, but the freedom to make more decisions and spend more time alone. In a classic proxemics study, Edwin Hall observed a South American ambassador follow a U.S. diplomat down the entire length of a huge hall while they talked. The northerner (like most of us) wanted two to three feet between him and his companion. The southerner was more comfortable with six inches. The one sensed his personal space being invaded, whereas the other felt a great chasm unless they were close.

Touching, grabbing, pushing, and embracing, all standard in some cultures, can cause war or at least a police report in others. Have you visited a home where no one ever closes the bathroom door and everyone opens each other's mail? Assumptions about privacy suddenly disappear. Experiment even slightly with "space sanctity" in elevators, grocery lines, and waiting rooms, and it becomes clear how deeply ingrained are our biases regarding appropriate behavior.

*How do these beliefs translate into audience proximity, movement patterns, gestural ranges, relationships to properties, entrances, and exits?* How large do people think they are? Never mind their literal height, weight, or strength. How do they *view* themselves? In most classical plays, individuals regard themselves as larger than we do. They need more space and fill more, simply to exist in all their personal glory, exuberance, anguish, or spirit.

### Place: Surface and Safety

*Is the setting rural or metropolitan? Urban or remote? Coastal or inland? Protected or exposed? Confined or open? Is the setting new or old? What influence do surface, terrain, flora, fauna, and weather have? Does the setting have a specific or generic character?* Location and proximity influence belief and behavior. Thoughts about the future are not the same in a sleek, modern environment as in one where history is around every corner. Isolation can add to inflexibility or invite transcendence. Linguists maintain that the rolling hills of Ireland influence both the lilt of speech and constant shifts of mood, just as the plains of the Midwest lead to flat sounds and relative stability. A recent empirical study (The Whims of Bicoastal Dining) focused on successful restaurants in L.A. and New York that decided to open a branch restaurant in the other city. Owners soon learned that they could not re-create their success without making significant adjustments in the menu, wine list, decor, food preparation and presentation, portions, turnover, and service.

*How aware of other places are the people? How provincial in perspective? Are they citizens only of this specific spot, or are they citizens of the world? What is their relationship to nature? To what extent is the environment controlled, altered, accepted, owned?* Do the people focus only on themselves and their friends, or does their vision extend to global concerns and causes? Is their ideal to batter Nature into obedience or to pay her obeisance? Is Mother Nature nurturer or enemy?

---

**E X E R C I S E**

**Change Place**

1. Pick a simple activity and, in pairs, perform it as if you were French; English; Russian; Italian; German; Southern; a native New Yorker (Big Apple); in Los Angeles (Big Avocado); in Washington, D.C.; in the nearest big city; in your college town.
2. Take the same plot elements in the Same Plot, Different Time exercise, and apply them to this exercise.

**E X E R C I S E**

**Place and Space Games**

Keeping the same rules and procedures in the Time Games exercise, go through the process after making the following choices:

definition: literal, spiritual, abstract
bubble: large and inflexible, highly flexible, small and inflexible
invasion: anything goes, no touching, affection but no violence
audience: huge and distant, small and close, medium and varied

1. Pick four cultural characteristics from the list to create a new society.
2. Perform immediately the Time Games sequence, up to the point where the group feels fully aware of the influences. Decide as a group when it is time to stop and go on.

---

## Values: Truths and Beliefs

*What are the beliefs most widely shared? What ideals? Which truths are assumed to be self-evident? What are the traditions, and how large is the commitment to them? How are friendship, family, trust, and community defined, and how are these bonds broken?* Can you recall the first time something you thought true was contradicted by someone else? Worse yet, did the person regard your "truth" as silly and not even worth considering? Devastating—to be thought both wrong and insignificant.

All groups share beliefs, which in times of trouble can bring the group back together. They constitute the culture's core. Beliefs form habits, which become customs, which surround the basic birth, marriage, and death rituals and are taken seriously. There are cultures in which it is traditional for the host to offer his daughter to a visitor for the night and those in which the violation of the host's daughter would be the most loathsome act possible. Every traveling salesman had better know the territory. In some cultures, a son is expected to challenge his father in battle. In our own, a record number of children have no firsthand knowledge of what a father *is*.

*What is the predominant mood? Who are the role models, heroes, idols? What are the shared fantasies and ideal futures? How do people define sin, consequences, forgiveness, ethics, justice?* Are these people happy, euphoric, melancholy, pensive, despondent, indifferent, or volatile? How comfortable, genuine, or forced is the dominant mood choice? Who are placed on pedestals? Whom do they envy, imitate, and emulate? What do they dream about? How close are their lives to their dreams? Are their heroes real or from legend and literature?

Even the most tolerant societies define certain acts as sinful. Thieves have their own code of honor, as do drug barons. How are social errors handled? How do you redeem yourself? Is any act beyond the pale? Behaviorists agree that if you live outside your own beliefs, with knowledge and awareness, you pay high prices. You can change your behavior or your beliefs. If you do neither, there are inevitable, profound consequences.

*What gets attention? What holds it?* Audiences now like laconic, nonverbal types who make a strong physical impression and open their mouths only for one-liners. Most classical drama favors orators, masters of rhetoric who elaborate and soar on any subject. Characters in Elizabethan drama speak in brilliant iambic pentameter because that is the only way anyone will listen.

*What value is placed on money? What is the place of God and the church in life? Are these two ever confused?* Feelings are always strong where bucks are concerned. Filthy lucre or key to happiness? Is money embraced, rejected, pursued, tolerated, or worshiped? How, beyond obvious personal gain, can it change life?

How much theology, doctrine, structure, and power surrounds the god of choice? Mythologist Joseph Campbell called the computer an unforgiving Old Testament God. Some of us have a relationship with our computer like that of Lot and God, with keyboard as altar. Others feel that "if God had meant us to take this life seriously, She wouldn't have created it that way."

*What kind of humor dominates? What role has laughter in society?* Laughter is the great lubricant of life. Some groups have no lubricant. What do these people think is funny? When is it appropriate to laugh? Is the humor wry, witty, elevated, broad, slapstick, vulgar, social, political, personal, kind, nurturing, vicious, satiric? Is laughter a primary means of dealing with pain? Does it get people through life or help them avoid it?

*How is fear defined? What are its sources, and how do people cope with it? How and to what degree is emotion expressed? How is it suppressed? How is it repressed?* Who are the monsters, demons, and dragons in this world? What do these people think is the worst thing that might happen to them? Invasion from a neighboring country, being alone, being ridiculed, the bogeyman? Is fear met head on or avoided? Is it dealt with collectively or privately?

---

**E X E R C I S E**

**Value Ceremony**

1. Work in teams of three.
2. As a team, take one of the following and arbitrarily pick a shared value for your society: ideals, family, mood, idols, sin, attention, money, God, humor, fear.
3. Write the standards on the board.
4. What kind of culture emerges? Can you begin to act these people?
5. What ritual or ceremony would be most meaningful to this group? Cast the leaders, and enact it for the rest of the class. See how close they come to guessing the values behind the act.

---

## Structure: Control and Change

*Who are the leaders? Who rules, and who follows? How easy is it to bring about change? How tightly or loosely structured is the society? How absolute is authority, and what is the voice of the individual? What is the governmental system?*

*How is justice brought about?* Nets surround societies—some hard, rigid, and indestructible; others soft, stretchable, and roomy. In most period plays, the net is more rigid than in our own world. Poor farm boys do not grow up to be emperor. A misplaced word can result in a misplaced appendage. The capacity to change one's destiny is limited to a golden few.

In our country, by contrast, we know how to sue, appeal, protest, plea bargain, and pursue a suspended sentence or parole. We have options, but many still feel utterly powerless within the system.

*How is the pattern of daily life ordered and followed? How are family and marriage defined? How much sanctity do they have? How are manners, etiquette, and rules set? How flexible are they? What is the level, type, and emphasis of education? Is education for both sexes? How wide is its impact?* What happens on a typical day? Is the family part of daily ritual? Do spouses bond for life or just for the season? To what extent is infidelity, separation, bigamy, or divorce tolerated?

Is knowledge seen as a means to freedom? Who goes to school, for how long, and what do they study? Do schools reinforce rules or encourage innovation? What is considered inexcusable ignorance?

*How are groups created and identified? Which are most powerful? What professions dominate, and how is work viewed? How is information gathered and spread?* Many classical plays do not involve "work" as we think of it. Characters do not have a "job" and pursue a "career." What replaces this use of time and energy? Remember that in classical drama being a homemaker may mean managing a staff of a hundred people.

---

1. Pick a simple activity and, in pairs, perform it as if you were members of the following groups: army, evangelical fundamentalists (God Squad), bikers, surfers, the Mafia, Skinheads, yuppies, street people, theatre people.
2. Take the same plot elements for the Same Plot, Different Time exercise, and apply them to this exercise.

**E X E R C I S E**

**Change Group**

1. Pick a simple activity and, in pairs, perform it as if you were acting in the following genres: musical comedy, silent movie slapstick farce, sitcom, gothic romance novel, Agatha Christie murder mystery, Sunday cartoon, network news broadcast, buddy movie, soap opera, *Masterpiece Theatre,* Western, horror flick, martial arts film, foreign film, documentary, game show.
2. Take the same plot elements in the Same Plot, Different Time exercise, and apply them to this exercise.

**E X E R C I S E**

**Change Genre**

1. Work in five groups, each group going back and arbitrarily choosing or inventing one significant characteristic of time, space, place, values, and structure.

**E X E R C I S E**

**Five Factors**

2. Share the results, and write them on the board.
3. With this entirely new group of characteristics in place, choose three candidates for leader. Give them five minutes to mix, campaign, and shmooze. Then hold the election.

---

### Beauty: Models and Expression

*What is the look most aspired to in this group? Who are the contemporary ideals of male and female perfection? What are the most coveted skin types, hair colors and styles, and physical proportions?* Each age favors a pattern in dress, hair, body, skin, and adornment, all reflecting how people think they want to look. At this writing, Mel Gibson and Michelle Pfeiffer (senior division) or Tom Cruise and Julia Roberts (junior division) would be strong contenders for being named as the cultural ideals. Instead of accepting these choices, debate among friends about who reigns as most people's physical ideal. How do others who do not meet that standard feel about themselves? Identify the ideal height, weight, shape, features, and colors. *The Journal of Personality and Social Psychology* recently reported that most women regard big eyes and a square jawline as attractive in a man; so the extremes (jaw—Clint Eastwood, exemplifying vigor and sexual power and eyes—Paul McCartney, exemplifying nurturing and compassion) are highly attractive, but those who combine these two (Tom Selleck, for example) eclipse the others in appeal.[4] What standards are used, and what factors can cancel others out? Know how close or distant each character in the play is from the desired look.

*What part does physical fitness play in physical attractiveness? What is the relationship between beauty, health, and comfort?* In our era, high muscle tone, low body fat, healthy consumption, and cardiovascular fitness are serious considerations for personal attractiveness. To what lengths will people go to achieve the ideal look? People now are willing to go through *enormous* discomfort ("No pain, no gain") for long-range attractiveness but very *little* discomfort (painful undergarments, girdles, high heels, stiff fabrics, starched collars, rollers, elaborate make-up) for temporary attractiveness.

*Which colors, shapes, textures, and silhouettes are favored? How important is fashion? How fast does it change? To what degree do people alter nature to create a thing of beauty?* Every catalogue seems to feature such colors as aubergine, papaya, sandpiper, or mist. Nothing is blue or red anymore. Day-Glo has been reborn as neon. What do these color choices say about us? Notice how people choose to package themselves and how long new looks last. A few years ago, wearing an "oversize" garment made people think you had borrowed clothes from a large relative, and "gym clothes" at the supermarket would have been out of the question.

Is the natural look pursued, or is the look flagrantly artificial in persons, homes, lawns, and meeting places? How is beauty expressed? Do people paint, draw, sculpt, compose music, write poetry, design objects? Are these talents cultivated from an early age? Are they encouraged or (as in mandatory piano lessons) enforced? In what contexts is the word "beautiful" likely to be employed?

---

1. Select a panel of three judges. Everyone else competes and/or tries to influence the judges. There will be five quick contests from five eras: the fifties, sixties, seventies, eighties, and nineties.
2. When a judge calls out the new era, take thirty seconds to change yourself into what you consider the ideal of that time. Then parade around the room. Judges may request turns and ask questions, but each contest lasts no more than three minutes.
3. When all five winners are chosen (one person may win more than one contest), they tell why they think they won. How does everyone else feel?

**E X E R C I S E**

**Beauty Contest**

The standard way for a man to react to an attractive woman varies in different countries. Note these examples:

Brazil—put imaginary telescope to the eye for a closeup look.
Greece—stroke the cheek.
France—kiss the fingertips.
Arab world—grasp the beard.
Italy—rotate forefinger on check.

1. Share any other such regional or time-bound customs you have noticed.
2. Let a woman walk through the room, and have the class respond to her attractiveness.
3. Let a man do the same.
4. Discuss which responses were "appropriate" given the times and which were unacceptable or vulgar. What cultural biases determine these behaviors?

**E X E R C I S E**

**Hey, Beautiful**

---

## Sex: Recreation and Procreation

*How significant a part of the collective consciousness is sex? What do most people consider turn-ons and turn-offs? Which areas of anatomy are revealed, concealed, emphasized? What are the sexual stereotypes?* For many years, Audrey Hepburn had a lucrative wig modeling contract in Japan because her neck was considered astonishingly attractive in a society prizing necks. Although she has had a successful career in the United States, her neck was not the reason. One campus bookstore currently sells five different calendars, all with the title *Buns*. Is that the current body part of choice?

*How is sexuality acceptably communicated? How is seduction defined? Is the emphasis on the act or the chase? On pleasure or procreation? What is the standard courtship ritual and its significance?* Because engaging in sex is something that both people and animals do, groups find rules to set us apart from animals. Between an elaborate, lengthy mating dance and a curt "Your place or mine?" what constitutes accepted foreplay? Is sex a diversion, game, sacred trust, sin, inconvenience, bore, or the reason for living? Do individuals have any freedom in choosing their spouses? How much tolerance is there for love at first sight?

*How great is the tolerance for deviation? What are the accepted attitudes toward infidelity and promiscuity? To what degree is sexuality suppressed or expressed?* Is experimenting with sexual preference, partners, positions, and potions appropriate? Two terms, once commonly used, have disappeared from conversation: "nymphomaniac" and "frigid." Why? What changes have made these terms passé?

In some Latin American cultures, men and women openly smolder and flaunt themselves, because family protection around unmarried women is so strong that breaking the barrier is nearly impossible. The unlikelihood of consummation allows the display of sexual energy. The film *The Accused*, with Jodie Foster, demonstrates the potential danger of innocent expression of sexuality in our society. What is possible without losing society's support? Where is the line drawn?

---

**E X E R C I S E**

**Sex Roles**

In this exercise, the class becomes a society that exhibits the following characteristics:

- Bisexuality, with women as the aggressors, is the norm.
- Women like experienced, knowledgeable women and chaste, virginal men. Many prefer one of each for a ménage à trois.
- Elbows and eyebrows are considered hot.
- Women are supposed to brag and strut. Men are supposed to be relatively silent and appreciative audiences.

1. Imagine that everyone is horny, and it is last call. When everyone has a partner or gives up, the game is over.
2. Discuss how it felt to exist in this world.

---

### Recreation: Doing and Watching

*What is most people's idea of fun? What would be an ideal social occasion in this world? What is most people's vision of an enjoyable evening, vacation, or day? To what degree do people participate? Are they doers or watchers? What is the intellectual life? Are the people thinkers or mindless hedonists?* A party is filled with style signals. What are parties like in this world? Are they formal or casual, planned or spontaneous, structured or open-ended, elaborate or simple, intimate or massive? Are they purely social gatherings, or does business go on? What is the attitude toward athletics and physical activity? In our own society, there seems to be a dichotomy: Reebok says, "Life is not a spectator sport" and Nike "Just do it," but couch potatoes disagree.

Is an *idea* fun? Are intellectual discussions and debates part of personal enjoyment? Do people grapple with cosmic questions or avoid analysis at all cost?

*What are common shared hobbies, pastimes, and concepts of what constitutes a good time? Do these vary between the sexes? What about consumption? What are the favored and coveted meals, drink, drugs, snacks? What role does food play in social interaction? What is the relative importance of recreation in life? What is the standard view of indulgence?* Food fads reflect perceptions of the good life, and each age has its own image of a good, healthy meal. Your parents remember when Americans called pasta "noodles" and were worried that it was unhealthy because it was too "starchy." What will replace pasta, mineral water, and frozen yogurt?

## Sight: Looks and Image, Movement and Contact

*How do all of the above factors manifest themselves in the way the world of the play looks, in the shapes and angles, in light and shadow, in dominant patterns of movement and gesture? In clothing, furnishings, props, hairdos, and jewelry?* Visual style signals reflect the society's shared beliefs. We may notice that everyone in a culture extends the pinky while drinking tea and holds the cup gingerly between the first finger and thumb, but it's crucial that the actor understand *why*. Is there a proper way to stand and sit, and, if so, for what reason? Which facial expressions are desired? Which gestures, and with what frequency? Is there an appropriate way to walk that reflects a sense of self? Do these behaviors change in public or private? How do people touch?

How do people approach each other? Are there standard bows and curtsies? How do these reveal the way people feel about space, both their own and that of others? Are special skills needed to maneuver inside this world?

## Sound: Speech and Song, Music and Dance

*How are the shared beliefs reflected in common speech, nonverbal communication, and the degree to which listening and speaking are prized?* Patterns of speech emerge out of shared feelings. Note the degree to which speech is encouraged at all. We happen to live in a visual, nonverbal time when vocabularies, writing skills, and literacy scores are dropping. Consider not only *what* people say but also how often, with what variety, and with what additional noises. How well do they each hear what others are saying, and what the role is of silence?

What vocal quality is most desired, rewarded, and emulated? For what reasons? What sense of timing is considered most acute? Is there a standardized pronunciation or great variance? Which part of the pitch register is employed, and how often? Are the words chosen vague or direct? Do nonverbal signals enhance, refine, or contradict the verbal signals employed?

Beyond speech, what is the role of music in life? How do people express themselves through song and dance? Which composers and instruments are popular, and what does that say about life?

## KEYS TO THE WORLD

To get into the new world, it helps to have keys—quick reminders to help you feel part of the new reality. Images (evocative stimuli for the senses), social success and suicide (extremes of rewarded and punished behavior), masking (knowing which faces are put forward), production (placing historical information in the context of a theatre event), and contemporary parallels (connecting you own world to this one) can all help.

### Images

What most vividly brings out the feelings of the culture? Is there a painting, sculpture, building, novel, essay, fad, landmark, concerto, invention, philosophy, custom, or quotation that captures the essence of the era? Here as examples are some images of the past four decades:

> The 1950s: jitterbug, hula hoop, Sputnik, TV dinners and TV trays, low-slung "blond" furniture, the Baby Boom, Norman Rockwell, cars with fins, Eisenhower, Elvis, poodle skirts, ponytails, ducktails, Jell-O, beatniks, bowling, "The Hit Parade," Howdy Doody
>
> The 1960s: free love, Vietnam, love beads, communes, acid rock, bell-bottoms, the Beatles, the Kennedys, tie-dyeing, folk music, Haight Ashbury, *Easy Rider*, "Laugh-In," mod, miniskirts, psychedelia, op art, roach clips, munchies, Black Power, peace symbols, the generation gap
>
> The 1970s: self-help, personal space, the Me Decade, the women's movement, Watergate, disco, homemade anything, gas lines, the Bee Gees, logo T-shirts, designer jeans, stir fry, jiggle, cults, vege-

tarianism, environmentalism, running shoes, quiche, "Saturday Night Live," *Saturday Night Fever,* white wine

The 1980s: surrogate mothers, prenuptial agreements, designer water, yuppies, stress, insider trading, glasnost and perestroika, self-esteem, aerobics, greed, homelessness, trickle-down theory, personal computers, Nintendo, AIDS, Tex-Mex, codependence, dietary fiber

Which images would you add to make life in each decade leap out? Here are "forbidden" words of the nineties—those so overused or perverse that writers have called for their death. Which do you think will survive? What do you predict will replace them?

Words to avoid in the 1990s: bimbo, careerist, claymation, cocooning, codependence, dirty dancing, dramedy, dweeb, high- or low-concept, infotainment, minimalism, mommy track, neo anything, New Age, Ninja, postmodern, post anything, power breakfast or lunch (or anything), sound bite, wannabe, wilding, wuss, anything from hell

---

1. Divide into five groups: the fifties, sixties, seventies, eighties, and nineties.
2. Try to be the first group to come up with five additions to the lists above.
3. Whenever one group reaches five, all of you share what you have with everyone else.

**E X E R C I S E**

**Lingering Images**

---

## Social Success and Suicide

How do you climb to the top? What guarantees downfall? What is the single most devastating thing one person could possibly say or do to another (the ultimate insult)? What is the very highest validation (the ultimate compliment) anyone could bestow or receive?

---

1. Work in the same groups as in the previous exercise. Determine what would be, in your decade, the ultimate compliment. Establish how the line would be phrased, who would say it and where, and who would be listening.
2. Once one group has an answer, all of you share what you have come up with.

**E X E R C I S E**

**Ultimates**

3. Then do the same with the insult.
4. Discuss what the two lines say about life in your decade.

---

### Masking

Each world has acceptable faces presented in society and onstage. In some, literal masks and veils are worn, as they are in ours only at Halloween or Mardi Gras. Usually, however, the mask is symbolic, as in the lyrics "Put on a happy face" or "Smile though your heart is breaking." In public, what is most likely to be hidden, revealed, acquired, affected, or cultivated? How complex is the preparation, and how easy is it to puncture the mask? Under what circumstances might it become transparent, translucent, reflective, gilded, chameleon, or fully opaque? How much is the mask acknowledged? To what degree is the difference between mask and face no longer understood?

### The Production

How are all of these factors likely to emerge in performance? As we match cultures, what are the trade-offs? Because only men appeared onstage until the mid-1600s, will our production feature an all-male cast? Will the Greek play be performed in an amphitheatre and the Shakespeare be done in a replica of the Globe? Knowledge of how the play was done originally, there and then, helps us make intelligent adjustments on how to do it here and now.

### The Perfect Audience

How should we (classmates, other cast members, crew, rehearsal visitors, and ultimately the public) behave in order to create audience rapport comparable to that of the original actors? How and where do we sit? Do we move and circulate during performance? Do we interrupt? With what kind of remarks or displays? Are there refreshments or other diversions? How do we acknowledge work well done? Do we offer verbal criticism? How much are we like or unlike what is being portrayed?

### Contemporary Parallels

What is going on in our society now that matches the new world? A silly fad can be as valuable as a major belief, if it provides a bridge. Conversely, where does this world diverge from ours? What must we leave behind in order to cross over? Where can connections be found?

### Summary Style List

The complete list of the preceding investigation categories is located inside the front and back covers of this book. Obviously there are many more questions than anyone would care to answer. Use the ones we've provided as a guide to help you explore the relevant issues in the particular world you wish to enter.

The following exercise combines all of these questions into a single acting experience in familiar styles. For the story to be true, each of the issues above needs to contribute to the lives of the characters. Because the basic story line is set, the creative space is all style.

---

**E X E R C I S E**

**Family Lies**

Place: France, England, Russia, Italy, southern United States, New York, L.A., Washington, D.C., your town
Time: fifties, sixties, seventies, eighties, nineties, prehistory, the future
Group: army, God Squad, bikers, surfers, the Mafia, Skinheads, street people, theatre people
Genres: musical comedy, silent slapstick, sitcom, gothic romance, murder mystery, cartoon, soap opera

Draw from two different categories. Work on the story out of class for a few hours. The scene involves three actors, with both sexes represented:

1. A is at home, exercising and fixing dinner. (*What is "home" like? How is the nest defined? What value is placed on exercise, and what is the currently popular way to stay fit? What kinds of foods are valued, and what kinds of rituals of preparation are involved?*)
2. B arrives (they do not know each other) with something that has been mistakenly delivered to the wrong address. (*How do strangers approach each other? How is the sanctity of the home invaded? What is considered a hospitable response to unexpected visitors?*)
3. A and B discover they are both married to (or living with) C, who has been keeping two separate households across town from each other. (*How much shock, rage, and hurt can be shared appropriately with someone one has just met? How do these people deal with wild, primary emotions at this moment? What is considered civilized behavior?*)
4. A and B resolve to confront C (who is expected momentarily) and to force C to make a choice. (*How easy or difficult is confrontation, how much a part of life? How fearful are they of losing C altogether? How solid or tentative is this joining of forces?*)
5. C arrives, is shocked at being found out, gets the ultimatum, but then presents another solution. (*How strong a factor is guilt at this moment, and*

*how humbled is the offender likely to be? What proportion of threat and charm
tactics are likely to be employed?)*

   6. Some kind of resolution occurs, which may please all, some, one, or none
of the above. (*Who leaves? Who stays? Do all three go their separate ways? A
ménage à trois? Something in between these extremes?*)

---

## FINDING THE WORLD

When you are dealing with a real play, your investigation should start with
the text itself. Remember not to confuse the world the playwright is *creating* with the world in which he or she may have been *living.* When Shakespeare creates the Athenian forest in *A Midsummer Night's Dream* or the
witches' lair in *Macbeth,* he is writing about a world very different from
that of Elizabethan London. Moreover, the primitive world of *King Lear*
is strikingly different from the whimsical one of *Twelfth Night.* Some elements connect all Shakespeare's plays, but each must be examined more
deeply on its own. So each script should be approached for the reality it
alone creates. Each new play is a new world to be discovered. It is the
*imaginative* world that is of interest to the actor/adventurer.

---

**E X E R C I S E**

**Playwrights' Worlds**

Each of these playwrights share a period. They are contemporaries:

David Mamet and Wendy Wasserstein
Tennessee Williams and Arthur Miller
Noel Coward and Eugene O'Neill
George Bernard Shaw and Anton Chekhov

   1. Discuss how each writer's work is reflective of the time in which it was
written. Then discuss how the world of one writer is different from that
of the other writer and how it is not reflective of the lives lived by most
people during that era.
   2. Take a universal situation (example: husband discovers wife has been
unfaithful and tells her he is leaving her). Meet in small groups, create
the scene in the style of that writer, and present it.

---

Style research moves from general to specific. You wish to consider
these factors:

- The period itself
- The world the playwright creates, which may be close to or far
from the one he or she lives in

- The world for this particular script, which may be like or unlike others the playwright has written
- The life of your character, who may be typical or unusual among the majority of characters

At each trip through the list, your knowledge gets more specific. Some fact about life in Restoration London may or may not directly illuminate your production of *The Way of the World*. If you discover something about Electra, you must ask, Whose Electra? She is godlike to Aeschylus, heroic to Sophocles, and human to Euripides.

The same principles that help you get inside a character in a play will help you adjust to a new neighborhood, town, country, or planet. The living world is less *set* than that in a script, but both worlds need to be investigated. Your skilled detective work can yield great rewards; by careful research, you earn the right to make things up. A great deal of the world of the play is a world of play.

# 3

# MASTERING STYLE
## The Classical Actor

## TESTS OF TIME

Real actors long to act in great classical drama. These scripts, having passed the test of time themselves, now test the actors. Can the performers transform themselves? Can they transport their audience out of modern America to Long Ago and Far Away, Once Upon a Time, and Days of Yore? Can they become larger than life and still be real? Those who can are much admired. Great plays, surviving the test of time, also carry the power of time. There is actor magic in them.

The next four chapters are devoted to the periods when drama rose to unparalleled heights. Although there are other instances of great surviving drama, these chapters deal with the periods and playwrights that are most likely to enter an actor's life:

Ancient Greece, 500–400 B.C: Aeschylus, Sophocles, Euripides (Chapter 4)

Elizabethan England, 1550–1620: William Shakespeare, Christopher Marlowe, Ben Jonson, John Ford, John Webster (Chapter 5)

Restoration England, 1660–1710: William Wycherley, William Congreve, George Farquhar, George Etherege, Aphra Behn (Chapter 6)

Neoclassic France, 1660–1700: Molière, Jean Racine, Pierre Corneille (Chapter 7)

Georgian England, 1775–1800: Richard Brinsley Sheridan, Oliver Goldsmith, John O'Keefe (Chapter 7)

James Edmundson (King John) and Dan Kremer (Cardinal Pandulph) in *King John*, Oregon Shakespeare Festival

Actors who excel in period style works do the same in

> Displaced drama, 1900–present: Maxwell Anderson, Peter Shaffer, Christopher Fry, Jean Anouilh (Chapter 8)

Displaced plays, also called costume drama, are relatively new and therefore not included in the category of classical drama; nevertheless, these plays demand of the actor the same skills of transcending time and space. The author writes from our century but looks back to re-create another. The language is less difficult, simply because it is formed for twentieth-century ears.

## PERIOD STYLE ACTORS

What makes a good period style actor? Some actors are less bound to their own time and space than are others. Without reading ahead in this chapter, try the following exercise:

---

**E X E R C I S E**

**Classics vs. Contemporaries**

1. Choose five actors whom you have not seen perform Shakespeare or other great works but whom you imagine would be good at it. Choose actors you yourself would hire for a full season of classical repertory. Select well-known actors with instantly recognizable names. (Call this your A list.)
2. Choose five actors whose work you respect but whom you do not consider highly castable in the classics, that is, actors whom you consider good, but not right for the kinds of roles involved. (Call this your B list.)
3. Remember that both lists must consist of performers you admire. Go back and cross out anyone who, on further reflection, you don't think is all that good.
4. Now write a short phrase (no more than four words) explaining your choices.
5. Do the same for the choices you eliminated.
6. Compare your lists with those of your classmates. Are there names that emerge with regularity on each list? Discuss these.
7. Are there some actors who appear on *both* lists, for different classmates? Why?

---

Over a thousand theatre professionals and students have taken the "quiz" above. The following names were most frequently mentioned:

*The A List*

| | | |
|---|---|---|
| Jane Alexander | Glenn Close | Richard Dreyfuss |
| Kenneth Branagh | Daniel Day Lewis | Faye Dunaway |
| Richard Chamberlain | Colleen Dewhurst | Albert Finney |

| | | |
|---|---|---|
| Audrey Hepburn | James Earl Jones | Peter O'Toole |
| Katharine Hepburn | Ben Kingsley | Vanessa Redgrave |
| Charlton Heston | Kevin Kline | Jane Seymour |
| Anthony Hopkins | Angela Lansbury | Maggie Smith |
| William Hurt | John Lithgow | Meryl Streep |
| Jeremy Irons | Mary Elizabeth | Jessica Tandy |
| Amy Irving | Mastrantonio | Max Von Sydow |
| Glenda Jackson | Irene Papas | Robin Williams |
| | Michelle Pfeiffer | |

*The B List*

| | | |
|---|---|---|
| Alan Alda | Henry Fonda | Eddie Murphy |
| Woody Allen | Jane Fonda | Bill Murray |
| Roseanne Arnold | Michael J. Fox | Paul Newman |
| Kathy Bates | Melanie Griffith | Jack Nicholson |
| Carol Burnett | Tom Hanks | Al Pacino |
| Cher | Goldie Hawn | Sissy Spacek |
| Kevin Costner | Holly Hunter | Tom Selleck |
| Tom Cruise | Diane Keaton | James Stewart |
| Geena Davis | Steve Martin | Lily Tomlin |
| Matt Dillon | Bette Midler | Bruce Willis |
| Michael Douglas | Liza Minnelli | Debra Winger |
| Sally Field | Mary Tyler Moore | |

You may disagree with some choices (as do I), but these are the names offered most often. There are more British actors on the A list, more comics on the B. Many think the British possess a classical dignity that most comedians lack. More A-list than B actors have stage experience. But beyond these first generalities, other patterns emerge. A-list explanations tend to include these words:

| | | |
|---|---|---|
| poise | boldness | stature |
| grace | size | intensity |
| class | sensitivity | focus |
| power | eloquence | clarity |
| sophistication | depth | mystery |
| presence | control | universality |
| versatility | command | majesty |
| voice | | |

B-list reasons often involve the adverb *too,* followed by these words:

| | | |
|---|---|---|
| limited | crude | insensitive |
| rough | small | weak |
| flat | light | subdued |
| low-class | ethnic | simple |
| conventional | informal | monotonous |

|          |         |          |
|----------|---------|----------|
| shallow  | slow    | internal |
| comedic  | modern  | awkward  |

Are the A-list names better actors than the B-list names? Not necessarily. The genius of some actors is to capture the time and place they are *in* and to reflect it *back* to their audience. Henry Fonda and Jimmy Stewart are important examples. These actors exemplify small-town Americana—decency, simplicity, virtue, the pioneer spirit, homespun wisdom—our country from the mid-nineteenth to the mid-twentieth century. This is an extraordinary gift. But their gift is also their shared limitation. The idea of Henry Fonda in tights and doublet, speaking a sonnet, or James Stewart in powdered wig and brocade, indulging in wicked gossip, is hard to imagine, except as satire. Neither actor seems made for time travel.

One reviewer suggested that Michelle Pfeiffer had proved that she cannot do the classics because she played Olivia in Shakespeare's *Twelfth Night* for the New York Shakespeare Festival to devastating reviews. Critics said she lacked vocal power and clarity in a large outdoor theatre. You can take hope and encouragement in this. Were Michelle Pfeiffer to train for the stage and to study vocal technique (two things she hasn't done), most observers would probably maintain that she has the *potential* to do this kind of work. She has the basic A-list qualities. Training may also be the only thing between *you* and classical power on the stage. So don't underestimate yourself.

---

**E X E R C I S E**

**A's vs. B's**

Try isolating those qualities in yourself that are right and wrong for classical theatre:
1. Read the B-list reasons to yourself. As you say each word, mentally cast it aside as though it did not describe your acting style. Identify those that you cannot dismiss so easily.
2. Read the A-list reasons, giving yourself permission to accept or to take on those qualities in yourself. Go ahead and feel larger, stronger, wittier, and more of a force to be reckoned with. Which words do not fit so well?
3. Go back and deal with the resistant words. Recognize and explore what may be blocking you. Promise yourself to become comfortable with the desired characteristics and to exorcise those in the way.

---

Sometimes directors do not want actors to develop classical qualities. To make the play more accessible to the audience, the director may decide to minimize the differences between performer and observer. In some cases, the director alters the whole world of the play for this purpose, for example, setting *The Taming of the Shrew* in the Wild West or *Lysistrata* in the Vietnam era. An actor must develop the capacity to go with the production concept, whatever it is. Take none of the information that follows, therefore, as rules; there are many right ways to do the classics. In productions like those above you do not *need* to change worlds, because the directors are bringing the play into your world or a familiar one. Most productions of the classics, however, are traditional, and that type is our concern here.

## COMMON THREADS

Actors who are adept in the classics are like chameleons; by taking on the characteristics of the world of the play, they can take us back in history or forward into fantasy. To be taken *seriously* as a knight, princess, witch, wench, god, or sorcerer, you need to weave these threads of the classical world into your performance.

*Time.*  Time moves less predictably, veering wildly between breathtaking speed and a careful, deliberate pace.

*Space.*  Personal space is larger. You need more room just to stand, sit, and move. Your concept of self radiates, sparkles, and flashes; when you make an entrance, you fill a void. When you invade another's space, you usually do so directly and suddenly (for example, sweeping lovers into your arms and kissing them or boldly striking opponents), without hesitating or sneaking around. Space is there for you to take.

*Place.*  Settings are both grander and simpler. You may be in a palace, forest, temple, battlefield, sea, or public square. You may be on an island or mountaintop. A more mundane spot, such as a drawing room, is merely suggested rather than elaborately staged—no small clusters of furniture, no small props; you are less likely to have something to lean on, sit on, or play with. You are likely to acknowledge the presence of the audience occasionally. You rely more on your imagination than on scenic devices to indicate a change of place.

*Values.*  People take history more seriously, tend to believe in the divine right of monarchs, and rely on miracles rather than scientific inquiry to explain events. Following one's own destiny is mandatory, and one's destiny is often also the destiny of others. Characters tend to have many people dependent on them, so their acts have great consequences. No one gains or keeps attention without speaking well. It is more important to live life fully and forcefully, even in sin and error, than safely and softly.

*Structure.*  Who you are when you are born is vital to who you will be when you die. Rulers (both of countries and of families) are less often questioned. You either play by rules or change them, often the latter. Order comes from the stars and the fates, not from generator and battery.

*Beauty.*    Beauty is more abstract, and the *expression* of it even more prized than the *possession* of it. You create beauty in your speech and create yourself when you go into the world. You handle far more fabric and accoutrements, and it helps to have features strong enough to match the clothes.

*Sex.*    At times, sex drops from consideration because the issues at hand are much more significant. At others, it becomes the focus of life. In general, sex is dealt with more frankly and enthusiastically, with less humor or embarrassment. Sex does not hide or cower.

*Recreation.*    Public celebrations are more common. Shyness is less tolerated. Life is envisioned as a banquet. The capacity to overindulge is more tolerated, even honored. Each person is expected to contribute to the entertainment, to help form the event, to make the party happen.

*American actors seem to have a fear of words and of language as apart from emotions. I want to drop the intimidation factor. What American actors are frightened of is a sense of discipline and technique. But these things need not negate the emotional work. They don't end the mystery of acting, they preserve it.*

—KENNETH BRANAGH

*Sight and Sound.*    Stillness and economy of movement alternate with bursts of physical boldness. You can do absolutely nothing and still pull your listener deep into your consciousness. You are also able to reach out to the back of the theatre and embrace everyone there in energy and power. You speak clearly, crisply, and cleanly, giving maximum attention to consonants as *shapers* of sound. Listeners never have trouble understanding you, yet your speech does not seem affected. You are able to speak at greater lengths, with more complexity and authority.

You can probably think of exceptions to the list above—brilliant classical performances that do not fit the mold—but these are the qualities required more often than not. What follows are the areas where young American actors in classical plays are most often asked to make adjustments. By mastering these very technical details, you can ultimately gain the freedom for full emotional expression.

What follows, although it looks like a list of rules, should be viewed as *possibilities*. These techniques are frequently requested and useful to have in your repertoire.

---

**E X E R C I S E**

**Classical Warm-Up**

Supplement or integrate this exercise with a standard physical and vocal warm-up that already works for you.

1. Sit in a kneeling position. Bring your head forward, so that your forehead touches the ground in front of you, while moving your arms straight backward, so that they rest at your side. Press your arms against your legs, with your palms facing upwards. The position will feel like total supplication.

2. Breathe deeply, and let your spine relax and stretch comfortably in this position.

3. Rise to a standing position very slowly: Move your arms in a half circle forward across the floor; then, turn palms downward and move them close to your knees to support you, and rock back onto your heels as the soles of your feet touch the floor. Keep your head low and your back rounded, in a fetal position. Again, breathe and release the spine.

4. Move into a puppet or rag doll position, but raise the tailbone so that it is the highest part of your body off the ground. Let your knees bend slightly. Test the freedom of your upper body by swinging your arms and head back and forth, left and right, like an ape.

5. As you very slowly stand, you should feel a pull at your tailbone and at each vertebra along your spine. As you rise, imagine you are moving through an evolutionary phase, growing brighter, quicker, and more confident. Pass through the stage you consider your real self, and move beyond into a heroic mode you rarely allow yourself. By the time you are fully upright, you should feel that you have evolved into a powerful personage.

6. From a standing position, look up at the ceiling and beyond to the sky. Raise your arms above you, and extend one arm as far as possible. Release it slightly, then extend the other, alternating in a gentle, tugging stretch. Believe you can touch the stars and clouds with each reach.

7. Look in front of you, and drop your arms and shoulders. Feel tall, aligned, and open.

8. Begin to make giant circles with both arms, with the motion coming from the shoulder joint. First, move both arms to the right; then to the left; then to the center; then outward. Visualize gestures emanating from your center, which is strong, into a large space that you command.

9. Spread your legs apart, and lean to the right, with the right leg bent and the other straight. Feel a stretch in the hip joint, and circle the arms to the right. Do the same with the left side of the body.

10. Return to a neutral stance, and breathe deeply while circling your arms first inward, then outward.

11. Stand still. Begin humming. Turn the hum into a roller coaster of pitch, moving comfortably higher and lower in your range.

12. Let your voice turn into a magic chariot plunging down a mountainside over and over, so that it explores the bottom notes of your register. Yawn, then turn the yawn into a hum, and let the hum drop lower and lower, until you get off the chariot and onto a vast hidden valley, speaking a few lines from your favorite role.

13. Repeat (12) three times or until you are comfortable using these bottom notes and adding them to the others available to you.

14. Alternate circling your arms and leaning in opposite directions. As you move, repeat the B-list words, and cast the ones you don't want away from you as you speak them forcefully: *limited, rough, flat, low-class, conventional, shallow, comedic, crude, small, light, ethnic, informal, slow, modern, insensitive, weak, subdued, simple, monotonous, internal, awkward.*

15. As you speak the following words from the A list, develop your own pattern of circles to make yourself feel as though you are beckoning or

taking on these qualities as your own: *poise, grace, class, power, sophistication, presence, versatility, voice, boldness, size, sensitivity, eloquence, depth, control, command, stature, intensity, focus, clarity, mystery, universality, majesty.*

16. Either speak a speech that always makes you feel powerful, or move into one of the warm-ups (in subsequent chapters) for feeling Greek, Elizabethan, Restoration, Molièrian, or Georgian. Remember that there are always exceptions. Bottom (in *A Midsummer Night's Dream*) is low-class, Othello is ethnic, Iago is nonmajestic. Select images to suit circumstances.

---

## PHYSICAL LIVES: DIGNITY AND SIZE

To achieve a bearing that seems suited to greatness follow these guidelines (key words and phrases appear in italics):

*Sitting.* Furniture is intended for you to exhibit yourself; it is not plush or comfortable. Think of it as your personal pedestal. Sit on the edges, *perching* as you might on a stool or leaning against a wall. Keep your back straight.

Both *descend and ascend by using the legs,* allowing the upper body to float erect as if you are riding on a horse from the waist up.

*Keep legs uncrossed* if you are a woman prior to 1920 or a man prior to the late 1800s. Clothes make this movement uncomfortable, which is associated only with "brazen hussies or tarts." Men may make this move when ladies leave the room (for example, the gentlemen in *The Importance of Being Earnest* might cross their legs and light their cigars when they are alone together, but not when women are present.) Not until skirts shorten is the move associated with modest or proper deportment.

When you are seated, arrange yourself in an *asymmetrical pose,* with one foot at an angle slightly different from the other and one hand counterpointing rather than imitating the other. Enjoy the aesthetic picture you create as a seated work of art. Save symmetry for ritual (see Gesturing).

Visualize yourself sitting in a range of period clothes that demand of you an *erect, steady bearing.* Although flowing Greek robes seem as different as possible from tight, puffed Elizabethan doublets, both types encourage similar postural choices. If you wiggle and shift, the Greek garment will fall off, and the Elizabethan one will cause you pain. Economy of movement allows you to save energy for when it matters.

Whereas we tend to sit down to speak, classical characters tend to *sit down to listen* at the end of their speeches. Since the speech itself is often an extended public argument, sitting often symbolizes completion and readiness to hear from others, a final punctuation.

*Connecting.*   Instead of leaning in to make points, rise up to them, *lifting yourself into the action.* Put the energy that makes you want to lean into the words and into your eyes instead. Onstage leaning reads as a suppliant posture. You appear, no matter how strong your words, to be begging.

Free yourself from the need to punctuate each crucial turn of phrase with a forward jerk of the head, or "chicken neck." Instead, put this effort into *enunciating* expressive vowels and sharp consonants.

When you are in repose, listening or evaluating, remain absolutely *still,* free of tiny neurotic moves and shifts. When you feel the need to gesture, make large, fully committed gestures whose energy radiates all the way to the ends of your fingertips and beyond.

Your self-concept is closer to a god's. Let your *head float* high above your body like a helium balloon, but keep your shoulders relaxed. Since you will be tempted to raise your shoulders with your head, check periodically and release them. Instead of working on great posture, think of yourself in larger terms. If you have any chance to study Alexander technique, do so. Have someone who has studied this technique teach you a "shlump" and how to emerge from that defeated posture into something powerful, like a butterfly from a cocoon.

Decide to be *taller than your scene partners* even if there is no hope of ever achieving it. Decide to have a neck longer than anyone else's onstage, so that you will always "rise to the occasion."

The need to look at other actors, both when you speak and when you listen, is not as great. Your *focus* is intense, but it is just as often directed to ideas and images as to the person with whom you are conversing. You do not need to lock eyes constantly to make and receive points. Your vision moves frequently beyond the moment, into the possible.

Because speeches are longer, the *speaker needs to be upstage.* Relish this convention as both speaker and listener. Give up your modern ideal of sharing in favor of acknowledging the person who needs focus.

Once you connect with another actor by eye contact, embrace, or simple touch, sustain it fully instead of backing off quickly. Really *clasp* or gaze at the person, without apologizing or second-guessing.

*Gesturing.*   Because your personal space is large, the *full extension* of your arms and legs in any direction is the minimum amount of room you require for your comfort. Think of a large ball or bubble surrounding you from which your personal glow emanates.

Your *arms* cannot comfortably swing listlessly or drop to the side, because your clothing forbids it. The drape of fabric or droop of lace requires an *energized* and ready wrist. Move your arms frequently up and out so that your meaning can emerge from the bulk of your costume. Armholes tend to be small, so your arms are most comfortable when you hold them in a curve. Think of each gesture as a flash of light that illuminates what you have to say.

When you are in repose, imagine that there is an *air space under the arms,* giving them a sense of relaxed readiness. Don't press them against the torso.

The audience will automatically fail to comprehend some words and events, so use the *space to clarify* what may not be understood. Do not fear the literal if it supports meaning (for example, Hamlet can wipe off Ophelia's makeup when he speaks of women painting themselves). Locate the city, the buried dead, the gods, and any other important catalysts or forces through gesture. Think of the scene as a series of photographs, paintings, or sculptures, where visual clarity can compensate for archaic language.

*Save symmetrical gestures for moments of ceremony,* worship, and ritual. Recognize that one side of the human body rarely falls into mimicry of the other except when we are formalizing experience, which we do frequently in classical drama. Relish the perfect balance with which you are bringing the world temporarily into a state of complete order.

*Allow big gestures to unfold.* Slowly return to a neutral position instead of quickly retreating. Resist the temptation to take the shoulder into the move. The gesture may burst into being, but let it die naturally.

---

**E X E R C I S E**

**Simple Power**

1. Find a box, chair, or platform to sit on and a small space to explore.
2. While someone reads aloud the key phrases below, let yourself explore these techniques. Don't worry about getting them right; rather, try to discover the feelings behind them.
3. When the activity suggests the need to connect with someone else, turn to an actor near you briefly, then go back into your own sphere.
4. Make up dialogue to run silently in your head when it helps you create a moment. For the asterisked items, work with a partner and actual dialogue.

| | |
|---|---|
| perching | clasp* |
| descent/ascent with the legs | full extension |
| asymmetrical pose | energized arms |
| lifting into the action | air space under arms |
| enunciating* | clarify in space* |
| stillness | clarify in space* |
| head float | symmetry for ceremony |
| taller than others* | mony |
| focus* | unfolding gestures |

---

*Moving.* When crossing into another person's bubble, use clean, *strong invasions.* Either leave someone alone, or go in for the assault (whether romantic, sexual, violent, or sporting) with full commitment.

When you walk, keep the torso relatively motionless and let the hips do the work. Do not sway them right and left; rather, maintain a strong forward rotation. Transcend the "jeans" walk, which is all angled hips, rocking, and shifting of weight, in favor of the *rotation walk*. Remember that you probably have no pockets and that your pants (if that's what you're wearing) do not rest on your hips.

Imagine you are being drawn by *two pulleys,* one attached to the top of your head and the other to your chest, both in perfect synchronicity. Remember to "lead with your nipples."

Think in terms of *gliding* rather than clomping. One of the singular accomplishments of the classical performer is to move quickly and gracefully around the stage (even in a pair of boots or heels) without making noise. This involves lifting the upper torso and regarding the floor as an ice arena. Sound of movement should not interfere with line readings.

*Display yourself;* parade and pose for others onstage with you. Sometimes you may want to take the longest route possible around furniture and use the distance to enhance your points. Drop twentieth-century apology and (often false) humility in favor of regarding yourself as a work of art.

You cannot usually back up easily, because a long train, an awkward weapon, or some other impediment may be in your way. So, *move backward in curves;* think in terms of continuing your journey with figure-eights and figure S's, all of which are graceful alternatives. And avoid tripping over your own clothes.

*Match walk to speech.* Recognize a potential conflict between tempo and rhythm, and mesh them. Aim to complete a move on the last syllable, perhaps even the last consonant of your line. Deviations from this pattern should be deliberate.

Check the *relationship of the head to the body* periodically to make sure the head is floating high above the rest of the body. If this relationship is off, most other connections will be off, too.

Learn to do less and allow more, so that your movements are not labored but inevitable. When you are trying to relax one body part, it is very easy to tense up the parts adjacent to it. Check to make sure you *relax all adjacent parts.*

---

Repeat the process of the preceding exercise, this time drifting through space, weaving in and out of other actors' spaces until it is time to touch or connect with them. Let the key phrase motivate your own discovery of the attitudes that underlie the motion:

strong invasion (silently agree with your eyes which of you is the invader, then reverse)
rotation walk
two pulleys

**E X E R C I S E**

**Bodies in Motion**

gliding
display yourself
move backward
curves
match walk to speech
head/body relationship
relax all adjacent parts

In this exercise, you will be demonstrating one or more of the preceding suggestions by undertaking a brief scene from a classical play.

1. Work in pairs. Take any four lines of dialogue from a classical play.
2. First present the scene in as "inappropriate" or modern a way possible.
   Have fun with it.
3. Redo the scene in classical style.
4. Discuss how each scene looked and felt.
5. Ask the rest of the class for additional suggestions for mastering classical
   movement.

## VOCAL LIVES: CRISPNESS AND CURITY

Classical speech—sometimes called elevated, stage, aristocratic, heightened, midatlantic or transatlantic speech—is a universal, cultured sound
free of regional, ethnic, and faddish speech patterns. Mastering this style
of speech means dropping sloppy diction and speaking with great clarity
and dignity, so that you sound, without being affected, as if you could
comfortably wear a crown.

*Vowels.*  *Avoid flat vowels* (which Laurence Olivier called double vowels),
those conspicuously Western, nasal tones. The *a* is the most distracting,
with the word "flat" coming out "flaaaaat." As you make the vowel sound,
don't allow vocalized breath to come through the nose. The word "flat"
should sound the same when you say it while pinching the nostrils as when
you speak it ordinarily. Flat *a*'s tend to pop up in such words as "pan,"
"back," "rat," "hand," "can," "ant," "example," "sample," "damp," "tramp."
   Selectively sigh, or *aspirate,* on a vowel to achieve a lyrical or emotional
effect. Notice that if you really mean something from the heart, you tend
to elongate the vowel ("I *love* you," "I *mean* it," "I'm *serious*"), but it has
impact only if it contrasts with other vowels, ones that are not elongated.
As you elongate the word, you exhale very slightly. This is a subtle balance
between general breathiness and failing to use any expulsion of air to add
variety to your intonation. Find key words and images to color and inten-
sify with your breath; this vocal pattern, although widely used in life, is all
too often edited out of a performance.

*Honor each sound.* Tape yourself to identify where you tend to swallow or entirely omit sounds. Pay particular attention to the pronunciation of connective words: "tuh" for "to" (alone and in other words, such as "together" and "tonight"); "fer" for "for"; and "n" for "and." Do not compensate by punching up connectives, as in saying "ay" for "a" or "thee" for "the" ("the" is pronounced "thee" only when it precedes a word beginning with a vowel). Watch short verbs ("kin" for "can" and "git" for "get") and modifiers ("jist" for "just") as well. Although you should fully pronounce connective words, give them only a secondary, light stress.

Note substitutions, particularly *diphthong substitutions,* and watch for diphthongs that have become triphthongs. For example, in a number of regions, the word "now" is pronounced as though it had at least three vowels ("a-ah-oh"). The classic drill "How now brown cow" is meant to encourage the speaker to drop the jaw, which allows this sound to emerge in an easy, unextended fashion. Danger words: "now," "sound," "mouth," "vowel," "round," "town," "extend."

Try not to substitute "ah" for "aw," as in "normal," "horn," "all," "law," "chalk," "chock," "taught," "tot," "walk," "wot," "nought," "not." Look for this and other *vowel substitutions:* "ou" for "oo," as in "pore" instead of "poor," and also in the words "root," "roof," "route"; "i" for "e," as in "git" for "get" and these exchanges: "pin" for "pen," "min" for "men," "linth" for "length," "strinth" for "strength."

Let the *jaw relax* when you make sounds like "lot," "top," "taunt," "lawn," "father," "fop," "job."

Use the *liquid u* ("ew"), as in "duke," "tutor," "tuba," "tune," "tuna," "stupid," "Tuesday," "astute," "pulchritude."

For words with optional alternative pronunciations, choose the more *euphonic,* or the one that is more pleasing to the ear. One standard is pronouncing "either" as "eye-ther" rather than "ee-ther," which is almost universal in classical theatre. The former sound strikes most ears as more musical.

Avoid adding *unneeded vowels* in words like "mischievous," "athletic," "burglar," "business," "disastrous," "lovely," "ticklish," "bringing," "calm," and "wash."

---

Work with a partner, ideally someone you have already worked with on a scene assignment. Draw slips of paper with the following categories:

flat vowels
aspiration
honoring each sound
diphthong substitutions
vowel substitutions
relaxed jaw

**E X E R C I S E**

**Classical Vowels**

liquid *u*
euphonic choices
unneeded vowels

1. If you have a short (one-minute) scene excerpt featuring the sounds in question, use it. Otherwise, create one with about ten minutes' preparation time.
2. Present the scene in the least classical way possible, playing into the troublesome vowels fully.
3. Try to sound as phony and affected as you worry about sounding.
4. Find the golden mean, where you use the technique for both clarity and truth.

---

*Consonants.*    Clean and sharpen consonants. Think of a consonant as an extraordinarily swift conversational *weapon*, highly muscular, and, like a natural athlete, effortless in attack. Avoid hard, bludgeoning consonants that are like sledgehammers in favor of clean ones that are like *darts*. The most bludgeoned consonant is the overcolored *r*, which makes words like "word" and "letter" come across as excessive and harsh. Some people linger so long and heavily on a word like "rear" that it sounds almost as though it had three syllables ("er-ear-er"), and hearing a phrase like "deliveries in the rear, please" can make you feel caught in consonant pollution. Hard *r* words: "frame," "barn," "better," "better off," "better barn." A close second in pronunciation abuse is the hard *l*.

Spend time and attention on *terminal consonants*. Most of us do not speak the last consonant of a word. Classical characters use this final sound to twist or cap off their points.

Pronounce the *h* in words beginning with *wh*, for example, "where," "whine," "white," "which," "when," and "what." Pronounce "wh" as "hw."

Do not *swallow syllables;* that is, do not reduce two syllables to one in such words as "jewel," "gruel," "cruel," "duel."

Avoid the sound "chew" when connecting "can't you," "don't you," "did you," "what you," "might you," "remind you." End the first word with a tiny break before starting the second.

Give *multiple consonants* more weight to keep them from getting lost in a word like "would'st." The toughest include *dst, ths, sts, pts, fts, pths, lpd, lps, pnd, mpt,* and *cts,* in words like "swept," "slept," "leapt," "hold," "fold," "belt," "guilt," "helps," "whelp," "band," "hand," "last," "first," "soft," "lisp," "shirt," "eighths," "mists," "frost," "accepts," "lifts," "depths," "helped," "yelps," "opened," "tempt," "acts," "facts."

Do not drop *middle consonants* in words like "recognize," "realize," "definitely," "traveler," "vegetable," "accidentally," "naturally," "history," "memorable," "believe," "different," "family," "interesting," "several," "sentence," "dentist," "sentinel," "bitten," "little," "endless."

Do not substitute *voiced for unvoiced* consonants in words like "little," "better," "accept," "access," "dirty," "oaths." In particular, avoid inverting *d* and *t*.

Let the tip of the tongue, the lips, and the teeth do all the work in forming clean consonants. Do not *work the jaw* too much; this effort is useless and looks labored. Crisp speech is analogous to sharp mime work; do no more than is necessary, and work only what must be worked.

*Do not labor the upper mouth* to achieve crispness. Watch actors with superb diction. Notice that they move the top of the mouth very little. Practice looking in the mirror to identify just those organs involved in shaping the sound.

---

Follow the steps outlined in the previous exercise, drawing in these categories:

**E X E R C I S E**

**Classical Consonants**

    consonant as weapon
    terminal consonants
    "wh"
    swallowed syllables
    "chew"
    multiple consonants
    middle consonants
    voiced and unvoiced consonants
    overworked jaw
    labored upper mouth

---

*Sound.* Expand your vocal resonance by moving past the nasal resonators and head voice, which produce a thin, strident sound. Explore the full *range of resonating* space and surfaces available to you, not to cultivate a "pretty" sound, but to find a varied, textured one.

*Explore pitch,* from the top register to the bottom. Although you hardly wish to sound British, you can adopt the British practice of making full use of the highest and lowest notes of your register. Practice asking questions with a high inflection and dropping down the scale for definite responses. Do not edit your lower register in order to play youth or naïveté; instead, simply allow more ready access to your upper register.

Avoid sounding phony or British or even worse—*phony British*. Aspire to speech that is clear but in no way regional. Avoid dialects when you play rustic, eccentric characters. Find other ways to distinguish them from the aristocrats. It makes no sense for a Cockney character to appear out of nowhere in a show in which everyone else sounds American and which is set in Egypt anyway. Historical evidence indicates that the people of Shakespeare's time sounded more like Americans than twentieth-century British actors. Ponder the absurdity of taking dialects to its logical course, for example, doing *Romeo and Juliet* with heavy Italian inflection. (Well, isn't that how they talk in Verona?) To keep from sounding pseudo-British, avoid the following:

- pronouncing "been" as "bean"
- pronouncing "again" as "agayn"
- pulled in *-o* rounded at the end, as in "bow-uth" for "both"
- clipped *-ry* endings, as in "secretree" for "secretary"
- tapped *r* in the middle of words, as in "tellible" for "terrible"
- omitted *-r*'s at the end of words, as in "ratha" for "rather"
- broad *a,* as in "ahsk" for "ask"

Identify *regionalisms* in your own speech that may distract from an audience's sense of the universal. Seek critical listeners, ideally ones born outside your region. Create your own list of nonstandard pronunciations. Aim, not to change your speech completely, but to cleanse it.

Remember to include *nonverbal* vocalizations. Because great classical writing is so clean, you might not realize that the characters in the play grunt, groan, sigh, growl, hiss, moan, squeal, guffaw, and even belch. The writing is short on stage directions and embellishments; fill it out. Making nonverbal responses to the lines of others is common; a gasp of surprise, a slight intake of breath in delight, or a sputter of exasperation can add to the audience's understanding.

Experiment with *singing the lines* just a little more. Poetic verse is closer to music than modern conversational prose. It has a definite rhythm, and the words call for dips and glides.

Concentrate on rooting sound to attain *power without stridency*. When you need to let rip with anger or righteousness, don't let the sound go up in pitch and resonate in the mask; it will seem more shrewish or whiny than strong. Let the sound emanate from deep within the torso at such moments.

Be sure you are *consistent* in pronunciation, particularly of names or terms no longer in use and whose "correct" pronunciation is somewhat debatable. Remaining true to historical accuracy matters less than remaining true to the world you have created.

Compete with your partners to achieve the fullest, *richest sound and greatest variety.* This is a friendly match; appreciate others' tone, but be determined that no voice will be stronger and more versatile than your own.

---

**E X E R C I S E**

**Classical Sound**

Follow the same process as you did in the last two exercises, using these concepts:

range of resonance
pitch exploration

phoney British
regionalisms
nonverbal vocalizations
singing the lines
power without stridency
consistency
richest sound, greatest variety

---

*Phrasing.*　Classical playwrights tend to build points, using *lists of three,* sometimes more. In a line such as "I hate, loathe, and despise you," each verb is more powerful and deserves more punch than the one before it. Each list works up to the strongest item in it. Relish this progression.

Characters also often speak *emphatically,* making a point so strongly that they are clearly not open to negotiation. Practice delivering each line with finality, as if it were a curtain line. (There are many curtain lines in these scenes—each character *tries* to have the last word.)

Except for rapid-fire exchanges of one-liners (stichomythia,) speeches tend to be longer—much longer than most of us are used to. Single sentences of ten or eleven lines are not uncommon. However, avoid the temptation to chop up the thought in order to make it clearer. Your listener may well forget the subject of your sentence by the time you get to the verb! Work instead on developing enough control to *speak longer on a single breath* and to think faster, as the characters often do.

While all sounds should be sounded, all words do not have equal value. Once you recognize the requirements of diction, go back and orchestrate the line so that the connective words are weak and given much less emphasis. Pick out, as both speaker and listener, the *target words,* the zingers in each sentence that need greater stress, the ones that "get" your partner because they are so gorgeous, insulting, powerful, loving, or all of the above.

Most of us learned *punctuation* as a writing rather than a speaking tool. Now stop and consider how these familiar signs alter speech. In the long, convoluted sentences of classical drama, viewing punctuation as a traffic signal is vital for clarity. Tape yourself, and check that when each punctuation mark appears, you are finding a distinct way to let the listener sense the change.

---

Demonstrate the following, using the format of the past three exercises:

　lists of three
　emphasis
　speaking longer on a single breath

**E X E R C I S E**

**Classical Phrasing**

target words
punctuation

The audience is going to find some imagery obscure and difficult, but you can clarify it by using *onomatopoeia*. Much classical writing is poetic, full of metaphor, and begging to be spoken for sensual as well as intellectual meaning. Always have at least one rehearsal in which you make each evocative word sound like what it is. Many in the audience feel as removed from classical speech as you may from Latin or Japanese. Let the word transcend the language.

**E X E R C I S E**

**Onomatopoeia**

Imagine that the audience either does not speak English or may not know the meaning of the following words. Strive to speak each so that it will be comprehended. Experiment with deliberate technical choices to help make the words sound like their meanings. Try the words first by themselves and then in sentences so that they have a context.

| | | |
|---|---|---|
| abandon | dense | gorgeous |
| abnormal | dilate | grasp |
| abortive | dirty | great |
| absurdity | down | grind |
| acquiesce | dramatic | |
| affectation | drunk | hail |
| angularity | durable | halt |
| attractive | | hate |
| avenge | eat | heal |
| awe | ego | heroic |
| | elegant | hint |
| base | empty | hover |
| beginning | endless | howl |
| book | envy | hush |
| bosom | escape | hysterical |
| breeze | evil | |
| brittle | exaggerate | ice |
| buoyant | exude | illicit |
| burlesque | | immaculate |
| bury | fade | impotent |
| | fairy | inane |
| camouflage | familiar | incredible |
| candle | far | indifferent |
| caricature | fastidious | inhale |
| carve | fatal | insinuate |
| castrate | feasible | intangible |
| caustic | feast | |
| coarse | fire | jab |
| cold | freedom | jest |
| contempt | | jitters |
| cure | gallant | joy |
| | gaudy | jubilant |
| danger | giggle | juicy |
| dead | gloom | jump |
| delicious | glue | junk |

justice
juvenile

kaput
keen
kick
kidding
kill
kind
kinky
kiss
knickknack
knowledge

languid
lascivious
lavish
leap
loathsome
long
lost
lovely
lubricate

magnify
manipulate
marvelous
mean
meek
mellow
mist
mold
mope
multitude

naked
nauseous
nerd
nimble
nonchalant
nourish
nude
nuisance
numb
nymph

oblivion
obscene
obsessed
oily
old
opaque

opposition
orderly
ostentation
overwhelm

pagan
pain
pale
palpitate
paralysis
parched
pathetic
peck
pulverize
pungent

racy
radiant
ragged
reckless
recoil
relax
repugnant
revel
ripe
rotund

sad
saucy
scandal
scorn
secret
sensuous
serene
sharp
smooth
superb

talent
tarnish
tender
texture
tidy
toil
torrid
touch
truth
tub

ugly
ulcer
uncertain

undo
unique
untenable
uproar
used
useless
usurp

vacillate
vampire
vast
vehement
velvet
venomous
vigor
virgin
vision
voluptuous

wallow
wanton
wave
weak
weird
wheeze
wiggle
wind
wonder
worm

yawn
yeast
yell
yellow
yes
yesterday
yield
yoke
yonder
youth

zany
zealous
zenith
zero
zest
zigzag
zipper
zodiac
zoo
zwieback

This exercise really makes you think. There are many lines in classical theatre which audiences have heard before but which mean little to them beyond the familiar words. Your task is to place the line in its context with enough spirit and conviction to drive it home.

1. Working in groups of five, each team comes up with a list of ten commercial or political slogans, public service announcements, or any other lines that are heard frequently in broadcast.
2. A pair of actors from each team is handed another team's list. That list contains their lines.
3. The actors now perform a scene suggested by the audience, such as a pickup in a singles bar or a parent waiting up for a late son or daughter, clarifying the relationship, objectives, and action of the scene with the new dialogue.
4. The actors discuss what they had to do to make the scene work and how the line often had a life of its own.

## VERSE: LANGUAGE STRUCTURED AND HEIGHTENED

All the plays written up to the time of Shakespeare were in verse. Some continue to be, even in this century. Many classical repertory companies and training programs require verse speaking as part of the audition process for acceptance. Verse is higher, fuller, and more rhythmic than ordinary speech. But for the uninitiated, verse is shrouded in mystery and therefore intimidating.

So how is verse different? First, it looks different on the page. Whereas a line of prose goes all the way to the margin of the page, a line of verse continues for only a limited number of syllables and then stops. Whereas capital letters appear only at the start of prose sentences, they appear at the start of each new line of verse, whether that line begins a new sentence or not. Here is a verse speech:

> If music be the food of love, play on;
> Give me excess of it, that, surfeiting,
> The appetite may sicken, and so die.
> That strain again! It had a dying fall;
> O, it came o'er my ear like the sweet sound
> That breathes upon a bank of violets,
> Stealing and giving odor! Enough, no more!
> 'Tis not so sweet now as it was before.
> O spirit of love, how quick and fresh art thou,
> That, notwithstanding thy capacity
> Receiveth as the sea, naught enters there,
> Of what validity and pitch soe'er,
> But falls into abatement and low price
> Even in a minute! So full of shapes is fancy
> That it alone is high fantastical.

And here is the way it might look if it were prose:

If music be the food of love, play on; give me excess of it, that, surfeiting, the appetite may sicken, and so die. That strain again! It had a dying fall; o, it came o'er my ear like the sweet sound that breathes upon a bank of violets, stealing and giving odor! Enough, no more! 'Tis not so sweet now as it was before. O spirit of love, how quick and fresh art thou that, notwithstanding thy capacity receiveth as the sea, naught enters there, of what validity and pitch soe'er, but falls into abatement and low price even in a minute! So full of shapes is fancy that it alone is high fantastical.

There are many verse forms, but most dialogue in English verse drama is either blank (unrhymed) or rhymed iambic pentameter. The word *iambic* tells you that the basic unit, or foot, is an iamb—an unstressed syllable followed by a stressed. Thus, each foot has this rhythm: "da DUM." The word *pentameter* tells you that there are five iambs in one line. So, the beat of a line of iambic pentameter sounds like this: "da DUM da DUM da DUM da DUM da DUM."

The speech above (from *Twelfth Night*) is one of the most famous opening speeches in Shakespeare. Duke Orsino is trying to get rid of the curse of feeling in love. Love is making him miserable, and the woman he thinks he loves is not responding. In the opening line, he imagines he might be able to feed the love he feels with music, hoping it will be stuffed and satisfied and will fade away:

If music be the food of love, play on.

Showing unstressed and stressed syllables, the line might look like this:

if MUsic BE the FOOD of LOVE play ON.

This is a perfect iambic line (and most are imperfect), but the principles are simple. So what is all the fuss about? When I first heard a director use the term *verse,* I thought, "Who's she?" When I first heard the term *iambic pentameter,* I thought, "What a great stage name." An important early lesson in classical acting is not to be intimidated by the terms and to ask about anything you do not know. Most real artists will help you and respect you all the more for asking. Verse is frightening only because it is new. Don't assume that everyone else in the room knows all about it and that you are the only "verse virgin."

So why do authors bother to write in verse, which is obviously more difficult than prose? For some of the same reasons that songs are written to express what mere words cannot. Verse is somewhere *between* song and regular speech, not so musical or fanciful as the one, and not so ordinary as the other. For the actor, verse offers the chance to play with both subtlety and grandeur, often at the same time.

The extravagance of the imagery encourages you to do extravagant things, to be both big and honest. There is no definitive way to scan or speak a verse speech. Possible inflections and personal interpretations are many. Verse increases sensibility to words, rhythms, and meanings that come only from sound—unexplainable meanings, deeper than the conscious mind can fathom. Verse tends to stretch an actor toward greatness.

Since Shakespeare's generation invented the prose drama, which now virtually dominates theatre, his audiences may have found prose lines as strange as you may find verse on first contact. After two thousand years of nothing but verse, the first prose lines must have been startling, but they immediately became comfortably familiar, and so can verse for you.

*Scansion and Freedom.*    Here is the basic language of verse. You may have first encountered some of these terms in a literature course. Reconsider them now as tools to help you build your performance.

- *Blank verse:* Language formalized into unrhymed lines of equal (or nearly equal) length. The most common form is iambic pentameter (ten syllables, five feet, each foot consisting of an unstressed followed by a stressed syllable). Blank verse is middle-ground speech—more elevated than normal speech, but less so than some other verse forms. The rhythm in blank verse approximates the beating of the human heart.
- *Catalectic:* Line with some syllables deliberately dropped for emphasis or to indicate an entrance, an exit, or a reaction.
- *Compensation:* Repairing metrical omissions in a line of verse, usually by speaking a vowel that would normally remain silent. Most common types: *-ed* ending ("rememberED" for "remembered"), *-ier* ("solJEEer" for "soldier"), *-ion* ending ("indignaSHEEUN" for "indignation"). These vowels are pronounced to get the line to reach ten syllables.
- *Couplet:* Two rhymed lines of verse that become a single expressive unit. Shakespeare uses couplets sometimes to call attention to an important point within a speech, but more often to provide a striking ending to a speech or scene. Characters feel proud that they have conceived a couplet.
- *Distributed stress:* Effect produced when two consecutive syllables share the stress, instead of one being heavily accented while the other is barely touched. The emphasis is distributed equally between the two. Instead of "da DUM," you may have "Da Dum," with neither being hit too softly or too hard.
- *Elision:* Omitting a syllable to make a line conform to a metrical scheme. Examples: "o'er" for "over," "th'incestuous" for "the incestuous," "'gainst" for "against," "on't" for "on it," "heav'n" for "heaven," "dev'l" for "devil." Elision may or may not be transcribed by an editor. Again, the idea is to get the line to speak at ten (or at the most twelve) syllables.

*Endings:* The last syllable in a line of verse may be stressed (*strong*) or unstressed (*weak*). In blank verse, a weak ending usually consists of an added eleventh syllable. Shakespeare uses weak endings to jolt the listener slightly or to guide the listener quickly into the next line. Strong endings are more common. Many traditional texts refer to strong and weak endings as *masculine* and *feminine* endings, respectively.

*Foot:* The basic unit of measure in verse, two or three syllables in length, with various stresses. In a phrase describing verse, the first word will identify the type of foot, as in *iambic pentameter.* The four most common feet are the iamb (unstressed-stressed), trochee (stressed-unstressed), anapest (unstressed-unstressed-stressed), and dactyl (stressed-unstressed-unstressed). Adjectives are *iambic, trochaic, anapestic,* and *dactylic.*

*Meter:* The number of feet in a line of verse, the overall pattern by which a line is parceled into divisions of time. The second word in a phrase describing verse indicates meter: *monometer,* one; *dimeter,* two; *trimeter,* three; *tetrameter,* four; *pentameter,* five; *hexameter,* six; *septenarius,* seven.

*Metrical pause:* Tendency to stop at the end of a line of verse, even though there is no punctuation to indicate a pause. Also called *end stopping,* this understandable but irritating habit prevents building up ideas within a speech and interferes with the audience's capacity to hear a lengthy sentence as a single unit.

*Personification:* Common practice of giving human characteristics to objects, emotions, or abstractions so that they appear to have a life and a will of their own. Standard choices are Love, Fortune, Reason, Nature, and Time.

*Poetry:* Use of elements from both speech and song to express feeling, ideas, and imagination; language full of imaginative power, effectively condensing experience by capturing evocative phrases. *Poetry* is too often mistakenly used interchangeably with *verse:* poetry is an imaginative use of language, which may or may not be formalized, whereas the formalization, if it exists, is verse.

*Pronominal mode:* Use of "thee" or "you" to address another. "Thee" most often indicates familiarity (which may or may not be supportive, as in relationships between siblings), warmth, or closeness, whereas "you" is more likely to be used in situations involving anger, coldness, unfamiliarity, high regard, or simple formality. These are generalizations, not rules. The distinction is roughly like the French use of "tu" or "vous" in showing the degree of intimacy the speaker shares with the listener.

*Recessive accent:* Stress that falls on a syllable other than that which would normally be accented. The recessive accent was especially common in the Elizabethan period because the language itself was changing so rapidly; shifts in emphasis were only one small part of the vast sphere of word experimentation. One example is this line spoken by the Chorus in *Romeo and Juliet:* "Temp'ring extremities with EXtreme sweet." The recessive accent is potentially useful in drawing attention to key words by twisting them slightly.

*Rhyme:* Repetition of the same or similar sounds for emphasis. *Historical rhyme* refers to words that used to be pronounced the same but are no longer (for example, these lines spoken by Dumaine in *Love's Labor's Lost:* "Through the velvet leaves the wind, / All unseen can passage find.")

*Rhythm:* Recurrence of any beat, event, or sequence with enough regularity that the time intervals seem equal and the overall impression is one of balance. Rhythm causes the audience to maintain a sense of pulse and the actor to keep the play moving along in a livelier, less indulgent manner.

*Scansion:* Close analysis of the metrical pattern of lines of verse. An actor scans lines to figure out how they should be read aloud, which syllables are stressed and which unstressed, what elisions or compensations are necessary, and so on. A line reading is said not to scan if it fails to meet the metrical demands of the speech. The act of scanning provides multiple clues for interpretation and emphasis.

*Split line:* Several characters speak, but so briefly that a single line of verse is the result. Example:

1st Lord: Was't you, sirrah?
2nd Lord:            Not I.
3rd Lord:                  Nay, it was I.

By using a split line, the playwright indicates that no pause should occur at all, that the lines should come just as quickly as if all three had been spoken by one person. Notice that the "conversation" involving three people still consists of a total of ten syllables.

*Stress:* Intensity of emphasis placed on an individual syllable. In a perfect line of iambic pentameter, the second, fourth, sixth, eighth, and tenth syllables are stressed, while the odd-numbered syllables are unstressed. Also called *accent*.

*Tempo:* Speed of delivery. Although verse makes strong rhythmic requirements, actors are comparatively free to manipulate tempo. Varying the tempo can be a great help in keeping the rhythm from seeming predictable.

*Verse:* Arrangement of language into formalized structure, usually iambic pentameter. It is sometimes said that verse is the grammar of the speech, whereas poetry is its soul.

1. Sit in a circle with your classmates.
2. Go around the room reading aloud, in your best possible classical speech, each of the terms and definitions in this section.
3. Let each reader complete a term. Then tell that person both what seemed genuinely classical to you and what you lost in terms of vowels, consonants, sound, and phrasing.
4. Enter the reading, not with a fear of being "caught," but with the understanding that others will be giving you gifts that your own ear cannot pick up.
5. When everyone has read, try to summarize the major successes and difficulties of this particular group. Agree to listen closely for these last items so that you can all help each other.

**EXERCISE**

**Classical Speech**

With one class period to prepare, review these terms from the previous section, drawing slips of paper with your assigned term. Your job is to demonstrate that concept.

**EXERCISE**

**Versifying**

| | | |
|---|---|---|
| blank verse | foot | rhyme |
| catalectic | meter | rhythm |
| compensation | metrical pause | scansion |
| couplet | personification | split line |
| distributed stress | poetry | stress |
| elision | pronominal mode | tempo |
| endings | recessive accent | verse |

1. Sitting in a circle, demonstrate rather than explain each term. Any actor may be called on to make any term clear. You may arm yourself with the complete works of Shakespeare or any other source, but after no more than five minutes, you must be able to demonstrate the concept.
2. Discuss afterwards what became clear and how.

In some plays, verse and prose alternate. Shakespeare uses verse about 72 percent and prose 28 percent of the time. Hamlet himself speaks about 60 percent verse and 40 percent prose. Why would one switch? Verse is more likely to be spoken

- By a character of high rank
- To a parent, ruler, or stranger
- In public and on formal, ceremonial occasions
- When speaking of love, truth, honor, the meaning of life, or any of the higher subjects

Prose is more likely to be spoken

- By a rustic, comic, humble character
- By someone who feels momentarily rustic, comic, or humble

- In broader, earthier circumstances
- When dealing with more mundane or bawdy subjects

Notice that during intense moments of your own life you fall into rhythms not unlike verse: "If YOU don't CUT that OUT, I'll PUNCH you OUT," or "Get IN the HOUSE this MINute OR no SUPPER!" Try to recall recent circumstances where you were in emotional states and note the patterns you fell into.

Should you pound out the stressed syllables relentlessly? No; that would be stultifying. Verse is like a pulse of the human heart, just under the surface but always present. It is there all the time and can be brought forward as in moments like those above. In rehearsal, it is often useful to work in the extremes, sometimes beating out the rhythm too forcefully, other times ignoring it to go for meaning, almost forgetting that the speech is not prose. Gradually bring these widely divergent styles together so that the speech is both rhythmic and natural.

---

**E X E R C I S E**

**Beating the Drum**

1. Get together with a partner, and create some drums for each of you.
2. Choose a scene, and speak it in as laborious and throbbing a way as you can.
3. Redo the scene as though it were prose.
4. Discuss what you like from each approach and what might help.
5. Try to blend all that you have learned.

**E X E R C I S E**

**Class Rhythm**

1. Pick a common group activity, such as announcements, readings, discussions, warm-ups, or critique sessions. The activity should be comfortable and familiar.
2. Do the activity in the basic rhythm of each of the following: an evangelical service, a cheerleading rally, a marriage ceremony, a political rally, rap.
3. Find other dominant rhythms to try.
4. Discuss the effect of the new rhythm on the familiar activity. What did you learn about the old rhythm of the activity?

---

Here are some of the most beloved verse passages from Shakespeare to use in the exercises that follow.

As an unperfect actor on the stage,
Who with his fear is put beside his part,
Or some fierce thing replete with too much rage,
Whose strength's abundance weakens his own heart,
So I, for fear of trust, forget to say
The perfect ceremony of love's rite,

And in mine own love's strength seem to decay,
O'ercharged with burden of mine own love's might.
O let my books be then the eloquence
And dumb presagers of my speaking breast,
Who plead for love, and look for recompense
More than that tongue that more hath more expressed.
O learn to read what silent love hath writ;
To hear with eyes belongs to love's fine wit.

(Sonnet 23)

       For within the hollow crown
That rounds the mortal temples of a king
Keeps death his court, and there the antic sits,
Scoffing his state and grinning at his pomp,
Allowing him a breath, a little scene,
To monarchize, be feared, and kill with looks,
Infusing him with self and vain conceit,
As if this flesh which walls about our life
Were brass impregnable; and humored thus,
Comes at the last, and with a little pin
Bores through his castle wall, and farewell king!

(*Richard II*, III, ii)

Romeo: If I profane with my unworthiest hand
      This holy shrine, the gentle fine is this:
      My lips, two blushing pilgrims, ready stand
      To smooth that rough touch with a tender kiss.
  Juliet: Good pilgrim, you do wrong your hand too much,
      Which mannerly devotion shows in this:
      For saints have hands that pilgrims' hands do touch,
      And palm to palm is holy palmer's kiss.
Romeo: Have not saints lips, and holy palmers too?
  Juliet: Aye, pilgrim, lips that they must use in prayer.
Romeo: O, then, dear saint, let lips do what hands do;
      They pray, grant thou, let faith turn to despair.
  Juliet: Saints do not move, though grant for prayer's sake.
Romeo: Then move not, while my prayer's effect I take.

(*Romeo and Juliet*, I, v)

---

1. Sit again in a circle, and let each actor take two lines of verse.
2. First, scan each line heavily. Assume that it is a perfect set of iambs.
3. Go back and identify where adjustments (elision, compensation, trochees, and so on) may be made so that the line flows more naturally and fits the meter.
4. Reread the completed line.
5. Help any actor who is having difficulty, but let him or her try the lines alone first.

6. Discuss those instances in which there appear to be more than one way to scan the line effectively.

1. Ten actors go to the front of the class. Two others wait in the wings stage left.
2. Observers suggest very famous lines from Shakespeare.
3. The group tries to physicalize the line, with each person becoming a stressed or unstressed syllable by standing or kneeling. For the line "If music be the food of love play on," for example, the odd-numbered actors kneel, and the even-numbered stand; there's no need for the backup team, because there are only ten syllables, not eleven or twelve. The actors then go back over the line and discuss how the stresses might vary. A syllable with very low stress might crawl into a fetal position, and strong stress might jump in the air. A strong stress with an exclamation point might leap in the air, thrusting the arms high above. If elision is needed, the actor might double over as if he or she had been hit in the stomach.
4. Each person speaks and physicalizes his or her syllable, first in a straight scanning for stressed and unstressed syllables. Then, the group does a more refined line reading, acknowledging other factors discussed in the previous section and accepting suggestions from the audience.
5. The actors let the meter guide them but also allow creativity full range in determining how to portray each syllable.

The ironic element of learning to speak verse is that at first it seems so overwhelming, but one day you suddenly get it, and then it seems so easy. Think of verse as a vehicle for *you* to drive to help you reach your destination. Verse is so packed with information, so powerful and so potent, that once you trust it, it demands less effort from you than does prose. Verse gives you a guide for phrasing, frequently telling you how to pronounce names, which word or syllable to point up, and where the emphasis needs to be. It shows you where shifts in relationships have taken place and offers both interpretive hints and stage directions. It is easier to memorize, because the rhythm helps you. It is also easier to retain, even after not working on it for a while. It gives you natural places to breathe. Well-spoken verse is highly pleasing to listen to and helps you keep the audience's attention. It is concise and exact in its shape and ultimately it helps you think faster. As you get caught up in its buildups and let it carry you, you feel greatly empowered.

Some of the most creative dance floor moves were seen during the disco craze of the 1970s. While largely forgettable in other ways, this period produced a certain artistic audacity, chiefly because the beat was so insistent that no one could possibly lose it. No matter how experimental or inspired or caught up in the moment the dancers became, they could al-

*Dance is a measured pace as a verse is a measured speech.*

—FRANCIS BACON

ways find the rhythm and return to it safely. Verse functions the same way. It throbs there, full of information, but encouraging you to swoop and leap and dazzle.

## SPIRITUAL LIVES: HEROIC DIMENSION

Theatre history is full of actors who were not blessed with impressive stature or resonant pipes but who rose to greatness because they possessed an extraordinary and hypnotic *internal* flame. Most classical characters think of themselves (therefore we think of them that way, too) as bigger, brighter, bolder, and more beautiful than mere mortals. They function in a larger emotional space, where laughter can be raucous and crazed, and where howling at the moon can be the only answer to the cruelty of the fates. The key to classical acting is acceptance of this mind-set. Accept that you have potential for greatness and grandeur. Accept that you deserve nothing less. Some specific guidelines follow.

*Variety of attack* gives you freedom. To reach the infinite variety within the characters, you must repeatedly explore more highs and lows, loudness and softness, beauty and harshness, danger and gentleness. Allow more *mercurial swings in strategy,* maneuver, and attitude. Fill the creative space.

An *unpredictable tempo* counterbalances the potential sameness in verse and archness in language. Although stresses in verse dictate rhythmic patterns, they do not limit tempo. Let passion guide you through time and timing.

*Sudden reversals* are common. Characters tend to follow a line of thought or an objective and then suddenly drop it and move in another direction. They tend to go deeply into an emotion, wring it quickly dry, drop it, and move to another. Accept this as part of the nature of *heroic perspective*.

Do not play the ending. Romeo and Juliet expect to win, to find a way out, to succeed every time they plunge down one more corridor of hell. Watching their hopes crushed is profoundly moving. For the actor, this means no whining and no generalized playing of mood. It means more *positive expectation,* more moment-to-moment playing.

Accept *archetypal reality* without judgment. You frequently represent Young Love, Insane Jealousy, Omnipotent Grandeur, Silly Servant, or any number of other types. By all means work out detail, but don't fight symbolic function. It is thrilling to play a character who represents broad spectrums of humanity.

*Do not judge* characters from a modern perspective and impose a reality that is not theirs. Ophelia (in *Hamlet*) is a weak and emotionally battered woman; to seek a modern strength in her is to judge her. Helena (in *All's Well That Ends Well*) falls in love with an arrogant, immature jerk. She is a bright and savvy woman. How can this be? Because he is the boy next door and a prince above her rank. This, in a fairy-tale reality, is reason enough. She is not lessened by her choices *inside* her particular world.

The *friendly competitions* in body and voice (noted earlier) are also present psychologically. Characters try to be wittier, sharper, more vibrant, more pained, or more pungent. They also acknowledge a point well made. They relish this competition. Winning is never more important than living fully and savoring the event. They always appreciate the qualities of others while attempting to top them.

It is too easy to forget the *basic principles of truth, focus, action, and objective* you learned back in your introductory acting classes. Far too many classical performances lack the basics, taking place in spaces that are neither hot nor cold, light nor dark, safe nor dangerous, public nor private. The characters are neither running late nor do they have all the time in the world. They are dying or in perfect health but nowhere in between. Make sure you deal with each question of relationship, objectives, and influences so that you establish a reality on which you can build the grand elements.

You often get *to be evil, lurid, violent,* and even utterly paranoid in classical theatre. *Embrace the opportunity.* Go for it. Let go of any ounce of embarrassment or temptation to soften. This is a great place to get these feelings out of your system. Here is where you can *be* what you only dream about in real life.

Learn to speak faster and more clearly by learning to *think faster.* These characters are quicker than many of us; their responses can often be like lightning bolts. By actually thinking more quickly, the words roll out with less effort.

Use the *blue flame* of anger at least as often as the red one. When a fire is blazing, it is vivid and bright but lacks the steady power of a pilot light or other focused fire. The most frightening anger can be that which is subtly directed, because instead of seeming to be out of control, the character seems to be in deadly earnest and unflinching.

Transform yourself into a *better you.* You are limited only by your willingness. If you believe it, the audience will. In your imagination, make adjustments that you could achieve if only you had enough time, dedication, surgery, therapy, or prayer. These roles allow full realization of your potential.

*Treat accidents as gifts.* If someone drops something or a feather falls off a hat, don't ignore it; react as your character would. The fates are giving you the chance to respond fully beyond the confines of the script. They are allowing you to explore heroically.

---

**E X E R C I S E**

**Catching the Spirit**

Write out the terms below on a card or in your journal. Keep the list where you can quickly look it over in rehearsal. Meditate regularly on how you are doing and promise yourself to acknowledge each one.

| | |
|---|---|
| variety of attack | basic principles |
| mercurial swings in | (truth, focus, ac- |
| strategy | tion, objective) |
| unpredictable tempo | embracing evil |
| sudden reversals | thinking faster |
| positive expectation | blue flame |
| archetypal reality | a better you |
| friendly competitions | accidents as gifts |

If time allows, draw cards with the above phrases, and demonstrate the concept before the class, using whatever scene or monologue you are currently rehearsing.

E X E R C I S E

**Shifting into Higher Gear**

1. Walk onstage as if you have just come out of a public building to return to your vehicle and find that
   (*a*) your three-speed has fallen over and landed in a puddle; (*b*) your battered VW bug has gotten another scratch in the side; (*c*) your Volvo has a dent on the front bumper; (*d*) your BMW has been totaled.
2. Let the class suggest two other series of disasters with a theme to connect them.
3. As a class, discuss the differences in behavior. The object is not to play as if you have a muddy three-speed when you have a totaled BMW. The situations in the classics, particularly tragedy, are often earth-shattering and monumental, requiring a reaction plane that most of us (we hope) stay out of most of the time.
4. Go through the process again, this time with four positive discoveries.
5. Continue to observe yourself in small disappointments or pleasures and ask how the event might have been intensified if the stakes were higher and you were living life in a higher gear.

E X E R C I S E

**Commanding**

*When you play a king, the first important thing to remember is that when you walk into a room, everything around you, you own.*

—KEITH MICHELL

Assume that you control your immediate universe. Enter and pass judgment on the mere mortals who surround you. Communicate your power and mood in a single sentence. Some possible lines:

"You have leave."
"Let the games begin."
"We are not amused."
"All rise."
"Off with his head."
"Cease and desist."
"Which of you has done this?"
"You may approach."

## SPECIAL SKILLS

Although each genre has its peculiarities (which will be addressed in sub-sequent chapters), there are some skills that all genres demand of the actor.

*Asides* are common. Right in the middle of a scene, one character may turn to the audience to confide in them, ask a question, give a knowing look, or in some other way quickly connect with them before returning to the scene. These are most effective if you treat them as sharp clicks. Keep your body facing the direction it was going, and simply snap your head out to face the audience—especially if the aside is very brief. If it is longer or more pronounced, try leaning sharply toward the audience. To punch it up one step more, dash quickly downstage to confide in the audience, then dash back to where you were and continue as if nothing has happened. If you are the partner of an actor doing an aside, look away at the moment of the aside to promote the illusion. Find something to occupy yourself, and go into slow motion or freeze. Never watch the actor do the aside. Help create the impression that, from your perspective, it never happened.

*Audience address* is far more common in general. Often only one character is onstage speaking. When you are in this situation, it is generally better to address the audience directly than to talk out loud to yourself introspectively. Because the action moves back and forth between overtly acknowledging and ignoring the audience, think of the audience as your collective best friend and confidant. You have the most open, sharing, and honest relationship possible. No one ever lies in a soliloquy; when you are alone with the audience, you speak the absolute truth (as you see it), and you speak it without embarrassment. The audience is Hobbes to your Calvin.

*Rehearsal garments* are fundamental to helping you get the feel of costumes to come. If they are not available, create them. Most characters handle a lot more cloth than we do. Capes, coats, trains, long and flowing sleeves, trailing ribbons, lace, petticoats—each age is different, but the garment is always challenging. The most important point is to wear the garment and not let it wear you. Flip it out of the way. Command it. You have a lot of fabric because you deserve it; you carry our own setting with you. When you lift the hem of a floor-length gown or robe, expend as little effort as possible. When you climb a staircase, use just one hand, and lift the hem only a few inches from the ground. You don't need to lift the hem at all when you descend a staircase. Recognize in each instance the least amount of effort needed to command the clothes.

*Bows, curtsies, and kneels* from some of the later periods can be learned. But for earlier periods for which we have no pertinent historical records, we often need to invent and ritualize such contacts as forming a marriage bond or contractual agreement, showing signs of respect, exorcising demons, calling on the gods, pleading for help, handing someone the message from an oracle—any maneuvers for which we have no evidence that shows how they were done back then. Answers emerge in improvisation and trial and error. Let the characters show you how they want these rituals performed.

*Cleaving* is common in all of the genres. Someone (usually male in these plays) grabs someone else (usually female), pulling her in for an embrace and possibly a kiss. This move is bold—when you cleave, you completely envelop your partner. A silly reminder of appropriate body positions is to go for "pee pee" kisses (crotch to crotch) not "teepee kisses" (in which only your lips connect, so that the two of you look like a tent on a reservation— in fact you look as though you have serious reservations about the whole thing). At the point in the play where this occurs, nothing short of the audacious will work. Leave your modesty at home.

Characters are always pretending to be someone else, and the actual disguise is so flimsy that you wonder why other characters wouldn't recognize them. This is a convention stemming from eras that had no films, photos, or close-ups that indelibly locked a person's image in the audience's mind. Promote the convention by seeing the character anew, investing the cape, hood, hat, or other minor disguise with power.

The capacity to handle weapons believably and to fight well is important to the classical actor. It is important to start early and work actively outside rehearsal to improve *combat* skills. Just achieving enough finesse to make sure the sword at your side does not stick into you or someone else requires time. Combat scenes are rehearsed twenty times as much as any stretch of dialogue. Here are some basic principles:

- Often, a fight is a scene about two people trying to kill each other. Remember, at heart it is a scene, with objectives and evaluations.

- Pauses in the action not only give you a break but also are often the most interesting.

- In most sword fights, there are only five basic cuts (attack moves) and parries (defense moves) which are then repeated in limitless combinations. These moves are not difficult to learn, and fights are then less complex than they seem at first glance.

- Even the blows themselves break down into three distinct parts: the windup (whose size and speed show the audience how strong the blow is), the hit (followed by a split-second pause), and the reaction, or follow-through (which shows how hard the blow struck).

- Each stage is helped by nonverbal orchestration (grunts, howls, clashing, blades, gasps, observer reactions, and so on), and the blow is the least important part. The windup and reaction send the clearest signals. Do not let feelings of intimidation prevent you from experiencing the great fun of getting to die and kill without consequences. This skill is highly learnable.

## SHARPENING CLASSICAL AWARENESS

Most actors who do the classics well also have a strong sense of mimicry, know how to do types, can speak dialects, and have some experience or aptitude in musical theatre. Why? Because these are all skills that demand a clean, direct, and powerful attack. Each is a possible path to enhancing your availability to the classics.

You can learn style through studying archetypes or cultural clichés. Some people are so tied to a culture that they are what one student once called "culturally bound and gagged." All stereotypes are unfair, and many are inaccurate, but actors need to understand types. The cultural cliché stems from true human behavior. Because of potentially obscure language, you need to sharpen your ability to make clear when you walk onstage who you are and what you feel.

Many actors cast as such extremes as prostitutes or nuns, are so anxious to avoid stereotypes that the resulting performance is unclear. It looks like the actor is busy *avoiding*. Instead, try to *master* the cliché first, getting every detail down pat, and then modify and refine the character step by step. You can't conquer a cliché by ignoring it. You have to *know* it first.

---

**E X E R C I S E**

**Mastering Types**

1. Draw slips of paper from one or both columns below, and combine them into this simple scenario:
   a. Enter a crowded room, and respond to the people around you.
   b. Sit down, and interact with at least one other imaginary person.
   c. Rise and leave.
2. Let class members guess out loud the age, emotion, and type of character. Discuss choices that met or violated their expectations.

| *Emotions* | *Types* |
| --- | --- |
| amused | nun/priest |
| angry | king/queen |
| shy | tycoon |
| euphoric | playboy/playgirl |
| sad | prostitute/hustler |
| bored | cowboy/cowgirl |
| disgusted | jock |
| frightened | punk |
| hopeful | hippie |
| disdainful | police |
| in love | politician |
| in lust | rock star |
| nervous | movie star |
| despondent | librarian |
| transcendent | reporter |
| hateful | comedian |
| cocky | gangster |
| indifferent | centerfold |
| grateful | hermit |
| cheerful | professor |

Now try adding dialogue to the scenario from the previous exercise. Go back and speak whatever you feel the character would in the given situation. Each actor is almost certain to utter lines typical of the character. For example, what style is represented by these lines?

"As long as you're living under my roof. . . ."

"Money doesn't grow on trees, you know."

"You're old enough to know better."

"*I'll* give you something to. . . ."

"Who was that on the phone?"

"What did you learn today?"

"Because I'm the___, that's why."

"Who's going to be at this party?"

This is known as the parent style. Can you take your type and find five lines that are so style bound they are impossible to avoid?

---

There can be no doubt that our most popular stylized entertainment is the musical. Our country has given the world one of the strangest forms of theatre. But it is strange only if you stop to pick apart its conventions and compare them to normal human behavior. Since most of us grew up on the musical, it seems the most natural thing in the world.

There are important connections between musical theatre and highbrow classical drama. Both types of plays often

- Combine the intimate and the spectacular.
- Blend the oratorical and the naturalistic.
- Move back and forth between representation and presentation.
- Feature characters alone onstage pouring their hearts out in soliloquy or song.
- Have large casts representing entire cultures.
- Involve public scenes full of ritual and ceremony.
- Embrace the shared mythology of the audience.
- Feature archetypal and often heroic characters.
- Are set in an exotic locale and/or a remote time period.
- Catch characters at their brightest and most intense with minimum vacillation, indecision, or exposition.
- Have a finale full of pomp and spectacle.
- Serve as a vehicle for pouring out intense, heartfelt emotion without embarrassment or hesitation, allowing the actor to play both *big* and *honest*.

E X E R C I S E

**Make It into a Musical**

1. Agree on one of the following events: (*a*) the Family Lies scenario (see Chapter 2); (*b*) a current news story; (*c*) the plot of a popular film; (*d*) a great historical event; (*e*) a classical myth or legend.
2. Working in threes, convert the event into a musical of no more than ten minutes' length. Use known popular songs at appropriate points. Change the lyrics slightly if necessary.
3. Consider the full range of musical conventions and styles. If enough people are involved, have one group do it as a Gilbert and Sullivan operetta, another as a 1920s Busby Berkely tap show, and others as a Rodgers and Hammerstein, Stephen Sondheim, and/or British "high concept" musical.
4. You may wish simply to describe some of the events instead of acting them all out, the way composers might pitch a show to potential backers. Narrate some passages and show others.

Why spend time on an art form so different, for example, from Greek tragedy? Because it is similar at the core. Once you learn to accept the reality of jumping up and breaking into song as a "normal" part of life, you have no trouble with the strangest conventions in the classics. If you can imagine a world where everyone in the laundromat breaks into synchronized song and dances atop the washers and driers, you can probably imagine anything else. If styles you encounter in subsequent chapters seem weird, remember that to the uninitiated, *nothing* would seem weirder than the American musical.

## MOVING INTO SCRIPTS

Now that you have played with familiar styles and recognized that you know more about the subject than you thought, it's time to take this confidence into acting in the classics.

E X E R C I S E

**Style Scenes: First Encounter**

1. Start working on your assigned scenes by assessing everything you *do* know already. Study the script and put together a basic character analysis based on evidence you find there. Go back and do everything you did the first time you seriously worked on *any* scene. What you know will surprise you, and you will be more sure of what you do not know.
2. Don't worry for the moment about the customs of that society or the staging conventions of that period. These are all worth researching, but resist the temptation to jump too quickly to the unfamiliar.

3. Get all the evidence you can from the script, and start committing the script to memory.

4. Approach the character as human to human, then move on to refining your sense of period and genre. Think of the character as someone you want for a friend, ideally a friend for life.

5. Are there other nonspeaking or barely speaking characters—guards, attendants, messengers—in the scene? How do you get the number down to two or three actors? If these imaginary others must be addressed, consider placing them in the audience. This convention works fairly well and certainly beats talking to empty spaces onstage.

6. Cut scenes down to no more than ten minutes, just enough to give you a good workout. Consider bleeding longer speeches, but also think about beginning the scene at a moment of high tension or simply working up to a suspenseful moment and then freezing. You do not need to do an epic to learn to act with epic scope. Keep the scene manageable.

7. The very first time you present the scene, try to take a curtain call in the appropriate style of the scene itself. Invent a bow if you do not have information on the proper way to take a bow. Let the class respond to the *feel* of what you do rather than its accuracy. This will give you an important opportunity to practice bows and a tantalizing preview of what it might actually be like to do this role in full performance. If possible, present scenes at least twice, the second as a showcase in which other classmates and guests try to interact with you. Because so many of these plays are presentational, explore a direct actor-to-audience relationship.

8. Surround yourself with images and other sensory stimuli as you rehearse. Find paintings, sculptures, music, scents, foods—as many ways of stimulating your own senses as you possibly can. Because these are so powerful, they can serve as keys into a style. Seek out and record a piece of music that could introduce your scene and in some cases underscore it.

9. Remember that these plays are great because they are not easy. They provide a tremendous mountain for you to climb and an amazing view once you get there. But be kind to yourself; realize that this is big-league material and that mastering it will take time. Shoot for perfection, but settle for excellence, and give yourself credit.

10. Use critiques to encourage each member to trust his or her intuition. It is perfectly acceptable to say that an actor's choice strikes you as too modern but that you are not sure why. Maybe others can help you name the problem. Divide the critique session into two distinct parts. First, identify what is working so that you give the actors a sense of what they can build on. Second, discuss what is not working, but state these problems in terms of highly possible accomplishments. When critiquing a Greek scene, you might call the two parts "Laurels" and "Javelins"; an Elizabethan scene, "Roses" and "Thorns"; Restoration and Molière scenes, "Kisses" and "Hisses"; a Georgian scene, "Cheers" and "Jeers." (The reasons why will soon become obvious.)

## PERIOD PERSONALITIES

The next four chapters take the issues of time, space, place, values, structure, beauty, sex, recreation, sight, and sound into the periods in history whose plays are most produced today—the eras you are likely to enter if you become a classical actor. In each chapter, an imaginary person from that time is interviewed on these topics. The following conventions shape the interviews. The subject

- Knows all about our era as well as his own.
- Cannot tell us anything not available to us in our own library or through research (that is, he cannot reveal secrets hidden in history).
- Chooses not to reveal any personal details.
- Has not informed his peers that he has elected to do this interview, so he is participating on the sly.
- Is a citizen of the world created by most of the *writers* of the era, not necessarily a citizen of the *real* world of the era.
- Has indicated that he may be called back at any time and may need to terminate the interview quite suddenly.

# 4

# GREEK PERIOD STYLE
## Three Generations of Tragic Vision

## THE WORLD ENTERED

Powerful differences exist between the civilized world of the plays' first audiences and the primitive world of the plays themselves. The scripts were written in the Classical period but are set in the Bronze Age, seven or more centuries earlier. The original audience is a patriarchal Athenian democracy. The plays dip into history and myth, sometimes back to a matriarchal Myccnacan monarchy. Almost all surviving production evidence is from the Hellenistic age, a century or more *after* the plays were written.

Are you confused? When you read about and study ancient Greece, always stop and ask *which* ancient Greece is being discussed. Let's present these problems in a more familiar context. Imagine that centuries from now, scripts from the 1940s and 1950s are discovered and considered great. Imagine that these plays are set, not in their own era, but in one much earlier, say the time of Robin Hood, and that they are about Robin, Richard the Lionhearted, Prince John, and the Crusades. Adding to the confusion is the fact that the only surviving production information is from the years 2040 to 2060, when solar power and laser lighting are standard staging devices.

You could get depressed about how little we know of ancient Greeks in performance, or you could revel in the fact that because we know so little, we have the freedom to create. Why not choose the latter?

Between the first major drama festival in 534 B.C. and the defeat of Athens in 404 B.C., the theatre virtually soars to greatness, along with every other form of artistic expression and investigation. Only 3 percent of

James Edmundson (Creon), Ted D'Arms (Oedipus), Nicole Adstrom (Antigone) and Mary Graham (Ismene) in *Oedipus the King*, Oregon Shakespeare Festival

all drama written in that century is left: thirty-three tragedies, eleven comedies, and one satyr play. Three playwrights stand as the first giants of drama. Each presents the actor with a distinct set of exciting challenges.

|  | *Aeschylus* | *Sophocles* | *Euripides* |
|---|---|---|---|
| *Dates* | 525–456 B.C. | 496–406 B.C. | 484–406 B.C. |
| *Plays* | 90 | 123 | 92 |
| *Extant* | 7 | 7 | 18 |
| *Drama Festival Victories* | 13 | 24 | 4 |

Aeschylus, who lived long enough to remember tyranny but died in a democracy, is particularly remembered for introducing the second actor, reducing the chorus from fifty to twelve members, inventing the trilogy, making the dramatic part of the performance as important as the choral, writing the most magnificent choral odes, and developing wildly effective satyr plays.

Sophocles is known for introducing the third actor and later the fourth (in *Oedipus at Colonus*), increasing and standardizing the chorus at fifteen members, discovering serenity in tragic vision, adding subtlety and suppleness to drama, discovering the power possible in quiet moments and internal conflict, achieving the most poignant and moving of climaxes, developing the arts of plot and characterization, developing scenes into full acts with choral divisions, and providing the model for Aristotle's definitions of classic drama.

Euripides, the youngest, is known for increasing the number of characters and roles (but not actors), showing that drama can focus on the individual and on specific social questions, developing interest in abnormal psychology and its origins, disconnecting the chorus from the main action, combining realism and pathos in one event, breaking traditions, and embracing controversy, innovation, courage, and independence.

Imagine being the first to accomplish any of their feats. Most of us would be thrilled to be remembered for any one of them. Together, Aeschylus, Sophocles, and Euripides give us visions of grandeur, serenity, and honesty, respectively. Half of their surviving scripts are about one family: the House of Atreus. As you read the plays, remember that Clytemnestra and Helen of Troy are sisters-in-law. No dynastic soap opera ever produced a family so fascinating or two women more capable of unsettling their world and changing the course of humanity.

How would a poet and seer of the time respond to our basic questions? The subject of our interview knows sympathetic magic, drama festivals, and how to summon an oracle. The subject also claims to be related to a god and to have survived a visit to the underworld.

Time: Pre-Homeric Mythology to the Fifth Century B.C. [Mycenaean period 1700–1100 B.C.; Archaic period 800–480 B.C.; Hellenic/Classical period 480–323 B.C.; Hellenistic period 323–146 B.C.]

**We live in the wide shadow of our past.**

*At what point in history are the plays set, written, and performed? How do these factors interact?*

We act our own history, known and imagined. When you act the stories of your George Washingtons and Christopher Columbuses, and then go farther back for your Christs, and further still for your Adams and Eves, you come close to what we feel.

*How far does the audience or play move out of its own time?*

A strong production is freed of time. Some in your century use what you call formal wear and even space suits. Both, for you, give a clean, universal feeling, so I do not object. Look less to your archaeologists and more to the plays themselves for help. Answers lie in the poet's words.

*How rapidly does time move for most people? How conscious are they of its passing?*

We have time for a good, thoughtful argument—always. We are deliberate and careful. We are less conscious than you of minutes, hours, and days, more so of harvests passed, festivals held, or famines survived.

*How do you record time? How long does the action last?*

Time is periods of war and peace, tempo stately, rhythm steady. The place of the sun, movement of stars, size of moon, and length of shadow are guides. Our plays are short by your terms, running perhaps an hour and a half (we present four or five in one day). Most honor the unities (time, place, and action) with one location and cycle of the sun.

*Do people focus on the moment or the lifetime? On the future or the past?*

Resolving the past is our task. Our plays begin near the end. The event—prophecy, curse, war, or betrayal—has occurred. Now it is revealed and understood. The future at the end of our tragedies is uncertain, bleak, close to unbearable.

*The life so short, the craft so long to learn.*

—HIPPOCRATES

*What is your attention span?*

We can listen long with care. Rhetoric is our invention. Many are illiterate, so hear all and remember. When we deliver a message, we commit the words to memory and repeat it to the recipient without change.

*Is age revered or feared?*

If lived honorably, life is rich in old age, with winter years full of respect and reward. Sophocles, our most honored poet, created his masterpiece at age ninety, Demosthenes, the great speaker, moved in his life through three names. In his youth, the people called him Batalus (effete flute player), then Argas (snake, or one vicious with words), but finally The Orator (wise speaker) when all finally learned to listen. Thespis was called Dangerous One when he created this creature called actor. At the end of his life, he was honored as City Dionysia Victor, a poet's highest achievement. Honor comes when you are ready.

## Space

*I am the universe, and my sphere is cosmic.*

*How is space defined and viewed? Is space literal or abstract?*

Space is soul, mind, body, and senses. Gods rule the sky and underworld. Man can be transported and transformed.

We see all twice. We see stars, but also a bear, lion, swan, giant, or bull *in* the stars. We see a sunset, but also a chariot driven across the sky. We see rising waves *and* dancing sea nymphs, rustling trees *and* dryads dancing in them, bubbling brooks *and* naiads leaping across them. We see life through the god. When thunder explodes, Zeus is angry, a volcano erupts as smoke arising from the smithy of Hephaistos, a tree or flower grows, to honor the god who seeded it.

*How large is one's personal bubble? What is privacy?*

We carry a large circle. We honor circles of others. We are not cold, but prize power and majesty. We are not small or uncertain. Within the home is strong privacy of quarters. We do not knock upon a chamber door—we scratch. All brutal acts occur offstage.

Yet, our plays are in public places with the chorus, ever visible and acts accountable. A life must bear scrutiny.

*What are attitudes toward invasion and force?*

War hovers always. Justice deals with violation within city walls, but not at its gates. A man prepares himself to be a powerful soldier, but speaker too. Words try mightily to prevent blows.

*When you produce the greatest effect upon the audience ... are you in your right mind? Are you not carried out of yourself?* —SOCRATES

*Be what you would seem.* —PLATO

## Place

*The jury is always present.*

*Is the setting rural, urban, or remote? Coastal or inland? Protected or exposed? Confined or open?*

All, except confined. We are just outside the palace, shrine, city gates, temple, or sacred place in Greece, Asia Minor, Crete, Cyprus, Phoenicia, or Egypt, or on another island. Someone arrives here always from a great journey.

We live outside. Our buildings are part of the surroundings, with columns beckoning the eye beyond. Your modern churches enclose the faithful to create sanctuary. Our altars are in the open air.

*What is the influence of geography and the relationship to nature?*

Seas surround hills, hot and dry with abundant fig and olive trees. Thyme and sage scent the hillsides. The sound of cicadas fills a night more clear and cloudless than yours. We worship Nature. We try to persuade her by offerings, by supplication, by a libation of wine, honey, or oil. We then accept the course she takes.

*Are you aware of other places? Are you citizens of the world?*

You use "idiot" to mean low in intelligence. For us, "idiot" means leading only a private life, with no service to the community. We are tied to our city-state, but we are members of the family of man. We also have slaves.

*Man is but a shadow of a dream. Yet if the gods bestow upon him but a gleam of their own radiance, bright flame surrounds him and his life is sweet.*     —PINDAR

## Values

*Life of balance, death with honor.*

*What are the beliefs most widely shared?*

Self-knowledge, harmony, and wisdom. Nothing in excess, until the time demands it. Then only unbridled fire will serve! Justice. Death before dishonor.

We must reach high, yet fear *hubris* (excessive pride and ambition, as of a man who would take for himself that which is of the gods), which leads to downfall. Truth is not to be hidden—no matter how painful. We come to the theatre to face our worst fear. The play begins with something very wrong, not yet understood. The veil of appearance is then lifted. Truth in full agony and beauty is revealed. Truth is sought like joy. Suffering is the path to wisdom.

Our words have changed with time. Here are five of the most important to help you understand us. What have you done to them?

*This ground is holy: here the brave are resting.*
—SIMONIDES OF CEOS

Justice (*dike*): path or expected events (no moral judgment)
Virtue (*arete*): efficiency or skill (no assumption of right or wrong)
God (*theos*): a force free of death (not always a persona; whereas
    Christians say, "God is Love," we say, "Love is as god")
Irrational: freed from rational thought (not always undesirable)
Ecstasy: a state beside oneself, filled with emotion too powerful for
    the body to contain (not the same as happiness)

*How do you believe the world began?*

Earth (Gaia) mates with sky (Uranus). So jealous is he of their offspring,
that he tries to stuff all back into her womb. Her youngest son, Kronos,
helps her by cutting off his father's genitals and throwing them into the
sea. Three drops of genital blood fall upon Gaia, causing the birth of the
Furies, while the genitals float away and form Aphrodite! Far from learning compassion from his own experience, son Kronos takes his own sister,
Rhea, as wife, and swallows all *their* children. But the sixth child, Zeus,
escapes, returns as a man, disguises himself as a cupbearer, feeds his father
a dreadful potion, and makes him disgorge the older brothers and sisters
of Zeus. These form the ruling gods. Sex and violence are at the core of
the creation.

*What are the traditions? How are bonds made and broken?*

Whom Zeus would de-
stroy, he first makes mad.
    —SOPHOCLES

Ritual, festival, and debate—chances to act out and reaffirm belief—are
our traditions. Community comes before family, then friendship. Man's
word is his honor. Break it, and you welcome death and destruction.
Swear by the dark river Styx, which must be crossed in the underworld, as
the most sacred of oaths. Fail to honor a god for sparing your life, sending a good wind, or granting wisdom, and the god will avenge. Vengeance most feared is to the mind.

*What is the predominant mood?*

Passionately reflective.

*Who are idolized?*

First, the gods; second, the heroes of myth (Theseus, Jason, Ajax, Perseus,
Herakles); third, achievers. Most beloved of goddesses is Demeter, whose
Eleusinian mysteries are the most sacred and secret. But our largest cults
are for the youngest and most handsome: Apollo the light and Dionysus
the dark. Our greatest hero, Herakles (Hercules) is, though mortal, accepted on Olympus. In addition to his standard heroic endeavors, he honors King Thespius one night by sleeping with all fifty of the king's daughters!

*What is sin, and what is justice?*

We do not turn the other cheek. We believe in full, public reckoning and
the power of a curse. Betrayal of the state is death. A curse, if not

avenged, descends from parent to child until atonement. When young Teiresias by chance views Athena, virgin goddess, bathing, she strikes him blind. This is merciful; the price for looking at a god is death. Because he meant no harm, she grants him the gift of prophecy. Still, one look means no eyes. None fails to pay the price.

*What gets attention? What holds it?*

Magnificence in mind and body. Those who excel are listened to. An actor will be listened to provided he has a rib cage as vibrant as the box of a lyre.

*What value is placed on money? What are its uses?*

Wealth means responsibility. Rich men of course pay for the theatre. Drachmas should serve Dionysus.

*What is the place of God and the church?*

The gods *connect* us to the unknown. Religion is practical, tangible, constant, not entwined in ethics, but tied to sex. Our gods are close. Unlike your Jehovah, they have shown us their vulnerability, vengefulness, and carnality. We prefer gods we can understand. Your Jehovah is too perfect. Our heaven is ruled by a beautiful, terrible divine family whom we offer sacrifices and mock behind their backs. We are the mortals and they the immortals. Immortality is not above vanity or deceit.

*What are the requirements to be a god?*

You must have a god for your father. Your mother, if not a goddess, must be at least a nymph.

*What kind of humor dominates?*

We laugh openly at stupidity and ineptitude, satirizing anyone who is prominent. None are above criticism or mockery; it helps them avoid hubris. We believe there are separate times for laughter, tears, and stoicism. Our City Dionysia ends with a comedy, after a day of tragedy, like dessert after a full meal.

*How is fear defined? How is emotion expressed?*

We fear defeat, slavery, disgrace, infamy. We believe in clear, unfettered emotion. We suppress petty jealousy. We ward off the evil eye with a necklet of blue beads or dose ourselves with Lethe water to escape the past. Spit quickly, if you look too far into the future. It is bad luck to price the unborn calf.

We hold these animals sacred: peacock, eagle, tiger, stag, snake, boar, white bull, cat, mouse, swan, owl, tortoise, and dolphin. Sympathetic magic, a connection between a thing and its name or symbol, guides us. As some of you use a doll (pricking it with pins) to torture a person, we believe your name means as much as your limb. If I write your name, curse it, and bury it—consigning it to the powers of the underworld—I may be killing you. So I speak your name and touch your objects with care.

*What happens when you die?*

It may not be the end. Our dead are stretched out on a bier, feet to door, in case. The family cuts its hair short to the skull. Visitors cut locks of their own, tie them in black ribbons, and hang them by the door. This may be repeated at a burial place. A death is honored with feasting and funeral games, not quiet seclusion. If you lived with honor, a bard may sing your name, and children may be taught your deeds. If so, though you have crossed the River, who would say you do not still live?

## Structure

### The Gods are vengeful but known.

*Who rules, and who follows?*

> The tyrant drinks his cup of pride
> And climbs beyond our sight,
> Then, blazing like an evil star
> Falls into endless night.
> —SOPHOCLES

In the Athens of my life, a Council of Five Hundred (resembling your House of Representatives) and a Main Assembly of fifty members (similar to your Senate) hear and make law. In our plays are rulers (king, archon, despot, oligarch, or ephor) with power to order death. But even the most powerful must win the approval of the citizen/chorus to survive. There is no absolute authority.

> Poetry is higher than history, for poetry expresses the universal, history merely the particular.
> —ARISTOTLE

We invented history (from *historia,* or investigation) as the first to tell truth with reason and not to revise and glorify our past. I see that some in your age have reverted to the old ways. We value the historian, but *revere* the artist.

He who rules is called the Shepherd of the People, because he stands between the wolf and the flock.

*What is daily life like?*

Time is given each day to develop mind and body. Blood relations are strong and volatile. Marriage is arranged for life. Instead of your furry little creatures, every residence has a house snake for luck.

*How are manners and etiquette set?*

We respect custom, our own and that of others. We believe in guest friendship, ritual, gifts, and rules about who goes first. We are quick to note and honor your rules, if they differ from ours.

*Who is educated, and how?*

> The unexamined life is not worth living.
> —SOCRATES

Privileged males learn mathematics, philosophy, literature, music, athletics, ethics, persuasion, and dance outside the home; women, artistic skills, spinning, and weaving within. We look for learning everywhere.

The playwright/poet is expected to be a *didaskolos,* or teacher on being alive.

### What professions dominate, and how is work viewed?

The city-state is foremost. Service bonds one to the state. Some offices are filled by lot. Profession of leader or public servant dominates. Later, acting becomes a profession. Praise singers, seers, prophets, shamans, and priests are revered. Actors are exempt from military service and have diplomatic immunity and so may be asked to carry secret communication between heads of state as they tour.

## Beauty

### *Nothing matches the human body in the sun.*

### What is the look most aspired to? Who are the contemporary ideals of male and female perfection?

Strong, statuesque, and proud, with keen intelligence in the eyes—eyes that are stern, radiant, gracious, without sentiment. Power in the limbs. Cleanliness, smooth skin, vitality, hair that is curled. Mesomorphic, symmetrical physical dimensions, well-muscled, with the effortless stillness and grace of the natural athlete. Sappho, whom Plato calls "the tenth muse," laments being short and dark, while rejoicing in her blonde "golden flower" daughter, Cleis. Sappho praises other women for pale delicacy and grace. Golden hair is chosen for characters of great beauty. The Olympians are models—Aphrodite, Eros, and Apollo in particular.

And yet, Dionysus, the newest and most dangerous god, is dark, with exotic eyes and lithe, sinuous limbs. He *defies* the ideal and is thought by many to be the most beautiful.

### What part does fitness play in attractiveness?

The body must be fit for an ordered self and for beauty. Vibrant good health, unrestricted garments, and little artifice are most desired. Athletic prowess is beautiful, most so in those who master many. Unlike your Olympics, at ours the pentathlon (one man mastering five events) is the highest honor. The physique of this athlete is most coveted.

We take physical beauty as seriously as any philosophical issue. I believe you take it seriously but pretend to find it unimportant.

### Which colors and shapes are favored?

We choose vibrant, solid-colored (indigo, scarlet, purple, green, black, and saffron) garments, many with bold trim in a key, stripe, or other geometric pattern. In theatre, colors are symbols—green for mourning, red for procurement, white with purple border for royalty. A hat indicates a traveler. Only the basic male himation and clothing of the poor are likely to be all white, a color chosen for mourning as often as black. The body is draped simply with cotton or linen for grace of line.

We love fragrances and scent as adornment. Jewelry, particularly that with a tinkling musical sound, is much loved. Earrings are for warding off evil spirits, before they are loved for beauty alone.

### *How is beauty expressed in daily life?*

Pots, vases, urns, bowls, and cups are used for storing oil, water, and food or for mixing or drinking wine, but their surfaces tell of our lives and legends. For some occasions, pots are commissioned, even a grave pot to honor the dead. A host might invite you to his home to celebrate your triumph and have you drink deeply from a cup, which shows in its interior a god in a situation like yours. After the final toast of the evening, the host may personally dry the cup and present it to you as a remembrance.

Tapestries and sculpture, both statues (especially *kouros* [nude male youth] and *kore* [draped maiden]) and reliefs, express our spirit. Music and dance are part of every ceremony. The drama has never received such support before or since. The poet's gift is worshiped.

## Sex

**The planting of seed is fundamental to life.**

### *How significant a part of life is sex?*

Sex is a chance to touch the god in us; it is part of life, renewal, like breathing; it is free of shame. It is more and less important to us than to you.

### *What are considered turn-ons and turn-offs?*

Excellence! Those with victor's laurels will be sought after. Strength, dexterity, and will are desired. Obesity, indecisiveness, and cowardice are not. The body is seen: Our athletes, some dancers, and all male children appear nude. Undergarments are uncommon. The torso is honored in sculpture, but never upstages force from the eyes.

The best way to ensure being able to mate with anyone of your choice is to be a god. But that is probably true in your world as well.

### *How is sexuality communicated, and how is seduction defined?*

We do not tease. We honor desire. Sex is union. If spirits meet, bodies may. Sex with the gods shapes belief. Your Jehovah pleasured himself with only one human, the mortal Mary, correct? Ha! Our Zeus has had everyone! Sisters, aunts, cousins, nymphs, and legions of humans! He is insatiable and able to take on any seductive form, from white bull to cuckoo. He threatens to seduce his mother when she tries to stop his marriage to his sister. Is he irresponsible and immoral? He is Zeus! Until you have had sex with a god, do not dare to judge, mortal.

*What is the courtship ritual? How much is deviation tolerated?*

Marriage is a business contract, with courtship left to negotiators. A male's first sexual experience is likely to be with another male. The bond formed may involve partnering with one's lover in battle as well, a bond believed to increase chances for victory. When you marry, your former lover may become godfather to your children and protector to your wife. If you die and he is not wed, he is the one most likely to marry your widow.

Orgy may be part of a celebration. A giant phallus, symbolizing renewal, appears at public gatherings. When Aphrodite and Dionysus, two of our more carnal gods, mate, they produce Priapus, an ugly child with enormous genitals. Most of us have small statues of Priapus in front of our homes. Aphrodite's cult is made up of honored priestess-prostitutes, known as protectors of the city.

*Hush, man, most glad indeed am I rid of it all, as though I had escaped from a mad and savage master.*

—SOPHOCLES, when asked if he still had sex during his advanced years

## Recreation

*Dionysus must have his due.*

*What would be an ideal social occasion?*

The Dionysian Festival is the height, but more often we choose quieter pleasures, such as dining and discussing ideas with friends. We seek balance between Apollonian wisdom and Dionysian inspiration. Nine is the perfect number, small enough for talk, large enough for diversity. We invented the "symposium," but you have again changed the word. Ours is livelier and more ribald than yours.

*Wine goes in and tongues let out. Gentlemen observe a mean, Tippling, with good songs between.*

—ANACREON

*Intellectual life?*

Even our wildest rites are based on inspiration. You desire surprising plots; we know our plots. We want irony, subtlety, new motives and causes for old deeds.

*Food?*

Thick red wine is watered down according to time of day and occasion. Sharing a cup is a ritual of trust, pouring wine on the ground a ritual of honor. We recline at meals, where fruits (figs, raisins, currants, olives) are always served with flat bread. Honey, almond cakes, and chestnuts are treats. A humble meal is barley bread and goat cheese.

*How important is recreation in life?*

Your saying "All work and no play make Jack a dull boy" sums up our Apollonian/Dionysian balance, or golden mean. Pleasure, rest, and celebration are vital to free work, study, and thought. Apollo brings peace and music. He likes tears no more than the sun likes rain. He understands your pain and will take it away. He will slay the darkness and help you stir men's hearts and minds, if you offer him song. His is a calming love. And Dionysus? [*Suddenly the subject stops and looks away as if in a trance.*]

Hermes waits to escort me to my world. There is a goat to be sacrificed and a friend in need of an oracle. I will leave you some writings. Read of Dionysus yourself if you dare. I pour you this libation [*taking a bowl of wine that seems to have just appeared*] to honor your search and assist your discovery [*splashes wine suddenly*]. What were your thoughts just now? Were you worried about stains on the carpet? The waste of fine wine? The propriety of this happening in your office? You need not concern yourself. The stain will disappear with me. The wish remains: May you more often drop small thoughts and let the god emerge inside you. [*The subject points outside the window. I look and see nothing. I turn around, and the Greek is gone, leaving this story of Dionysus behind.*]

### Dionysus

The youngest god has long dark hair, wears garlands of ivy, and is the only god with a mortal mother. He is ecstasy and horror, vitality and savage destruction. He is the god of the theatre, whom we worship when we perform.

Dionysus is created when Zeus seduces Semele, a mortal woman of astonishing beauty. Semele is tricked by Zeus's jealous wife, Hera, into asking him to give her one wish and to swear on the river Styx not to refuse. She asks to see him, but no mortal can view a god without dying. He has no choice. As she bursts into flames, Zeus cuts open her womb and his own thigh, where he keeps Dionysus full term. Dionysus goes through so many trials that he is born three times.

When Hera recognizes Dionysus, she makes him mad. He journeys through the east with an army of satyrs and maenads. He teaches men to make wine. His grandmother, Rhea, cures him and initiates him into the secret of women's mysteries. He decides to teach women how to celebrate him. When Ariadne, the great love of his life, dies, he places her crown among the stars, now known as Corona Borealis.

Worship of Dionysus is pure release of inhibition, resulting in union with nature and the creative force. He offers wine and sex as paths to ecstasy. Kings oppose him because he threatens law and order. Hera is his mortal enemy because he calls on women to forget their usual roles and is her husband's "bastard" son by a gorgeous mortal. He is the only god to rescue and restore women instead of diminishing or raping them. He prefers their company, having been raised for a time as a girl, in one of many efforts to protect him.

The grapevine each year is severely pruned, lies dormant, and then sprouts new life. Dionysus is thus tied to nature, suffering, and women. His festivals (Rural Dionysus, Leneas, Anthesteria, and City Dionysus) connect seasonal planting, tending, harvesting, and wine making. Tradition involves singing over the sacrifice of a goat, a disguise in which the god was once murdered by Titans. The term *tragedy* emerges, meaning goat song.

Dionysus, in your own life, may be a mystic, musician, or murderer. In the darkest world he has Charles Manson's hypnotic deadliness. He is eternal youth, shifting moods, and passions. Jim Morrison, Mick Jagger, David Bowie, and Prince are public Dionysian figures. Dionysus uses disguise more than any other god: stag, goat, lion, bull, dolphin, and especially panther, leopard, and lynx—the most graceful and savage of cats. Remnants of his worship take hold at Halloween, Mardi Gras, and some concerts and parties. Dionysus is the one your mother hates when he comes to the house to pick you up. And not without reason. You ride away with him (on his motorcycle?), feeling free and dangerous. Does he lead you to impending doom or to inspiration? It depends on you.

## SIGHT

*Human gods walk the proud Earth.*

Productions in ancient Greece took place in the open air before an audience of up to thirty thousand people on stone bleachers in a hollowed-out hillside surrounding two-thirds of the stage. We cannot expect to recreate these circumstances. We can only strive to elicit in our audience the *feelings* the ancient Greek audience experienced on watching actors literally circling each other in attack and examination. There will probably be no altar (*thymele*) of Dionysus onstage, or anything as profoundly meaningful for the audience. How can you capture the feeling of serving the god there? What is the most revered place in your town? Imagine a blend of championship fight and court trial in such a place, and endow your theatre with such power. State your case clearly and fairly if you have any hope to win. Verbal boxing, legal holds, and logical knock-outs are all performed under the watchful eye of the town's wisest citizens. Minds and hearts are out for world championships. You have four choices to make regarding your costumes:

1. You can try to match the original production by wearing an ornate costume consisting of a long robe under a short mantle, an *onkos* (ornate headdress indicating the sex, age, and status of character), and a mask of cork or linen (*prosopon*). These restrict sudden or sharp movements, require that you keep your head upright, and severely limit your peripheral vision. You must turn your entire head to face the object or person you wish to see and take each step with great care. If you are a prophet, you may wear a robe of open netting. If you are a chorus member, your costume may resemble normal attire. "Modified original" productions are common, employing half masks, masklike makeup, or some other softening of the full mask/*onkos* effect.

2. You can try to look like a member of the original audience by wearing a *chiton* (inner garment) and possibly *himation* (outer). The chiton, a rectangular garment open at the right side and caught at both shoulders, may be short or long and belted in various ways around the torso and waist. The himation is a rectangular wrap draped around the body restricting the freedom of one arm. If you are a Stoic or a philosopher, you wear *only* the himation. A *chlamys,* or short square cloak, may be worn by younger men and warriors.

   If you are woman, you may wear a Doric chiton, a rectangle of wool folded over at the top and draped around the body, with the front and back attached at the shoulder with a *fibula* (a large clasp resembling a safety pin) and girded under the breasts or at the waist. The overfold is a peplos. Or, you may wear an Ionic chiton, a wider garment with no overfold, often with a pleated or crinkled effect. A fibula or buttons fastens the garment along the top of the arms, creating a sleevelike appearance. You may also add a himation or a *diplax,* which is much like the male chlamys). Athenian women sew up the open side of their chiton and consider Spartan women, who do not, sluts.

   Men's hair is short. Younger men are clean-shaven, and older men have healthy well-tended beards. Women pin their hair up, often in braids, and cover portions with a band or coronet. Both men and women may have hair curled over the forehead and sides of the face. Jewelry adorns the body. Indoors, feet are bare. Outdoors, a sandal or a leather boot or buskin is worn.

3. You can look as the characters probably did when they lived. In the Minoan-Mycenaean period during the reigns of Agamemnon and Menelaus, women wear bell-shaped, tiered skirts, tight girdles at the waist, some type of headdress, and long curls down the back. They bare their breasts. Men wear a girdle, loincloth, a tunic with sleeves, greaves, and helmets with animal trims (such as tusks and tails), plus metal studs and leather fringe. Hair and beards are very long and crimped into serpentine tresses.

4. You can achieve the look your designer and director create. This is the most common choice. You may look like a Roman or the citizen of some future world. Or, the director may decide to go for a military look or simply invent a fanciful antiquity.

There are no featherweights in Greek drama, no airy, delicate, flighty, people. Therefore, the best costumes, regardless of details, help the performers achieve a tall, dignified, commanding, godlike presence.

## Movement and Contact

Hypnotic stillness alternates with extravagant gestures and full, forceful crosses. Because ritual is valued, symbolic and formal movements can be juxtaposed with less studied gestures. The torso is kept erect, with head upright. Gestures have clearly defined beginnings, middles, and ends and are held for the duration of the thought. The arms do not move stiffly but refrain from making small distracting movements. Imagine that all nonessential qualities (mannerisms, old habits, tiny movements) have been stripped away so that only what is clean and necessary remains. These characters are archetypal, not particularized. They have been *simplified* to the point of purity and basic humanity and then *amplified* by the enormity of their circumstances and the magnitude of their plight.

We have no evidence indicating how ancient Greeks bow, except for actions implied in the scripts.

1. When you are supplicating, go all the way down to the ground, and prostrate yourself. You may be extended anywhere from a kneeling position, hands down on the floor, to fully lying face down before the honored one. You might kiss the garment of the person before you. If you fall to your knees, pull forward as you do so, with some of your energy pulling you up (not unlike sliding into home plate). This helps you avoid injury and accomplish the move soundlessly.

2. When you kneel, step forward as you bend, ending with the other knee on the ground and the one with which the move started now bent. Allow room between yourself and those to whom you are paying obeisance.

3. Open your palms to indicate the power of the person addressed, and take the hands of this person with your palms up. You might proceed to place the hands of the honored one against your forehead.

4. Invent codes with your scene partners or fellow cast members. Decide on a curse, a gesture of thanks, an invocation of the gods for help, a warding off of the evil eye, a silent signal forbidding someone to come closer, and other symbolic actions. This is opportunity for creating a world.

5. Express grief by covering your head and face and, sometimes, by raising a veil over your head.

6. Men *show friendship* by grasping each other's forearms near the elbow. A man further emphasizes the commitment by placing the other hand on the friend's shoulder. This gesture (which evolves into our handshake) demonstrates that you do not have a weapon. You come open and unarmed into contact. Women are more likely to clasp hands.

7. With the above exception, there need be no significant difference in the way the sexes move. There is a directness and simplicity in the words that should be supported by movements.

8. The forehead can be used for a variety of moves. A clenched fist pressed to the brow is a gesture of homage to a god or person of great importance. Touching the hand to the brow and extending the arm up in the air is a salute, as is a fist across the chest. Touching two or more fingertips to the brow and lowering the head slightly indicates paying honor without extreme obeisance. A soldier may press a spear or other weapon to the brow as a gesture of respect or to pass someone through an entrance.

9. References to gods may involve extending the arms toward the god's home, palms up for the Olympians and palms down for Poseidon, Mother Earth, and the underworld. When you address the gods, first look toward their home and then look out all around to acknowledge that the god may be anywhere.

## SOUND

*I speak for the ages.*

*The proper method of delivery can change the speech. We must pay attention to it because we cannot do without it.*

*—ARISTOTLE*

An aptitude for complicated lines of thought is to be cultivated. Experience with debate, forensics, and oratory is helpful, because these arts originate here. A slow to moderate tempo often works. Awareness of the rhythmic shifts within the dominant tempo is essential. Resist the temptation to give every image great weight and to fall into a ponderous delivery; the best arguers are full of surprises. The statues may be carved in marble, but the lines are being invented as you speak.

Aristotle and other thinkers continually refer to the need for a well-trained voice. Sophocles's retirement from acting because of the weakening of his voice is an open acknowledgment that the arts of the poet and actor are not the same. A fully rooted, resonant sound with generous attention to the lower notes in the register is crucial—an unsupported voice will not be listened to. The capacity to give consonants great weight, to be able to twist, turn, dart, and spit them without worry of affectation, is another aspect of mastering speech. There is an animal boldness to words that asks for the force of a lion or an eagle.

Feel free to sing, chant, intone, declaim, and explore other ways to express words through sound beyond simple speech. This is not just a scene; it is ritual and may shape destiny. The poets admire lean lines and spare sentences supported by firm, direct delivery.

The tragedy consists of five parts:

1. *Prologue* (exposition)
2. *Parados* (processional entrances)
3. *Episodes* (individual characters in action; five or six sections)
4. *Statismon* (lyrical sections involving singing and dancing, in which the chorus passes comment on the action or the issues each character raises)
5. *Exodus* (summary, frequently with a message, and choral exit)

Emotionally the play will move through four stages:

1. *Agon* (conflict)
2. *Pathos* (suffering)
3. *Threnos* (lamentation)
4. *Epiphany* (revelation of transcendent truth, spirit, godhead)

By their nature, each part can take a different vocal attack. Some passages demand highly poetic, lyrical speech. Others (the famous messenger speeches) need storytelling, tale-weaving vivid description. Debate sections demand a lawyer's command of issues and language. Lamentation speeches need an operatic release. The quick one-line exchanges, called *stichomythia,* need sharp timing and crisp attack.

Ancient Greek does not translate easily. What is elegantly concise in the original takes many words to express in English. Verse lines seem, to Western ears, to be in a perpetual state of unresolved half-tones. Language, structure, prose, and verse vary so much among translations (see Chapter 8) that the same play can be nearly unrecognizable. The originals have a pure simplicity and directness of language, but many flowery translations exist, so beware.

## Music and Dance

The ancient Greeks believe that music can spur action, strengthen the spirit, undermine mental and spiritual balance, completely suspend will-power, and produce magic. Many scholars believe that performances were more like song and dance than realistic behavior, that all movement was ritualized and speeches chanted. Greeks understand harmony and have three key modes: Dorian (strong and masculine), Phrygian (passionate), and Lydian (lascivious and effeminate). The following instruments are popular:

- *Lyre.* The lyre, the definitive Greek instrument, consists of five to seven spun-silk strings struck with a plectrum. Sometimes the player uses a turtle shell for a sounding board. The lyre is used to

Depicted are representative elements of Greek style. The layering of circles in the Greek theatre evokes the feeling that the actors are gathering for a ritual. The lamp (on the footed pedestal) offers a delicate glow and can be placed almost anywhere, and the lyre is the instrument of choice and sacred to Apollo. Next to the lyre is a chair and foot stool that reflect a tendency to command a large amount of space in sitting or reclining. Vases are practical works of art, revealing both heroic deeds and patterns for stage move-

ment. Women reflect a range of adornment, but always exhibit a graceful simplicity of line. Notice the sharp contrast between our vision of the classical Greek look and the tightly girdled look actually worn during the period in which most of the plays are set. The young athlete/warrior dresses for action, the monarch/statesman for contemplation and dignity. Open, loose, flowing clothing may be fastened with a fibula, a large clasp resembling a safety pin. Sandals may be worn, but bare feet are also common.

accompany poetic and choral passages. An oversized version, called the *kithara* or *phorminx,* is similar to a celtic harp or dulcimer. Hermes, it is said, made the first lyre while he was still a small child, to lull his mother to sleep so that he could go out to play wherever he wanted.

- *Aulos.* The aulos is a double- or single-reed instrument spanning three octaves. Its rich, low, resonant sound accompanies solo passages. Today an oboe, clarinet, or a bagpipe chanter can be used.
- *Percussion.* Cymbals and drums establish rhythms and guide choral moves. A modern percussion section can punctuate movement and shifts of action.

What emerges is a sound of haunting simplicity. Imagine a delicate string, low reed, and simple drumbeat underscoring speeches, offering subtle, evocative accompaniment, with descending notes in simple, monophonic patterns. Synthesizer music is often used because it creates a timeless, compelling, and not quite identifiable sound.

Dance is responsible for the very life of Zeus, god of gods, and it is so honored. (To prevent Kronos, his father, from eating him alive, the Curetes danced over baby Zeus in a wild, leaping, noisy, shouting, sword-and-shield display, so that Kronos would not hear Zeus crying.) To the ancient Greeks, dance means any rhythmic movement: juggling, tumbling, ball tossing, and movements of the hand, foot, head, and eye. Evidence suggests Greek dance involves more hand movement and less foot movement than ours. Dances may be ritual (sacrifice, prayer, exultation), funereal (slow, curvilinear dirges), processional (lines, chains, small clusters), warlike (vigorous attack and defense moves), or Dionysian (planned wild, disordered chaos suddenly emerging into surprising patterns).

## KEYS TO THE WORLD

### Images

The names of gods fill the plays and serve as evocative models. Some may be more familiar to you in their Roman versions:

| Greek | Roman | Identity |
|---|---|---|
| Zeus | Jupiter | King of all the gods |
| Hera | Juno | Wife to Zeus, goddess of marriage and children |
| Poseidon | Neptune | King of the sea, god of horses |
| Demeter | Ceres | Goddess of planting, harvest, rebirth |
| Athena | Minerva | Goddess of wisdom and courage |

| Greek | Roman | Identity |
| --- | --- | --- |
| Hestia | Vesta | Elder sister to Zeus, goddess of the home |
| Apollo | Apollo | God of healing, arts, the Sun |
| Artemis | Diana | Goddess of the moon, hunting, chastity |
| Aphrodite | Venus | Goddess of love |
| Eros | Cupid | Her son |
| Ares | Mars | God of war |
| Persephone | Proserpina | Daughter of Demeter, queen of the underworld |
| Hades | Pluto | King of the underworld |
| Hephaistos | Vulcan | God of fire, crafts |
| Hermes | Mercury | Messenger of the gods, patron of travelers, transporter of souls |
| Dionysus | Bacchus | God of wine and inspiration |
| Kronos | Saturn | Father of Zeus, Hera, Demeter, Poseidon, Hades; ruler of first generation of gods |

Try this invocation.

**EXERCISE**

**Greek Warm-Up**

> Aphrodite, give me beauty and freedom.
> Apollo, give me harmony and clarity.
> Ares, give me courage and power.
> Artemis, give me vision and light.
> Athena, give me wisdom and strategy.
> Demeter, give me growth and renewal.
> Eros, give me love and magic.
> Hades, give me intuition and objectivity.
> Hephaistos, give me skill and creativity.
> Hera, give me nurturing and commitment.
> Hermes, give me swiftness and connection.
> Hestia, give me safety and identity.
> Poseidon, give me loyalty and feeling.
> Zeus, give me strength and will!
> And Dionysus, to whom my art is dedicated,
> Dionysus, give me inspiration and passion!!!
> Now all the gods fill me with fire.
> Drive me to destiny and wonder.
> Help me go beyond the real and into ecstasy.
> Help me find the god in me.
> Let me understand. Let me act.

Here are other organizing principles of the Greek world:

Nothing in excess (Not every day is a Dionysian rite)
A balanced life (Humility balances pride, passion balances reason,

mind balances body, human limitation balances ideal vision, civi-
lization balances barbarity, rationality balances irrationality, law
balances ecstasy)

Wisdom above all else, and above all other knowledge, self-
knowledge

The polis (city-state) as center of life

Any simple act may have infinite reverberations and catastrophe

Fertility of soil and fertility of woman mean survival

The Acropolis (Cult sanctuary of Athena, the place of the owl, the
snake, the sacred spring, and the cave)

Evocative art: Battle of Lapith and the Centaurs, Exkeias's Dionysus cup, Eupronios's Karator, Kirtios boy, The Bronze warriors

To ask of every act, Is my honor in this? Was this well done?

### Social Success and Suicide

You attain success by doing things that earn you the ultimate compliment:

> You are a balanced human. You bring honor to your people.

You achieve balance by reaching beyond personal vanity to service. To excel so that you reflect glory *back* on those you represent is the ideal; so, you
top the accolade above if you can add,

> And honor to my home as well.

Your failure in this world comes from doing things that earn you the
ultimate insult:

> You are selfish and unworthy.

To be Greek is to serve and to deserve to serve. Only small creatures are
too preoccupied with themselves to do so. Some who are selfish can still
give, but to be self-absorbed *and* inadequate to the task earns you vilifica-
tion. Here is another strong contender for the ultimate insult:

> You have set yourself above your fate. You have become an offense to the
> gods.

This means that the recipient has succumbed to *hubris* and will pay.
To be successful, you must

- Develop your mind, body, and skills to their fullest.
- Give to the city-state with a generous heart.
- Find ways of achieving excellence.
- Find the god in you to move with force on earth.
- Allow both your passion and your reason full expression.

You commit social suicide by

- Becoming full of yourself (*hubris*), offending a god, and subjecting yourself to retribution (*dike*).
- Leading a private life with no concern for the general well-being.
- Allowing yourself excess in any of the appetites of life.
- Being disloyal.
- Being stupid.

### Masking

The play is meant to be performed by masked actors, so rehearse in mask at least once. Spend time choosing your mask, study it, and wear it for brief periods of time. Let the power of the god enter you, along with the power of actors who have taken on this character before. If you can spend time in the storage area of your theatre or in a shop that sells masks, try on several. Let the spirit of each mask enter your spirit while leaving it intact. Let the mask itself tell you how to respond. As you wear the mask, you will discover that your limited peripheral vision encourages you to maintain a stately bearing and to pivot your entire body in any direction and towards any listener. Speak to the mask, addressing it at first as "you" and then, once you feel part of it, as "I."

There are only seven surviving vase paintings known to show fifth-century masks. These masks are softer, more natural, and less tortured than our earlier impressions of ancient masks. The mouths are only slightly open. Their expressions have endlessly shifting meaning. The Greek term for mask (*prosopon*) is also used in everyday conversation to refer to one's own face. Regard the mask as life-giving, not life-taking, as offering revelation, not concealment.

Characters also mask themselves in Righteousness. All choose to think themselves correct and resistent to negotiation. Recall those times in your own life when you have taken on this attitude. In modern therapy, a common goal is to give up the need to be right all the time; the Greeks, however, never give this up.

### The Production

Rehearsing in a large outdoor space and in full mask helps you understand the power and openness the performance brings. Your actual set will probably be clean and simple, an exterior with sky beyond and a large open space for choral movements. It should attempt to capture timeless dignity and raw power.

*There is no function more noble than that of the god-touched Chorus, teaching the city in song.*          —ARISTOPHANES

What is to us the strangest ingredient in Greek tragedy made it most moving and involving for the original audience. The chorus is the ideal spectator for the event. Instead of appearing in the strangest costumes and doing the most peculiar acts, the chorus is supposed to comfort and guide the audience by reacting to the events as the audience would. The chorus is there to express the conventional attitude of the average citizen of this community, to introduce new characters and question them, admonish or chastise characters behaving inappropriately, offer comfort and sympathy to characters who are victims, explain puzzling events, establish facts, and clarify motives. The chorus may pray, lament, celebrate, contemplate, or share ironic observations. It has a group identity, but each member also has a single identity, not unlike a modern chorus in a musical. When the chorus appears, we feel comforted and connected.

The chorus declines in importance as the drama moves forward. The choruses of Aeschylus are involved and committed; those of Sophocles are concerned but detached. The choruses of Euripides (with the stunning exception of *The Bacchae*) are ironic and remote, sometimes even in counterpoint to the event.

### The Perfect Audience

The audience arrives full of the anticipation of having the human experience illuminated for them. They go to the play, not just to have a wonderful time and experience spectacle and wonder, but to gain insight, much as people today go to church, concerts, or therapy. If you are approximating the original audience as part of a class or rehearsal exercise, indicate your displeasure by hissing and by knocking your heels against the seat or platform on which you are sitting. You will probably choose not to throw olive pits, much less stones, despite precedent. Applaud by clanging objects, such as cups on tables and weapons against shields.

### Contemporary Parallels

Although much of the Greek world may seem alien to you, there are elements that connect that world to ours:

- A preoccupation with the body and physical fitness, a belief in the relationship between fitness and other excellence and the association of beauty with strength.
- The nude or seminude male (for the Greeks, in person and sculpture; for us, in print and film) as a symbol of beauty, at least equal to that of the female.

- A desire for natural, unspoiled elements in food, clothing, and possessions; the desire to keep things simple.
- A powerful desire for comfort in everything worn, touched, or reclined on.
- The impulse to work hard and then party hard, to categorize life experiences.
- An obsession with sports events bordering on the maniacal.
- A belief in democracy, the rights of the individual, and the need to protect those rights.
- A commitment to open debate as the means by which issues can be settled.
- A feeling that each life phase has its own rewards and wonders, so that neither youth nor age is perfect.
- A constant reexamination of authority, with all power figures ready targets for satire.

It is too easy to think of the Greeks as distant from us. But the sky full of constellations named for them still watches over us. Most of the areas of human endeavor were originated by the Greeks, from the Olympics to mathematics, astronomy, engineering, architecture, medicine, money, law, literature, and scientific inquiry. They believe in magic, it is true, but there are still some things for which we have no better explanation.

## PLAYS AND PLAYWRIGHTS

The following plays are those most often produced:

| | |
|---|---|
| Aeschylus | *The Suppliants* (490 B.C.) |
| | *The Persians* (472 B.C.) |
| | *Seven Against Thebes* (469 B.C.) |
| | *Prometheus Bound* (460 B.C.) |
| | *The Oresteia: Agamemnon, The Libation Bearers, The Eumenides* (458 B.C.) |
| Sophocles | *Ajax* (450 B.C.) |
| | *Antigone* (442 B.C.) |
| | *Oedipus Rex* (409 B.C.) |
| | *Electra* (409 B.C.) |
| | *Philoctetes* (409 B.C.) |
| | *Oedipus at Colonus* (401 B.C.) |
| Euripides | *The Cyclops* (438 B.C.) |
| | *Alcestis* (438 B.C.) |
| | *Medea* (431 B.C.) |
| | *Hippolytus* (428 B.C.) |

Euripides (cont.)     *Andromache* (427 B.C.)
                      *Hecuba* (413 B.C.)
                      *The Suppliants* (421 B.C.)
                      *Ion* (417 B.C.)
                      *The Trojan Women* (415 B.C.)
                      *Electra* (413 B.C.)
                      *Iphigenia in Tauris* (414 B.C.)
                      *Orestes* (408 B.C.)
                      *The Bacchae* (405 B.C.)
                      *Iphigenia in Aulis* (405 B.C.)

## SCENES

If only two or three actors take part, lines assigned to the chorus may in some instances need to be cut or reassigned to the character closest to that point of view.

*Agamemnon*
Clytemnestra, Aegisthus, Chorus
The unfaithful queen and her lover attempt to justify their murder of her husband to the representative of the people of their city.

*Antigone*
Ismene, Antigone
Defying the orders of her uncle, Creon, that her brother, who sought rebellion against Creon's government, not be given burial, Antigone meets secretly with her sister to ask for her help in carrying out a deed certain to bring about Antigone's execution.
Creon, Haemon
Father and son face the disintegration of their relationship as they differ over love and loyalty.

*The Bacchae*
Pentheus, Dionysus
Failing to honor the god, the city's leader has him captured and refuses to recognize his divinity until it is too late.

*Electra*
Chrysothemes, Electra, Clytemnestra
One sister warns another against confronting their mother about the death of their father, but Electra, in her pain, approaches the queen at the altar of Agamemnon's grave. (Also can be performed as two separate two-character scenes.)

*Iphigenia in Aulis*
Clytemnestra, Iphigenia, Achilles
Can the queen sacrifice her daughter to avoid war?

*Iphigenia in Tauris*
Orestes, Pylades, Iphigenia
On a remote island, separated for many years, brother and sister are unexpectedly reunited. She is now a priestess, he a fugitive.

*The Libation Bearers*
Orestes, Electra
Meeting at the tomb of their father, brother and sister lament the indignity of his death and plot vengeance on their mother for her part in it.

*Medea*
Jason, Medea
Medea avenges her betrayal and exile by her husband, poisoning his new wife and then slaughtering their two children. Jason encounters her and the bodies of their offspring.

*The Trojan Women*
Hecuba, Helen, Menelaus
Troy is defeated. All Hecuba's children and grandchildren are dead, except one daughter, who is insane. The Greek king has come to Troy to claim his unfaithful wife, who has been the cause of the war.
Talthybius, Andromache, Hecuba
The Greek captain is a caring man, but there is no easy way to separate the queen, her daughter-in-law, and her grandson, each destined for a separate horror.

---

Members of the class play the gods in this exercise. You might choose either to select the actors you feel are right for each part or to draw, in which case men and women draw separately.

1. Find a spot in the room according to your station. Arguing and negotiating with the other actors is fine.
2. Those left over come as suppliants before the gods with a request. Keep the request simple, and make it something you really would like, such as an A in the class or glorious weather for the coming weekend.
3. The gods discuss their part in the request: whether it should be granted; who should become the patron of this suppliant; and how, if the act is granted, each might contribute to bringing it about.

**E X E R C I S E**

**God Meeting**

1. Select someone no longer living or something no longer a part of your life. You may choose someone close to you, a public figure you admire, a custom or courtesy no longer practiced, or some quality of life that is missing.
2. Spend the time between one class period and the next devising a simple offering and statement honoring the dead. Ask for the care and protection of Dionysus, Apollo, or any other god of your choice.

**E X E R C I S E**

**Homage to the Dead**

3. Perform the ritual of honor, sacrifice, and speech at a designated altar in the room. Everyone else listens very closely and tries to support each suppliant. Don't make any effort to sound Greek; just speak simply and from the heart.

**E X E R C I S E**

**Movement Cycles**

In this exercise, the actors explore the basic movements in acts of survival. These acts may include planting the seed, nurturing, harvesting—anything that all people at all times have done.

1. With several designated side coaches calling out the event, mime it and interpret it into a simple rhythmic move.
2. At a signal from the coaches, look around you at the different movements, and silently agree as a group on a modification or combination so that everyone is doing the same move.
3. Note that modification, and move on to another. Go through several cycles of movement. The coaches then repeat the words while the actors visualize each move.
4. Go back and attempt to repeat the entire set of cycles, connecting with the other actors.

**E X E R C I S E**

**Choral Interpretation**

Take the basic idea for the exercise above, but use a choral passage from a script instead. Use the same kind of silent collaboration to refine the movement.

1. First, simply explore the movement while the side coaches read the lines.
2. Then, stand still and repeat the lines after the coaches read them.
3. Finally, go back and integrate movement and speech.

**E X E R C I S E**

**Mask Day**

1. Wear masks as you arrive to class, and go about normal class business for at least a full half hour.
2. Perform familiar tasks, such as a well-known warm-up or critique session.
3. Designate teams to accomplish new tasks, such as describing and demonstrating the colors in the room, the lighting system, or the different acoustic surfaces.
4. Discuss the effect the mask has on bearing and sound.
5. Sit in small circles of five or six people. Pick up an imaginary mask in front of you, and while everyone watches, demonstrate it and put it back down.
6. Next, pass each mask around the circle. Everyone's mask should be worn by everyone else.
7. Select the one mask of all those available that you all will wear. Put this one on, and circulate among the other groups, letting the mask direct you.
8. You may use sound to communicate, but try to avoid words.

**E X E R C I S E**

**Stadium Play**

1. Organize a trip to a football stadium. Estimate how much of the space would be used in a classical Greek production.
2. Using that space, have some students perform down on the field and others form the audience.

3. Start with a simple discussion, class announcements, or questions about an upcoming assignment. Fill up the amount of space you're using.
4. If you are working on a Greek scene, present it in the space. Repeat the Choral Interpretation exercise above. Make sure each actor has the opportunity to speak and move in the space as well as to watch and listen.

After Eris was rejected from Mount Olympus, she sent the gods a golden apple inscribed "For the most beautiful." Hera, Athena, and Aphrodite all claimed it, and Paris, son of the king of Troy, was chosen to act as judge in the dispute. He ultimately chose Aphrodite because she promised him Helen, the most beautiful woman in the world. These events led to the Trojan War.

**E X E R C I S E**

**She Who Is Most Beautiful**

1. Cast the five roles, and enact the story in a ritualized manner with improvised dialogue. If you are Athena or Hera, really try to get the story to end differently this time. If you are Paris, consider all arguments carefully. Believe that the story is actually being created right now.

## SOURCES FOR FURTHER STUDY

Adler, Mortimer J. *Aristotle for Everybody*. New York: Macmillan, 1978.

Anderson, M. J., ed. *Classical Drama and Its Influence*. New York: Barnes & Noble, 1965.

Bickerman, Elias Joseph. *Chronology of the Ancient World*. Ithaca, N.Y.: Cornell University Press, 1980.

Bieber, Margarete. *The History of the Greek and Roman Theatre*. Princeton: Princeton University Press, 1961.

Bolen, Jean Shinoda. *Goddesses in Everywoman*. New York: Harper & Row, 1985.

———. *Gods in Everyman*. New York: Harper & Row, 1990.

Brooke, Iris. *Costumes in Greek Classic Drama*. London: Methuen, 1962.

Earp, Frank Russell. *The Style of Sophocles*. New York: Russell & Russell, 1972.

Gagarin, Michael. *Aeschylean Drama*. Berkeley, Calif.: University of California Press, 1976.

Graves, Robert. *Greek Gods and Heroes*. New York: Dell, 1960.

Grube, George M. A. *The Drama of Euripides*. London: Methuen, 1973.

Guthrie, W. K. *The Greek Philosophers*. New York: Harper & Row, 1950.

Hamilton, Edith. *Mythology*. Boston: Little, Brown & Co, 1942.

Hope, Thomas. *Costume of the Greeks and Romans*. New York: Dover, 1962.

Johnson, Robert A. *Ecstasy*. San Francisco: Harper & Row, 1987.

Kirkwood, Gordon Macdonald. *A Study of Sophoclean Drama*. Ithaca, N.Y.: Cornell University Press, 1958.

Kitto, H. D. F. *The Greeks*. Chicago: Aldine, 1964.

Oates, Whitney Jennings. *The Complete Greek Drama*. New York: Random House, 1938.

Pickard-Cambridge, A. W. *The Dramatic Festivals of Athens*. Oxford: Oxford University Press, 1953.

Sweet, Waldo E. *Sport and Recreation in Ancient Greece*. New York: Oxford University Press, 1987.

Taplin, Oliver. *Greek Tragedy in Action*. Berkeley, Calif.: University of California Press, 1978.

Webster, T. B. L. *Greek Theatre Productions*. London: Methuen, 1970.

———. *The Tragedies of Euripides*. London: Methuen, 1967.

Wellesz, Egon, ed. *Ancient and Oriental Music*. London: Oxford University Press, 1936.

## VIDEOS

**Electra, The Trojan Women, Iphigenia** (Michael Cacoyannis)     Cacoyannis is considered perhaps the premiere contemporary interpreter of Greek tragedy on film. The work of Vanessa Redgrave in **Trojan Women** and Irene Papas in **Iphigenia** is particularly striking. Any of the three would be a good first exposure to the style.

**Oedipus Rex** (Tyrone Guthrie)     This highly effective Stratford Festival production with masks is at least as austere, ritualistic, and formal as the original productions probably were.

**Medea** (Zoe Caldwell)     A dramatic, intense adaptation of Euripides's play by Robinson Jeffers, effective in its full-out attack and force.

**Songs of Sappho** (New York Greek Drama Company)     An attempt to authentically recreate the performances of poetry accompanied by dance as they might have been done in the poet's own lifetime.

# ELIZABETHAN PERIOD STYLE
# Theatre of Earth and Stars

## THE WORLD ENTERED

Over two thousand years pass before unquestioned greatness returns to the theatre. Plague, war, and famine have wiped out much of the world's population and, for a time, theatre itself. Then a mighty England emerges as ruler of the known globe, guided by a queen of majesty and diplomacy. The English language explodes; vocabulary increases by one-fourth, with over ten thousand new words added in less than a century. Never, before or since, has a language grown so astonishingly. The drama is where the new words soar. The term *Elizabethan* is not limited to the era between the birth and death of Elizabeth I. E. M. W. Tilyard identifies it as "meaning anything between the ages of Henry VIII and Charles I akin to the main threads of Elizabethan thought." Prior to Elizabeth's reign, laws are passed forbidding noblemen to raise private armies, encouraging trade instead. By the time she takes on the crown, the emphasis has already shifted from power struggle to commerce. The feudal system is dead. Because her father, Henry VIII, broke with Rome and created his own church, Elizabeth, at her coronation, becomes both head of state and head of the Church of England. She has no higher allegiance than her own vision. Although the Renaissance begins in Italy, it flourishes in an emancipated England.

The English can now do no wrong, accomplishing feats formerly thought impossible, among them Drake's voyage around the world, Raleigh's exploration of North America, and an astonishing naval victory over the Spanish, who previously had claimed title to the greatest naval

Barry Kraft as The Chorus in *Henry V,* Oregon Shakespeare Festival fleet in the world. Elizabethans have already found "more things in heaven and earth" than ever previously dreamed of. They regard the world as *theirs*.

Although it provides an important backdrop, the Elizabethan era is not what most of the plays are about. The playwrights opt for more exotic choices. Living in an extraordinary world, they often place their plays in worlds even more extraordinary. Understanding this style means entering the *imaginary* lives of the writers, beyond their day-to-day existence. It also means acceptance of miracles.

What follows is an interview with an expert familiar with court, country, and city life. A close friend of Ben Jonson and William Shakespeare and a dabbler in the occult, our expert has lived in the plays themselves (in such kingdoms as Shakespearia and Jonsonia), as well as in London. The interview was set up with the help of alchemy and witchcraft. The speaker lapsed occasionally into blank verse or rhymed couplets, claiming that any other form of expression would be inadequate. The subject felt informal that day and therefore addressed me consistently as "thou." I was never quite certain why; perhaps the expert liked me or felt the disdain for me that one might for a servant. Immediately after the conversation, the expert disappeared in smoke.

Time: 1550–1625

*Love alters not with his brief hours and weeks,*
*But bears it out even to the edge of doom.*

*In what point in history are the plays written, set, and performed?*

Written in the years 1550–1625, our plays be *set* in times ancient, all the way forward to times not yet lived. They be not about a moment in time but about *all* time. E'en the "history" plays alter fact to suit vision. And what vision! Our poets do play with time, so thou be'est ne'er certain how many days or years have gone by in our plays. Time will seem different in performance than it doth appear on paper. Our writers are magicians.

*How far does the audience or play move out of its own time?*

If moved far out of the Renaissance, they lose majesty. But lose power? Not a whit! Our plays fit every period known or imagined by man!

*How does time move?*

Semper Eadem: Ever the same through all alteration.
—MOTTO OF ELIZABETH I

We stride forth in glory, and every prospect doth exist on our horizon. We do take more time than thee to smell the rose. The clock has been perfected, and we note tolling of church and tower bells, but still watch sun and moon as truest guides. Whilst change be ever constant, so be our queen.

*How do you record or note time?*

A fortnight past, when our glorious queen did visit the estates of Lord Leicester, the clocks were stopped for the duration of her stay, since, quoth his lordship, "Where Virginia is, there time stands still." She doth have such power o'er her lords and we, her subjects, have such power o'er the world! Time is oft' times capitalized, spoken to, personified. Ay, marry, no other subject is addressed more often in our plays. Father Time is a powerful man with two strong daughters, Fate and Truth.

*What is the dominant tempo/rhythm?*

Blank verse captures our lives, like unto the cantering of our horses, the beat of our tabors [drums] and the pulse of the human heart.

*Where do people focus?*

Past be merely catalyst to future. We dwell not on deeds done, but thrust ahead. Yet, if ye wrong us, think not our memories be so short that we shall fail vengeance, no matter how bloody or long it take. We do think of lifetimes and generations to come. Ye can always imagine the *next* scene at the end of our plays, be it wedding celebration, reunion feast, or funeral procession.

*What attention spans do your people have?*

We listen not unless thou speak'st boldly and beautifully, with pride in thy heart and vision in thy tongue. Those worthy of attention receive it, by commanding it. If thou speak'st well, we will stay with thee. If not, see to thyself.

*Is age revered or feared?*

Youth is a sadly brief and fleeting time, like unto the lives of flowers. Childhood, as thou know'st it in thy time, doth not exist in ours. Children dress and act as we do, are expected to be interested in philosophy and to make worthy conversation at table. Silliness be not tolerated. Our poets are as infatuated with the last days of boyhood as the first dawn of womanhood. Boys and women be seen as similar, the oncoming of beard and drop in voice regarded with some sadness.

## Space

**I stand amidst the spheres, and I stand tall.**

*How is space defined?*

Britannia doth rule the world, and her cathedrals thrust toward heaven!

*All places are distant from Heaven alike.*

—ROBERT BURTON

*How large is personal and private space? How flexible?*

Huge! We fill the universe with self. The higher thy class, the larger thine own space. Yet, space alters oft' betimes. We embrace heartily and seize what we want, and then spheres burst. A man may seek to be alone when not fit company. When in public, be expected to *take part,* and save thy contemplation for anon.

*What are attitudes towards invasion and physical force?*

Grant me a moment to gather my thoughts [ *pause* ]:

> No where is man more noble than in war,
> Provided that he fight for noble cause.
> 'Tis England's turn as lion now to roar.
> And vanquish any who oppose our laws!

*Our swords shall play the orators for us.*
—CHRISTOPHER MARLOWE

Did serve? 'Twas extempore. Forgive me. The muse captured me. Space is invaded forthrightly—grabbing a woman and kissing her full, slapping a glove across an opponent's face or thrusting a dagger into his body. Word or blade may confront ye at any time.

Yet, be forceful *and* eloquent in execution, for invasion without grace be ill thought of.

*How do these ideas affect the theatre space?*

Our theatre symbolizes the universe, from trapdoors (hell) up to canopy (heaven), so all elements exist within the Globe. Our four famous theatres be all located within a few streets of one another in south London, *far* from palaces and cathedrals. Nearby be Klink Prison (a term ye have stolen to mean *any* prison) and other jails. Thieves, prostitutes, vagabonds, and beggars do live here, so those who cross the bridge do journey to the wrong side of the Thames. In this dangerous darkness, magic rises, and all manner of humankind cross paths.

## Place

*My home is the world, and where I am I own.*

*Where are the plays set?*

Our scope is epic. Our settings may be throne room, hovel, peaceful garden, or raging tempest. Our plays sweep through the known world, both tamed and wild, and magical, imaginary lands, new minted in our minds. Scenery changes little; the *lines* make powerful suggestion, and the rest, my friend, be acting!

*And space in daily life?*

Our population has grown from three to four million in under sixty years (more new people e'en than words), with massive movement to London and new debate 'tween country pleasures and with those o' the city. New inventions (the chimney! carpenter's tools! glass!) allow smaller rooms, windows, light, and more indoor time, and houses now are oft' built in the shape of an **E**. Can'st supposition why? The most important new space be the Long Gallery, a place of exercise, dancing, and music, with fireplaces and family portraits o'erlooking the garden. Home now is center of life, for better or worse.

   Our pride and joy be our flowers and time to tend them! Garden be as vital as gallery for walking our footpaths of knotted ribbon mazes.

*What is your relationship to nature?*

Nature may give trial and torment or peace and safety. Natural order and goodness can be corrupted, but we believe in the Noble Savage.

*How aware are you of other places?*

Though England be the sceptred isle, we are entranced with Italy and the Machiavellian mind. We are torn 'tween revolutions in science, philosophy, and politics whirling 'round us. We do cling to simple superstition *and* yearn for reasons. Many are disturbed by the new theory of Copernicus, which says the earth be not center to the universe (with all spheres circling us), but that it doth forsooth revolve around the sun!! We explore land and sea as readily as mind and soul.

*Charity and beating begins at home.*
—JOHN FLETCHER

## Values

*One man in his time plays many parts.*

*What are the beliefs most widely shared? What are the ideals? Which truths are assumed to be self-evident?*

I will teach thee to become an Elizabethan! A person worthy of Shakespeare and the stars. Stand up. No, taller, Bartonio! Is that not thy name? Well, I *choose* to call thee Bartonio. Up, man! Now this be what thou call'st a "warm-up," a thing we do not require as *we* are always ready! Stand tall, sirrah. Speak these words and believe them!

   My spirit lifts me high above the ground.
   I have an answer ready for any man.
   I have the wit to jest even with saints.
   I am as true as flesh and blood may be.
   I was not born to sue, but to command.
   The heavens blazed with light upon my birth.

Shown are representative elements of Elizabethan style. While still open to the heavens and circular in feel, the Elizabethan theatre is more enclosed and holds about one-tenth of the audience of its Greek counterpart. Chairs are solid, massive, rigid, and uncomfortable. The most popular instrument of the time is the delicate, stringed lute, although the less versatile virginal is also greatly coveted. The covered, longer look in the clothing of the earlier period continues to be favored by women in the country, but it is replaced by a wider, more spectacular look at court. The display of strong

legs is fundamental to the young, swaggering male, as is bulk of fabric to the older statesman. The ruff around the neck and the bun roll around the middle create a sense of expanded space. The magnificently detailed gloves may be used for falconry, warmth, challenging someone to a duel, or simple display. La volta is a popular dance which looks singularly athletic and odd to our eyes. The lord is lifting the lady by the base of her rigid fatheringale.

I am part of a glorious cosmic order.
I stand assured and firm upon the earth,
And am called up by an unfolding star.
I walk one tiny step below the angels.
I move with confidence toward godliness.
I am the bridge between all matter and spirit.
I am a courtier, adventurer, poet, swordsman,
A wit, philosopher, musician, and gentleman (*or* lady)
I sing and dance to the music of the spheres.
I know that music both heals and transforms.
I hunger for my life and will devour it.
Upon this garden earth, I plant my seeds.
My thoughts are great, and so will be my deeds!

Well done! Now, doth answer thy question? Say these words aloud daily, and someday, perchance, thou wilt be worthy to be called Elizabethan.

### What is your dominant mood?

Ours do swing like pendulum from dark to light, laughter to tears, and back. We are open to emotion and welcome change. We do place comedy in e'en the most tragic plays—as the Porter, forsooth, in *Macbeth* and the gravedigger in *Hamlet*—welcoming irony, counterpoint, and antithesis. A sad lament will have a humorous turn of phrase. A joyous paean will be shadowed with dark, disturbing images. We do savor all the turns the heart can rightly urge, *save two*. Whining and sullenness we do not countenance. These must be supplanted with turns more lively. 'Tis better to be merry or weep than chide or pout.

### Are there forces beyond your control?

Four humors of the body (melancholy, phlegm, blood, and choler) dominate moods, and the position of the stars change fortunes and feelings. Harmony is sought and Chaos avoided.

### Who are your idols?

*They are never alone that are accompanied with noble thoughts.*
    —SIR PHILIP SIDNEY

Gloriana sets the tone for majesty. Her favorites (Essex, Raleigh, Leicester) be briefly imitated 'til out of favor. Exemplary lives find lasting admiration. Belike the most admired man of our era is Sir Philip Sidney, who did die generously at war and was regarded as th'epitome of chivalry at court.

### What do you admire most?

*Silence is the virtue of fools.*    —FRANCIS BACON

Verbal eloquence be honored above all other accomplishments. To have another man say, "Roundly replied!" is to have won the day!

*What do you hope for?*

Our capacity to dream of honor, glory, wealth, and advancement knows no bounds. Why should it, when our lives exceed most men's dreams?

*How do you define sin?*

Sin is the corruption of God's creation. Man *is* corrupt and may attain salvation through living generously and faith. Sin is failing to battle for the seven virtues to win over the seven vices inside thyself.

*And justice?*

The word of a gentleman is oft' accepted in court of law without oath, so rank indeed hath privilege. Yet, for thousands of years, a poor man would ne'er be heard. Now at least he may speak. Pray he speak well, if he is in the right. And that the gentleman will show him mercy.

*What gets attention?*

Effectiveness of assertion!

*What are the value and uses of money?*

No character, in our plays, lacks sufficient means to survive. Money doth beget information, reward a service or a servant. 'Tis meet to have gold to travel painlessly or provide dowry. Greed is a sign of corruption. Our favorite money? 'Tis called a Sovereign.

*What is the place of God and the church in life?*

We believe in God and pray each day. He is not to be questioned. His servants are: Pope and Church of England, Catholics and Protestants forever arguing doctrine! Enough! God gave us his word, but 'tis not oft' well spoken.

*What kind of humor dominates?*

Laughter is our defiance of war, plague, age, and oppression. Laughter bursts forth as raucous, hearty, joyous release. During our most solemn event, some detail will go wrong and provoke laughter. Later we may well recall that moment as the best! We do love puns and language tricks, but love what thou call'st a "groaner" as much as more elevated and ironic turns of phrase. We take not ourselves too serious.

*How is fear defined?*

The greatest fear is desperate silence. We wear our hearts, not on our sleeve alone, but in our words. Our greatest *shared* fear is Chaos, which can bring down the whole of creation. We fear God, the Devil, evil spirits, the wrath of our Monarch and lesser leaders. We fear disease, famine, and death. We no longer fear the Spanish.

> 'Twas God, the Word that spake it,
> He took the Bread and brake it;
> And what the Word did make it,
> That I believe, and take it.
>                    —ELIZABETH I

*Whether I am doomed
to live or die, I can do
both like a prince.*

—JOHN WEBSTER

Fear, when the moment comes, giveth a man the change to prove his mettle.

## Structure

*Order exists. Humans must needs find it.*

### Who rules, and who follows?

Each species hath a natural leader. For us, 'tis Elizabeth; for the angels, God; for animals, the lion; for birds, the eagle; for trees, the oak; and down through the Great Chain of Being, to plants and basest minerals. Each of us doth know where we stand 'twixt Elizabeth and scullery maid. The body human has three monarchs: liver, heart, and brain. The world is made up of four ruling elements: earth, water, air, and fire. Each class excels all others in some single way. E'en the lowly stone hath the glory t'exceed the rest in strength and durability. The chain looks thus:

| | |
|---|---|
| God | perfection |
| angels/ether | pure understanding |
| stars | fortune |
| elements | being |
| man | feeling and under-<br>    standing |
| animals | sensation |
| plants | growth |
| metals | durability |

*I have the body of a
weak and feeble
woman, but I have the
heart and stomach of a
king, and of a king of
England too.*

—ELIZABETH I

Man is in the middle, without perfection or durability, but central to the chain. His position is most difficult *and* most full of recompense. Our men be led by a woman, and we believe in the Divine Right of Kings.

Justice runs quick and brutal to slow and soft, but it will come. Beheadings are widely viewed and worthily bethought as reminders of consequence! Nobles be beheaded, low-class felons hung.

### What is the pattern of daily life and family?

Our country's women be much freer than those of Europe. Visitors are shocked that they may kiss our wives and daughters in friendship and find it antic that 'tis not customary t'invite a man to dine without also inviting his wife. Women may go out (in groups) unescorted, yea, e'en to public ale houses. Widows assume full ownership and control of property. Some run businesses. Women be legal equal of men betimes, 'til they marry. At that time they become property.

*How is etiquette set? How flexible is it?*

True spirit of courtesy exceeds how a man stands or holds his knife. We ask ourselves if the behavior was honorable, not if it broke some rule.

*And education?*

For the first time, half our population is literate! School hours are long, with arduous copying major means for learning. Boarding schools are new, teaching Latin, English grammar, music, logic, rhetoric, geography, history, mythology, Hebrew, Greek, Italian, French, penmanship, reading aloud, and drawing. Queen Elizabeth is master of all of these, yea, and Spanish and astronomy besides! Her work with her tutor, Roger Ascham, did begin when she was three, and she is superior to most men in learning.

*There is not such whetstone to sharpen a good wit and encourage a will to learning as is praise.*
—ROGER ASCHAM

*What professions dominate?*

'Tis an exacting office being lord or lady, with huge staff to lead and lands to tend. Work doth involve foreign service, collecting of debts, leasing of lands, and military obligations. Below nobility is merchant class, working class (artisans, shopkeepers, actors) and underclass (servants, laborers, shepherds, vagabonds). The Black Death moved us from farming to shearing sheep, where one man can fill the space of twenty if he but tend flocks instead of crops.

## Beauty

*Where'er light shines is beauty to be found.*

*What is the look most aspired to?*

Fair be favored over dark. Some heroes fall in love with raven-haired beauties but ask themselves, "Wherefore?" Both sexes wish to deport themselves tall. Long waists, legs, and necks are envied. Men must have strong, well-formed legs.

*Who are the contemporary ideals?*

The Queen do be much envied for her slim waist, kept all these years. Hair most coveted is red or blonde curls. Ye should by now know why. 'Twill ne'er hang from a woman's head nor touch her face, but be swept up and decorated. Wenches' faces strive for fair, pale, smooth skin, high forehead, widow's peak, red lips, and startling, lively eyes. Within the volume of fabric worn, graceful hands and feet gain much attention when they emerge. Perchance because we see so little, we cherish each glance. Men's hosed legs be the only full appendage exposed.

*What part does fitness play in attractiveness?*

We be active, dancing and riding for hours on end, practicing with spirit to excel at both. In our parlance, the word "proper," by the by, as in "he will make a proper man," doth note the physical attributes of the man, not his manners. Elizabeth, with ever eye to the future, exercises each morning by dancing our most strenuous dance, the galliard, six to seven times.

*Which colors and shapes are favored?*

Splendor is beloved—gold, black, white, and silver—heavily bejeweled. Dark silks and velvets reflect and absorb light, like the lining of a jewel box. Brighter colors flash through slashed openings or from attached precious stones. 'Tis not meet to look less than thou art. The new looking glasses (of polished metal) are in high favor.

*Is nature altered in order to create beauty?*

Belike the issue can best be summed up by this exchange 'tween Viola and Olivia in *Twelfth Night*. Olivia unveils herself and, quoth she, "Tis not well done?" Viola doth reply, "Excellently done, if God did all." Olivia, after a moment of recovery from this sly retort, and the inevitable laugh it doth provoke from the audience, assures her it is natural and, quoth she, "will endure wind and weather." Often, in truth, 'tis excellently well done, but 'twill not endure wind and weather. Enough said.

*How is taste defined, and what artistic expression is favored?*

True love is a durable fire,
In the mind ever burning,
Never sick, never old, never dead,
From itself never turning.
—SIR WALTER RALEIGH

Fie on thy word "taste," Bartonio. If 'tis done well enough, 'tis done well! Nothing is deemed vulgar, crude, or unseemly, if it hath great accomplishment. By this hand, all should'st be able to write a sonnet, sing a madrigal, play a lute, declare a position, or ride a horse. Those with imagination move beyond these trifles. A pox on any who fool who would do less!

## Sex

*In life's great banquet, sex may be any course,*
*In sooth, it may perchance replace the meal.*

*How significant a part of the collective consciousness is sex?*

Only a worthy quest will replace lewd bawdry in our lives. Mating be openly talked and joked about. E'en our young virgins do oft' engage in ribald repartee.

*What are considered turn-ons and turn-offs?*

Men learn to swagger and display with grace and must be quick of wit and strong of body. A woman is soft of demeanor, but sharp of mind, quick of tongue, lively of spirit, and graceful of movement. Both must appear modest *and* assertive. The shrinking violet hath no place in our garden.

### *What is the courtship/seduction ritual?*

Each man doth court the Queen at all times. Thus, the "courting" of the mistress of any manor be accepted ritual. Serenading, music, poetry, flowers, tokens, missives, and passionate declarations abound. There is no tactic ye employ now in a pinch that we do not employ as a matter of course. Speak foreign languages to woo thy beloved, and perfumed sheets may keep her in thy bed, which be a massive, carved oak masterwork, costly and elaborately furnished, often with an embroidered canopy. 'Tis passed on to future generations or friends, *not* to one's spouse. Yet, a patch of grass will do as well. A merry chase is good sport, and consummation devoutly to be wished.

### *How much tolerance is there for infidelity?*

Our plays talk of horns, meaning cuckolds. We jest about unfaithfulness and believe if a man does not "serve" his woman well, she may leave him with horns on his head growing longer at each of her indiscretions. Infidelity between a man and woman each married to others be not likely. Servants be more in danger than the lady or lord of the manor nearby. If thy mate do tire of thee, watch more for poison in thy cup or help falling down the stair than for divorce court.

### *Is there any suppression of sexuality?*

We have such tolerance for excess and appetite that few would judge another as desiring too much. We call our brothels "stews." Elizabeth hath decreed a woman cannot be a prostitute before the age of forty. There be prudes aplenty, but be they beloved of our playwrights? Not a whit.

## Recreation

### *Each triumph doth deserve a celebration.*

### *What is most people's idea of fun?*

At a stroke, merriment can transport an ordinary moment into nimble playfulness, word game, wit, delightful tune, or joke reverberating in the public square. "Fun" (as thou call'st it, a tiny word for such bountiful pleasure) doth await 'round every corner, eager for discovery. Every person plays an instrument, singing rounds is common family pastime, and dancing so honored that Elizabeth hath promoted courtiers for no other deed save brilliant leaps and turns.

### What would be an ideal social occasion?

Rejoicing o'er a recent victory—our ships at sea, our wits at court or our swains at wooing—is cause for celebration. A nuptial? 'Tis e'en greater cause! We celebrate many festivals you do not—The Vigil of St. John the Baptist (Midsummer's Eve), Harvest, Lord of Misrule (Twelfth Night), Feast of the Virgin, Shrove Tuesday, St. George's Day, Tournament Day, and May Day. And, Lord warrant us, we *create* occasion for more! The Puritans do hate it when we dance around the Maypole. Fie on them.

### Are you doers or watchers?

We devour life. The hunt (deer and hare) is sport of Kings, alas, of outlaws and poachers as well. Hyde Park be still wild enough for Elizabeth to hunt therein. Though every boy over age seven must, by law, be taught how to shoot bow and arrow, 'tis now practiced for pure pleasure. Hitting of bull's-eye with arrow or tongue—we like it well. We love to watch blood shed: cockfighting (two game cocks let loose on a chained animal), baiting (divers dogs let loose on a chained bear, bull, or badger), or public executions (hangings, beheadings, and burnings). Thou might'st spot thirty heads o'er the bridge on the way to the theatre and amuse thyself attempting to identify them! Baitings cost a penny. Hangings are free.

Elizabeth composes music and verse and plays the virginal. Sit and wait for *others* to entertain her? Fie! 'Twould not do for our good Bess! Since 'tis not thought seemly for nobility to sign their name and be credited, all do thus for pure joy, without thought of honor.

### What are common shared pastimes?

Lord warrant us! Outdoors there be donkey and horse racing, cudgeling, wrestling, tennis, eating contests, sack and wheelbarrow races, lawn bowling, boxing, greased pig chases, and silly sports, such as grinning through a horse collar—with funniest grin winning.

Football is violent by your standards. We bother not with team number limits, lines, or penalized fouls. In fact, it suffice us to forego most rules altogether. Entire villages and districts may challenge each other. If the Spanish had watched us play football, they would ne'er e'en have considered war. Falconry is high sport among the gentry, and pets are loved. Our queen has six lions, one lioness, one wolf, one tiger, and e'en a porcupine. Tamer mortals have tamer creatures.

Inside we play bells, board games, dice, and cards. Sewing (crewel, lace, tapestry, appliqué, quilting, braid, and embroidery) hath reached undreamed-of heights. Yet list, the most loved pastime of all, I warrant thee, is going to the theatre! Nie unto twenty thousand, or one-tenth of the population, attend public performances, and a like number private ones.

### What foods are eaten, and what is food's role in society?

Potatoes (from Raleigh's American expedition), figs, apricots, and currants newly visit our gardens. At eleven o'clock in the morning we devour hot food—beef, mutton, lamb, veal, hare, eel, salmon, duck, rabbit, pheasant, pigeon, rook, pig, turkey, quail, partridge, woodcock, capon, seagull, blackbird, lark, peacock, meat pies, sausages, breads, butter, cheese, boiled vegetables, fruits, and puddings served on pewter or silver service. Forks are still rare. Jupiter! Was not piercing the animal once, when we killed it, enough?! A vexation to keep stabbing it, say I!

*And beverages?*

Wine and sack are now oft' imported, but ale houses exist on every corner and beer is the true beverage of our people. By my troth, I have a great thirst. Methinks this 'interview,' as you call it, sufficient reason for celebration. Invite thy friends, and we shall feast! Let all who come ask away! We shall dine and dance and 'interview' 'til the lark beckons the dawn! We shall . . . ah, no, I cannot. I hear my muse calling me. Forgive me, friend. I must return to my time and seek my destiny. I will leave some jottings to assist thee in the rest, Bartonio! Myself must write a sonnet for my beloved and deliver it myself upon the moors. Fare thee well. Rest you merry. I go! [*Exit in smoke.*]

## SIGHT

*As we do march forth, all the world takes note.*

Our most dazzling rock star could be eclipsed, both in personal adornment and in sense of self, by a resplendent Elizabethan lord or lady making an entrance. Only a few comedies are likely to be costumed in authentic Elizabethan garb, because the extravagant padding, called *bombast,* makes actors resemble hockey players. Elements included in most productions, usually with modifications, follow.

1. Men
   - *Head.* Hair is collar-length. Trimmed beard and mustache are for mature men; young men are clean-shaven. Hats are worn inside and are flat and usually round, with notched brims. A stiff ruff frames the throat.
   - *Torso.* A white oversized shirt, shirred at the neck and wrists, may be worn under a *jerkin,* a type of sleeveless vest. A *doublet* (close-fitting jacket) may top a waistcoat. The *codpiece,* which originates innocently as a practical triangle that fills the crotch area between the tops of hose, is tied to the waist by *points* (laces). Codpieces develop, however, into ostentatious, extravagant works of art, often stuffed and sometimes slashed, bejeweled, and bedecked.
   - *Overgarments.* Older characters may wear a long overcoat with a huge collar, often a fur collar. Capes of various kinds—long,

Possible Elizabethan looks. Most Elizabethan productions are set in earlier periods because the look is more graceful to a present-day audience. Costumes can range from the early Gothic period through High Renaissance

(probably the most popular choice) and the Tudor period preceding Elizabeth's reign.

short, draped, or stiff—are often worn over one shoulder. Usually they are shaped like full circles. A soldier often wears one small piece of his armor to remind others of his profession.

- *Feet.* Shoes are made of soft leather or velvet and may be flat, with no heels. Boots are loose enough to turn down or reach to the upper leg and are held by straps to the doublet.

2. Women
   - *Head.* Women in the early Elizabethan period part the hair in the middle and wear a heart-shaped cap. At the end of the period the hair is curled, ribboned, plumed, and bejeweled. Wigs are popular. Ruffs, the major distinguishing feature of the period, develop from one inch to nine. Wrist ruffs often accompany.
   - *Torso.* The garment consists of a chemise with low bodice and a kirtle (petticoat) stretched tightly over stays and hoops. A *farthingale* (hooped petticoat supporting the shape of the skirt), *basquine* (corset to shape the bodice), and a stomacher (embroidered or jeweled center front section) may be among the encumbrances. Corsets are called *bodies,* later to become *bodice.* Some are made of steel! A combination of overskirt and underskirt may also be worn. Early in the period, the overgown is bell-shaped; later, the enormous farthingale look becomes popular. Sleeve treatment changes from wide openings pulled back at the elbows (*angel wings*) to puffed leg o'muttons.
   - *Feet.* Soft slippers are gradually replaced by heels to add stature.

3. Both sexes
   - Pieces of clothing may be tied together with points.
   - Earrings, brooches, chains, and rings are favored by both sexes, the male wearing one earring, often a pear-shaped pearl drop. Rings may be worn on all four fingers and thumbs.
   - Anyone might carry a flat fan, decorative money pouch, or a *pomander* (an orange or apple stuffed with cloves to keep "bad aires" away). These items may hang from the waist.
   - Gloves are works of art, with gauntlet cuffs that are heavily embroidered, often bejeweled and fringed, in leather of many possible colors. Gloves are also favored gifts.

### Movement and Contact

An enormous sense of self and the bulk of fabric contribute to assertive, direct and commanding moves. Anything inconsequential would be altogether lost across the room and fail to suit the spirit of the times. The following bows and curtsies are often used in production. They bridge the gap of several centuries.

*Men's Bow.*   Step forward on the left foot, and lift the torso high to signal that the bow is about to take place. Keeping the left leg extended and relatively straight in front, "sit" on the bending right leg (which has formed a forty-five-degree angle), keeping the torso lifted. Keep the eyes on the person to whom you are bowing. At the last minute, dip the eyes down, and depending on the amount of obeisance being paid, bow the head, upper torso, or more. Return the upper portion of the body, the eyes first, and then move to a standing position. Resist the temptation to incline the upper body too early and too far and to stick the buttocks out. For much of the bow, you appear in upper body, as though you were on horseback. You may use the hand crossing the body to remove and replace the hat during this maneuver. The other hand may guide the sword at your side up and back, so that it does not scrape the floor. The free hand may also indulge in a salute or personal flourish of some kind.

*Women's Curtsy.*   Hold the upper body as described above. Keep the torso high, and let the legs do almost all of the work until the curtsy is nearly complete. After the initial step forward, move the right leg close behind and beneath the left. The left will be bent when the curtsy is completed; the right supports the body's weight, either just beneath the left or with the right knee touching the floor. Face the arms inward, and either move them up and out like wings as the bow is completed or hold them in and keep the palms also facing. Hand moves may be personalized.

Bows and curtsies range from deep and close to the floor (in honoring the monarch) to slight (with only the smallest tilt of the head and a quick lowering of the eyes) in a perfunctory acknowledgment of an equal or of someone of whom you are suspicious and with whom you wish to lose eye contact only momentarily.

*Hand Kissing.*   Keeping the arm rounded, the woman offers her hand, palm facing downward. The man takes it lightly in his own. He kneels very slightly, his eyes locked on hers. He lifts the hand to his lips and looks down only at the instant of hand to lip contact. (In history, the lips sometimes did not actually touch the hand, but in production they usually do.) Then he reverses the movement exactly. The temptation is to lean too far inward and dive for the hand instead of lifting it toward the body or to spend too much time looking at the hand and not enough time looking into the eyes of the lady.

*Reverence.*   Kissing one's own hand (or pretending to with an air kiss) and extending it to another is a highly respectful tribute or greeting. It is

Elizabethan bows and curtsies. These movements are theatrical exaggerations often chosen in production. Note that the bows may be modified or exaggereated by the depth of the dip and the size of the flourish. The Elizabethan bows provide the basis for those employed in subsequent periods.

---

always done at the start and end of a dance but may be done at countless other moments. The *top* of the palm is kissed, and flourishes may be added.

## SOUND

*This Mother tongue resounds second to none.*

The authentic sound of the period is a guttural, full, earthy dialect. Great weight is placed on consonants, including rolled hard *r*'s, and vowels are intensely colored. Pitch often changes on the vowel. Elizabethan speech sounds like a thick Scottish brogue mixed with American Appalachian. It bears *no* resemblance to modern upper-class British speech, often called *received* or *Oxfordian speech*. Elizabethan speech is highly expressive; words are both caressed and punched.

Would you like to sound like a real Elizabethan? Here are the basics to try in a speech. Remember to employ hard consonants and high energy.

1.  Replace the "aw" sound with "aa." For example, "want" rhymes with "pant" and "water" with "hatter."
2.  "Take" sounds like "tek" ("make" like "mek" and "table" like "teble"). Draw out the "eh" sound.
3.  "Head" sounds like "haid" ("dead" like "daid," "bread" like "braid").
4.  "I" sounds like "uh-ee" ("my" like "muh-ee," "fly" like "fluh-ee").
5.  "Mercy" sounds like "maircy," with a very hard *r*.
6.  "Fair" has a flat *a* and "uh-ee" sound: "faa-er."
7.  "Neither" sounds like "nayther."
8.  "Day" has a long *i* and short *a*: "daa-ee."
9.  "Lord" sounds like "loord" ("word" like "woord," "come," like "coom").
10. "Down" sounds like "duh-oon" and "house" like "huh-oos."
11. "Cup" sounds like "coop" ("up" like "oop," "cut" like "coot").
12. "Love" sounds like "luv."

Read aloud a speech you are working on (or use one from Chapter 3) with the above sounds. Remember the force and relish when you return to standard speech, and let it help you exorcise once and for all any attempt to sound high-tone.

*[A player] adds grace to the poet's labours: for what in the poet is but ditty, in him is both ditty and music.*

—JOHN WEBSTER

## Elizabethan Language Guide

Anywhere you go, you try to learn the local way of speaking to fit in and communicate. Here are some examples from Shakespeare and his contemporaries.

### *Forms of Address*
**Respect**

| | | |
|---|---|---|
| My lord (My lady) | Friend | Young gentleman |
| Reverend sir (madam) | Most worthy sir (madam) | (Fair lady) |
| Gracious__ | Lad *or* Youth | Learned, honored__ |
| | | Gentles |

**Honor**

| | | |
|---|---|---|
| Your grace | My commander | Great King or |
| Your worship | Your highness | Queen |
| Most royal majesty | Dear sovereign | Most honored lord |
| My liege | | |

**Familiarity**

| | | |
|---|---|---|
| Wench | Fellow | Kinsman |
| Mate | Sweet | Cousin *or* Coz |

**Disdain**

| | | |
|---|---|---|
| Fool | Clown | Dunce |
| Sot | Wretch | Wretched one |
| Strumpet | Harlot | Hag |
| Whoreson villain | Foul devil | Viper |
| Minion | Idle creature | Dissembler |
| Knave | Rogue | Pedant |

*Greetings*

| | | |
|---|---|---|
| What ho? | Holla! | Hark! |
| I pray you . . . | Save you! | How now? |
| Well met | Happily met | Well o'erta'en |
| How dost thou? | Good morrow | Good day |
| Salutations | Happiness | Hail |
| Good day | Good even | Gooden |
| Good dawning | Good time of day | God save you |
| I bid you welcome | Joy and comfort | Greetings to you |

*Good-byes*

| | | |
|---|---|---|
| Farewell | Fare thee well | Peace be with you |
| Rest you merry | Give you good night | May we meet again |
| I take leave | | I will anon |
| We will haste us away | I have done | I go from hence |
| | Presently away | I will hie |
| We will here part | I go | I must attend |
| To__will I | I am resolved | Come ho |
| Let us thither | Let us after | Let us not lack thy company |
| Follow me thence | Let us remove | |

*Dismissals*

| | | |
|---|---|---|
| Be gone | Tarry not | I acquit thee |
| Get thee gone | You have leave | Go tread the path that thou shalt ne'er return |
| Depart | Get thee from my sight | |
| I alone will stay | | |
| I weary of you | Dispatch | |
| Remove thyself | No longer stay | |

*Commands*

**Action**

| | | |
|---|---|---|
| Fetch him (her, them) hither | Call her hence | Give him tending |
| | Call them forth | Proceed |
| Bear them thence | Lend thy hand | Stand forth |
| Attend him | Let him approach | Apply thyself to our intent |
| Approach | Prove it so | |
| Bid them welcome | Provide yourself | I charge thee speak |
| Look to 't | Hie thee hither | |

**Pause**

| | | |
|---|---|---|
| Peace | Stir not | Relent |
| Forbear | Pause awhile | Cease |
| No more | Disturb me not | Leave_____ing so |
| Speak not | Vex not | Press me not |
| Mend your speech | Mark me | Mark you that |
| Hear me | Give me audience | A word |
| Give us leave | Stay your thanks | Tarry |
| Behold | Repair thy wit | |

**Mood**

| | | |
|---|---|---|
| Be of good cheer | Be merry | Live in hope |

*Disagreement*

| | | |
|---|---|---|
| 'Tis not so | No, nor is it meet | I think not so |
| Thou'rt made to say it | A false conclusion | I do defy thee |
| | Thou liest | I know not that |
| Believe not all | 'Tis to be doubted | 'Tis none of mine |
| That follows not | It cannot be | Not a whit |
| Never | Talk not so | Fie, fie |
| I do protest | Go to | I will none |
| That is no matter | I care not | Tempt me not |
| You do mistake your business | 'Twould not do | Nay |
| | I'll no more | |
| I am for no more | Never so | |

*Agreement*

**Praise**

| | | |
|---|---|---|
| Fairly spoke | Nobly spoken | Well said |
| Well urged | Worthily be-thought | Roundly replied |
| Excellent! | | Thou hast hit it |
| I do commend thy choice | A nimble wit | Amen |
| | 'Tis most credible | |

**Assent**

| | | |
|---|---|---|
| Perchance | Most like | 'Tis thus |
| We are agreed thus | 'Tis so then | I think it so |
| It likes me well | It pleaseth me | It shall suffice me |
| I am resolved | I embrace it | Yea, at all points |
| We judge no less | I doubt not that | Yea, in good faith |
| My physic says aye | I believe thee | 'Tis probable |
| 'Tis as thou sayest | That ever holds | I think it well |
| So shall I | I shall see it done | So be it |
| I am for you | Ay, marry | Amen |

*Questions*
**Who**

| | | |
|---|---|---|
| Who calls? | Of what parentage art thou? | Who hath done this? |
| What's he comes here? | Of what person-age? | From whom come thou? |
| Who's within? | Who servest thou? | |

**What**

| | | |
|---|---|---|
| What cheer? | What find I here? | What would you? |
| What is your will? | What wilt thou do? | What make you here? |
| What news? | What sayest thou? | Thy request? |
| What means this? | What is thy pas-sion? | |
| What sport to-night? | | |

**Why**

| | | |
|---|---|---|
| Why so? | Where's your argu-ment? | Why dost thou? |
| Why_____you so? | Thy reason? | Thy purpose? |
| Thy cause? | How follows that? | |
| Wherefore? | | |

**Where**

| | | |
|---|---|---|
| Where were you bred? | Whence camest thou? | Upon what ground stand we? |
| Whither bound? | What place is this? | Upon what ground stand we? |

**How**

| | | |
|---|---|---|
| How fair you? | How know you? | How camest thou hither? |
| How is't with you? | How now? | How say you? |

**Others**

| | | |
|---|---|---|
| Wilt come? | Dost call? | Art thou resolved? |
| Shall'st go_____? | Did'st note? | Is't come to this? |
| Dost thou hear? | Must it be so? | Say you so? |

*Oaths*

| | | |
|---|---|---|
| Alas! | Alack! | Jove! |
| Jupiter! | Zounds! | Cupid have mercy! |
| Od's my life! | Gramercy! | Woe the while! |
| Vexations! | Lord warrant us! | O ye gods! |
| Christ's mother! | A god's name! | A pox on you! |

*Parentheses*

| | | |
|---|---|---|
| As I do live | As I bethink me | By mine honor |
| In faith | By my troth | In good earnest |

I warrant you        I'll stand to 't        By yonder___
If there be truth in  By this hand          In sooth
  sight              Sirrah                So please you
If fortune please     Marry sir
Albeit               Whilst we breathe

*Other Common Expressions*

| **Modern term** | **Elizabethan term** |
| --- | --- |
| Mr. | Master |
| Ms. | Mistress |
| Female (*familiar but not at all insulting*) | Wench |
| Ladies and Gentlemen | Gentles |
| Please | Prithee *or* Pray |
| No kidding *or* really | Forsooth |
| Excuse me | Pardon *or* Cry you mercy |
| Before | Ere |
| Wow | Marry |
| Maybe | Belike |
| Various *or* all different | Divers |
| Later | Anon |
| Nag, rag, scold | Chide |
| Bizarre *or* crazy | Antic |
| I said | Quoth I |
| She said | Quoth she |
| You (*intimate; as sentence subject*) | Thou |
| You (*intimate; as object*) | Thee |
| Your (*intimate; before consonant*) | Thy |
| Your (*intimate; before vowel*) | Thine (*same with* my *and* mine) |
| Thou *or* you *plural* | Ye |
| Buddy, Pal, *or* Buster (*insult addresses to strangers*) | Sirrah *or* Fellow |

## Music and Dance

Every well-educated person in this period can sight-read music, which is often printed on a grand scale so that several singers can read it at once. Minstrels are common both at court and in the countryside. Extraordinary music, from glorious sacred madrigals to bawdy tavern rounds, pervades daily life. Composers work in all forms. Thirty-two of Shakespeare's thirty-seven plays have direct references to music.

The most popular form of music is the *ayre,* a song composed for single voice, often self-accompanied by lute or viol. The *madrigal* is a complicated piece for two to eight voices sung a cappella, often around a table, as part of a social function. Also popular are the consort, or chamber music, and contrapuntal, polyphonic, and homophonic compositions.

One popular instrument is the *recorder,* a vertical flute that produces a soft, woody sound. It comes in various sizes—soprano, alto, tenor, and bass. The most common of all instruments and the most popular instrument for the home is the *lute,* a small pear-shaped harp with six to thirteen strings, some doubled. The *virginal* resembles a small harpsichord and is often played by young women (or "virgins," including You Know Who). The *viol,* a forerunner of the violin, is suitable for polyphonic music. It has four to five strings and is held in the crook of the arm instead of under the chin. Other popular instruments are the *cornetto,* a loud processional instrument with clarinet body and trumpet mouthpiece that produces a buzzing sound; the *cithern,* the *bandore (pandora)* and the *mandolin,* forerunners of the guitar that have long necks and hollow-sounding boxes; the *sackbut,* a forerunner of the trombone; and the drum, tambourine, harp, and organ. In the theatre, the most popular musical choice is the *broken consort* with wind and string instruments mixing tone colors for expressive, exciting, and moody effects.

Dancing varies from loosely organized activity on the village green to an art practiced at court under the tutelage of experts. Popular slow dances include processionals such as the *basse,* a French promenade led by musicians; the *pavane,* a grave and majestic dance, which literally means "parade"; and the *allemande,* a stately German dance whose moves range from a pronounced goose step to a lighter, more delicate triple-time step. Faster dances include *la volta* (a risqué Provençal dance in which men thrust women into the air), *corranto* (faster Italian dance, light and lively and low to the ground), *galliard* (the dance most representative of the Elizabethan spirit, with leaps and pliés in the air; Shakespeare calls it the *syncopace*), and *canaries* (challenge dances, in which each sex tries to outdo the other). Ring and round dances, such as the *bralle,* the jig, and Morris dances, complete this rich tapestry of dance, from dignified to bawdy.

Dance is symbolic of the universe. Leaps and turns represent the cosmos, circles the continued passage of the globe and the circling of the sun. Because it is believed that the sun moves clockwise, each dance begins on the left foot, and circles move to the left. Only witches dancing in covens move counterclockwise, the "wrong" way.

## KEYS TO THE WORLD

### Images

When the word *Elizabethan* comes to mind, contradictory and lively images emerge:

*When the iron is hot, strike.* —JOHN HEYWOOD

Virile men and graceful women
Men and women who are dignified, hearty, robust, expansive, energetic, intimidating, bold, both formal and informal, bawdy, flirtatious, sensual, powerful, fluid, balanced, and vigorous
Life as a cause for celebration
Violence as daily and inevitable
Heavy perfumes, sauces, and fabric; rich, dense, voluptuous sensations
Blood and guts, thunder and lightning
Exquisite quiet dawns after turbulent nights
Famous theatres: Rose, Swan, Globe, and Fortune
Vocal music with echoes, alternations, and oppositions
Machiavelli's *The Prince*
Leonardo da Vinci's pageant costume designs
Raphael's Vatican frescoes
Hatfield House
Benvenuto Cellini's *Saltcellar of Francis I*
Tintoretto's painting *The Last Supper*
Furniture designs of Giovanni Nossemi
Madrigals of William Byrd, Thomas Morley, Thomas Tomkins, Thomas Weelkes, and Orlando Gibbons; harpsichord compositions of Byrd and Morley
John Dowland's exquisite creations for the lute
Individuality, virtuosity, zest, adventure

### Social Success and Suicide

The capacity to praise is so vital to simple social survival that there are many possible choices for the ultimate compliment. This is perhaps the best choice:

The heavens such grace doth lend thee, that thine eyes can cure the blind.

This line is the best choice because it establishes a connection between the recipient and heaven, which gives the recipient the power to perform miracles with *very little effort*.

In the devastating war of words, the following might be designated the ultimate insult:

In his sleep he does little harm, save to his bedclothes about him.

This insult is more cutting than an overtly venomous, vituperative remark, because it characterizes the recipient as inconsequential and silly, not even worth addressing directly. The subject probably drools and wets the bed. The insult is a throw-away remark tossed en route to more significant altercations.

All aspire to excel at praise and verbal warfare. Here is a collection of the lowest insults and highest praise from an age in which everyone is expected to master both:

*Insults*
You cream-faced loon
You bloody, bawdy villain
You whoreson, clap-eared knave
You remorseless, treacherous, lecherous, kindless villain
You decrepit wrangling miser, you base ignoble wretch
You dwarf, you minimus
You brawling, blasphemous, uncharitable dog
You gross lout, you mindless slave
You caterpillar of the commonwealth, you politician
You worshiper of idiots
You dull, unfeeling barren ignorance
You whimpering, whoremaster fool
You mangled work of nature, you scurvy knave
You ignorant, long-tongued, babbling gossip
You old, withered crab tree
You irksome, brawling, scolding pestilence
You base, vile thing, you petty scrap
You filching, pilfering snatcher
You injurious, tedious wasp
You common gamester to the camp
You country copulative
You tiresome, wrangling pedant
You fawning greyhound, you petty trafficker
You base, fawning spaniel
You infectious pestilence
You untutored churl
You son and heir of a mongrel bitch
You smiling, smooth, detested parasite

You lunatic, lean-witted fool
You painted Maypole
You thing of no bowels
You silly, sanctimonious ape of form
You low-spirited swain, you base minnow
You unlettered, small-knowing soul, you shallow vassal
You rank weed, ready to be rooted out
You puffed and reckless libertine
You lascivious, fat-kidneyed rascal
You ugly, venomous toad
You foul defacer of God's handiwork
You tainted harlot, crammed with wickedness
You living dead man
You dull and muddy mettled rascal
You impudent, tattered prodigal
You contaminated, base, and misbegotten sot
You close contriver of all harms
You cold porridge
You botcher's apprentice
You base, ignoble wretch
You juggler, you canker blossom, you thief of love
You puppet

*Praise*
Age cannot wither thee, nor custom stale thy infinite variety.
Thou dost teach the torches to burn bright.
Thy beauty's majesty confounds the tongue and makes the senses
    rough.
Thou art far fairer than any tongue can name thee.
The all-seeing sun ne'er saw thy match since first the world begun.
To thine honors and thy valiant parts, I both my soul and fortunes
    consecrate.
Nothing ill can dwell in such a temple as thou art.
Thou hast the courtier's eye, the scholar's tongue, the soldier's
    sword.
Thou art as wise as thou art beautiful, as strong as thou art kind.
Thou walkest in eternal grace and with each step thy tread doth
    bless the ground beneath.
I gaze upon thee, adoringly, as the moon upon the water.
Thou mak'st each coming hour oe'rflow with joy, each minute full
    of wonder.
Thou art a lion that I am proud to hunt.
If thou wilt not love me, I will not love myself.
My love for thee is dearer than eyesight, space, or liberty.
Thou art as wise as thou art fair and true.
My wild heart could'st be tamed to thy loving hand.

The instant I first saw thee did my heart fly to thy service.

The four winds blow in from every coast renowned suitors, all vying for thy hand.

Thy hand is fair, yea whiter than the paper it writ on.

I bow to thee as a true subject to a splendid new-crowned monarch.

For you I would be trebled twenty times myself, a thousand times more fair, ten thousand times more rich.

I am giddy at the expectation of thy touch. Anticipation whirls me round and doth enchant my sense.

The silver moon shines not half so bright as doth thy face in giving light.

No book provides a study of such excellence, as doth the beauty of thy face.

Thine eyes sparkle the promethean fire and nourish all the world.

To serve thee doth make labor pleasure and turns mean tasks into noble delight.

Thou art perfect and peerless, created out of every other creature's best.

'Tis fresh morning with me when thou art by at night.

I might call thee a thing divine, for nothing in nature I ever saw so noble.

Except I be with thee, love, in the night, there is no music in the nightingale.

At the altar of thy beauty, I sacrifice my tears, my sighs, my heart.

Thy life is as tender to me as my own soul.

When my eyes did see thee first, I thought thou purg'd the air of pestilence.

Mine ear is much enamor'd of thy throat, so is mine eye enthrall'd to thy shape.

I'll pluck the wings from painted butterflies, / To fan the moonbeams from thy sleeping eyes.

Each act of thine is crowned in present deeds / So that, my love, all of your acts are queens.

Had I force and knowledge more than was ever man's, I would not prize them, without thy love.

Were I crown'd the most imperial monarch, I would not prize my crown above thy love.

Two of the fairest stars in all the heaven, having some business, do entreat thine eyes to twinkle in their spheres til they return.

Come what sorrow can, it cannot countervail the exchange of joy that one short minute gives me in thy sight.

To thine honors and thy valiant parts, I do my soul and fortunes consecrate.

More welcome are ye to my fortunes than my fortunes are to me. I give up all to have thy company.

I will live in thy heart, die in thy lap, and be buried in thy eyes.

Here comes my love, now heaven walks on earth.

O, thou that dost inhabit in my breast, leave not my mansion so long tenantless. Repair me with thy presence.

My thoughts do harbor with thee nightly. / Oh, could their master (mistress) come and go as lightly.

When I do look on thy perfections I lose all reason and I am struck blind.

Did my love til now? Forswear it sight.

For I ne'er saw true beauty till this night.

---

1. Divide into two teams, one called the Sun and the other the Moon.
2. Devise a competition to see which team is the superior deliverer of Elizabethan reviews.
3. Have an interlude first for praise, then for insults.
4. Either draw one of the phrases above, or have an uninvolved party point to the remark you are to speak just before you deliver it. Work with minimum preparation time and maximum inspiration.
5. Have a team of judges call each encounter between two insulters or two praisers, so that everyone knows the score as the competition continues.
6. Variation: Divide the list in half, providing each team its own remarks. Assign lines, and have each actor rehearse at least overnight, so that all encounters are between two well-prepared adversaries.
7. Discuss what means of delivery, beyond the words themselves, brings about victory in this type of exchange.

**E X E R C I S E**

**Praise and Insults**

---

To be a social success, you must

- Excel in all Renaissance virtues: scholar, soldier, poet, lover.
- Make music and verse at a moment's notice, with minimum provocation.
- Master Italian, Spanish, and French fashion and philosophy while claiming to prefer plain English virtue.
- Do all things fully, whether high or low, delicate or vulgar, angelic or animal. Go the distance.
- Create a giant circular glow around yourself. Make yourself resplendent any way you can.

You commit social suicide if you

- Have an opportunity to speak but fail to think of anything to say.
- Get caught being false or feigning in your vows of love or get caught breaking any promise.
- Shrink away from a challenge or be discovered as a coward.

- Fail to honor and reward excellence and royalty in others.
- Break your place in the cosmos and defy the stars.

## Masking

Elizabethans do not wear theatrical masks except in a masque, a peculiar combination of mummery, pageant, and entertainment, which offers an excuse for court nobles (who are not otherwise supposed to "act") to dress in elaborate disguise and honor the monarch. The plot is always allegorical, with the queen, compared flatteringly to some classical mythological figure, triumphing over evil. The grande finale is a spectacle of choreographed dances in which Gloriana herself makes occasional appearances. With the exception of great ladies, who wear a mask attached to a cord around the waist to protect the face from the sun, Elizabethans do not wear masks in daily life.

Elizabethans value feelings, desire to share them, and hide them when they are not ready to express them *well*. Fear, cowardice, and indecision are most hidden because least rewarded. Social masks give identities to live up to. Elizabethans portray themselves as *more* idealized and *less* vulnerable. The character always unmasks when alone with the audience in soliloquy.

Disguise is rampant. The five "breeches" heroines in Shakespeare (Rosalind, Viola, Imogen, Julia, and Portia) masquerade as boys (Ganymede, Cesario, Fidele, Sebastian, and Balthasar) for a portion of the play. The Navarrian lords in *Love's Labor's Lost* woo their ladies as Russians. Petruchio in *The Taming of the Shrew* masks himself in boorish attire for his wedding. The masked Montague boys crash the Capulet ball in *Romeo and Juliet*. Beatrice in *Much Ado about Nothing* uses her mask at the ball to talk about Benedick to his face. The mask of night is used for changing bed partners in *Measure for Measure* and *All's Well That Ends Well*. Edgar in *King Lear* disguises himself as Poor Tom to keep from being killed. Duke Vincentio in *Measure for Measure* pretends to be a friar so that he can examine at close quarters the corruption in his city. Disguise is always for a good end; a character must don the new identity to save a life, uncover evidence, or fulfill destiny. Deception is a path toward freedom.

## The Production

Current plans involve reconstructing the Globe Playhouse on its original site. Until this project is completed, we will not know what it feels like to perform in the original space—a great open stage nearly forty feet wide and twenty-nine feet deep, with up to seven entrances and exits, where every corner of one's field of vision is filled with up to three thousand spectators, none farther away than sixty feet and some close enough to touch. There are rough reconstructions of the *stages* of the Elizabethan period, but not of the *houses* surrounding them; actor/audience proximity is therefore still partly a mystery. Among modern spaces, a thrust stage with a large audience rake comes closest to the feel of the original.

Most productions are done on unit sets with platforms, staircases, and ramps but with no attempt to suggest locale. Scenes overlap; some actors exit while others enter. Lighting and music are used to smooth transitions, carve space, and shape time. Costuming is likely to be High Renaissance or another period whose style features a more relaxed and universal silhouette than Elizabethan. Costumes are likely to be the single most important visual element in the production.

### The Perfect Audience

The robust enthusiasm and active interaction of a modern rock concert or athletic event come closest to exemplifying the relationship between Elizabethan actors and their public. The reverent, intimidated audience at a present-day Shakespearean performance is remote from the spirited original. Actors, although spared the rude interruptions and distracting quarrels among the groundlings, may miss the vitality of an audience that knows it is not in church.

In some of your rehearsals, include interruptions from both ignorant louts and educated skeptics (played by other cast members, the director, and the staff) to get the feel of what could happen at any moment. Think of tiers of people—some who have paid one penny to stand in the pit, others two pennies to sit in the galleries, and still others three pennies for private boxes. You need passion and intensity to satisfy the groundlings but must be noble and dignified enough for the private boxes. Imagine them all eating and drinking freely. Then consider that if you are not sufficiently involved, eloquent, or interesting, your audience might stop you, turn to their own conversations, or even leave. Infuse the audience with boldness. Ask the questions in the soliloquies as though you really wanted an answer. Make the audience members feel as though they were absolutely your best friend. They will reward you with energy and power, carrying your performance to new heights. Imagine listeners who virtually insist on electrifying action, and give it to them.

### Contemporary Parallels

The late twentieth century shares these conditions with the late sixteenth:

- Music as a constant part of life, moving from background to foreground, but ever present, influencing and shaping events.

- A great love of exploration and adventure, a genuine pioneer spirit alert for new lands, planets, or galaxies to discover, conquer, and settle. Those who venture into unknown realms and return become heroes.

- An understanding that basic body chemistry determines to a remarkable degree one's physical and mental health and that "you are what you eat." For years we regarded the Elizabethan's theory of body humors as quaint and naïve. Now we know that fundamentally they were right.

- Huge energy and expense placed in entertainment and an almost manic sense of creating (even working at) fun.

- The existence of a plague that defies scientific knowledge and control, devastating a major portion of the population and creating unprecedented fear and paranoia.

- The belief that large cities are the center of life, along with the idealization of the beauty and peace of the country; constant turmoil over which we prefer and where we want to be.

- Living comfortably with contradictions as science and a high level of technology flourish along with astrology and spiritualism; being at ease with both rational thought and superstition, looking in all directions to explain life, feeling no need to be the same all the time.

- The importance of self-knowledge as a subject for study and of self-esteem as a goal.

- Belief in the individual and in assertiveness, spirit, and speaking out.

- An explosion of information. The early printing press parallels the computer in gathering and expanding knowledge. The languages (English then, computer language now) seem to have unlimited possibilities.

## THE OPEN SCENE: US AND THEM

One way to embrace the Elizabethan age is to experience an event from our world in their terms. The open scene is a common exercise in acting and directing classes. It stimulates imaginative *subtext,* since text is minimal. The contemporary lines can adapt to almost any situation, most obviously leaving home, substance abuse, or suicide, but myriad contexts are possible. In Elizabethan England, with magic, murder, royalty, and wonder in the air, possible situations for the Shakespearean lines compound even more.

| *Contemporary Open Scene* | *Shakespearean Open Scene* |
| --- | --- |
| "Oh." | "Alas." |
| "Yes." | "'Tis so." |
| "Why are you doing this?" | "Why dost thou this?" |
| "It's the best thing." | "'Tis foremost among choices." |
| "You can't mean it." | "Thou cans't not speak from the heart." |
| "No, I'm serious." | "Nay, I am in earnest." |
| "Please." | "Prithee, note me." |
| "What?" | "Wherefore?" |
| "What does this mean?" | "What meaning has this?" |
| "Nothing." | "None." |
| "Listen." | "Hear me." |
| "No." | "Nay." |
| "So different." | "'Tis wondrous strange." |
| "Not really." | "Not in truth." |
| "Oh." | "So." |
| "You're good." | "Thou art good." |
| "Forget it." | "Think not on't." |
| "What?" | "How now?" |
| "Go on." | "Proceed." |
| "I will." | "I shall" |

Elizabethan language differs from ours not only in word choice but also in the frequent choice of verse over prose:

*Shakespearean Open Verse Scene*

"You're here, I see. I had not thought to find you."
"I am intent to do the thing I must."

"Why do you feel that you must take this course?"
"It is the best that is now open to me."

"You cannot mean this truly in your heart."
"I mean it with my heart and my soul, too."

"I ask of thee that thou wilt hear my words."
"What can'st thou say that I do not now know?"

"What meaning can this have to change our lives?"
"It means no more nor less than simply nothing."

"I do implore that thou wilt hear my plea."
"I do refuse because I am decided."

"This is most strange and unfamiliar."
"Not so in truth. It merely is the same."

"I see what is, and that I must accept."
"You are as good as any human born."

"I do not wish for you to think on this."
"What shall I, then, my friend, if not on this?"

"Go now, and may God save you then from fright."
"I go, and strong, for I am in the right."

---

**E X E R C I S E**

**Open Scenes**

1. If you have never done an open scene project, devise a situation in contemporary language for the first scene above, concentrating on the subtext behind the text.
2. Identify what does and does not seem Elizabethan about the scene, and adapt it for the second scene. If you have already worked with open scenes, start here and devise an encounter within the world you have just learned.
3. Put the same scene into verse, so that you now have full lines of iambic pentameter written in Elizabethan language. Let your imagination run wild and tap into a whole new world.

---

## PLAYS AND PLAYWRIGHTS

Here are those scripts most often produced. Almost any play by Shakespeare is more likely to enter your life than any single script by any other writer of the period. Do not discount his brothers, however; the rest of Elizabethan drama offers some genuine thrills and chills.

| | |
|---|---|
| Beaumont, Francis, and John Fletcher | *The Knight of the Burning Pestle* (1607) |
| | *The Maid's Tragedy* (1667) |
| | *The Two Noble Kinsmen* (1594) |
| Dekker, Thomas | *The Shoemaker's Holiday* (1599) |
| Ford, John | *'Tis Pity She's a Whore* (1625) |
| Heywood, Thomas | *A Woman Killed with Kindness* (1603) |
| Jonson, Ben | *The Alchemist* (1610) |
| | *Bartholomew Fair* (1614) |
| | *Every Man in His Humour* (1598) |
| | *Volpone* (1605) |
| Kyd, Thomas | *The Spanish Tragedy* (1592) |
| Marlowe, Christopher | *Doctor Faustus* (1588) |
| | *Edward II* (1590) |

|  |  |
|---|---|
|  | *The Jew of Malta* (1588) |
|  | *Tamburlaine the Great* (1587) |
| Middleton,<br> Thomas | *The Changeling* (1623) |
| Shakespeare, Wil-<br> liam | *All's Well That Ends Well* (1602–1604) |
|  | *Antony and Cleopatra* (1605–1606) |
|  | *As You Like It* (1599–1600) |
|  | *The Comedy of Errors* (1588–1593) |
|  | *Coriolanus* (1607–1608) |
|  | *Cymbeline* (1609–1610) |
|  | *Hamlet* (1601–1602) |
|  | *Henry IV, Part 1* (1597–1598) |
|  | *Henry IV, Part 2* (1597–1598) |
|  | *Henry V* (1598–1599) |
|  | *Henry VI, Part 1* (1590–1592) |
|  | *Henry VI, Part 2* (1590–1592) |
|  | *Henry VI, Part 3* (1590–1592) |
|  | *Henry VIII* (1612–1613) |
|  | *Julius Caesar* (1599) |
|  | *King John* (1596–1597) |
|  | *King Lear* (1605–1606) |
|  | *Love's Labor's Lost* (1588–1594) |
|  | *Macbeth* (1605–1606) |
|  | *Measure for Measure* (1604) |
|  | *The Merchant of Venice* (1596–1597) |
|  | *The Merry Wives of Windsor* (1597–1601) |
|  | *A Midsummer Night's Dream* (1594–1596) |
|  | *Much Ado about Nothing* (1598–1600) |
|  | *Othello* (1603–1604) |
|  | *Pericles* (1608) |
|  | *Richard II* (1595) |
|  | *Richard III* (1592–1593) |
|  | *Romeo and Juliet* (1594–1596) |
|  | *The Taming of the Shrew* (1593–1594) |
|  | *The Tempest* (1611) |
|  | *Timon of Athens* (1605–1608) |
|  | *Titus Andronicus* (1592–1594) |
|  | *Troilus and Cressida* (1601–1602) |
|  | *Twelfth Night* (1599–1600) |
|  | *Two Gentlemen of Verona* (1593–1595) |
|  | *The Winter's Tale* (1610–1611) |
| Tourneur, Cyril | *The Revenger's Tragedy* (1607) |
| Webster, John | *The Duchess of Malfi* (1612) |
|  | *The White Devil* (1608) |

## SCENES

### Elizabethan Scenes

Although plays of this period are rarely produced (those of Shakespeare obviously excepted), they are virtual gold mines of material. The works as a whole may not suit the tastes of late twentieth-century audiences, but these isolated scenes are dynamic, hot, and startling in any time.

*The Changeling*
Beatrice, De Flores
The beautiful Beatrice and her disfigured servant play a game of sexual obsession.

*Doctor Faustus*
Faustus, Mephistopheles
As one of his experiments with magic, Faustus enters a dark grove where he conjures up a devil dressed like a friar.

*The Duchess of Malfi*
Duchess, Antonio
In spite of her brothers' warnings, the widowed duchess decides to remarry and chooses her humble secretary.
Duchess, Bosola
Hired by her wicked brothers, Bosola brings more terror to the Duchess than she had imagined possible.

*Edward II*
Edward, Isabella
The king rejects his queen in favor of his "favorite," Gaveston.

*The Jew of Malta*
Barabad, Abigail, Ithamore
Not even the innocent love of his daughter can stop the ruthless ambition of unscrupulous Barabad.

*The Maid's Tragedy*
Evadne, King
Forced to become the king's mistress, even in the presence of her own husband, Evadne vows to kill the king, using her known relationship with him to get past his guards and take his life.

*The Revenger's Tragedy*
Vendice, Hippolito
Because of the violation of his sister, the revenger undertakes to even the score.

*The Shoemaker's Holiday*
Lacy, Rafe
Disguised as a humble shoemaker, Lacy is able to enter the mayor's home and pursue his beloved.

*'Tis Pity She's a Whore*
Giovanni, Annabella
A brother and sister confront the fact that their love for one another is far more than the love of siblings.

*Two Noble Kinsmen*
Arcite, Palamon
Sick of Thebes and the rule of Creon, the two kinsmen decide to leave.
Arcite, Palamon
Imprisoned, the two men profess undying loyalty to each other, then proceed to quarrel over a woman they see.

*Volpone*
Volpone, Mosca, Voltore
A consummate miser and his crafty servant dupe a suspicious visitor out of one more gift, which Voltore gives in the hope of being remembered in Volpone's will.

*The White Devil*
Vittoria, Brachiano
A duke makes the deadly mistake of falling in love with a famous Venetian courtesan.

## Shakespeare Scenes

Because actors are ever in search of Shakespearean material, are often required to find it, and are most intimidated by it, the following list is offered. For other periods and playwrights, only the best known have been listed. Here everything that might do for an audition or showcase is included, because "undiscovered" or rarely performed Shakespeare is, in some contexts, more admired than the familiar. Where an asterisk appears, some cutting of other characters or piecing from various parts of the scene is necessary.

*All's Well That Ends Well*
I,i Helena, Parolles
An immoral rogue and a clever heroine debate the relative use of virginity.
I,iii Helena, Countess
Though below his station, Helena confesses her love for the countess' son.
III,vii Helena, Widow

Disguised as a pilgrim, Helena plots to trick her unworthy husband into getting her pregnant.

*Antony and Cleopatra*
I,i Antony, Cleopatra
Antony is too besotted with Cleopatra's taunting to attend messengers from Rome.
I,iii Antony, Cleopatra
Feeling very sorry for herself, Cleopatra acknowledges that she must allow Antony to pursue business in Rome.
II,v Cleopatra, Messenger
Pity the messenger whose job is to inform Cleopatra that Antony has wed Octavia.
IV,xiv Antony, Eros
His servant holds the sword on which Antony, having false report of the queen himself, elects to kill himself.
IV,xv Antony, Cleopatra
A wounded Antony is brought to Cleopatra and dies in her arms.
V,ii Cleopatra, Clown
The clown delivers the basket of figs with the asp that will enable the queen to take her own life.

*As You Like It*
I,iii Rosalind, Celia, Frederick
Two princesses joke merrily about the one falling in love. Next moment the twisted father of one and uncle of the other expels his niece from his kingdom. Rosalind and Celia vow to stay together and to travel in disguise.
II,iii Orlando, Adam
His faithful old servant informs Orlando of his older brother's plot on his life. The two agree to escape and to share their lives together.
III,ii Touchstone, Corin
The city clown lords it over the country shepherd, but the old man more than holds his own.
III,ii Rosalind, Celia
Celia, disguised as Aliena, has spotted the beloved of Rosalind (now disguised as a boy, Ganymede) in the very forest to which they have escaped.
III,ii Rosalind, Orlando
Rosalind/Ganymede tries out her disguise on the man she loves, and he doesn't recognize her. In fact, he agrees to allow her/him to help cure him of his love for this person named Rosalind.
IV,i Rosalind, Orlando
Orlando learns how to woo and even pretends to wed his teacher.
III,v; IV,iii Rosalind, Phebe, Silvius
In trying to get vain shepherdess Phebe to accept the wooing of her young

shepherd swain, Rosalind misfires, and Phebe falls in love with her/him instead.

*The Comedy of Errors*
I,ii Antipholus of Syracuse, Dromio of Ephesus
Master beats the wrong servant for losing or stealing his money, not knowing that the servant has a twin.
II,ii Antipholus of Syracuse, Dromio of Syracuse
Master quarrels with other servant (his own), not realizing that this time he has the other twin.
III,ii Luciana, Antipholus of Syracuse
He tries to seduce her; she is shocked, thinking he is her brother-in-law, not realizing it is his twin.
III,ii Antipholus of Syracuse, Dromio of Syracuse
Servant informs master of his encounter with Nell, a woman of global proportions.

*Coriolanus*
I,ix Coriolanus, Cominius
After a brilliant victory at Corioli, Marcius is given his new surname of honor, Coriolanus.
IV,v Coriolanus, Aufidius
Banished from Rome, where he was formerly revered, a champion warrior offers his services to his old enemy to avenge himself on his ungrateful city.
II,i Sicinius, Brutus
Two tribunes plot to disgrace Coriolanus, whom they considered overproud.*
V,iii Coriolanus, Volumnia
As he is about to destroy Rome, the warrior's mother pleads with him on her knees to spare the city.*

*Cymbeline*
I,iv Iachimo, Posthumus
A crafty Italian bets a trusting Briton that he can seduce his wife, Imogen.
I,vi Imogen, Iachimo
Iachimo attempts to seduce Imogen. She rejects him outright, he claims only to have been testing her, then arranges to have himself delivered secretly to her bedchamber in a trunk.
II,iii Imogen, Cloten
The princess rejects the romantic advances of her crude stepbrother, and he vows revenge.
II,iv Iachimo, Posthumus
Iachimo presents falsely acquired but overwhelming evidence of Imogen's unfaithfulness, a bracelet she vowed to Posthumus never to take off and knowledge of a mole on her left breast.

III,iv Imogen, Pisanio
The servant of Posthumus reveals that he has been ordered to kill Imogen, falsely believed by her husband of being unfaithful. They plan a way to save her life.

*Hamlet*
I,ii Hamlet, Horatio
Horatio tells Hamlet about seeing his father's ghost on the castle watch.
I,v Hamlet, Ghost
Hamlet meets his father's ghost, who informs him of his murder by his own brother.
II,i Polonius, Ophelia
Ophelia tells her father about Hamlet's wild appearance in her chamber.
III,i Hamlet, Gertrude
Called to Gertrude's closet, Hamlet upbraids her for her marriage, kills Polonius, thinking he was Claudius, and is visited by the ghost of his father.*
III,i Hamlet, Ophelia
Ophelia tries to return Hamlet's gifts. He responds by destroying the last threads of hope for their relationship and advising her to "get thee to a nunnery."
IV,iii Hamlet, Claudius
Hamlet taunts Claudius about the murder of Polonius and is ordered out of the kingdom.
V,i Gravediggers
While working on Ophelia's grave, the two clowns joke about death.
V,i Hamlet, Gravedigger
The prince discovers the grave and skull of the court jester, Yorick, he knew as a boy.

*Henry IV, Part 1*
I,ii Hal, Falstaff
The prince of Wales and his large, dissolute friend trade friendly insults.
I,iii Hotspur, Worcester
Hotspur and his uncle plan a rebellion against the king. The older man handles most of the strategy, the younger most of the anger.*
II,iii; III,i Hotspur, Lady Hotspur
Lady Percy argues with her husband because he will not tell her his plans, they reconcile in their way, and bid each other good-bye.
II,iv Hal, Falstaff
Learning that a rebellion is being mounted against the king, the two tricksters take turns imitating him.

*Henry IV, Part 2*
I,ii Falstaff, Lord Chief Justice
The lord chief justice of London advises Falstaff to stay away from the prince.

II,ii Hal, Pointz
The two friends tease each other about their position in the world and read an outrageous letter from Falstaff.
III,ii Silence, Shallow
Two old codgers discuss the good old days.
IV,iv Hal, King Henry
On his deathbed, the king and his son reach a final reconciliation.

*Henry V*
III,iv Alice, Katharine
Speaking mostly French, the princess and her gentlewoman attempt an English lesson.
IV,i Henry, Williams
Henry disguises himself at camp the night before the Battle of Agincourt and argues with a soldier about the lives of kings and troops and their obligations to each other.
V,i Pistol, Fluellen, Gower
Troublesome Pistol gets a deserved comeuppance and is forced to eat a leek.
V,ii Henry, Katharine
Though more soldier than master of love or languages, Henry manages to woo and win the French princess.

*Henry VI, Part 1*
I,ii Joan La Pucelle, Charles
Joan of Arc wins over the French dauphin by literally proving she has more skill at swordsmanship than he.
II,iii Countess, Talbot
The countess has ambitious plans to capture the rebel leader until she finds how strongly supported he is.
IV, v Talbot, John
Father and son both die on the battlefield, one of wounds, the other of a broken heart.
V,iii Margaret, Suffolk
Sent to woo for the king, Suffolk finds himself strongly drawn to Margaret.

*Henry VI, Part 2*
I,ii Eleanor, Gloucester
Husband and wife reveal their dreams and boundless ambitions to one another.
I,iii Margaret, Suffolk
Suffolk is banished. The queen, who is in love with him, vows that she will somehow see him again.
IV,x Iden, Cade
A starving man is killed for breaking into the garden of another.

*Henry VI, Part 3*
III,ii Edward, Lady Grey
Lady Grey refuses to sleep with the king, then accepts his offer of marriage.
V,vi Gloucester, Henry
King Henry VI is killed by the future Richard III.

*Henry VIII*
I,i Norfolk, Buckingham
Two lords respond differently to the pomp displayed by the cardinal.
II,iii Anne, Old Lady
Henry's eye has fallen on Anne, and her old friend claims she will not refuse the crown.
IV,i Wolsey, Cromwell
Completely fallen from power, the cardinal tries to assess his life and pass some wisdom on to his secretary.
IV, ii Katharine, Griffith
Ill and no longer queen, Katharine tries to envision some kind of peace in her life.

*Julius Caesar*
I,ii Brutus, Cassius
Cassius attempts to get Brutus to join the conspiracy against Caesar.
II,i Brutus, Portia
Reminding him that she is Cato's daughter and knows politics well, Portia asks to be told what her husband is up to.
II,ii Caesar, Calpurnia
Because of troubling omens in the night's storm, Calpurnia begs her husband not to go the senate today.
IV,ii; IV,iii Brutus, Cassius
Great strain is put on the friendship of the two leaders as the Battle of Philippi approaches.

*King John*
IV,i Hubert, Arthur
An imprisoned young prince persuades his keeper not to execute him.
IV,ii Hubert, John
Hubert reveals to the king that he has not obeyed his order to kill Prince Arthur, and John is much relieved.

*King Lear*
I,ii; II,i, Edmund, Gloucester
The bastard son fools his father into believing his brother, Edgar, intends to kill him. Later he gives himself a wound to "prove" his brother's treachery.
I,iv; I,v Lear, Fool
The old king's fool attempts to counsel and mock him and to help him avoid madness.*

IV,ii Albany, Goneril
Husband accuses wife of treachery, she accuses him of weakness, and each accuses the other of unworthiness.*
IV,vi Edgar, Gloucester
Disguised as Poor Tom, Edgar leads his blind father to Dover and makes him believe he has survived leaping from the cliffs.

*Love's Labor's Lost*
I,ii Armado, Moth
Fantastical Spaniard and precocious page discuss Armado's infatuation for a peasant girl.
III,i Armado, Moth
The page sings and jokes to offer solace to his lovesick master.
III,i Berowne, Costard
A courtier commissions a loud rustic to deliver a message to the woman he loves.

*Macbeth*
I,vii Lady Macbeth, Macbeth
Macbeth has second thoughts about committing murder to seize the crown, but the thane's wife both shames him and spurs him on.
II,ii Lady Macbeth, Macbeth
Between the two of them, Duncan is murdered and his guards implicated.
IV,iii Malcolm, Macduff
Loyal warrior recruits Duncan's rightful heir to return and seize the Scottish crown from Macbeth.

*Measure for Measure*
I,iv Isabella, Lucio
An impish rogue informs his friend's sister about his danger.
II,ii Angelo, Isabella
A young novice pleads with the deputy governor for the life of her brother, condemned to die for impregnating his fiancée.
III,v Angelo, Isabella
If she will offer him her sexual favors, he claims he will spare her brother.
III,i Isabella, Claudio
In prison, Claudio pleads with his sister to put his life above her virtue and to save him.
III,ii Vincentio, Lucio
Not recognizing the duke, who is disguised as a friar, Lucio slanders the duke relentlessly.
IV,ii Vincentio, Provost
A plan to save Claudio's life involves executing a reprobate drunk in his place.

*The Merchant of Venice*
I,i Antonio, Bassanio

The merchant agrees to lend funds to his young friend to help him court the beautiful Portia.

I,ii Portia, Nerissa

The lady-in-waiting of an heiress reviews with her the qualities of all the suitors who have pursued her since her father's death.

I,iii Antonio, Shylock

To secure a loan from Shylock, Antonio agrees to strange terms involving a pound of flesh.*

II,ii Launcelot, Old Gobbo

The incorrigible young Gobbo teases and confuses his blind old father at their reunion.

III,ii Portia, Bassanio

The suitor whom she loves passes her deceased father's test, chooses the right casket, and wins her hand.

V,ii Jessica, Lorenzo

On a beautiful night in Belmont, two newlyweds contemplate the power of moonlight and music.

*The Merry Wives of Windsor*

II,i Mistress Ford, Mistress Page

Two housewives realize they have received the same love letter from a large, aging lothario.

II,ii Ford, Falstaff

Pretending to be a Mr. Brook, Ford hires Falstaff to attempt to seduce his wife.

III,iii Mistresses Ford and Page, Falstaff

The ladies foil Falstaff by having him hide in a basket, which they then have dumped in a ditch.

III,v Ford, Falstaff

Falstaff reports to the disguised Ford about his seduction attempts and basket misadventures.

*A Midsummer Night's Dream*

II,i Helena, Demetrius

Helena pursues her beloved into the woods, but he will have none of her and pursues Hermia instead.

II,i Puck, Fairy

The rhyming servants of the warring king and queen of the fairies discuss the war.

II,i Oberon, Titania

The battling couple encounter each other, fail to negotiate, and go their separate ways.

III,ii Helena, Lysander, Hermia, Demetrius

A love potion plays mischief with four lovers for hysterical misadventures in the woods.

III,ii Oberon, Puck

The king checks the not altogether successful efforts of his servant.

*Much Ado About Nothing*
IV,i Beatrice, Benedick
Difficult as it was to admit their love for each other, Beatrice now presents Benedick with a very difficult challenge in order to prove his—he is asked to kill his best friend.
V,ii Beatrice, Benedick
The two battling lovers agree that they enjoy each other's company enormously and will probably continue taunting each other forever.
III,i Hero, Ursula
While Beatrice listens in hiding, her two friends "set her up" by pretending to discuss how much Benedick loves her.

*Othello*
I,iii; IV,ii Iago, Roderigo
While pretending sympathy for Roderigo's pursuit of Desdemona, Iago takes his money and fills him with false hopes.
I,viii Desdemona, Emilia
Her lady-in-waiting attempts to console Desdemona over her husband's wild jealousy.
II,iii Iago, Cassio
Iago lures Cassio into asking Desdemona to plea for him to save his reputation.
III,iii Othello, Iago
Iago subtly poisons Othello's mind and undermines his faith in his beautiful wife.
III,iii; III,iv; V,i Othello, Desdemona
Desdemona innocently pleas for the life of a captain and loses her handkerchief. Othello later asks her for it, enraged with suspicion that she has given it to the captain and that they are lovers. Finally, possessed, Othello takes her life.

*Pericles*
IV,iii Dionyza, Cleon
A queen confesses to her husband the ordering of the murder of Pericles's daughter because she so far outshone their own child.
V,i Pericles, Marina
Father and daughter are reconciled after being separated for almost all of her life.

*Richard II*
I,iii Gaunt, Bolingbroke
Father tries to ease the pain of banishment for his son.
II,iii York, Bolingbroke
The regent tries to dissuade the rebel from causing civil war in the king's absence.
V,i Richard, Queen
Waiting for him on his way to prison, Richard's queen bids him farewell for the last time.

*Richard III*

I,ii Richard, Anne

She begins by cursing him for the deaths of her father-in-law and husband and ends up seduced and won by him.

III,vii Richard, Buckingham

Richard and his ally in crime stage a public scene in which Richard is "persuaded" to accept the crown.

IV,ii Richard, Buckingham

The two plotters begin to realize they cannot trust each other.

IV,iv Richard, Elizabeth

Most of her children are dead because of him, and now he persuades her to woo her daughter for him.

*Romeo and Juliet*

I,iv Romeo, Mercutio

On the way to crash a ball at the Capulets', two friends make merry.

II,ii Juliet, Romeo

The star-crossed lovers declare their love in the balcony scene outside her chamber.

II,iii Romeo, Friar

At first balking at his request to marry them, the friar changes his mind and decides this may provide a way to end the dispute between the two households.

II,iv Nurse, Romeo

Juliet's nurse meets him and helps set up their wedding.

II,v Juliet, Nurse

Fretting over her nurse's lateness in going to meet Romeo, Juliet is then frustrated by her teasing and her petulance.

III,ii Juliet, Nurse

Bringing the dreadful news of Tybalt's death and Romeo's involvement, the nurse at last agrees to bring Romeo to spend one night with Juliet before his banishment.

III,iii Romeo, Friar

Romeo is frantic over his banishment, but the friar helps him realize those things for which he can be glad.

IV,i Juliet, Friar

The friar saves Juliet's suicidal desperation by agreeing to help her with a magic drug.

*The Taming of the Shrew*

I,i Lucentio, Tranio

New in Padua and infatuated with Bianca, Lucentio trades identities with his servant so he may be near her.

II,i Kate, Petruchio

Who is the immovable object? Who the irresistible force? This is their first meeting.

IV,v Kate, Petruchio
En route to her sister's wedding, Kate learns how to play Petruchio's game.

*The Tempest*
I,ii Ariel, Prospero
While acknowledging his success in creating a shipwreck, Prospero informs Ariel he will have to perform more services before achieving his freedom.
I,ii; III,i Miranda, Ferdinand
She has never seen a young man; he has never seen a creature so lovely. They fall in love.
II,i Antonio, Sebastian
The two plot to kill Alonso for the throne of Naples.
II,ii Trinculo, Stephano, Caliban
A monster and two clowns frighten each other, get drunk together, and agree to scheme together.

*Timon of Athens*
IV,iii Timon, Apemantus
Two old friends call each other names and try to one-up each other in terms of who is angrier against mankind.
II,ii; IV,iii Timon, Flavius
Too generous to all, Timon finds out from his servant he is bankrupt. His faithful servant finds him in the woods and attempts to offer him comfort.

*Titus Andronicus*
II,iii Tamora, Aaron
The queen and her lover plot death and rape for others.
II,iii Tamora, Titus
Disguised as Revenge, Tamora tries to get Titus to do her bidding.

*Troilus and Cressida*
I,i Troilus, Pandarus
Troilus's adoration of Cressida is both encouraged and mocked by her cynical uncle.
I,ii Pandarus, Cressida
While watching all the Trojan heroes march by, Pandarus praises Troilus. Pretending disinterest, Cressida admits later that she loves him.
I,iii Ulysses, Nestor
The two try to devise a way to motivate Achilles to action.
III,ii Troilus, Cressida
The two lovers, after much pandering by Pandarus, are brought together and declare their vows of faith.
III,iii Ulysses, Achilles
The famous warriors discuss the elusive nature of fame.

*Twelfth Night*
I,iv; II,iv Viola, Orsino
Disguised as a boy, Viola achieves service for the duke of Illyria and is sent by him to help him woo the countess Olivia, but she has fallen in love with him herself.
I,v Viola, Olivia
The countess is not interested in the duke's suit but is very smitten with his messenger.
III,i Viola, Olivia
This time she confesses her love for the page and is rebuffed.
III,i Viola, Feste
The clown and the disguised young woman discuss the strange ways of the world.
IV,ii Malvolio, Feste
Disguised as a crazed curate, the clown mocks the imprisoned Malvolio.

*Two Gentlemen of Verona*
I,i Valentine, Proteus
Two best friends part as the one leaves their hometown of Verona and the other seeks adventure in Milan.
I,i Proteus, Speed
Proteus cannot get a straight answer out of his servant about whether he did or did not deliver a love letter.
I,ii Julia, Lucetta
An intercepted love letter is the source of much banter and teasing between mistress and maid.
II,i Valentine, Speed
Speed offers his unique observations on Valentine's new love.
II,v Speed, Launce
Two comic servants discuss the women with whom their masters are in love.
III,i Speed, Launce
The two consider a letter regarding the attributes of a woman with whom Launce is in love.
III,i Duke, Valentine
The duke tricks his daughter's suitor into revealing his plans to elope with her, then has him banished.
IV,iv Julia, Silvia
Disguised as a boy, Julia, against her own heart, delivers a letter from her beloved to the daughter of the duke.

*The Winter's Tale*
I,ii Leontes, Camillo
A trusted adviser tries to persuade his king that his jealousy is unfounded.

II,i Leontes, Hermione
A possessed king accuses his noble queen of adultery and claims that the child she is carrying is that of his best friend.
III,ii Leontes, Paulina
Cursing him for his crazed jealousy, Paulina reveals that the king's wife is dead and shocks him into a recognition of his own madness.
III,iii Shepherd, Clown
Father and son find an abandoned baby and vow to give it a home.
IV,ii Perdita, Florizel
A prince dressed as shepherd and a shepherdess dressed as goddess pledge their love. Neither knows that she is actually a princess by birth.
IV,iii Autolycus, Clown
Counterfeiting himself as a victim of robbery, a rogue steals the purse of the man who helps him.

---

1. Cast one classmate as Queen Elizabeth I. Everyone else has two class periods to choose a poem in honor of the queen's coronation. Poems may be sonnets from Elizabethan poets or others, or your own!
2. Stand before the court, pay obeisance to the queen, and then read her offering.
3. Discuss what it felt like to be honored and to honor.

**E X E R C I S E**

**Sonnet for a Sovereign**

1. Work in teams of three. Each team is responsible for coming up with two entirely new terms not currently in the language. One term can be silly (such as *nairs* for nose hairs) and the other more serious and useful (such as *forback,* which describes the feeling of wanting to move on and retreat at the same time: "I feel forback").
2. Unveil your terms to the class and try very hard to use them during the next few weeks, both in and out of class.
3. Give some special reward or recognition to the person who employs the largest number of new terms and to the team who came up with the one the class finds most useful.

**E X E R C I S E**

**Invent Language**

To understand more fully how Elizabethans view life, create a literal chain with one person at the end of the room on the highest possible platform as God and another at the other end lying curled up on the ground as a rock. Discuss each step in the chain and who is the head of each group on the chain (lion for animals, and so on).

**E X E R C I S E**

**Chain of Being**

1. Draw the name of a classmate of the opposite sex.
2. Create a tribute to that person by either (*a*) writing and presenting a poem; (*b*) composing and singing a song; or (*c*) performing some heroic public deed.

**E X E R C I S E**

**Tribute For Two**

3. Keep the particular nature of the tribute secret until its unveiling in class. You may include some humor in the works, but there is to be no roasting or satire. It is a genuine tribute and gift.

**E X E R C I S E**

**Top and Bottom Halves**

Elizabethans are comfortable with a higher sense of elegance and music blended with a lower sense of animalism and earth. The pessimistic belief in man's corruption through sin is balanced by the optimistic belief in the hope for salvation through grace.

1. Present a speech stressing just music, then just earth, then pessimism, then optimism.
2. Let the pendulum swing wildly in each direction. Then go back and repeat, allowing each of the four a voice in the final product.

**E X E R C I S E**

**Shakespearean Spat**

1. With a partner, go over the Elizabethan vocabulary list.
2. Devise a scene of some disagreement between you. Each of you uses at least one term from each category (greeting, good-byes, disagreement, agreement, and so on).
3. Present your work with the idea of owning the terms.

**E X E R C I S E**

**Danger Games**

These Elizabethan party games all offer an element of risk and a high potential for losing dignity.

1. Pass the orange: Competing teams pass an orange under the chin, no hands allowed, preferably down a line and back.
2. Jingling: Blindfolded in a circle, players try to catch the one unblind-folded person present who continuously rings a bell.
3. Stool ball: A player in the center tries to hit others with a ball as they run from stool to stool. If you get hit, you are "it."
4. Jousting: Two men carrying rolled-up newspapers and riding on the backs of two others try to knock each other off.
5. Cock fighting: Two men in a circle try to push each other out by using their chests.
6. Shark Island: Like King of the Mountain, but played in the center of a circle.

## SOURCES FOR FURTHER STUDY

Aykroyd, J. W. *Performing Shakespeare*. New York: Samuel French, 1979.

Barton, John. *Playing Shakespeare*. London: Methuen, 1984.

Beckerman, Bernard. *Shakespeare at the Globe*. New York: Macmillan, 1962.

Bentley, Gerald E., ed. *The Profession of Player in Shakespeare's Time*. Princeton: Princeton University Press, 1984.

Berr, Ralph. *On Directing Shakespeare*. New York: Macmillan, 1977.

Berry, Cicely. *The Actor and His Text*. New York: Macmillan, 1988.

Bethell, S. L. "Shakespeare's Actors." *Review of English Studies,* 1950.

Birch, Dorothy. "Vocal interpretations with Reference to Shakespeare." In *Training for the Stage*. London: Pitman, 1952.

Boas, Guy. "The Speaking of Shakespeare's Verse." *Essays and Studies by Members of the English Association,* 1964.

Boyd, Morrison C. *Elizabethan Music and Musical Criticism*. Westport: Greenwood Press, 1962.

Bradbook, Muriel C. *Elizabethan Stage Conditions*. Connecticut: Archon Books, 1962.

Brissenden, Alan. *Shakespeare and the Dance*. Atlantic Highlands, N.J.: Humanties Press, 1981.

Brown, Ivor. *Shakespeare and the Actors*. London: Ivor Brown, 1970.

Brown, John Russell. *Shakespeare in Performance*. New York: Harcourt Brace Jovanovich, 1976.

Burtin, Elizabeth. *The Elizabethans at Home*. London: Secker & Warburg, 1958.

Burton, Hal. *Great Acting*. London: British Broadcasting System, 1967.

Cohen, Robert. *Acting in Shakespeare*. Mountain View, Calif.: Mayfield Publishing Co., 1991.

Davis, W. S. *Life in Elizabethan Times*. New York: Harper & Brothers, 1930.

Driver, Tom F. *The Sense of History in Greek and Shakespearean Drama*. New York: Holt, Rinehart, 1960.

Fletcher, Anthony. *Elizabethan Village*. Harlow: Longman, 1967.

Gurr, Andrew. *The Shakespearean Stage*. New York: Cambridge Press, 1980.

Harbage, Alfred. "Elizabethan Acting." *Publications of the Modern Language Association,* 1939.

Holmes, Martin. *Elizabethan London*. New York: Frederick A. Praeger, 1969.

Joseph, Bertram. *Elizabethan Acting*. London: Oxford University Press, 1951.

La Mar, Virginia. *English Dress in the Age of Shakespeare*. Charlottesville: University Press of Virginia, 1969.

Pearson, Lu Emily. *Elizabethans at Home*. Stanford University Press, 1957.

Playford, John. *The English Dancing Master*. London: Cecil Sharp House, 1651.

Reese, G. *Music in the Renaissance*. New York: W. W. Norton and Sons, 1959.

Reeves, Marjorie. *Elizabethan Citizen*. Harlow: Longman, 1961.

Tilyard, E. M. W. *The Elizabethan World Picture*. New York: Vintage Books.

Tyna, Kenneth. *He That Plays the King*. London: Longmans, Green and Co., 1950.

Welford, Enid. *The Court Masque*. New York: Russel and Russel, 1962.

Williams, Neville. *The Life and Times of Elizabeth I*. New York: Doubleday, 1972.

Wilson, J. D. *Life in Shakespeare's England*. London: Cambridge University Press, 1949.

Woodward, G. W. O. *Queen Elizabeth I*. London: Pitkin Pictorials, 1975.

## VIDEOS

**Acting in Tragedy** (Brian Cox), **Acting in Shakespearean Comedy** (Janet Suzman)    Master classes in which veteran performers coach novices and illuminate the extremes of Elizabethan performance.

**Henry V** (Kenneth Branagh) and **Henry V** (Laurence Olivier)    Seeing both films is a major lesson in changing tastes in Shakespearean performance over fifty years, since each represents its own era brilliantly.

**Playing Shakespeare** (John Barton)    Ten videos containing roughly the same text as the book by the same title and corresponding to chapter titles but with the invaluable addition of seeing some of the Royal Shakespeare Company's greatest actors in action.

**Macbeth** (Trevor Nunn)    This production embraces the ritual, high intensity and audience (camera) confidences favored by the Elizabethans.

**Romeo and Juliet** and **The Taming of the Shrew** (Franco Zeferelli)    No other filmmaker has captured the Elizabethan sense of festival, celebration, and unbridled excess as well as Zeferelli whose eye for lavish period detail is amazing.

## COMPARING GREEKS AND ELIZABETHANS

Greeks and Elizabethans share, in spite of scientific "progress," a belief in the possibility of magic and a connection to the elements. Theatre is largely outdoors, the audience surrounding the actor on three sides and on various levels. Nature, the world, and the cosmos are constant factors. As theatre moves indoors, largely at night, the concern also shifts from cosmic matters toward social relationships. Before we leave these two periods, let us compare them:

|  | *Greek* | *Elizabethan* |
|---|---|---|
| *Time* | | |
| Written | 5th century B.C. | Late 16th, early 17th century A.D. |
| Set | Mythology/13th century, B.C. to 5th century B.C. | Ancient Greece through imaginary times |
| Beginning | Story begins near the end and draws in past events | Story begins and ends |

|  | Greek | Elizabethan |
|---|---|---|
| Climax | High emotional intensity and mental struggle | Battle, duel, reconciliation—usually physical |
| Past | Binding us in necessity | Door to the future |
| Future | Difficult to bear | Full of promise |
| Change | Characters do not change; veil is lifted | Sometimes metamorphosis occurs; all become more of what they truly are |
| *Space* | | |
| Theatre | Up to 30,000 spectators | Up to 3000 spectators |
| Ritual | Formalized and ordered | Unbounded |
| Movement | Still | Active |
| Tension | Balance | Motion |
| Change | Action is to be feared | Action is highly desirable |
| *Place* | Single important gathering spot | Anywhere/everywhere on the globe |
| *Values* | | |
| Sin | Hubris, going against nature | Disloyalty to sovereign, people |
| God | Multiple, personal | Single Christian deity |
| Belief | Fate | Providence |
| Conflict | Good vs. good, or lesser of evils | Good vs. evil |
| Tone | High | High and low together |
| *Structure* | | |
| Script | Unities | Freewheeling five acts |
| Pattern | Event to knowledge | Knowledge to event |
| Scenes | Standardized | All lengths |
| *Beauty* | Statuesque | Polarized |
| Sex | Survival, seed, ecstasy | Bawdy, robust, deserved |
| Recreation | Categorized | Public celebration |
| Sight | Striking simplicity | Colorful splendor |
| Sound | Direct, clean, soulful, subject to translation | Eloquent, loquacious, mercurial |

# RESTORATION PERIOD STYLE
## Decadence as One of the Fine Arts

### THE WORLD ENTERED

An important brief interlude precedes this era. While the death of Shakespeare does not by itself send the English theatre into a state of mourning, his demise coincides with the theatre's downward spiral from greatness. Politics replaces art as the public's primary preoccupation. Those for and against the monarchy struggle for power. The execution of Charles I in 1649 proves just how strongly Parliament disagrees with him on the question of the divine right of kings. Oliver Cromwell and the Puritans take control, establishing the Commonwealth. A repressive atmosphere pervades—theatre is officially called corrupt and outlawed in 1652. But with Cromwell's death, the Puritans are no longer strong enough to control the Loyalists, and Charles II, who has been living in comfortable exile in France, is invited back to reclaim the throne for the Stuart dynasty. After years of upright self-denial, the longing for diversion and indulgence resurfaces. Weary of the black clothing of the Sin Squad Puritans, many now long for color. What follows is the reign of a king far more wild and licentious than his father ever was.

There are two classes now, "us" and "them." "We," the aristocracy, do not care enough about "them" to discuss them. Theatre is only for "us." The following interview is with a court insider. Aside from assurances of impeccable credentials, the expert wished no more details revealed.

Maggie Smith as Millamant in *The Way of the World,* The Stratford Festival

Time: 1660–1710

*We live in the eternal now. Nothing before us, or after, can measure up to what we are tasting.*

*How would you describe your sense of time?*

We have just survived a dreary period of *no* theatre. While it lasted less than twenty years, it *seemed* an eternity. Some dutifully wore those charming, if stiff, white collars, and tried to be as puritanical as Cromwell, but the effort was overwhelming and, quite frankly, tedious. Thank God the Protector (who was, just between the two of us, not all that attractive) has gone to heaven, where he will be much happier. Now, after wearing black forever, *our* idea of heaven is to play and to forget the consequences, in this life or the hereafter. Today is the Age of Possibility, with a new king, new court, and new set of rules.

*In what point in history are your plays set and performed?*

*The multitude is always in the wrong.*

—JOHN WILMOT,
EARL OF ROCHESTER

Our plays are set here and now because everything else is less interesting. This is what your century might call "country club theatre," theatre written by, played by, and presented to the elite in exclusive environs, safely remote from the ill-informed, unwashed masses.

*How far does the audience or play move out of its own time?*

If the current age is at all decadent (and yours is, my dear), our plays might be updated, but usually you, the audience, will be asked to travel all the way back. You will be privileged to pretend you are a wicked, worldly citizen of our own incomparable era.

*How rapidly does time move for most people?*

There never seems to be sufficient time to learn all the gossip or to engage in playful trifles. Life is a whirlwind. Only when I am trapped in the company of some bore does it suddenly stand still. Therefore, time moves rapidly when I am amused, and interminably when I am not. When I look long and hard in the mirror, I am suddenly sadly aware of the years. I can lose myself forever in the moment, but I see all around me those with brighter eyes, smoother skin, and (can it be true?) more alluring auras. I must remember only to stare at my reflection in candlelight.

*How do you note time? What is your tempo/rhythm?*

Time is arranged by periods of preoccupation or assignation, as chapters in a lurid memoir. Mostly we remember our lives according to love affairs or scandals of note. We must get on with life or we shall yawn, and yet . . . if the moment or temptation is sufficiently delicious, let the world go by, and let me savor. Life is an erratic game, whose pace veers from frenetic to languid, allowing delightful diversion before jumping back into the fray.

*Do people focus mainly on the moment or on whole lifetimes? On the future or the past?*

Absolutely on the moment! Forget the past and defy the future! You may quote me, at least among people of quality, and without using my name. What is the latest novelty there across the room? Our interest in the future extends but to immediate desires. The past is absolutely forgotten, with the exception, of course, of grudges and vendettas.

> *We all labor against our own cure, for death is the cure of all diseases.*
> —GEORGE VILLIERS, DUKE OF BUCKINGHAM

*What lengths of attention spans do your people have?*

What was that question again? Ah, yes. Well, it depends on how delicious or obscene the details, does it not? What were we talking about? Let me just say that if you are interesting enough, I will stay with you forever. Who is that divine creature who just walked into the room?

*Is age revered or feared? What is the relationship between youth and maturity?*

If only I could know all I do, without wrinkles, bitterness, and carping. Never mind, I much prefer knowing to *not* knowing, but wish I were still translucent. It does take longer to prepare to go out nowadays, it seems. God-a-mercy, look over there. Who invited those old crones? Take them away; they depress me.

> *Age is deformed, youth unkind,*
> *We scorn their bodies, they our mind.*
> —THOMAS BASTARD

*How important is this issue? How uniform are views?*

We endeavor not to think about time; that is how important it is. And we are, my dear, in complete agreement.

## Space

**How can I invade, and how shall I respond to invasion?**

*How is space defined and viewed?*

Wherever I am is the center of the universe, and all forces move out from this central force—*c'est moi.* We do delight in mind games, yet are infinitely more social than philosophical.

*In what ways do personal bubbles alter?*

We desire enough space to *display* ourselves, but also love to sidle up closely for flirtation, so the "bubble," as you so charmingly put it, is flexible, continuously "popping" and re-forming. We are secretive, but once discovered, no detail is considered beneath reporting. We often go out masked, desiring privacy *and* conducting our assignations in dangerously public places.

*How is space violated?*

The hands do wander, no doubt about it, but all must be done with beguiling delicacy and panache. Enough skill will avail you anything you desire.

*How do these beliefs translate into movement?*

I require considerable room around me to express myself sufficiently. Since, in performance, I am competing with socializing, what I do is pronounced, extroverted, presentational, and clear. I accomplish all this without seeming to push for effect or to overstate. I will prolong both my appearances and my withdrawals from the stage. It is more important to me to make a stunning, clear, and authoritative impression than to be believed.

　　Our theatres are intimate and small. Standing room is a thing of the past, benches are backless, but three galleries of boxes provide "comfort." The apron is the invention of this time period, and we are proud of it, so proud that we use little else. At last there is a special diminutive "stagette," if you will, to allow the actor closer proximity to the audience. All entrances are made through stage doors built right into the proscenium arch. All scenery is relegated to the upstage area, which is employed for little more. The actor may be fully, closely scrutinized and joined onstage. I note you have kept the apron all these years. A wise move.

## Place

*Every detail must be perfect, whether God created it thus or not.*

*Is the setting rural or urban?*

Pshaw! Need you ask? The city is the source of all worthwhile, the country intended for occasional diversion. One must maintain a home there, but seldom use it, except as a place for sport. We remove ourselves from the forces of nature in all matters.

*What influence does weather have? To what extent is your environment controlled?*

As little weather as possible, if you please. Our hedges say it all—painstakingly shaped domes, hearts, or diamonds, not simple vulgar vegetation. Our rooms are large and grand, with huge staircases, tiled floors, vaulted ceilings, and detailed surfaces. Furniture is not comfortable, but

*Love ceases to be a pleasure when it ceases to be a secret.*

　　—APHRA BEHN

*I must confess I am a fop in my heart.... I have been so used to affectation that ... what is natural cannot touch me.*

　　—SIR GEORGE ETHEREGE

rather an array of lovely display pieces, the more ornate and gilded the better.

*How aware are you of other places?*

We are infatuated with all things Oriental and adore travel. Chinese furniture and Peking scrolls upon one's walls will engender multifarious compliments. We do now acknowledge the French as style masters, particularly as our own monarch has so many French tastes, including the appearance of women onstage, a recent and titillating development. Many are altering their names to sound more French.

## Values

*Since I am the center of the Universe, my commitments are secondary to my desires.*

*What are the beliefs most widely shared?*

Life is a sumptuous, meticulously prepared meal, more enjoyable if nibbled than devoured. Self-gratification is to be pursued at all cost, unpleasantness to be avoided at all cost.

*How important is tradition?*

The restoration of the monarchy means a return to old customs associated with old rank and old money. *Noblesse oblige.* There are no other impediments to personal pleasure. Etiquette is all. You may do what you desire, if you do it with the correct statement, finger, or gift.

*When all is done, human life is ... but like a froward child that must be played with and humoured a little to keep it quiet, till it falls asleep, and then the care is over.* —SIR WILLIAM TEMPLE

*What is the predominant mood?*

Giddy, hedonistic playfulness.

*Who are your idols? What are shared fantasies?*

While the king and his current mistress set the tone, we greatly admire anyone clearly living out a life of limitless, but demurely pursued, pleasure. Perpetual amusement, youth, and gratification would be any notable person's view of rapture. Personally, however, I cannot abide anyone feeling better than I do.

*I can endure my own despair,*
*But not another's hope.*
—WILLIAM WALSH

*How do people define sin and forgiveness?*

We forget easily, but we do not forgive easily. Revenge for a personal slight is *de rigueur.* All else is negotiable.

*What gets and holds attention?*

Startling, devastating wit and beauty. The capacity to shock without offending. The ability continuously to surprise and delight. It is inappropriate for the actor, no matter what his character's plight, to ask that the audience pity him, feel compassion for him, or feel that their altruistic (pardon the word) natures have been broached. We abhor this cloying vexation. Instead, what we appeal to is the audience's libertine, rational, unsentimental side, their love for satire, their delight in the outraging of conventions and in tweaking the nose of piety. *Comprendez?*

*And money?*

Ah! A florin discreetly pressed into the appropriate palm. Money is freedom. Money is power. It can buy you anything, except youth. And it *can* buy you youths.

*What is the place of God and the church in your life?*

God has been, quite frankly, overrated, and the church can be a bore. The clergy is truculently myopic, and the services simply lugubrious. Everyone is a potential god, and life itself is to be worshiped.

*What kind of humor dominates?*

Wit is the means by which all is accomplished. Humor is cerebral, studied, arch, and biting. It is lovely to laugh at another's expense and, on occasion, useful to turn the laughter toward oneself. A slight titter is considered more appropriate than a howling guffaw. And it is far better to refer to another's "odorous fondness for breathing through his mouth" and "unpleasant, vaporous dampness" than to his bad breath and sweat.

*How is fear defined?*

Disgrace, public humiliation, poverty, disease, and pathetic old age are our terrors. Suppression, repression, and political maneuvers are survival tactics. We try not to dwell on fear, and we certainly do not acknowledge it, but all abhor the thought of the scorn of one's peers and the grave of a pauper. It is acceptable to express controlled delight and occasionally a finely edged rage, but never vulnerability, uncertainty, or vulgarity.

## Structure

*Those In the Know lead those out of it.*

*Who rules, and who follows?*

The aristocracy constitutes an exclusive fraternal order. We collectively decide the destiny of others, and the king decides *our* destiny. Since we are still reeling from an experiment in individual rights, we are quite reactionary and inflexible. One's only hope for advancement is noble birth, fortunate marriage, or fortunate "arrangement." The king at his discretion may

*For money has a power above*
*The stars and fate, to manage love.*

—SAMUEL BUTLER

*All men would be cowards if they durst.*

—JOHN WILMOT,
EARL OF ROCHESTER

pluck a title and estate from a recalcitrant antimonarchist, consign this person to oblivion, and place the awards in the lap of a favorite. Nell Gwynn, the best known actress of our era, begins as a lowly orange wench (a girl who sells oranges), achieves great stage success, leaves the theatre to become the king's mistress, and bears him children, whom he bestows with titles.

*How is justice brought about?*

While there is talk of a constitutional monarchy, at the moment it is absolute. The king or one of his deputies decides what is right. It is, in my opinion, a burden lifted.

*How is daily life ordered?*

The surprise of life comes, not by what one is doing at a given time, but with whom one is doing it and where. The day begins with an elaborate, lengthy ritual of preparation. In a sense, we are all actors in our own lives, and our attention to detail before venturing onstage is considerable. The entire morning is given over to one's *toilette*. The hair and face are mended endlessly, and one may entertain in one's own boudoir, even upon one's own bed, provided one has an appropriately attractive morning gown. Remember, the bed is the only comfortable piece of furniture in our home. Dressing is an arduous task. The rest of the day is spent in a combination of receiving and paying calls, in the hopes that the evening will produce an occasion.

*How are family and marriage defined?*

Must we speak of it?

*How are etiquette and education set?*

We look to the French court and to our monarch's whims for winds of change, but *volumes* are published on the appropriate way to go about almost any endeavor. Change slowly filters, ever so gracefully, down from the throne. The motions of classical education are pursued by both sexes of the aristocracy. Intelligence and literacy are greatly prized, but academic rigor is low, since these virtues are valued more for their resulting skill to charm and entertain than for their capacity to enlighten. Verses are no longer ends, but means.

*How are groups created and work defined?*

What you call the clique (and I prefer to call coterie) comes into full flower. Those with similar self-interests become allies in pursuit of influence and information—the closer to the throne, the stronger. Not to work is still *infinitely* preferable to work. It is the "work" (it pains me to speak the word) of the aristocracy to ensure that we will never have to work. That is why so many of our plays are all about the quite necessary

*The world is made up for the most part of fools and knaves.*

—GEORGE VILLIERS, DUKE OF BUCKINGHAM

*Such was the happy garden-state While man there walk'd without a mate.*

—ANDREW MARVELL

*Strange to say what delight we married people have to see these poor fools decoyed into our condition.* —SAMUEL PEPYS

*Here lies my wife; here let her lie! Now she's at rest, and so am I.* —JOHN DRYDEN

*Poetry's a mere drug.*

—GEORGE FARQUHAR

*She that is with poetry won Is but a desk to write upon.* —SAMUEL BUTLER

pursuit of fortune and estate. The professional actor and musician emerge. If one must have "work," this is the best category for getting near the elite, but one must not assume one will become part of it, Mme. Gwynn's good fortune notwithstanding. The ownership of land, managed by someone else, is absolutely the only acceptable way for a gentleman to earn an income.

### *How is information spread?*

The primary means, of course, is gossip. While word of mouth is astonishingly effective in our society, the use of hand-delivered notes is widespread, and news gazzettes (not unlike your scandal sheets) are relied upon, as well. To be the last to know is to feel deeply humiliated.

### Beauty

*Smooth, altered, and utterly, divinely calculated.*

*Her lips are two brimmers of claret,*
*Where first I began to miscarry,*
*Her breasts of delight*
*Are two bottles of white,*
*And her eyes are two cups of canary.*

—RAINS, FROM *EPSOM WELLS*

*Why hast not thou a (looking) glass hung up here? A room is the dullest thing without one.…*
*In a glass a man may entertain himself.*

—DORIMANT,
IN *THE MAN OF MODE*

### *What is the look most aspired to in this group?*

An elegance that defies one's sternest critics. In the latter part of your century, the phrase "drop-dead chic" effectively summarizes what we seek. A slender personage is desired, topped off by a mane of curly hair of similar length for men and women, the women's considerably more contained. Pale skin and delicate features are prized. A great beauty is like a fine wine.

### *What part does physical fitness play in attractiveness?*

Physical what? Do you mean fit to be tied? Just a little sex joke. Health and comfort are really quite irrelevant. One will endure anything for splendor. Men's garments happen to be an encumbrance, while women's corsets are merciless. We believe frequent bathing is unhealthy, and only a very few of us have lavatories. We do not brush our teeth until the end of the century, and then only the upper front teeth, because, of course, those are the ones seen. The newest rage from France is the silver toothbrush. I have two, each presented me by a different paramour. And, of course, one must examine one's countenance at regular intervals.

### *Which colors and shapes are favored?*

We love deep, rich jewel tones: greens, blues, vermilions, and crimsons in velvet, brocade, and satin. The feeling is of towering height gradually descending in a bell-shaped line. Fluttering ribbons, ruffles, feathers, fringe, and lace may cascade from almost any point, momentarily distracting attention as the eye descends. In both our persons and our surroundings, it is surprising that so much ornamentation can nonetheless communicate clear lines and spaciousness. Keeping up is simply essential, and speaking of up, the king is one of the tallest men in England. I believe this a cause for the desire we all now share to become longer.

*To what degree is nature altered to create beauty?*

Must we discuss nature again? Wigs, paint, and embellishment are fundamental. Nature did not leave the skin white enough or the other features bright enough, and one must compensate. And let me just say, while we are on the subject, that your plastic surgeons would be the most successful creatures at court if they could manage time travel. Part of the morning ritual is the application of heavy white zinc oxide, which reduces one's features to an immobile mask. For the many unfortunate, this is an attempt to cover the ravages of smallpox. The hands may be covered as well. The lips are painted Spanish red and the cheeks inlaid with a shiny red gum. Next, the definitive symbol of our vision of beauty—the patch, a little black taffeta cover (usually circular, but possibly in the shape of a star, moon, crown, or heart) which may cover pox marks or simply attract. One places the patch near the lip (for flirting), the nose (for roguishness), the eye (for passion), or, later, on either side of the face to indicate political affiliation (Whig or Tory). A lady's headdress may alter the shape of the head beyond recognition. We called it a "commode." Why are you smiling?

We use the term "undress" to mean any state short of full attire. A lady may be in undress when she is simply without her manteau (cloak), a gentleman without his wig. Undress is therefore a normal stage, and it is possible to be undressed out of doors. Since both sexes may employ obvious makeup in daily life, actors in your century face the challenge of making up for the stage so that both the character and the fact that the character is deliberately made up are clear to the audience. So much for nature.

*How is taste defined?*

Taste has nothing to do with morals and all to do with refinement. The approach must be refined, but not the appetite. Fluidity is fundamental. What you will call classical ballet is emerging as an art form, and much time is spent training with the ballet master on simple deportment for life, as well as the dance. Ladies should be able to sing and play either harp or harpsichord. The instrument creating the most interest is the viola da gamba. Men who compose music and paint are highly regarded. An intellectually facile mind and a way with words are considered artistic accomplishments.

## Sex

*The chase is far more important than the act.*

*How significant a part of the collective consciousness is sex?*

We think about it constantly. We talk about it unceasingly. We believe in pleasure. Have I said that?

*What do most people consider turn-ons and turn-offs?*

Verbal facility and music are captivating, as are long, swanlike necks, exquisitely shaped shoulders, and lovely breasts for the women, and curly manes of hair and strong, well-shaped calves for the men. Any of these may be aggressively displayed. A sudden twist of a gallant's leg may send a damsel swooning. A little glimpse of her ankle *en passant* is truly provocative. The décolletage, often teasingly enhanced by Venetian lace at the edges of the bodice, is employed to store letters and other small, secret items. We are, as you so bewitchingly put it, "turned off" by dullness, prudery, age, shyness, and overt, unrefined vulgarity.

In our time, it is a rare play which does not at some point feature the leading lady in male disguise so that all may see her hips, calves, and ankles.

The king was most clever in quenching the howl of Puritan protest at this phenomenon. He argued that it is at least as offensive for the male sex (*à la* the clergy) to wear skirts in public, as for the female to display herself. As I was saying to him just last Tuesday week, "Sire, you are a fount of wisdom and gladsome cunning."

While we seem artificial to you, and our men do bedeck themselves with ornament, our desire is still for male virility and female delicacy. We have great tolerance for fops and crones, but tolerance is not the same as "turn-on."

*How is seduction accomplished?*

The veil and mask exist in words, looks, and moves. The *double entendre* and hidden agenda are deeply appreciated. The fan sends out a series of provocative messages. Secrecy is essential. Seduction is a game of skill, intended for the masterful.

The chase is so sweetly savored that achieving success is very near, albeit not quite, disenchantment. Yet, even as your beloved acquiesces and the rapturous Act of Oblivion grows near, you do not go hastily toward consummation, but precede it with well-paced tiny kisses, caresses, nibbles, and teasing words.

*Is the emphasis on pleasure or procreation?*

Pleasure is deserved; procreation a mere responsibility. We are not fond of children, but the world must go on.

---

*Sidebar quotes:*

"Women let me with the men prevail,
And with the ladies as I look like male.
"Tis worth your money that such legs appear;
These are not to be seen elsewhere:
In short, commend this play, or by this light,
We will not sup with one of you tonight.

—EPILOGUE FROM
THE GENEROUS ENEMIES

Perhaps the kind attendant [damsel] shall display
Her waving handkerchief, to court your stay.
If the white flag flies waving to the field,
The warrior knows the charming fort will yield.

—CHARLES HOPKINS

*What is the courtship ritual?*

A lengthy series of notes, gifts, and delicate gestures juxtaposed constitutes the pursuit. Steps forward and backward and shifts of strategy are all common. Courtship is an endlessly fascinating game of cat and mouse. One proves oneself a worthy lifetime adversary and companion in the game of life.

*Courtship to marriage, as a very witty prologue to a very dull Play.*
—WILLIAM CONGREVE

*Are deviation, infidelity, and promiscuity tolerated?*

We are an overwhelmingly, some would say exhaustively, heterosexual society. It is our primary interest, and our fops are very interested in assignations with women. We would probably tolerate almost anything done discreetly, however. Infidelity is almost inevitable. Promiscuity is tolerated in women and all but expected of men.

*To what degree is sexuality suppressed or expressed?*

I have no idea what you mean. Come sit closer and explain it to me carefully.

*Her arms by her side are so formally posted, She looks like a pullet trussed up to be roasted. The swell of her bubbies, and jut of her bum To the next brawny stallion cries, "Come, my dear, come!"* —NED WARD

## Recreation

*Gossip, intrigue, flirtation, nibbling, tasting, and testing are the delights which make life tolerable.*

*What is most people's idea of fun?*

We love to play, without innocence. We love to be bad boys and girls. The words "naughty" and "saucy" come into widespread use in our era. We love a large gala and a private rendezvous better than anything in between and particularly enjoy mixing these two. Creating one in the midst of the other is pure bliss.

*What would be an ideal social occasion?*

An all-day celebration at Whitehall Palace, with continuous feasting, culminating in a magnificent masked ball, would be perfection. Falling in and out of "love" with someone and finding a new "love" would be "lovely." Since clothes and lovemaking are the two great pleasures of life, the delectable day should involve both.

   A less auspicious, but equally enthralling, day would include extensive discussions of my wardrobe with my valet or boudoir maid, my milliner, seamstress, and shoemaker, all of whose lives are devoted to my own personal splendor. I would accomplish taking dancing, music, or fencing lessons and receiving as guests some members of the royal inner circle. I may even ask them to join me in my withdrawing room. (I am told you have now dropped the "with" from the designation. Do you use the room for

*I cannot think God would make a man miserable only for taking a little pleasure out of the way.* —CHARLES II

*Men are but children of a larger growth.*
—JOHN DRYDEN

sketching now?) I would somehow manage to take in the court, royal park, salons of friends, a coffee shop, an eating house, the theatre, and some card game. I would promenade, employ my own carriage or a sedan chair—the newest and most prestigious French import—or hire a hackney coach. One keeps oneself amused.

*Are you doers or watchers?*

We do both, although we would rather do and be watched than watch and not do. Our refinement requires allowing others to take a turn.

*And your intellectual life? Are you thinkers or mindless hedonists?*

*I am always of the opinion of the learned, if they speak first.*

—WILLIAM CONGREVE

But, my dear, thinking can be hedonistic. You must *have* ideas in order to *fulfill* them. To feast and to indulge, one must know all that can be ordered from life's menu. Intellectual *playfulness* is requisite. Endless philosophizing, ethical pondering, and metaphysical maundering are as boring in their ways as an utter vacuum.

*What are the common shared pastimes?*

Beyond the musical endeavors I have described, we love to write letters and to promenade. Cards are now accepted addictions; the gambling table beckons like a demon. Ladies enjoy experimenting with magic potions designed to subdue or bring out the ribald in their gentlemen. Ladies do whatever gentlemen do, but with greater anonymity or more elaborate disguise. Everyone seems, of a sudden, to have a little dog. The king has eighteen, and they have their own court physician. His favorite and mine (dog, not doctor) is named Bibillou, but in confidence, I must tell you it elates me His Grace allows me to call the darling creature BiBi and occasionally even Lou-Lou.

*What food and drink are favored?*

Consumption is both sensual gratification and art form. The dining hour is now quite late—two or three o'clock in the country, and four or five in the city. We largely reject implements in favor of eating with our fingers, making art a necessity. And delicate dribblings on chins and breasts are irresistible. Our small meals involve four courses, average ones up to twelve, and a true celebration must have twenty-four. Such an occasion would last five to twelve hours and move through separate rooms for fish and soup, roasts and fowl, sweets and desserts (I adore marzipans!). Then, after games in the salon, coffee, hot chocolate (recently the rage) or liqueurs in yet another room. Ten fine wines are minimal if you wish to set a good table, and the recent invention of the bottleneck (corkscrew) has vastly expanded the range of ports, sherries, burgundies, champagnes, and punches to savor.

We prefer richer and heavier food and drink than you and would find your chardonnays and your salads pathetic. A pleasing light snack? Some claret and sweetmeats and perhaps a fig or two. Or one of the very new white wines, accompanied by the latest invention, a delectable cheese produced in the otherwise quite boring village of Cheddar.

*And the importance of recreation in life? The standard view of indulgence?*

Pshaw. Life *is* recreation, so I never indulge myself. If my purpose is pleasure, how could any act I commit be construed as self-indulgent? I prefer to think of it as simply measuring up to my responsibilities. Now, I have some scribbles to share with you, but I would prefer you read them in the next room, so I may have a moment of reflection in solitude. When you return, I will have something utterly delicious to tell you.

[*I acquiesce. When I return, the subject has disappeared and has not, at this writing, returned.*]

## SIGHT

*Painted, bright, shameless, and proud of it.*

Personal splendor must be attained at any cost, and artifice is certainly expected. Wigs become more common than natural hair as the period progresses. Think of yourself as a work of art that must be re-created daily and put on active exhibition. Appearance is such a vital part of life that it forms the basis of the following exercise.

---

A few more touches, and I think I may
Be ready to embark upon my day.
My wig's resplendent, to perfection curled,
My face a masterpiece to show the world.
And this new glorious garment which I wear
Is very near too exquisite to bear.
When out upon the promenade I tread,
My enemies will wish that they were dead.
They all will feel so plain, so drab, so mortal
I must make certain they don't see me chortle.
Though I have often hovered near perfection,
There has been no day in my recollection,
When I looked so alluring, fine, and bright.
I know this will be my day and my night!
Although the day has not quite yet begun,
I feel my battles are already won.
I've ordered new hats, lace, shoes, songs, and coats.
I've sung, danced, primped, fenced, gossiped, and sent notes,
And most important, in one slight endeavor,

**EXERCISE**

**Restoration Warm-Up**

Learned some information that may sever
From off a pedestal a libertine,
Whom I have always known to be obscene.
When I so subtly share this tiny fact
The court from top to bottom will react!
I'm armed, festooned, prepared in every way,
I now make haste to leap into the fray!

---

### Women

- *Head.* Hair is arranged in ringlets and is longer in the back than in the front, sometimes in a style similar to what we call pigtails. Long curls off the face (*heartbreakers*) and short curls on the face (*confidents*) may be embellished by ribbons, pearls, feathers, or *fontage,* (a headdress of lace and wire resembling a Spanish mantilla).

- *Torso.* The neckline is cut low, wide, and revealing. The corset is boned in front and laced in back; the *manteau* (gown) is bell-shaped. The long, full skirt is open and caught up in the front, revealing an underskirt and perhaps a small, heavily laced apron, and either pulled into a bustle or draped over small *panniers* (hoops used to expand the skirt at the sides). Sleeves come only to the elbows, so that the lace of the chemise is visible below them. Rings may be worn over elbow-length gloves. A train is likely to be worn in public, not at home.

- *Feet.* Stockings may be brightly colored and are held by garters just above or below the knee. Shoes generally have half-inch heels and are closed with a bow, but the first high heels, which cover only the toe and instep, appear during this period.

- *Personal props.* The most fundamental prop is the fan. When going out, women may carry a *reticule* (drawstring bag), pomander, and parasol. If the weather threatens, a *fichu* (triangular scarf), hood, and muff may be added, and, of course, a vizard mask.

### Men

- *Head.* Hair is loose and long beneath a splendiferous, beplumed hat. Wigs change from tousled (spaniel) to corkscrew formal (high horned) as the century ends. The face is clean-shaven, except for a possible thread mustache.

- *Torso.* The men's costume is an oversized prototype of the three-piece suit. The long embroidered coat is loosely shaped to the body and reaches down to the knees, as does the vest. Cuffs are wide, and pockets are large. The shirt is embellished with lace and ribbons. Breeches come to the knee. The look grows tighter as the period progresses, moving from full breeches to narrow.

- *Feet.* The shoe is the same height as the ladies' but somewhat larger in shape. A prominent buckle may top it off.

- *Personal props.* Any or all of the following may be carried: snuff-box, handkerchief, perfume vial, walking stick (with elaborately carved head and perhaps a loop for ribbons), round or egg-shaped watch hung from a neck ribbon, and a small dress sword hung from a *baldric* (a belt worn over one shoulder).

### Both Sexes

Both sexes may carry muffs, also hung from the neck. For royalty, the heels and tongues of shoes may be red. Ladies are known to adapt gentlemen's clothing with great abandon for walking, riding, hunting, and shopping. For rehearsal, women should purchase a fan that snaps open and shut with great ease. For rehearsal clothes, a pillow can stand in for the bustle; strap the pillow to the posterior by splitting the pillow case open at each end and slipping a belt through. Men can wear a large open overcoat or rain-coat, a scarf, and a hat with a large brim. For both sexes, a handkerchief is useful—the larger the handkerchief and the heavier the material, the better. Ladies' character shoes and men's heeled shoes from the late sixties and early seventies can substitute.

### Movement and Contact

Because artifice is desired, you need not fear being called unnatural. Calculate each maneuver, thinking of yourself as moving from pose to pose to pose. Each time you change positions, rearrange yourself as a display. We have all practiced being models in private; imagine, however, that all models are trained in classical ballet and that they use only positions derived from ballet. The Restoration is the first period in which the feet are turned outward, with the chest as the center of energy. Fourth position is considered the most graceful. Other widely approved positions are long or short (feet apart or close) second position for the man and first position or short second position for the woman. Give some thought to allowing the hands to be governed by the feet in imitation or attractive counterpoint.

A lady moves in sweeping curves, head held high, and heels slightly off the ground so that the moves are silent. Hold the skirt only so that it rises ever so slightly off the ground. You are expected to lead with the bosom, as if the breasts were the first and foremost work of art in the moving gallery that is you. The steps are tiny and smooth, as if any move from one

Shown are representative examples of Restoration style. The relatively intimate Restoration theatre (seldom even one-third the size of the Elizabethan theatre) uses the apron almost exclusively. Because audiences are seated onstage in boxes and chairs, the line between performer and patron all but disappears. Chairs are all flourish and decoration, with no possibility of comfort. Even the popular harpsichord is frequently ornamented in every available space, in contrast to the more subdued alternative solo instrument of choice, the viola da gamba. The male periwig reaches outlan-

dish proportions, and the term *bigwig* is introduced. The ladies' mask and muff symbolize the infatuation with disguise and indulgence. Shoes are resplendent and high. Note the contrast between the coutier and the Puritan and the gradual move toward longer coats favored by the king. Ladies compete with gentlemen for the most ornamental accoutrements. Ladies' headdresses become taller, trains longer and the fan is as important to non-verbal communication as punctuation is to verbal communication.

location to another were part of a dance. Leave a pose by pivoting on the ball of the foot.

A gentleman must command his clothing by strongly flicking lace ruffs off the hands and the hair off the shoulders. Power shines through embellishments. The flourish abounds. The costume can easily make you look like a box with head and legs sticking out each end, so if you are a gallant, tame your costume. Never allow the hands to hang at your sides, because the hand disappears into a sea of lace. At every possible occasion, "make a leg" (flash a calf) without appearing to notice that you are doing so. Men now often remove hats indoors. After doffing the hat extravagantly, subtly showing off the clean interior, turn it inside toward yourself, and place it under the left arm or in front of the left hip. Stand up when a lady enters the room or approaches you, and open and close doors for her.

Although there is little mobility from the shoulder, circular movements of the elbow, the wrist, and the joints of each finger colorfully enhance an impression of delicate refinement. Everyone aims to be irresistible. Movement is like a sentence, and stopping is like punctuation, with each stop as different as a comma from a question mark. For the first time in history, an acting book (written by Thomas Betterton) appears. It is highly prescriptive, to the point of dictating which hand to put over your heart when you speak of yourself. Betterton concentrates, however, on the playing of tragedy, because everyone sees himself as playing a comedy all the time and therefore in need of no instruction.

*Fanning: The Language of the Fan*   The fan is a primary tool and even, on occasion, a weapon. The following signals have evolved historically and are worth practicing, but what matters is that you and your partner understand each other. Invent your own signals; command your fan and communicate clearly with it.

*You can do almost anything with a fan, except fan with it.*   —EDITH EVANS

| | |
|---|---|
| Tip of fan touching the lips | "Hush!" |
| Touching fan to the right cheek | "Yes!" |
| Touching fan to the left cheek | "No!" |
| Touching fan to the nose | "I do not trust you." |
| Yawning behind fan | "You bore me." |
| Pointing fan to heart | "You have my love." |
| Hiding eyes behind fan | "You attract me." |
| Brushing open fan toward person | "Go away." |

| | |
|---|---|
| Carrying fan in left hand | "I desire your acquaintance." |
| Placing fan near left ear | "You have changed." |
| Twirling fan on left hand | "I wish to get rid of you." |
| Drawing fan across forehead | "We are watched." |
| Shut | "You have changed." |
| Carrying fan in right hand | "You are too willing." |
| Drawing fan through hand | "I hate you." |
| Twirling fan in right hand | "I love another." |
| Drawing fan across cheek | "I love you." |
| Closing fan | "I wish to speak." |
| Carrying fan in right hand before face | "Follow me." |
| Drawing fan across eyes | "I am sorry." |
| Opening and shutting fan | "You are cruel." |
| Dropping fan | "Let's be friends." |
| Fanning slowly | "I am married," or "I am relaxed." |
| Fanning fast | "I am engaged," or "I am upset." |
| Touching handle to lips | "Kiss me." |
| Open wide | "Wait for me." |

*Snuffing: Taking Snuff*   Hold the box, which, if worthy, is made of gold and encrusted with jewels, between your thumb and index finger, and tap a bit of snuff onto the back of your hand or wrist, or pinch some out with your fingers. Inhale. Close the box, return it to your pocket, and flick errant particles from wrist, cuff, or sleeve. If offering the box to a lady, who does not carry her own, allow her to take it in her fingers and snort the snuff into each nostril.

*Handkering: Handkerchief as Weapon*   You heavily perfume yourself to guard against your own body odors (remember, you rarely bathe) as well as those you encounter on the street. You virtually douse your handkerchief with scent and employ it as a kind of machete in your journey. You store the handkerchief in your generous cuff or pocket or catch it in your ring, and when you are confronted with odoriferous unpleasantness, you whip it out and twirl it. There are elaborate guidelines about which fingers the point should protrude between, which side of the hand the lace should appear on, and how to maneuver (most of the moves are circular). Do not place the handkerchief the same way to remove it as to replace it but, instead, keep reversing positions. As long as it is out, why not punctuate a few of your remarks with it? Again, consistency and clarity among the cast are more important than historical accuracy.

*Typing: Playing into Your Image*   Your character's name is likely to reveal a dominant characteristic: Bull, Sir Clumsey, Constant, Lady Fanciful, Lady Fidget, Foible, Mrs. Frail, Heartfree, Horner, Loveless, Manly, Sir Novelty Fashion, Petulant, Pinchwife, Lord Plausible, Lady Pliant, Scandal, Mr. Smirk, Snake, Sparkish, Mrs. Squeamish, Sullen, Tattle, Waitwell, Lady Wishfort, Witwood. Delve into the trait, punching up animal images or high emotional states. You probably have a function (gallant, rogue, prude, fop, courtesan, wit, cuckold, gossip, plain citizen, wooer, philandering wife, rich uncle, jolly old knight, country bumpkin, city sophisticate) that allows you to follow a tradition. This typing can free creativity. Like verse rhythms, the type gives you a safe place to start.

*Descending: Sitting and Reclining*   Some sources allow a man to hold the back of a chair while seating himself; others are adamant that the chair must never be acknowledged. Flip up your coattails and correct the fall of your sword as you sit. As you lower yourself, press the back of one leg against the chair, and slip the other leg, toe pointed, under the chair to steady the descent. You may then reverse the positions of the feet once you are seated to finish off the action nicely. When you rise, reverse the whole action. Ladies sit and rise in plié.

*Showing Reverence: Bowing and Curtsying*   Since physical etiquette is taught by ballet masters, many maneuvers in the salon resemble those of the dance. Sources regarding the correct bows are contradictory. What follows is a frequent production choice.

### Men's Bow

Sweep the hat off with the right hand, and transfer it to the left under the arm. The bow itself begins when the hat is at shoulder height. Slide the right foot forward in a half circle a step before the left, with both feet turned out and both legs straight. Incline the body forward from the waist, keeping the spine and neck straight. Now bend both knees outward, keeping the front leg straighter than the rear, which in turn takes most of the body weight. Keep the feet flat on the ground. Now sweep the right leg back behind you in a half circle, before shifting your weight there. The right arm may sweep forward and down to your side. As you rise, shift your weight onto the front foot and move into third position. One of many possible variations is to place either your hat or your hand on your heart (as if to say, "My heart is yours") and then to sweep it gracefully toward the floor, turning the palm or rim of the hat upward (as if to say, "And I lay it at your feet"). Another variation is to kiss your hand in the direction of the lady to whom you are bowing.

In the Restoration bow and curtsies, the steps are more calculated and precise than those usually employed in Elizabethan staging. Eye contact and careful attention to symbolic choices are far more desirable than individual flair or bravado.

*Women's Curtsy*

Take a step to either side, and before continuing make certain that this move calls attention to you. Now return the foot you have just moved back to the other foot, heels touching as in first position. Bend knees smoothly and slightly outward, inclining the body a bit forward. Allow the arms to fall easily at your sides. Heels remain on the ground, unless the curtsy is particularly deep, in which case they rise slightly. The move resembles a plié. If it is executed "en passant," you needn't stop moving for more than a split second to do it; just dip as you pass the recipient. A common variation is to sweep one foot, as in the man's bow, forward for the forward curtsy, back for the back curtsy, and in either direction for the deep curtsy, quite similar to that used by the Elizabethans.

Touching and being touched are matters of great care. The fingertips are primed and alert and may brush gently against another person or object before darting away. You are acutely sensitive to shifting maneuvers. The bulky clothing presents a challenge for getting close, but it is just that—a challenge. All the maneuvers of hand kissing, cleaving, and embracing (described in Chapter 5) hold true, except that before you carry out the action, the object of the action will likely give you some signal to indicate compliance.

## SOUND

*Sly, playful, acerbic, sharp.*

Although Restoration characters may appear preoccupied with themselves, listening is terribly important. Not to have heard or understood is deplorable. You must have a lucid response, but it must *be* a response. Calculated nonverbal responses (sighs, vaguely stifled yawns, laughter, subtle purrs, growls, and even hisses) embellish verbal responses. Those nonverbals associated with basic body functions are, however, deplorable. Language is elevated, and the use of euphemism is raised to a high art. Full use of the top head voice and the bottom chest voice and musical dancing between the two are essential for expressing refinement and playfulness. Allow freewheeling melodic patterns and inflections. Refine consonants to razor sharpness to score points. The feeling of gracefully gliding vowels arranged between dartlike, clear consonants makes for devastatingly elegant speech.

The following skills of delivery, although not exclusive to the Restoration, are most heavily employed in this style. They overlap.

1. *Counterpoint.* Speech requires a balance between nonchalance and precision. Speakers make their points with pin-sharp crispness

but always leave the impression that they are exerting very little effort.

2. *Asides.* Whereas the Elizabethans also do asides, theirs are generally shorter and less digressive. To drive your interjected point home to the audience, you need a complete shift in focus and upsurge in energy. Then you return to your scene partner, pretending the aside never happened.

3. *Double entendres and pointing.* Innuendo is constant. Words usually have both an innocent and a sexual meaning. Usually the double entendre needs just the slightest break or pause just before and after, with some vowel extension and perhaps a change in quality to help load your statement. The more sexual the remark, the more likely you are to use false pause, stopping just before selecting the key word.

4. *Verse interludes.* Restoration plays are mostly prose, so instances of verse must be savored with pride and shaped with care. Remember, these people create verse not for its own sake but to achieve something and congratulate themselves on the effort. Play intention and pride in creation. The most common interlude is the *epigram,* a short piece of verse (rarely more than eight lines) ending in a clever summary and involving puns, antitheses, paradox, or ironic counterpoint. Some sort of setup and a surprising payoff are built into the rhyme.

5. *Negotiation.* Contracts and deals are regularly made in Restoration plays. Note the tone of negotiators and barterers in real life; theirs is unlike any other conversation. They constantly present themselves as powerless, so that the slightest compromise seems like a major sacrifice. Learn to martyr yourself to win the game.

6. *Echoing.* Often you repeat your partner's line back to him or her with the slightest variation and continue this game in series. You must give back as good and better than you get. Repeat each crucial word with a mimic's bite, and then insert the *new* word with the extra twist that tops the choice your partner made.

7. *Love masks.* Characters often claim to be enamored of someone to whom they are actually indifferent, or vice versa. The audience is allowed a glimpse of what you feel, but your partner is not. What you say is for two different listeners, each of whom takes a different meaning.

8. *Repartee.* Speaking cleverly for the sheer pleasure of doing so means a sensual tasting of language, an enormous relish in winning points, a sense of building triumph as you develop an argument, a virtual caressing of your favorite images, and small or-

gasms of alliteration. This is particularly essential in building the longer speeches.

9. *Excessive politeness*. Maggie Smith is one of the most accomplished living performers of Restoration comedy. She moves past civility into a state of delicate endurance of the crudeness of others that is hysterically funny to watch, in part because she always appears to be somewhat sorry for the other person to whom she is speaking—sorry that the person is so crude, so limited, so lacking in imagination. This attitude colors line readings and takes the vicious edge off biting lines. It is as if she simply has no choice but to put down the poor things with whom fate has forced her to interact; she insults them out of a great sense of charity.

10. *Prologue and epilogue*. Almost every Restoration play contains a prologue and an epilogue. The prologue is usually spoken by a man, the epilogue by a woman. These speeches are usually in rhymed couplets and contain messages to ponder. They require intricate shaping and a very direct relationship with the audience. The actor generally relates to the public directly rather than in character.

11. *Undercuts*. The technique of deflating your partner by moving underneath his or her point is highly useful in Restoration dialogue. Usually, your partner feeds you something in a bright tone and perhaps in a high pitch, and you respond, without seeming to push for effect, in a lower pitch and with a clear rejection of what has been said. You come in almost right away; just as the other actor's point starts to take flight, you ground it.

12. *Arcs*. Arcs are lengthy speeches that build in intensity and hilarity quite slowly. They require elaborate phrasing with careful attention to breath, thought, and voice. Only practice will develop this skill, but it is useful to think in terms of planting items around the room, which you will pull together into some glorious creation when you are ready. You drop a point to your audience and/ or partner, make certain they have received it, and subtly promise them that you will get back to it and that it will be worth their while to hold on; then, you sharply launch into your next point. This way, you build and sustain interest until you complete your work of speech art.

## Music and Dance

During the Restoration, music discovers an inventive, buoyant, self-confident spirit. For the first time, the publication of sheet music makes tunes available to anyone. Operas are loved, as are oratorios, cantatas, fugues, preludes, sonatas, suites, and concertos. Composers are becoming more attracted to (*a*) writing for one particular instrument or solo voice; (*b*) writing music for the first time in measures; (*c*) writing elaborate musical ornamentation; (*d*) expressing a wide range of emotion, so that for the first time such feelings as rage and disdain are given full musical (controlled) expression; and (*e*) showing off, that is, displaying virtuosity for its own sake. Favored keyboard instruments are the spinet, pianoforte, and—perhaps the definitive instrument of the period—the harpsichord. Gaining attention are the oboe, cello, and viola da gamba, for winds and strings now come into their own. The full orchestra also now flowers, and art songs emerge.

Music matches ideals associated with speech—careful, exquisite tone and timing, assertiveness, buoyant attack, and a blending of French and English customs. The embellishments are called *baroque,* which literally means "irregular as a perfect pearl." Both speech and music are full of unexpected trills countered by long smooth swells.

While ballet influences offstage movement profoundly, the social dance of choice, the *minuet,* captures shared feelings about being alive. The style is formal, but the steps are quick and light and demand control, balance, clean lines, and poses. Stately, graceful moves are interspersed with pauses. Although the minuet demands correct deportment, it is emotionally full of searching and evading, with partners now facing, now side by side, now gliding past each other in elusive courtship. The floor pattern moves historically from a figure **8**, to an **S**, to a **2**, to a **Z**. Skill in the dance is so highly prized that statesmen who cannot master it place their careers and credibility in jeopardy. Both partners begin, as in dances of the past century, on the same foot; in the minuet, however, they begin on the right. Other popular dances are the *saraband* (in which the entire body moves and arm movements are controlled), the *gigue* (a gentler version of the galliard, with hopping steps), and the *gavotte* (another adapted French peasant dance, in which each couple dances alone in the center and then each partner kisses all participating members of the opposite sex). Moves are now more limited and stylized, with less room for individual choice and more emphasis on correct form.

## KEYS TO THE WORLD

### Images

Something one dislikes : "loathsome"
Something one likes: "charming"
Elegance
Sensuous informality
Decorous self-display

*Next to coming to a good understanding with a new mistress, I love a good quarrel with an old one.* —DORIMANT, IN *THE MAN OF MODE*

Calculated casualness
Studied nonchalance
Disguised artifice
Consummate ease
Effortless urbanity
Brittleness
Satire
Flirtatiousness
Veiled emotions and intentions
Wickedness
Delight
Proud, preening, brilliantly plumed exotic birds
Architecture of Christopher Wren, particularly St. Paul's Cathedral
   and Hampton Court
Discoveries of Isaac Newton
Paintings of Peter Lely
Philosophies of René Descartes, John Locke, Immanuel Kant, and
   David Hume
Acerbic observations of Jonathan Swift
Music of Henry Purcell foremost; runners-up: Vivaldi, Lully, Scar-
   latti, Bach, Corelli, Torelli, Handel
Actors: Thomas Betterton (most distinguished), Charles Hart,
   Elizabeth Barry, Anne Bracegirdle
Evocative words and phrases:
"He who wins with the least effort—wins."
"Nothing is more important in life than to please in conversation."
"True victory is the result of innate superiority."

### Social Success and Suicide

You can quickly rise or fall from favor in a genuinely fickle environment
such as the Restoration world. You will know you have succeeded if you
should happen to receive the ultimate compliment:

> Your effortless wit has left me speechless, and your beauty has left me breath-
> less. Allow me to bestow upon you any favor you desire.

*When you part with your
cruelty, you part with
your power.* —MILLAMANT,
   IN *THE WAY OF THE WORLD*

Your disgrace will be complete if someone to whom you happen to be
particularly attracted bestows upon you the ultimate insult:

> You are dull and old. [*stifled yawn*] Please remove yourself immediately from
> my path and permanently from my life.

To be a social success, you must

- Look stunningly and effortlessly turned out at all times.
- Make appearances at the best soirees with desirable companions
  and make everything done or said there look easy.

- Know gossip before anyone, or at least appear to.
- Be quoted with some frequency; be quoted often enough to be misquoted.
- Develop a reputation beyond your own actions or, even better, beyond human endurance.

You commit social suicide by

- Speaking directly, explicitly, and absolutely to the point.
- Exposing your rural origins and animal tendencies through bodily noises or clumsy maneuvers.
- Have attention given you and somehow "drop the ball" by saying nothing, nothing noteworthy, or something stupid.
- Revealing your vulnerability in public.
- Get caught working, studying, trying too hard, being utterly faithful, enjoying the country, or cheating at cards (any other type of cheating is acceptable).

### Masking

Socially, wearing a vizard out on the street is commonplace, as is remaining masked for the entire evening at a ball. There has never been such validating of hiding while in public. Although actors rarely play scenes masked, the idea of disguise is most popular. One employs a deliberate, calculated presentation of self. Fans and other accoutrements noted earlier may literally hide one while evaluation, recovery, and maneuvering occur. The best mask, of course, is to appear to have none.

*A gallant ought always to testify an ardour and impatience: and though he be ice, he ought always to say, he burns.*

—ANONYMOUS AUTHOR OF *THE ART OF MAKING LOVE*

*No mask like open truth to cover lies,*
*As to go naked is the best disguise.*

—WILLIAM CONGREVE

---

Repeat the masked activities suggested in the previous two chapters, with this basic change in perception: The veneer *never* comes off in Restoration plays. The audience might get a fleeting glance beneath, but that is all. The relentlessly nonsentimental mask will vary—now opaque, now translucent or even scrimlike—but it stays on. Restoration playing is thus about how skillful, interesting, and varied your mask is rather than about when you choose to put it on. Covering up is admired and naked emotion abhorred.

**E X E R C I S E**

**Always On**

---

### The Production

Most Restoration productions attempt to recreate the ambience of one of the original performances, which featured a consort in the gallery playing music before and after the play as well as during interludes. Present-day productions employ unrealistic wing and drop sets and make some attempt to create, through lighting, the effect of candlelight, footlights, and chandeliers. Sometimes boxes are built onto the sides of the apron for aristocrats to sit in. Dandies may appear on the stage itself. The actor generally acknowledges the audience as "my public" and plays in a presentational way, even singling out favorite members of what might be termed his or her personal fan club. Proximity to the audience requires that actors come right to the lip of the stage for crucial speeches and asides. Not infrequently, the beginning and end of the performance is embellished by such touches as orange wenches and others peddling wares and themselves. A recent production always singled out the highest university official in the audience, and a wench publicly delivered an assignation note to him from one of the actresses, who would then peek around the curtain to blow him a kiss. Often, actors dressed as the king and his entourage enter and are seated with honor. The more the audience is made to feel like the original audience, the more they will succumb to the playful, prurient spirit and leave prudery in the lobby.

## The Perfect Audience

*Damn me, Jack, 'tis a confounded play, let's to a whore and spend our time better.* —BULLY BEAU, QUOTED BY TOM BROWN

At no time in history has the action portrayed onstage been more perfectly matched to the daily life of the audience. There are two kinds of perfect audience. One captures absolutely the overwhelming challenge to original actors. The other captures this feeling in a more subtly supportive way. You must experience the first to develop the second.

Audience members of the first type come to the theatre as much to be seen, hunt for prey, socialize, and pass the time as to see the play. They come to "chatter, toy, play, hear, hear not." They not only flirt outrageously and sometimes ignore the action of the play, but also attempt to top it. As Sparkish in *The Country Wife* says, "The reason why we are so often louder than the players, is, because we think we speak more wit, and so become the poet's rivals in his audience." Those who feel more clever than the play sit in Wit's Row (onstage or right up front) or find other distraction. A scene rehearsal with this interaction, while unnerving, can sharpen your attack and get you to win your audience and score points. Remember, however, that this audience does not *oppose* you. It may lose interest in you or decide to top you, but it is not hostile or adversarial.

*Lords come hither [to the theatre] to learn the à la mode grin, the antic bow, the new-fashioned cringe, and how to adjust their phiz to make themselves as ridiculous by art as they are by nature.* —TOM BROWN

Audience members of the second type let a flirtatious eye fall on the actors and only occasionally scan the room. They see the action onstage as a direct reflection of their own daily lives and participate in it, verbalizing agreement with the performers or complimenting their charms. Men indicate approval by beating their walking sticks or staffs on the floor. Women applaud with the fan and use it to signal the players and occasionally actually venture so far as to applaud with both hands.

## Contemporary Parallels

The 1990s offer the following connections to the 1690s:

- Preoccupation with "me first" at all costs, so that feeling good about oneself becomes the basis for major life decisions.
- Conglomerates devoted to maintaining beauty and the illusion of youth.
- Belief and resignation that corruption in high places is commonplace and almost inevitable.
- Resemblance of the ritual of snuff use to that of cocaine, both in appearance and in the fundamental desire for a quick fix (snuff, however, is less addictive).
- Establishments (for example, singles bars, some fitness clubs, dating agencies, television programs, classified ads) devoted primarily to bringing strangers together. In these spaces, the great opening line is all.
- Greed as rewarded behavior.
- Theatre-related social events (cast parties, receptions, awards banquets) where full bitchy artifice sometimes rules.
- Preoccupation with food, combined with a desire for the very best, leading to such items as gourmet ice cream bars and hot dogs.
- How-to books that avoid ultimate ethical questions in favor of formulas for success.
- A general softening of society, so that hard physical labor is unknown to many and fitness must be achieved through equipment.

## PLAYS AND PLAYWRIGHTS

Here are those scripts most often produced:

| | |
|---|---|
| Behn, Aphra | *The Rover* (1667) |
| Congreve, William | *Love for Love* (1695) |
| | *The Way of the World* (1700) |
| Dryden, John | *Marriage a la Mode* (1672) |
| Etherege, George | *Love in a Tub* (1664) |
| | *She Would If She Could* (1668) |

|  | *The Man of Mode* (1675) |
| Farquhar, George | *The Recruiting Officer* (1706) |
|  | *The Beaux Stratagem* (1707) |
| Vanbrugh, John | *The Relapse* (1696) |
|  | *The Provok'd Wife* (1697) |
| Wycherley, William | *The Country Wife* (1675) |
|  | *The Plain Dealer* (1676) |

## SCENES

*The Beaux Stratagem*
Mrs. Sullen, Archer
Broke and seeking his fortune, Archer aims at the conquest of a young, neglected wife. Though strongly attracted to each other, they feel compelled to pretend they have entered the gallery adjacent to her boudoir merely to "admire the art."
Dorinda, Mrs. Sullen
A young woman married to a drunken brute meets with her sister-in-law to decide what to do with and about him.

*The Country Wife*
Margery Pinchwife, Mr. Pinchwife
Fearing cuckoldry, Pinchwife tries to force his young wife to write a letter to her lover that will end their relationship.

*The Man of Mode*
Dorimant, Lady Loveit
The affair is over, and Dorimant feels compelled to make certain his former love understands this in no uncertain terms.

*The Plain Dealer*
Manly, Lord Plausible
A man of character tries to get rid of a fop with none.

*The Recruiting Officer*
Captain Plume, Captain Brazen
Two recruiters in search of soldiers find more than they bargained for in a small English town.

*The Rover*
Willmore, Angelica
A rover and a rogue, Willmore attempts to persuade Angelica, a high-priced courtesan, to bestow her wares upon him free of charge.

*The Way of the World*
Millamant, Mirabell
In this drama's first prenuptial agreement scene, two sophisticates meet to negotiate the precise conditions of their future life together.
Mirabell, Fainell
Over a lively game of cards, two social climbers explore the foibles of the aristocracy and the need to hide one's true feelings in order to play the game.

*The Relapse*
Lord Foppington, Young Fashion
On his way to the theatre, a consummate fop is visited by his pleasant but cunning younger brother, who is in need of funds.

---

1. Take turns standing in the center.
2. Everyone else gets up and walks around you and examines you, not by touching but still very curiously.
3. Revel in the attention. You are a world-class model, and they should be eating their hearts out.
4. Shift your position occasionally to show yourself off to better advantage or to give them a little peek.
5. Discuss what tempted you to feel intimidated and what helped you get past it.

**E X E R C I S E**

**Check Me Out**

1. Work in couples while appropriate music from the period plays in the background.
2. Calling on impressions of ballet moves, the man offers the woman his arm, and the two of you promenade around the room as if you were ballet stars on curtain call.
3. Assume you are the most dazzling couple, but acknowledge the others as you pass. Give yourself plenty of room and focus on jointly executed S curves, C curves, 8s, and as many graceful maneuvers as possible, all the while keeping in promenade.

**E X E R C I S E**

**Promenade**

1. Keeping in the Restoration mode, go outside with your partner for fifteen minutes.
2. Find as many things as possible that can be improved on nature in order to fit your Restoration sensibilities.

**E X E R C I S E**

**Messing with Mother Nature**

3. Return to class and share your findings. You must have not only targets but also specific plans. How do you want it cut, painted, draped, or altered, and how do you feel your suggestions will improve life?

**E X E R C I S E**

**Chic It Out**

1. Come to class one day dressed in what you consider your most sensational, knockout outfit.
2. Take turns parading around for applause and approval.
3. At an agreed upon break, go out and change, so that the body part or parts that you feel most proud of are exposed or emphasized.
4. Come back and repeat the exercise, showing off what a phenomenal specimen you are. Those who break up have to go out and start all over until they develop the requisite eat-your-heart-out attitude.

**E X E R C I S E**

**Double Dish**

1. Agree on a task that the whole class can accomplish, such as cleaning up the classroom or rearranging the furniture.
2. Designate someone to start a rumor, which everyone tries to spread without being caught.
3. Arrange an assignation with someone, and try not to let others catch you doing so.
4. You have a three-part task: the group activity, the gossip, the assignation agreement. If you think you are the first to achieve all three tasks, stop the action. Find out who knows what and with whom. Discuss the concentration necessary to carry out these divided tasks.

**E X E R C I S E**

**Entendre**

Sit in a circle. Try to have a group discussion in which every remark can be taken two ways. Load each statement, and employ all of the techniques discussed. If you cannot devise a double entendre, pass and let the next person pick it up. Agree on a topic or agenda that you are motivated to discuss so that you put your effort not into keeping the conversation going but into keeping up with both the literal meaning and the innuendo.

## SOURCES FOR FURTHER STUDY

Avery, Emmett. "The Restoration Audience." *Philosophical Quarterly,* January 1966.

Baur-Heinhold, M. *Baroque Theatre.* New York: McGraw-Hill, 1967.

Blitzer, Charles. *Age of Kings.* New York: Time-Life Books, 1967.

Boehn, Max Von. *Modes and Manners.* Philadelphia: J. B. Lippincott Co., 1929.

Boswell, Eleanore. *The Restoration Court Stage, 1660–1702.* Cambridge, Mass.: Harvard University Press, 1932; New York: Benjamin Blom, 1960, 1965; New York: Barnes & Noble, 1966.

Bracher, Frederck, ed. *Letters of Sir George Etherege*. Berkeley, Calif.: University of California Press, 1974.

Brown, John Russell, and Bernard Harris, eds. *Restoration Theatre*. New York: Capricorn Books, 1965.

Bryant, Arthur. *The England of Charles II*. London: Longmans, Green and Co., 1935.

Callow, Simon. *Acting in Restoration Comedy*. New York: Applause Books, 1992.

Cunningham, C. W. and Phyllis. *Handbook of English Costume in the 17th Century*. London: Faber and Faber, 1955.

Dobree, Bonamy. *Restoration Comedy, 1660–1720*. London: Oxford University Press, 1924.

Elwin, Malcolm. *The Playgoer's Handbook to Restoration Drama*. London: J. Cape; New York: Macmillan, 1928.

Fujimura, Thomas H. *Restoration Comedy of Wit*. Princeton: Princeton University Press, 1952.

Gilder, Rosamond. *Enter the Actress: The First Women in the Theatre*. Boston: Houghton Mifflin Co., 1931; New York: Theatre Arts Books, 1961; Freeport, N.Y.: Books for Libraries Press, 1971.

Henshaw, N. S. *Graphic Sources for a Modern Approach to the Acting of Restoration Comedy*. Ph.D. diss., University of Pittsburgh, 1967. (ETJ5-68-157-70)

Hopkins, Charles. *The Art of Love. Dedicated to the Ladies*. 1700. R. Wellington, 1704.

Hotson, Leslie. *The Commonwealth and Restoration Stage*. Cambridge, Mass.: Harvard University Press, 1928; New York: Russell & Russell, 1962.

Knutson, Harold C. *The Triumph of Wit*. Columbus: Ohio State University Press, 1988.

"The Language of the Fan." *American Heritage Magazine,* February 1966.

Lester, Katherine Morris, and Bes Viola Oerke. *Accessories of Dress*. Peoria: The Manual Arts Press, 1940.

Lewis, W. H. *The Splendid Century*. Oxford: William Morrow and Co., 1954.

Loftus, John, ed. *Restoration Drama*. New York: Oxford University Press, 1970.

Lynch, Kathleen M. *The Social Mode of Restoration Comedy*. New York: Macmillan, 1926; New York: Octagon Books, 1965; New York: Biblo and Tannen, 1965.

McCollum, John. *The Restoration Stage*. Boston: Houghton Mifflin Co., 1961.

Paine, Clarence S. The Comedy of Manners (1660–1700): *A Reference Guide to the Comedy of the Restoration*. Boston: F. W. Faxton, 1941.

Palmer, John. *The Comedy of Manners*. New York: Russell & Russell, 1962.

Powell, Jocelyn. *Restoration Theatre Production*. London: Routledge & Kegan Paul, 1984.

Seyler, Athene. "Fans, Trains and Stays." *Theatre Arts* 31, 1947.

Styan, J. L. *Restoration Comedy in Performance*. Cambridge: Cambridge University Press, 1986.

Swedenberg, H. T., Jr., ed. *England in the Restoration and Early Eighteenth Century*. Berkeley, Calif.: University of California Press, 1973.

Wideblood, Joan, and Peter Brinson. *The Polite Society*. New York: Oxford University Press, 1965.

Wilson, J. H. *A Rake and His Times*. Oxford: Oxford University Press, 1952.

## VIDEOS

**Acting in Restoration Comedy** (Simon Callow)     Master class with scenes from *The Relapse* coached for ultimate clarity of language and varying levels of humor. Companion to text of the same title.

**The Draughtman's Contract** (Peter Greenaway)     Perhaps the only commercial film set in the appropriate time (1694), it is racy, arch, and filled with detail on daily life during the period.

**The Way of the Word** and **The Country Wife** (BBC educational series)     Shortened scripts without most subplot action, these films are nevertheless effective in recapturing the period and are literally the only versions available of Restoration plays on film.

**Dangerous Liaisons** (Stephen Frears)     While set a hundred years later, this film is very much in the Restoration spirit of addictive decadence.

# 7

# RELATIVES OF RESTORATION PERIOD STYLE
## Morals and Manners

## CRUSTY UNCLE AND CONSERVATIVE GRANDCHILDREN

Two groups of plays resemble those of the Restoration but are different enough to merit a separate look. The term *comedy of manners* is often applied to all of the plays of the Restoration, Molière, and the Georgians. In fact, the term often designates *any* play involving witty banter among the elite. Because the setting is often a salon or parlor, a room designated for talk, the term *drawing room comedy* is also used. Some refer to any play of this kind as a Restoration work; however, the term denotes a specific English historical genre depicting a unique world never quite duplicated in any other time or place.

What ties the three groups of plays together is a newfound concern for appropriate behavior as the subject for plays. Questions of little interest to the Greeks and the Elizabethans are now considered important. What constitutes good manners? How important is it to have them? How do you get them? How do you display them? How far can you stretch them? These replace the cosmic issues of destiny and the meaning of life that preoccupied earlier eras. The Greeks and Elizabethans defy mere rules or create their own; these later groups maneuver safely within structure. They play by the rules.

Whereas the Restoration involves elegant corruption, its two closest relatives are considerably more wholesome. Both Molière and the Georgians are interested not simply in what behavior works but in what behavior is morally *right*. They are interested in the overall good of society at least as much as the individual in it. They find in this struggle of self versus society

Pat Galloway (Dorine) and William Hutt (Tartuffe) in *Tartuffe,* The Stratford Festival

a strong source of laughter. Molière *precedes* and influences the Restoration. He writes from France during the earliest part of the movement and inspires most of the Restoration writers. The Georgians *follow* the Restoration by nearly one hundred years, during which time enough sweeping changes take place in the world to give rise to a distinct kind of comedy involving the middle class.

The three share many characteristics. Molière could be called the uncle of Restoration, the crusty but benign influence, always amusing but with strict ideas about what is right. The Restoration takes his mordant wit and removes it from any discernible moral stance. The Georgians could be called in turn the grandchildren of the Restoration. A little embarrassed by their profligate ancestors, the Georgians become highly concerned with what is proper and much less concerned with aristocratic privilege. The following discussions are short, dealing only with answers that are different from those in the preceding chapter. If a topic is not mentioned, assume there is no significant difference from the Restoration. Even the strangest families share genetic traits.

To distinguish these worlds clearly, you may wish to refer regularly to the comparison chart on page 245.

# MOLIÈRE:
# Moral Lessons Sweetened with Laughter

## THE WORLD ENTERED

Why a section on a single playwright? Molière is easily the second most produced playwright in the world and most observers' choice for second greatest. Whereas Shakespeare is surrounded by a half dozen other brilliant writers, Molière stands alone. Like Shakespeare, he steals or borrows plots from a wide variety of sources, uses plots merely as something on which to attach his ideas, and embraces characters from the aristocracy all the way down to country bumpkins. In fact, Molière sometimes makes the play *about* the bumpkin. Also like Shakespeare, he died in his fifties after creating over thirty plays and working primarily with one established company under royal patronage. Both were investors or part owners of their companies, and both were actors: Molière even acted on the night of his death in 1673, playing, ironically, the title role in *The Imaginary Invalid*. No one in his time and place touches his genius. And *absolutely* no one shares his particular voice. Today, Théâtre Français is rightly called the House of Molière.

Three important influences make Molière's work unique. First, he writes during the period in which a movement called *neoclassicism* dominates France. Theatre is required to achieve a sense of decorum and appropriateness. Plays must not offend the sensibilities of audiences. Characters must behave properly. The play must be ultimately morally uplifting and adhere to the basic Greek unities. Molière manages to work within this framework and still write comedy. In fact, he is the first to give comedy true respectability, raising it to the level of esteem previously reserved for tragedy. He manages to inject subtle nuances in an art form thought to be loud, broad, and indelicate. He surprises audiences with the idea that comedy can actually be polite. He creates social satire as we know it today. He manages to get his audience to laugh at itself while being admonished.

Second, Molière also writes from the tradition of the *commedia dell'arte*, which employs the very broadest comic and improvisational ingredients in performance. The commedia dell'arte had been a famous Italian acting company led by the great Tiberio Fiorelli, also known as Scaramouche. The term gradually came to refer to the entire Italian improvisational movement. At one time, Molière's company shared a space with theirs. They worked with stock characters, plots, and pieces of business—pratfalls, slapstick, and most of what we now see in broad farce, cartoons, and clowns. To be done well, this kind of comedy must be clean and sharp. Molière observes and uses the great precision of the Italian performers, carefully refining it and giving it sophistication.

A third significant influence on Molière is the reign of Louis XIV, a monarch with an incomparable ego and great love for pageantry, laughter, and dancing. He appeared early in his reign as the Sun King in the Ballet de Nuit and the name stuck. He desired more vehicles for more guest appearances. After first performing for the twenty-year-old Louis at the Louvre on October 24, 1658, Molière spent much of the rest of his life creating plays, interspersed with music and dancing, featuring His Radiance.

*Has God forgotten all I did for Him?* —LOUIS XIV

Imagine a playwright of the twentieth century managing to draw from vaudeville and the circus, honor the strictest rules of etiquette and most repressive lobbying groups, serve the whims of a major tycoon who believes himself to be the center of the universe, and still write strong satire. This is the genius of Molière.

Our interview is with a member of Molière's own acting company, first called the Illustre Théâtre. The actor has worked with the playwright from his humble days touring the provinces through his glory days at the Palais-Royal.

## Time: 1658–1673

*My friends, we're wasting time which should be spent*
*In facing up to our predicament.*
—CLÉANTE, IN *TARTUFFE*

*How does this time influence your work?*

*Mon Dieu!* This age [Molière's life 1622–1673, court performances 1658–1673] is full of changes. We first performed in Paris and were a flop. We toured the provinces and learned our craft. Now we are the most renowned company in Paris! The vastly overrated Conferie de la Passion [*subject stops here to pretend to spit ferociously on the ground* ] cannot even touch us. But we have many enemies, and each day is a new test. *C'est formidable!* Everyone walks on eggs, and the situation could always change. This is equally true of our actors and our characters. Our plays, because they are about, how do you say, universal foibles, can be done anywhere, anytime. There is always some group as ridiculous as the ones my dear Jean-Baptiste mocks in his plays.

Age is reviled, and youth is connected with innocence, virtue, and a good heart. Both youth and age need to learn temperance! The old characters are often the most bigoted and easily duped, often exploding and yelling. Youth is sweet, but headstrong. It is not so wonderful to be young, but it is much worse to be old, *n'est-ce pas?* The disastrous Thirty Years' War, from 1618 to 1648, has wiped out half the people of Europe, so young or old, we are just grateful to be alive, you know? Time moves swiftly in our plays. Conflict is direct, with all action stripped down to bare essentials and the story strongly driven forward. A Molière play is lively and brisk. One needs to stay sharp or otherwise miss it.

*We come too late to say anything which has not been said already.*

—JEAN DE LA FONTAINE

## Space

*How is space defined and violated in the plays?*

No one has any privacy, even at home, where visitors pop in constantly! Spying is common. Space is immediate, literal, social, interior, close, and familiar. For long stretches our characters give each other amounts of space, and there are many who never, ever touch. *Pas du tout.* But then just when you think it is all talk, the commedia (you know the Italians, *mon cher*) leaps in, and out comes the slapstick, cudgeling, delirium, physical jokes, *lazzi* (which you sometimes call "bits" or "shtick"—much more vulgar words, but then you are Americans, *n'est-ce pas?*), malaprops, echo reply, and repetition of business. Molière's mentor and teacher has been Fiorelli, just as Molière has been mine.

While we were reduced for a time to renting tennis courts to play, our space at the Great Hall of the Hôtel du Petit Bourbon, adjacent to the palace of the Louvre, is forty-five feet square. The theatre at the Palais-Royal, our permanent home since 1660, is *magnifique,* and *aujourd'hui* we are accustomed to playing to audiences of up to a thousand.

## Place

*What is the setting like?*

The play is set in someone's home or just outside in the garden or street. We need several doors and places to hide for full effect, but little in the way of props. We are *artistes!* And remember, *mon cher,* we survived thirteen long years on the road and every *petite ville* from here to Marseilles! [*Subject stops to make the sign of the cross and look to the heavens, shaking head as if to say, "Never again, please."*]

*How aware are people of other places and people?*

Casts are small. Characters have a narrow circle of acquaintances. Plays never expand beyond immediate community, neighborhood, court, or the circle in which the protagonist moves. It is Molière who takes comedy inside to the salon. As it moves inside, comedy focuses more on character, less on situation alone.

## Values

*What beliefs are shared, and what is the source of humor?*

A war wages between decorum (natural elegance of thought, speech, movement and conduct) and baser behavior. At one extreme, *The Misanthrope* is dominated by aristocrats and stays quite dignified, except for the invasion of one crazed servant. At the other, *The Doctor in Spite of Himself* is all rustic bumpkins and license for lazzi. Characters in Molière's plays often deny reality out of blind egotism or stupidity and seek to impose false visions of themselves.

> *Common sense is not so common.* —VOLTAIRE

The humor comes from the way characters vigorously contrive to frustrate each other's plans. *Beaucoup de* tricks are played! Molière pokes fun at mistaken ideas of what is dignity, and the servant is often far more sensible than the master of the house. This character walks through the play taking *plaisir* in pricking the balloon of pretension in others. Remember, the balloon is our invention. The clever brothers Montgolfier created it and Molière metaphorically pricks it. *C'est magnifique!*

Shared truth is that everyone can be frail and stupid, but the best thing to do is laugh at these human foibles. You cannot help liking even that Tartuffe, who is what you would call a "sleaze." This is a glorious role, and I could be glorious in it, if only Jean-Baptiste would . . . never mind. There is a forgiveness in the plays that makes even the harshest judgments tolerable. Most of our characters are ridiculous in some way but quite to be respected in others. We do not think of good and evil at their extremes. In the world of our plays, good means reasonable, not necessarily heroic. Evil means hypocritical and mean-spirited, not necessarily corrupt. *Le roi* does not wish the subject of death discussed, *ever*. Are we alone just now?

Molière (not his real name, you know—it used to be Pocquelin—he changed in order not to disgrace his *famille*) has known what it is to fail and to deceive the self. His *père* was one of eight court upholsterers, but Jean-Baptiste would not go into the family business! Who would? To make love to a chair? *Pas moi!* He also dropped out of law school and spent time in debtor's prison after our first failed performances. Well, so did I, to tell the truth [*again stops to cross self and clasp hands, this time shaking them at heaven*]. He tried repeatedly to play tragedy, but to no avail. My beloved Jean-Baptiste has a slight lisp, speaks very quickly, and has short legs, wide-set eyes, a peasant face, swarthy skin, and heavy, black, active eyebrows, not unlike your beloved Groucho. He has managed to turn all his liabilities into grand assets, but not without some pratfalls along the way!

It was *difficile* almost beyond endurance. Just as Molière was released on bail, another creditor had him imprisoned again! Finally, we borrowed 522 livres and pawned everything, even our theatre wardrobe, our main working asset. So we took to the provinces at a low point. If we are now at the top, we have, as you say, "paid our dues."

We saw every type of person on the road! Then we came back, and Molière saw Paris with an eye sharpened by absence and experience. So the high and the low are all *stupide,* but what can you do but love them? And we are a huge success now, in part, because for twenty-five years, people have forgotten farce, and now we make them remember. And we show them persons like themselves, with all their *petit* quarrels and foibles, and they are delighted to look into our mirror. Our work makes them laugh, makes them think, and sometimes makes them a little sad. This is as it should be.

### Structure

*Who leads, and who are idols?*

Louis XIV dictates everything. Few kings have ever lived longer or ruled more powerfully. He took the throne at age five and has coined the phrase *L'etat, c'est moi,* or "I am the state." The patronage of the king is essential to life, especially in a society that regards acting as a sinful profession. The king has even served as godfather to Molière's first *enfant,* who, it breaks my heart to say, died within the same year. *Pauvre petit bébé.* But past *le roi,* there are few deities. We see through the flaws in all and sometimes suspect it is better to be a peasant.

*What are the family and daily life like?*

The family! Ha! *Cherchez la femme!* My poor Jean-Baptiste has married one of the most flirtatious, spoiled, and least affectionate women in Paris! And she is less than half his age. They fight continuously, and worse yet— oh, it is the worse *scandale!*—many think that she is his daughter!! *C'est effrayant!* Years ago, his mistress was Madeleine Béjart. This coquette, Armande Béjart, has been presented as her sister, but the tongues wag. *Tout le temps,* they wag! Our archrival, Monfleury, he of the ranting and bombast [*a quick spit here*], has actually made the unspeakable accusation before the king! *Mon Dieu!* Well, enough of this petty gossip! Is it true? I

*It is an odd job, making decent people laugh.*

—MOLIÈRE

*One is never as unhappy as one thinks, nor as happy as one hopes.*

—DUC DE LA ROCHEFOUCAULD

*The people have little intelligence, the great no heart.... If I had to choose, I should have no hesitation. I would be of the people.*

—JEAN DE LA BRUYÈRE

*No man is a hero to his valet.*     —MADAME CORNUEL

know not. Does the frustrated relationship of the playwright and his *mari* enter the plays? Ha! All you have to do is read them!!

*How are the plays themselves structured?*

The structure, like the content, is monitored by an ever vigilant intellectual police, full of suggestions.

Plays are required to have four or five acts, each of similar length and form. Verse is for tragedy and prose for comedy, so even in this category my brave Jean-Baptiste pushes the limits and innovates. Language is required to sing sonorously and to be appropriate. Certain subjects are forbidden. There are strict boundaries, let me tell you. Our plays are structured so differently from yours that we invent something called the "French scene." A new scene always begins with the arrival or departure of a character, so our plays have many scenes even without changes of time, place, and action. There is always an opening exposition scene in which two characters explain all. The second is a demonstration of what they have been discussing. In the third comes a series of cascading complications. And fourth and last, a group scene with the cast all present for the ending. *C'est parfait, n'est-ce pas?*

*What is the role of friendship and trust?*

Our plays are full of concerned good friends (*raisonneurs*) trying tirelessly to save foolish central characters from self-destruction, offering patient, measured advice and comfort. The plays juggle excess against common sense, low farce with high wit, and emotion with reason. Of course, the advice is *never* taken, and the central character rarely grows or changes.

Molière has a close and lasting bond himself with the celebrated Cyrano de Bergerac, who has championed him on a number of occasions. (A play about their friendship—now *that* would be worth seeing, *n'est-ce pas?* Why does no one write it?) And our company understands true friendship. In all these years, only one actor has left us, and we have the *best,* including the brilliant comedy of Jodelet and L'Espy, plus no fewer than five members of the great theatrical family Les Béjarts.

We view the world somewhat closer to type. This is partly a carryover from the commedia, partly our love of order. And speaking of order, justice is always, *always* done in Molière's plays. Everyone gets just what he deserves. Family members often mistreat each other the most and are taught to forgive.

The types we play are as follows [*subject strikes a different delightful pose as each title is announced*]:

Pantalone (duped father, often lecherous)
Good Friend (adviser)
Good Wife
Ingénue (both boy and girl)

*Let a single completed action, all in one place, all in one day, keep the theatre packed to the end of your play.*

—NICOLAS BOILEAU

*It is impossible to please all the world and one's father.*

—JEAN DE LA FONTAINE

Coquette (flirt)
Précieuse (learned lady)
Prude
Nagging Wife
(Zanni) Tricky Servant
Honest Servant
Stupid Servant
Honest Courtier (a type I hope to meet someday!)
Dottore (doctor)
Marquis Capitano (braggart soldier)
Tricky Lawyer

These characters are more than your clichés. We artistes think of them as classic forms to be filled, instead of played flatly. Names mean little, and Molière often uses the same name for a single character type from play to play.

### Beauty

*What look and modes of expression are favored?*

For the entire reign of Louis, France is first in the world in art, literature, war, and statesmanship. We have a taste for grandeur and a complex ceremonial style that never makes it to England in the Restoration. We invite more people to the party. And we expect them to behave better!

*The maid of the précieuse is always putting her spoke in the conversation.*  —MOLIÈRE

Our plays tend to feature the fluffier, larger, looser look of the period. We have a greater fondness than the English for the girl-woman who is not so sophisticated, or at least does not appear to be. While many in our society consider *les précieuses* (privileged young women who relish poetry, euphemism, and highly elevated talk as part of lovemaking—Roxane in *Cyrano de Bergerac* is of this group) beautiful and fine, not Molière! How can such women be taken seriously? Women who call a chair "a commodity of conversation"? Be serious. Their idea of beauty is for love to move through the following stages, quite slowly [*again, strikes a pose for each phase*]: Indifference, Disinterested Pleasure, Respect, Assiduity, Inclination, the City of Tenderness, and—at last—the Dangerous Sea!!! Now how could Jean-Baptiste not make fun of them? And no wonder it is often a "simple" servant who jabs!

We are not attracted to those who violate social standards, and our sense of the beautiful is rather refined. We can amuse ourselves readily holding salon and have a fondness for extensive moral philosophizing. Somewhere in most of our art will be a symbol of *le roi*. It shows the highest praise that Molière is called by his contemporaries *le peintre*, or the painter. His pen draws pictures with a beauty and clarity comparable to any executed in oil.

## Sex

*How is sex viewed and communicated?*

Sex is, of course, *magnifique,* but also a bit funny, don't you think? And it can make you act *très* foolish. On the stage, *maintenant,* it must be handled, if at all, with the utmost delicacy. We are limited by an edict, penned by Richelieu, forbidding us on pain of dismissal, fine, or exile (only *le mort* is worse, *mon cher*) against the use of "lascivious words," *phrases à la double entendre* and "indecent words or gestures." We are required on the stage to remain "completely free of impurity." So be it.

*Cover that bosom, girl.*
*The flesh is weak*
*And unclean thoughts*
*are difficult to control.*
*Such sights as those can*
*undermine the soul.*

—TARTUFFE

*I could sooner reconcile*
*all Europe than two*
*women.* —LOUIS XIV

## Recreation

*What pastimes are favored? How do people have fun?*

Fencing catches on with us in a way that never captures the hearts of the English. I believe they are fonder of greater brutality. The deft, quick touch, all dependent on the slightest flick of the wrist, gives us endless *plaisir.* And, of course, we never fatigue of discussing what is morally right. It is best, however, to say it quickly and sharply and leave a bit unsaid.

*The way to be a bore is*
*to say everything.*

—VOLTAIRE

But what is the most fun of all? Why, to laugh, of course. It is the only answer for the reasonable man. Irrationality and excess are the best subjects for humor. I have mentioned *les précieuses.* Molière loves to mock complacency, extravagance, self-absorption, and vanity. He hates pedants and quacks. Oh, and the doctors, whom everyone else takes so seriously and whom many fear. Such targets for the pen of Molière!! [*shouting forcefully at passersby*] Down with *les médecins*!!! [*stopping, cringing, sitting*] *Pardonnez-moi.* I was momentarily carried away.

*A learned fool is more*
*foolish than an ignorant*
*one.* —MOLIÈRE

While the pious and the indignant are always trying to stifle our company, fortunately the king's idea of recreation is seeing others annoyed. We do that well. Only, *entre nous, le roi* has lately been seen in the company of the austere and oh so religious Madame de Maintenon. I hope her influence isn't great. Oh, and that Lully. He writes the music *magnifique,* but I do not trust him, either. One must be ever vigilant.

## Sight and Sound

*What shapes, movement, and speech patterns are favored?*

We make a greater distinction between our stage costumes and those worn in life than do the English—brighter, bolder colors, with more reflective surfaces. We shine back on the audience a slightly more brilliant and vivid version of themselves. We actors must be verbal and physical acrobats in our capacity to move instantly back and forth between prankish contrivance and refined observation. Rhythms are often stichomythic rapid-fire exchanges involving repetitions, gradual exaggeration, setups, pauses, 'straight man' responses, comic topping and undercutting, and general verbal warfare. Molière writes some plays in verse and some in prose and does not mix the two, as does Shakespeare. The wild farces tend to be in prose. Jean-Baptiste's favored form of verse is the *alexandrine,* a line of four anapests, or anapestic tetrameter, which simply does not translate to the English-speaking ear. A line of iambic hexameter comes closest in stress. *Mon Dieu!* Let me try to demonstrate:

> I will now try to share with you the way in which
> Molière arranges his thoughts into lines which switch
> After twelve syllables, which may have an inner pause.
> After the sixth syllable, a caesura will cause
> A slight break in the total line of verse. They are
> Called alexandrines. Six iambs can somehow jar
> Your ears accustomed to Elizabethan lines,
> Which have only five feet and also fewer rhymes.
> Iambic hexameter might be the name to give
> This verse through which Alexander the Great still lives.
> He is a favorite subject of many a French romance,
> But somehow his verse, when translated, does not dance!

*Anyone may be an honorable man and yet write verse badly.*

—MOLIÈRE

Phew! *Quelle* task! It is, remember, *s'il vous plaît,* Molière who is the playwright and the poet, not I. I am only an actor. What am I saying? [*stops, hugs self, jumps up*] I am blessed and proud and ready to fly as an actor! And I am late for rehearsal as we speak, so if I wish to continue I must bid you *adieu. Bonne chance avec votre représentation de Molière!* [*exits running*]

## KEYS TO THE WORLD

### Images

French words for standards in the theatre: *bienséance* (propriety) and *verisimilitude*
A point made in quick rhyme: the couplet
Music of Jean-Baptiste Lully
Paintings of Nicolas Poussin
Gerard Terborch's *Portrait of an Unknown Man*
Nicolas de Largillière's portrait *Louis XIV and His Family*
Coysevox's bronze bust of Louis XIV
The Hall of Mirrors in the Palace of Versailles
The serious side of the period: plays of Jean Racine and Pierre Corneille

Jacques Callot's commedia sketches
Eustache Lorsay's *Molière in Theatrical Costume*
Alexandre Le Blond's Scaramouche engraving
Melingue's *Molière and His Troupe*
The engraving *Players of the Hôtel de Bourgogne*

### Masking

Molière's plays are fundamentally about *un*masking. Molière takes a long hard look at his characters' pretenses and strips them away. At the same time, he derives inspiration from the masked tradition of the commedia dell'arte, which involves inflexible, predictable masks and characters who do not necessarily learn from experience. Many of Molière's characters begin as simplified types and then in the unmasking are simplified *further,* so that we recognize what is most basic and universal about them.

The commedia troupes wear masks, which are immediately recognizable to the audience, based on types listed earlier. The French of this period are even more fond of wearing masks than the English. Farce involves pulling things *off* one way or another; stealing, hiding, deception, uncovering, gags, and practical jokes abound. Polite masks (spirit) are peeled away to show primitive urges (flesh). Undoing arrogance, causing embarrassment, generating belly laughs, inverting authority (servants suddenly telling masters what to do, important matters suddenly being treated as insignificant), even crucifying oneself by blurting out the truth without thinking, all are common. The *undoing* of others is crystallized by these mildly violent traditional pieces of business: the gifle (a small slap) in the face or the slapstick (a paddle split down the middle) used to spank or strike. Characters are often symbolically slapped or spanked into reality.

*Greatest fools are oft most satisfied.*

—NICOLAS BOILEAU

Take any twenty lines of dialogue. Any period of script will do, provided that two actors know the lines well enough to play with them.

1. Create and demonstrate two lazzi or pieces of comic business.
2. Present the script, finding every opportunity to perform the traditional commedia business.
3. Go back, and remembering decorum, perform the script with an aristocratic sense of precision and purpose.
4. Attack the scene a third time, combining the elements of (2) and (3). Shoot for grandeur, then shoot that grandeur down, and then aspire to it again. Find the tension between decorum and slapstick.
5. Discuss and analyze how the seemingly disparate elements might blend.

**E X E R C I S E**

**Commedia vs. Court**

M<sup>r</sup> de Moliere

Selected elements specific to Molière's works. Molière wrote in the early
stages of the Restoration, so the two styles share many visual elements.
Traditional commedia dell'arte characters, called *masks,* provide the basic
types, which Molière develops and humanizes. Molière's own features lend
themselves to bemused comedy, and the commedia influence shows in his

performance as Sganarelle. New interest in the peasant / servant class surfaces in the plays of Molière. Notice the wider, fluffier look for both classes
at this point in the century. Actors are accustomed to adjusting performances between such extremes as a small public theatre and a vast open-air
court shell.

## The Production

The major verse plays work best in a period which allows some aristocratic ennui or languor, where the look and feel of the designer's world is one in which people have the time and money simply to hang out and engage in taunting debate. The earthier prose farces are often set in a generic fairy-tale world, not unlike the setting in a staging of *Jack and the Beanstalk*, with a timeless sense of a more innocent world. Unlike Restoration comedy, a Molière play is very likely to be placed in the present time or near to it, because almost every element translates into present-day life.

## Contemporary Parallels

- The hypocrisy of network censorship, which allows the broadcast of programs dealing with the most sordid topics just as long as certain words are not used and certain body parts are not revealed.
- Exposure of the sanctimonious prude (for example, catching television evangelists in the most lurid personal circumstances).
- Accepted belief that common workers often know a lot more than those at the top.
- Tolerant but condescending laughter at marriages or "arrangements" between persons of different generations.
- A strong desire for entertainment that is wrapped up with a message as well as a bow; a wish to be both amused and enlightened.
- A strong interest in exposing the failings of those in positions of power.
- A comfortable juxtaposition of philosophical discourse with circus antics (for example, on a talk show, an innovative thinker may share air time with trained seals).
- A tendency to type and generalize others based on one's first impression.
- A desire for comedy over anything else, to have everything served up with the honey of laughter.
- An awareness that we all need to forgive each other, recognize each other's shortcomings and idiosyncrasies, and still invite each other to dance.

## PLAYS

Here are those scripts most often produced:

*The Bourgeois Gentleman* (1671)
*The Doctor in Spite of Himself* (1666)
*The Imaginary Invalid* (1673)
*The Learned Ladies* (1672)
*The Misanthrope* (1666)
*The Miser* (1668)
*The School for Wives* (1662)
*Sganarelle* (1660)
*Tartuffe* (1667)

## SCENES

*The Bourgeois Gentleman*
Jourdain, Music Master, Dancing Master
Desperately desiring to be regarded as a gentleman, Jourdain hires professionals to teach him the right qualities.
Cléante, Covielle
A wily servant advises his young master on how best to win his beloved from his disapproving father.

*The Doctor in Spite of Himself*
Martine, Sganarelle
A woodcutter and his wife perpetually try to outdo each other in tricks and insults.

*The Learned Ladies*
Armande, Henriette, Clitandre
Two sisters strongly disagree regarding matters of the head and the heart.

*The Misanthrope*
Arsinoe, Celimene
Celimene, the toast of Paris, is visited at her salon by less youthful and popular Arsinoe, who wishes to tell her rumors of her "dear friend's" reputation.
Clitandre, Acoste
Two idle courtiers debate which of them comes closer to perfection of person.
Alceste, Celimene
The misanthrope tries desperately to get some degree of faithfulness from the hopeless coquette with whom he is infatuated.

*The Miser*
La Fleche, Harpagon
A sharp-tongued servant, whose name means "arrow," is searched by his ever-greedy, ever-paranoid master.

*The School for Wives*
Arnolphe, Agnes
Arnolphe has selected and all but imprisoned an uneducated naïve woman much younger than he. He hopes to prepare her to be his wife, but a young handsome man has "found" her.

*Tartuffe*
Elmire, Orgon, Tartuffe
The head of the household refuses to believe his wife's claims that his pious best friend tries repeatedly to seduce her. So, she has her husband hide under the table and invites the "friend" in to prove it.
Mariane, Dorine, Valère
An outspoken maid helps the daughter of the head of the household defy her father's wishes regarding whom she should marry.

Michelle Morain (Kate Hardcastle) and William McKereghan (Squire Hardcastle) in *She Stoops to Conquer*, Oregon Shakespeare Festival

# GEORGIAN:
## Theatre Welcomes the Middle Class

### THE WORLD ENTERED

The population of England nearly doubles between 1650 and 1800. The most procreating group? The middle class. Powerful citizens, who are neither upstairs nor down, emerge. They struggle to design their place in society, embracing some aristocratic and some lower-class virtues. Plays of the period are often called *comedy of goodwill*. Most of the scripts are cloyingly sentimental, but two writers represent the period's true strengths. Richard Brinsley Sheridan and Oliver Goldsmith both react against the treacle of the times and in so doing reflect the best of the times.

In 1772, Goldmith publishes his famous "Essay on Theatre," which decries sentiment and cries out for "laughing comedy." He does more than criticize: the next year, he produces a work that embodies what he requested, *She Stoops to Conquer*. This play has so little in common with others of the time that only through the influence of the powerful and popular Samuel Johnson does it get produced at all. Both Goldsmith's plays and Sheridan's place more emphasis on character than Restoration theatre while retaining some of the biting wit. They identify the difference between real and feigned virtue. By our standards, however, there is plenty of sentiment in both playwrights' work—goodness is inevitably rewarded and gentility supported.

Our interview is with a member of the newly formed middle class, a person immersed in commerce and the arts and often mentioned in the columns of the *Tatler*. The subject was at pains to make certain I noticed the impressive coach and four in which our guest arrived. We discussed the quality and cost of the horses' bridles at some length before I could get the subject to turn to the issues of the interview, which was then embraced enthusiastically.

Time: 1755–1800

*Time for toys.*

*Where do people focus their energy now?*

Your most obedient servant is pleased to reply. Egad! What a time this is! I vow, it seems not possible to me that any time ever could have been better! An astonishing number of recent inventions and discoveries has made the world our oyster: hypnosis (by Mesmer), public clinics, the spinning mill (by Arkwright), the cast iron bridge, the steam engine (by

*The arrogance of age must submit to be taught by youth.* —EDMUND BURKE

Watt), and both hydrochloric and sulfuric acids (by Priestley)! We even have the first encyclopedia, so it is now possible to look up all manner of learning. The young are lucky to be alive, say I, and they know so much!

The time not spent with these lovely new gadgets and such is spent planning parties, picnics, and balls. Even funerals have become lavish displays and major occasions. Zooks! Got to do the dead right, you know! Do them up proud, say I. The plays are fast moving and lively. You must keep up. You just must.

*All that is human must retrograde if it does not advance.*

—EDWARD GIBBON

## Space

### Human being as ship afloat

#### How is personal space defined?

*What a pity it is that we can die but once to serve our country!*

—JOSEPH ADDISON

Zounds, but we feel big! We have big wigs, the ladies have big hips, we explode in every direction as if we've been shot out of a cannon. Nowadays, we don't touch so easily and thoughtlessly as in the past. Only a thoughtless booby fails to show respect. But we all most definitely know how to put on a show of ourselves! A man's home is his castle, and his country is his pride. We would do anything to save the two.

#### How has the performance space altered?

*We that live to please, must please to live.*

—SAMUEL JOHNSON

The new theatre reduces the apron, and good riddance, say I. The lighting is much improved, so our scenes move upstage, creating a much larger distance between actor and observer. We can sit back and see the whole picture, not feeling intruded upon. And audience members are removed from the stage. It don't seem proper for a man to sit on a stage, so I'm devilish glad for the departure. No real man would deign show himself so. The theatres are getting larger and larger, and we are filing them, to be sure. Mercy and miracles! Great scenic wonders are being displayed—cut out set pieces, fancy painting—much of it actually having something to do with the time and place of the *play* being performed in front of it! And we the people know what we like to see there, that let me tell you. We are The Public, and you'd best serve us prudently.

## Place

### On the road.

*The way to ensure summer in England is to have it framed and glazed in a comfortable room.* —HORACE WALPOLE

#### What is your relationship to nature, and how aware are you of other places?

Well, now, we finally put those old roads in order and made 'em more tolerably passable. It happens that travel and a new contrivance called the "vacation" are emerging as common practice. We are only just beginning to name the streets and put some numbers on a few houses. I protest it don't seem right to me to have a number on a man's castle, but it is starting to happen, no matter. I own we most enjoy fixing up nature. Our sets are lavish, like our homes, and we take our love of scenery into the backstage. 'Fore Gad, we now know all manner of ways to oil things up and get 'em on and off in a dandy way. Since the most important and fashionable of the arts is architecture, it happens every gentleman wants to know about it. I confess we give more care to our interiors than our exteriors, with attention to every detail in mantles, doorways, and panels. I'll be sworn, we love domes. And we're painting everything white! If only it were possible to force the weather to be constant.

## Values

### God as Engineer.

#### *What are the shared beliefs?*

The word that sums up how we feel about life, my boy, is Benevolence. Ay, this is what runs the universe, and it is the basic guiding human quality. We don't ridicule vice anymore; we glorify virtue! Bad behaviors (even by that minx, Lady Teazle) are simply mistakes in manners. Put a little charity in your face, say I. We are obliged to make manners better and to enlighten those less fortunate.

In our time, God is seen in material rather than spiritual terms. He's the main engineer who designed the universe, set its laws—and started it running, by the by. Lud, the answer to all our problems lies in reason, and we call our time the Age of Enlightenment. Oh, we still believe in sin, but we also believe man can move to enlightenment through reason. You will have to forgive me. It is *not* good manners to talk of this, son, so we must change the subject.

I own that not everyone thrives in this system. And what about those who do not? Heigh-ho! We put 'em away. Debt is now an imprisonable offense, and the prisons are overcrowded. Since 'tis needful to pay gaoler's fees to get out, many just go there and disappear! And the world is a cleaner place, say I. Only a very low paltry set of fellows would allow themselves into such a state of affairs.

And as to our theatres, there has been admirable atonement, and they are no longer the sinful citadels of cynicism and debauchery they were a century ago. They appeal to good, hardworking people, not just a drinking, philandering gentry. Our comedies have all the humor of the Restoration, without its decadence. Our greatest interest lies in the natural man. A new, simpler, more direct human being defies the stuffy, arch old aristocratic order and ushers us into the future. Whereas many of our

*To whom nothing is given, of him can nothing be required.*
—HENRY FIELDING

*Religion is by no means a proper subject of conversation in a mixed company.*
—PHILIP DORMER STANHOPE, EARL OF CHESTERFIELD

*The murmuring poor who simply will not fast in peace.* —GEORGE CRABBE

characters still have names that type them, we now have some fine young people, worthy of approbation, called Charles, Maria, or plain simple Kate, who are pitted against the foibles and frivolities of the Snakes and the Sneerwells. Enough of trolloping and roguery, say I!

## Structure

### A rule for everything.

*Who leads, who follows, and how is daily life ordered?*

*A precedent embalms a principle.*   —LORD STOWELL

Heyday! For the first time in history, even the *French* attempt to emulate British art, fashion, and government! And goodness, do we teach those who are too Frenchified a thing or two! Now, we did take their ideas of decorum and proper behavior and proceeded to made them all keen issues in our lives. I daresay we keep busy making up laws about what's proper and what's not, what's been done before and what must be done next. Such concerns can lead to vexations.

*Where there is marriage without love, there will be love without marriage.*

—BENJAMIN FRANKLIN

Now the Americans are a different matter. The impertinence! Wanting to be governed by themselves?! Plague me! Let me say that the only man from the Colonies (and I intend to use that term to my dying day, no matter what they call themselves), the only one worth a ha'penny is jolly Ben Franklin. And the only reason Mr. Franklin is enlightened, in the humble opinion of yours truly, is due to the time he spent on *this* side of the ocean. So say I. The revolutions in France and the Colonies, while lacking forbearance and good nature, have, I grant, prompted many to argue over the subject of freedom. And an interesting subject it is. There are still arrangements and mergers among families, but we all hope to find that we can think of our spouse as more than a business partner.

*There is no art which one government sooner learns of another than that of draining money from the pockets of the people.*   —ADAM SMITH

Lud, our government is grand. For the first time we have a Prime Minister (Robert Walpole), a House of Lords (titled landowners), and House of Commons (elected officials). Alack! Our huge middle class has economic and social power, but no real political clout yet. "The two hundred" as we call 'em, still own everything. Eh? Who are they? Zounds! The aristocracy, the two hundred or more families who really run the country. Pshaw! Ha'n't you read your history? In fact, 5 percent of the population own 95 percent of the land. Firstborn sons take over the land. Secondborn sons pursue careers in politics or the church. Only later sons have much choice.

*Beware you be not swallowed up in books! An ounce of love is worth a pound of knowledge.*

—JOHN WESLEY

Young boys now attend Eton and other public schools (what you in America call private schools) away from home, then try to go on to Oxford or Cambridge. Then, I daresay, having completed their education, the young men must go abroad for a year to tour the Continent. Finishing schools are for young ladies, who must know all manner of frippery to get on in the world. Depend upon it though, what we want to know is how things work. What we seek are ways to make *others* work. We have no wish to get caught in a theory that just sits there as a confounded thought.

Oh! And how I love my paper! Newspapers have gained massive popularity. I confess I am at a loss to recall how life was contrived before they came to pass. 'Tis fashionable to get your name in the columns, and political cartoons are a new delight, provided they are not about *you*. The reporter's own viewpoint is still evident in news stories. Egad, none of your twentieth-century pretense of objectivity.

Advances in industry and science, some but yesterday, lead us to believe the world can be controlled.

*And how are these changes influencing the theatre?*

Even *acting* becomes a respectable profession! Fewer ungrateful libertines take up the call. Our much admired Mr. Garrick has helped structure the process of the theatre, demanding far more and regularly scheduled rehearsals than in the past, forcing actors actually to listen to each other and to find natural rhythms. The theatre is less haphazard than hitherto for his contribution, although some do not take with his desire to have the actor use his own personality instead of fitting a general heroic mold. On the one hand, we prefer things tidy and positive, so the plays themselves end happily, with all the loose ends tied up in a neat bow. To my vexation, the structure of the performance, on the other hand, is a might sloppy. Sometimes the author writes the prologue or epilogue. Sometimes it may be a separate author altogether, even an actor! Sometimes there is no prologue at all! We've some need for care and circumspection, if I may say so. This is the beginning of what you will call a "star." We go to the theatre to see our favorites! We cheer for them! In fact, we mostly think the player's persona far more important than the play.

## Beauty

*What looks are aspired to, and how is beauty expressed?*

Now that even the French are looking to us, why all proper persons are aware of image, so we prudently pay attention to the details all around us and fix things up proper. Topiary reaches even greater heights. Our bushes sometimes look like animals, chess pieces, even statues! But for real beauty, the new tree of choice is the elm!

Each person probably looks to you, my man, like an inflated balloon about to burst. A goodly portion of trumpery is needed to make a good showing. A woman's hair can add three feet one way (up), her panniers easily that the other (sides), then her train another (back). Women appear as great ships sailing slowly in harbor. Men also add width with coats, higher heels, and wigs. By the laws, who would have thought a single human being could take up so many square inches!

It does not follow that we are baroque! We like lines cleaner, straighter,

*Life is too short to study German.*

—RICHARD PORSON

*Authors owe more of their success to good actors than they imagine.*

—JOHN HILL, IN *THE ACTOR; OR, A TREATISE ON THE ART OF PLAYING*

*Fashion—a word which knaves and fools may use,
Their knavery and folly to excuse.*

—CHARLES CHURCHILL

more recognizably geometric than the curly, serpentine ones of the past century. No more unnecessary curves, if you please. A movement called *associationalism* affects our art. We want art to touch our emotions, and we want to know what it has to do with *us*. And, to be sure, each of us has opinions about what art is, which we will express in a minute. Good art moves us, and bad art does not. So be it.

## Sex

*How are sexuality and seduction expressed?*

*The Duke returned from the wars today and did pleasure me in his top-boots.*

—DUCHESS OF MARLBOROUGH

You alarm me with your questions. Well, truly a hearty sort of eroticism exists, although a clear separation is made between women of quality and tarts! Make no mistake. Though a need is a need, if I may say so.

O death! There is something new called burlesque, where women are hired to dance naked for men in private clubs. And Lud! There is a salacious interest in the memoirs of both the Marquis de Sade and Casanova. No one I know admits to reading them, of course, but the shops are always out of copies. Or so I have been told.

*A miss for pleasure and a wife for breed.*

—JOHN GAY

Whereas a young man's training may now involve a professional to get him ready for the duties of husbanding, adultery is no longer a fit subject for discussion. Once harnessed together in matrimony, if passion cannot be founded in duty, then let discretion be your tutor.

## Recreation

*A man indeed is not genteel when he gets drunk, but most vices may be committed very genteelly. A man may debauch his friend's wife genteelly and he may cheat at cards genteelly.*

—JAMES BOSWELL

*Everything from restaurants to strippers.*

*What are favored pastimes and ideas of fun?*

Odd's heart, there is nothing to surpass a ball done proper. Unless it's a good game of lawn bowling. The newest diversions include cricket, horse races, fox hunting, and golf! Oons, gambling is so popular that even at a ball, a gaming room is provided for those who prefer the table to the dance floor. It is important to enjoy oneself in a proper way and to take liberties like a gentleman.

Prizefighting is the sport of choice for young dandies. Lud, they often take lessons from the leading fighters of the day to spruce up their skills. Ladies do not participate in any outdoor sports, except shopping! Shopping as diversion is new, and none of the shops of Europe can compare to ours! I understand you have eating places all over? Well, the restaurant as you now know it is just emerging. Tea is giving chocolate truly a run for its money as drink of choice. Serving tea is becoming a prescriptive art. Zounds, what a fuss in how each thing involved is held and used just so. Plague me if I can remember just how to hold the pot and my pinky all at

*A man may surely be allowed to take a glass of wine by his own fireside.*

—RICHARD BRINSLEY SHERIDAN, ON BEING ENCOUNTERED DRINKING IN THE STREET WHILE WATCHING HIS THEATRE, DRURY LANE, BURN DOWN

once. People have always slipped gold pieces to servants, but we invent the real custom of tipping! In our coffee houses are placed boxes with the words "To Insure Promptness," eventually shortened to "tip." Please don't hate us for it.

Women now often continue their singing lessons well into adulthood. Every family who can afford one hires a dance master to teach steps and deportment. He tells us how to walk and even how to embrace! Good breeding, you see, is in itself considered an expression of beauty. When being unkind, contrive always to appear to be discussing others not present.

*You should always except the present company.* —JOHN O'KEEFE

There's no denying it, we have even contrived fashionable maladies. If you wish to get ill with style, there are "the spleen" among men and "the vapors" among women. Lead poisoning, from both makeup and household items, is common. The London season, fall to spring, is now established, with summers in the country, at Brighton or Bath, please. Nothing else will do. We even have country clothes, which are cut with more room to allow movement, and, of course, we have country pleasures.

*God made the country and man made the town.* —WILLIAM COWPER

And now that I peruse my watch . . . see this? The finest gold and the best in craftsmanship, if I may be allowed to say so. Every time I wind it, I feel proud. Avarice is the vice of the age, I must confess, but who would be a lackey when he may contrive not? . . . What was I saying? Ah, yes! My bags are packed, and, I'm afraid, I cannot give you any more of my time. Brighton awaits me. Time is money, you know. I must wish you a good morning. Heigh-ho!

*[Subject summons coach and four, which has been equipped with new livery, and shows it to me with pride, even exposing the teeth of one of the horses so I will know what a quality steed it is. Subject jumps in, and the carriage lunges forward. Subject waves heartily from the window as carriage disappears around the corner and out of sight.]*

## SIGHT

The look is large and pale, with powdered wigs, pastel garments, and a human silhouette sometimes nearly as wide as it is high. Makeup is still acceptable for both sexes, and fops might carry fans, but there is a strong movement against the use of both. Pearls, lockets, and jeweled buckles become popular again. Colors are softer and lighter. There is a move to a feminine sensibility. You might call the total look "more is more."

### Men

- *Head.* Men's hair is always tied back, and wigs are less common at the end of the period than at the beginning. Earlier

Visual influences on the actor of laughing comedy. Georgian's love of all things round, symmetrical, and ordered is reflected in this gazebo. Improved lighting and architectural skills make scenic depth possible as well as larger houses. Chairs are almost ludicrously small and delicate when contrasted to the human torso, almost like a small pedestal for the human to perch on. Ladies' headdresses compete for size only with panniers,

which take the hips to counterbalancing proportions. The parasol is an extremely popular aid in keeping skin utterly white. A certain corpulent self-satisfaction is suggested by some Georgian gentlemen, although clothing is designed for elegance and display. Ladies' wear may range from flamboyant ball gowns to the softer, more pastroal look, with feathers somehow managing to top almost any ensemble.

on, men wear tricorn hats. Later, an early type of top hat becomes popular.

- *Torso.* The waistcoat, the least comfortable piece of clothing, is shorter and buttoned all the way to the neck. A short sword and cane are frequently carried. A jabot (a lace or cloth ruffle worn on the shirtfront), tight knee breeches, and gartered stockings are standard. Cravats are worn high, and, later, collars on shirts stand way up.

### Women

- *Head.* Women wear linen caps or large hats. Their hair is whitened and enlarged to great proportion. Above the hair, some great object, such as a bird or ship, may be placed. Over this extravaganza may be worn a *calash,* a large foldable hood resembling the top of a Conestoga wagon. Later, hair is worn in loose curls, with shoulder scarves and enormous straw hats to form a softer look.

- *Torso.* Heavy corseting restricts the upper body altogether. Use of *busks,* strips of whalebone or other material inserted into corset pockets, forces posture; removal of them allows some freedom. (A lady's beloved might personally carve and present her with a busk so that his handiwork may be close to her heart.) Panniers, a variation on hoops, project strongly right and left. Flowers made of fabric are added to trim gowns, and floral patterns are widely used. A wide, deep neckline filled with light scarf and elbow-length sleeves with ruffles are favored. Later in the period, emphasis shifts from sides to back: the hoops and panniers disappear and are replaced by a bustle arrangement. Women begin to choose plainer fabrics.

A man's wife is now considered a primary showpiece for his wealth. The finer and more elegantly dressed she is, the richer he is considered to be. Country clothes are cut with more room and comfort. In production, extremes may be used for comic effect; "natural" women might dress more like our collective image of Martha Washington, whereas "extravagant creatures," such as Lady Teazle, Mrs. Hardcastle, or Mrs. Malaprop, might be festooned in the high excesses of a Marie Antoinette.

*I chose my wife, as she did her wedding gown, not for a fine glossy surface, but such qualities as would wear well.*

*—OLIVER GOLDSMITH*

### Movement and Contact

Men may not approach married women directly, but they may approach marriageable women with great discretion and minimal contact and do anything they wish with servants. Public displays of affection are not considered appropriate. Matrons are like monuments. The stereotype of women fainting originates in this period, not as a result of their "weakness," but because the corseting allows only small shallow breathing and impairs circulation. Maneuvering in panniers requires short, mincing steps.

Men greet with handshakes or slight bows, as do women, who may also embrace. A lady takes a gentleman's arm, not hand, when walking. The fashion is to extend the back leg before taking the next step and to lift the heels slightly between steps. Armholes are particularly tight, restricting full range of motion. For this reason, arms are never held straight at the sides but are curved in various degrees, and most gestures are made between the waist and the shoulders.

*Bowing and Curtsying*   Bows are highly varied in this period, as they are starting to disappear. Some men simply bend forward slightly at the waist, a bow that is not much more than a nod, and ladies do no more than a small dip. If you are playing a more traditional gentleman, move the right foot to the side and put weight on that foot, allowing the left merely to be supported by the toe. Take off your hat and move it to the side, inclining the back slightly. As you rise again, move the left foot up behind the right in the fourth position. The tricorn hat is removed in a robust and extroverted way. Extend your arm out nearly straight as you lift it to remove the hat. Let the thumb touch the forehead as you take the hat off, and straighten the arm as you remove it, exposing the hat's interior to others around you.

The most casual curtsy is made by sliding into fourth position, bending the back knee, and rising on the front leg without bending the body. This curtsy is easy and fast and can be made while in motion, without really stopping. Many other styles of curtsy abound.

There is more fussing with clothing now, partly because of the sheer bulk, partly because so many people are new to dressing up. It is acceptable and even recommended in behavior guides for men to grasp a chair before sitting and rising in order to support themselves and avoid ripping their breeches and for ladies to take their skirts in their hands and rearrange them periodically. Unlike the svelte Restoration skirt, the Georgian hoop will not make it through a door unless you lift each side to narrow your silhouette or slide in sideways. Early practice is advisable. In one production, the rented costumes arrived only just in time for a preview performance. An actress put on her panniers and entered wearing them front to back, so she looked like she was riding a horse. Fortunately the play was a comedy.

Although people fuss over how to greet *appropriately,* such concerns do

*Sir I look upon every day to be lost, in which I do not make a new acquaintance.*

—SAMUEL JOHNSON

not prevent this gregarious, outgoing, exhaustingly social group from greeting *enthusiastically*. The Georgians love to meet new people.

## SOUND

*We should constantly use the most common, little easy words, pure and proper, which our language affords.*

—JOHN WESLEY

*(Actors) who have feeling without fire are not able to express that very feeling; and those with whom spirit gets the better of sensibility, always run to excess.... Insipidity is the general character of the inferior performancer and extravagance is too much that of the superior ones.*

—JOHN HILL, IN *THE ACTOR; OR, A TREATISE ON THE ART OF PLAYING*

In comparison to the language of the Restoration, Georgian language is consciously simple and direct. Decorum is important, but so is a collective need to drop pretension and speak clearly. The effort to avoid indelicacy in language often results in avoiding eloquence as well. Except for an excessive use of silly expletives and fractured grammar, the language is becoming very much as it will be for the next several hundred years.

The many guides to speaking and acting stress the need for a natural, unforced, unaffected delivery. What is uncertain is exactly what would be considered natural by these exuberant, puffed up, extroverted people. It seems less likely that they mean a subdued or reserved delivery than a rather open, robust, and unpretentious one that strikes a balance between bombast and boring.

### Music and Dance

Music becomes fully available to the common man. Classical music becomes what it is today. Both opera and the mass grow in popularity. Haydn and Mozart perfect the symphonic form. Clarity, balance, order, refinement, control, and restraint replace Baroque excess. Folk music spreads, and composers take popular street melodies as themes to use in symphonies. The age sees the rise of the professional dancer. There is more exhibition dancing. Everyone, however, takes part in contra-dances. Popular ones include the *cotillion,* in which four couples dance in a circular, weaving pattern, often at weddings, and the *rigaudon,* or *rigadoon,* another circle dance with hopping, pliés, and alternating leaps.

The real dance of choice and singular invention of the times is the *waltz.* Couples embrace and do turns about the room for the first time. The dance moves up from the middle class to intoxicate the aristocracy. At first the waltz is a slow dance in ¾ or ⁶⁄₈ time still under the shadow of the extremely popular minuet. Dropping rules and formality, however, the waltz encourages individual expression. Whereas the minuet emphasizes social distinctions, the waltz breaks down all barriers. Moralists are quick to point out the danger of a dance which allows young women to be grasped by their partners, thrown into the air, and twirled about. Another similar and even livelier partner dance, the *polka,* becomes popular. The polka involves a simple uptempo slide to the side, turn, and hop.

## KEYS TO THE WORLD

### Images

Architecture of the innovative Adams brothers, Robert and James
Covent Garden and Drury Lane
Operas of Gluck
Symphonies and oratorios of Haydn and the vast body of music of
    Mozart
Handel's *Messiah* and *Coronation Anthems for George II*
Paintings of Gainsborough and Watteau—large canvases with per-
    fect skies and clouds
Dequevauviller's *L'Assemblee au Salon*
Fragonard's *The Swing*
Portraits by Lely and Kneller
Engravings by Bosse, Hogarth, and Boucher
The bombé chest, which features a curved, convex outline compa-
    rable to the human silhouette that was fashionable at the time
Chippendale furniture
Fielding's novel *Tom Jones* (and Tony Richardson's film)
Swift's *Gulliver's Travels*
Outstanding actors: David Garrick, Charles Macklin, Soranger
    Barry, Thomas Sheridan, William Powell, Sarah Siddons, Han-
    nah Pritchard

### Masking

While the wearing of real masks declines in popularity, the new social mask of choice is Middle Class Respectable, invented and shaped by the period. A solid outward show is favored. Lewd and power-mad impulses are carefully concealed and suppressed in favor of good-hearted decency. Everyone creates an appearance of joviality and good humor. Sentiment is often used as a personal mask, an increasingly popular choice among women. The Middle Class code requires a shocked look for some moments, a deeply sympathetic one for others, and stern disapproval for quite a few. The concern for personal image and outward appearance is as great as at any time in history. "What will the neighbors think?" is not an idle question but a guiding principle. Taste becomes a matter of study.

*Taste does not come by chance: it is a long and laborious task to acquire it.* —SIR JOSHUA REYNOLDS

### The Production

Most productions attempt relative authenticity. The spirit of the shows is comfortable enough that the peculiar clothes and props are not off-putting to an audience. Some allowance for the actors' comfort is, however, frequently made. These plays present fewer language demands than earlier plays, and character analysis is straightforward. Characters are not difficult to understand, so much of the challenging fun in performance comes in the wigs, panniers, and general life as a human barge. Their motives are clearer and can be played with absolute directness.

### Contemporary Parallels

*Life is a jest, and all things show it.*
*I thought so once, but now I know it.*
—JOHN GAY (HIS OWN EPITAPH)

- The charge of government during the period is to "decrease the taxes of the rich and increase national defense." (Sound familiar? Has any administration within memory been accused of having these goals?)
- Newspapers blur fact and opinion.
- Many regard the entire world from an economic point of view.
- Those with new money will go to extravagant, even ludicrous, lengths to display it and to prove they have the right to it.
- An anti-intellectual aura combines with an interest in learning. Learning focuses on how things work, not why.
- The natural human form is expanded. Teasing, mousse, shoulder pads, oversized clothing, and pumping iron parallel wigs and panniers.
- The high-tech industry dominates; machines and gizmos are virtually a national addiction.
- There is a strong ambivalence toward sentiment. It is at turns rejected and embraced to the point where it becomes downright cloying.
- Plays are forerunners to modern sitcoms and screwball comedies in their formula plot, broad characterization, and hearty, robust humor.
- The expanded middle class dominates the culture.

### PLAYS AND PLAYWRIGHTS

Here are those scripts most often produced:

| | |
|---|---|
| Gay, John | *The Beggar's Opera* (1728) |
| Goldsmith, Oliver | *She Stoops to Conquer* (1773) |

| Lillo, George | *The London Merchant* (1731) |
|---|---|
| O'Keefe, John | *Wild Oats* (1791) |
| Sheridan, Richard Brinsley | *The Critic* (1781) |
| | *The Rivals* (1775) |
| | *The School for Scandal* (1777) |
| Tyler, Royal | *The Contrast* (1787) |

## SCENES

*The Critic*
Dangle, Mrs. Dangle
A drama reviewer's spouse wishes he would give up his calling so that her house may be free of all sorts of riffraff, including actors.
Dangle, Sneer, Puff
An entrepreneur without scruple turns his hand to the calling of playwright.

*The Rivals*
Mrs. Malaprop, Jack, Lydia
Captain Jack Absolute (alias Beverly) has come to call on the niece of the woman more prone than any in history to misuse the English language.
Julia, Faukland
Two lovers insist on allowing pride and decorum to get in the way of their love.

*The School for Scandal*
Sir Peter, Lady Teazle
A much younger wife plucked from the country has learned all too well how to spend her much older husband's money in the city.
Snake, Lady Sneerwell
A leading gossip mongerer, with the help of her hissing servant, prepares to take on the world.

*She Stoops to Conquer*
Kate Hardcastle, Marlow
(two scenes) Marlow is desperately shy in the presence of ladies but bold in the presence of wenches. Discovering his malady, Kate disguises herself as a maid in order to ease their courtship.

*Wild Oats*
Rover, Harry
A nobleman has been trying on the life of an actor but now feels compelled to end his "vacation."

**E X E R C I S E**

**Creating Commedia**

1. Using the list of commedia types as a starting point, identify what you consider modern parallels. Which of these types exist in our world and popular entertainment? Put the new list on the board.
2. Create contemporary lazzi or comic situations. Which funny encounters happen often enough to be called classics?
3. Cast two or three of the scenes, and with no more than five minutes' preparation present them for the class.

**E X E R C I S E**

**Warm-Ups for Relatives**

1. Review the basic classical warm-up and those for the Greek, Elizabethan, and Georgian periods.
2. Discuss what would be helpful in a Molière and a Georgian warm-up.
3. Divide into two teams, and within each team delegate responsibility to write a certain number of lines on a particular topic or to come up with a physical maneuver.
4. Meet with the other team, and then teach the warm-up to the other half of the class.

**E X E R C I S E**

**Accepting the Middle Class**

1. Divide into two groups: old-school aristocrats and middle class.
2. You are meeting for the first time because the aristocrats need the middle class's money and help, and the middle class wants culture and status. Negotiate.

**E X E R C I S E**

**Contrasts**

1. Work in threes in front of the class.
2. Discuss a topic the audience gives you.
3. Each time you speak or react, do so first in a dignified and intelligent way, and follow it with a crude, low-level response. For example, you might say something terribly polite and then stick your tongue out behind the other person's back.
4. Try not to get caught by your two partners in the low-life pranks.
5. Discuss the contrasts and concentration necessary

**E X E R C I S E**

**Fencing Words**

Take an actual set of foils if you have the protective gear or, if not, any other gentler battling items, such as foam bats. Improvise a spat in which you tap your partner each time you make a point. Then move on to actual dialogue, letting the weapon sharpen your delivery.

**E X E R C I S E**

**Family Reunion**

1. Select two students to represent each of the three periods: Restoration, Georgian, and Molière. Divide the rest of the class into three cheering squads.
2. You are actually family members. The Molièrians are the uncle and aunt of the Restorations, who are the parents or grandparents of the Georgians. The topic of discussion is "What is the proper way to behave?" Debate, discuss, and attempt to compromise.
3. Alternative topic: "What is the best way for us to conduct our next family reunion?"

Start with the basic premise of the Family Lies exercise (Chapter 2), one of the other encounters set up earlier between the sexes, or a new one invented by the group. Any number can participate, but three per group is a good number.

1. Place the story in the Restoration, as written by Molière, and in the Georgian period. Begin by discussing with your group what will be exactly the same and what will have to be different.
2. Select names. These may be either based on your own names, on personal characteristics, or both. For example, some recent class choices follow.

*Restoration names with clear innuendo*

Sir Wellington Worthit (a potential lover, slow to coax, but ultimately highly satisfying)
Mistress Quickly-Compromised (no explanation necessary)
Sir Randy Rutting (no explanation necessary)

*Molière names based on current social stereotypes*

Bimbette de Florette (an actress known to space out)
Madame Demande (someone who always gets what she wants)
Walkmande (an actor always accompanied by his personal cassette player and off in his own world)
Alternative: French versions of actual names, such as Barbi, which imply certain personality traits.

*Georgian names based on more exaggerated, less sly, or overtly sexual qualities than those in the Restoration*

Lady Snickersnort (actress with an unusual snorting laugh)
Mrs. Buxombounty (actress with enormous breasts)
Sir Joshua Sloshedalot (played by an actor known to drink more than a little)
Alternative: Combine with Georgian type names some simple, plain ones for unaffected characters.

3. Proceed through a basic analysis of the customs and rewarded behavior to devise the details of the scenario.
4. Create your text by referring to actual scripts from each style for syntax, word choices, and rhythms.
5. After presenting the work in class, discuss in greater depth the areas where the three seem to intersect and where they are, in fact, worlds apart.

Given your cumulative knowledge of each era, invent specific answers for these world-entering ideas:

1. Social Success and Suicide—Molière and Georgian
2. Ultimate Compliment and Insult—Molière and Georgian
3. Ideal Audience—Molière and Georgian

As a group, discuss ideas for (1), then work in pairs demonstrating (2) while the class attempts to respond as (3).

## SOURCES FOR FURTHER STUDY

### Molière

Baur-Heinhold, M. *Baroque Theatre*. New York: McGraw-Hill, 1967.

Chapman, R. A. *The Spirit of Molière*. Princeton: Princeton University Press, 1940.

Ducharte, Pierre Louis. *The Italian Comedy*. New York: Dover, 1966.

Gordon, Mel. *Lazzi*. New York: Performing Arts Journal, 1983.

Grimarest, De. *The Life of Molière*. Paris: Isidore Liseux, 1877.

Gross, Nathan. *Aesthetics and Ethics in Molière's Comedy*. New York: Columbia University Press, 1982.

Howarth, W. D., and Merline Thomas, eds. *Molière: Stage and Study*. Oxford: Clarendon Press, 1973.

Hubert, Judd D. *Molière and the Comedy of Intellect*. New York: Russell & Russell, 1972.

Lawrenson, T. E. *The French Stage in the Seventeenth Century*. Manchester: University of Manchester Press, 1957.

Lewis, W. H. *The Splendid Century: Life in the France of Louis XIV*. Oxford: William Morrow and Co., 1954.

Matthews, Brander. *Molière: His Life and His Works*. New York: Scribner's, 1910.

Mongredien, Georges. *Daily Life in the French Theatre at the Time of Molière*. London: George Allen, 1969.

Oreglia, Giacomo. *The Commedia dell'Arte*. New York: Hill & Wang, 1968.

Tilley, A. A. *Molière*. Cambridge: Cambridge University Press, 1936.

Wilcox, John. *The Relation of Molière to Restoration Comedy*. New York: Benjamin Blom, 1964.

Wiley, W. L. *The Early Public Theatre in France*. Cambridge, Mass.: Harvard University Press, 1955.

Wright, C. H. C. *French Classicism*. Cambridge, Mass.: Harvard University Press, 1920.

## VIDEOS

**Aspects of the Commedia Dell'Arte** (Giovanni Poli)    Clear demonstration of stock character types which so heavily influenced the writing of Molière.

**The Misanthrope** (Edward Petherbridge)    Employing Richard Wilbur's translation, this production is highly stylized and compelling.

**Tartuffe** (Jean Meyer)    In French, but newly issued with English subtitles. Thought to be very similar to the production style employed by Molière's own company.

**Tartuffe or The Imposter** (Anthony Sher)    A striking RSC production translated by Christopher Hampton in which the language is superbly spoken.

## The Georgians

Boswell, James. *Life of Samuel Johnson*. 1791. New York: Random House.

———. *On the Profession of a Player*. 1770. London: Elkin, Matthews, and Marrot, 1929.

Chesterfield, 4th earl of (Philip Dormer Stanhope). *Letters to His Son*. 1771.

Cunningham, C. W. *Handbook of English Costume in the 18th Century*. Boston: Plays, Inc. 1972.

Downer, Alan S. "Nature to Advantage Dressed: Eighteenth Century Acting." *Publication of the Modern Language Association* 58 (December 1943).

Gay, Peter. *Age of Enlightenment*. New York: Time-Life Books, 1965.

Gray, Chalres H. *Theatrical Criticism in London to 1795*. New York: Benjamin Blom, 1966.

Hill, Aaron. *The Art of Acting*. London: J. Osborn, 1746.

Hill, John. *The Actor; or, a Treatise on the Art of Playing*. 1755. New York: Benjamin Blom, 1972.

Lloyd, Robert. *The Actor, A Poetical Epistle*. London: Dodsley, 1760.

Melville, Lewis. *Stage Favorites of the Eighteenth Century*. New York: Benjamin Blom, 1969.

Murphy, Arthur. *The Life of Garrick*. 1801. New York: Benjamin Blom, 1969.

Rude, George. *The Eighteenth Century*. New York: Free Press, 1965.

Shaftesbury, 3rd earl of (Anthony Ashley Cooper). *Characteristicks of Men, Manners, Opinions, Times*. 1711.

Southern, Richard. *The Georgian Playhouse*. London: Pleiades Books Limited, 1948.

Thaler, Alwin. *Shakespeare to Sheridan*. Cambridge, Mass.: Harvard University Press, 1922.

Wildeblood, Joan, and Peter Brinson. *The Polite Society*. New York: Oxford University Press, 1963.

## VIDEOS

**Tom Jones** (Tony Richardson)     Probably the consummate Georgian film in spirit and robust comedy, this adaptation of Henry Fielding's famous novel won an Oscar for Best Picture the year (1963) it was released.

**Barry Lyndon** (Stanley Kubrick)     While more somber and cold than plays of the era, this film is filled with visual information and provides an indelible lesson in the class structure of the times.

**Amadeus** (Milos Forman)     Particularly in the numerous party and opera performance scenes, this film demonstrates period dress, manners, sensibilities, and pastimes.

**The Rivals, She Stoops to Conquer, The School for Scandal, The Critic**
(BBC)     Lively, well spoken renderings of all four plays are offered in these productions mounted for television. Each captures the peculiar balance of genteel exaggeration and proper audactiy characteristic of the period.

## COMPARISON OF RESTORATION, MOLIÈRE, AND GEORGIAN STYLES

Manners plays share a concern with social issues over cosmic ones, an interest in concrete daily reality over mysticism, and a desire for a stable society over twists of fate. Because characters are completely preoccupied with themselves, scripts are always contemporary and local. Here are some areas of contrast:

| | *Restoration* | *Molière* | *Georgian* |
|---|---|---|---|
| *Time* | 1660–1710<br>Mercurial, quixotic | 1658–1673<br>Rapid, impulsive, occasionally stately | 1755–1800<br>Brisk, lively |
| *Space* | Intimate<br>Displays, poses | Court to court (tennis to king's) | Large, well-lighted<br>Scenic developments |
| *Place* | Elegant, urban | Neutral, social | Any city/country spot |
| *Values* | Personal gratification | Reason without hypocrisy | Benevolent good humor |
| *Structure* | Languid elite class<br>Erratic<br>Exclusive | Absolute monarchy<br>Unities imposed<br>All strata | Representative government<br>Ordered, tidy<br>Middle class |
| *Beauty* | Long, lean, painted | Charming, demure, sprightly | Fresh, fulsome, open |
| *Sex* | Yes, please<br>Assignations | Inappropriate topic<br>Ridiculous | Categorized<br>Male outlet |
| *Recreation* | Gossip<br>Flirtation | Trickery<br>Deception | Social events<br>Decoration |
| *Sight* | Curls, ribbons, feathers<br>Decorative | Same as Restoration | White, wide, symmetrical<br>Architectural |
| *Sound* | Arch, crisp, sly | Sharp, bright, relished | Simple, direct, proper |

# 8

# DISPLACED STYLE
## Plays Out of Their Time

To some extent, every play is displaced when it is performed anywhere outside the place or group for which it is intended. In productions of classical drama, it is always an option to pull the play's audience back in time and to make them feel much like the original audience. But what about plays that do not reflect their own time to begin with? Or plays that do not travel well? Or that change radically, depending on which translator, adapter, or editor gets hold of them? Displaced plays, like displaced persons, are searching for a home.

## BLENDING STYLES

The audience comes with one set of answers to the questions in the ten style categories (see Chapter 2). The playwright, unless the script is hot off the presses, supplies another. Even if it *is* just off the presses, the playwright may have chosen answers from the imagination instead of basing them on his or her own society or culture. The play may be set in an era where a third set of answers exists, and sometimes the producer decides to set it in yet *another* time and place. How to get the recipe right? Blending all the points of origin is a task to challenge any actor. And it is the actor, ultimately, who blends with the audience. Here are some suggestions:

1. Research into all contributing worlds is important. Each must be acknowledged in some way because each contributes some part of the final product, even if only a small part. Knowledge of these

Henry Woronicz (Cyrano) and Michelle Morain (Roxane) in *Cyraro de Bergerac,* Oregon Shakespeare Festival

**247**

worlds enables the director and actor to appreciate vital influences.

2. The actor and director need to discuss candidly the purposes of the production, beyond simply serving the script. If the director is doing *The Taming of the Shrew* to show the systematic brainwashing and abuse by which spirited women in our society are violated, everyone involved deserves to know. If the director's purpose is to prove that men are stronger, wiser creatures and that the world is more civilized if these strong, wise men make all of the important decisions, everyone should know.

3. Reverberations from current events and controversies should be examined. A news story can suddenly change the impact of a play. If a war is declared, the play may suddenly take on unexpected dimensions. The overthrow of a government, the emergence of a new fad, or the release of a national life-style statistic can make for a different play. Moreover, shifts in taste can affect audience response.

4. Doing the show exactly as it was done originally needs to be honestly explored. How much do we *know* about the original? How much of this is genuine knowledge, and how much is the educated guess of scholars? What are the fundamental differences between us/now and them/then? Each of the time periods in previous chapters has been discussed in terms of mounting an authentic production, and it is clear that the closer the time of writing to the time of playing, the more likely the director will opt for this choice. Georgian and Restoration plays are staged similarly to the originals far more often than are Greek or Elizabethan. The farther away in both time and space, the more mist surrounding the originals, and the more differences in cultural perspective, the less likely the play will be staged authentically.

5. The director and actors need to scrutinize every piece of historical research in terms of its relevance to the production. An actress playing Titania, queen of the fairies, once stopped rehearsal to ask me whether rushes were still spread across the stage floor at this time in history. Good for her for reading about old-fashioned floors, but does that have anything to do with her performance? She is the queen of the fairies; she may be walking on gossamer speckled with soft diamonds, illuminated by fireflies, and spread like a carpet of spider webs in her path. In this instance, an imaginative choice is more useful to the actor than a scholarly one.

6. Remember that each successful production creates its own world. What starts out looking like a hopeless muddle may end up a fascinating mixture that reveals a universe unto itself. Sometimes this comes about as the result of active debate and exchange of ideas; sometimes it comes about by magic. I once acted in a

*It's a dumb first movie, full of kids, animals, first-time actors speaking in a foreign language. And on top of that, a period piece!*

—KEVIN COSTNER, JOKING WITH THE PRESS BEFORE THE OPENING OF *DANCES WITH WOLVES*

Shakespeare festival production of *Twelfth Night* in which the producers had held three national competitions to select costume and set designs and original music for the show. The winners were given contracts with the festival to supervise their designs. However, *each* competition had had separate judges. The chosen costumes were called "Fairytale Flamingo" (hot and Spanish!), the sets "Delicate Oriental" (wispy fishnets, tiny baskets, and tinkling bells), and the music "Quasi-Elizabethan" (synthesizer galliards). Although the cast members were horrified, we plunged on ahead, and because *Twelfth Night* is a play of wild abandon and surprise (and because its setting, Illyria, is a magical place), all of these disparate elements came together, and audiences and critics were rapturous over the final product. A world was formed by the fates.

The following plays "out of time" were written in one time and place and are set in another, often in an earlier time. Most classical plays are also set in eras *prior* to their dates of authorship (see Chapter 3). The ancient Greek playwrights were not much interested in fifth-century Athens as a source of drama. Only Aeschylus's *The Persians* is contemporary to his time, and only Aristophanes's satires are "local." The only Shakespeare play that seems to be at all about Elizabethan daily life is *The Merry Wives of Windsor.* The past then, as now, seems an irresistible source of inspiration.

The time of Shakespeare and the four hundred years before him (1200 to 1600) are the most popular settings in which modern writers "displace" new plays. Historical personages from these periods are as colorful as any fictional character. Also, most of us look to these eras for our own Once Upon a Time fantasies.

## DISPLACED PERIOD PLAYS

### Displaced Greek

| | |
|---|---|
| Anouilh, Jean | *Antigone* |
| Giraudoux, Jean | *Electra* |
| | *Tiger at the Gates* |
| Jeffers, Robinson | *Medea* |
| | *The Tower Beyond Tragedy* |
| Sartre, Jean-Paul | *The Flies* |

### Displaced Medieval, Renaissance, and Elizabethan

| | |
|---|---|
| Anderson, Maxwell | *Anne of the Thousand Days* |

| | |
|---|---|
| | *Elizabeth the Queen* |
| | *Joan of Lorraine* |
| | *Mary of Scotland* |
| Anouilh , Jean | *Becket* |
| | *The Lark* |
| Bolt, Robert | *A Man for All Seasons* |
| | *Vivat! Vivat! Regina!* |
| Bond, Edward | *Lear* |
| Eliot, T. S. | *Murder in the Cathedral* |
| Fry, Christopher | *The Lady's Not for Burning* |
| | *A Yard of Sun* |
| Gibson, William | *A Cry of Players* |
| Giraudoux, Jean | *Ondine* |
| Goldman, William | *The Lion in Winter* |
| Gressieker, Hermann | *Royal Gambit* |
| Herman, George | *A Company of Wayward Saints* |
| Osborne, John | *Luther* |
| Shaffer, Peter | *The Royal Hunt of the Sun* |
| Shaw, George Bernard | *Saint Joan* |
| Stavis, Barry | *Lamp at Midnight* |
| Synge, J. M. | *Deirdre of the Sorrows* |

## Displaced Manners

| | |
|---|---|
| Balderston, John | *Berkeley Square* |
| Bond, Edward | *Restoration* |
| Hampton, Christopher | *Les Liaisons Dangéreuses* |
| Hirson, David | *La Bête* |
| Rattigan, Terrence | *A Bequest to the Nation* |
| Rogers, David | *Tom Jones* |
| Rostand, Edmond | *Cyrano de Bergerac* |
| Shaffer, Peter | *Amadeus* |
| Shaw, George Bernard | *The Devil's Disciple* |

| | |
|---|---|
| Thomas, Eberle | *The Three Musketeers* |
| Weiss, Peter | *The Persecution and Assassination of Jean-Paul Marat as Performed by the Inmates of the Asylum of Charenton under the Direction of the Marquis de Sade* (usually referred to as *Marat/ Sade*) |
| Wertenbaker, Timberlake | *Our Country's Good* |

## Blends

Some plays are clearly neither within the genre of contemporary American realism nor directly inspired by a single historical period or culture. They are eclectic combinations blended somehow into a single script, or they are set in a time that has never existed. A knowledge of historical acting styles is helpful because these plays make many of the same demands on the actor. Even those set well into the twentieth century hearken back to other customs and are enhanced with a knowledge of period style. Musical plays, in addition to their own distinct conventions, present, if they are set in the past, the same demands as authentic period pieces. Some of these plays are set in modern times but written in verse, which is hardly the modern voice of choice. All create very specific style demands and opportunities. All create their own worlds.

| | |
|---|---|
| Barnes, Peter | *Red Noses* |
| Barrie, James M. | *Peter Pan* |
| Camus, Albert | *Caligula* |
| Coward, Noel | *Blithe Spirit* |
| | *Hay Fever* |
| | *Private Lives* |
| Daniels, Sarah | *Byrthrite* |
| Dunlap, Frank, and Jim Dale | *Scapino* |
| Eliot, T. S. | *The Cocktail Party* |
| Fry, Christopher | *A Phoenix Too Frequent* |
| | *Venus Observed* |

| | |
|---|---|
| Kopit, Arthur | *Oh Dad, Poor Dad, Mama's Hung You in the Closet and I'm Feelin' So Sad* |
| Lerner, Alan Jay, and Frederick Loewe | *Camelot* *My Fair Lady* |
| Miller, Arthur | *The Crucible* |
| MacLeish, Archibald | *J.B.* |
| Molnár, Ferenc | *The Swan* |
| Richardson, Howard | *The Dark of the Moon* |
| Rodgers, Richard, and Oscar Hammerstein II | *The King and I* |
| Shaw, George Bernard | *Androcles and the Lion* *Arms and the Man* *Caesar and Cleopatra* *Heartbreak House* *Man and Superman* *Pygmalion* |
| Stoppard, Tom | *Rosencrantz and Guildenstern Are Dead* |
| Webber, Andrew Lloyd, and Richard Stilgoe | *Phantom of the Opera* |
| Whiting, John | *A Penny for a Song* |
| Wilde, Oscar | *The Importance of Being Earnest* *Lady Windermere's Fan* |
| Wasserman, Dale | *Man of La Mancha* |

## DISPLACED SCENES

*Amadeus*
Constanze, Salieri
Mozart's wife requests a teaching position for her husband. The court composer offers her terms that she at first rejects but later reconsiders.

*Anne of the Thousand Days*
Anne, Henry
Shortly before her execution, the king visits his wife to determine once and for all whether the adultery for which she stands convicted is actually true.

*Becket*
Becket, Henry
(two scenes) Young king and best friend frolic together with boyish abandon, then meet years later when "the honor of God" has made them adversaries.
Becket, Gwendolyn, Henry
After promising his king and friend to return him an equal favor, Becket is asked to sacrifice his mistress, a conquered aristocrat, the thing he loves most in the world.

*The Crucible*
Elizabeth, John
Puritan wife searches her heart to find forgiveness and understanding for her unfaithful husband.

*A Cry of Players*
Will, Anne
Young Shakespeare can no longer endure the stultifying Stratford life and begs his wife to let him go to seek his destiny.

*Cyrano de Bergerac*
Cyrano, Roxane
He has loved her since their childhood, but she is beautiful, and he is a source of constant ridicule for the size of his nose. She has asked for a secret meeting, and his hopes are high.

*Elizabeth the Queen*
Elizabeth, Essex
The queen visits her rebellious young lover to persuade him to recant his treasonous acts and save his life.

*The Importance of Being Earnest*
Gwendolyn, Cecily
When city sophisticate makes a sudden visit to the country home of her fiancé, she is greeted, much to her surprise, by a young, attractive, and not altogether naïve young woman.
Jack, Algernon
Two London dandies debate appropriate behavior and the chances of the one to marry the other's cousin.
Jack, Lady Bracknell
A suitor for the hand of the formidable Lady Bracknell's daughter is interrogated as to his qualifications for marriage.

*La Bête*
Prince Conti, Valere
A consummate performer persuades his monarch that the court theatre cannot survive without him.

*The Lady's Not for Burning*
Alizon, Richard
A young, convent-raised girl rejects her arranged marriage to a wealthy dolt and chooses instead a poor clerk whom she has just met today.
Jennet, Thomas
He wants to be hanged, but no one will take him seriously. She wants to live but is about to be hanged for witchcraft. Together they find something larger than death—love.

*Les Liaisons Dangéreuses*
Valmont, Mertuil
Two decadent members of the French aristocracy plan new ways to corrupt the innocents around them.

*The Lion in Winter*
Henry, Philip
Philip, the young French king, devastates the old English one by informing him that Henry's son seduced Philip as a boy.
Eleanor, Alais
The two women in Henry's life try to repair their own relationship and move beyond the battle of who is to be his queen.
Henry, Alais
The king awakens his young mistress and promises to take her to Rome for an annullment, which will free them to marry.

*A Man for All Seasons*
Henry, Thomas
A dangerous, volatile king debates the relationship between church and state with his devout, principled, careful "servant."

*Mary of Scotland*
Mary, Elizabeth
A rebellious, passionate queen is imprisoned by a politically crafty one. Now jailer visits prisoner.

*Ondine*
Ondine, Hans
A young knight falls in love with a beautiful water sprite and unknowingly seals his own death warrant.

*Saint Joan*
Joan, Dauphin
A peasant girl becomes the driving force behind the reticent young ruler and inspires him to action.

*Tiger at the Gates*
Cassandra and Andromache, opening scene
The prophetess sister of the victorious general and his pregnant wife disagree on the prospects for peace in the land.
Hector and Helen
The Trojan War is about to take place. The Trojan general is determined to stop it. The woman who has caused it all is indifferent.
Hector and Ulysses
The two generals meet to see whether Helen's infidelity is sufficient cause for war.

## PERIODS AND PLAYS LESS CHOSEN

The first major omission you may have noticed is Greek comedy. Aristophanes was a comic genius on a par with the big three tragedians of the first flowering of drama. Of his eleven surviving scripts, the most popular (and the subjects of their satire) are the following:

| | |
|---|---|
| Greek—Aristoph-anes | *The Frogs* (Euripides)<br>*The Clouds* (Socrates)<br>*The Birds* (city life)<br>*Lysistrata* (war) |

The last, in which wives withhold sex from their husbands until the men stop fighting, is produced frequently because its humor and wisdom is universal. Aristophanes manages to offer serious criticisms through rollicking wit and great fantasy. His plays are about his *own* city in his own time, but when they are done well, the *current* president, mayor, policies, issues, and fads are satirized. The plays are almost always updated so that the current *parallel* to the past target is zapped. The result is an acting style that is more of a blend of the Marx Brothers and "In Living Color" than classical.

No other periods have produced more than isolated instances of great vehicles for acting. The following scripts stand out. They are all worth your attention and may enter your life at some time.

| | |
|---|---|
| Roman—Plautus | *The Menaechmi*<br>*Amphitryon* |

These Roman plays have been adapted many times, with the device of mistaken identity used over and over. They are akin to the work of Aristophanes but cruder, louder, more frantic. Acting in them feels like doing circus vaudeville with a plot.

| Medieval—authors unknown | *The Passion Play* |
| | *The Second Shep-herd's Play* |
| | *Everyman* |
| | *The Nativity* |
| | *Master Pierre Pate-lin* |

The anonymous ancestors of Shakespeare ground their plays in liturgical form and fill them with biblical characters. The plays remained popular in Elizabethan England until the queen banned them as Catholic propaganda. Most have been adapted into very modern-sounding texts, but the originals offer all the challenges and much of the beauty of classical verse. They are far more simplistic than the work of Shakespeare, but they bequeath him a legacy of blending comedy and tragedy in the same play. Like the Greeks, the Medievals write for audiences who know the plot and so watch the play to understand motivation (why did Cain do that to Abel, anyhow?) and to find reflections from their sacred history to apply to their own lives. These works are folk drama. They are like folk music that precedes and inspires grand opera.

| Neoclassic—Jean Racine | *Phèdre* |
| Eighteenth-century Italian—Carlo Goldoni | *The Mistress of the Inn* |
| | *The Servant of Two Masters* |

Racine's work stays within the Neoclassic confines and has much of the power of a Greek tragedy written from a seventeenth-century perspective (he is a contemporary of Molière). The two Goldoni plays have much in common with Molière in their commedia influences, stock characters, dominating busybody servants, and lively, nonstop action. They also share a Georgian robust good humor and simplicity. Both hold up extremely well in twentieth-century production.

## EASTERN VISION: KABUKI ON THE HORIZON

As a culture, we tend to stay focused on our own tradition, often missing a wealth of style wonders. From Japan, however, we have received theatrical forms that are entering the actor's life more and more often, particularly in production concepts for Western plays. There are four fascinating styles: Noh, Bugaku, Bunraku, and Kabuki.

Noh is the oldest (early 1300s) and most delicate, with short, serious, subtle, distant works in which a chorus chants a story while masked actors dance and perform pantomime. Zeami, its founder, suggested that theatre should be like a flower blooming from the imagination. Symbolic simple gestures convey complex meanings. Noh is tragic in tone, with characters that have remained the same for centuries, although contemporary writers, such as Yukio Mishima, have adapted the form into modern settings. Bugaku is a stately and elegant form of dance, and Bunraku involves giant puppets. All of these present a specialized appeal but offer fresh ways to stylize modern works. The easiest style for Westerners to understand is Kabuki.

Kabuki is a livelier and longer form of dancelike drama dating back to the 1600s. *Kabuki,* from the verb *kabuku,* means "incline," "slant," "tilt," or "trend." An outrageous and eccentric female dancer, Izumo-no-Okuni, performed in male garments and wore a wooden cross around her neck. Her adaptation of religious dance, called *numbutsu odori,* included an erotic interlude. Her audience called her *kabuku* and *kabukumono,* meaning "weird" and "flashy." From its beginning, the form has been associated with the fashionable avant-garde, so it has lent itself to surprising new twists. It has come to mean, in popular usage, a break with the past.

*Time*  Although Kabuki began as seventeenth-century religious parodies performed by women, it has ironically developed into male-only theatre designed for demonstration of actor versatility. Kabuki has a sensational history. In 1629, women were banned from Kabuki because of accusations of prostitution and were replaced by young boys (*wakashu*), also accused of prostitution in 1652. For a time, their forelocks were shaved to make the boys less attractive. Finally, a censored, all-male adult company was established. The form changed continuously until after World War II, when it was frozen for about thirty years. Now the leading Kabuki artist, Ennosuke Ichikawa III, is again stretching the limits, reviving lost traditions of clowning and audience interaction and adding new and spectacular stunts. The plays are epic and play fast and loose with history and historical personages. Kabuki involves lightning-fast costume changes and freezes and poses juxtaposed with rapid, energized moves.

*Values*  Kabuki is popular because it deals with the joys and sorrows of common people living in a remote and fascinating past. It blends tragedy, comedy, realism, and romanticism all into one performance. Among its traditions, the art of a male actor impersonating female characters is called *onnagata,* and specialization in rough male roles is called *aragoto* or *otokagata.* The acting techniques, called *kata,* are passed from one generation to the next. The first Kabuki actors were called *yakusha,* signifying one who officiates at a religious ceremony. The plays always teach some moral lesson.

There are eighteen famous classical Kabuki plays, together called the *juhachiban,* and over two hundred plays in all. Performance always relies on dance, music, and elaborate vocal effects. A guiding principle is *yatsushi,* in which the old is presented but at the same time modernized and parodied. Kabuki is a *yatsushi* of Noh, as haiku poetry is a *yatsushi* of waka, or tanka. Famous characters may appear in outrageous modern garb and predicaments.

**Space and Sight**    Narrators, called *joruri,* frequently act as the chorus for the play, and stage assistants, or *koken,* dressed in black act as invisible helpers, handing props to actors, holding garments out for display, and sometimes acting as scenery. Black is the color of nonexistence, so a black curtain symbolizes night. Makeup also involves color symbolism; for example, red represents justice or strength, and blue evil or the supernatural. Costumes and headgear can put tremendous pressure on abdominal muscles and the temples. If these items are used, the actor should either modify them or work with them for some time prior to performance.

Kabuki theatre uses a ninety-foot proscenium opening, and important entrances are made on a *hanamichi,* a runway through the audience from the back of the auditorium. The chorus (*joruri*) traditionally sits upstage on a raised platform. The traditional stage is made of cypress scrubbed with bean curd, which greatly aids movement on the resulting surface. A pull curtain (*hikimaku*) is standard, although revolving stages, lifts, and other spectacular effects are in view of the audience.

**Structure**    Entrances and exits are made from the audience left, traditionally believed to be superior to right. Those entering on the *hanamichi* are of high rank or in some way due serious attention. *Hanamichi* exits are powerfully rhythmic. There are a great many rules and conventions in Kabuki. An *onnagata* is seated a half pace behind an actor in a male role, and an actor always faces the audience for an important speech. Male characters always start with the left foot, women with the right. Great beauty of stage picture is sought, and each scene ends with a striking pose called a *mie.* The *mie* can also occur during the scene and is preceded by energetic motion, then offset by the sudden stillness. This convention crystallizes the striking contrast within the form between intense drama and utter tranquility. Acting veers from the stylized (*jidai-mono*) to the realistic (*sewa-mono*).

**Sound**    Music and percussion are heavily used to reinforce the actors' performances. Stick drum, wooden clappers, and flute may accompany recitation. The flute is traditionally believed to have the power to bring back departed spirits.

Modern Kabuki has added everything from acrobatics to giant puppets to high technology. The scripts are not performed word for word but are instead thought of as libretti or simply a blueprint for performance. Kabuki scripts are rarely performed by American actors, but the style itself is increasingly being used in mounting other scripts, especially Shakespeare and Greek tragedy. Greek tragedy with its mixture of drama, poetry, music, and dance, is particularly suited to the stylistic devices of Kabuki. Kabuki is often compared to Shakespeare because of its sweep, grandeur, and sheer scope. For those Shakespeare scripts involving magic, storms, and high ritual (*The Tempest, Macbeth, A Midsummer Night's Dream, King Lear,* and *Titus Andronicus* among others), the form offers an ideal way of handling these elements through striking theatrical conventions instead of high technology. A forest suddenly created and dissolved by *koken* and a wind depicted by swirling chiffon are simple, highly theatrical possibilities.

## ADAPTATIONS AND EDITIONS: CAN THIS BE THE SAME STORY? CAN THIS BE THE SAME SENTENCE?

Myths and legends are fair game. Anyone may retell the story of Hercules, Arthur, or even your Aunt Tillie, if she is legendary. If the author significantly revises an old story, it is regarded as a new play. Each of the three Greek tragedians, for example, writes an Electra startlingly different from that of the others. An editor prepares a work for publication, often altering punctuation, spelling, and the arrangement of the words on the page for purposes of clarification. Editors are often not actors, directors, or playwrights. They are often not even theatregoers. They read the line, not necessarily as it might be spoken, but rather as it might be silently read.

*It is important to be aware of all the editing that has gone on. The word we're revering may not be the playwright's intended word.*

—REX RABOLD

A Shakespeare festival director once instructed each of us in the cast to go back to the First Folio (the earliest collected works of the playwright) and check for differences between what appeared in that massive volume and the single script paperback copy, which we, for convenience, had been using in rehearsal. I was amazed at how many differences there were and at how often, after looking at both choices, I found the original more speakable and more intriguing as a line to be delivered. So whenever you are in a play or doing a scene that has appeared in different editions, check out as many editions as possible. Every change involving a comma or colon may reveal some clue to meaning.

Do the same with any word that is not precisely clear to you. Words not only were being invented during many of these periods but also often had multiple meanings. Because the first dictionary (*A Table Alphabeticall . . . of Hard Usuall English Wordes*) did not appear until 1604 and the first dictionary of *all* English words did not appear until 1721, there is no standard guide to definitions prior to these dates. Moreover, Elizabethan and Restoration writers are particularly fond of puns; key words, therefore, may have multiple meanings.

## TRANSLATIONS: CAN THIS BE THE SAME SCRIPT?

Here are some samples of ways in which translators have dealt with the same speech. This is the very first speech of Sophocles's *Antigone,* perhaps the most performed of all the Greek tragedies. The play is a universal debate between the youthful desire for what is morally right and mature desire for a balance between personal justice and justice for all. Antigone has buried her brother in direct defiance of her uncle, Creon, ruler of Thebes. Because her brother had been fighting against the government (in a battle with her other brother), he has been denied the rights of burial. She is asking her sister, Ismene, if any more grief could come to their family.

> Ismene, O my dear, my little sister, of all the griefs bequeathed us by our father Oedipus, is there any that Zeus will spare us while we live? There is no sorrow and no shame we have not known. And now what is this new edict they tell about, that our Captain has published all through Thebes? Do you know? Have you heard?
>
> (Shaemus O'Sheel)

> My sister, Lov'd Ismene, of the ills
> Which sprung from Oedipus conceives there
> One, by the hand of Jove, not brought on us
> His sole-surviving children? There is nought
> That sinks the soul with anguish, deep distress,
> Shame, and disgrace, but in thy ills and mine
> I see it all. E'en now what new decree
> Is rumour'd by the Chief as late proclaim'd
> Through all the city. Know'st thou? Hast thou heard?
>
> (R. Potter)

> Ismene, sister mine, one life with me,
> Knowest thou of the burden of our race
> Aught that from us yet living Zeus holds back?
> Nay, for nought grievous and nought ruinous,
> No shame and no dishonour, have I not seen
> Poured on our hapless heads, both thine and mine.
> Uttered, men say, to all this Theban folk?
> Thou knowest it and hast heard?
>
> (Robert Whitelaw)

> O sister! Ismene dear, dear sister Ismene!
> You know how heavy the hand of God is upon us;
> How we who are left must suffer for our father, Oedipus.
> There is no pain, no sorrow, no suffering, no dishonour
> We have not shared together, you and I.
> And now there is something more. Have you heard this order,
> This latest order that the King has proclaimed to the city?
>
> (E. F. Watling)

> Ismene?
> Let me see your face:
> my own, only sister,
> can you see
> because we are the survivors
> today Zeus is completing in us the ceremony

of pain and dishonor and disaster and shame
that began with Oedipus?
And today, again:
the proclamation, under the rule of war
but binding, they say, on every citizen . . .
Haven't you heard?
(Richard Braun)

Ismene, dear sister,
You would think that we had already suffered enough
For the curse on Oedipus:
I cannot imagine any grief
That you and I have not gone through. And now—
Have they told you of the new decree of our King Creon?
(Dudley Fitts and Robert Fitzgerald)

Ismene listen. The same blood
Flows in both our veins, doesn't it, my sister,
The blood of Oedipus. And suffering,
Which was his destiny, is our punishment too,
The sentence passed on all his children.
Physical pain, contempt, insults,
Every kind of dishonor. We've seen them all,
And endured them all, the two of us.
But there's more to come. Now, today . . .
Have you heard it, this new proclamation,
Which the king has made to the whole city?
(Don Taylor)

Have actors read these seven versions of the speech. Close your eyes, and let the differences in the words act on you. Discuss the differences. Ancient Greek is a strongly inflected language with verse lines roughly equivalent to trochaic hexameter (a line of six feet, each with a stressed followed by an unstressed syllable). This rhythmic pattern is all but impossible to translate literally into our language. It sounds tentative, uncertain, and overly inflected to our ears. The result is that many translations veer so far from the original that they seem like adaptations. There is almost every form of translation available: rhyming couplets, blank verse, free verse; flowery and curt, vague and blunt, romantic and sardonic, elevated and basic. In one current translation, the messenger calls Antigone a "bitch."

The differences among translations are even sharper in exchanges between two characters. Experiment the same way with the following tense confrontations from *Medea* and *Electra*. Prior to the following exchange from Euripides's *Medea*, Jason has married another woman, and Medea has retaliated by killing their two children. This is their first confrontation after the murder.

M: Think of thy torment. They are dead, they are dead!
J: No, quick, great God; quick curses round thy head!

*For such is our pride, our folly and our fate,
That few, but such as cannot write, translate.*
—SIR JON DENHAM

M: The Gods know who began this work of woe.
J: Thy heart and all its loathliness they know.
M: Loathe on. . . . But, Oh, thy voice. It hurts me sore.
J: Aye, and thine me. Would'st hear me then no more?
M: How? Show me but the way. 'Tis this I crave.
J: Give me the dead to weep, and make their grave.
M: Never!

Gilbert Murray

M: The children are dead. I say this to make you suffer.
J: The children, I think, will bring down curses on you.
M: The gods know who was the author of this sorrow.
J: Yes, the gods know indeed, they know your loathsome heart.
M: Hate me. But I tire of your barking bitterness.
J: And I of yours. It is easier to leave you.
M: How then? What shall I do? I long to leave you too.
J: Give me the bodies to bury and to mourn them.
M: No, that I will not.

Rex Warner

M: See, they are no more:
    I can hurt you too.
J: They'll live, I think
    in your tormented brain.
M: The gods know who began
    this whole calamity.
J: Yes, the gods know well
    your pernicious heart.
M: Hate then: I spurn
    the wormwood from your lips.
J: As I do yours; so let us
    be rid of one another.
M: Yes, but on what terms?
    That's also what I want.
J: Let me have the boys—
    to mourn and bury them.
M: Never!

Paul Roche

M: The children are dead. That will sting you.
J: No! they live to bring fierce curses on your head.
M: The gods know who began it all.
J: They know, indeed, they know the abominable wickedness of your heart.
M: Hate me then. I despise your bitter words.
J: And I yours. But it is easy for us to be quit of each other.
M: How, pray? Certainly I am willing.
J: Allow me to bury these bodies and lament them.
M: Certainly not.

Moses Hadas and John Harvey McLean

In this scene from Sophocles's *Electra,* the title character encounters her mother at the grave of her father. Clytemnestra has murdered Agamemnon and taken a lover, Aegisthus. Electra is deep in mourning for her father and full of hatred for her mother.

E: The enmity on thy part, and thy treatment, compel me in mine own
  despite to do thus: for base deeds are taught by base.

C: Thou brazen one! Truly I and my sayings and my deeds give thee too
  much matter for words.

E: The words are thine, not mine; for thine is the action; and the acts find
  the utterance.

C: Now by our lady Artemis, thou shalt not fail to pay for this boldness,
  so soon as Aegisthus returns.

E: Lo, thou art transported by anger, after granting me free speech, and
  hast no patience to listen.

C: I hinder not—begin thy rites, I pray thee; and blame not my voice for I
  shall say no more.

R. C. Jebb

E: Only your acts and your hostility
    Force me to this behaviour. Infamy
    Is got by contact with the infamous.

C: Insolent creature! I, my words and acts,
    Make you so loudly overeloquent?

E: It is your fault, not mine; you are the doer,
    And deeds find names.

C:                                  Not mine by Artemis,
    Who is my mistress, when Aegisthus comes
    Shall you escape, for this audacity!

E: See, now you fly into a frenzy! First
    You let me speak my mind—then, you'll not listen!

C: Will you not let me sacrifice, without
    Words of ill omen, after suffering you
    To say all that you can?

E: Go, sacrifice!
    I let you! Nay, I bid you! Censure not
    My mouth again, for I shall say no more.

George Young

E: But it is your heartlessness that forces me;
    Crime is quickly learned from crime.

C: A monstrous nursling! She preaches on me
    As her text; on what I do, on what I say!

E: It is you who talk. It is your deeds that talk.
    Even in my words it is your deeds that talk!

C: Artemis! Queen! Witness! When Aegisthus comes
    She shall diminish this impudence!

E: Do you see?

> Having given me leave to say what I would
> She will not listen.
>
> C:  And so, though you have had your say,
> You will keep my from sacrifice by screaming?
>
> E:  Go. I invite you. Sacrifice.
> Do not blame my tongue, for I say no more.
>
> Frances Fergusson

> E:                Your treatment
> Forces me to answer hate with hate.
> Evil breeds evil—I learned from you.
>
> C:  That's enough! Such insolence! You talk
> Too much of what I do and what I say.
>
> E:  No! Your own words, your own actions,
> Speak for themselves. They need no words from me.
>
> C:  Artemis, queen of heaven! When Aegisthus
> Comes home, you'll suffer for this.
>
> E:  You see? You allow me to speak, and then
> You lose your temper and refuse to hear.
>
> C:  I've heard enough, allowed enough!
> Now hold your tongue, and let me sacrifice.
>
> E:  Yes, sacrifice. I'll hold my tongue
> I've said my say: there is nothing more.
>
> Kenneth McLeish

Which of the translations above is best? It depends on the kind of production planned. Is the production going to be formal, with masks and highly theatrical costumes? Is it going to be simple, with minimal makeup and subtle playing? Wildly experimental? Text and production should match. When you are choosing a translation for a scene or monologue, consider your purpose. What is the impact you wish to make? If you are putting together an audition with two monologues, what do you need to show? A capacity for artifice? A direct, strong attack? Facility with language? Raw honesty? Many actors stop at the first translation they find. Many are disappointed, because having been told that a certain work is deeply moving, they find it leaves them cold. But it may be the translation that leaves them cold. These are great plays; they are survivors. Keep looking until you find the version that suits you. Prominent translators of the Greek poets include Peter Arnott, Countee Cullen, Dudley Fitts, Moses Hadas, Edith Hamilton, Robinson Jeffers, Richard Lattimore, Gilbert Murray, Paul Roche, Philip Vellacott, and Rex Warner.

The works of Molière nearly match the Greek tragedies in the number and variety of translations. Originally in French, of course, some of the plays are prose, but more are in a form of verse, called alexandrines, which does not quite translate (see Chapter 7). Molière's works were translated into English almost immediately, and they significantly influenced Restoration writers. William Wycherley even adapted *The Misanthrope* into *The Plain Dealer*.

What follows is speech by Alceste, the title character in *The Misanthrope*. He is criticizing, as he frequently does, hypocrisy. He is unhappy when people claim to like someone whom they do not care for at all. The original speech reads:

> Une tell action ne saurait s'excuser,
> Et tout homme d'honneur s'en doit scandaliser.
> Je vous accabler un homme de caresses,
> Et temonger pour lui les dernieres tendresses;
> De protestation, d'offres et de serments,
> Vous chargez la fureur de vos emrassements:

Note how various translators render the speech:

> I call your conduct inexcusable, Sir,
> And every man of honor will concur.
> I see you almost hug a man to death,
> Exclaim for joy until you're out of breath,
> And supplement these loving demonstrations
> With endless offers, vows and protestations.
> (Richard Wilbur)

> . . . there's no excusing such an action, and every man of honour ought to be shocked at it. I see you stifle a man with caresses, and profess the utmost tenderness for him; you overcharge the transport of your embraces with protestations, offers and oaths.
> (H. Baker and J. Miller)

> There can be no excuse for such an action!
> A man of honor should be scandalized!
> I watch you load a man with compliments,
> With protests of the tenderest affection;
> You put your arm around him, uttering vows
> Of aid and comfort and profound esteem.
> (Morris Bishop)

> There is no excuse for such behavior: every man of honour would shrink from it. I see you overwhelm a man with caresses and show him the utmost affection; you burden the wealth of your embraces with protestations, offers and vows of devotion.
> (A. R. Walker)

> . . . there is no excuse for such behavior, and every man of honour must be disgusted at it. I see you almost stifle a man with caresses, show the most ardent affection, and overwhelm him with protestation, offers, and vows of friendship.
> (Waldo Frank)

Here is a lover's spat from *Tartuffe*. Mariane's father insists she marry a man she loathes instead of her beloved Valère. Her maid, Dorine, attempts to help the two lovers, but their pride and stubbornness provide as much of a barrier as her father's plans.

V:  Of course! You never really loved me at all.

M:  Alas! You may think so if you like.

V:  Yes, yes. I may indeed: but I may yet forestall your design. I know on whom to bestow both my hand and my affections.

M:  Oh! I don't doubt that in the least, and the love which your good qualities inspire . . .

V:  Good Lord! Let's leave my good qualities out of it. They are slight enough and your behaviour is proof of it. But I know someone who will, I hope, consent to repair my loss once she knows I am free.

M:  Your loss is little enough and, no doubt, you'll easily be consoled by the change.

V:  I shall do what I can you may be sure. To find oneself jilted is a blow to one's pride. One must do one's best to forget it and if one doesn't succeed, at least one must pretend to, for to love where one's love is scorned is an unpardonable weakness.

M:  A very elevated and noble sentiment, I'm sure.

V:  Of course and one that everyone must approve.

John Wood

V:                                    I'm sure
    you never really loved me.

M:                                    You're entitled
    to your opinion.

V:                                    Yes, I am entitled;
    and I may manage to forestall your plan,
    by taking my proposal somewhere else.

M:  I wouldn't be surprised; you're so goodlooking . . .

V:  God, let's leave my looks out of it, shall we?
    They can't be that good, as you've just yourself
    demonstrated. But there is somebody,
    who feels kindly for me and, now I'm free,
    won't be ashamed to remedy my loss.

M:  Your loss seems far from great, I'm sure you'll have
    no difficulty finding consolation.

V:  You may be confident I'll do my best.
    Being abandoned puts us on our mettle;
    we must make every effort to forget
    the person who's responsible, and even
    if we can't quite succeed, we must pretend to:
    to show oneself in love with someone faithless
    would be the most unpardonable weakness.

M:  What an exalted, lofty sentiment.

V:  I don't think anyone could disapprove.

Christopher Hampton

V:  Doubtless, and you never had any true love for me.

M:  Alas! You may think so if you please.

V:  Yes, yes, may think so; but my offended heart may chance to be beforehand with you in that affair, and I can tell where to offer both my addresses and my hand.

M: I don't doubt it sir. The warmth that merit raises—

V: Lack-a-day! Let us drop merit. I have little enough of that, and you think so, but I hope another will treat me in a kinder manner; and I know a person whose heart, open to my retreat, will not be ashamed to make up my loss.

M: The loss is not great, and you will be comforted upon this change easily enough.

V: You may believe I shall do all that lies in my power. A heart that forgets us, engages our glory; we must employ our utmost cares to forget it too; and if we don't succeed, we must at least pretend we do; for to show a regard for those that forsake us, is a meanness one cannot answer to one's self.

M: The sentiment is certainly noble and sublime.

V: Very well, and what everybody must approve of.

H. Baker and J. Miller

V:                          And I now see
That you were never truly in love with me.

M: Alas, you're free to think so if you choose.

V: I choose to think so, and here's a bit of news:
You've spurned my hand, but I know where to turn
For kinder treatment, as you shall quickly learn.

M: I'm sure you do. Your noble qualities
Inspire affection . . .

V:                          Forget my qualities, please.
They don't inspire you overmuch, I find.
But there's another lady I have in mind
Whose sweet and generous nature will not scorn
To compensate me for the loss I've borne.

M: I'm no great loss, and I'm sure that you'll transfer
Your heart quite painlessly from me to her.

V: I'll do my best to take it in my stride.
The pain I feel at being cast aside
Time and forgetfulness may put an end to.
Or if I can't forget, I shall pretend to.
No self-respecting person is expected
To go on loving once he's been rejected.

M: Now, that's a fine, high-minded sentiment.

V: One to which any sane man would assent.

Richard Wilbur

Again, have eight actors read the speech, and listen for the differences. Whereas critics, actors, and directors disagree about which translations of Greek plays are the best, there is a wide consensus that the Molière translations of Richard Wilbur are the most effective. They are highly actable and come closest to both the meter and the rhyme scheme of the original. The translator opts for a five-foot line compatible to our ears, the next best choice to the original. Wilbur's lines flow sharply and crisply on the tongue. However, besides *The Misanthrope,* he has translated only three other scripts: *The School for Wives, Tartuffe,* and *The Learned Ladies.* Other Molière translators of note include John Ozell, Katherine Wormeley, Curtis Hidden Page, F. C. Green, Bermel (whose versions of the prose one-act plays have been widely praised), Miles Malleson, Donald Frame, and John Wood. Your choice of translator depends on your style of presentation. A highly physical commedia-inspired performance with lots of slapstick will require a different text than an arch, still, and elegant presentation in the manner of the Comédie Française.

When making a translation choice, consider each of the following:

- Speakability (Trippingly on the tongue, or just tripping?)
- Form (Rhymed, free, or blank verse, prose, a mix? Similar or removed from the original?)
- Phrasing (Short or lengthy? Smooth or choppy?)
- Vocabulary (Common, elevated, clear, inaccessible?)
- Characterization (Distinct, or do all speak similarly?)
- Translator's notes (Are alternative line readings provided and meanings explained?)

When tracking down multiple translations, start with both the title and author listings in the library catalogue. Then check *Play Index* to locate translations in anthologies. Next, check the *Chicorel Theatre Index* for possible omissions in the above. The play script catalogues from major publishing houses (Samuel French, Dramatists' Play Service, and Dramatic Publishing Company) may each list several separate translations. The volume *Books in Print* will indicate which are still in print and whether any new editions have been recently published. Additional information regarding the original production of a translation can be pursued through the *Arts and Humanities Index, The New York Times Theatre Reviews, New York Theatre Critics Reviews, Book Review Index, Book Review Digest,* or a reference librarian. If all else fails, you could translate or adapt the work yourself.

## PLACING VERSUS DISPLACING

How do you get over the linguistic and cultural hurdles involved in period style production? As the language changes, literacy and vocabulary scores drop, and visuals replace conversation, it is the actor who has the stewardship of keeping the classical plays alive and vital. The actor needs to keep the words immediate and make them impossible to ignore. One of the first ways to go about this task is to return to a point of innocence regarding the play so that you can rediscover, step by step, the spirit and relationships at the heart of the play. One way is to imagine that the play has not yet been written. It is unformed, a mere gleam in the playwright's eye. Here is an exercise to help you return to the beginning.

---

Perform the exercise with a playwright from each of the major periods and one twentieth-century writer. The example that follows shows how the exercise could be done if Shakespeare were the playwright selected.

**E X E R C I S E**

**Persuade the Playwright**

*Casting*

Director, teacher, or other staff member: Wm. Shakespeare

Others on staff: Members of Shakespeare's acting company (Burbage, Condell, Hemming, and so on)

Everyone else: The characters they are performing in the show or in their scene assignments

The highest authority figure in the play(s) chairs the event.

1. Version A: All actors are characters in the same play, which has yet to be written (and could end up quite different from the one the actors know). Word of the event itself (for example, the shocking deaths of the Capulet and Montague kids) has reached the world's greatest playwright, William Shakespeare, who appears as an honored guest. He has expressed interest in writing a script based on the event. It is six months after the end of the story. All participants have agreed to meet in some neutral space (including those returning from the grave) to share with Shakespeare and company their versions of what occurred. Shakespeare has sent word to all involved that he is highly intrigued with the story itself but somewhat puzzled by individual motives, unclear about where he should place primary and secondary focus in his play and uncertain about how serious or light the treatment should be. Since the play has yet to be written even though the events have occurred, the potential for change is great and the stakes for each participant are high. All are strongly motivated to make certain they are accurately represented. For example, in *Romeo and Juliet,*
   • Tybalt's role could be greatly expanded.
   • The entire story could focus on the prince and the troubles he faces in ruling Verona.
   • The story could emerge largely as Lady Capulet's personal tragedy.
   • Benvolio's struggles to be a good Montague may become the focus.
   • The story could center on the friar's experiments with potions.
   The title itself could naturally change, as well.
2. Version B: Four or five delegations from different plays compete to capture the author's imagination and become his or her next script. The action is the same as above except that actors are competing not only for the portrayal of truth as their characters see it, but also for their funda-

mental story to be regarded as the most immediately worthy or compelling in the eyes of the writer.

3. Variation: The characters persuade a director to stage their play as his or her next production. In this version, actors performing scenes from a variety of periods may compete, arguing not only the value of their play but also the benefits of staging it in their period.

**E X E R C I S E**

**Theatre Sports Period Drama**

1. Using the standard format for theatre sport competitions and working in teams of four or five, select one of the major categories: Greek, Elizabethan, Restoration, Molière, or Georgian.
2. Let the audience call out and suggest a place, an object, and a situation.
3. The team immediately creates a scene in the style in question, combining the three elements and attempting to resolve the problem. Because this exercise forces you to think on your feet using the archetypes and point of view of each period, you gain the experience of thinking and writing lines as a character would. Don't give in to the temptation to lampoon the style but instead let the humor arise from the situation itself.

---

## PLACING THE PLAY: THIRTY STEPS TO CLASSICAL ACTING

Style plays are always potentially strange to an audience and potentially intimidating to an actor. Displacement is always in the air, ready to invade both sides of the footlights. Many actors are assigned a period style monologue or scene and spend weeks "hating" it because they do not yet understand it. Or they get the general idea, but not the moment-to-moment riches. Here is the best way I have found to place the work so that it makes perfect sense to both performer and observer. Some of these ideas were introduced in Chapter 3 as general principles. Try them here as rehearsal exercises connected to a specific text. These thirty steps will clarify the script and enlighten you. Some can even thrill you.

1. Scansion: Honor the meter.

If the play is not written in verse, you can obviously skip this step. Otherwise, sit down with the script as if it were a musical score and count it out. The laborious effort of identifying stressed and unstressed syllables, elisions, compensations, trochees, and iambs will pay off in a clear rhythmic pattern that supplies much information about pronunciation and interpretation. Once you understand the stresses, you can let the script's pulse work on you and free you (see Chapter 3).

2. Stanislavsky-based character analysis: Unearth circumstances and motives.

The following are the principles of the Stanislavsky system.

These elements are always present in any clear, sharp performance. Can you answer these questions as your character would?*
For any single encounter, consider the following:

- Relationship: What do characters mean to each other?
- Objective: What do I want?
- Obstacle: What is in the way?
- Strategy: What is my game plan to achieve my objective?
- Tactics: What are my plays within the overall game plan?
- Relationship between text and subtext: What do I speak out, and what do I hide or imply?
- Interior monologues: What is the "tape" running in my head saying?
- Evaluations: What do I consider and reject each time I choose something else? (Some of an actor's most interesting work relates to the choice pondered but not taken.)
- Beats: What transactions occur in this scene? How many are there? What points are won? How does the encounter break into smaller encounters?

For the full life of the character, ask yourself the following:

- Given circumstances: What are the major influences shaping me?
- Magic "if": What do I, the actor, need to project or change so that I can play this person without judgment?
- Objective hierarchy: What do I want most to least? In what order?
- Line of actions: What is the arc of my behavior? How do my actions pull together into a pattern?
- Score of script. How can I, the actor, mark and shape the script to help me map my work? How can I make it my musical score?
- Endowment: Which props and people do I need to imagine? What do I need to enhance and fill in?
- Recall (What can I, the actor, use from my own experience to illuminate that of the character?)
- Images: How can I, the actor, tap my senses to bring the performance to life?
- External adjustments: What do I, the actor, need to change about my persona to play the role and serve the script?

---

*Further discussion of these fundamental terms may be found in the three basic volumes of Konstantin Stanislavsky (*An Actor Prepares, Building a Character, Creating a Role*) or a thorough introductory acting text.

- The creative state: How can I, the actor, relax and make myself available to inspiration?

The most common complaint from coaches and directors working on the classics is that their actors skip these steps instead of adding new ones. What is the good of pointing your toe correctly if you don't know what time it is and what you want?

3. Recording while reading from the script: Check memorization periodically.

The use of a cassette recorder can open your ears. First, it will help you memorize your lines. You want to get the words right, especially because some of these plays are so well known that some audience members can recite them with you. The more you work on a role, the less likely you are to look at the text and see the unfortunate rewrites you are speaking. If you record the script *early,* word for word, you will not only see how far you have come with time but also ensure that you are text-perfect. Play the tape while you do other activities at home. Let the words come to *you.* They will.

4. Reference room research: Unearth new clues to meaning.

### OED *and Lexicons—Multiple and Contradictory Meanings*

Find every meaning every key word has ever had. Do not neglect the words you think you already know. You need to know which convey double, triple, or more messages. You need to know whether a word lost some twist of meaning in time so that you can punch it to help the audience. *The Oxford English Dictionary* (often just called the *OED*) is the most highly regarded authoritative source and contains a wealth of historical detail. *Webster's Third New International Dictionary,* with over 450,000 entries, is the most complete. Check them both. What seems like a purely scholarly exercise will reveal a wealth of suggestions for new line readings.

### Other Editions of the Script—Punctuation, Spelling, Phrasing Hints

Check out other editions and translations in addition to the one you are using. One comma can change the meaning of an entire important line. Learn how these "traffic signals" can redirect and guide you.

### Production Histories—Traditions in Interpretation

Knowing what other actors did with the role is important. Keeping yourself pure is arrogant. As Bertolt Brecht said, steal from the best. Do not study these actors' work relentlessly, but look at it once on video, or track down details about the production history in such works as the Shakespeare *Variorum,* a volume that summarizes the primary performance choices actors have made throughout history. Keep what excites you. Then make it your own.

5. Regular taping and playback: Gain permission to do more.

    Many actors are afraid to tape themselves because they hate what they hear. Listen to yourself often enough to get past that first coy embarrassment and reach an objective assessment of that voice. What most actors discover in playback is that they are doing much *less* than they thought they were. You may think you are making a tremendous drop in pitch to strengthen a given moment, only to hear that you have merely dropped a few notes. Taping and listening gives you permission to do more. You accept the need to go the distance. Access to video equipment will give you all the more feedback. Tape most of the following as you try them.

6. Antitheses: Try to overdo.

    Classical writers set words in opposition to each other. A word is introduced, and then another comes along to match it, slap it, or knock it down. Sometimes four or five sets of words knock out or counterbalance each other. You clarify this relationship by punching the first word and then giving its companion or adversary some of the same emphasis. The audience senses the connection. Consider this sentence: "The *actors* in *white* at the *back* are more interesting than the *jocks* in *lime* at the *front*." There are three sets of contrasts. Each requires a slight punching. The first word is pointed slightly, and its "mate" is given a similar twist to reveal the connection and point up the contrast. Most actors have found this exercise the single most effective technique for clarifying classical speeches. Practice speaking antithetically offstage to develop your sense of words in opposition.

7. Key words: Punch up even more in long passages.

    Audiences hear about 70 percent of what is spoken from the stage and fill in the rest. In classical drama, this percentage drops considerably because of the obscurity of the language. It is likely that you are being too restrained in kicking the most important images. Fight the tendency to play general emotion and meaning instead of finding each image anew. Serve up the images like great gifts.

8. Adjectives: Give them value and let them modify, qualify, and change nouns.

    If the writer has added a word before a noun, the word is probably intended to *change* that noun in some way. Let it. Resist the temptation to dive into the phrase and get through all the modifiers as quickly as possible. Take a long look at how each modifier acts on the noun in question. Many modifiers act *against* the noun or alter it almost past recognition. Honor the adjective for its power, and use it.

9.  Metaphors: Mentally set off in quotation marks, underline, or use capital letters.

    When you are not speaking literally but using metaphor, your delivery needs to help the listeners so that, for example, they don't think you're really talking about your dog when you mean the kingdom. Adding quotation marks, underlining, or using capital letters for the figures of speech can separate these thoughts from the more direct ones. If as you speak these words you imagine that you are setting them off with quotation marks, you will hold back slightly before and after the phrase and thrust it forward as you speak. If you imagine you're putting a line under it, you will stretch and sweep the phrase deliberately from beginning to end, finishing it off quite sharply. If you imagine you're using capital letters, your attack on the initial letter of each word will be bold, big, and precise, as though you were putting it up on a marquee. All three techniques grab attention. Each gives a different edge to the line.

10. Coining each word and phrase: Refuse to play summaries or generalizations.

    One of the biggest temptations is to speak famous words as if they have been written in granite and recited many times. To your character, however, they have *never* before been uttered. When you begin the most famous soliloquy, you have *no idea* how you will end it. Mint the words and evaluate them as you move through each thought. Think of yourself as the playwright. The more familiar the material, the more important it is that you do this. Always consider what your character might have said but chooses not to. Almost choose to. This technique can lead you to startling, original readings.

11. Alliteration: Try to overdo.

    A series of words with the same first letter or sound is worth punching. Your character delights in the capacity to do this. Relish, twist, and turn the sound instead of backing off from it. A series of matched sounds is just that—a series. Savor it.

12. Verbs: Punch up and relish.

    Alec Guiness has said that the verbs are the most important and most neglected part of any speech. Classical sentences are long. The trip from subject to predicate can seem interminable. By the time you reach the period, you may well have lost the drift. By thinking of the verb as a truly active word, breathing and full of energy, you can bring the whole sentence to life. Grab each verb, feel it, and free it.

13. Humor and irony: Unearth all kinds, isolate with same techniques used for metaphor, and add quickness to irony.

    Don't forget the jokes. These characters are wittier than you and I. They see sly smiles at every corner. The lines have not been written in granite, nor are you a somber statue simply reciting. Identify the kind of humor in the speech: humor shared with the audience, with other characters, with both; humor hidden from other characters; humor overtly mocking other characters; self-deprecating humor. What makes a script survive is its reverberation and nuance, the little digs, undercuts, and twists that further delight us on each hearing. The three techniques suggested for metaphors work equally well for irony because it too says one thing and implies another. Explore each of the possibilities above, and then learn to say the ironic phrase *faster*. When you first discover irony, you will be tempted to take forever with the figure of speech, just in case anyone missed it. Once you become adept at handling irony, you can use a light touch. These are little sparks and will not light if you smother them.

14. Audience relationship: Find the right balance between introspection and confiding in the audience.

    Classical theatre acknowledges audiences more overtly than fourth-wall theatre. Trust the audience completely; treat your listeners as you would the people who are always there for you, no matter what. When you are alone onstage, the speech will most of the time come to life if you turn to your listeners and share it with them. This will not always happen, but never deny them their participation. Try going deep into yourself at one extreme in the speech, then try thrusting the words out in a very public way. Then blend the two approaches, recognizing that even while you are confiding in a best friend, you sometimes turn inward and think to yourself. The audience is there to help you at every turn. In aside or soliloquy or other moments, look for chances to let the audience help you shape the play. When you turn inward, do so with the knowledge that the audience will come inward with you.

15. Sense of first time: Expect the opposite of what you get.

    Even if the play is a tragedy, the characters rarely expect it to turn out that way. Most people live in a state of hope. No matter what disaster has befallen, today may bring a solution to all of our problems. Forget that you have read the play; instead, work your way moment by moment through the character's life, just as you do your own. The tragic impact is far more powerful if the character reaches for hope yet one more time. This also frees you from a sense of self-importance. Speak each sentence from a point of innocence.

16. Interruptions: Speak as if audience heckling were possible at any moment.

   The original audiences were undoubtedly more rowdy than ours. Although few listeners today will heckle you, learn to play as if that were a possibility. Imagine that your thoughts are sound, that the audience believes in you as a person, but that they may take issue with any of the particular twists and turns of your observations. Really good friends do this. This technique will give you energy, a sense of immediacy, and the impetus to keep moving.

17. Exits: Speak as if audience departure were possible at any moment.

   In any moment of life, the person you are speaking with may end the "scene" just by leaving. In classical theatre, where every moment seems more vital, the possibility is even greater. Rehearse as if each line may indeed end the scene. See what happens. A dynamic is set up when you realize that you need to be vital and compelling enough to keep your partner from moving on to other pastures.

18. Bottoming out: Go for mumbled, naturalistic, scratch-and-itch delivery.

   The classic Marlon Brando delivery is not what is expected in style work, but it can reduce high-flying affectation to simple, direct, basic communication. Just speak the speech without conveying any sense of the world of the play and with a strong need to express the truth here and now. Take the speech "down"; find out what to throw away and what simply to let happen. The most electrifying performances are those with surprise, variety, and sudden unexpected contrast. Great actors know when to drop the grandstand play and get simple.

19. Going over the top: Go for old-fashioned oratorical delivery full of bombast and overplaying.

   If you can, get hold of recordings of actors of the past century (Julia Marlowe, E. H. Sothern, Ellen Terry, Otis Skinner, Edwin Booth, and others). Listen and learn. What was once thought brilliant may easily seem ludicrous to you now, but imagine yourself in an enormous opera house with an audience desiring the full romantic unleashing of dramatic passion. Let it rip. Feel the rush of going over the top, of giving the top balcony its money's worth. Discover those moments in which nothing less than full-out bravura, razzle-dazzle, and tour de force will do. This style of delivery is incredibly freeing; it can be very funny but a great rush, as well. Almost everyone who tries this finds isolated moments in which they realize that "diva delirium" is just what they need.

20. Speed-through: Listen to tape and determine whether you have earned each pause.

    Actors who work on the above techniques can be tempted to belabor their performances. There are so many elements demanding the actor's attention that the performer tends to go into slow motion. To avoid this problem, speak the part as rapidly as possible. In a speed-through, you may sacrifice projection, but keep the other elements in place. Although you may at first feel like an old-time movie, resist the urge to burlesque. Video can be crucial at this stage; you will naturally tend to think that you are moving as fast as you can, but once you view the video, you will marvel at all the dead air.

21. Music: Sing the play as though it were an original musical or opera.

    Most of the language of classical drama is more elevated than day-to-day speech. Some of it is *much* more elevated. The words, rhythms, images, and phrases come closer to song than speech at given moments. Polarize into that sphere. Imagine that the play is either opera or a modern "sing-through" musical. Let your pitch, volume, quality, and phrasing know no bounds where music is concerned. Afterwards, identify where this felt and sounded good and which operatic elements might enhance your performance. In ritualized drama, such as Greek tragedy, you may literally wish to chant, intone, or sing certain passages.

22. Changes. Use shifts in moods, meanings, tactics, and attack. One of the big traps in long speeches is to play "in general." Avoid this by naming each section of the speech so that it is clear how the character is different than she was just a moment earlier.

23. Layering: Add conditioning forces, imaging, private audience, grouping, rehearsed futures, suppression.

    These following elements relate to the Stanislavsky system but were developed by subsequent research in behavioral sciences. They can "layer" a performance to give it shape.

    • Conditioning forces: How hot or cold, familiar or unknown is the space? How light, safe, and comfortable? How late are you? What thoughts may be distracting you?
    • Imaging: To make each line bright, what pictures, scents, sounds, and touches should you be considering?
    • Private audience: Which people in your character's life haunt that person no matter what? Which are always present? Who

is this person's god, mentor, idol, deadly enemy? How are these the same as or different from your own?

- Grouping: What does the character think of the groups around him or her? Which groups does the person judge, and which does he or she join?
- Rehearsed futures: How does the character fantasize and plan the future? What are the person's fears and dreams about the future?
- Suppression: Which impulses does the character sublimate, feeling they are not appropriate to unleash?

24. Onomatopoeia: Try to overdo it.

Since archaic language and convoluted phraseology can limit a modern audience's enjoyment of the play, your job is to get these people past the barriers. Imagine that the show is written in a foreign tongue, and try to make each word and sound comprehensible. Shape and taste each image. Then, go back and try to do all of this as fast as you can. When you first learn the technique, you will leave large gaps between words as you recover from the effort of bringing forth one image and begin to form another. Push yourself to eliminate these gaps so that your speech is bright and seamless.

25. Apprehension: Give the audience an understanding beyond simple comprehension by adding rhythm, sound, and texture.

The most abstract of all these steps is recognizing that much of what is going on will not be clear to the audience on a direct, cognitive level. Get them to feel and sense the language as you do. Try to get them to experience what you are living on an apprehending level beyond simple cognition. Brilliant writers put together speeches that depend much less on a conscious recitation of facts than on an almost magical combination of rhythm, music, and sound. Let the magic work through you.

26. Contemporary paraphrase: Adapt entire scene to modern lingo.

One of the best ways to bridge the language gap is to make certain that the subtitles in your own head are complete and accurate. If you know every word in your own terms, your chances for making those words clear to your audience are greater. The most effective exercise is to take the text and "translate" it yourself. Present your scene or monologue in entirely modern language. Update the situation, and use as much slang or jargon as you wish. Paraphrase word by word and phrase by phrase; don't just go for the general gist of the line. Go through the script once for what comes easily. Note places you have just skimmed and haven't a clue what you are saying. These are the passages that really need work.

Here is an example from *Richard III*,I,ii. Richard has murdered Anne's husband and has the audacity to show up and try to stop his burial.

> A: Avaunt thou dreadful minister of hell!
>    Thou hadst but power over his mortal body,
>    His soul thou canst not have; therefore, begone.
> R: Sweet saint, for charity, be not so curst.

Now note this paraphrase of the passage:

> A: Go away, you disgusting monster!
>    You killed him.
>    You can't do him any more harm. So just leave.
> R: Sweetheart, give me a break and lighten up.

Also, resist the temptation to lampoon the script. After a few inevitable collapses of laughter, move past the absurdity and work toward simple word-by-word clarity. Try the exercise two ways. First, perform the entire scene or act in paraphrase and then go back and run the lines as written. Next time, alternate paraphrasing individual lines and speeches with speaking the originals. Say the paraphrase until you are comfortable and then go back and speak the original, coining the words.

27. Rhymes: Say them with extra pride and relish in your own cleverness.

    When your character completes a couplet, instead of backing off from the artificiality of rhyming, enjoy it. Cap the endings. When you say brilliant things in conversation, don't you savor them? So does your character. If it is a significant source of pride to alliterate, it is an incredible rush to rhyme! Instead of feeling put off, the audience will begin to share your appreciation and almost feel they are writing the couplet with you.

28. Monosyllabic lines: Give them air; never rush them.

    A line that consists of words of only one syllable requires a deliberate, measured delivery, like a drumbeat. No matter how light and mercurial your delivery has been, this kind of line is a signal to measure each word and allow it to breathe. This style of delivery can offer an electrifying contrast to polysyllabic complexity. Do not try to make the line sound like the more baroque speeches.

29. Ambiguities and contradictions: Look for them and play them.

    If your character analysis does not produce a tidy package, be delighted and intrigued. Find each moment in which your character is headed in one direction but veers toward another. The very qualities that are most frustrating are often ultimately the most compelling. Each of us is a series of contradictions, and we all have facets no one can figure out. Big, brilliant characters will also have complex edges, so don't try to get them to fit perfectly into your notebook.

30. Truth + poetry + character = good classical acting: Keep all three balls in the air.

Keep each of these three at your fingertips. Rehearse them in alternate patterns. Speak and move with total honesty. Then, shape the verse and the curtsies brilliantly. Finally, work on the details of this particular human being down to the slightest mannerism. Honor each of these three elements at various rehearsals, recognizing that if you do, they will all eventually honor each other in your performance.

---

The preceding approaches are summarized here for you to use as a checklist. Take a scene or monologue and determine the amount of time you have before you are to present the material in class or in performance. If you have a month, work with one classical step each day between now and then. If you have two weeks, work with two each day. Chances are that the ones you feel most resistant to at first glance will be those in which you will experience breakthroughs.

1. Scansion: Honor the metre.
2. Stanislavsky-based character analysis: Unearth circumstances and motives.
3. Recording while reading from the script, check memorization periodically.
4. Reference room research: Unearth new clues to meaning (*OED,* lexicons; translations/editions; production histories, other meanings and interpretations).
5. Regular taping and playback: Gain permission to do more.
6. Antitheses: Try to overdo.
7. Key words: Punch up even more in long passages.
8. Adjectives: Give them value and let them modify, qualify, and change nouns.
9. Metaphors: Mentally set off in quotation marks, underline, or use capital letters.
10. Coining each word and phrase: Refuse to play summaries or generalizations.
11. Alliteration: Try to overdo.
12. Verbs: Punch up and relish.
13. Humor and irony: Unearth all kinds, isolate with same techniques used for metaphor, add quickness to irony.
14. Audience relationship: Find the right balance between introspection and confiding in the audience. Soliloquys—be introspective, then with audience as confidant, trust audience completely. Scenes—explore audience/chorus relationship, asides, performer awareness.

15. Sense of first time: Expect the opposite of what you get.
16. Interruptions: Speak as if audience heckling were possible at any moment.
17. Exits: Speak as if departure were possible at any moment.
18. Bottoming out: Go for mumbled, naturalistic, scratch-and-itch delivery.
19. Going over the top: Go for old-fashioned oratorical delivery, full of bombast and overplaying.
20. Speed-through: Listen to tape and determine whether you have earned each pause.
21. Music: Sing the play as though it were an original musical or opera.
22. Changes: Find character shifts, avoid generalizations.
23. Layering: Add conditioning forces, imaging, private audience, grouping, rehearsed futures, suppression.
24. Onomatopoeia: Try to overdo it.
25. Apprehension: Give the audience an understanding beyond simple comprehension by adding rhythm, sound, and texture.
26. Contemporary paraphrase: Adapt entire scene to modern lingo.
27. Rhymes: Say them with extra pride and relish in your own cleverness.
28. Monosyllabic lines: Give them air; never rush them.
29. Ambiguities and contradictions: Look for them and play them.
30. Truth + poetry + character = good classical acting: Keep all three balls in the air.

# GENRE STYLE
## The Isms

In a store, the term *generic* refers to a low-cost, non-name-brand product. In general usage, *generic* means "average" or "typical." Period and genre are the two most common ways to approach a play. In drama, the term *genre* refers to type, class, form, movement, or category. The individual play within the genre may or may not be "ordinary."

In our century, realism is the dominant genre. The term *realism* did not emerge until the 1850s. In a way, however, the dramas of all periods are "realistic," because the performances onstage reflect the way each period sees itself—not necessarily the way its people really look or live, but their collective self-concept. Every period has its own vision of realism. That vision can look quite "unreal" from the perspective of time.

The predominant genres, or isms, emerged during the nineteenth and twentieth centuries in approximately this order:

Romanticism, early 1800s
Realism, 1850s
Naturalism, 1873
Impressionism, 1874
Symbolism, 1890–1920
Expressionism, 1910 (or 1901)
Futurism, 1910–1930
Dadaism, 1916
Constructivism, 1921
Surrealism, 1924
Didacticism, 1927
Absurdism, late 1940s

Jessica Tandy (Mary) and William Hutt (James) in *A Long Day's Journey into Night,* The Stratford Festival

Feminism, late 1960s
Postmodernism, 1980s

Although most isms are no longer produced in their pure form, elements of them continue to influence both playwrights and productions. Why should an actor know this? Because the terms are batted (and battered) around by directors, designers, and critics attempting to explain what a show is striving to accomplish. Often, a script is not written within a particular genre, but the production team decides to present it in that form. Sometimes this approach illuminates the text. Other times it destroys it. Some isms began in art, music, literature, politics, or philosophy. Because the terms are not understood the same way by everyone in these disciplines, confusion can easily arise when these terms pop up. You need to know enough to communicate well with others involved in a show, and you need to know enough to protect yourself within the show. Many isms are not actor concepts at all, but it is the actor who is expected to function within the framework of the genre.

Most isms begin with a manifesto, or public declaration of principles, brought forth by someone who does not like the status quo and feels it is time for a change. Each manifesto is summarized here and is followed by the movement's historical background, sight and sound characteristics, and distinctive images to help you grasp the genre. Where relevant, skills required of the performer and representative play titles are listed.

## ROMANTICISM

**A rejection of classical order in favor of imagination and emotion.**

*Manifesto.*    Feelings are more important than thoughts. Anything that is natural is good. A true hero is often forced to stand outside society in order to live life as passionately and fully as it should be lived. Beyond mere earthly life lies a higher truth that is found through art and feeling. True happiness can be found only in the spiritual realm. The sublime in nature and art must be worshiped. Everything exotic and picturesque has value. Even something ugly and grotesque has worth, if it elicits a powerful response. We long for the past.

Our heroine or hero often must die by the final curtain as a result of following her or his heart in an uncomprehending world too full of reason, machines, and rules, a world that has become spoiled by moving too far away from its natural state. Still, to die and leave the physical world is not too great a price to pay for being true to oneself.

*Background.*    By the late 1700s, the Neoclassical movement (see Chapter 7) is losing ground. Strictly ordered works depicting the ideal, rather than the natural, are declining in appeal. A group of German writers dominated by Goethe, Schiller, and Klinger develop a school of writing called Sturm und Drang (Storm and Stress), which espouses the rights of the individual, the glory of nature, and the power of emotion. The English poets Coleridge, Wordsworth, and Forrest catch the drift. A form of drama evolves that is still, in some ways, with us today.

### Images

Terror of the self
Music of Chopin, Liszt, Wagner, Tchaikovsky
Love through death
Byron's poetic drama *Sardanapalus*
Poetry of Shelley and Blake
Brighton Pavilion
Honor and duty above all practical consideration
Society as an evil establishment trying to crush passion
Delacroix's operatic paintings
Turner's landscapes
Rich, lush, heavy, sensuous, operatic

*Sight.* Large casts and spectacle are common. Settings are often long ago and/or far away. Bold and fluid movements, grand, graceful, majestic maneuvers, and great sweeping curves predominate. While Romanticism is influential in bringing about historical accuracy in costuming, the look is likely to be flamboyant: Flowing garments, thick capes, scarves, billowing fabric. The vision of nature focuses on glorious sunrises and tornadoes, not the humdrum or everyday. A romantic hero need not be beautiful but should somehow be extraordinary. Almost every Barbra Streisand film has strong elements of romanticism.

*Sound.* The plays are in verse or poetic prose on a grand level. Great variety of expressiveness and a large vocal range are desired. Delivery should be defiant and sentimental without becoming strident and cloying.

*Skills.* Romantic acting is tour de force bravura playing, demanding great bravado and expressiveness, a willingness to hit operatic heights and a soulful and expansive nature. Training in classical ballet and great beauty of tone help. Can you suffer deeply and defy society? Of course you can. Romantic drama is basically full-blown melodrama and is not for actors who take a half-hearted approach or who giggle easily.

### Works

| Dumas, Alexandre | *Camille* |
| Goethe, Johann Wolfgang von | *Faust* |

| Hugo, Victor | *Hernani* |
| | *The Hunchback of* |
| | *Notre Dame* |
| | *Les Misérables* |
| Rostand, Edmond | *Cyrano de Bergerac* |
| Shelley, Mary | *Frankenstein* |
| Shelley, Percy | *Prometheus Un-* |
| | *bound* |

## REALISM

Art based on nature and real life, without idealization or distortion.

*Manifesto.* It is time to reject the impractical and visionary. Theatre should show how everyday people react to their environments. Characters should be multidimensional, internally motivated, and believably portrayed. Human psychology and the five senses should be employed to explore relationships onstage. Only drama that is directly relevant to the *life* of the viewer has genuine *meaning* to the viewer. We have had enough plays about kings and lords, rebels and visionaries. What about grocers? Social and domestic problems are experienced by us all and need to be illuminated on the stage.

*Background.* The French Revolution, industrialization, and Darwin's and Comte's theories of evolution sequentially lead to an interest in bringing social themes and scientific inquiry to theatre. By the mid 1800s, the extravagant characters and callow insights of melodrama are declining in popularity. Freud's work on the clinical analysis of personalities, Ibsen's scripts of carefully crafted social import, and Stanislavsky's acting system all reflect an interest in seeing life portrayed onstage as it is lived offstage. The term achieves full validation when the Moscow Art Theatre names its Fourth Studio "The Realistic Theatre." For the first time in history, plays do not focus on people who are absolutely exceptional by title, power, beauty, intellect, or eccentricity of personality. For the first time, characters onstage could be the people next door.

*Images*

Selected truth
The well-made play
Relevance
Democratic Individualism
Writing about what you know

Life as model
Explore, then reduce
Photojournalism
Paintings of Philip Pearlstein
Novels of Steinbeck and Faulkner
Poetry of Sandburg and Frost
U.S. folk music

*Sight.*   All scenic elements are as accurate as possible, with some editing of irrelevant details and some partial or skeletal sets. Settings look like modifications of actual locales. An attempt is made to create the feel of a real living space, and the use of props is considerable. Largely through the influence of Émile Zola, the box set develops, although sometimes several settings are represented with a cinematic overlapping of action. Costumes and properties are true to both historical period and character personality. Movement is true to life and therefore can be hesitant, unobtrusive, and occasionally random. Movement strives to appear motivated and honest.

*Sound.*   The use of pauses, nonverbal responses, incomplete thoughts, informal sentence structure—all the characteristics of speech on the street or in the home—characterizes realistic drama. Scripts are prose and barely heightened from normal conversation. Declamatory artifice in delivery is completely rejected, but clarity is maintained.

*Skills.*   Capacity for public solitude and strong sense of natural interaction with other actors, props, and setting. Strong believability. Ability to tap internal resources and find truth. Working on character from motivations. Eye for contemporary detail, shading, and nuance. No ham actors allowed. Minimal scenery chewing allowed.

*Works.*   Earliest and most influential plays and playwrights:

| | |
|---|---|
| Chekhov, Anton | *The Three Sisters* |
| | *The Cherry Orchard* |
| | *Uncle Vanya* |
| | *The Seagull* |
| Ibsen, Henrik | *A Doll's House* |
| | *Hedda Gabler* |
| | *The Wild Duck* |

Most of the works of the two most revered twentieth-century playwrights, Arthur Miller and Tennessee Williams, are realism. Elements of realism are also strongly present in the contemporary works of Wendy Wasserstein, Michael Weller, Lanford Wilson, Marsha Norman, Tina Howe, A. J. Gurney, Aaron Sorkin, Beth Henley, and August Wilson.

## NATURALISM

**Life with details, including the ugly, the distracting, and the irrelevant.**

*Manifesto.*　Realism only *begins* to oppose artificial theatricality and does not go far enough! It chooses which elements of life it wishes to present. What is needed in the theatre is stark reality, with no compromise. The keys to all truths are scientific method and careful scrutiny. Individuals cannot be held responsible for what they do, because heredity and environment overwhelm them. Plays should be more human and less social in orientation. No characters are specifically sympathetic; they just *are.* Plays do not need to progress rapidly, be briskly paced, or have clear climaxes. Endings can be pessimistic, ironic, cynical, and even disappointing, like life. Actors should *live* the life of their characters onstage rather than *play* them.

*Background.*　All the forces influencing realism, with the addition of a rising interest in socialism and the average working man, combine to form naturalism. Emile Zola coins the phrase "slice of life" (Can we assume that realism was merely a bite or sip of life?) and writes *Thérèse Raquin,* the first consciously conceived naturalistic drama. His introduction for that play is the true complete manifesto of the movement. The movement catches on in France (André Antoine and the Théâtre-Libre), Germany (Otto Brahm and Freie Bühne), and Russia (Stanislavsky and the Moscow Art Theatre). Jack Thomas Grein's Independent Theatre and George Bernard Shaw attempt to establish the movement in England, but the British don't care for it. Eventually, filmmakers adopt the attention to detail necessary for naturalism, but the movement's impact remains in the theatre today. Naturalism is the alley behind realism's street.

*Images*

Warts and all
Don't look away
Man as victim
Effects of environment
David Belasco's sets
Scientific scrutiny
Théâtre-Libre
Degas's last works
Documentary
Tight closeup
White noise
The uncensored mind
Who needs an ending?
Eavesdropping

*Sight and Sound.* Set detail may be extensive—water runs, stoves cook, and (in a famous Antoine production) real flies buzz around real beef hanging in a meat market scene. A highly contained box set is frequently employed. Real clothes are better choices than costumes, which require minutely accurate detail. No gels and no makeup are preferred. The environment is a major character and has more influence than any human in the play. Movement needs to seem spontaneous. The fourth wall is very much in place, and the audience is never acknowledged. Actors are less likely to cheat or use open turns and are more likely to turn their backs to the house and generally drop theatrical conventions in favor of accuracy. All movement comes from inner experience.

One of the most vivid touches of naturalism in television history was the sound of Archie Bunker flushing the toilet on "All in the Family." This was not a naturalistic show, but that was a naturalistic moment. When we hear a flush on network television, we think about all the offstage noise and life sounds usually edited in performance. When "Roseanne" was first broadcast, audiences realized that it had been a long time since they had seen anything but tidy kitchens and svelte families on the tube.

Speech in naturalistic plays may be muffled or even mumbled if it is true to character. Language is basic, gritty prose, often lower class in syntax. Conversations do not necessarily go anywhere. Snatches of dialogue may be lost or drowned out by background noise or distractions.

*Skills.* Naturalistic acting demands great subtlety and a complete lack of artifice. The performer must have a willingness to dispense with charm, charisma, and the need to command an audience. A simplicity that belies technique is essential. Naturalistic acting is much more difficult for most actors than it first seems, because they so accustomed to editing themselves for performance. A complete concentration and a highly developed ability to play *in* the moment and to go *with* the moment are needed, as are deeply rooted psychological comprehension of character, strong empathy and ability to play complexity of personality, sense of ensemble, and the willingness to "let it all hang out." A director I once worked with referred to a role as "scratch and itch and belch and fart" part. He meant that it was a naturalistic role. How does Ibsen, the father of realism, feel about this?

> *Zola descends into the cess-pool to take a bath, I to cleanse it.*
>
> —HENRIK IBSEN

*Works*

| | |
|---|---|
| Gorky, Maxim | *The Lower Depths* |
| Hauptmann, Gerhart | *The Weavers* |
| Steinbeck, John | *Of Mice and Men, Grapes of Wrath* |
| Strindberg, August | *Miss Julie* |
| Zola, Émile | *Thérèse Raquin* |

## IMPRESSIONISM

A higher world, artificially created and emotionally sublimated.

*Manifesto.*   Theatre should attempt to capture the moment through feeling, mood, and atmosphere. We accept some aspects of realism but reject its need for identifiable motives and dramatic plot elements. There is no need for a clear-cut climax, beginning, or end. Characters may be generally bewildered and indecisive, because that is what we all are. Human desires are half formed and our impulses rarely followed through. Violence and rage often smolder and remain unreleased. Art should reflect our pervasive passive and/or helpless state.

*Background.*   The movement evolves from a famous painting, *Impression: Sunrise* by Claude Monet and develops first into a school of painting, beginning in Paris in the mid 1870s. Next, the movement develops in music. Impressionism's influence remains strongest in the scenic elements of a production. In performance, impressionism is a reaction against the nearly strident intensity of romanticism. It lingers in theatre in the form of mood pieces without recognizable structure.

### Images

> Fleeting light
> Rough brush strokes
> Spontaneity
> Repetition of hue
> Small planes of color
> Quick rendering
> Filtered boulevard, distanced landscape
> Vantage point
> Juxtaposition
> Paintings of Pissarro, Cailleboote, Cassatt, Morisot, Renoir, Bazille, Sisley
> Cafe Guerbois
> Scrim

*Sight.*   The foreground disappears into the background. Movement tends to be tentative, half-formed, and incomplete and is often juxtaposed with tableaux. The emphasis lies completely in the creation of mood.

*Sound.*   Overlapping dialogue, isolated fragments of speech, and heavy use of background sounds may be employed and orchestrated. In the purest form, voices blend with each other and with other sounds to become at times indistinguishable.

*Skills.* Impressionistic drama demands that the actor be able to sustain a mood effectively and perform compellingly without a recognizable through-line or sense of character development and to blend with the environment, both physically and vocally, when required to do so. Because impressionistic works often contain elements of realism and expressionism, the actors may be asked to blend elements of all three. This ism is more likely to involve the design team than the actors.

### Works

| | |
|---|---|
| Maeterlinck, Maurice | *Pelléas and Mélisande* |
| Strindberg, August | *The Father* |
| Zola, Émile | *Nana* |

## SYMBOLISM

**Poetic, dreamlike theatre seeking the profound or mysterious in life.**

*Manifesto.* Mood and atmosphere are far more important than plot or action. Let us drop the simpleminded cause-and-effect mentality. There is no need for characters to have personalities of their own, because they are symbols of the poet's inner life. Ambiguity is the key. What appears onstage is not necessarily a *clear* symbol the audience will recognize; rather, it is symbolic of the author's *consciousness*. Legend, myth, and spirituality come together to produce evocative theatre. Suggestion is far more powerful than explicit representation. Theatre should seek the profound and the unfathomable experience. The life shown in realistic theatre should be either changed or transcended. Let us turn our backs on objective reality and move strongly into the subjective and intuitive. The autonomy of art frees it from any obligation to deal with social problems in political terms. Art needs to move beyond truth.

> *Lying, telling beautiful, untrue things is the proper aim of Art so that life will imitate art.*
>
> —OSCAR WILDE

*Background.* Maurice Maeterlinck and Edward Gordon Craig begin the movement in the 1890s, and it remains popular until the 1920s. Symbolism is a reaction against the growing popularity of realism. Maeterlinck is heavily influenced by Stéphane Mallarmé and Paul Verlaine. Adolphe Appia and Max Reinhardt also dabble in this movement, through lighting and set design respectively. The paintings of Gauguin, Rousseau, Toulouse-Lautrec, and De Chirico reflect the basic values. Wagner tries to fuse all the elements—music, dialogue, color, light, shape, and texture—together in performance. Impressionistic symbolism and expressionistic symbolism combine these three movements. Film, because of the control it affords, embraces elements of this movement after it falls away from the theatre. The use of a single, monumental, symbolic (though not necessarily comprehensible) set decoration remains common today.

### Images

Irrational self
Bizarre juxtapositions
Projected light
Mood music
Filters
Mixed analogies
Your wildest dreams
Aurélian-Marie Lugné-Poe
Edgar Allan Poe
Alfred Jarry
Claude Debussy
Decadence glorified
Federico Fellini
Omnipresence

*Sight.*   Movement may be enigmatic and often accompanies music. Static poses may alternate with ritualized, frenzied, whirling moves. The space is full of shadows and mists, possibly mirrors, with an undefined, dreamlike quality. Costumes draw on a range of tribal and cultural influences and are often draped and gauzelike. Much modern dance, specifically in the Isadora Duncan tradition, relates strongly to symbolism.

*Sound.*   Strong emphasis on the voice and its music. Present-day New Age music suits a symbolist production. Language may be full of mysterious references. Statements may consist only of simple nouns with adjectives rather than complete sentences. Lines tend to be rhythmic, possibly even poetic, with an electrifyingly hypnotic use of cadence and intensity to build emotion.

*Skills.*   Actors must function on a high level of abstraction to play situations associated more with dreams than with waking experience. They must be able to play larger than life, personify a quality or trait, and sometimes function like a puppet. Symbolist theatre demands a willingness to drop clarity, practicality, and definition in favor of distortion and exaggerating for effect.

### Works

Andreyev, Leonid        *He Who Gets Slapped*

| | |
|---|---|
| Jarry, Alfred | *Ubu Roi* |
| Maeterlinck, Maurice | *The Intruder* |
| | *The Blind* |
| | *The Blue Bird* |
| | *Pelléas and Mélisande* |
| O'Casey, Sean | *Within the Gates* |
| O'Neill, Eugene | *The Emperor Jones* |
| | *The Hairy Ape* |
| Strindberg, August | *The Dream Play* |
| | *The Ghost Sonata* |
| Wedekind, Frank | *Spring's Awakening* |
| Wilde, Oscar | *Salomé* |
| Yeats, William Butler | early plays |

## EXPRESSIONISM

**Life seen through a single set of subjective emotions.**

*Manifesto.* Most other isms are too passive and specialized. We need theatre that is forceful, urgent, and emotionally charged. Theatre needs to capture the inner spiritual struggle each of us goes through to develop into the New Person of the future. Creating a character is much less important than presenting a strong argument onstage. Nightmarish, anti-industrial, deliberate distortions of reality are perfectly acceptable ways to deliver a harsh truth. Real theatre is not literary drama, but instead an exploration of consciousness through living performance. Dreams are a major source of truth, and the portrayal of the dreamlike state may illuminate life so that the subjective can be objectified. The real heroes are hidden among the common workers, stifled by a dangerous, dehumanizing, and deadly system. The values of the older generation are useless. It is time for fresh subjectivity that mirrors inner psychological realities instead of outer physical appearances. It is time to get serious.

*Background.* Expressionism originates in the paintings of Auguste Herve, exhibited in 1901 under the title *Expressionismes* and eventually influences all of the arts. Although Herve intends his works to oppose those of the impressionists, the movement ultimately revolts against naturalism and romanticism as well. Vincent van Gogh and Edvard Munch are the best known expressionist painters, and George Kaiser is the leading dramatist working exclusively in the form, although the later visionary works of Strindberg and Ibsen make significant contributions to the genre. The theatre embraces expressionism most fully in the twenties. Vsevolod Meyerhold and his "biomechanics" theory of acting (involving gymnastics, ballet, and acrobatics) have some influence, as do Freud's ideas regarding the analysis of dreams. The idealism regarding change that characterizes the movement in its early days gives way after World War II to utter disillusionment, and expressionism eventually becomes more a mode of production than of playwrighting.

### Images

Author's message, author's message, author's message
Sharp contrast and intense distortion
Spirit, soul, mind
The sources of truth
Martyrdom
Moody, atmospheric lighting
Diagonal lines
Leaning walls
Colored light
Leopold Jessner
Nightmares
Later dances of Nijinsky, Cunningham, and Graham
Music of Igor Stravinsky

*Sight.* Sharp angles and harsh and startling lighting and color distinguish the look. Walls may slope, windows and doors may be deformed, dark shadows may be juxtaposed with shafts of bright light. Platforms, ramps, scaffolding, and unexpected elements (such as a trapeze) may enter the playing space. Geometric images dominate. Movement may involve stark groupings of actors and choreographed histrionic business. Actions may be fragmentary, disconnected, puppetlike, or robotlike. Some use of masks and Oriental stage technique may be employed. Costumes and props may be grotesquely exaggerated.

*Sound.* The explosive language of expressionism features a startling contrast between lyrical passages and staccato, almost amputated dialogue. The genre calls for the full range of sound, including nonhuman noises, shouting, chanting, and barking. Movement and dialogue may be repetitious and mechanical, with tempos shifting dramatically.

*Skills.* Expressionism demands volatile emotional playing representing an alienated state of abstraction; highly theatrical, sometimes flagrantly presentational playing representing the subconscious and the spiritual; and the capacity to remove a human quality (such as greed or lust) from your characterization or to become the quality incarnate.

*Works*

| | |
|---|---|
| Čapek, Josef and Karel | *The Insect Comedy* |
| Čapek, Karel | *R.U.R.* |
| Kaiser, Georg | *From Morn to Midnight* |
| Rice, Elmer | *The Adding Machine* |
| Shaw, Irwin | *Bury the Dead* |
| Strindberg, August | *The Road to Damascus* |

## FUTURISM

Actor as machine; totally integrated theatre.

*Manifesto.*   Reject the past, and glorify progress. Anticipate a great industrial future! Theatre needs to give formal expression to the energy and movement the new machinery has provided. We need strong, broad emotions. Technology must rescue theatre from its deadly museumlike atmosphere and literary, logical bias. Machines and wars can be a source of great beauty. In fact, war is the world's hygiene, cleaning out unfortunate vestiges of the past. Barriers between arts, actors, and audience need to be smashed.

*Background.*   Founded by Filippo Tommaso Marinetti, futurism is the forerunner of dadaism, although its purposes are quite different. Marinetti's *Manifesto of the Futurist Synthetic Theatre* is the document that most clearly defines the movement's purposes, including the effort by some Italians to wake up their country and propel it into the industrial age. The concepts later influence Italian fascists. The movement runs from about 1910 to 1930. Eventually, Ionesco employs some of the techniques, as does performance art today.

*Images*

War games
Ideas that kill
Kinetic sculptures
Utilitarian objects
Designs of Depero
Psychology of machines

Leather, chains, steel, cement
Mechanical ballets of Silvio Mix
Electric currents and colored gases
Scenography of Enrico Prampolini
Mad Max macho movies

*Sight.*   Futurist productions are multimedia, high-tech wonders with multiple focuses and simultaneous action. Costumes favor straight lines, metallic surfaces, and loose fit, basically turning the human silhouette into a mechanical one, although the face, arms, and legs are often left uncovered. The actor is totally integrated into setting. The setting may be controlled, or the event may occur as street theatre. The look is macho mechanical.

*Sound.*   Almost anything may be asked of the actor. Language tends to be blunt, simple, and direct. The sound is masculine and militaristic. Lines may involve ideological diatribes, manifestoes, shouting, and mechanical noises, mostly delivered in presentational fashion. The actor is the director's robot and may be asked to perform in a highly geometric, machine-like fashion, uttering just noises rather than lines. "Music" may be created out of sirens, machine guns, and other war sounds.

*Skills.*   The actor needs highly developed technical skills and great patience and must let go completely the desire to portray realistically. The ability to eliminate your own idiosyncratic, detailed behavior in favor of total integration into the surroundings and a strong masculine attack, along with the stamina to endure sustained violent, high-energy, repetitive sequences, are crucial.

### Works

| | |
|---|---|
| Balla, Giacomo | *Disconcerted States of Mind* |
| Canguillo | *Detonation* |
| Marinetti, Filippo Tommaso | *Feet* |
| Settimelli | *Sempronio's Lunch* |

## DADAISM

**Theatre dedicated to contradicting expectations.**

*Manifesto.*   Nothing is sacred! Theatre should take a nihilistic approach to life and a revolutionary attitude toward art. Anti-art is the way to think;

"creative" acts are worthless. Audiences should be infuriated, enraged, and moved beyond rationality to passion. All elements of the past need to be destroyed. All beliefs have no reason. The future smacks of death, so the moment is all that matters. Spontaneity is the closest anyone can come to creating; the more shocking and violent the better.

*Background.*  Inspired by the writings of Franz Kafka, the movement is conceived in Zurich by Tristan Tzara and spreads to France, led by Hugo Ball. Dadaism itself defies the keeping of records, so its progress is only randomly transcribed. The Dada Gallery is established in 1916, and the ideas remain prominent until 1922. More a means of creating a theatrical event than for writing scripts, dadaism does not produce a body of work. It tends to be favored at private entertainments, soirees, or Happenings.

*Images*

    The Sex Pistols
    Anti-art, Antireason, Antithought
    Kurt Schwitters
    Terrorism
    Fingernails scratching a screen door
    Eating garbage, worms, and excrement
    Your own personal worst gross-out
    Nonsense
    Car horn locked into honk
    Freewheeling, unconnected, nonverbals

*Sight and Sound.*  Dadaism is largely improvisational and spontaneous. Dialogue is incongruous, full of nonsequiturs, shouting, singing, berating, gibberish, and obscenities. Space tends to be vast, bare, unlocalized, and abstract, but it may be littered with irrelevant items. Laughing at the audience is a common mode of attack.

*Skills.*  Dadaism demands a willingness to humiliate yourself and others aggressively; an imaginative sense of what will strike others as obscene and sacrilegious; audacity; and a confrontational, defiant nature.

*Works.*  The concepts that underlie dadaism discourage scripting. Some elements of the movement appear in these works: Peter Weiss's *Marat/Sade,* Tom Stoppard's *Travesties,* Sam Shepard's *Unseen Hand,* e. e. cummings's *Him,* and Gertrude Stein's *Four Saints in Three Acts.*

## CONSTRUCTIVISM

Build a story; don't tell it.

*Manifesto.*   Sentimentality and individual feeling have no place in the theatre. Theatre has been too interested in illusion, and it is now time to strip all that away. The unsightly clutter of the naturalistic stage needs to be replaced. An architectural vision will wipe out a pictorial. It is time for acting to turn back outward, replacing psychological and emotional nuance with gymnastic and acrobatic precision. A play is just a vehicle for examination and revelation.

Constructivism precedes today's deconstructivist theatre, in which a play is taken apart with no regard to the playwright's intentions, to reveal a theme of current interest. The script may then be reconstructed in a new configuration.

*Background.*   A joint project between sculptor Lyubov Popova and director Vsevolod Meyerhold in 1921–1922 produces the idea for a "machine for acting." Meyerhold develops an accompanying approach to acting, called *bioenergetics*. Frederick Winslow Taylor's research into efficiency finds a theatrical corollary. The movement reacts against the Moscow Art Theatre in its attempt to go as far away from detailed, lengthy, painstaking internal work as possible. Meyerhold takes an engineer's approach to the stage, demanding purely functional use of space. Although the acting approaches do not remain popular, the use of a "bare bones" skeletal set is still common. Deconstructivism now focuses not on mechanical elements of production, but rather on pulling apart the mechanics of the text.

### Images

Popova's sculpture and stage designs
Costumes by Goncharova
Vsevolod Meyerhold
Message above text
Biomechanics in action
Social masks in relationships
Script as mere libretto
El Lissitzky, Naum Gabo, Kazimir Malevich
Vladimir Tatlin's *Model for Monument to the Third International*

*Sight and Sound.*   A production may involve circus techniques, acrobatics, highly physical performances, and machinelike sets that strip away traditional decor and illusion. The entire support structure is clearly in view, and all platforms are unfaced and unadorned. A curtain is never used, and the entire set is completely in view from the time the audience arrives until it leaves. Sets of ramps, wheels, ropes, pulleys, elevators, and conveyor belts may all be employed. Actors may be asked to use exaggerated, rhythmic, repetitive movements. Garments may be geometric creations or work uniforms. Sound is dominated and determined by movement. The sounds of wheels, pulleys, conveyor belts, or hammers may all be imitated by the actor.

*Skills.*   Constructivism calls on the actor's circus techniques and broad, farcical caricature ability; skills in gymnastics, acrobatics, and mime; dance training; an intensely controlled, precise, athletic body; and the capacity to step out, examine, and then dive back in.

*Works.*   Because constructivism is a production concept only, there are no scripts. The most famous early production was Meyerhold's mounting of Fernand Crommelynck's *The Magnificent Cuckold*. Any current deconstructivist production will be controversial, because it will not be the same play many arrive expecting to see. A highlight of the recent One Minute Play Festival was a response to a famous director's deconstructionist production of Shakespeare's *Twelfth Night*. The one act play consists entirely of Shakespeare walking onstage wearing a pair of six-shooters and asking the audience politely, "Can anyone tell me where I can find (director's name)?" and then pulling out both guns and walking off.

## SURREALISM

Spontaneous creation without interference from reason.

*Manifesto.*   Insanity is often true sanity. Freed from the need for reason, morals, or aesthetics, the artist's mind is finally capable of creation. The subconscious mind is the source of the most significant perceptions. Once your logic and ego are neutralized, truth has a better chance to surface. Those elements which appear at first glance to be opposites can in hypnotic or dreamlike states actually be reconciled into a new vision. Great theatre has plasticity (freedom to manipulate appearances) and musicality (freedom to allow the subjective mind to explore). Under these circumstances, the spirit can be liberated from the flesh, and the unreal can become real. True theatre has the power to disturb viewers to the depths of their being.

*Background.*   Antonin Artaud, working in the 1930s, is the major figure associated with this movement, but its origins go much farther back. Alfred Jarry's 1896 production of *Ubu Roi* strongly influences the surrealists, as does Freudian psychology. The term is first coined by the French poet Guillaume Apollinaire in 1917. The manifesto is written in 1924 by Andre Bréton, who claims that surrealism rises out of the ashes of dadaism.

Under Artaud, the movement evolves from one that places emphasis on words to one that invents a new language to express psychic experience. He breaks away from others and creates a "Theatre of Cruelty," in which actor and audience are asked to suffer a painful psychic transformation in order to achieve purification. His work influences Jean Genet, Albert Camus, Jerzy Grotowski, and subsequent tribal, communal theatre experiments.

### Images

Jean Cocteau's blends of ballet and drama
Pablo Picasso
Salvador Dalí
music of Pierre Boulez
Grotesque as path to liberation
Spontaneous gesture as key to true inner self
Guillaume Apollinaire
André Breton
Léonide Massine
Psychic automatism
Plasticity
"Twin Peaks"

*Sight.*   A dream world and a realistic world are often both explored for contrast. A high level of distortion, optical illusion, objects in sizes, and unexpected juxtapositions are all possible. Scenes occur in unusual locations, and two seemingly unrelated scenes may be played back to back. A strong sense of lyrical ritual emerges.

*Sound.*   Dialogue favors poetic imagery, but verse is free, without specific meter. Characters do not tend to answer each other directly; one person's shared internal monologue may motivate but not otherwise connect with another's. Language is used, not for communication, but for exploration, interweaving, and ritual. Musical tones may dominate. Artaud develops an entire nonverbal vocabulary. Sound attempts to free itself from the traditional slavery of the written word into full exploration of the nonverbal.

*Skills.*   The capacity to play archetypes and to blend sexual characteristics is helpful. Characters are often androgynous or hermaphroditic. A full range of sounds beyond language may be tapped. A priestlike total commitment to the process is required.

### Works

| Apollinaire, Guil-laume | *The Breasts of Tiresias* |

| Artaud, Antonin | *Jet of Blood* |
| | *The Philosopher's Son* |
| | *The Burnt Belly* |
| Cocteau, Jean | *Antigone* |
| | *Orpheus* |
| | *Parade* |
| | *The Ox on the Roof* |
| García Lorca, Fed-erico | *The Butterfly's Spell* |
| | *Blood Wedding* |
| Jarry, Alfred | *Ubu Roi* |
| Vitrac, Roger | *The Mysteries of Love* |
| | *Victor* |

## DIDACTICISM

**Narrative theatre for the intellect rather than the emotions (also called Epic or Brechtian Theatre).**

*Manifesto.*   Theatre should make you think and act. Actors should present characters instead of inhabiting them. Audiences should always remain aware that they are watching a performance and never lose themselves in the lives of the characters. Essentially, theatrical illusion is to be destroyed; the action must be frequently interrupted so the audience can remain emotionally disengaged and able to view the work intelligently. Critical watching discourages passivity; audiences should feel they have the power to change a society that is not working. This disengagement is known as *alienation;* specifically, the play's *subject matter* is what is alienated (the term does not mean to be "offended" or "angry.") The original German word is *Verfremdung,* which is to see things in a new light, to step back and look again at what has become familiar.

Drama should deal with human beings caught in the midst of social or political conflict. The best theatre spreads social ideology. Naturalism is to be rejected because it fails to portray man within the general landscape of the whole society. Other forms of theatre encourage audiences to embrace idealistic attitudes that have no relevance to real life. The stage is meant to narrate (not embody), to demand decisions (not feelings), to communicate knowledge (not experience), to present arguments (not suggestions) and to appeal to our reason (not instincts). *Gestus* is the key word for the concept. It involves the revelation of a relationship by deed, word, or look—the way all connections between people can be suddenly illuminated by some movement of the body, tongue, or eye. This is achieved through productions that are epic in scope, with a loose narrative form. Numerous separate episodes are sometimes presented in the past tense.

*Background.* Erwin Piscator conceives of the idea of a "proletarian drama," which Bertolt Brecht develops and extends. Brecht, who becomes the movement's main theorist and dramatist, is strongly influenced by the expressionists but works in a far more cynical mode. He experiments briefly with Dadaism and the ideas of Karl Marx. He develops a dramatic economy, simplicity of language, mature vision, and depth of expression seldom seen on the stage before this time. Eventually he refines his work through his own company, the Berliner Ensemble. His arbitrary ideas modify with time. Brecht's later writings reject the rigidity of his earlier statements. Delight becomes a major concern, but he defines delight as the pleasure that comes from discovering new truths about oneself and the world, which he calls the perfect reconciliation between teaching and pleasing. His theories are subjected to many conflicting interpretations but continually stimulate directors throughout the world.

### Images

Being forced to make a decision
Clarity, strength, and reserve; nothing wasted
Social significance above all
Political focus
Complete control
Moving within and outside the mask
Cartoons of George Grosz
Edvard Munch's *The Scream*
*Gestus*
Helen Viegel, Kurt Weill, Lotte Lenya

*Sight.* Didactic theatre is best presented in a proscenium space with a blank screen on which images can be projected. In keeping with the central idea of *Verfremdung,* actors may carry placards to describe scenes and remove suspense, and auditorium lights may be left on. Conspicuously theatrical props (such as a paper moon) may indicate time. The scenery is likely to be constructivist—simple stairs, scaffolding, revolving stages. The same devices originally intended to remind observers of the theatrical work are common stage conventions in our era. Because present-day audiences tend to disregard the naked mechanics of a show, these traditional choices may be replaced by any constant reminder (cameras, amplification, multiple screenings) that the event is a theatrical one and not real life. The movement runs the spectrum from realistic to highly stylized. Changes in time and place are frequent and abrupt.

*Sound.* The language in didactic theatre is clear, distinct, strong, and often harsh. Dialogue is mixed with narration and singing interludes, which have a vaudeville-like feeling. Music is used to neutralize emotions instead of intensifying them, the opposite of its usual function in theatre. Dialogue may be poetic in a blunt, colloquial way, full of both malice and wit. Strident prologues and epilogues are common. Audiences are frequently addressed directly, and a wide range of dialects may be employed.

*Skills.* Actors may be called on to use their capacity to step in and out of character, to comment and "demonstrate" character with some flexibility, and to make an idea crystal clear rather than enforcing emotional involvement. Training in mime, clowning, and oriental acting techniques is helpful. Brecht recommends that actors develop the ability to think of their characters in the third person and to "quote" the behavior of the character, with the same immediacy as someone who has experienced an accident and now feels compelled to recreate the event for listeners. The distancing, therefore, is by no means to be equated with the dropping of commitment.

*Works*

| | |
|---|---|
| Brecht, Bertolt | *Mother Courage and Her Children* |
| | *The Good Woman of Setzuan* |
| | *The Threepenny Opera* |
| | *The Caucasian Chalk Circle* |
| | *Galileo* |
| | *The Resistible Rise of Arturo Ui* |
| Kipphardt, Heinar | *In the Case of J. Robert Oppenheimer* |
| Tabari, George | *Brecht on Brecht* |
| Weiss, Peter | *Marat/Sade* |

## ABSURDISM

An irrational world where truth is unknowable and life is nonsensical.

*Manifesto.* Understanding is impossible. Sudden changes of mood and motive are what life is about. All laws of probability and physics are suspended. Sartre's statement is probably the most optimistic statement associated with the movement. Man's *only* freedom is the exercise of his conscious mind. He is in a state of moral paralysis. There is no illusion or light left in the universe; there is only metaphysical anguish. (*Absurd* is used

*If man can recognize and accept the simultaneous existence of his absurdity and his responsibility to give himself definition through choice and action, there is hope.*

—JEAN-PAUL SARTRE

here in a broader, sadder sense than "ridiculous." It is derived from the original musical term for "out of harmony.") Life has lost reason, logic, and propriety. Man has lost touch with his roots, so existence is useless and meandering. The laughter that may emerge comes from a deep state of pain. Laughter is a coping tool, often the only coping tool. It is difficult to communicate with others, so we need to fill time, as if life were spent in a waiting room with no inner office, by playing games, joking, dancing, singing, and indulging in silly routines or escapes. Space, linear time, and conventional structure are to be abandoned; plots are therefore often circular (everything that happens has happened before), and the play ends exactly where it began, with the ever-expected explanation never arriving.

*Background.*   Although the first absurdist plays are written in the 1940s, Samuel Beckett's *Waiting for Godot* (1953) is the genre's first major success. The ideas of futurism, dadaism, and surrealism culminate after World War II in the brutal awareness that humanity is perfectly capable of destroying itself. Continental Europe has experienced the greatest devastation of this war, with massive human, economic, agricultural, and architectural loss everywhere. Fatigue and disillusionment are rampant, and the idea of life as meaningful is suspect. Memories of the concentration camps and gas chambers are vivid. This is the canvas for absurdism. Philosophers Albert Camus and Jean-Paul Sarte (and the whole philosophy of existentialism— using will instead of reason to deal with problems arising from a hostile universe) begin to influence playwrights. Another major influence is the work of silent film comedians, including Buster Keaton, Charlie Chaplin, Keystone Kops, and later Laurel and Hardy and the Marx Brothers, who exist in an often nightmarish black-and-white world beyond their comprehension. The movement is popular in the fifties and early sixties. Some writers point to Samuel Beckett's short play *Breath* as the official end of absurdism, but absurdist elements are present today in some of the works of Sam Shepard, David Mamet, and David Rabe.

### Images

Mind games
God is dead
Pet rocks
Tackology
A roomful of beepers
Toddler résumés
Politics
Quality time
Hiroshima
Greed evangelists
President Quayle

The comic strip "Life in Hell"
PBS fund-raising
Zen vacuum
Irrational man
*Le Néant,* the Void
Insurance

*Sight and Sound.* Absurdist plays may be realistically mounted, so that the absurdity comes out of setting up false expectations, or they may be staged on a cartoonlike level. Because humans, animals, and objects are interchangeable in this world, they may be given each other's qualities. Characters may be complex and multidimensional or completely stereotyped. Casts are mostly small, and effects are minimal. Speech is disconnected, noncommunicative, and rambling. People never seem to listen to each other. Rushes of sound are followed by unexpected and sometimes interminable silences. The mood changes just as it appears to establish itself.

*Skills.* Actors must be able to make rapid-fire changes, produce massive variety, and use pauses and silence to surprise the audience. Having many voices and attacks, high energy, and imagination are helpful. Physical demands may include acrobatics, silent film technique, song and dance, vaudeville, circus tricks, quick breaks between presentational and nonpresentational audience relationships, and the capacity to be real and unreal in sharp juxtaposition. It is no accident that a major Broadway revival of *Waiting for Godot* in 1989 featured three of the world's most brilliant clowns, Robin Williams, Steve Martin, and Bill Irwin. All three do comedy that is mental and unpredictable and use their intense physical dexterity to punctuate. Can you comfortably launch into gibberish, a robotlike monotone, a political dialectic, a catatonic trance, or high, ruthless rage while doing a soft shoe? This may be your ism.

## Works

| | |
|---|---|
| Albee, Edward | *The American Dream* |
| | *The Sandbox* |
| Beckett, Samuel | *Waiting for Godot* |
| | *Krapp's Last Tape* |
| | *Happy Days* |
| | *Endgame* |
| | *Footfalls* |
| Camus, Albert | *Caligula* |
| Genet, Jean | *The Maids* |
| | *The Balcony* |

|                      | *Deathwatch* |
|----------------------|--------------|
|                      | *The Blacks* |
| Ionesco, Eugène      | *The Bald Soprano* |
|                      | *Rhinoceros* |
|                      | *The Chairs* |
|                      | *The Lesson* |
| Kopit, Arthur        | *Oh Dad, Poor Dad, Mama's Hung You in the Closet and I'm Feelin' So Sad* |
|                      | *The Day the Whores Came Out to Play Tennis* |
|                      | *Chamber Music* |
| Pinter, Harold       | *The Dumb Waiter* |
|                      | *The Birthday Party* |
|                      | *The Caretaker* |
|                      | *No Man's Land* |
|                      | *Old Times* |
|                      | *The Homecoming* |
| Pirandello, Luigi    | *Six Characters in Search of an Author* |
| Sartre, Jean-Paul    | *No Exit* |
|                      | *The Flies* |
| Shepard, Sam         | *Buried Child* |

## FEMINISM

**Theatre by, for, and about women.**

*Manifesto.*   Women have a voice, too long neglected and pushed inside, which must be released and heard. Drama has been dominated, to our great loss, by male perceptions. Fewer than 10 percent of plays are written by women, and less than one-fourth of the roles in plays are for women. Invaluable insight and artistic expression come out of women's lives. Not only are women in no way inferior or less important than men, but their lives offer extraordinary theatrical richness. Woman's experience must be considered in any future decisions for this art. Old plays need to be reexamined, and new works must be generated from a feminist perspective. Inadequate patriarchal forms must give way, through cultural revolution, to new forms that serve a new perspective. We must move from self-destructive misogyny to creative justice. Women must have freedom to set their own life patterns. Theatre must reflect this freedom.

*Background.* The roots of feminism are political rather than artistic. Out of the woman's suffrage movement of the nineteenth century (in which the United States drags far behind New Zealand, Australia, and the Scandinavian countries in granting women the right to vote) grows the feminist movement of the last half of the twentieth century. The early movement, whose leaders include Mary Wollstonecraft, Sarah M. Grimke, Lucretia Mott, Elizabeth Cady Stanton, Susan B. Anthony, and Lucy Stone, is associated with antislavery. The later movement takes inspiration from civil rights activism and is a recognition of subtler enslavement, in terms of the deprivation of economic and social rights. Feminism is precipitated by women filling the labor force while experiencing job discrimination. The influential works of Simone de Beauvoir (*The Second Sex*) and Betty Friedan (*The Feminine Mystique*) finally bring the term into universal use by the late 1960s, and 1973 is a watershed year with the publication of *Ms.* magazine. Feminism has been co-opted, merged, redefined, and expanded beyond its essentialist origins towards pluralism and diversity. Materialist (Marxist), Ecological (environmentally based, formerly cultural) and radical (separatist) feminist movements now approach the issues from diverse perspectives. The arena of identity politics involves multiple feminist perspectives.

Although many regard Nora in Ibsen's *A Doll's House* walking out the door and leaving her family as feminism's first step in the theatre, the movement has no clear playwrighting history, and its issues are only beginning to be fully explored. Deconstructionist production, performance art, choral plays, and dramatic collages are the most common forms through which the movement from disenfranchisement to empowerment are explored.

*Images*

Affirmative action
NOW
ERA
Fighting words: Sex Object
Myth: Women are weak, passive, dependent, overemotional
"Domesticity Deadens"
Landmark titles: *A Vindication of the Rights of Women; Equality of the Sexes and the Condition of Women; Our Bodies, Ourselves.*
Issues: reproductive freedom, contract/property rights, economic/ policy power, independence, child care, equality, autonomy
Inclusive language

Sarah Daniels
Gloria Steinem
Balance of power
Rachel Rosenthal's performance art
Ground-breaking theatre troupes: Split Britches and At the Foot of
the Mountain
From oppression to autonomy

*Sight and Sound.*   At this writing, more and more productions are carefully considering each of the issues above. Women are likely to look and sound stronger. There are likely to be more of them in any cast as all roles are reexamined and alternative casting seriously considered. Most productions of scripts that deal directly with the issues are simply mounted, with a minimum of technical effects and maximum feeling. The direct audience address monologue is common, as is narration interspersed with episodes. Close attention is being paid to the natural rhythms of women's speech. Language is likely to be vernacular and associative. Preconceptions of what is appropriate are dropping in favor of what women actually share. As in the early phases of naturalism, there is the laughter of recognition as moments in life appear onstage and we wonder why it took so long.

*Skills.*   Actors in the genre require ease in breaking the fourth wall; the capacity to play simultaneity and drop linearity; the ability to discover and enlarge creative, impassioned rituals; the capacity to work in communal, nonhierarchical collaboration; and a flair for transformational playing, with immediate embracing of new identities, contexts, and actions.

**Works**

*I found God in myself and I loved her. I loved her fiercely.*

— NTOZAKE SHANGE

| | | |
|---|---|---|
| Churchill, Caryl | *Top Girls* |
| Cryer, Gretchen | *Getting My Act Together and Taking it on the Road* |
| Fornes, Irene | *Fefu and Her Friends* |
| Kennedy, Adrienne | *Funny House of a Negro* |
| Lamb, Myrna | *Apple Pie* |
| Norman, Marsha | *Getting Out* |
| Shange, Ntozake | *for colored girls who have considered suicide when the rainbow is enuf* |

| Terry, Megan | *Transformations for Three Women* |
| Wolff, Ruth | *The Abdication* |

## POSTMODERNISM

New and old make …

*Manifesto.*   Play with the past without embracing nostalgia. See life with quotation marks around it. Place the new up against the old. The present sells; history is dead; ideals are illusion. Forget consistency, continuity, originality. Embrace splicing and blurring of forms, stances, moods, and cultural levels. Enshrine the discontinuous. Challenge all arbiters of good taste. Undermine seriousness with kitsch. Respect all uncertainties. See erosion as art. Theatricalize the mundane; politicize the theatrical. Replace declarations of faith with declarations of skepticism. Aspire to ambiguity. Avoid all systems.

*Background.*   Postmodernism first appears as a rebellion against modernism in architecture, then painting, then dance. The term is coined by J. Hudnut in 1949, and the major first work is Robert Venturi's *Complexity and Contradiction in Architecture,* followed by Susan Sontag's "Notes on Camp" (1964) and Charles Jencks's *The Language of Post-Modern Architecture* (1977). Modernism, existing roughly from 1450 to 1960, is based on production in the factory, capitalist society, linear time, nationalist orientation, and bourgeois culture. Postmodernism replaces these with production in the office, global society, changing/cyclical time, pluralist orientation, and taste-centered culture. It is essentially a reaction to the 1960s, when our collective belief in progress explodes and old values are shattered but none move in to replace them. The term is not really used in theatrical circles until the 1980s. *Postmodern* is now used as indiscriminately as *Gestalt* was in the 1970s.

*Images*

Lite dog food
Radicchio
Bill Irwin
Mabou Mines
The Woosere Group
David Byrne
music of Philip Glass
Fredric Jameson

*The post modern aesthetic is fundamentally theatrical…. one form masks, disguises, hides itself within or behind another.* —KARI TOEPFER

*Postmodernism is a self-imposed, cultural anesthesia. It is anticipatory shell shock.* —TODD GITLIN

*Basically, postmodernism is whatever you want it to be, if you want it bad enough. Chevy Chase is the postmodern Bob Hope.* —BRUCE HANDY, *SPY* MAGAZINE

The global village
B & Bs
Ecological art
Julina Schnabel and Bad Painting
Selfhypnosis
Tanning clinics
Directors
"Moonlighting"
Tadeusz Kantor and Ariane Mnouchkine
Sam Shepard
Warhol's multiple-screen images
Tom Wolfe
Twyla Tharp
*The Gospel at Colonus*
Laurie Anderson
Spalding Gray
Fiction by Bret Easton Ellis, Anne Beattie, Tama Jonowitz
Cyberpunk
*Sharper Image* catalogue
David Letterman
Jennifer Blande's sculpture-photo blends
Mark Kostabi's hired out original paintings
Movies that use clips from old movies
Photos of photographers
The Portland Building

*Sight.*    Designs are likely to evoke the past and present simultaneously, with period detail executed in new and unexpected materials, colors, and shapes. A first impression will alter with extended viewing, through quirky, informed touches and sly insertions.

*Sound.*    Old sounds reverberate with new cadences. The tone is blasé, exhausted, bemused, and self-conscious. It helps to be a devastatingly accurate mimic of celebrities.

*Skills.*    Postmodern theatre calls on the actor to express enthusiasm for any phenomenon while simultaneously mocking it; to ferret out humor and irony and find political implications in every possible source; to balance the raucous and disrespectful with the bland and the meek; and to develop vocal technique to convey a feeling and its alternatives. Knowledge of television, shopping malls, garage sales, and suburbs as sources of information also helps. Although postmodernism is rooted in disillusionment, it is not a hostile performance style; rather, the performers show delight in the invention of themselves and respect for their differences. Actors turn to address the camera occasionally.

## Lingo

Reflexivity—authorial confession or intrusion into a work
Intertextuality—mixing traditions, genres, texts
Pastiche—ironic collage
Appropriation—stealing or heavy modeling (e.g., Madonna's Monroe)
Androgyny—resistance to gender codes for normative behavior
Neologism—an invented word that defies definition (like *postmodern*)
Deconstruction—reading against the grain for what is latent or unsaid

> *I have forced myself to contradict myself in order to avoid conforming to my own taste.*
>
> —MARCEL DUCHAMP

## Works

| | |
|---|---|
| Churchill, Caryl | *Cloud Nine* |
| Cogdan, Constance | *Tales of the Lost Formicans* |
| Durang, Christopher | *Laughing Wild* |
| Guare, John | *House of Blue Leaves* |
| Hwang, Henry David | *M. Butterfly* |
| Lapine, James, and Steven Sondheim | *Sunday in the Park with George* |
| Lucas, Craig | *Reckless* |
| Mann, Emily | *Still Life* |
| Shepard, Sam | *Cowboy Mouth* |
| | *Angel City* |
| Wagner, Jane | *The Search for Signs of Intelligent Life in the Universe* |

## ISMOLOGY: Tacking Qualifiers onto the Isms

Potentially confusing terms are often used in combination with *other* terms that qualify, limit, expand, or distort original meaning:

| | |
|---|---|
| neo- | New and different from (neo-absurdism) |
| retro- | Backward (retro-absurdism) |
| proto- | First in time, the beginning of (proto-absurdism) |
| quasi- | In some sense or degree (quasi-absurdism), often a put-down |

| semi- | Partly or incompletely (semi-absurdist) |
| ultra- | Beyond the limit and then some (ultra-absurdism) |
| post- | After, subsequent to (postabsurdism) |
| pre- | Earlier than, prior to (pre-absurdist) |
| -esque | In the manner or style of (absurdesque) |

My advice: If a director starts talking about a neo-absurdist expressionistic production with semidadaistic retroromantic elements, see if it's not too late to get out of town. Otherwise, talk to the director and see how the concept affects you, the actor.

---

**E X E R C I S E**

**Ism Tableaux**

1. Working in groups of five or six, draw one of the isms.
2. Without any talk, arrange yourselves into a pattern that you feel captures the ism. Remember this so that you can recreate it.
3. Discuss what the manifesto and the works mean, and collaborate on a more sophisticated tableau that all agree on.
4. Return to class and present both. Discuss the differences.
5. Let the class direct or modify your group into yet another tableau that captures the ism more completely.

**E X E R C I S E**

**Big Moments**

1. Working in small groups, draw one of the isms. Meet very briefly before coming back into class and presenting
   a. a marriage ceremony in your ism
   b. a brief death scene
2. Discuss how the genre alters the major event and the crucial difference between the happy and sad event.

**E X E R C I S E**

**Genre Lingo**

1. Agree as a whole group on the relationship between two characters and a topic of discussion, which will be the same in all scenes.
2. Between one class and the next, come up with a short stretch of dialogue, no longer than an open scene, that you feel absolutely captures your ism.
3. Discuss the differences in presentations and your own feelings about the feasibility of reviving this ism in the future or using it as part of a production concept.

**E X E R C I S E**

**Ism Visualization**

1. Working in teams of three, have each person find a photo, sketch, cartoon, painting, etching, or advertisement that pulls together most of the ism's ideas.
2. Bring these to class, and arrange them as a collage.
3. Establish an amount of time for everyone to circulate without speaking.
4. Gather in a circle and guess each ism. Go back and discuss any that provoked some disagreement.

1. Working in groups of three, draw an ism. Write a one-sentence version of the full manifesto that will speak to today's audience.
2. Brainstorm during one class session, and go home and sleep on the tentative line. If your team members disagree, do each line each person feels needs to be spoken.
3. Stage the line so that you make a statement not only with words but also with a picture and with your interpretation of lines.

**E X E R C I S E**

**Berlitz Manifesto**

Draw an ism, and go to the grocery store. Find the single item that most embodies the ism. Place your item with those chosen by classmates who have drawn the same ism. Discuss the still lifes.

**E X E R C I S E**

**Ism Shopping**

1. Draw an ism. Either assume the identity of its most famous spokesperson, or invent a new identity for yourself. Remember that you are the most adamant proponent of this theatrical concept.
2. Come to class, and debate your ideas with four other ismologists.
3. Discuss which ism most easily dominated and what it felt like to assume a position not necessarily your own.

**E X E R C I S E**

**Meeting of the Minds**

Within our predominant ism, we tend to subdivide.

1. Take either a contemporary realistic scene in progress or one devised through improvisation, in which actors are cast close to age and type. Change it so that it could be called
   - comedy
   - drama
   - farce
   - tragedy
   - tragicomedy
   - dramedy
   - political drama

   Discuss the changes, particularly what caused the scene to become less "realistic."
2. Try the scene again, this time making it:
   - fantasy
   - melodrama
   - satire
   - burlesque

   Discuss the isms (other than realism) that were touched when the scene entered these realms.
3. Devise a basic comic situation and perform it realistically. Then take the exact plot and have the scene become a comedy of
   - character
   - intrigue
   - manners
   - morals
   - romance

   Where does the scene leave realism, and what historical periods does the treatment begin to resemble?

**E X E R C I S E**

**Realism Isms**

# PERSONAL STYLE
## Creating Reality

We use groups to define ourselves, but we are not just joiners. People who are forces to be reckoned with are more than their memberships. Those who possess, master, transcend, create, or influence style find a personal signature to autograph the world. Group style is shared. Characterization gives distinct inner life. But *personal* style is how you leave your mark.

This chapter explores ways of personalizing each style we have studied so that you can carry some of that style into your life. It also explores defining your own style, recognizing when it fits, and knowing when it needs modification. Your personal style suits some periods and genres, just as it suits some groups and towns, better than others.

### DEFINING YOUR OWN STYLE

To understand others, you must first know yourself. If you have experienced difficulty becoming Greek, Elizabethan, or Molièrian, it may be that you are not clear about your own style habits. To understand your own style, look at your world-entering choices. Having studied style analysis, classical acting, five different period styles, displaced style, and genre, would your answers to the questions first raised in Chapter 1 now be any different? Has the new information influenced how you see yourself? How do the questions we use to approach entire worlds apply to you? Remember that some of the most interesting style characteristics are those that fall short of perfection.

*What a man is, rather than what he knows, will at last determine his style.* —E. B. WHITE

*Style reflects idiosyncrasies. Your personality is apt to show more to the degree that you did not solve the problem than to the degree that you did.*
—DESIGNER CHARLES EAMES

Demetra Pittman (Beatrice) and Jon Pribyl (Benedick) in *Much Ado About Nothing,* Oregon Shakespeare Festival

### Time

1. What is your own personal tempo/rhythm? How close or removed is it from those around you? Are you time bound? Is there anything about you that has failed to evolve?

2. Have you ever felt you were born in the wrong time? Do you have a particular affinity for one bygone era, as if you lived then in another life? For more than one?

3. Which time periods speak to you enough to influence your style choices? Which would you most love to visit?

### Space

1. What is the size, flexibility, and scope of your personal bubble? How easily does it adjust?

2. How do you connect with and use the space, surfaces, and shapes around you?

3. Do some rooms get too small for you as you suddenly realize that you are overbold and overloud? Does the reverse happen? How sensitive are you to the space needs of others?

### Place

1. Do your attitudes, behaviors, and vocal and physical lives reflect where you came from, no matter where you are? Are you place bound? To what extent do you recognize and adapt to the place you are in?

2. What sorts of places do people associate with you, even if they are not part of your actual experience?

3. Where do you feel most at home? Most stimulated? Where do you really belong?

### Values

1. Do you have beliefs that are not widely shared? Do some beliefs make you feel almost as though you were from another planet?

2. Which assumptions about right most strongly influence your interactions?

3. How clearly do you communicate your values through your presentation of self? How often are you misinterpreted? Do you bite your tongue and keep your own counsel, or do you impose your thoughts regularly?

### Structure

1.  What is your relationship to authority? How likely are you to accept, defy, or manipulate the power of others? Where do you present yourself between rebel and conformist?

2.  How easily do you move between social, economic, political, spiritual, and cultural groups? How aware and flexible is your sense of appropriate behavior?

3.  How do you impose structure on the lives of others?

### Beauty

1.  Where do you place yourself on the beauty scale, and how have you responded to that? Are your own tastes or preferences outside the norm? Do you reveal this? Under what circumstances?

2.  How do you change your looks when you appear before others? Where do you work hardest to adjust/improve yourself?

3.  Other than theatre, what are your favored modes of artistic expression?

*Wouldn't this be a great world if insecurity and desperation made us more attractive?*

—ALBERT BROOKS

### Sex

1.  Are you aware of what is sexually attractive about you? Of what is not? Do you exploit this in any way?

2.  Do you emphasize, reveal, or hide parts of your body?

3.  Do you express your sexuality? Are you embarrassed, intolerant, or defiant of "normal" courtship behavior?

### Recreation

1.  Do you find certain things fun that others find boring or difficult?

2.  Which of your pleasures are shared or unique? Are there "national pastimes" you find impossible to comprehend? Are there some to which you are addicted?

3.  Where are you on the doer/watcher, thinker/feeler, celebrant/meditator scales?

### Sight and Sound

1.  How do your vocal mannerisms help you and limit you? Where are you most bound?

2.  How do your physical habits affect these same factors?

3. Does your speech or movement fit better into some genres or periods than others?

### Music and Dance

1. What is your theme song? Which is your dance?
2. Which style of music reflects you best?
3. To what extent do you use music and dance to express yourself?

### Images

The abstract form first introduced in Chapter 1 can be helpful (fabric, animal, beverage, mode of transportation, city, tree, color, play, scent, song, type of day, decade or era, film or TV series, landmark or building, snack, mythological or fantasy figure, spice, musical instrument, painting or photo, toy).

1. Which answers jumped out at you the first time you saw the list, and which have taken more time?
2. In which categories did you fear what others would choose? Which images do you really *wish* were associated with you?
3. Where do people's images of you most strongly disagree?

### Masking

1. Which are the faces you wear in public?
2. When does your facade drop most readily, and when can it be counted on to appear?
3. Which of your masks work well for you? Which get in the way?

### The Perfect Audience

1. What groups are you best with? Who admires you most? What kinds of audience response do you have the most trouble dealing with?
2. What kind of audience are you? A good listener? Do you howl with laughter? Actively empathize? How generously do you respond?
3. Which members of your private audience are always present?

### Social Success and Suicide

*All styles are good, save the tiresome kind.*
*—VOLTAIRE*

1. What have been your greatest public triumphs and tragedies?
2. When you felt victorious and larger than life, what was it that made you so good?

3. Is there a pattern in the times you are hot and times you are not? Can you trace circumstances and signals that may help you to more success and less suicide in the future?

---

1. Write a brief phrase in response to each of the three questions in the categories of time, space, place, values, structure, beauty, sex, recreation, sight, and sound.
2. Also briefly summarize your style choices in these areas: images, masking, perfect audience, and social success and suicide.
3. Underline those answers you are comfortable with, and highlight those you wish to do something about.
4. Make some decisions about what to own, accept, develop, or change.

**E X E R C I S E**

**Analyzing My Style**

---

Don't rush to change. It is important to remember that very few styles were well received when they first appeared. Maybe you are a pioneer.

## YOUR PERIOD STYLE SELF

Part of the joy of acting in classical plays is getting to live long ago and far away. Creating a whole new identity for yourself in another time and place is great adventure. A period style alter ego can help you define yourself and also serve as a path to playing a character in a play. Some actors are able to grow in a style if they can function as a character of their own creation, one who is free of the constraints of text. Ask yourself, What would be the Greek me? Elizabethan me? Restoration me? Molière moi? Georgian me? How would any of these personages answer the following questions?

- *"My name is . . ."* Note how names are formed, how this differs between the sexes, and what the differences tend to imply. Pick a name that still has something of your own in it—some letter or syllables—so that your classmates or other cast members can remember it. This also helps you symbolically keep some of the present you as part of the new you. Remember, the Elizabethan guest dubbed me Bartonio. If I were Greek, I might be Baresius. Who are you?

- *"I was born in . . ."* You were not necessarily born on this earth. You may have been born in an entirely imaginary kingdom, in an undiscovered province, or on a star. You need only choose.

- *"My titles are . . ."* If your twentieth-century origins are humble, don't necessarily buy into that for your period self. Who are you in your soul? Who were you *meant* to be?

- *"My primary possessions include . . ."* You may own vast lands, fleets

*Original styles almost always look crude and excessive: Picasso's in painting ("My three-year-old could draw better!"), Brando's in acting ("He's got marbles in his mouth!"), Elvis' in music ("Photograph him from the waist up!"), Lenny Bruce's in comedy ("Book him!"). In their first outrageousness, these artists seemed to signal the end of the world; instead they were heralding a new one.*

—MARY CRONIN

of ships, cities, magic potions, magic objects, and chests of jewels. You may own people. What gives you power and inspiration beyond your own drive?

- *"The people for whom I am responsible are . . ."* Whose lives change because of your decisions? Do you have a primary adviser—a shaman, priestess, prime minister, or wizard? For how many and what kind of sheep are you the shepherd?

- *"A physical description of me is . . ."* Start with what you really look like. Adjust that in your imagination. You may choose to square your jaw line, add more hair, grow a few inches, or make your coloring more striking. Keep the changes close enough that as you walk around you can believe that this is you, and if you returned to your regular life you would not be unrecognizable.

- *"The most crucial event in my life up to now was . . ."* Let your imagination soar. A profound experience or twist of fate may have changed your destiny. It could be an encounter with a god or a glimpse into the crystal ball. Who knows?

- *"Above all else, I believe . . ."* Devise a statement to adopt as your personal credo. It marks what you would fight to the death for, the point beyond which you will not be pushed. It guides you on life's adventure.

---

**E X E R C I S E**

**My Other Selves**

Who would you be if you lived in the world created by the playwrights of these periods? If you had an ancestor, what would he or she have been like? If you are living there now, in a time warp, as you *also* live here, what kind of creature are you?

1. Devise a Greek, Elizabethan, Restoration, Molièrian, or Georgian persona.
2. Create an alter ego for yourself in that world, based on what you know about that world. Approach it either as if you lived then or as if you still do. Test your knowledge of the period as seen by the playwright. What you are unsure of, make up. Remember that you know who you are better than anyone else does.
3. Complete the statements: "My name is . . ."; "I was born in . . ."; "My titles are . . ."; "My primary possessions include . . ."; "The people for whom I am responsible are . . ."; "A physical description of me is . . ."; "My most crucial life event up to now was . . ."; and "Above all else, I believe . . ."
4. Introduce yourself to the class or cast, sharing crucial information from the list above.
5. Let them ask you questions, and trust yourself to respond.
6. Variation:
   a. Repeat the exercise as a character from a play, but take to the process some of the confidence from your own imagination.

b. Have the class interview a series of characters from different scenes or plays. It helps if the characters share something; for example, all are kings, all want revenge, or all are unfaithful.

1. If you are showcasing scene work, have created characters introduce real ones and interact between scenes or monologues.
2. Plan an event, such as a Grecian harvest festival, a celebration of the queen's birthday, or a welcome soiree for the king's new mistress. Cast the essential historical roles, but allow everyone else to play in the identity each has chosen.
3. Combine the two above, and alternate improvised activities with the presentation of scripted material.

**E X E R C I S E**

**Alter Ego into Character**

## PERIOD STYLE DAYS

Set aside a class meeting devoted to bringing one period to life. Your goal is to help the participants feel as if they have entered the world of the plays and briefly lived there and to give them a personal experience with the style. You are creating an educational theme party. Initial considerations include the following:

### Occasion

What is the cause for gathering and celebrating? Which of the many reasons these people find to celebrate creates this particular celebration? Choose something that excites you, that you yourself would love to be invited to.

### The Senses

What stimulates the senses of sight, sound, smell, taste, and touch? Consider the following:

1. How can you alter the classroom in terms of shape, light, and space?
2. What music or sound effects can serve as background and enhance mood, and what kinds can call attention to you when you want it?
3. What aromas, perfumes, incense, scents, or food smells might permeate the air?
4. What food and drink might you serve? How might the serving of the refreshments be ritualized?
5. What surfaces, fabrics, or objects should be touched? In what ways might people touch each other as part of the experience?

### Costumes

What is the simplest yet most evocative way for classmates to dress, wear their hair, and look for the day? Review suggestions for rehearsal garments. How can the participants change enough to feel that they live in this world? What personal props should actors carry?

### Images

Find picture books with examples of buildings, artwork, clothing, undergarments, furniture, and basic props. Find photos of actors playing the roles being performed by classmates and paintings of the dominant personalities of the period. Use the Images section of each chapter to help you select your choices. Consider setting up these items around the classroom as you would at a museum, fair, or festival. Consider presenting a slide show as well.

### Admission

How do people get in? Must they show an invitation? A calling card to be dropped off? Must they bring an offering? Will only a weapon work? Or only a poem?

### Activities

Devote some energy to each of these activities:

1. A warm-up (physical, vocal, and mental) to help the class let go and enter the world you are offering them.
2. Family lies in this period. Carry out the simple three-character bigamy scenario from the Family Lies exercise in Chapter 2, but adopt all cultural assumptions and theatrical conventions of this particular style. This is a highly revealing and important exercise because the class now *knows* the story and can appreciate it as pure style. Like the original Greek audiences, who know what is coming next, the class can savor what it means.
3. Improvisations and sketches involving time, space, place, values, structure, beauty, sex, recreation, sight, or sound. Select the areas in which you feel as a team that these improvisations or theatre games will help the concept come to life.
4. Lessons in success and failure in the worlds of the plays, including perhaps some masked activity.
5. Some hints on ways to wear clothes and not let them wear you. If the costume shop is willing to cooperate, borrow items of clothing that must be experienced firsthand, such as corsets and trains, in sufficient quantity for everyone.

6. Learning some basic steps for the most evocative dances of the time. Keep it simple; avoid painstaking detail in favor of a quick feel for the dance as an expression of how people feel about being alive.

7. A chance to bow, pay obeisance, touch, and make contact in the period. Set up a social interaction in which these activities can be practiced automatically rather than as part of problem-solving contexts.

8. Experience in becoming the perfect audience. Arrange for side coaching and cheerleading, and have some classmates perform and others play ideal observers.

9. Brief readings from different translations or adaptations so that everyone can hear the range of scripts available for the same work and can distinguish various qualities and types of translation.

10. Select displaced examples for the period—writers, actors, films, plays, and people in the community whose attack on life evokes the period in question. For example, Dorothy Parker is a twentieth-century writer whose sensibility seems quite Restoration, and Tony Randall is a modern actor who could slide comfortably into that period. It can be very helpful for actors to see examples of another era existing in some form within their own.

### Guidelines

To maintain the spirit of the day, agree to function within these basic rules:

1. Keep the entire presentation in the present tense, and use the first person (for example, "We worship Dionysus," not "They worshiped Dionysus").

2. Have each person assume a distinct identity different from his or her usual self, and at some time present each person or provide the person the opportunity to introduce himself or herself. Have people stay in character.

3. Allow a time-out for questions if people are confused.

4. Sacrifice historical accuracy in favor of the spirit of the plays; enter the world *envisioned* by the playwrights, which may not be that *lived in* by the playwrights.

5. Make sure that all activities involve tasks to be *accomplished* and are not just a means to pass the time. For example, we are not just here to honor a god; we are here to select the virgin to be sacrificed. This creates a dynamic. It is always easier for actors to focus on pursuing an objective. Keep the gathering active and purposeful.

6. Combine tasks. For example, play an actual party game from the

period that both teaches the standards of beauty and also requires actors to use key phrases from the language of the time.

7.  Provide victories for the participants, and make them feel valued and successful. Let all involved know that they can and will master this style, and let them see in what areas they are making progress.

8.  Encourage all participants to think of themselves as inhabitants of a province or precinct with its own customs. This way, you can't do anything wrong; if you botch up a bow, the reason is that people bow differently where you come from. Any strange word you speak (such as "wow" or "10K") is a peculiar term used by your people. In fact, you might honor classmates who do these bloopers for bringing such diversity to your celebration and for sharing their customs. This will quickly relax your classmates and help free them from fear of failure.

9.  Give your audience/participants a theatre program listing each interlude and the appropriate lengths to help guide them through the experience. This provides structure for the event and helps you use the time to best advantage.

10. Hold a debriefing session in which all class members can talk about what they got from the occasion and which issues are still unresolved for them.

*In matters of grave importance, style, not sincerity, is the important thing.* —OSCAR WILDE

If you are not involved in a class or rehearsal, you can still give yourself many of these sensory experiences. This is basically dress-up and "let's pretend." You are limited only by your own willingness and imagination.

---

E X E R C I S E

**Period Style Day**

Draw from the checklist those activities you wish to plan, and allot a specific time period for each. Remember that this can be merely a taste of the world; each actor can make many promises to go back and explore each factor in depth later. Keep the basic principles listed below in mind.

| *Checklist* | *Principles* |
| --- | --- |
| Warm-up | Present tense |
| Family lies (or possible variations, such as proposals or pregnancy announcements) | Distinct identities |
| | Time-outs allowed |
| | Spirit over accuracy |
| | Purposeful activities |
| Music, slides, and food—senses work | Combined tasks |
| | Many possible victories |

Improvisations
Social success and
 failure lessons
Clothing sugges-
 tions
Dance steps
Bows
Perfect audience
 coaching
Translation read-
 ings
Displaced examples

All are experts
 from their region
Program providing
 clarity and struc-
 ture
Debriefing session

---

## YOUR ISM SELF

Ask yourself which of the isms speak most directly to your own sense of the world, to your vision of what art, music, and theatre should say and do. You may choose a name that is similar to that of your favorite painter (Van Bart?) or composer (Bozart?). The entire class could come to one class session as their ism alter egos. Develop your adoption of this into a complete look, sound, and attitude.

Use these questions to help you find your ism:

1. What is your own manifesto? What is going on now that you tend to protest? What do you choose to advocate for the future?

2. How does your background lead you to your own convictions? Do your parents or ancestors espouse recognizable isms that you are either evolving or defying?

3. Which special skills are necessary to perform you? What would others need to work on to be responsive to all your shifts of behavior and perspective?

4. Of the images you leave, are any reminiscent of an existing genre? Maybe you are a whole new ism. Brechtian feminism? Postmodern naturalism? Dadaist romanticism? Now there's a thought.

## ISM DAY

Isms Day can be presented by a single report team or with pairs of actors each drawing one or two isms. Use as many of the basic ideas suggested for Period Style Day as possible with these modifications:

1. Present a collage instead of a sustained event, so that every five minutes or so the style changes.
2. Have the audience change location and configuration to suit the genre. Instruct audience members in how they should respond. Have fun determining who gets to sit or stand where and when people should howl support or sit on their hands.
3. Find a piece of music or series of sound effects that most supports the movement. Find visuals as well.
4. Read a brief snatch of representative dialogue, if it exists.
5. Act out a quick marriage proposal or other universal event for each ism, with the appropriate outcome for that genre.
6. Find a food image to show, and if edible, to share.
7. Comically demonstrate the actor pitfalls for going overboard with this ism.
8. Team members might dress in neutral black and then change just one element for each section.
9. Share five abstract images that capture the essence.
10. Move historically from romanticism into the future so that the class can experience the movements as they have occurred, are occurring, and will occur.

---

**E X E R C I S E**

**Alter Egos Unleashed**

1. Pick one of the characters you have created for yourself as a Greek, Elizabethan, Restoration, Georgian, or ism proponent.
2. Take this creation into the twentieth century for a four-hour period, staying in character and responding in kind. You may work with a partner or a small group, provided that you are all from the same period or genre.
3. Make sure that the excursion involves some interaction with present-day people and that you give yourself the gift of viewing the peculiarities of our society from another's perspective.
4. Report to the class, as your alter ego, what you learned in your journey and what you found most peculiar about twentieth-century Americans.
5. Variation: If time allows, have the entire class do the same period so that everyone would take his Greek character, for example, into the world and then return to the temple, conversing as Greeks on what you saw, on your opinions of twentieth-century Americans, their peculiarities, and in what respects, if any, they seem reasonable.
6. Bring an object back to the class from the modern age that your compatriots in history would find particularly miraculous, peculiar, or horrifying. This exercise takes some courage and works only if you stay in character. But it can also give you a sense of confidence and power.

Having found some other powerful selves in yourself, in what contexts might you use them? Meet and brainstorm with two other actors, and offer your suggestions to the group as a whole. As contexts are suggested by the team, others will come up. Jot down those that intrigue you, and promise yourself to try them out. Here are some examples:

1. Your Greek self can help you in a court of law, whenever you need to defend your position publically, and . . .
2. Your Elizabethan self can help you tap into your most romantic imagination when you want to win someone with music, verse, and worship and . . .
3. Your Restoration self can help you get the dish, teach you how to get revenge, and . . .
4. Your Molière self might show you how to prick the balloon of pretense, to recognize your own foolishness, and . . .
5. Your Georgian self might allow you to be as gregarious, polite, and cheerful at that reception as your parents always wish you would be, and . . .
6. Your ism self might change you just enough to help you fit into a group you normally butt heads with, and . . .

## MODELS: STYLING YOURSELF ON SOMEONE ELSE

We all look to role models. Some influence us briefly and lightly, others long and hard. We look and sound like their clones until we exorcise their influence and free ourselves. The personal style choices made by these people are so vivid that they have influenced those of others: Clark Gable, Marilyn Monroe, James Dean, Jacqueline Kennedy Onassis, Marlon Brando, Cary Grant, Farrah Fawcett, David Bowie, Coco Chanel, Sid Vicious, Michael Jackson, Madonna.

The fashion hall of fame recently came out with its all-time best-dressed list of people who have had the most influence on the rest of us. In addition to several on the previous list were the duke and duchess of Windsor, Audrey Hepburn, Harry Belafonte, Grace Kelly, David Niven, and Fred Astaire. Did you make the list? Neither did I.

Some of the names may seem like heroic figures to you, and others may seem laughable. Why? What names would you add to the list? This group has influenced mostly style, not substance. Which of them *have* exerted a more substantial influence? Which have influenced the way people think beyond the way they dress?

The models examined in the following exercises are the members of your faculty. They are not necessarily people you have attempted to emulate. In fact, the exact opposite may be true. You have, however, observed them at some length. The faculty of a theatre department is seen in class,

*The best classic line, according to Miss Manners, to use when you disapprove of the style choice made by another: "There is a time and a place for that sort of thing," the words "and this isn't it" being implied. . . . It is particularly devastating to those who were trying to shock, because the remark makes it clear that it is not the action itself that is being condemned, but the arena in which it has been performed.*

—JUDITH MARTIN

at rehearsal, in production meetings, in student conferences, in coaching sessions, working in the shop, supervising others, lecturing, and at receptions and parties. You see them in enough situations to be able to conjecture their style choices in other imaginary situations.

---

The subjects of this exercise are your own theatre faculty or any other group of authority figures with whom the whole class has regular contact. The "recipients" here are graduate students. If there is no graduate program in your department, substitute any level of student, and make any minor adjustments necessary. Working in teams of four, each team draws the name of one of your own theatre faculty.

Situation A: The graduate student's thesis or dissertation has been selected for publication, and she has been asked by a major repertory company to do a year's residence exploring the theories in the document. The teachers sought this award on the sly and are about to announce the good news to the lucky student.

1. Divide the group into three teachers and one recipient.
2. Take approximately fifteen minutes to prepare the outline of your improvisation.
3. Each of the three "teachers" adopts the style of a particular faculty member. (Imagine that at one time in your life, you decided that the way this person presented himself in the world was so admirable that he served as a genuine role model for you.) This is not a simple imitation or impersonation in the style of Rich Little. You are not trying to *be* the faculty member, just to adapt the person's *style* of presentation and communication.
4. Consider these questions:
   a. *Time.* How likely is it that the person would prolong the announcement, as opposed to popping right out with it? How anxious is the person to get on to other business?
   b. *Place.* Where would this person choose to break the news? A shop, office, conference room, hallway, auditorium, lobby, or some place off campus?
   c. *Space.* To what degree would the person employ physical contact or distance?
   d. *Beauty and sex.* Do these factors enter into this encounter in any way? To what extent are they always or never present in conferences with this person?
   e. *Recreation.* Is this meeting fun or just business as usual?
   f. *Structure.* How formal/informal would the basic situation be? How official does it seem?
   g. *Values.* What particular truths (if any) do these faculty members embrace that the recipient may or may not share?
   h. *Sight and Sound.* How do the above express themselves in the range of choices from ways of sitting and making eye contact to tone of voice and choice of images?

Situation B: The graduate student has been caught plagiarizing his thesis or dissertation, and the proof is absolute. As if this were not bad enough, the student has been caught naked in one of the faculty lounges with a freshman student of undisclosed sex. The faculty "team" must break the news that the student will be expelled and that there may even be a lawsuit.

Present both versions and discuss the style decisions made. When did the exercise descend into simple mimicry, and when did it most clearly stay in the realm of style? Which stylistic choices seemed most and least accurate to those who admire or emulate this faculty member? Remember that emulation is not the same as mimicry or impersonation.

Go back and do the exercise in the style of one of the influential personalities mentioned in this chapter or, by mutual agreement, another emulated celebrity.

**E  X  E  R  C  I  S  E**

**Celebrity Style**

Select someone in the group, and go through the process of trying to emulate this individual.

**E  X  E  R  C  I  S  E**

**Classmate's Style**

Imitation may be the most sincere form of flattery, but personal style models are still often overlooked for recognition. They are honored about as often as comic actors are at Oscar time. We easily forget our style inspirations. To help determine your own style, take time to honor those who have influenced it.

1. Go back into your own personal history, and try to pick out the person you most often tried to be like during these ages: 3–5, 5–10, 10–15, 15–21, 21–25. (Continue in four- to five-year cycles, depending on your age.)
2. Identify what you wore, said, moved, or in any other way changed to emulate your model.
3. Identify the most emulated person you knew during those times. Often this is somebody at school whose influence you never could understand but whose lead others seemed to follow. Where were you most and least in accord with others in their choices?
4. Who are the people you would right now give anything to be? Whose personal style do you most admire? Whose style do you emulate now?
5. How is the person you would like to become in the future different from the person you are now? What about you would you like others who follow you to try to emulate?

**E  X  E  R  C  I  S  E**

**Emulations**

## PRESENTATION CHOICES

Some people design themselves, reinventing and re-creating themselves from top to bottom. They often begin by choosing a new name. Here are the real names of some rock stars:

Huey Lewis (Hugh Anthony Cregg III)
Billy Idol (William Broad)
Elvis Costello (Declan Patrick McManus)
Jon Bon Jovi (John Bongiovi)

Three of the best known actresses in the world were not always called what they are now:

Meryl Streep (Mary Lou Streep)
Cher (Cherilyn La Piere)
Sigourney Weaver (Susan Weaver)

Try to picture Mary Lou and Cherilyn before they made their style choices and renamed themselves. How would you feel about Benjamin Franklin Goodrich tires; Scientifically Treated Petroleum; Leon Leonwood Bean clothes; Mars and Mars candies; Bradley, Voorhees and Day underwear; or shopping at James Cash Penney's store if initials had not been chosen by these icons? You may even have forgotten some of your own names; see the exercise that follows.

---

**EXERCISE**

**My Names**

1. Identify at least five names you have been called in your life: pet names, nicknames, or tease names others gave you. What were the circumstances? Which of your own choices in presenting yourself may have brought about the name?
2. Identify any name you gave yourself and tried to encourage others to use. Why? What were you trying to present?
3. If you had to change your name right now, perhaps because someone else in Actor's Equity had it or because some serial killer had it, what would you pick? Why? What would the new name put forth in the world that your old one does not?

---

Most of us do not change names. I have stuck with mine in spite of disliking it (Bob Barton sounds like a game show host), and most of us stay with what we have, fond of it or not. But whenever you even *think* about a change, you are considering a significant style choice. The name precedes you. It is the first message in your image statement. When people hear or read your name, what kind of person do you think they envision? Your name is followed by a series of choices by which you make yourself known; see the following exercise.

Complete each of these statements.

E X E R C I S E

I Choose

1. On a day off, I go out to eat . . .
2. For my favorite evening event, I wear . . .
3. If I inherited several hundred thousand dollars, I . . .
4. My idea of the perfect two-week vacation is . . .
5. If I were looking for a house, I would tell my real estate agent to find me . . .
6. If I were expecting a child, I would consider the names . . .
7. My first choice for a new car or vehicle would be . . .
8. If I decided to get a pet, I would choose . . .
9. If I subscribed to one new magazine, it would be . . .
10. My best friend will throw me any kind of birthday bash I want, so I choose . . .

Which of your choices are partially influenced by how you wish to present yourself in the world? Which not at all?

Another way to gather information about your style is to ask others what they think of when they think of you. What do you leave behind? The answer may be a literal one—your keys, which you are notorious for losing, for example—or as general as a lingering thought or impression.

E X E R C I S E

Leftovers

1. What do you tend to leave behind for others to remember you by?
   * Food? (Peanuts? Spilled coffee? Gum?)
   * Small objects? (Paper clips? Chocolate wrappers? Beer bottle caps?)
   * Scent? (Cologne? Mints? Body odor?)
   * Sound? (Welcome silence? Lingering rock music from your stereo? Screeching tires?)
   * Clothing? (Favored old shirt? Running shoes? Baseball cap? Earrings?)
   * Tracks? (Mud? Lipstick? Piles of laundry?)
   * Words? (Buzzwords? Favored phrases? Lingering lingo?)
2. What do others most strongly associate with you when you aren't there? Your book bag? Your car? Your dog? Your chatter? Your laugh?
3. Where do these images match and contradict your own sense of self?

Are there ways in which you never let others see you? Do you camouflage, enhance, or hide? Do you monitor language, moods, and vulnerability in order not to hurt or be hurt? Do you ever project something that is actually the exact opposite of how you feel or who you are? Have any of your masks become old habits, with no real protection value?

*When we see a natural style, we are surprised and delighted, for we expected to see an author and we find a man.*
—PASCAL

**E X E R C I S E**

**Unmasking**

1. Make a list for yourself of the circumstances and people before whom you mask.
2. Draw a cartoon of the mask or masks, or pick a symbol of what it or they represent.
3. Cross out the items on the list that are useless.
4. Put question marks next to those whose value you are going to investigate, with the idea of either removing or replacing the mask.
5. See whether you can put the symbolic act into actual practice.

**E X E R C I S E**

**My Personal Coat of Arms**

Does your family have a coat of arms? If so, examine it to see whether parts of it strike a responsive chord with you and feel right. If not, start from scratch.

1. Draw a circle, diamond, or a shield on a large sheet of paper.
2. Put on your coat of arms the images that reflect what you send out in the world. Don't feel any need to fit a heraldic mode; yours may feature a can of beer and a crayon box. Select as many as six visuals for the crest.
3. Explore what you want in terms of color, decoration, and general adornment.
4. You may wish to do several drafts. Forget artistic ability. If you don't draw well, then *your* coat of arms *should* have stick figures.
5. Hang the coat of arms on the wall, and let yourself enjoy what it says.

**E X E R C I S E**

**Motto and Vow**

1. Devise a statement to go with your coat of arms, one that sums up your philosophy, your wisdom, and your humor. Let this be a statement that you would like emblazoned on your tomb, because you believe it down to your bones.
2. Pick another statement based on what you would like to be. Give yourself an identity that you know you can achieve; anyone can tap the hero within if truly called. Choose something possible but not easy, something you wish were always the case and on good days *is* the case, but you would really like to reflect who you are all the time. Make the statement either about you, as in "Bob is . . .," or from you, as in "I am . . ."

**E X E R C I S E**

**Old Myth/New Myth**

Review all the fairy tales, childhood stories, childhood heroes, comics, old wives' tales, and myths that have influenced who you are. Which tales have always haunted you? Which images (for example, those depicting what a real man or woman should be) have plagued you, so that even after you decided they were a crock, they still influence the way you present yourself?

1. Pick the image or story that you feel is least helpful to you now. Recite it to yourself, and as you do so, revise the details to make it one you find nurturing, one that serves you better.
2. Write a new fairy tale, stealing shamelessly from all those you like, but creating an adventure that is full of glory. Work with all the familiar terminology: "Once upon a time, there was a handsome prince named Robert, who woke up one day and . . ."
3. Let the revision and the new tale guide you.

## PERSONAL STYLE DAY

This meeting is devoted to exploring issues and sharing answers raised in this chapter. The group should decide what it would like this day to be. Here are some possibilities.

*You find your style by finding yourself and you make something of it by putting yourself on the line.* —TRISH DEITCH ROHRER

### Pictures from the Past

Each person brings two photographs, a baby or early childhood picture and the worst photograph ever taken of that person. Place these at random around the room, and hold a guessing game. Be sure to tell *all* class members that they are just as adorable now as they were as babies and that the other photograph has got to be of someone else.

### Style Extremes Show

Each person brings two items reflecting how different or varied he or she can be in public. Two recent examples: A woman brought two red shoes, one a spike-heeled slide for her "babe" self, the other a high-top for her more funky side. An actor brought a comic book and the complete works of Shakespeare, the two things he was most often seen reading in the Green Room. Write up a commentary, like those in a real fashion show, to be read by the hosts. Get up and parade around, showing off your extremes while the narrative is read.

*True style comes from flaunting our own limitations.*

—PATRICK FRALEY

### Flaunting It

Pick what you consider your greatest limitation, and find a way to punch it up. If the class sits in a circle and you have the chance to get up and walk around in the center, what would you do or say to highlight for once—instead of hiding—what you consider a shortcoming? Decide to have fun and own it.

### Style Ritual

Write down on a slip of paper the one abstract image you would really like to lose, or at least put on the back burner until it can serve you. This one outrages you and depresses you, because you have to admit that it is both true and not the way you want to present yourself in the world. This is the one you are ready to do something about. Replace it with the image you like the most and would like to be worthy of in the future.

Set up the room with a waste basket onstage and a very nice basket containing little paper wishing stars or some other symbolic objects. With everyone watching, go up and read the word naming the image you want to dump, tear it up, and throw it in the waste basket. Take a wishing star and announce your commitment to your second image, after which the class will respond with tumultuous applause.

### The Great Hall

Hang up the coats of arms and mottoes. Circulate and admire them, especially if the artwork is atrocious. When everyone has had a chance to examine each shield fully, let all of the knights pick up their own, move in front of the group, and publically say their mottoes.

### Theme Songs and Leftovers

A designated team picks a song and a leftover to represent each person. While the exhibit is revealed and the tune plays, everyone else guesses. When the audience guesses right, go on to another artiste.

### Stage Names

All class members get up and quickly share the five names of the past, and then, to a drum roll or fanfare, announce the names they would choose if they wanted to change or had to in order to join Equity.

### Lowest Style Moment

All classmates attempt to re-create as closely as possible the very lowest period in their style awareness history, the worst look, attitude, demeanor, and/or sound they have ever chosen. This frequently unveils the nerd within. Try to inhabit the person fully as you describe that phase of your life. Variation: Confess your worst emulation choice, the person you once wanted to be like and now would not even consider as a model.

### Displacement Votes

Who *really* belongs in one of the periods of genre covered in this book? Prepare a ballot, vote, tabulate, and then announce which time each member of the class should choose.

---

**E X E R C I S E**

**Evolving Personal Style**

Here is a summary of the activities above. If you do not have a chance to perform them all in public, give yourself the experience in private.

1. Pictures from the Past
2. Style Extremes Show
3. Flaunting It
4. Style Ritual

5. The Great Hall
6. Theme Songs and Leftovers
7. Stage Names
8. Lowest Style Moment
9. Displacement Votes

---

## ADAPTING VERSUS ADOPTING

If you have studied style with a class, others have experienced your progress firsthand. Many have watched you for some time. They know where you were and where you now are. Class members are good at assessing each other and giving candid, humane feedback.

As an actor, you try to understand periods and genres for good style acting. You also try to develop an individual style while communicating effectively with the group and being a good colleague, a supportive partner, and an aggressive and challenging co-worker. You try to become an ensemble player who can fly solo when the occasion demands it. Because theatre is shared art, we all need to learn to compromise, collaborate, and challenge. We need to master diplomacy while not letting anyone out of his or her responsibilities. This style challenge is every bit as large and important as what occurs in front of the footlights. Many brilliant actors do not work much because their personal style is so abrasive that others cannot endure being around them. Others have modified their style choices to the point of becoming complete wimps—never asserting themselves and allowing themselves to grow, always in fear of being accused of having an "attitude," and ending up accused of having no courage. Others manage playful compromises and are able both to join and to remain independent.

Acting style and personal style are connected. And growth in one may feed growth in the other.

*Manners are a way to screw people over without their knowing it.*

*—P. J. O'ROURKE, IN MODERN MANNERS: AN ETIQUETTE BOOK FOR RUDE PEOPLE*

*I liked to push the system at school. I did it through clothes. We had a regulation grey suit and I managed to get mine lined with gold or burgundy material. The school didn't like it—but I was wearing their suit so they couldn't do anything about it.*

*—JEREMY IRONS*

---

Consider your own status in acting style and personal style. In each category, consider both evidence of progress and the need for growth. If time allows, draw the name of a classmate to analyze that person's status, as well.

1. Interview those who have worked with this person, particularly scene partners and directors, to get their ideas.
2. Check your own impressions with those of others in the class. Make certain that your conclusions are based on evidence and shared opinion.
3. Write out a list under each of the categories.
4. Share in class a brief summary of what you have learned. Be sure to speak to the actor in question. Make sure that your progress report expresses a sense of your interest in the person's growth. Make sure your suggestions

**E X E R C I S E**

**Style Growth**

are stated in positive and future-oriented terms. For example, don't say, "You need to stop being such a rude jerk"; instead, say, "I wish for you that in this next year you will find ways of asking for what you need instead of telling others." Remember that all valid criticism is a gift.

## STYLE FREEDOM

Know enough about what is going on to make informed *and* brave decisions. Your life is an adventure. You are constantly On Safari. You explore the wilds. You unearth wonders within yourself and all around you. Style is the parachute, submarine, or rocket by which you journey. It could be the three-wheeler, stroller, or skateboard. It can be the crystal ball, magic wand, or time capsule.

The more you understand your own style, the better prepared you become to play other styles. The more understanding you have of other styles, the more options you have as you continue to develop your own. The more options you have, the less likely you are to be intimidated.

Acting in style plays can be a renewal of childhood's "let's pretend," with all its power and conviction intact. A journey of the imagination is possible any time, any place. The great period plays are awesome avenues by which we can journey past the mundane into the heroic. And the more of these plays you perform, the more wonder you discover—or rediscover. To play a modern factory worker involved in a child custody suit and concerned about car payments has its own rewards, but the pleasure of playing a prince, a witch, a warrior, or a goddess wrestling with the future of the world is unparalleled. Style work expands your horizons and unleashes your vision.

Personally, style education helps you extend your own playground. It frees you from cultural prisons. You discover more ways to create reality. You recognize events as neutral and contexts as chosen. You learn to see imperfections as lovable and ownable. You see more right ways to do things.

The relationship between the plays and the actor's life is subtle and complex. By acting those who are witty, powerful, and great, you unquestionably have a chance to tap into your *own* wit, power, and greatness. Understanding the styles of the world offers you both more masks and more chances to unmask. You gain the ability to present or protect whatever part of yourself you choose. Your own style is richer and more expressive for tasting others. Style gives you choice. It helps you act your own life better.

*The size of the emotions in the classics is limitless, infinite, allowing you to explore great emotion within perfect literature.*

—ANNETTE BENNING

*I long to see American actors knock the socks off of British actors, so many of whom reek of, "I'm a proper actor, and there's that ass-scratching Method actor over there, mumbling into his boots."*

—KENNETH BRANAGH

*Those who excel have "kaleidoscopic" thinking. They can look at a routine, spin it around and suddenly put it in a different context.*

—ORGANIZATIONAL PSYCHOLOGIST ROBERT GANDOSSY

*We're born with biological hardware. But we can choose software.*

—PHILOSOPHER SAM KEEN

# INDEX